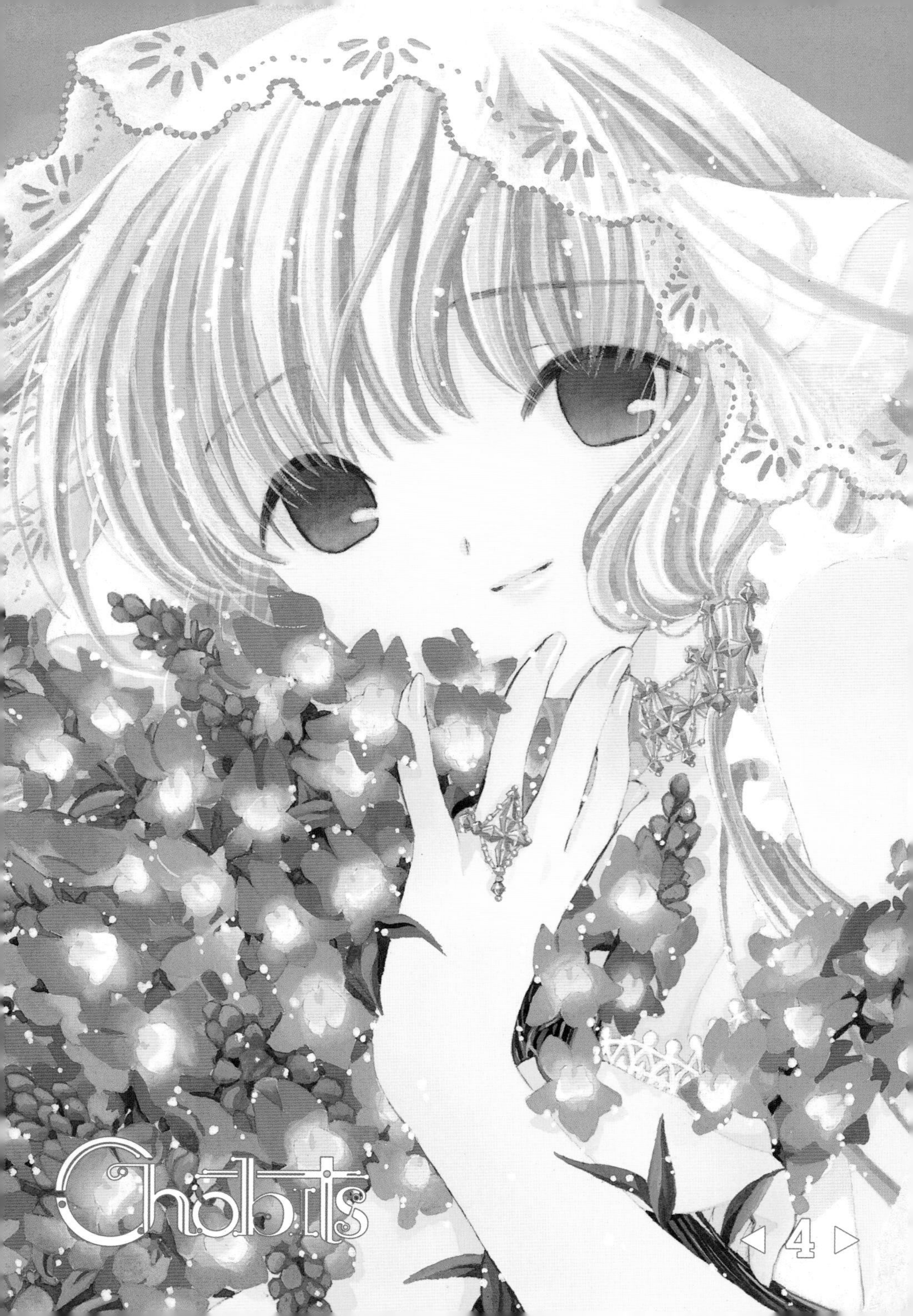
Chobits
4

# CONTENTS

◀ **CLAMP** ▶

SATSUKI IGARASHI
NANASE OHKAWA
TSUBAKI NEKOI
MOKONA

◀ Book design ▶
C L A M P

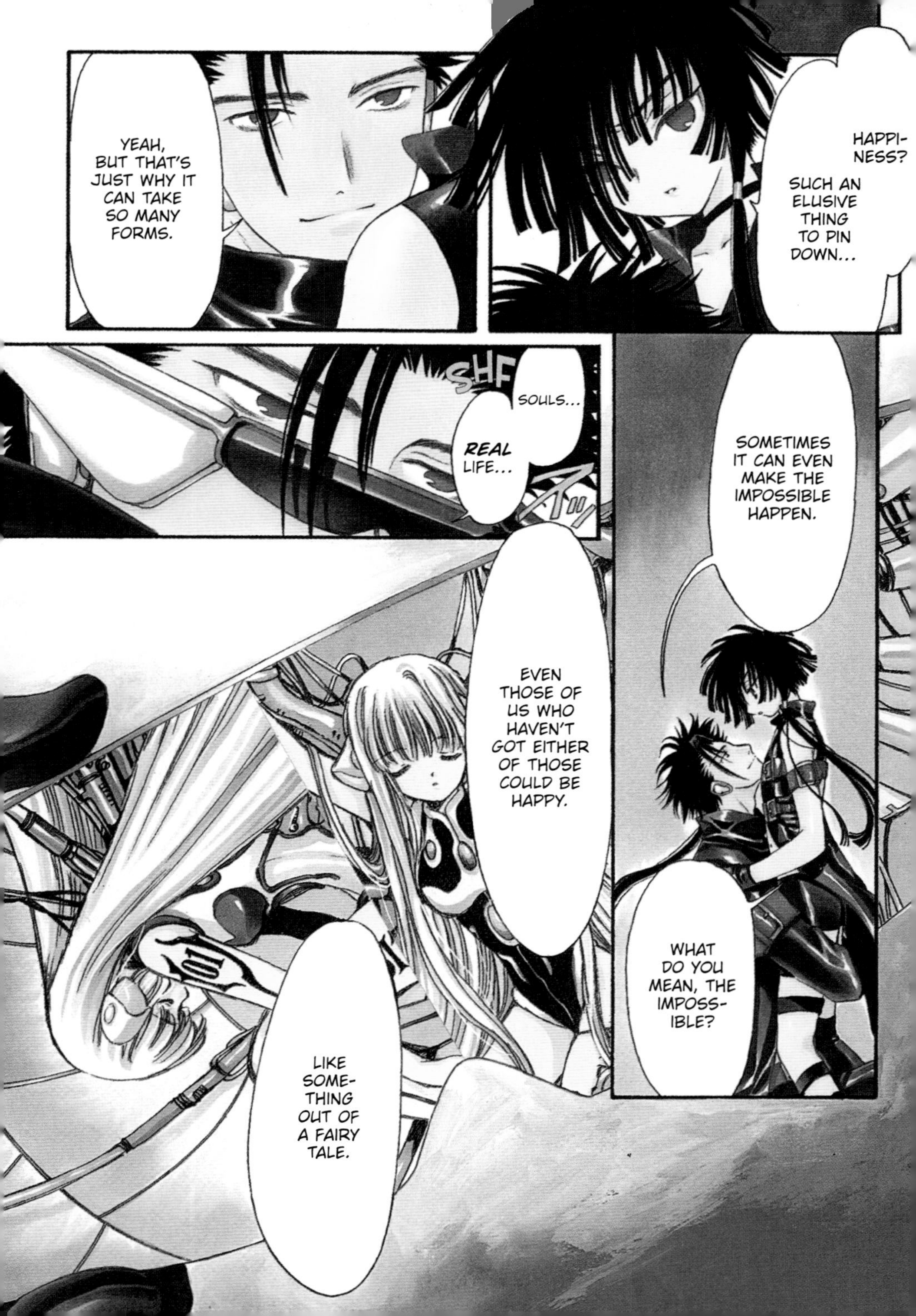

HAPPI-NESS?
SUCH AN ELUSIVE THING TO PIN DOWN...
YEAH, BUT THAT'S JUST WHY IT CAN TAKE SO MANY FORMS.
SHF
SOULS...
REAL LIFE...
EVEN THOSE OF US WHO HAVEN'T GOT EITHER OF THOSE COULD BE HAPPY.
SOMETIMES IT CAN EVEN MAKE THE IMPOSSIBLE HAPPEN.
WHAT DO YOU MEAN, THE IMPOSS-IBLE?
LIKE SOME-THING OUT OF A FAIRY TALE.

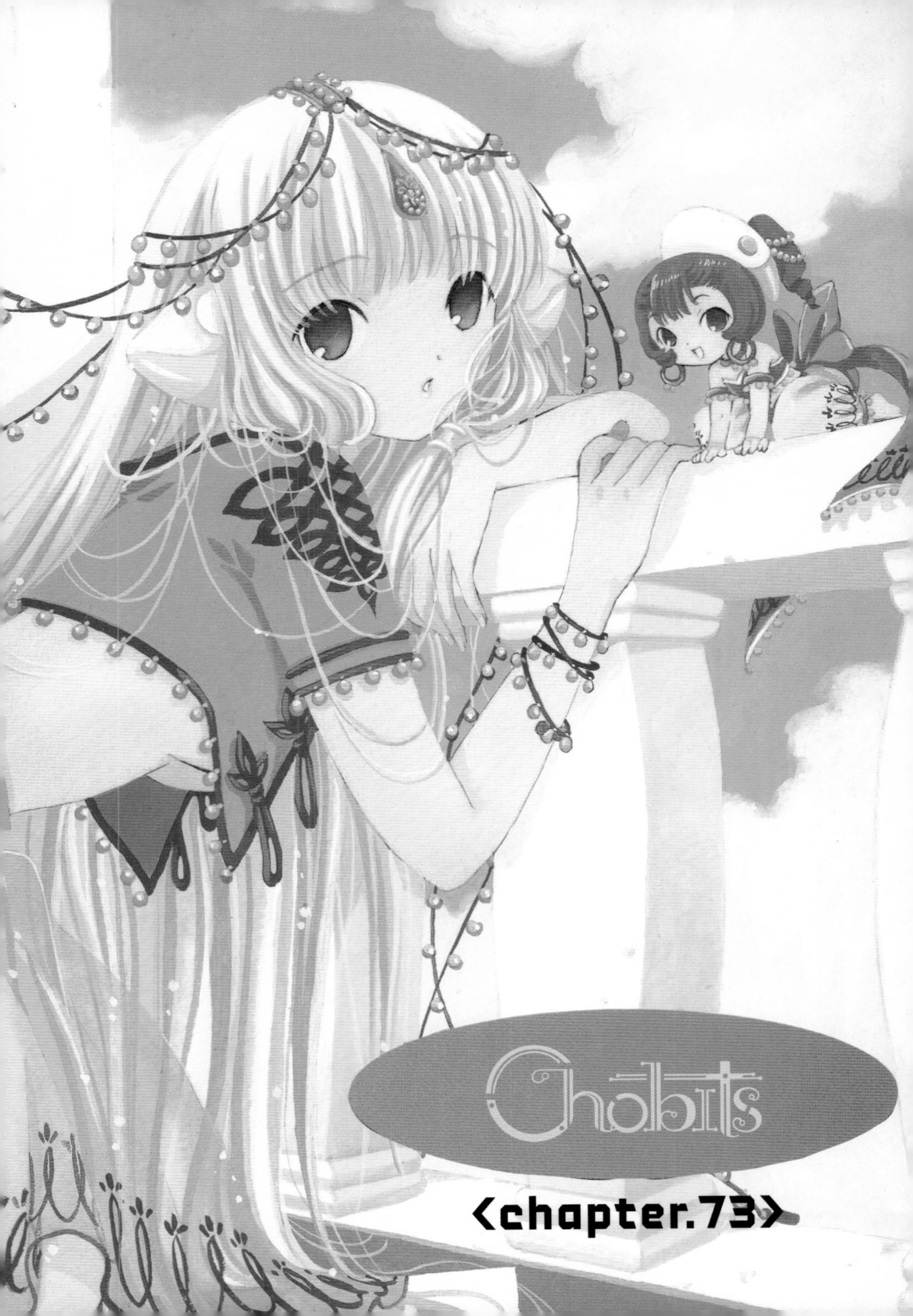
Chobits
<chapter.73>

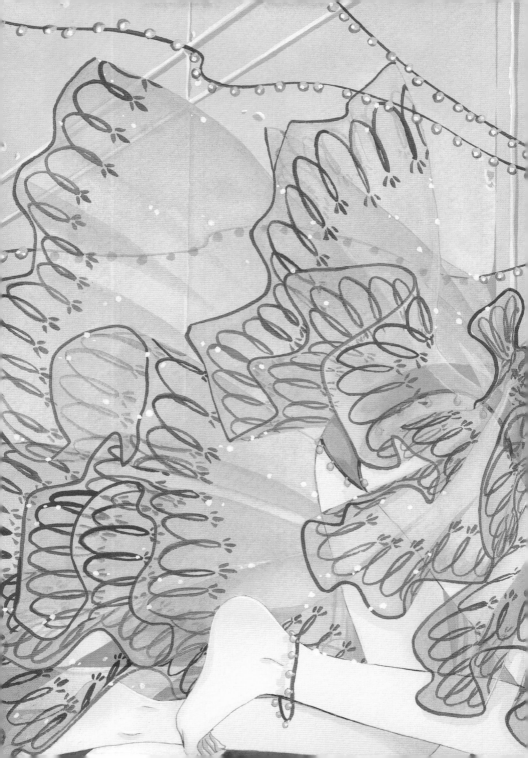

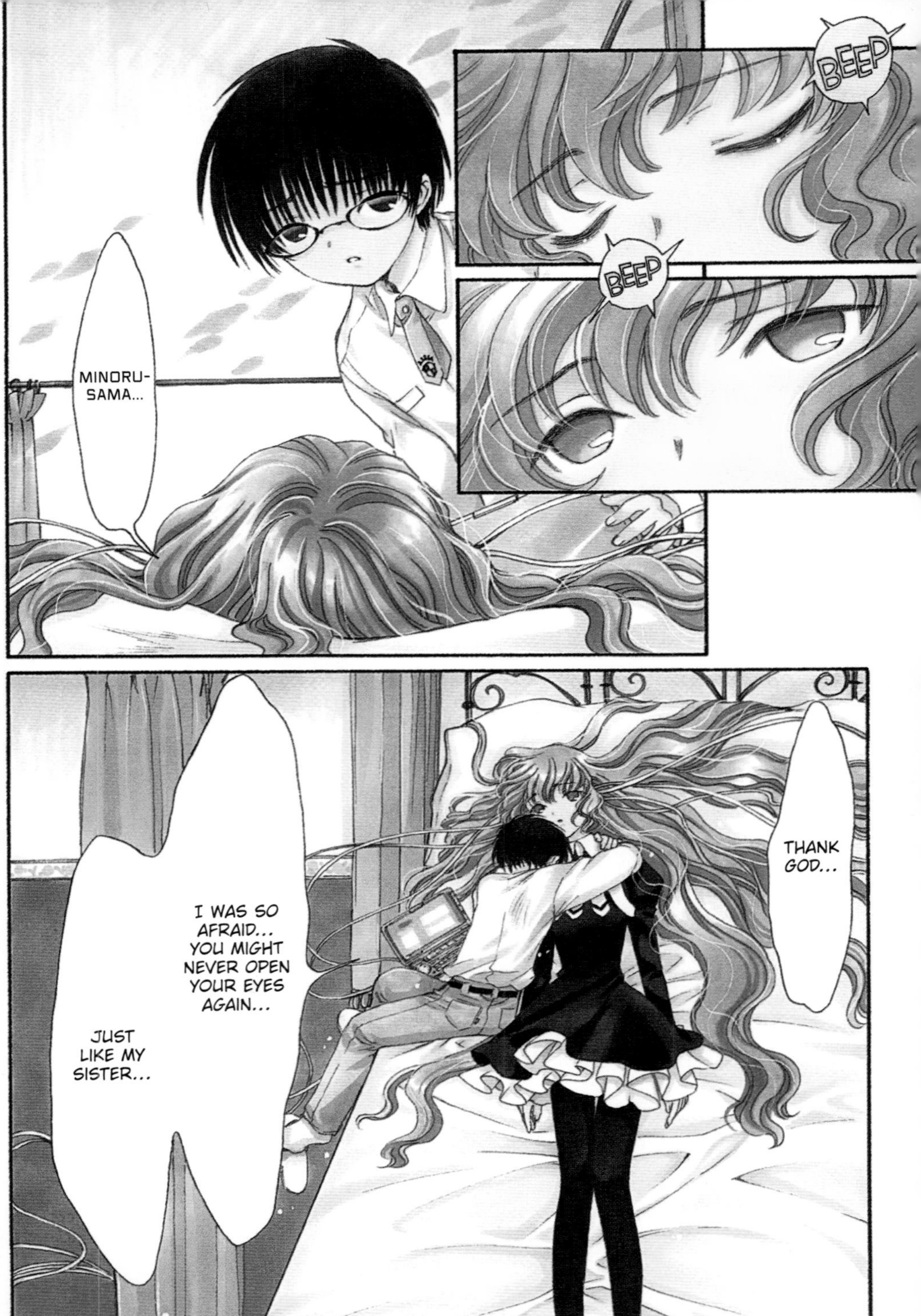
BEEP
BEEP
MINORU-SAMA...
THANK GOD...
I WAS SO AFRAID... YOU MIGHT NEVER OPEN YOUR EYES AGAIN...
JUST LIKE MY SISTER...

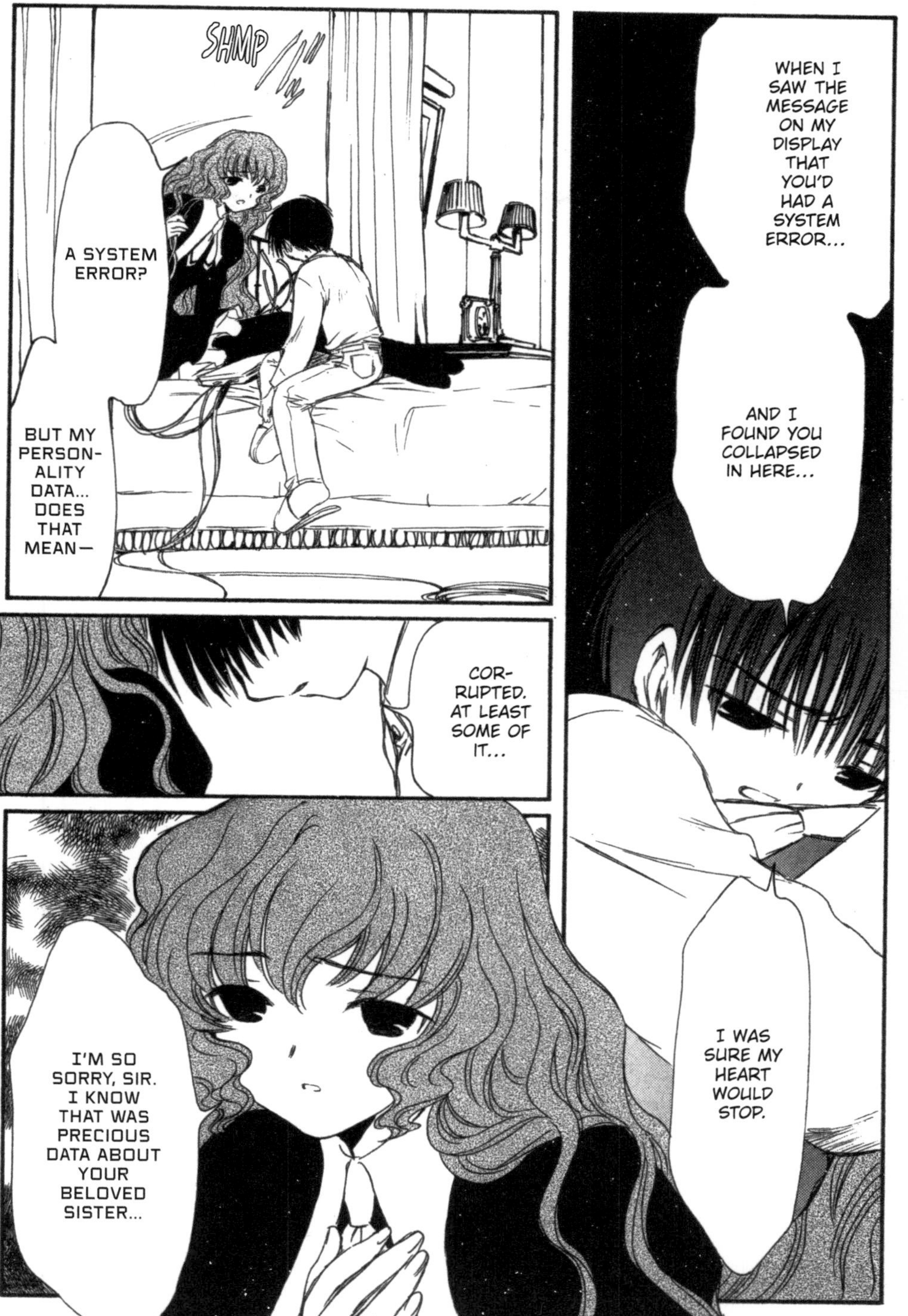
WHEN I SAW THE MESSAGE ON MY DISPLAY THAT YOU'D HAD A SYSTEM ERROR...
AND I FOUND YOU COLLAPSED IN HERE...
I WAS SURE MY HEART WOULD STOP.
SHMP
A SYSTEM ERROR?
BUT MY PERSON-ALITY DATA... DOES THAT MEAN—
COR-RUPTED. AT LEAST SOME OF IT...
I'M SO SORRY, SIR. I KNOW THAT WAS PRECIOUS DATA ABOUT YOUR BELOVED SISTER...

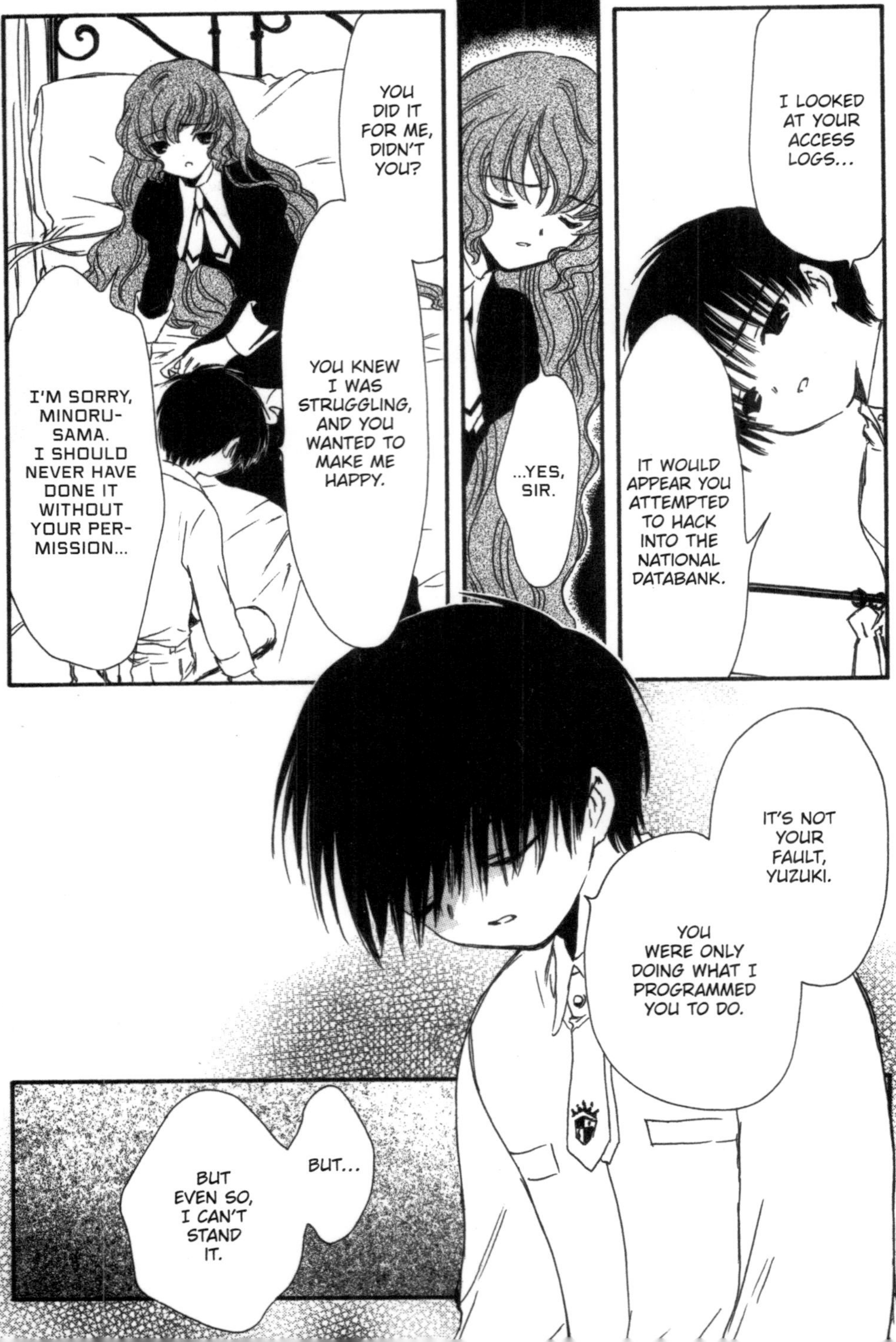
I LOOKED AT YOUR ACCESS LOGS...
IT WOULD APPEAR YOU ATTEMPTED TO HACK INTO THE NATIONAL DATABANK.
...YES, SIR.
YOU DID IT FOR ME, DIDN'T YOU?
YOU KNEW I WAS STRUGGLING, AND YOU WANTED TO MAKE ME HAPPY.
I'M SORRY, MINORU-SAMA. I SHOULD NEVER HAVE DONE IT WITHOUT YOUR PER-MISSION...
IT'S NOT YOUR FAULT, YUZUKI.
YOU WERE ONLY DOING WHAT I PROGRAMMED YOU TO DO.
BUT...
BUT EVEN SO, I CAN'T STAND IT.

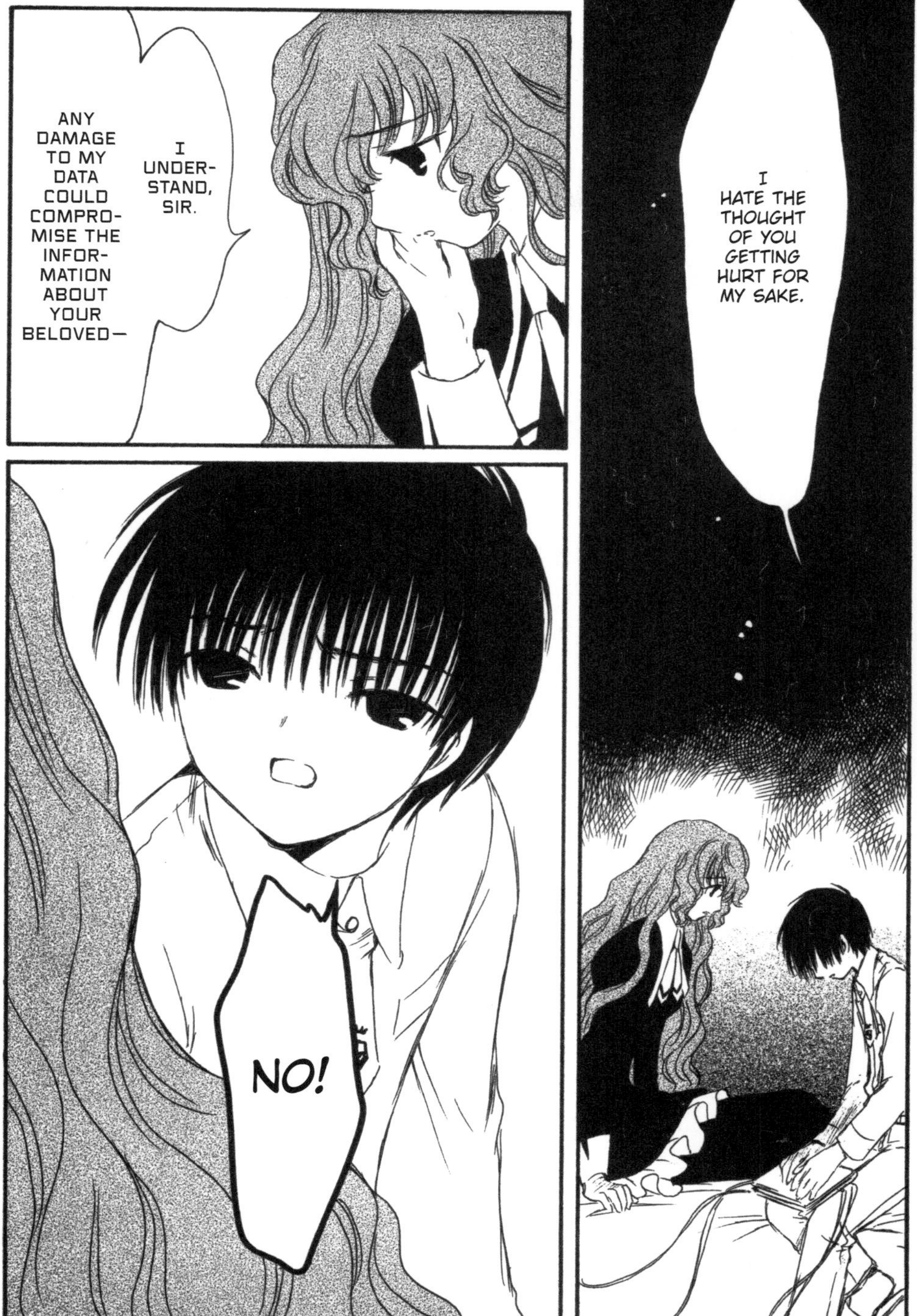
I HATE THE THOUGHT OF YOU GETTING HURT FOR MY SAKE.
ANY DAMAGE TO MY DATA COULD COMPROMISE THE INFORMATION ABOUT YOUR BELOVED—
I UNDERSTAND, SIR.
NO!

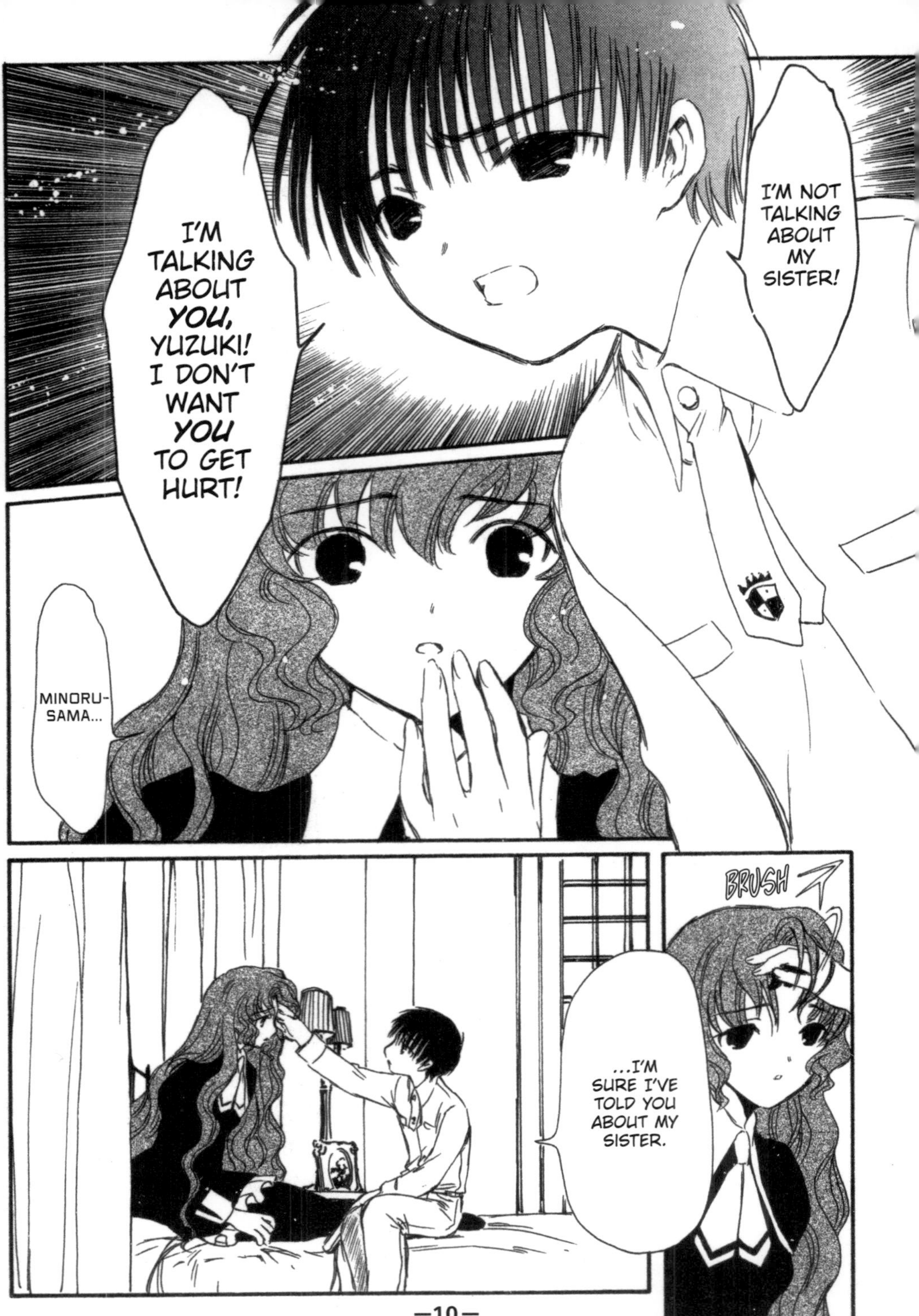
I'M NOT TALKING ABOUT MY SISTER!
I'M TALKING ABOUT **YOU**, YUZUKI! I DON'T WANT **YOU** TO GET HURT!
MINORU-SAMA...
BRUSH
...I'M SURE I'VE TOLD YOU ABOUT MY SISTER.

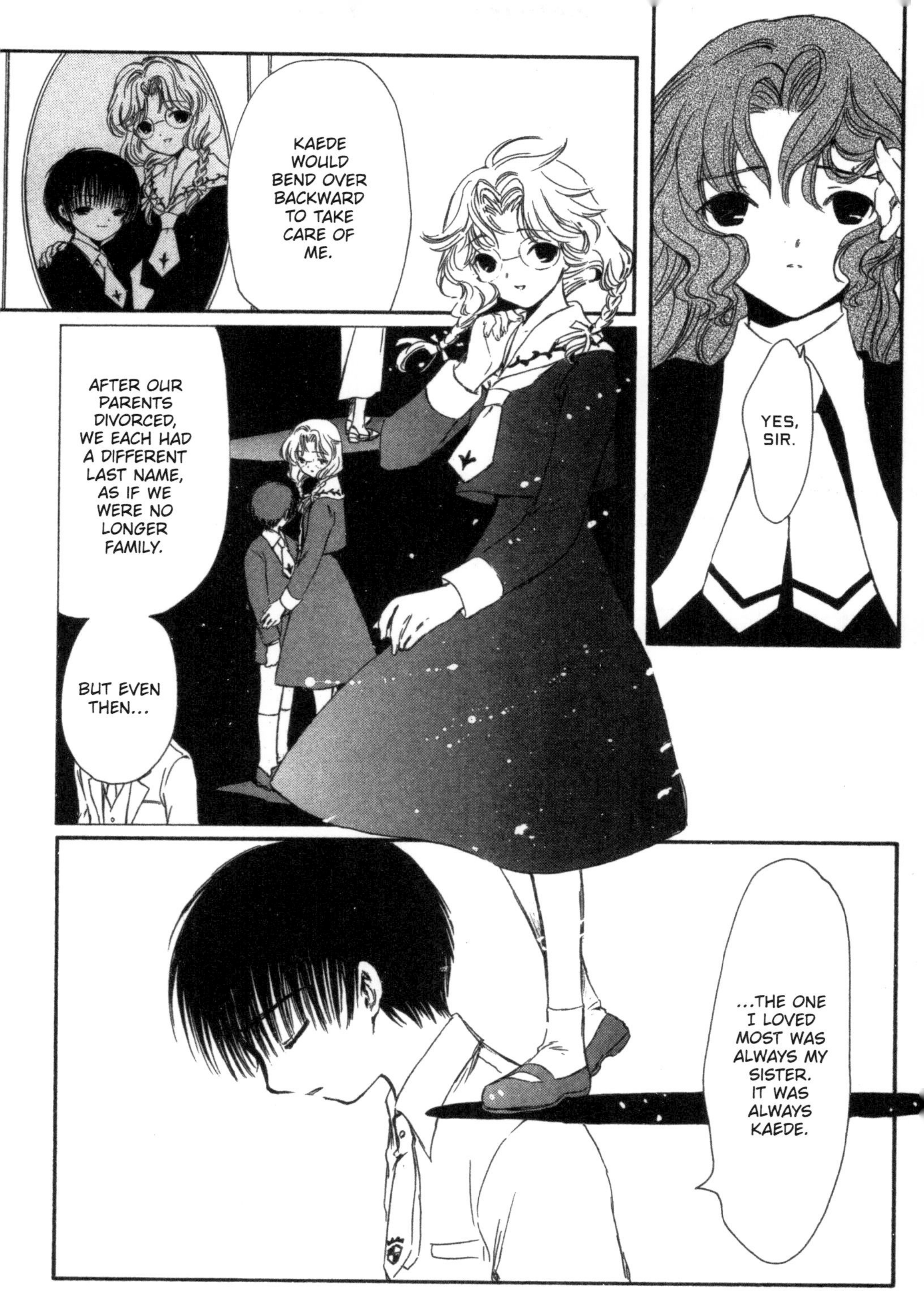
YES, SIR.
KAEDE WOULD BEND OVER BACKWARD TO TAKE CARE OF ME.
AFTER OUR PARENTS DIVORCED, WE EACH HAD A DIFFERENT LAST NAME, AS IF WE WERE NO LONGER FAMILY.
BUT EVEN THEN...
...THE ONE I LOVED MOST WAS ALWAYS MY SISTER. IT WAS ALWAYS KAEDE.

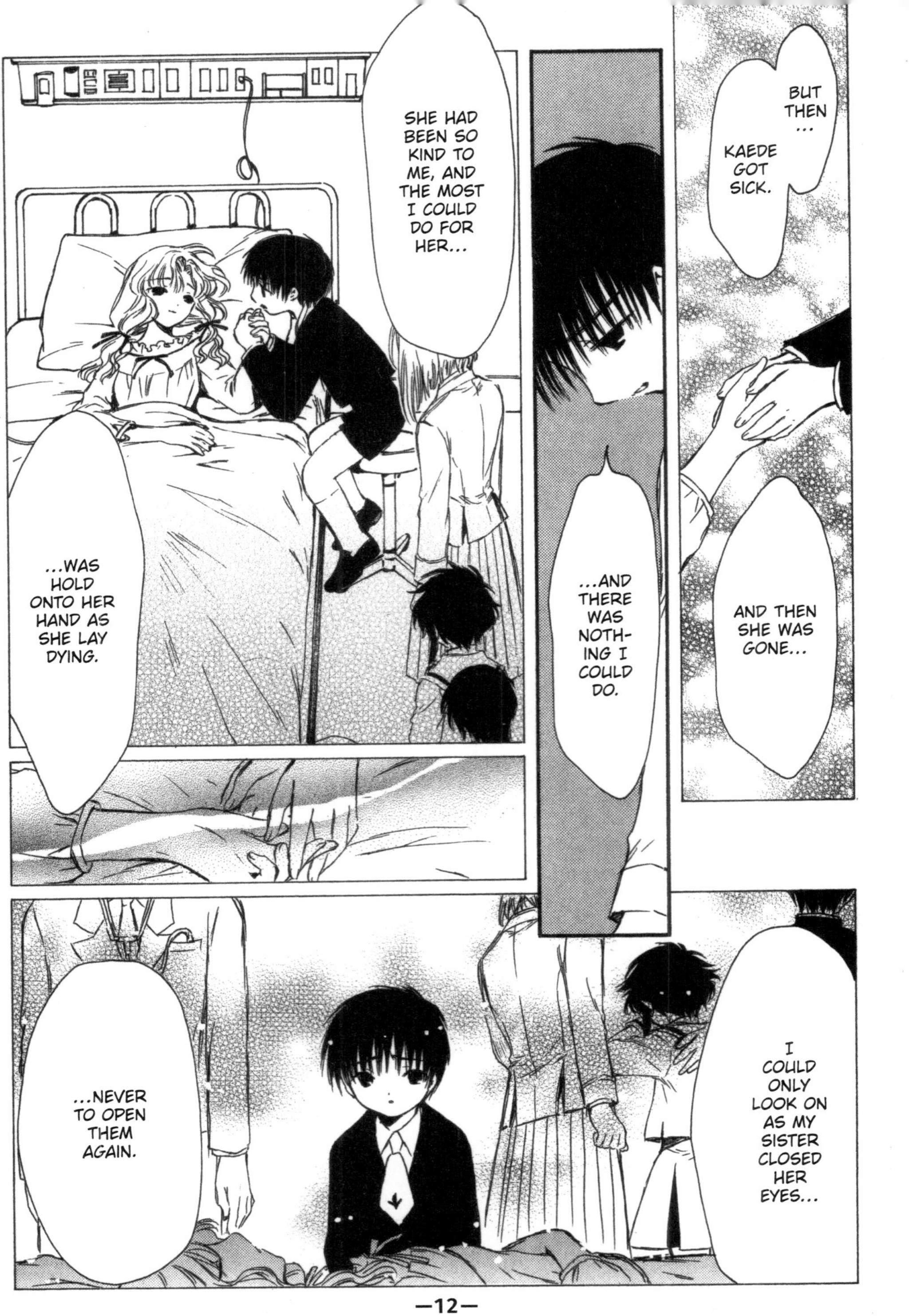
BUT THEN...
KAEDE GOT SICK.
AND THEN SHE WAS GONE...
...AND THERE WAS NOTHING I COULD DO.
SHE HAD BEEN SO KIND TO ME, AND THE MOST I COULD DO FOR HER...
...WAS HOLD ONTO HER HAND AS SHE LAY DYING.
I COULD ONLY LOOK ON AS MY SISTER CLOSED HER EYES...
...NEVER TO OPEN THEM AGAIN.

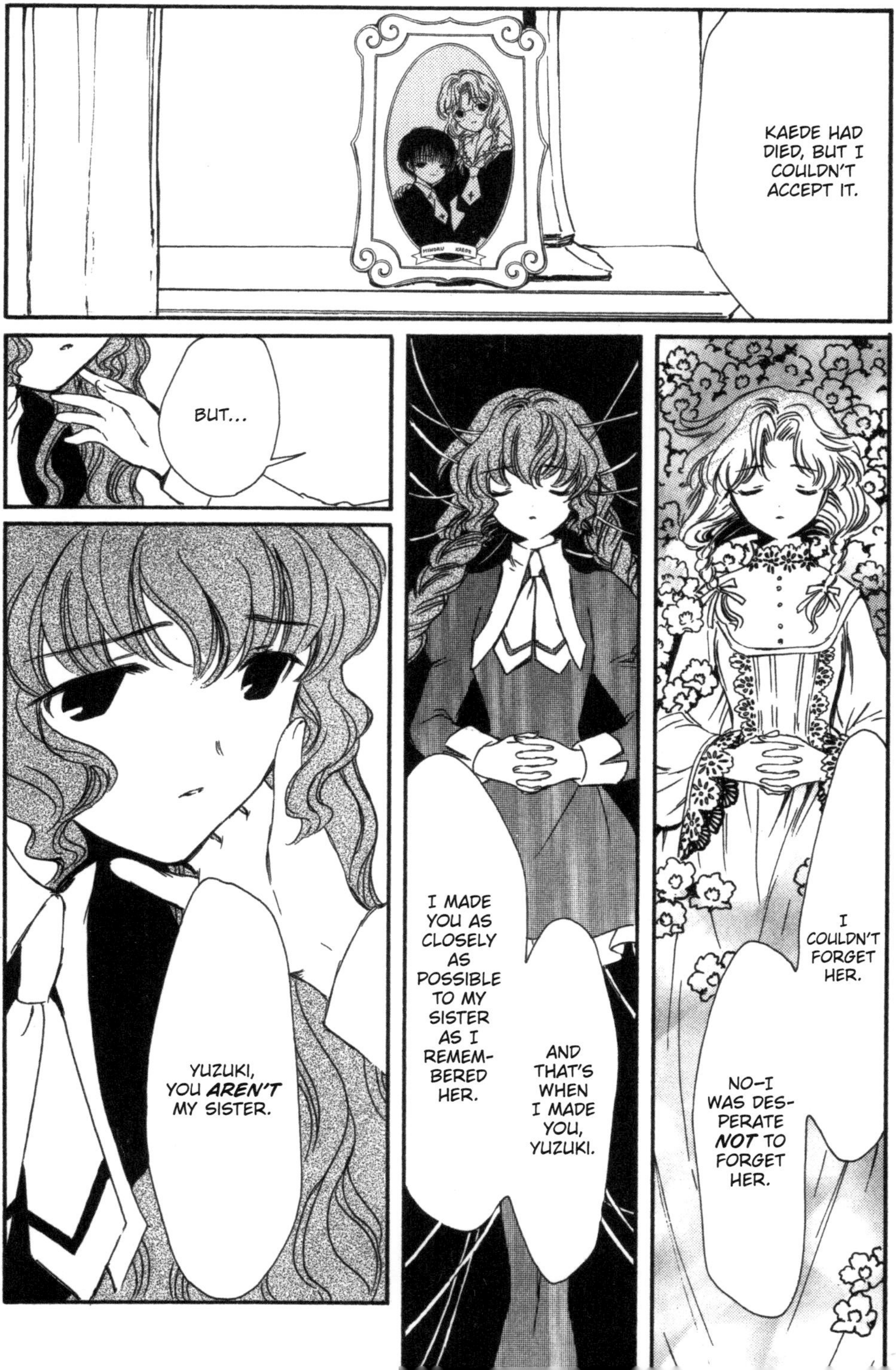
KAEDE HAD DIED, BUT I COULDN'T ACCEPT IT.
I COULDN'T FORGET HER.
NO—I WAS DESPERATE NOT TO FORGET HER.
I MADE YOU AS CLOSELY AS POSSIBLE TO MY SISTER AS I REMEMBERED HER.
AND THAT'S WHEN I MADE YOU, YUZUKI.
BUT...
YUZUKI, YOU AREN'T MY SISTER.

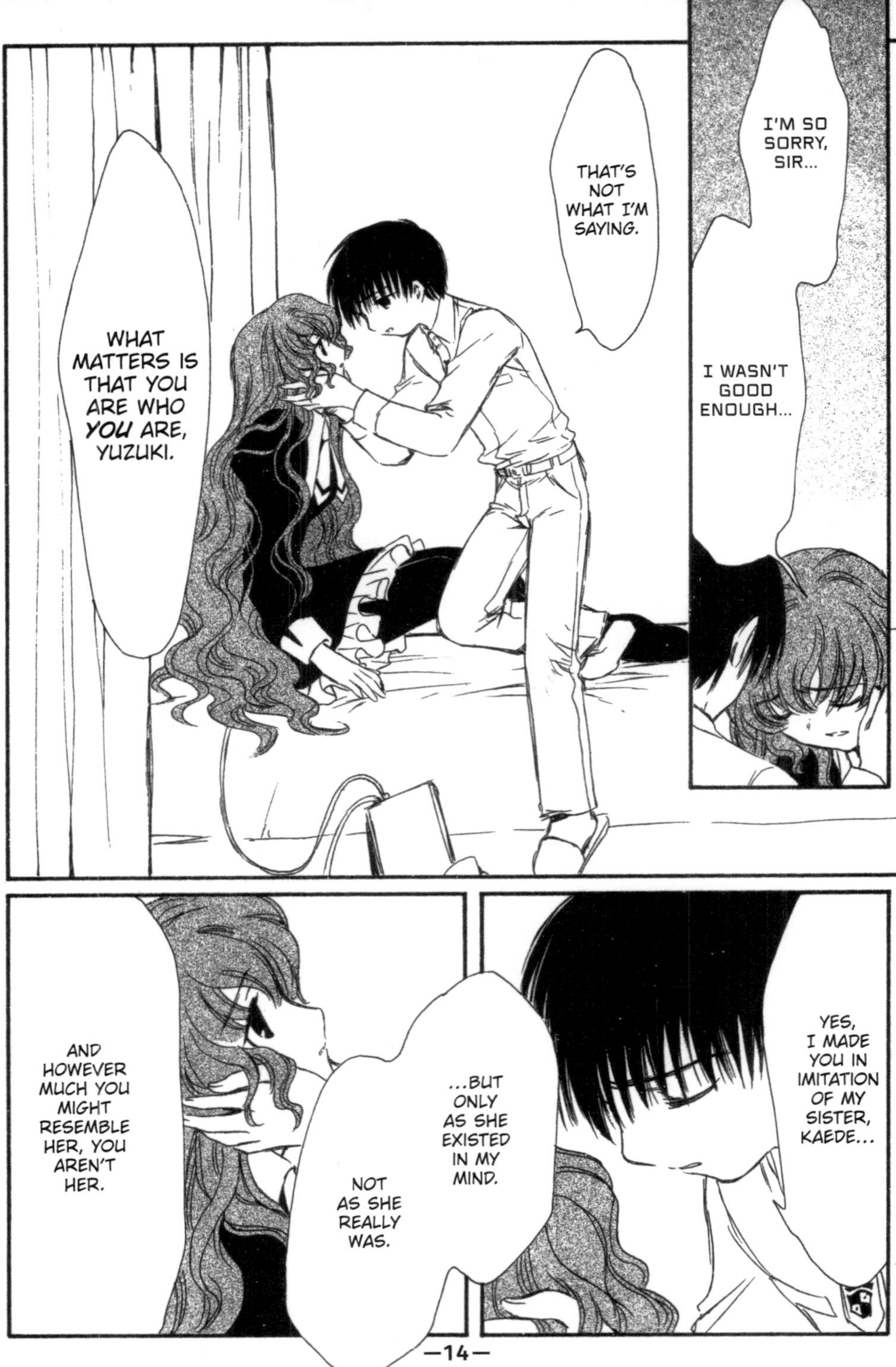
I'M SO SORRY, SIR...
I WASN'T GOOD ENOUGH...
THAT'S NOT WHAT I'M SAYING.
WHAT MATTERS IS THAT YOU ARE WHO YOU ARE, YUZUKI.
YES, I MADE YOU IN IMITATION OF MY SISTER, KAEDE...
...BUT ONLY AS SHE EXISTED IN MY MIND.
NOT AS SHE REALLY WAS.
AND HOWEVER MUCH YOU MIGHT RESEMBLE HER, YOU AREN'T HER.

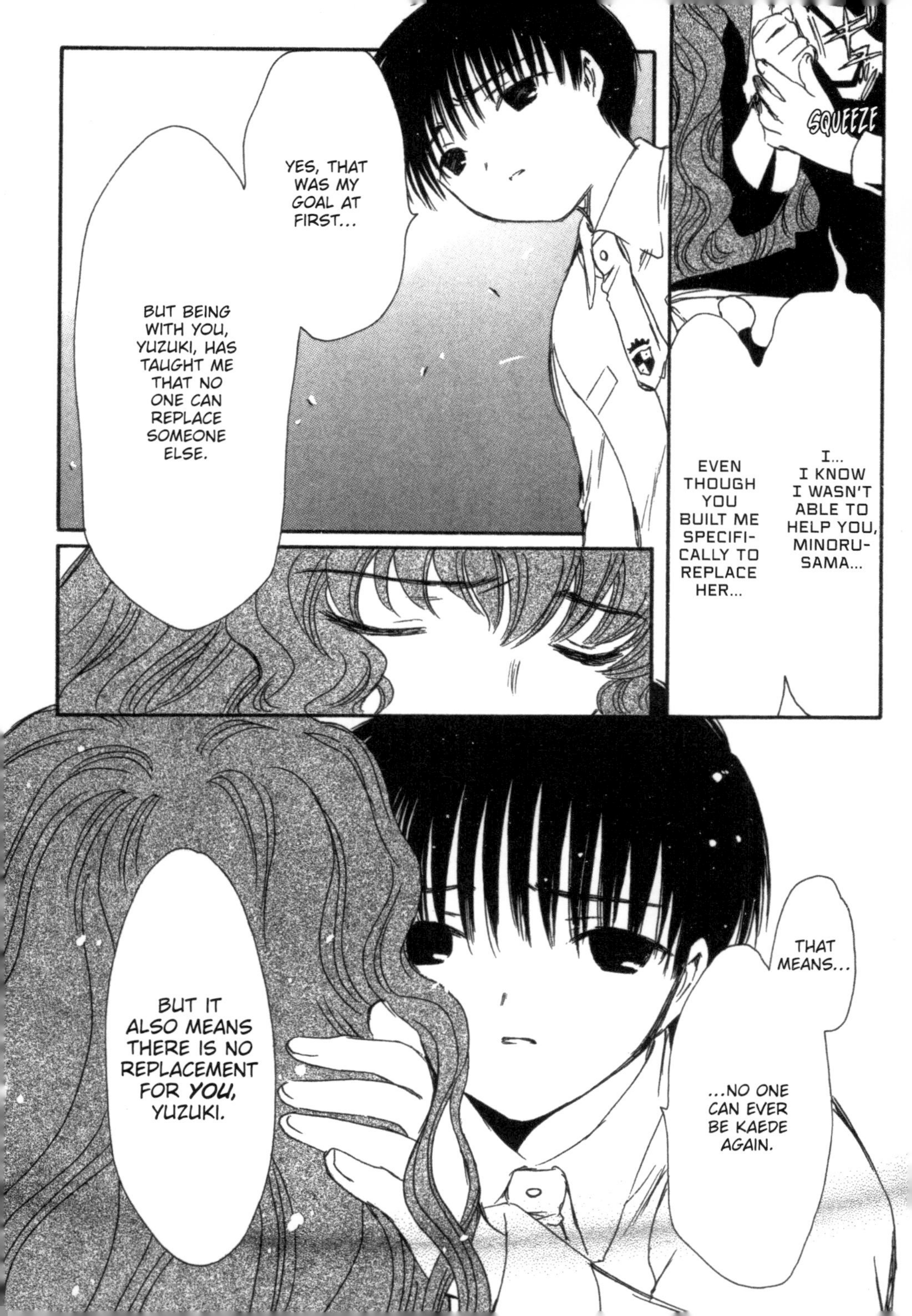
SQUEEZE
I... I KNOW I WASN'T ABLE TO HELP YOU, MINORU-SAMA...
EVEN THOUGH YOU BUILT ME SPECIFICALLY TO REPLACE HER...
YES, THAT WAS MY GOAL AT FIRST...
BUT BEING WITH YOU, YUZUKI, HAS TAUGHT ME THAT NO ONE CAN REPLACE SOMEONE ELSE.
THAT MEANS...
...NO ONE CAN EVER BE KAEDE AGAIN.
BUT IT ALSO MEANS THERE IS NO REPLACEMENT FOR *YOU*, YUZUKI.

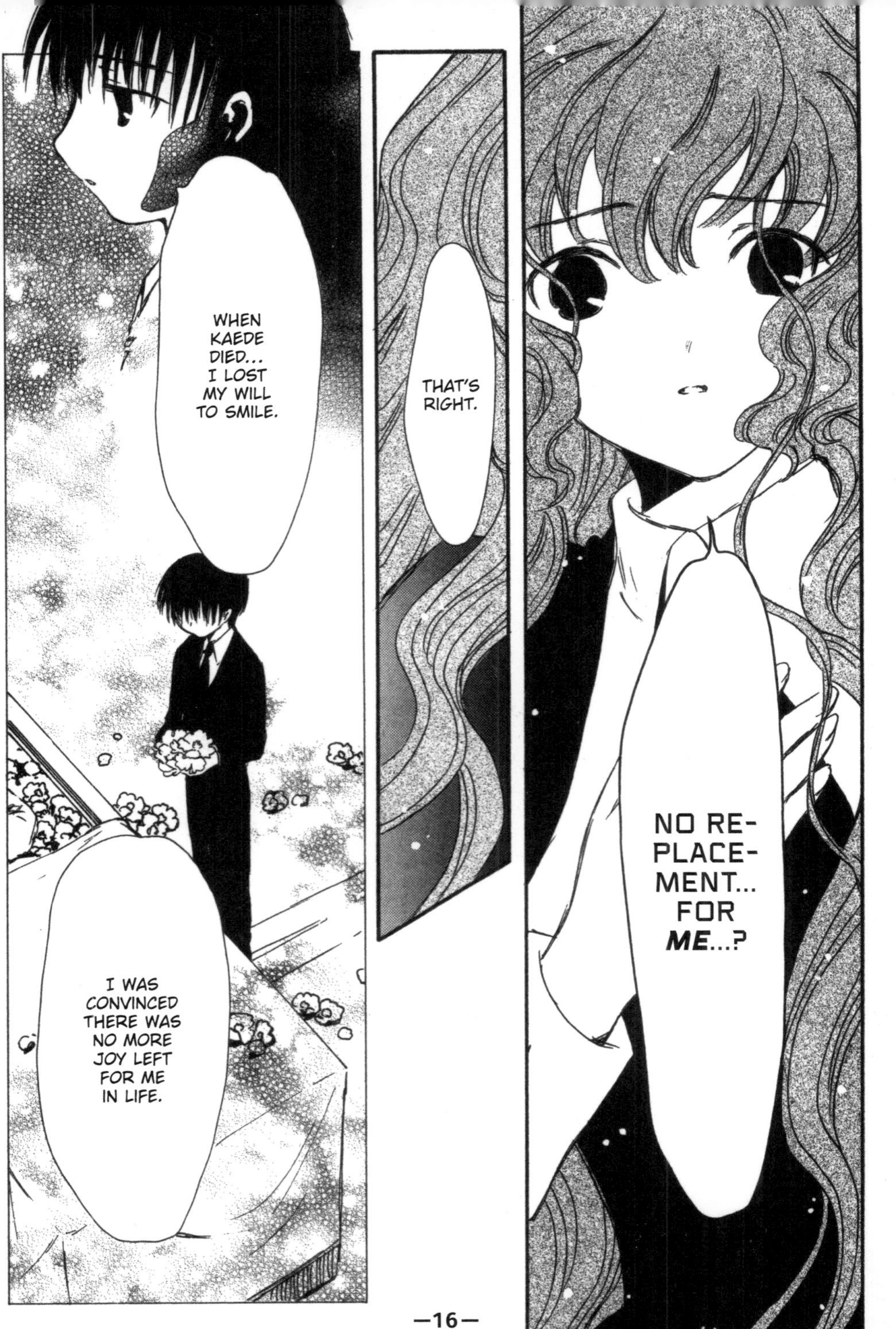
NO RE-PLACE-MENT... FOR ***ME***...?
THAT'S RIGHT.
WHEN KAEDE DIED... I LOST MY WILL TO SMILE.
I WAS CONVINCED THERE WAS NO MORE JOY LEFT FOR ME IN LIFE.

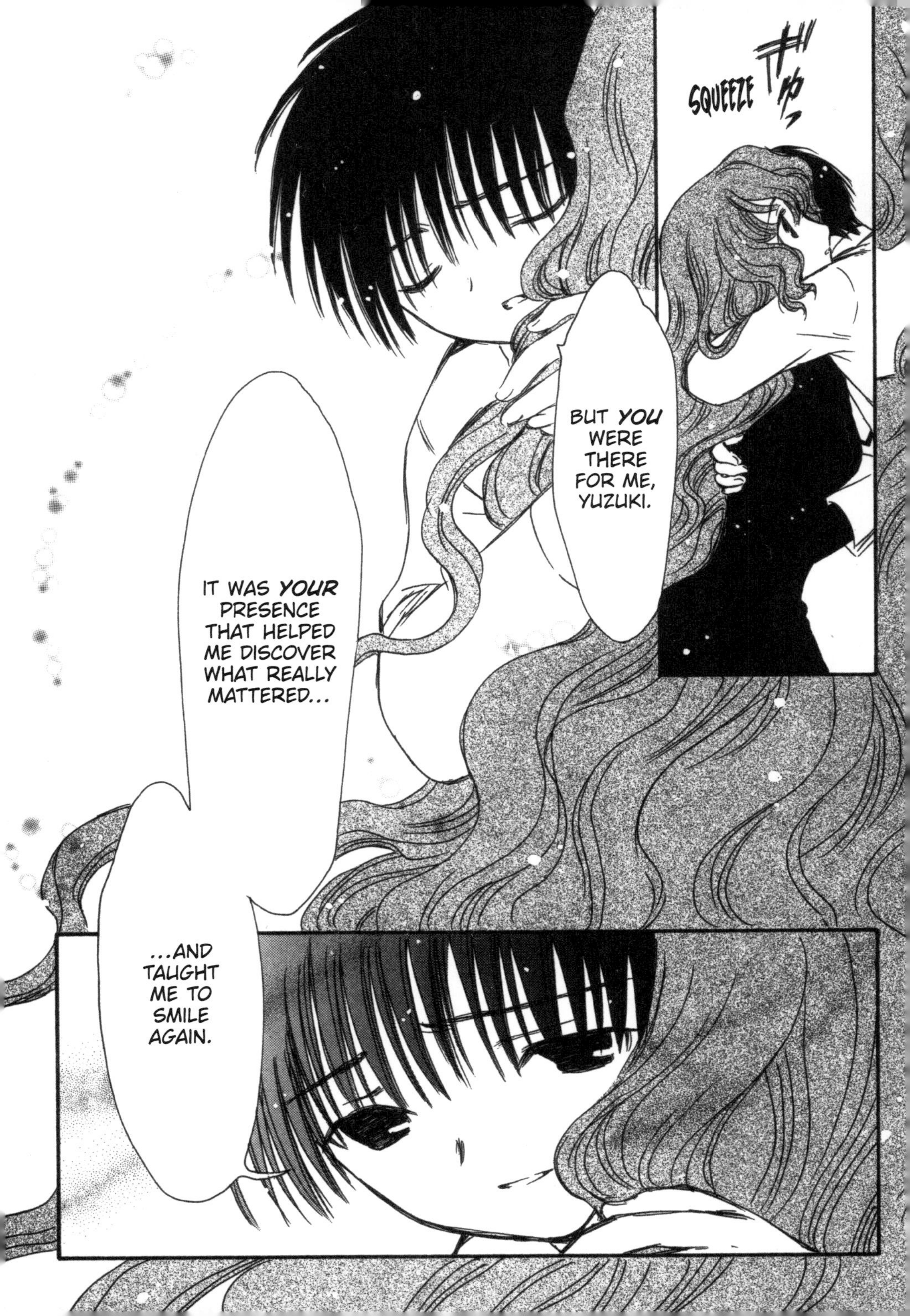
SQUEEZE
BUT *YOU* WERE THERE FOR ME, YUZUKI.
IT WAS *YOUR* PRESENCE THAT HELPED ME DISCOVER WHAT REALLY MATTERED...
...AND TAUGHT ME TO SMILE AGAIN.

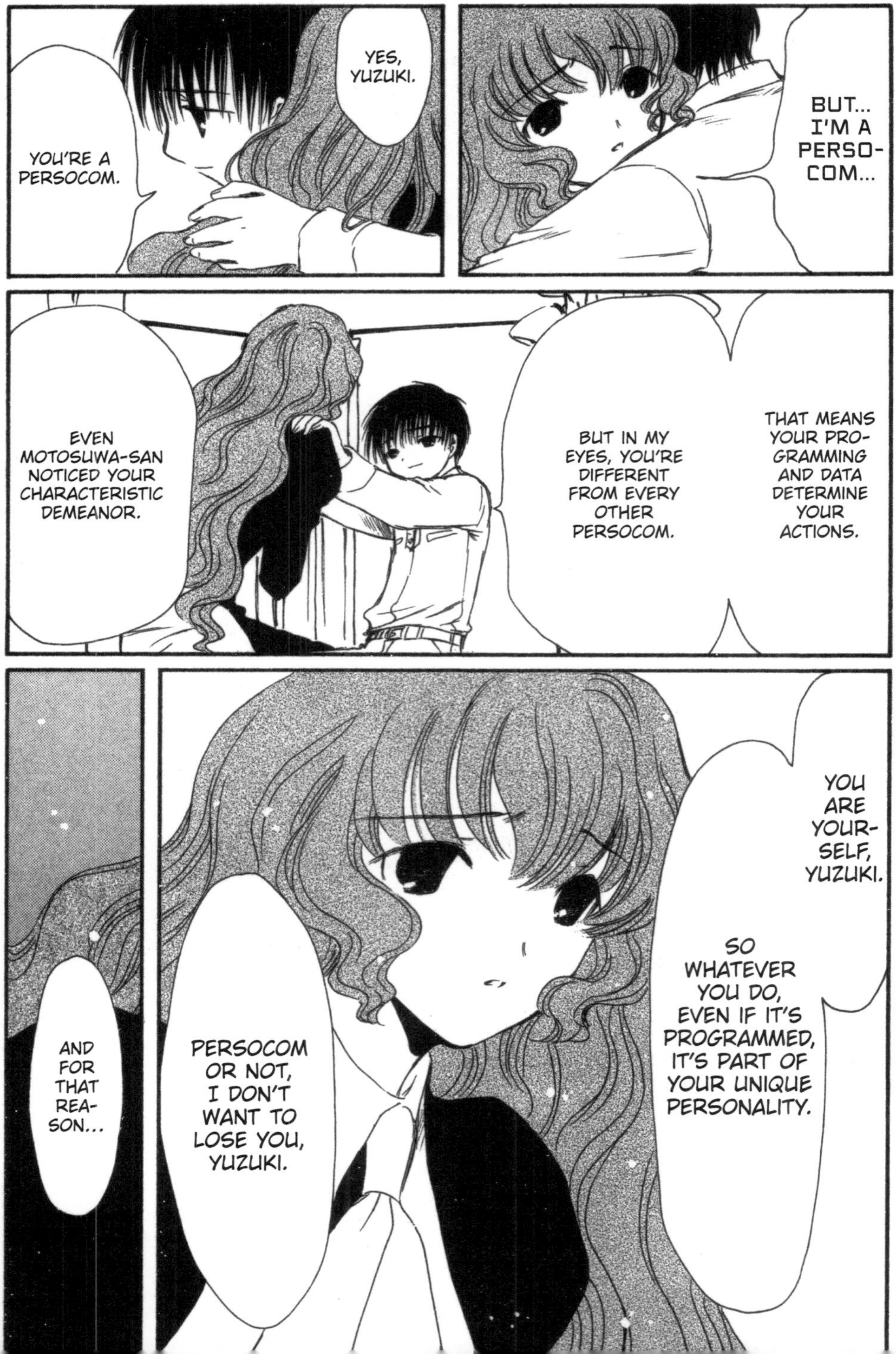
BUT... I'M A PERSO-COM...
YES, YUZUKI.
YOU'RE A PERSOCOM.
THAT MEANS YOUR PRO-GRAMMING AND DATA DETERMINE YOUR ACTIONS.
BUT IN MY EYES, YOU'RE DIFFERENT FROM EVERY OTHER PERSOCOM.
EVEN MOTOSUWA-SAN NOTICED YOUR CHARACTERISTIC DEMEANOR.
YOU ARE YOUR-SELF, YUZUKI.
SO WHATEVER YOU DO, EVEN IF IT'S PROGRAMMED, IT'S PART OF YOUR UNIQUE PERSONALITY.
PERSOCOM OR NOT, I DON'T WANT TO LOSE YOU, YUZUKI.
AND FOR THAT REA-SON...

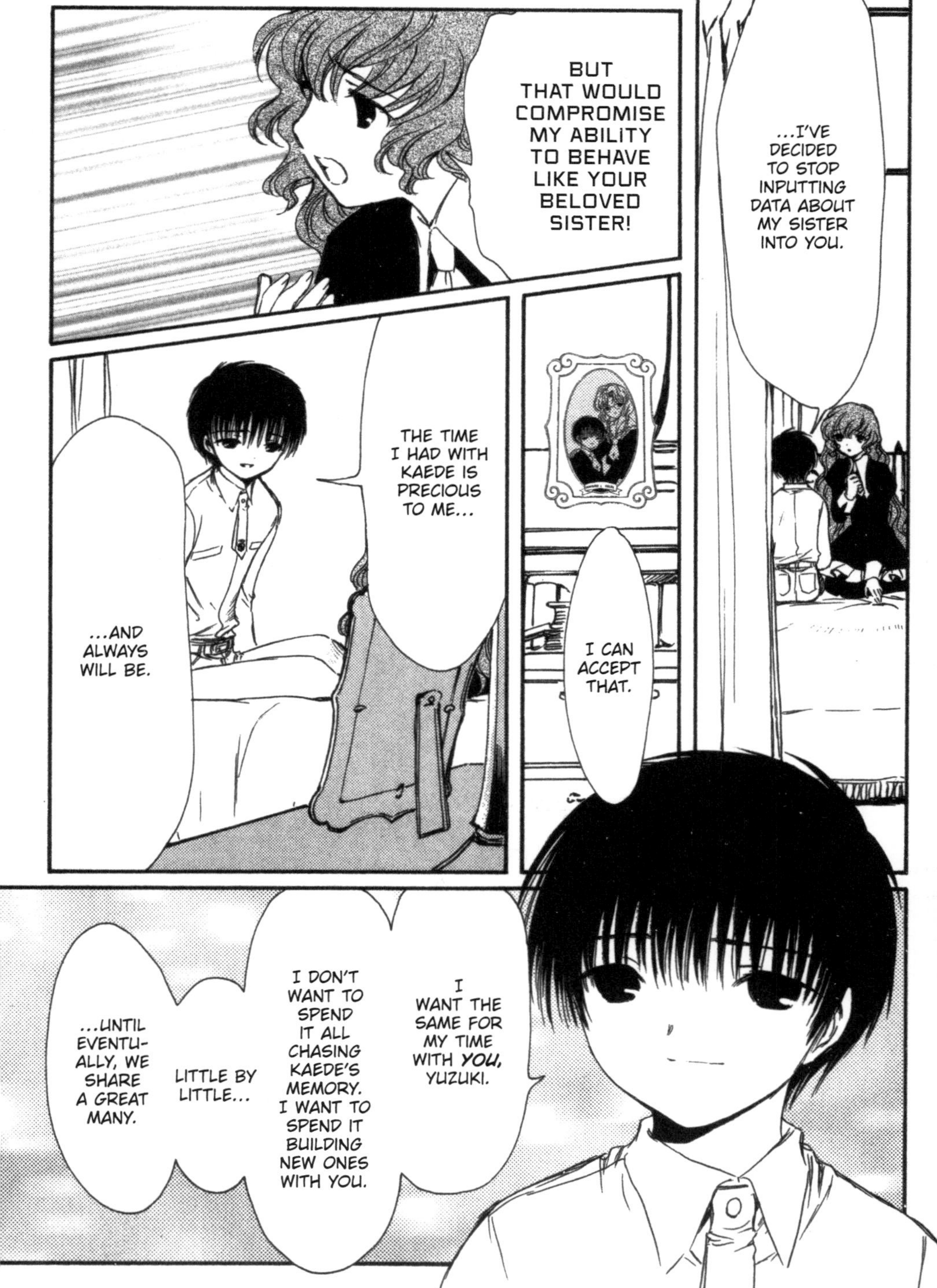
...I'VE DECIDED TO STOP INPUTTING DATA ABOUT MY SISTER INTO YOU.
BUT THAT WOULD COMPROMISE MY ABILITY TO BEHAVE LIKE YOUR BELOVED SISTER!
I CAN ACCEPT THAT.
THE TIME I HAD WITH KAEDE IS PRECIOUS TO ME...
...AND ALWAYS WILL BE.
I WANT THE SAME FOR MY TIME WITH *YOU,* YUZUKI.
I DON'T WANT TO SPEND IT ALL CHASING KAEDE'S MEMORY. I WANT TO SPEND IT BUILDING NEW ONES WITH YOU.
LITTLE BY LITTLE...
...UNTIL EVENTU-ALLY, WE SHARE A GREAT MANY.

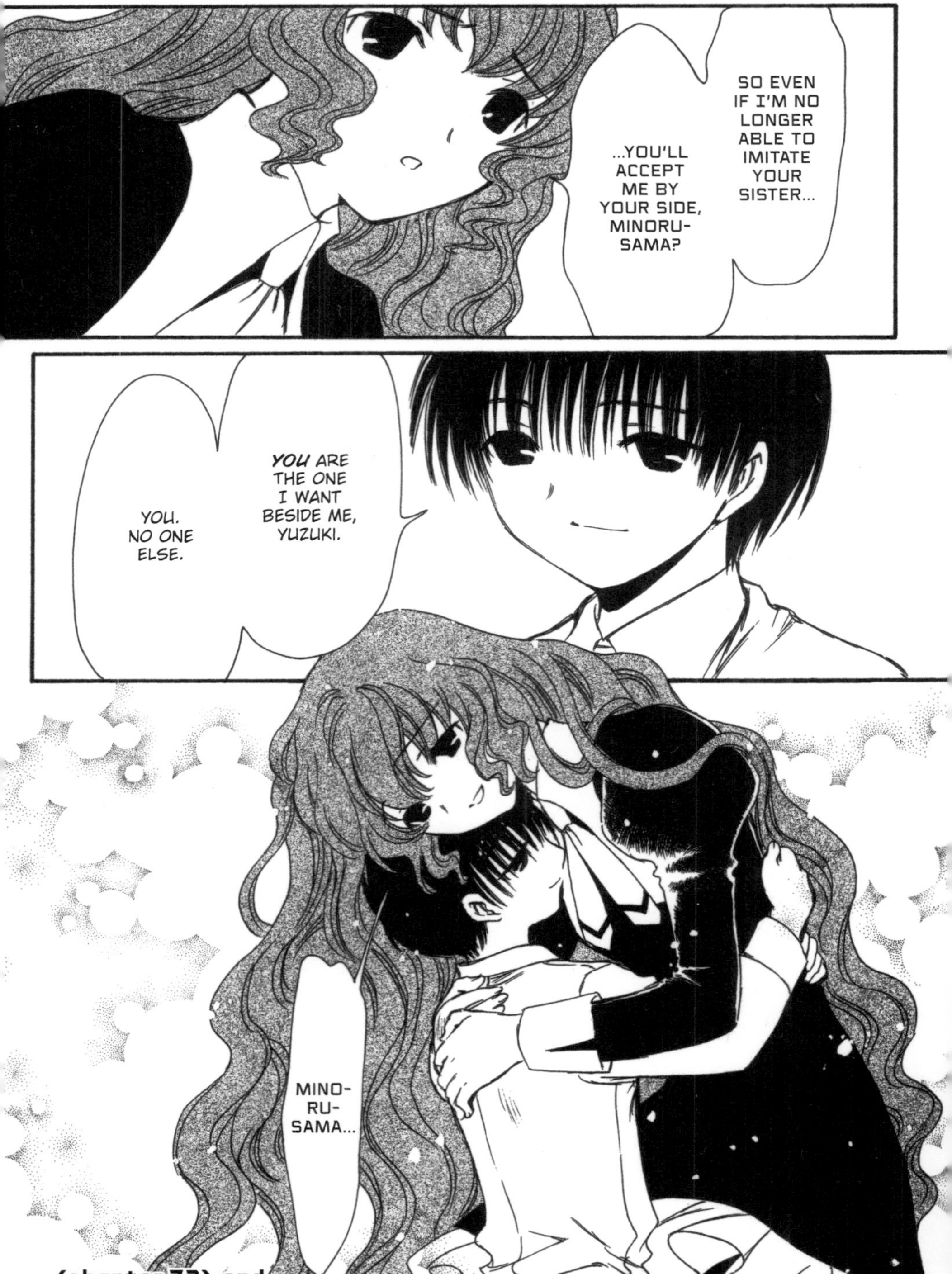
SO EVEN IF I'M NO LONGER ABLE TO IMITATE YOUR SISTER...
...YOU'LL ACCEPT ME BY YOUR SIDE, MINORU-SAMA?
YOU ARE THE ONE I WANT BESIDE ME, YUZUKI.
YOU. NO ONE ELSE.
MINO-RU-SAMA...
<chapter.73> end

**〈chapter.74〉**

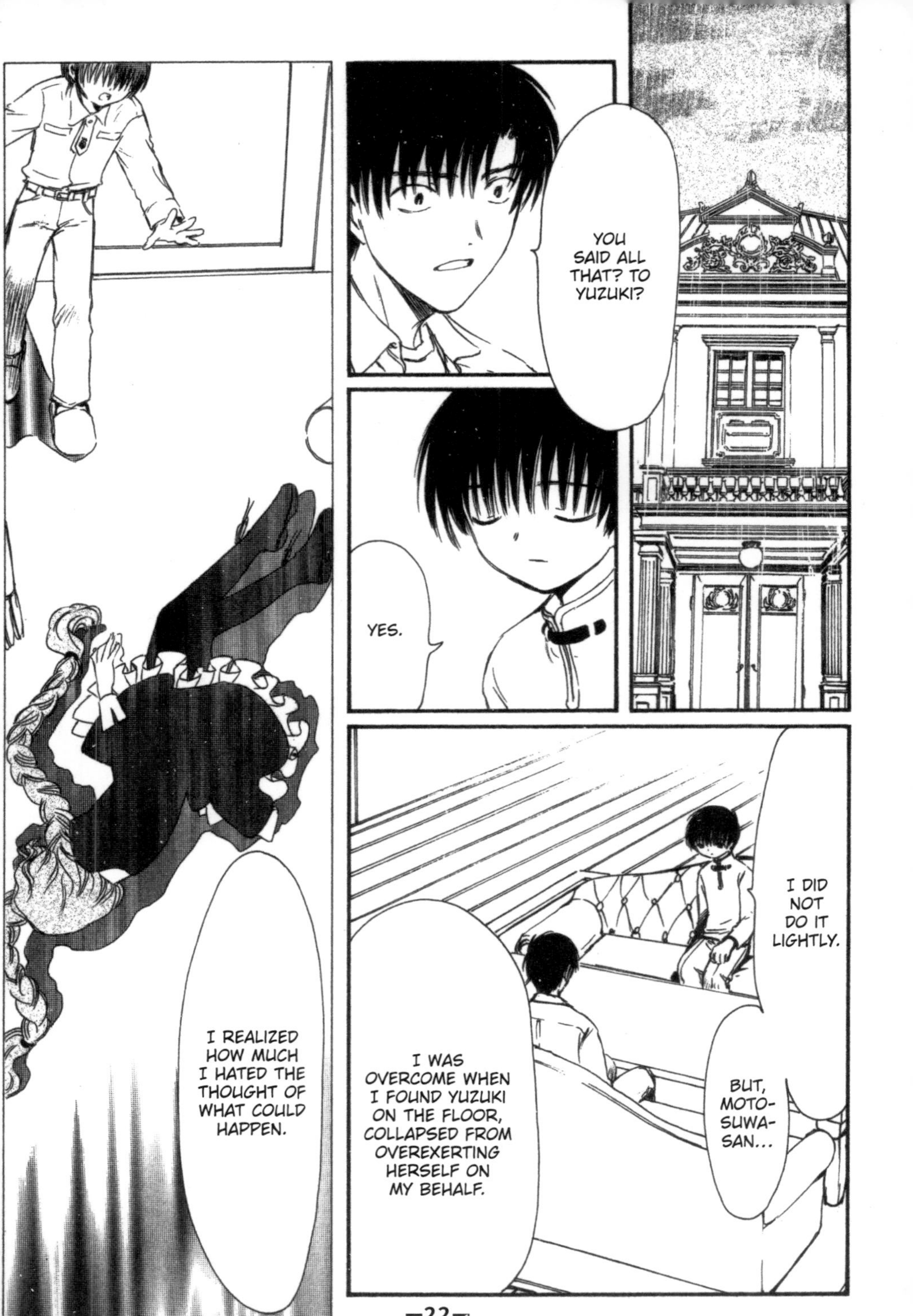
YOU SAID ALL THAT? TO YUZUKI?
YES.
I DID NOT DO IT LIGHTLY.
BUT, MOTO-SUWA-SAN...
I WAS OVERCOME WHEN I FOUND YUZUKI ON THE FLOOR, COLLAPSED FROM OVEREXERTING HERSELF ON MY BEHALF.
I REALIZED HOW MUCH I HATED THE THOUGHT OF WHAT COULD HAPPEN.

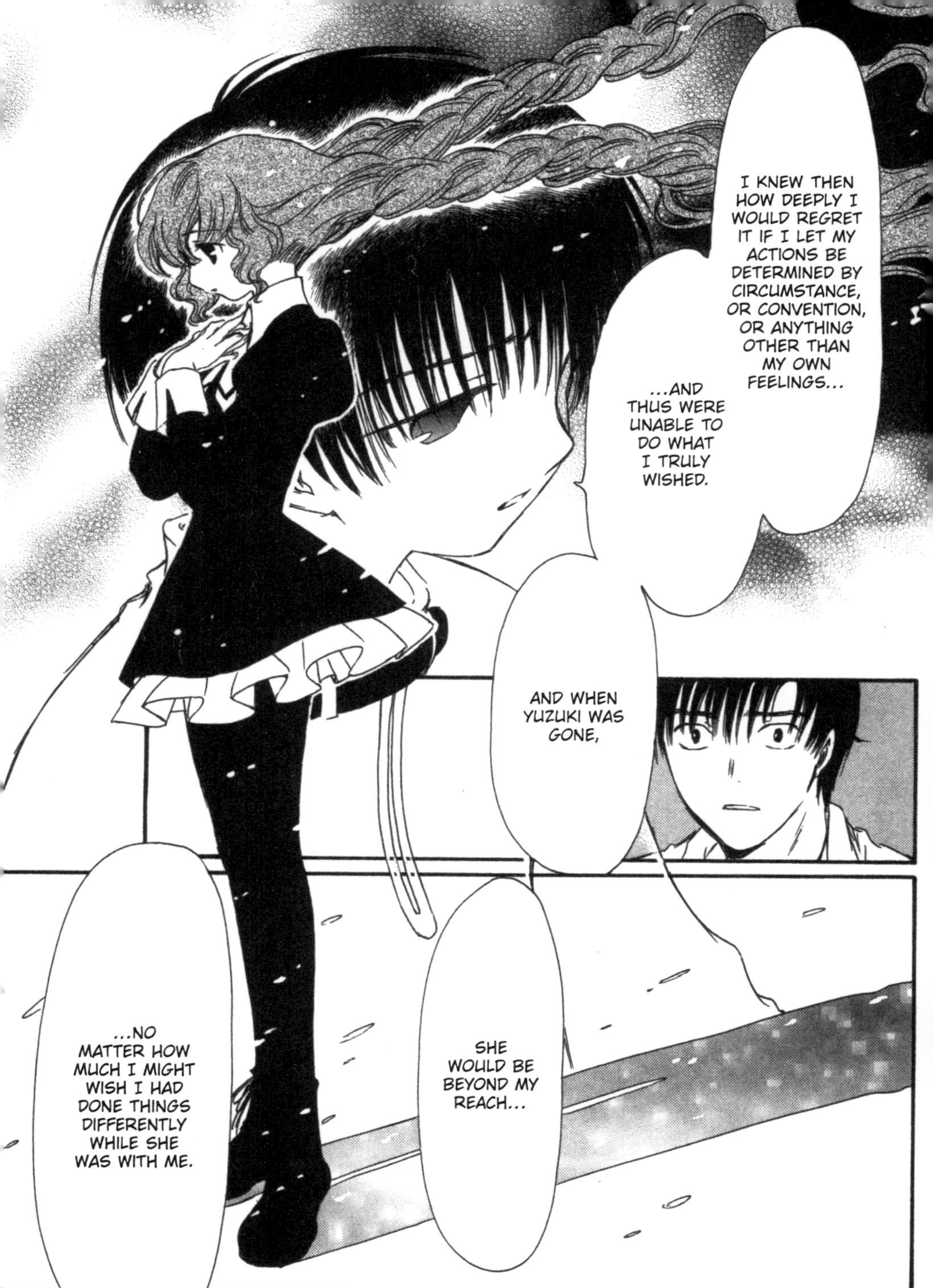
I KNEW THEN HOW DEEPLY I WOULD REGRET IT IF I LET MY ACTIONS BE DETERMINED BY CIRCUMSTANCE, OR CONVENTION, OR ANYTHING OTHER THAN MY OWN FEELINGS...
...AND THUS WERE UNABLE TO DO WHAT I TRULY WISHED.
AND WHEN YUZUKI WAS GONE,
SHE WOULD BE BEYOND MY REACH...
...NO MATTER HOW MUCH I MIGHT WISH I HAD DONE THINGS DIFFERENTLY WHILE SHE WAS WITH ME.

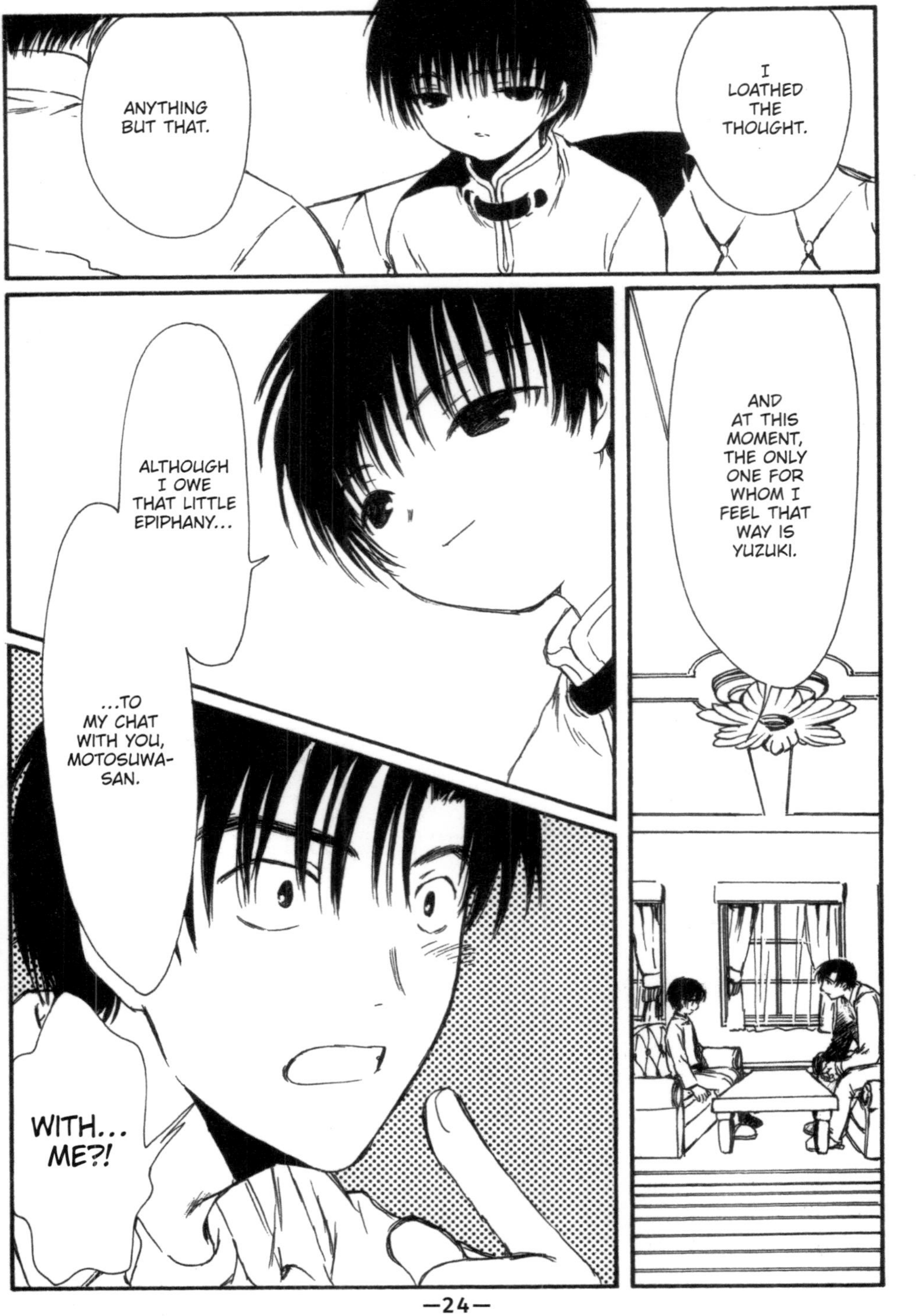
I LOATHED THE THOUGHT.
ANYTHING BUT THAT.
AND AT THIS MOMENT, THE ONLY ONE FOR WHOM I FEEL THAT WAY IS YUZUKI.
ALTHOUGH I OWE THAT LITTLE EPIPHANY...
...TO MY CHAT WITH YOU, MOTOSUWA-SAN.
WITH... ME?!

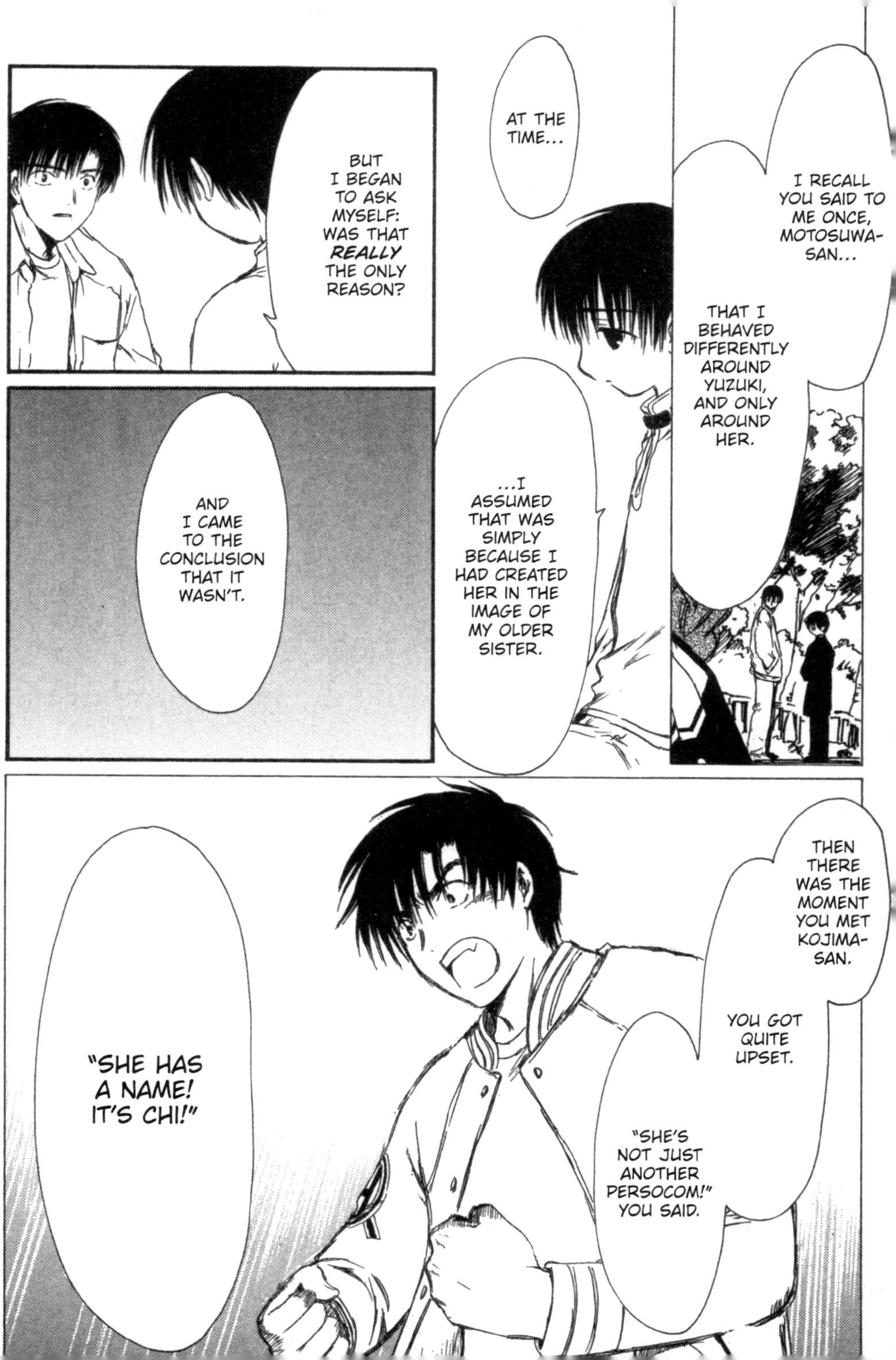
I RECALL YOU SAID TO ME ONCE, MOTOSUWA-SAN...
THAT I BEHAVED DIFFERENTLY AROUND YUZUKI, AND ONLY AROUND HER.
AT THE TIME...
...I ASSUMED THAT WAS SIMPLY BECAUSE I HAD CREATED HER IN THE IMAGE OF MY OLDER SISTER.
BUT I BEGAN TO ASK MYSELF: WAS THAT *REALLY* THE ONLY REASON?
AND I CAME TO THE CONCLUSION THAT IT WASN'T.
THEN THERE WAS THE MOMENT YOU MET KOJIMA-SAN.
YOU GOT QUITE UPSET.
"SHE'S NOT JUST ANOTHER PERSOCOM!" YOU SAID.
"SHE HAS A NAME! IT'S CHI!"

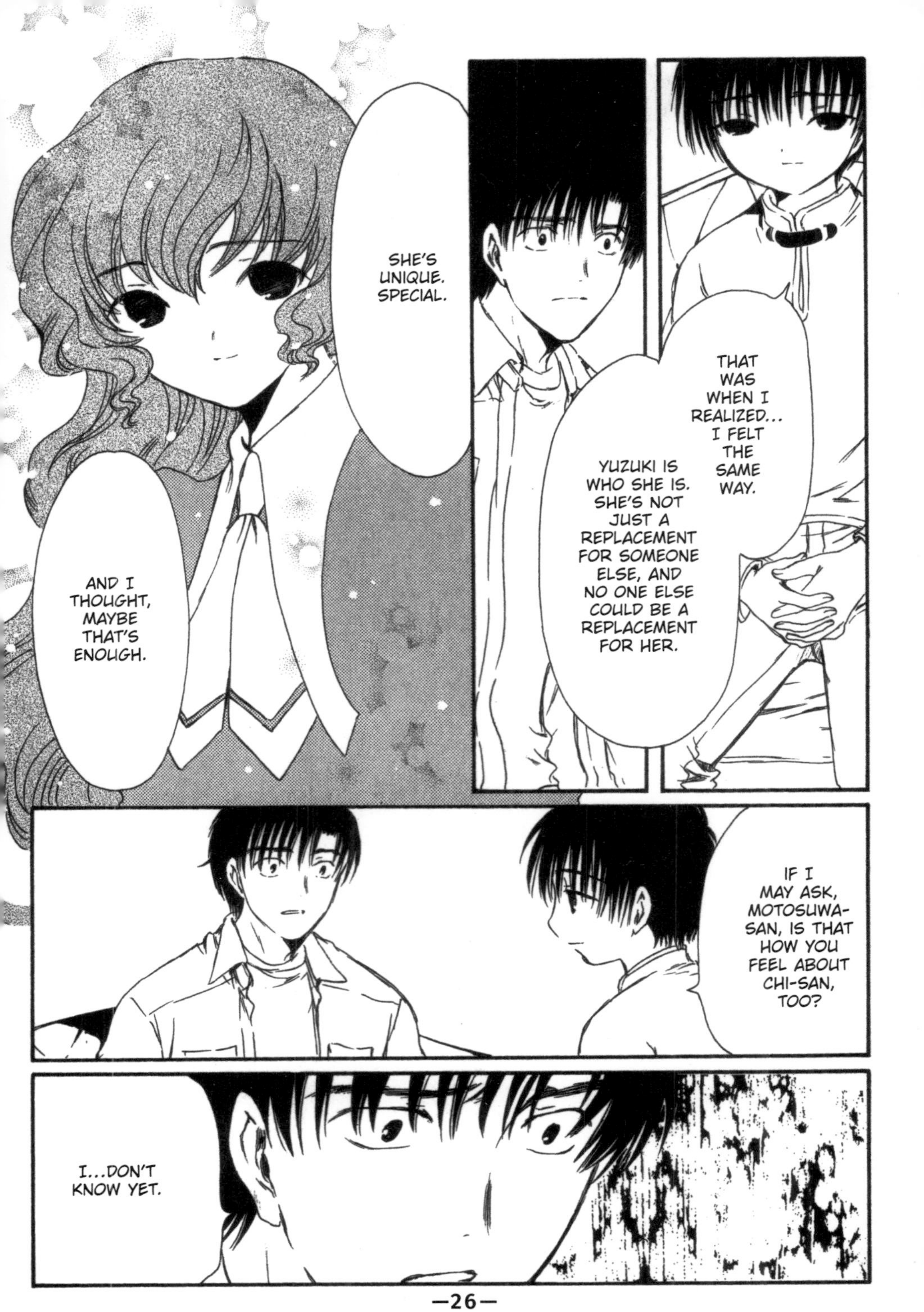
THAT WAS WHEN I REALIZED... I FELT THE SAME WAY.
YUZUKI IS WHO SHE IS. SHE'S NOT JUST A REPLACEMENT FOR SOMEONE ELSE, AND NO ONE ELSE COULD BE A REPLACEMENT FOR HER.
SHE'S UNIQUE. SPECIAL.
AND I THOUGHT, MAYBE THAT'S ENOUGH.
IF I MAY ASK, MOTOSUWA-SAN, IS THAT HOW YOU FEEL ABOUT CHI-SAN, TOO?
I...DON'T KNOW YET.

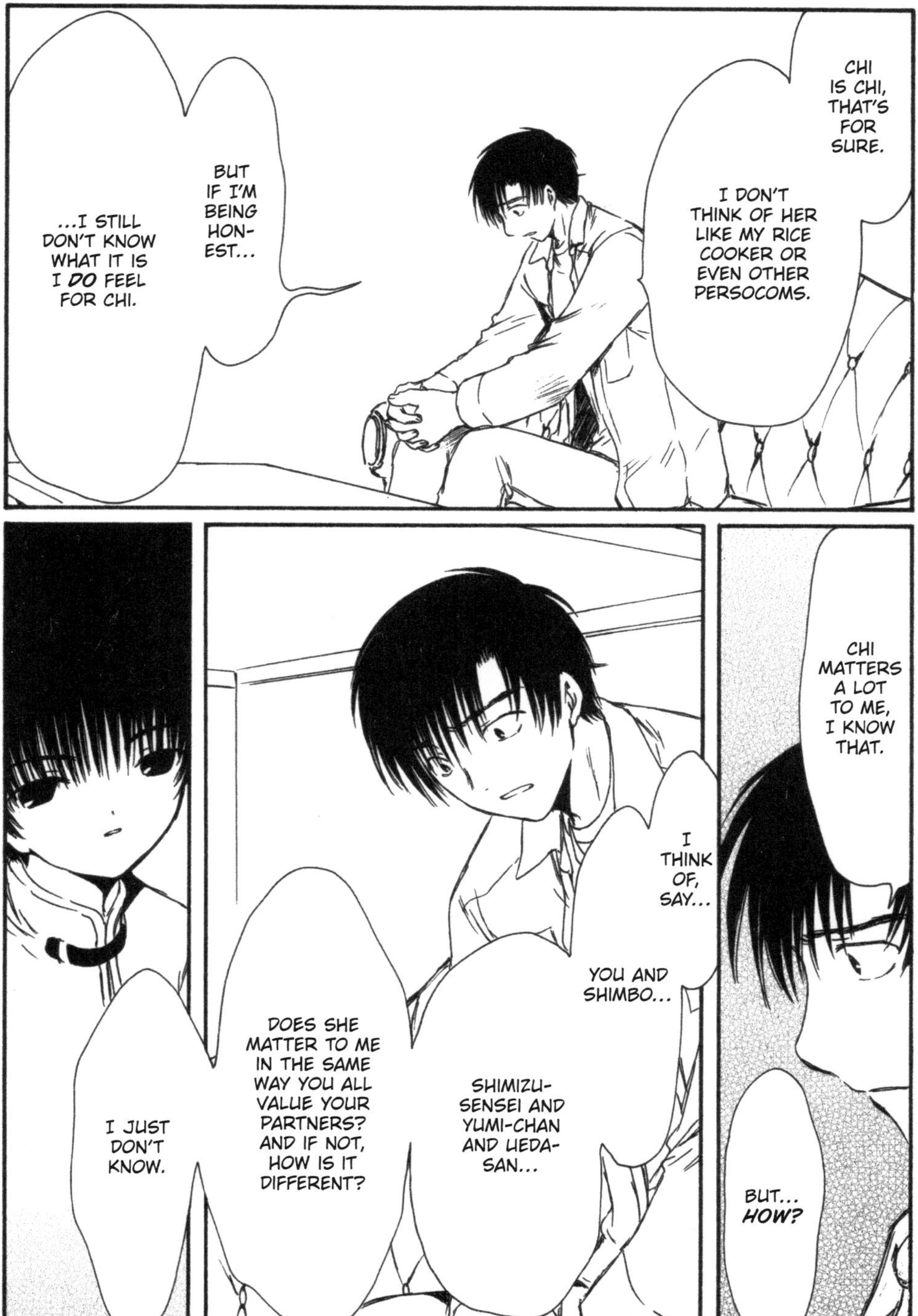
CHI IS CHI, THAT'S FOR SURE.
I DON'T THINK OF HER LIKE MY RICE COOKER OR EVEN OTHER PERSOCOMS.
BUT IF I'M BEING HON-EST...
...I STILL DON'T KNOW WHAT IT IS I *DO* FEEL FOR CHI.
CHI MATTERS A LOT TO ME, I KNOW THAT.
BUT... ***HOW?***
I THINK OF, SAY...
YOU AND SHIMBO...
SHIMIZU-SENSEI AND YUMI-CHAN AND UEDA-SAN...
DOES SHE MATTER TO ME IN THE SAME WAY YOU ALL VALUE YOUR PARTNERS? AND IF NOT, HOW IS IT DIFFERENT?
I JUST DON'T KNOW.

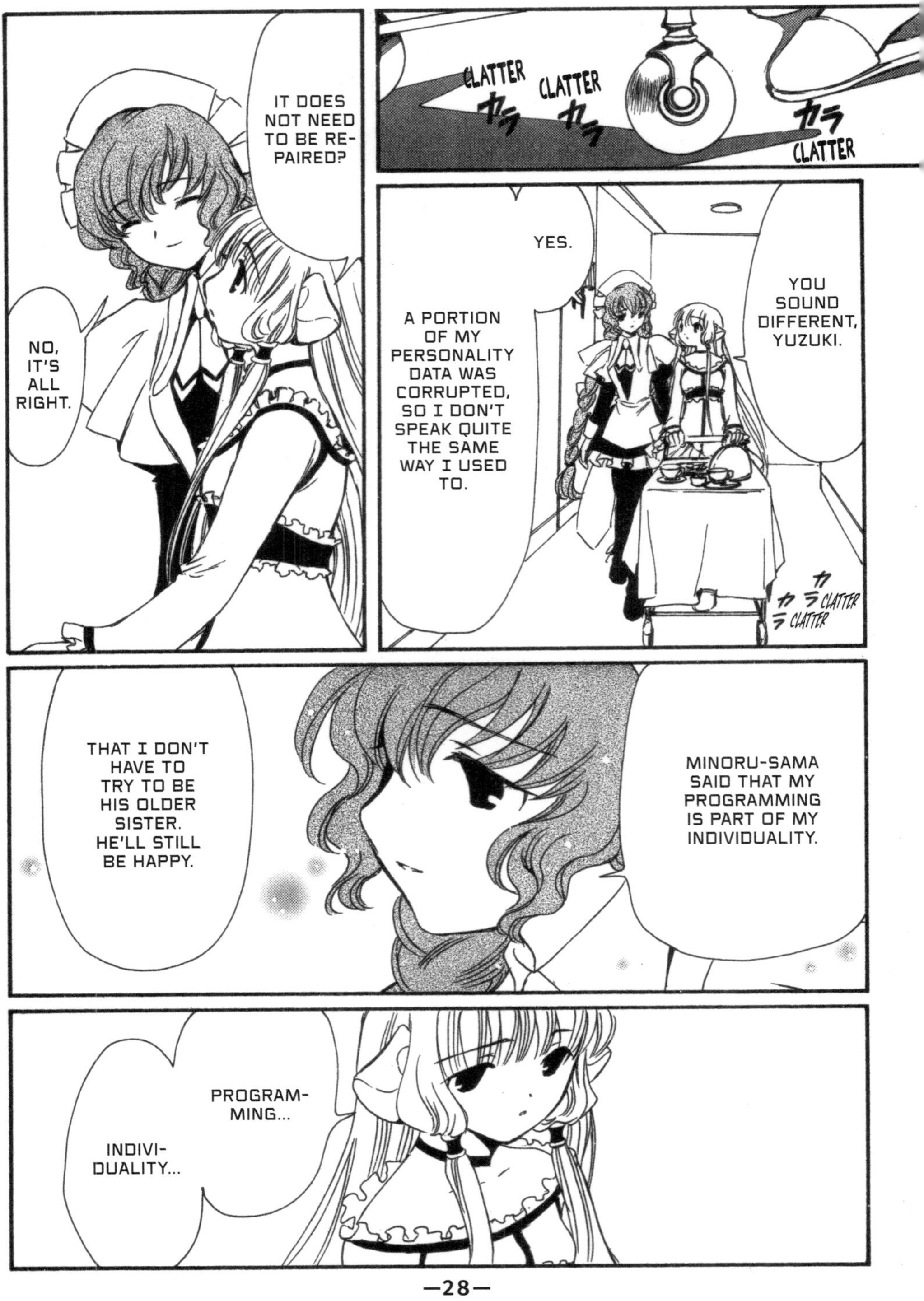
CLATTER カラ
CLATTER カラ
カラ CLATTER
YOU SOUND DIFFERENT, YUZUKI.
YES.
A PORTION OF MY PERSONALITY DATA WAS CORRUPTED, SO I DON'T SPEAK QUITE THE SAME WAY I USED TO.
カラ CLATTER
カラ CLATTER
IT DOES NOT NEED TO BE RE-PAIRED?
NO, IT'S ALL RIGHT.
MINORU-SAMA SAID THAT MY PROGRAMMING IS PART OF MY INDIVIDUALITY.
THAT I DON'T HAVE TO TRY TO BE HIS OLDER SISTER. HE'LL STILL BE HAPPY.
PROGRAM-MING...
INDIVI-DUALITY...

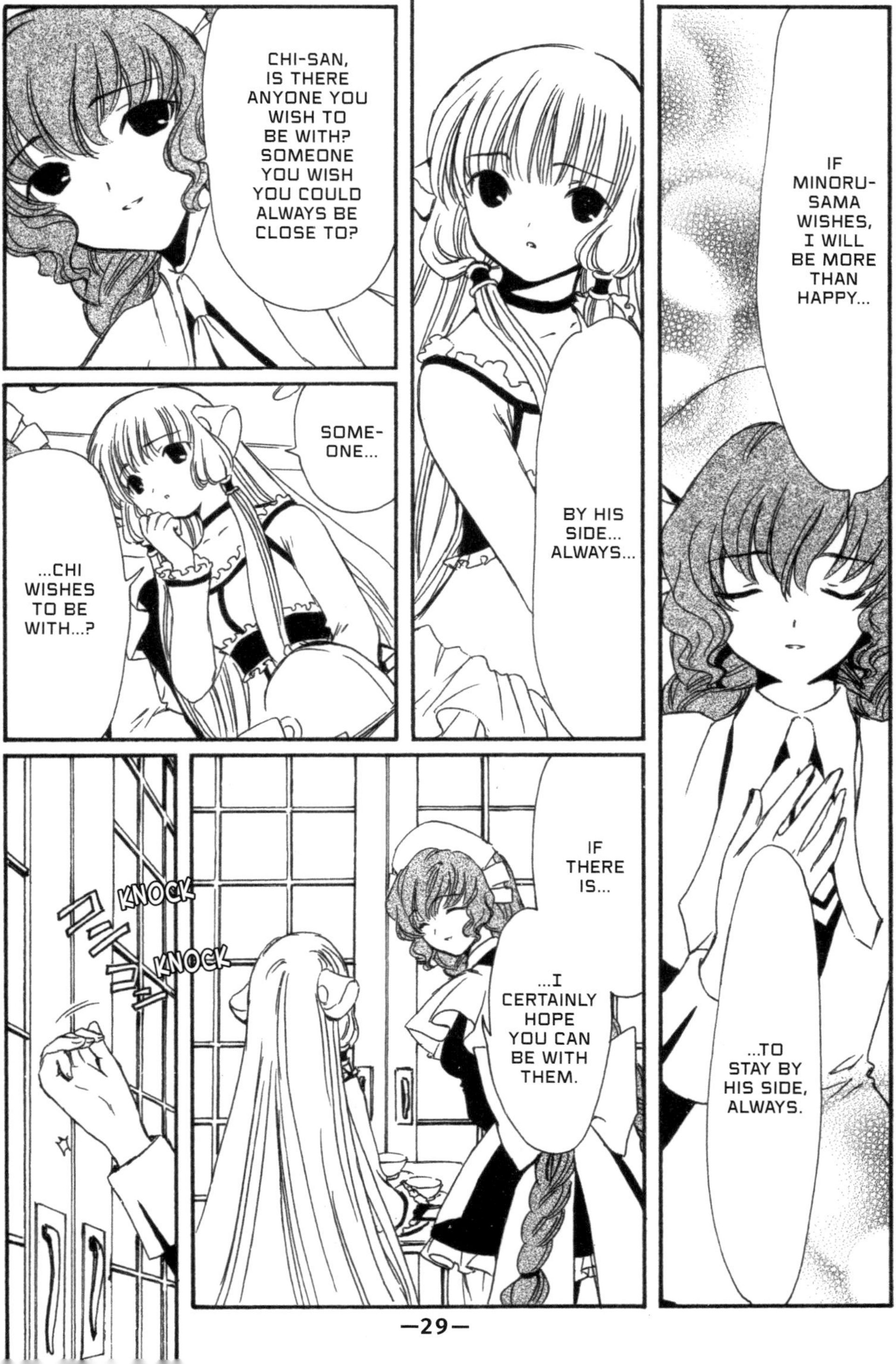
IF MINORU-SAMA WISHES, I WILL BE MORE THAN HAPPY...
...TO STAY BY HIS SIDE, ALWAYS.
BY HIS SIDE... ALWAYS...
CHI-SAN, IS THERE ANYONE YOU WISH TO BE WITH? SOMEONE YOU WISH YOU COULD ALWAYS BE CLOSE TO?
SOME-ONE...
...CHI WISHES TO BE WITH...?
IF THERE IS...
...I CERTAINLY HOPE YOU CAN BE WITH THEM.
KNOCK
KNOCK

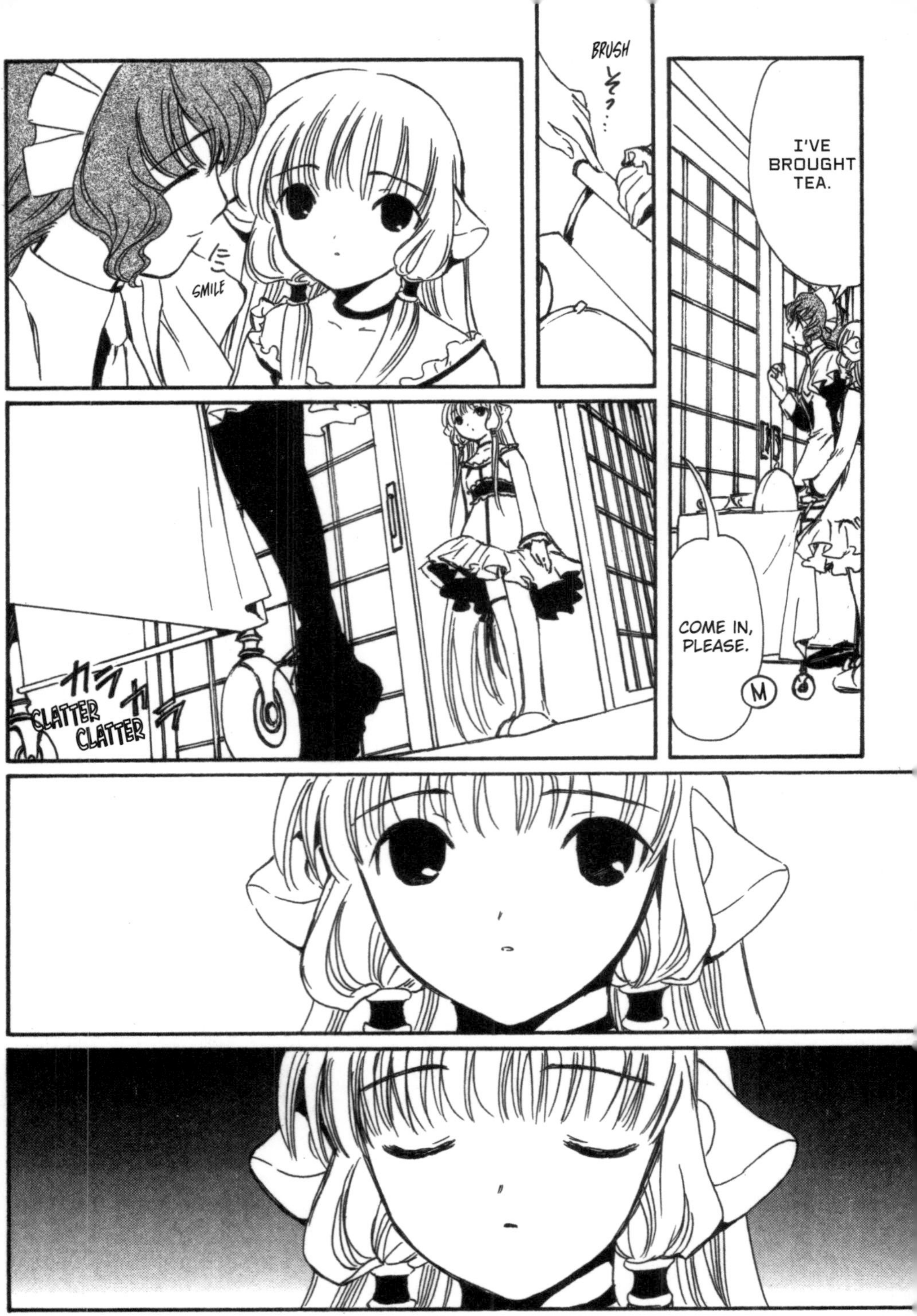
I'VE BROUGHT TEA.
COME IN, PLEASE.
M
BRUSH
SMILE
CLATTER CLATTER

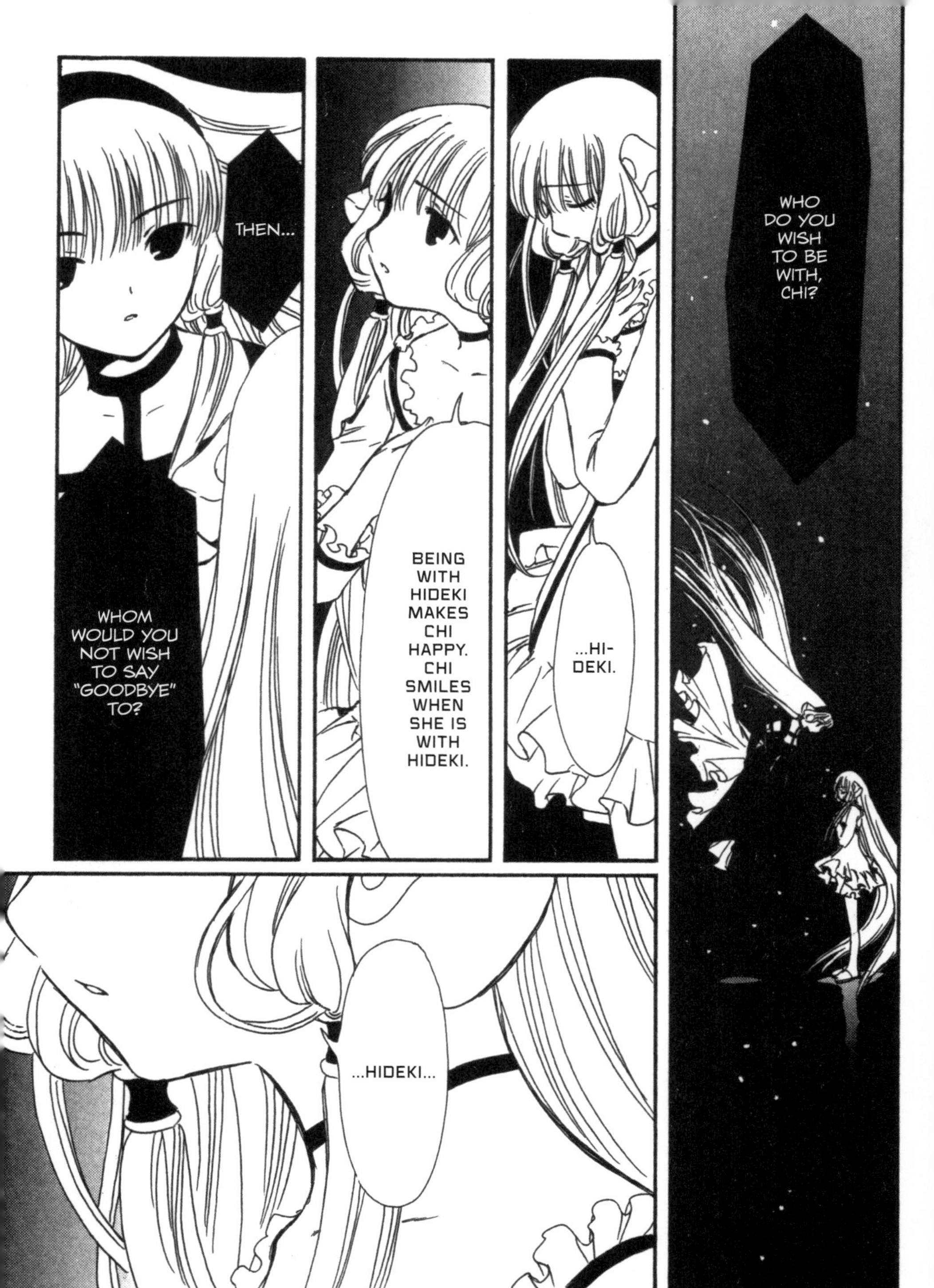
WHO DO YOU WISH TO BE WITH, CHI?
...HI-DEKI.
BEING WITH HIDEKI MAKES CHI HAPPY. CHI SMILES WHEN SHE IS WITH HIDEKI.
THEN...
WHOM WOULD YOU NOT WISH TO SAY "GOODBYE" TO?
...HIDEKI...

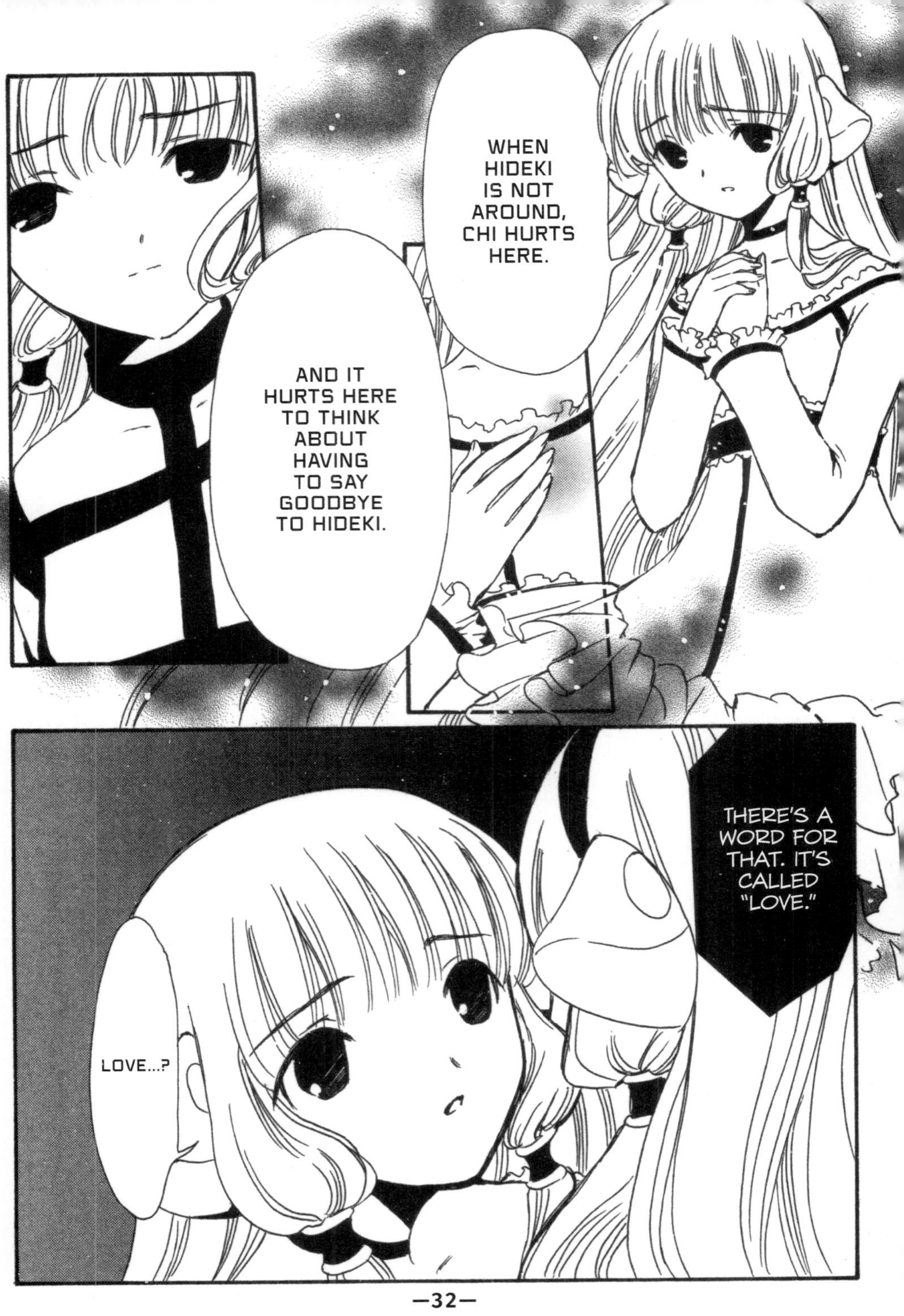
WHEN HIDEKI IS NOT AROUND, CHI HURTS HERE.
AND IT HURTS HERE TO THINK ABOUT HAVING TO SAY GOODBYE TO HIDEKI.
THERE'S A WORD FOR THAT. IT'S CALLED "LOVE."
LOVE...?

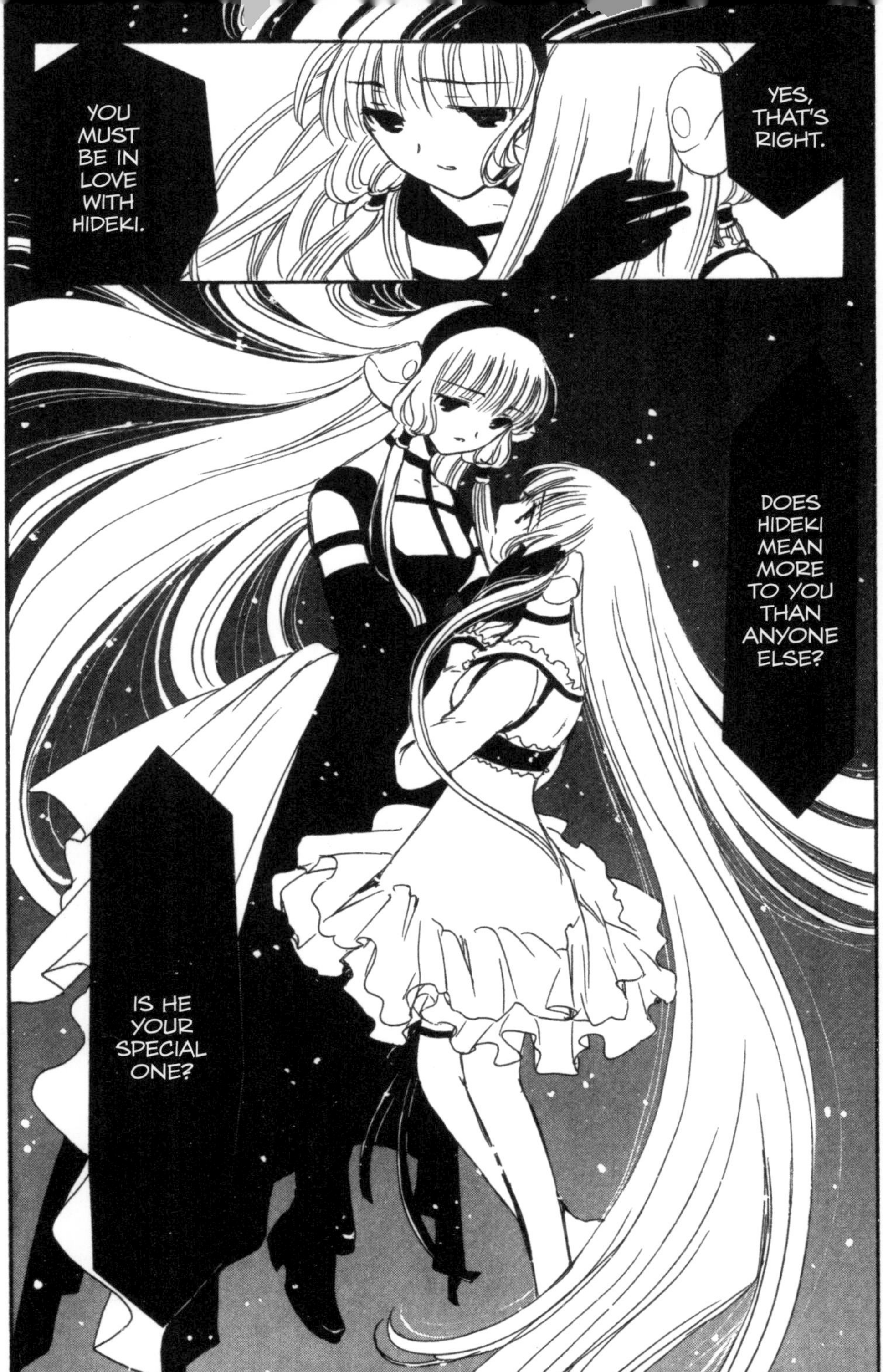
YES, THAT'S RIGHT.
YOU MUST BE IN LOVE WITH HIDEKI.
DOES HIDEKI MEAN MORE TO YOU THAN ANYONE ELSE?
IS HE YOUR SPECIAL ONE?

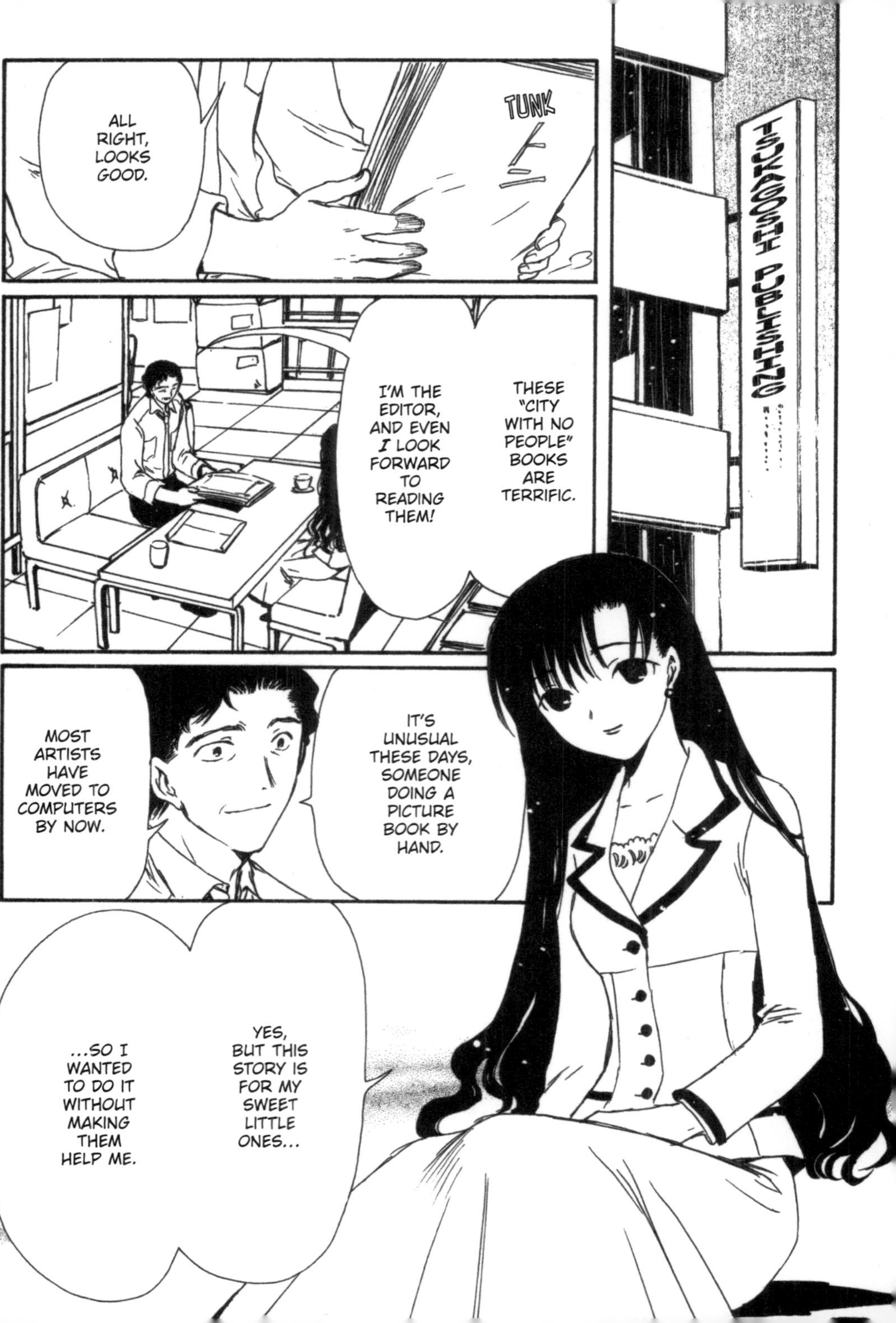
TSUKAGOSHI PUBLISHING
TUNK
ALL RIGHT, LOOKS GOOD.
THESE "CITY WITH NO PEOPLE" BOOKS ARE TERRIFIC.
I'M THE EDITOR, AND EVEN *I* LOOK FORWARD TO READING THEM!
IT'S UNUSUAL THESE DAYS, SOMEONE DOING A PICTURE BOOK BY HAND.
MOST ARTISTS HAVE MOVED TO COMPUTERS BY NOW.
YES, BUT THIS STORY IS FOR MY SWEET LITTLE ONES...
...SO I WANTED TO DO IT WITHOUT MAKING THEM HELP ME.

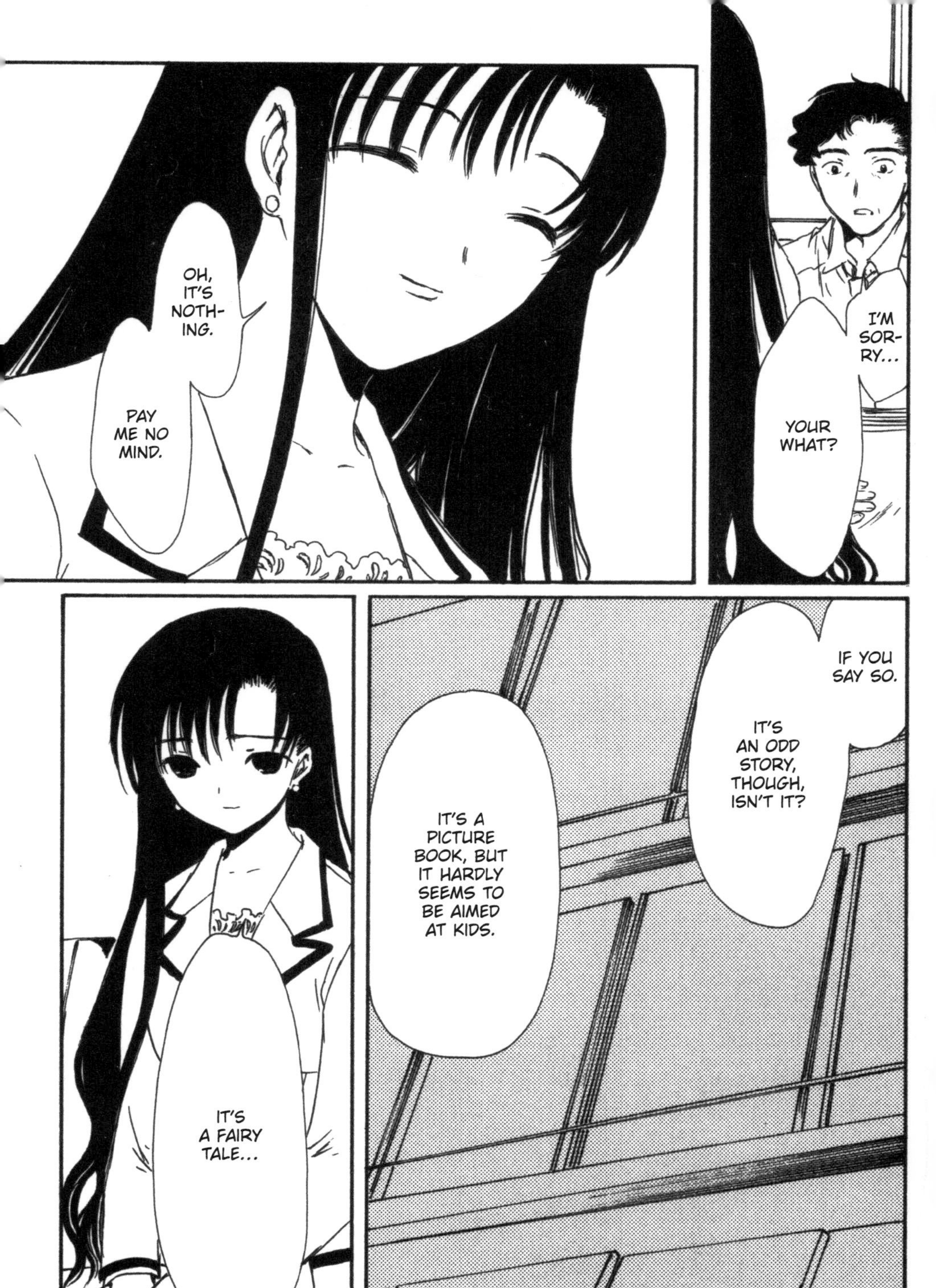
I'M SORRY...
YOUR WHAT?
OH, IT'S NOTHING.
PAY ME NO MIND.
IF YOU SAY SO.
IT'S AN ODD STORY, THOUGH, ISN'T IT?
IT'S A PICTURE BOOK, BUT IT HARDLY SEEMS TO BE AIMED AT KIDS.
IT'S A FAIRY TALE...

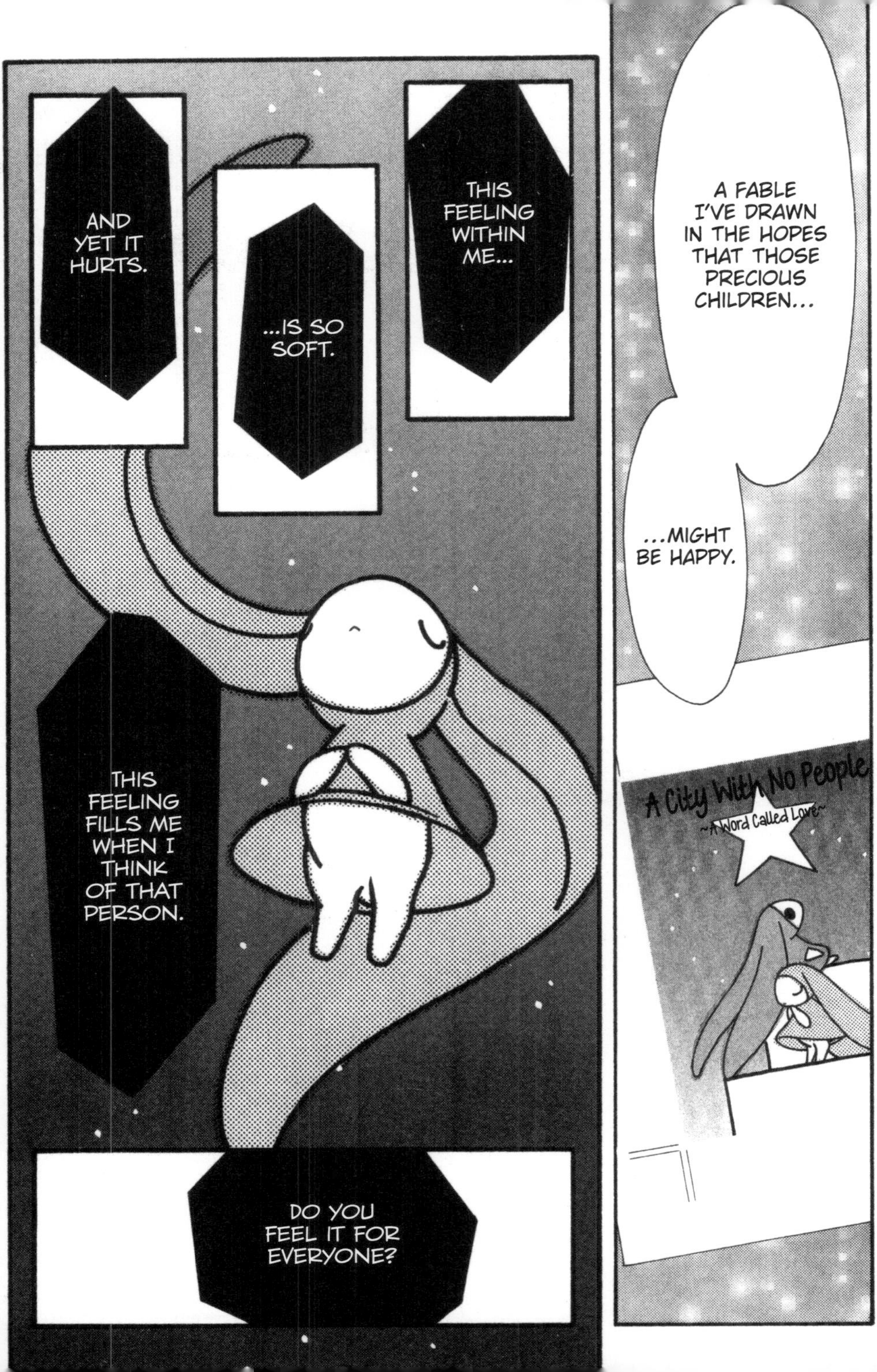
A FABLE I'VE DRAWN IN THE HOPES THAT THOSE PRECIOUS CHILDREN...
...MIGHT BE HAPPY.
A City With No People
~A Word Called Love~
THIS FEELING WITHIN ME...
...IS SO SOFT.
AND YET IT HURTS.
THIS FEELING FILLS ME WHEN I THINK OF THAT PERSON.
DO YOU FEEL IT FOR EVERYONE?

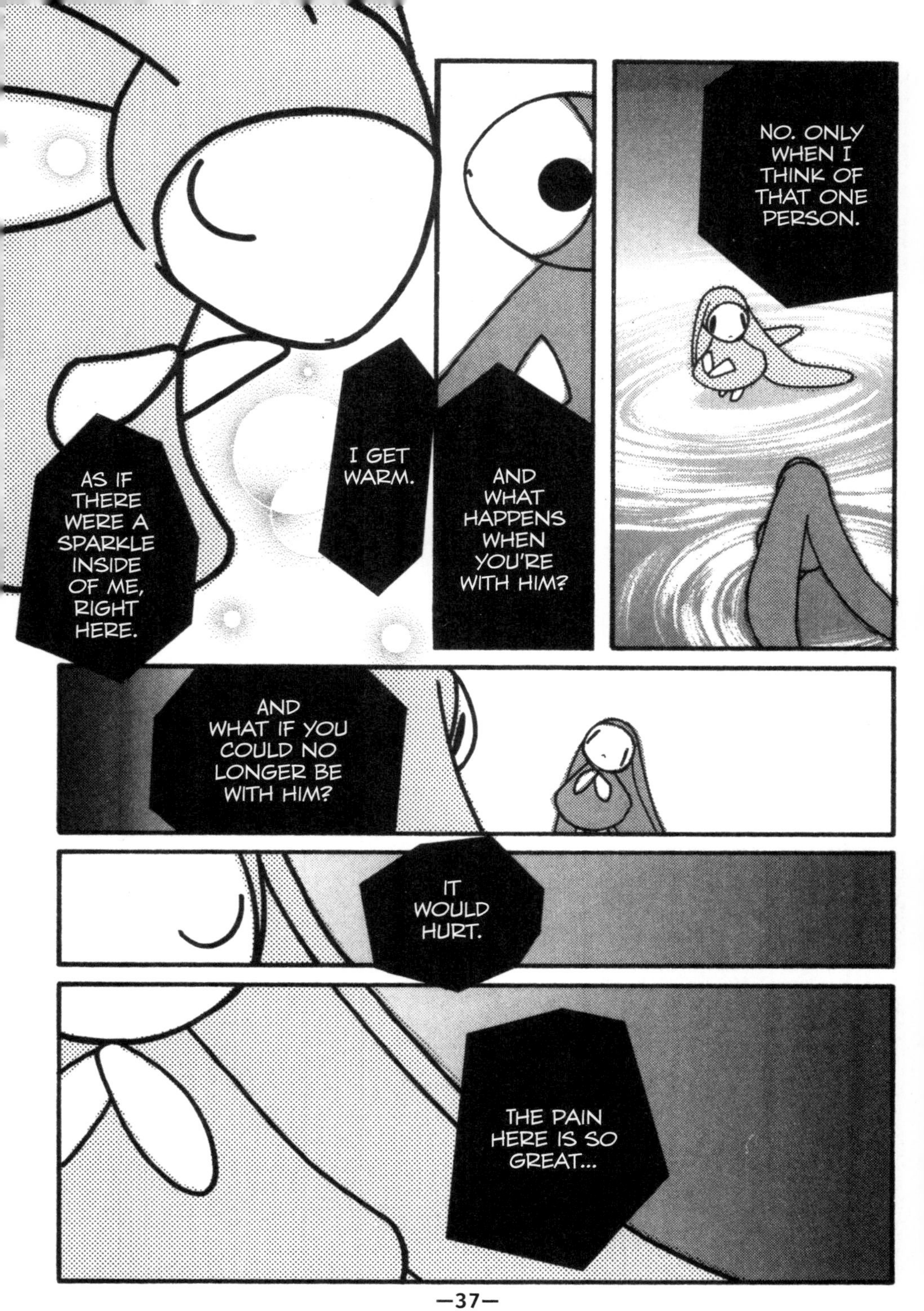
NO. ONLY WHEN I THINK OF THAT ONE PERSON.
AND WHAT HAPPENS WHEN YOU'RE WITH HIM?
I GET WARM.
AS IF THERE WERE A SPARKLE INSIDE OF ME, RIGHT HERE.
AND WHAT IF YOU COULD NO LONGER BE WITH HIM?
IT WOULD HURT.
THE PAIN HERE IS SO GREAT...

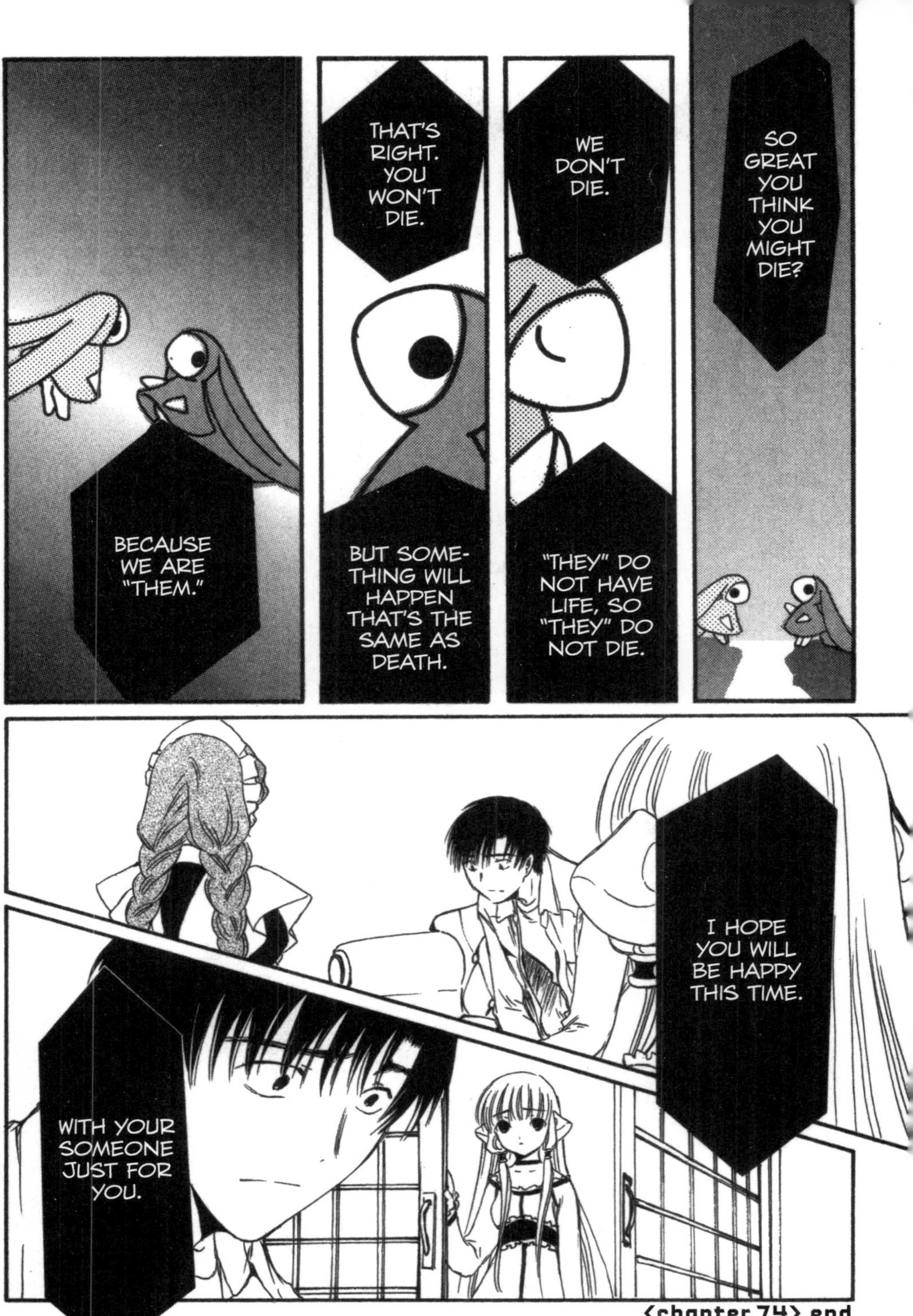
SO GREAT YOU THINK YOU MIGHT DIE?
WE DON'T DIE.
"THEY" DO NOT HAVE LIFE, SO "THEY" DO NOT DIE.
THAT'S RIGHT. YOU WON'T DIE.
BUT SOME-THING WILL HAPPEN THAT'S THE SAME AS DEATH.
BECAUSE WE ARE "THEM."
I HOPE YOU WILL BE HAPPY THIS TIME.
WITH YOUR SOMEONE JUST FOR YOU.

<chapter.74> end

## <chapter.75>

Chobits

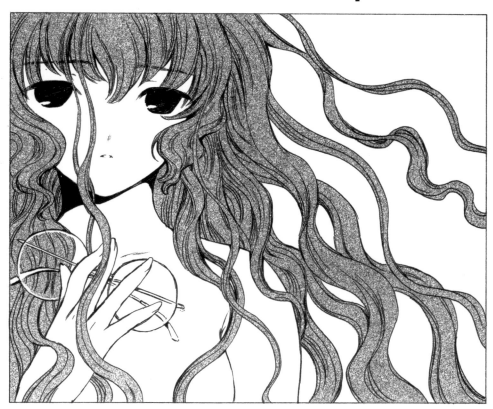

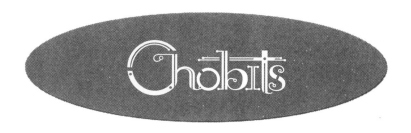

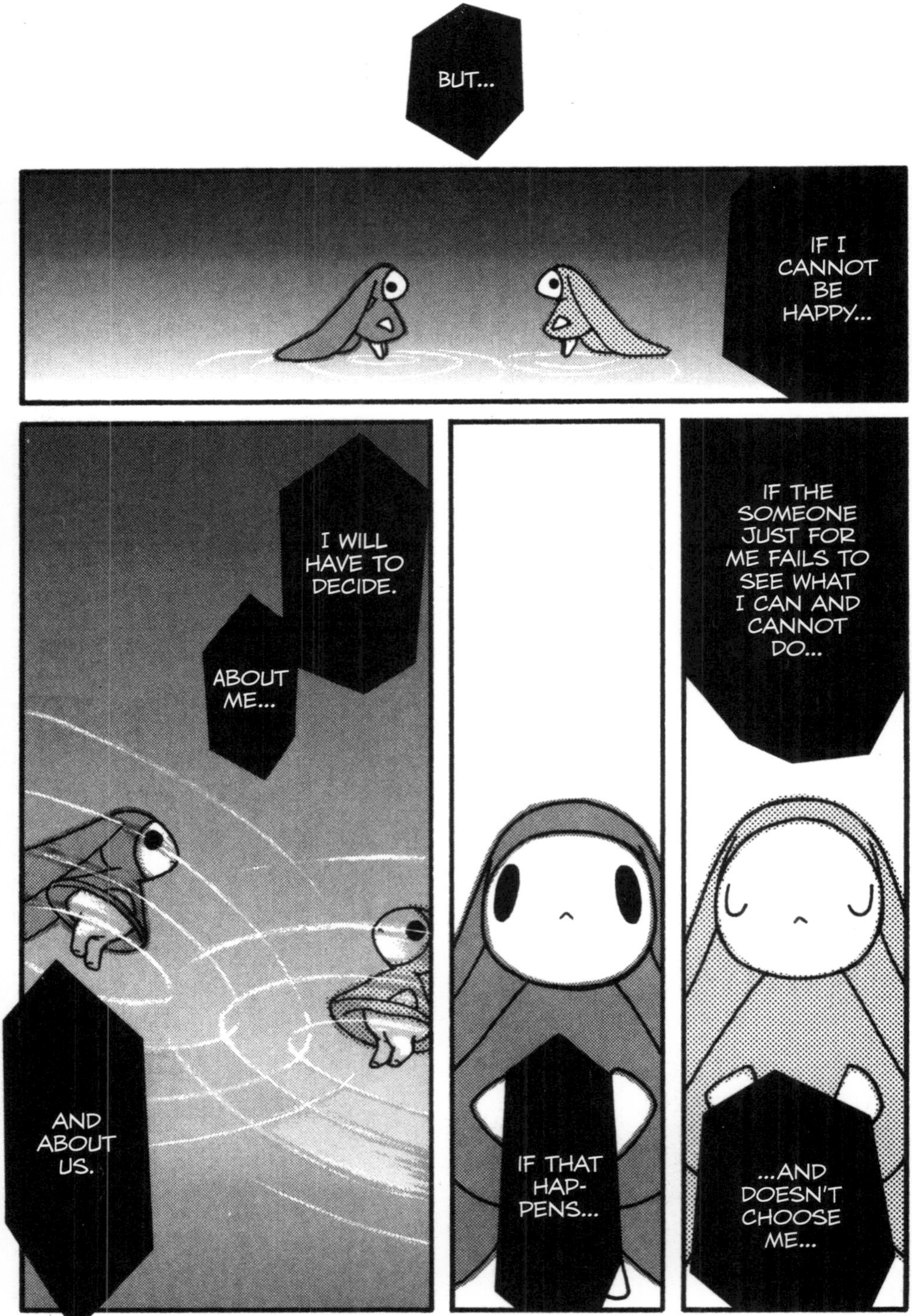
BUT...
IF I CANNOT BE HAPPY...
IF THE SOMEONE JUST FOR ME FAILS TO SEE WHAT I CAN AND CANNOT DO...
...AND DOESN'T CHOOSE ME...
IF THAT HAP-PENS...
I WILL HAVE TO DECIDE.
ABOUT ME...
AND ABOUT US.

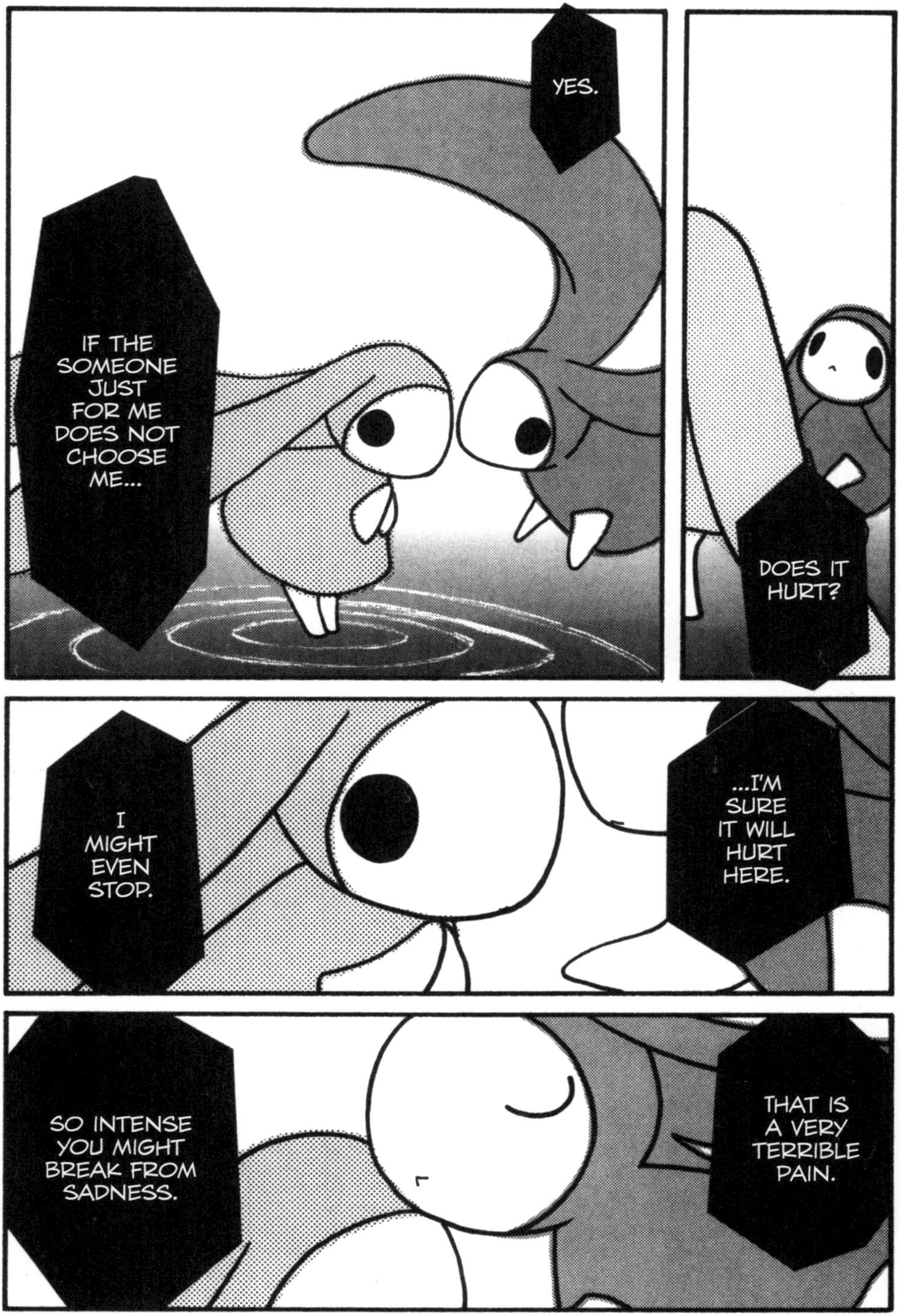
DOES IT HURT?
YES.
IF THE SOMEONE JUST FOR ME DOES NOT CHOOSE ME...
...I'M SURE IT WILL HURT HERE.
I MIGHT EVEN STOP.
THAT IS A VERY TERRIBLE PAIN.
SO INTENSE YOU MIGHT BREAK FROM SADNESS.

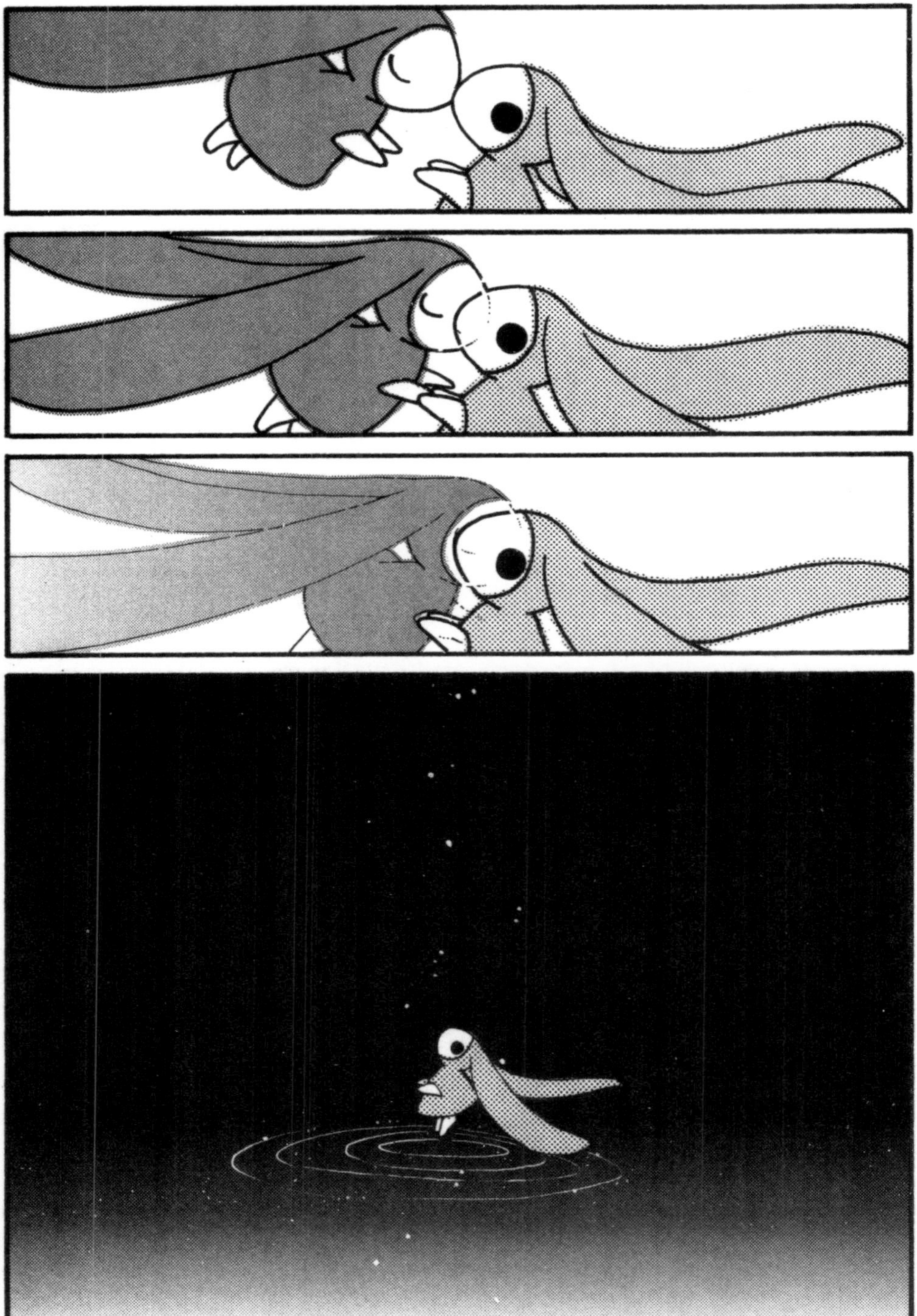

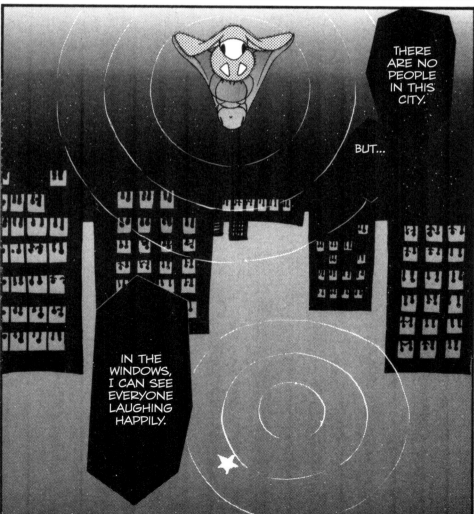

THERE ARE NO PEOPLE IN THIS CITY.

BUT...

IN THE WINDOWS, I CAN SEE EVERYONE LAUGHING HAPPILY.

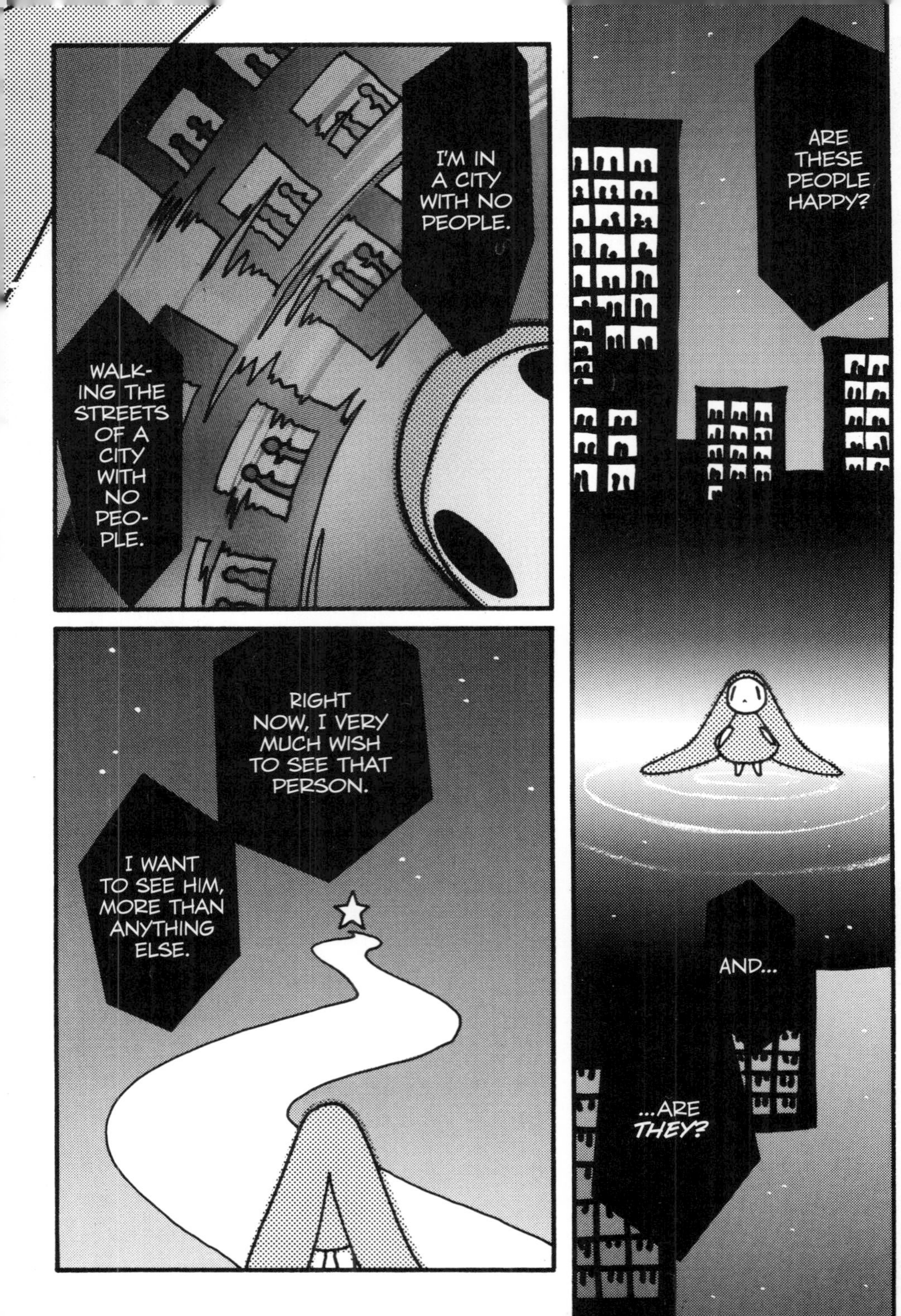
ARE THESE PEOPLE HAPPY?
AND...
...ARE THEY?
I'M IN A CITY WITH NO PEOPLE.
WALKING THE STREETS OF A CITY WITH NO PEOPLE.
RIGHT NOW, I VERY MUCH WISH TO SEE THAT PERSON.
I WANT TO SEE HIM, MORE THAN ANYTHING ELSE.

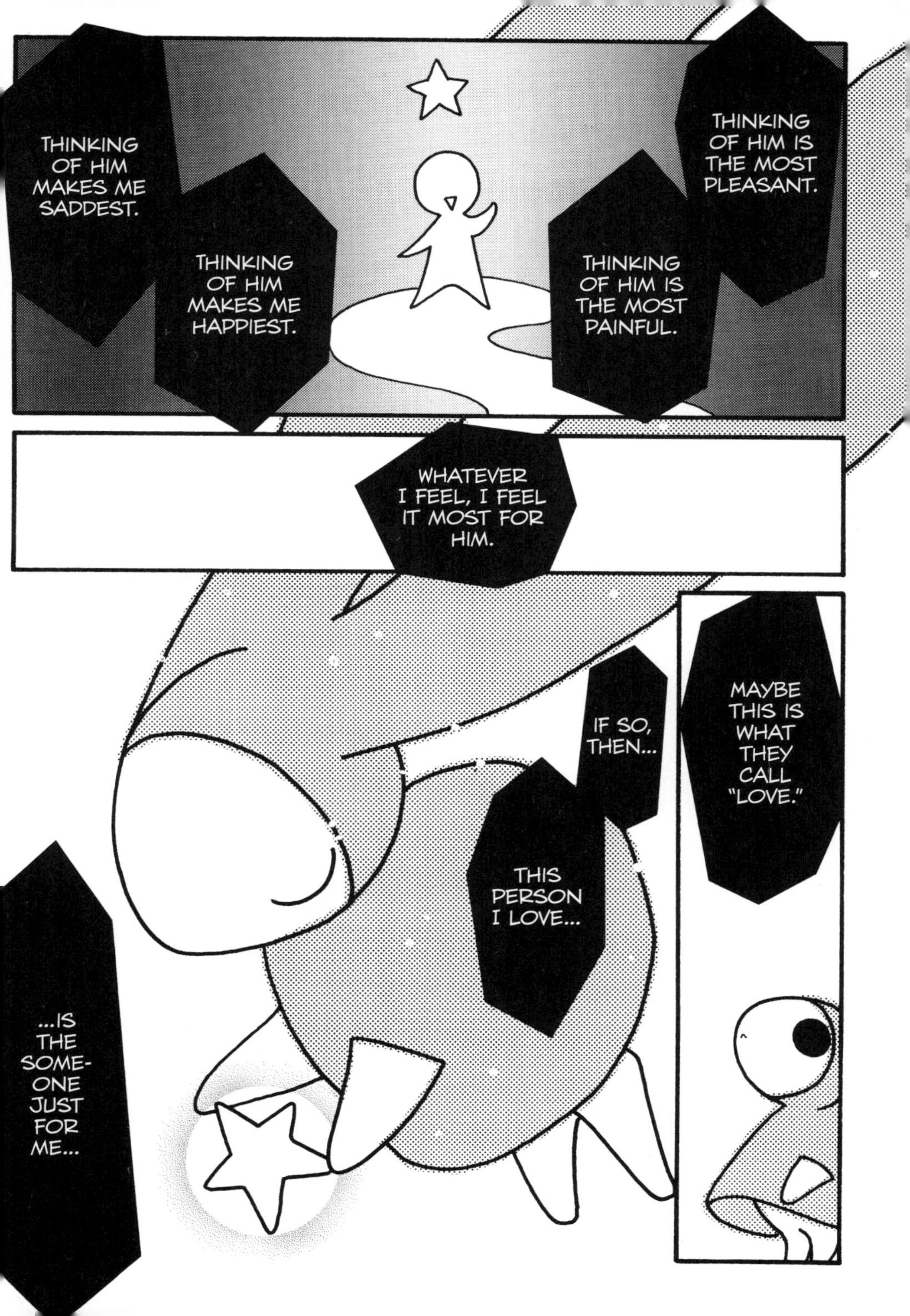
THINKING OF HIM IS THE MOST PLEASANT.
THINKING OF HIM IS THE MOST PAINFUL.
THINKING OF HIM MAKES ME SADDEST.
THINKING OF HIM MAKES ME HAPPIEST.
WHATEVER I FEEL, I FEEL IT MOST FOR HIM.
MAYBE THIS IS WHAT THEY CALL "LOVE."
IF SO, THEN...
THIS PERSON I LOVE...
...IS THE SOME-ONE JUST FOR ME...

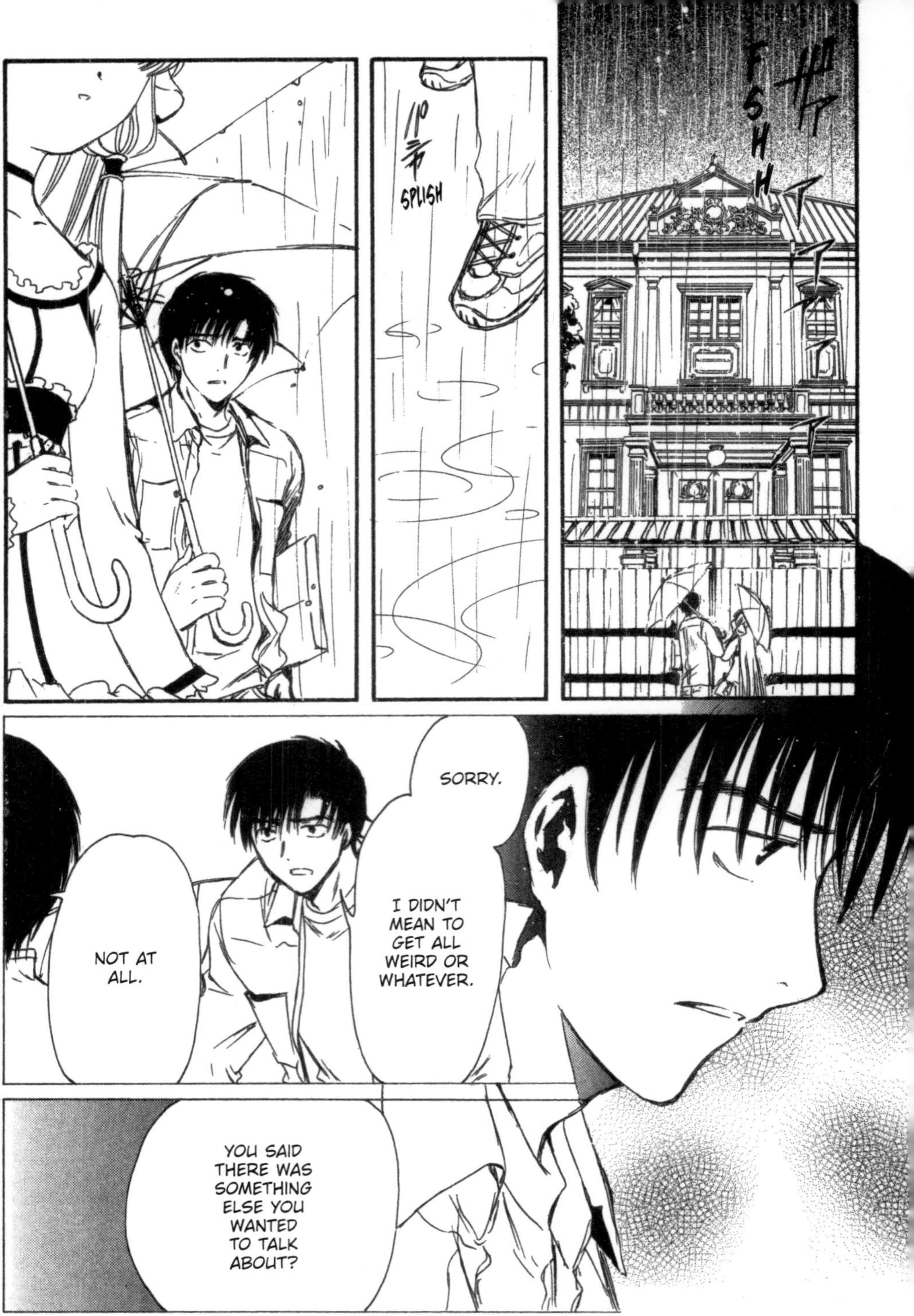
FSHHH
SPLISH
SORRY.
I DIDN'T MEAN TO GET ALL WEIRD OR WHATEVER.
NOT AT ALL.
YOU SAID THERE WAS SOMETHING ELSE YOU WANTED TO TALK ABOUT?

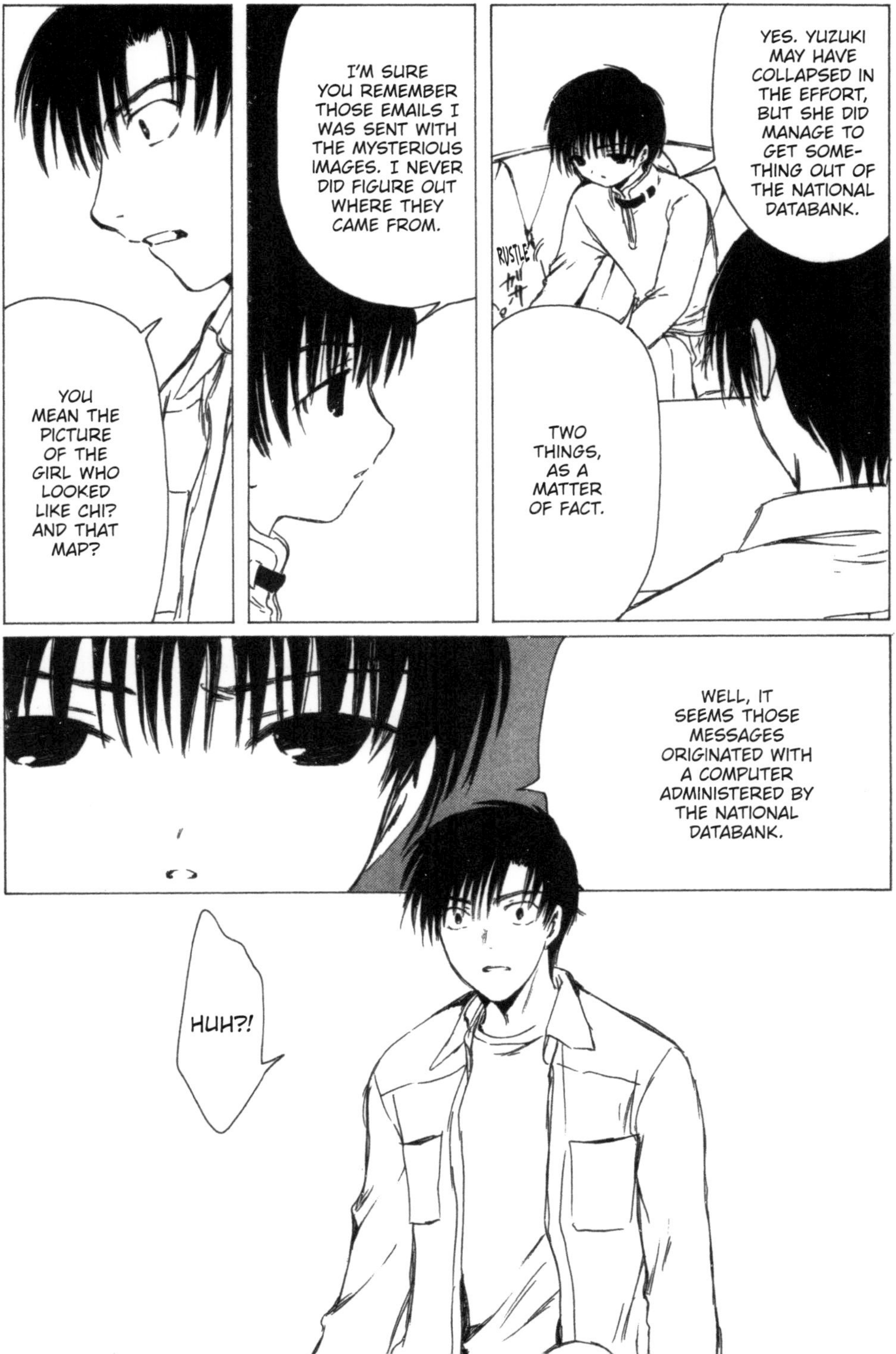
YES. YUZUKI MAY HAVE COLLAPSED IN THE EFFORT, BUT SHE DID MANAGE TO GET SOME-THING OUT OF THE NATIONAL DATABANK.
RUSTLE
TWO THINGS, AS A MATTER OF FACT.
I'M SURE YOU REMEMBER THOSE EMAILS I WAS SENT WITH THE MYSTERIOUS IMAGES. I NEVER DID FIGURE OUT WHERE THEY CAME FROM.
YOU MEAN THE PICTURE OF THE GIRL WHO LOOKED LIKE CHI? AND THAT MAP?
WELL, IT SEEMS THOSE MESSAGES ORIGINATED WITH A COMPUTER ADMINISTERED BY THE NATIONAL DATABANK.
HUH?!

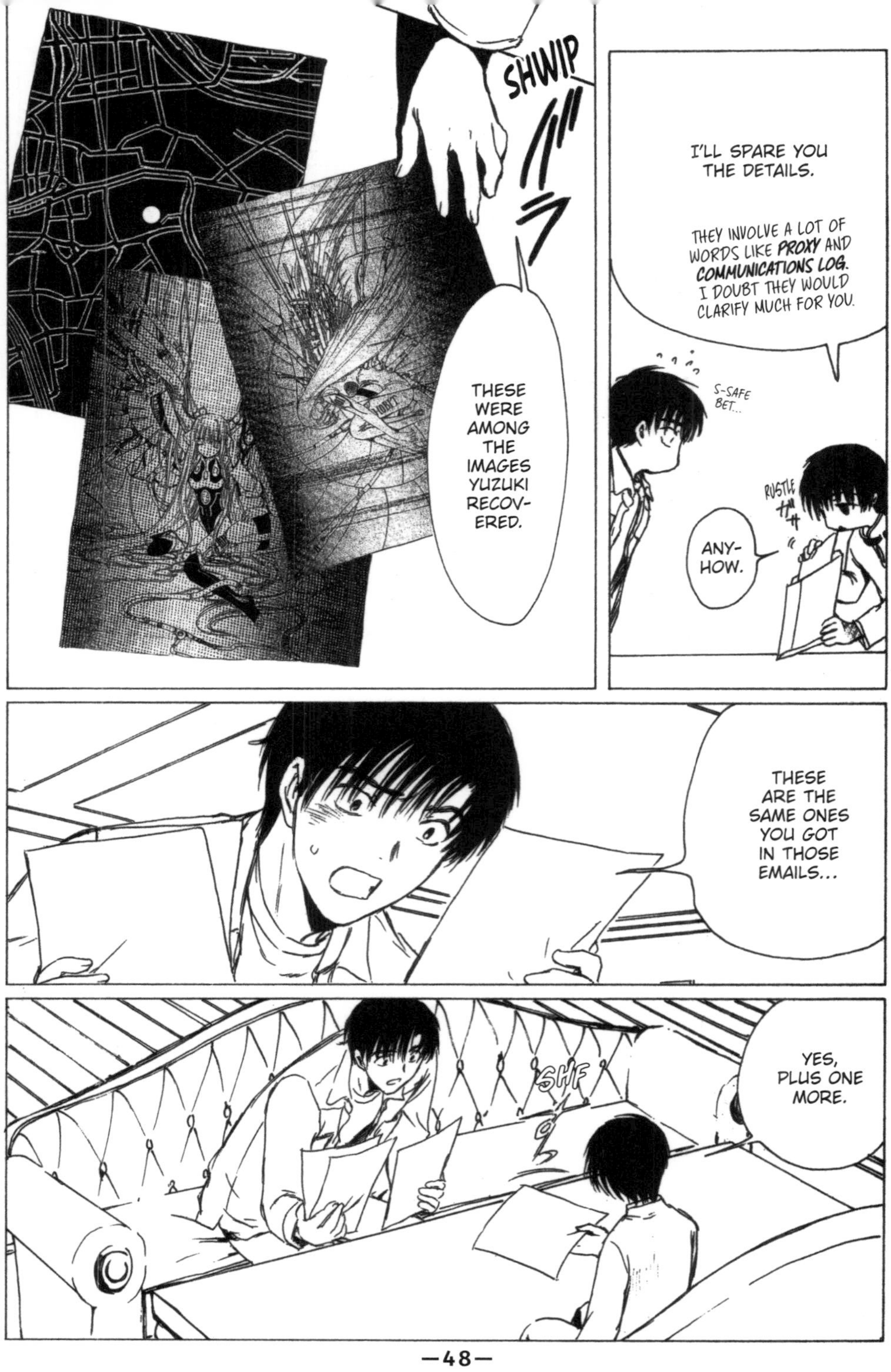
I'LL SPARE YOU THE DETAILS.
THEY INVOLVE A LOT OF WORDS LIKE **PROXY** AND **COMMUNICATIONS LOG**. I DOUBT THEY WOULD CLARIFY MUCH FOR YOU.
S-SAFE BET...
RUSTLE
ANY-HOW.
SHWIP
THESE WERE AMONG THE IMAGES YUZUKI RECOV-ERED.
THESE ARE THE SAME ONES YOU GOT IN THOSE EMAILS...
YES, PLUS ONE MORE.
SHF

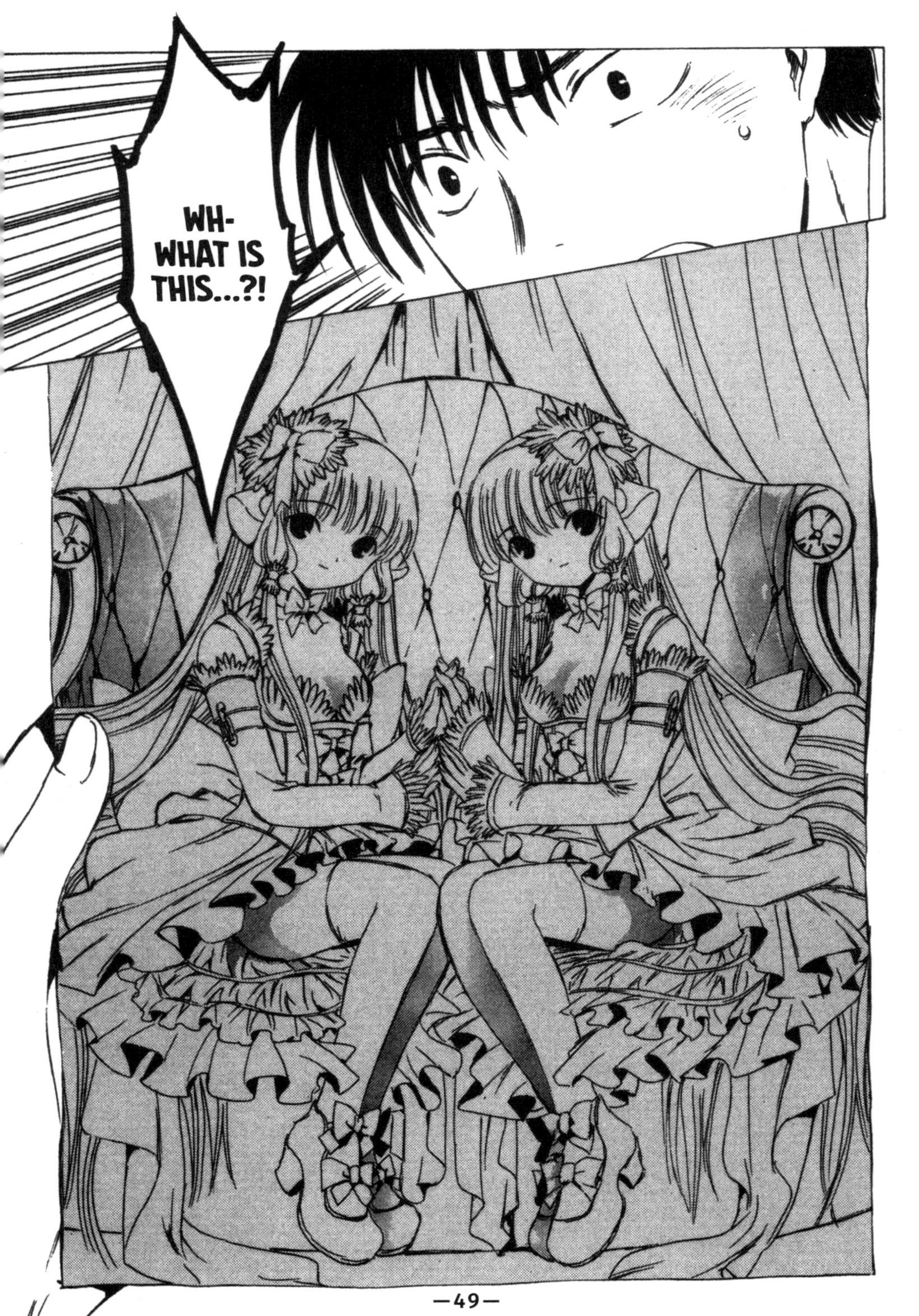
WH-
WHAT IS
THIS...?!

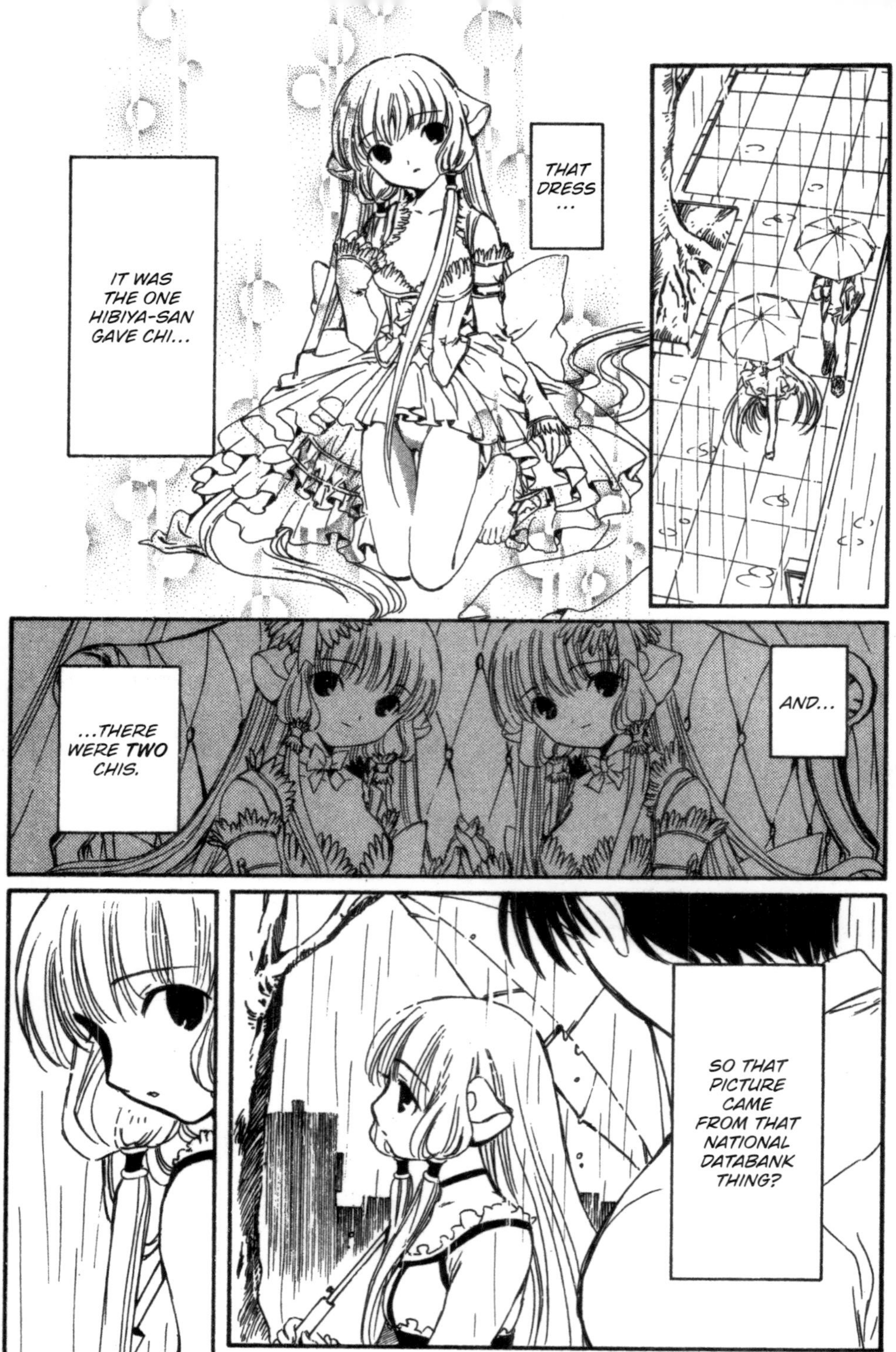
THAT DRESS ...
IT WAS THE ONE HIBIYA-SAN GAVE CHI...
AND...
...THERE WERE **TWO** CHIS.
SO THAT PICTURE CAME FROM THAT NATIONAL DATABANK THING?

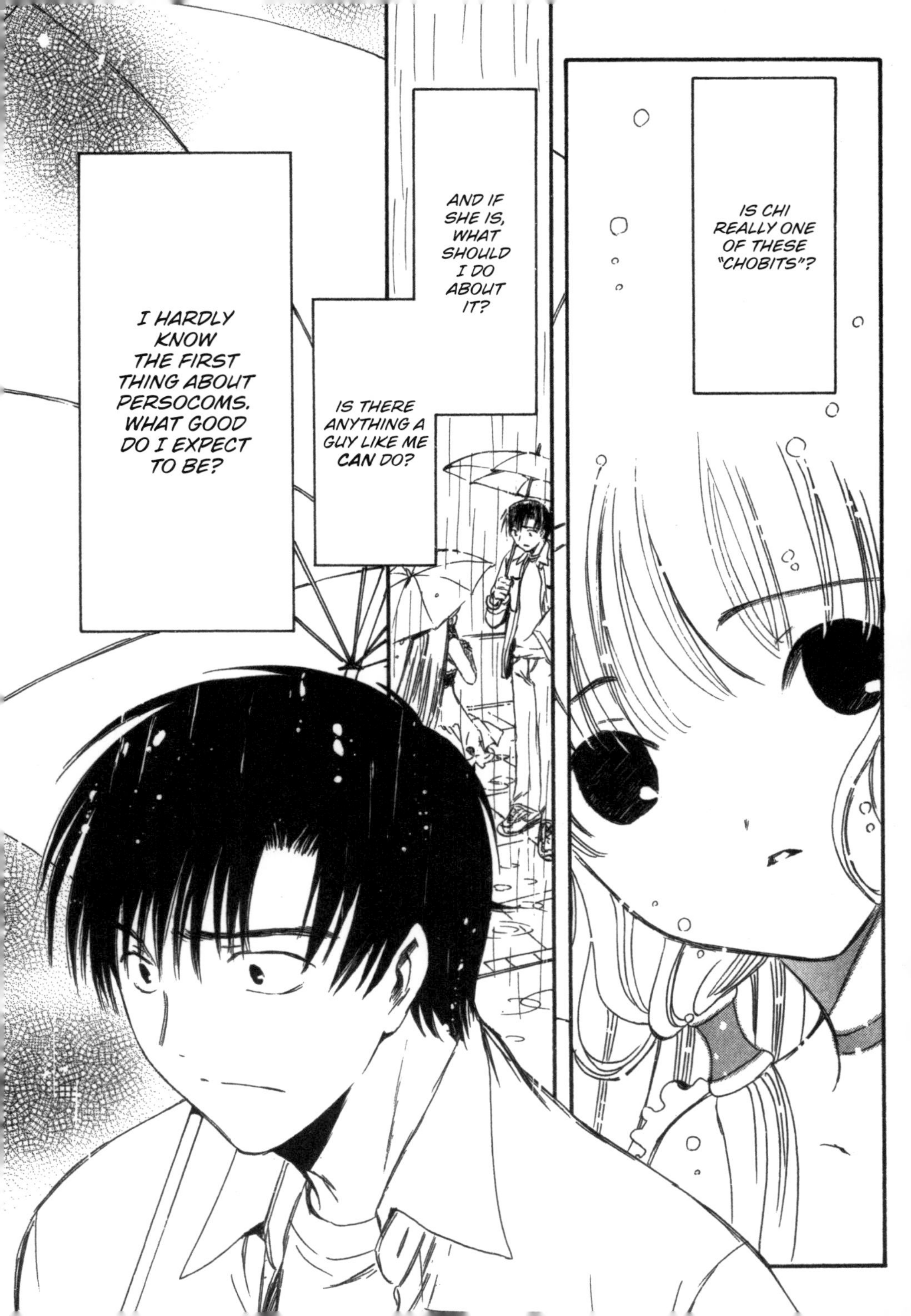
IS CHI REALLY ONE OF THESE "CHOBITS"?
AND IF SHE IS, WHAT SHOULD I DO ABOUT IT?
IS THERE ANYTHING A GUY LIKE ME **CAN** DO?
I HARDLY KNOW THE FIRST THING ABOUT PERSOCOMS. WHAT GOOD DO I EXPECT TO BE?

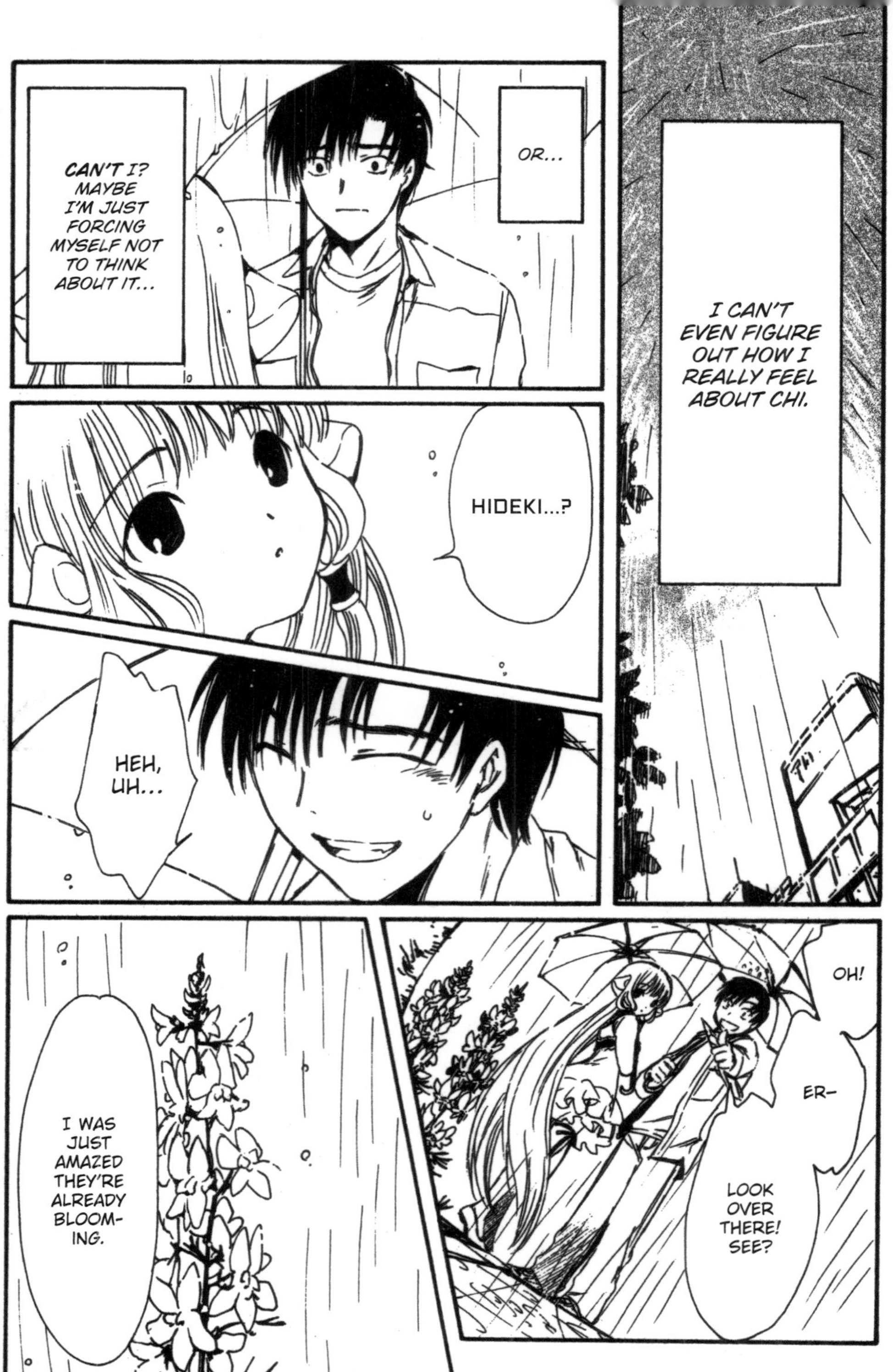
I CAN'T EVEN FIGURE OUT HOW I REALLY FEEL ABOUT CHI.
OR...
CAN'T I? MAYBE I'M JUST FORCING MYSELF NOT TO THINK ABOUT IT...
HIDEKI...?
HEH, UH...
OH!
ER–
LOOK OVER THERE! SEE?
I WAS JUST AMAZED THEY'RE ALREADY BLOOM-ING.

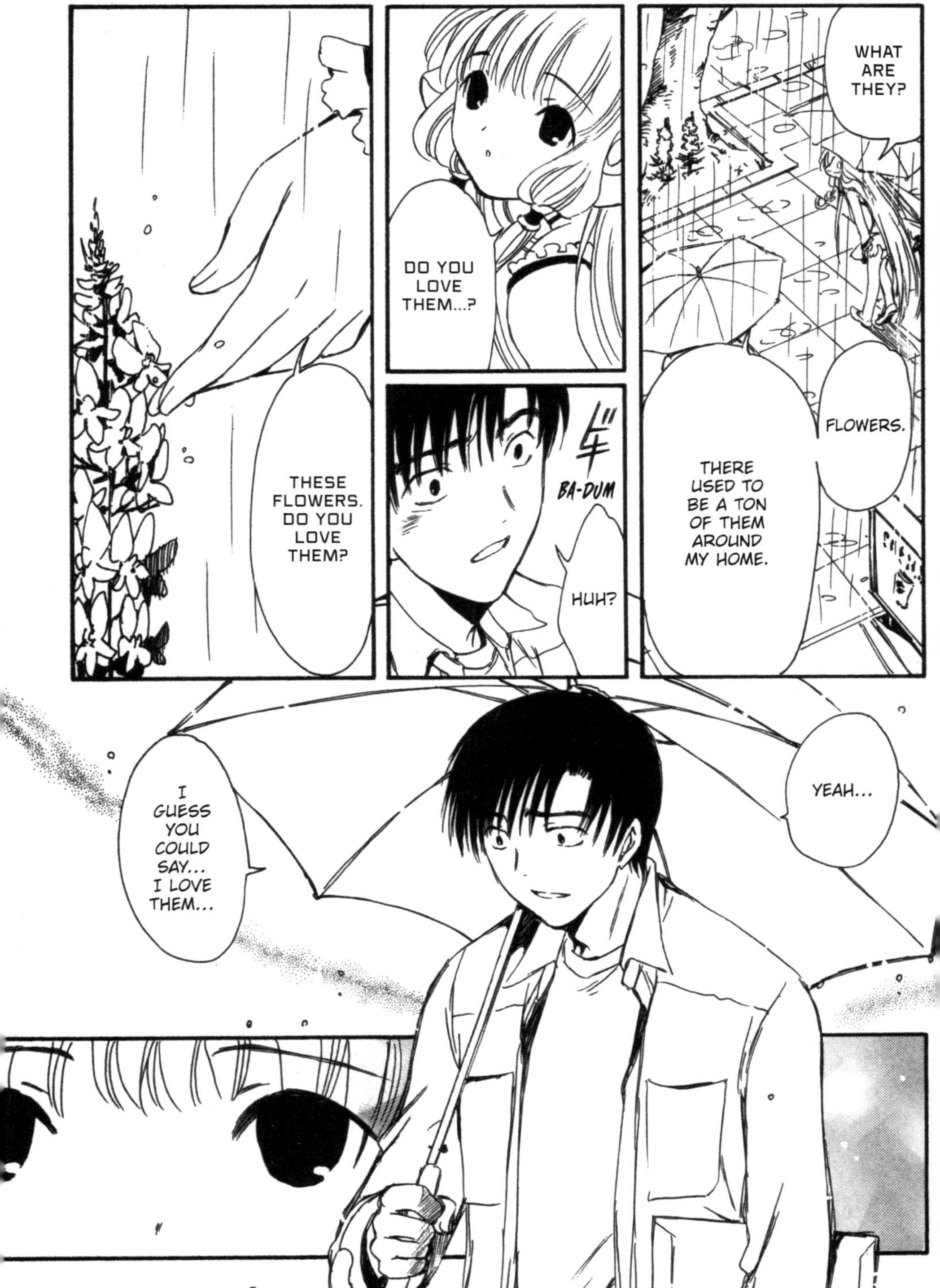
WHAT ARE THEY?
FLOWERS.
THERE USED TO BE A TON OF THEM AROUND MY HOME.
DO YOU LOVE THEM...?
BA-DUM
HUH?
THESE FLOWERS. DO YOU LOVE THEM?
YEAH...
I GUESS YOU COULD SAY... I LOVE THEM...

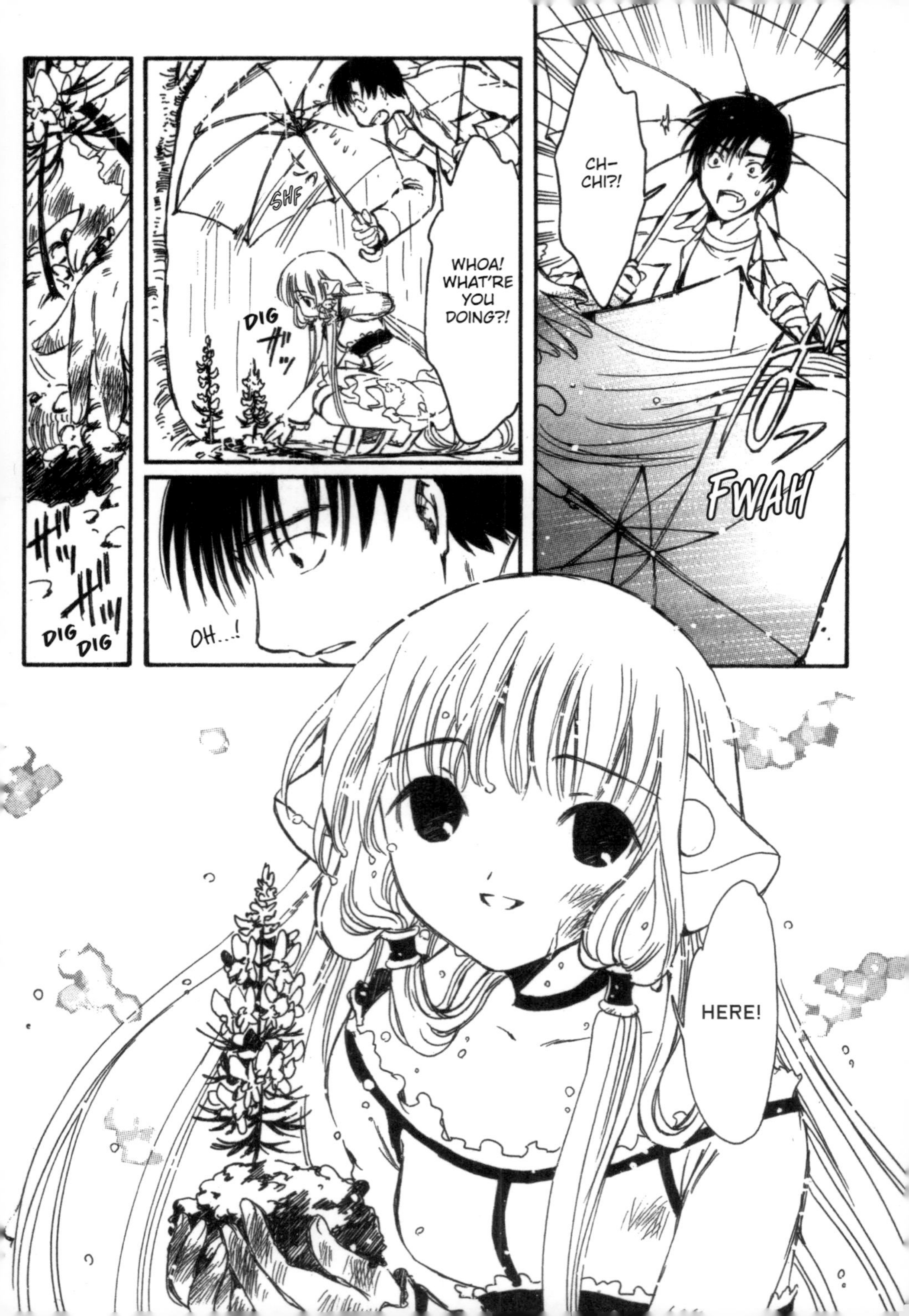
CH-CHI?!
FWAH
WHOA! WHAT'RE YOU DOING?!
SHF
DIG
OH...!
DIG DIG
HERE!

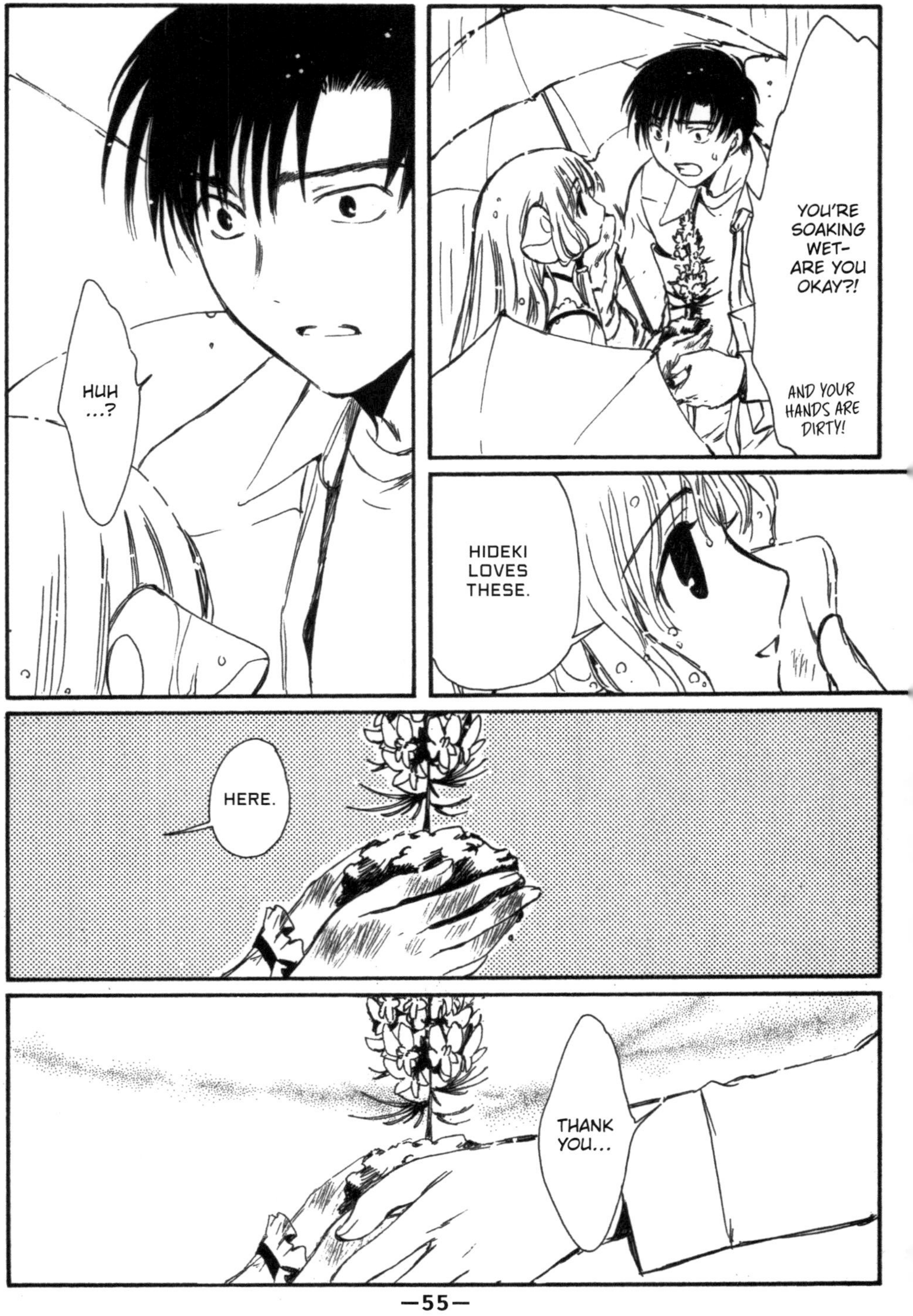
YOU'RE SOAKING WET- ARE YOU OKAY?!
AND YOUR HANDS ARE DIRTY!
HIDEKI LOVES THESE.
HUH ...?
HERE.
THANK YOU...

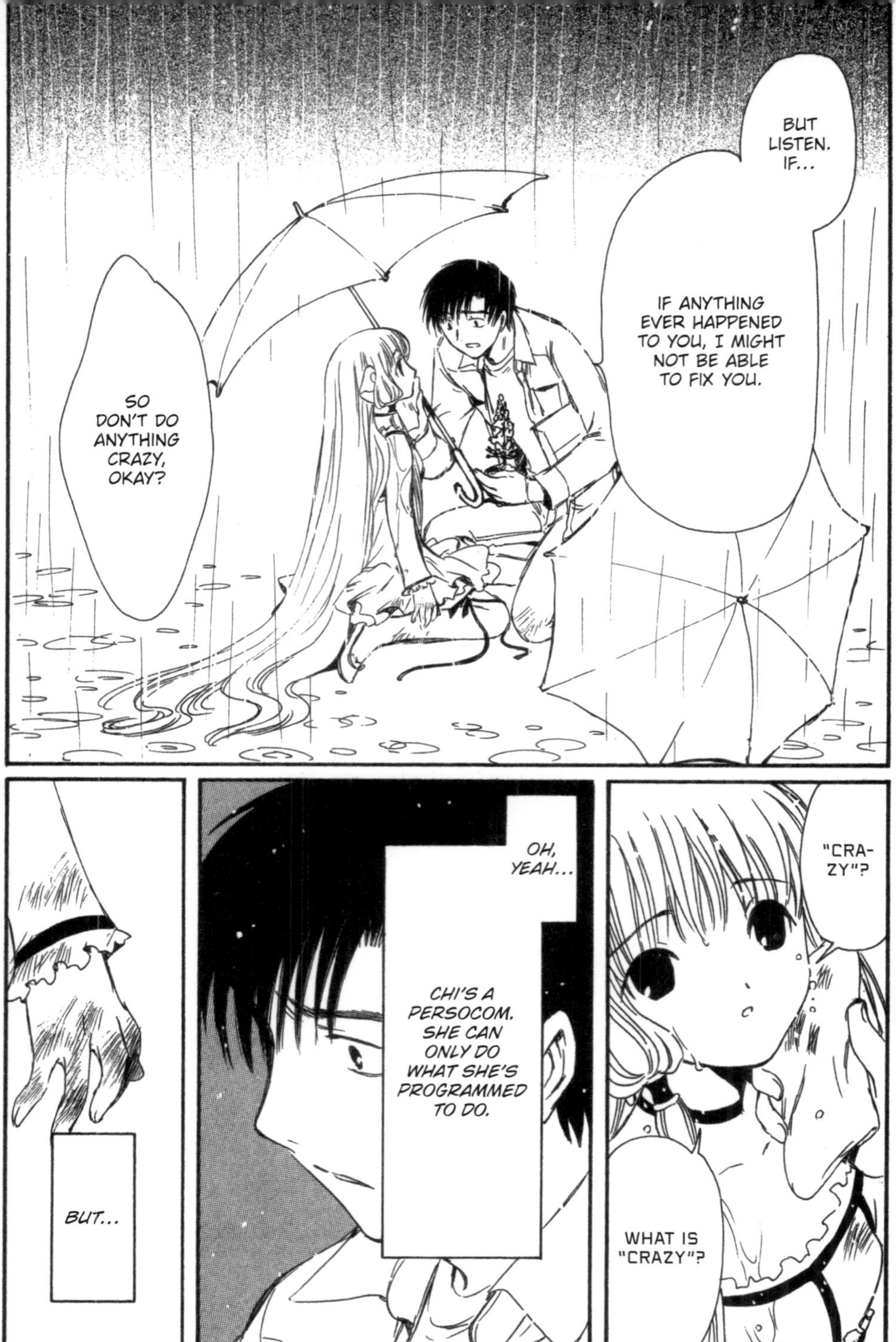
BUT LISTEN. IF...
IF ANYTHING EVER HAPPENED TO YOU, I MIGHT NOT BE ABLE TO FIX YOU.
SO DON'T DO ANYTHING CRAZY, OKAY?
"CRA-ZY"?
WHAT IS "CRAZY"?
OH, YEAH...
CHI'S A PERSOCOM. SHE CAN ONLY DO WHAT SHE'S PROGRAMMED TO DO.
BUT...

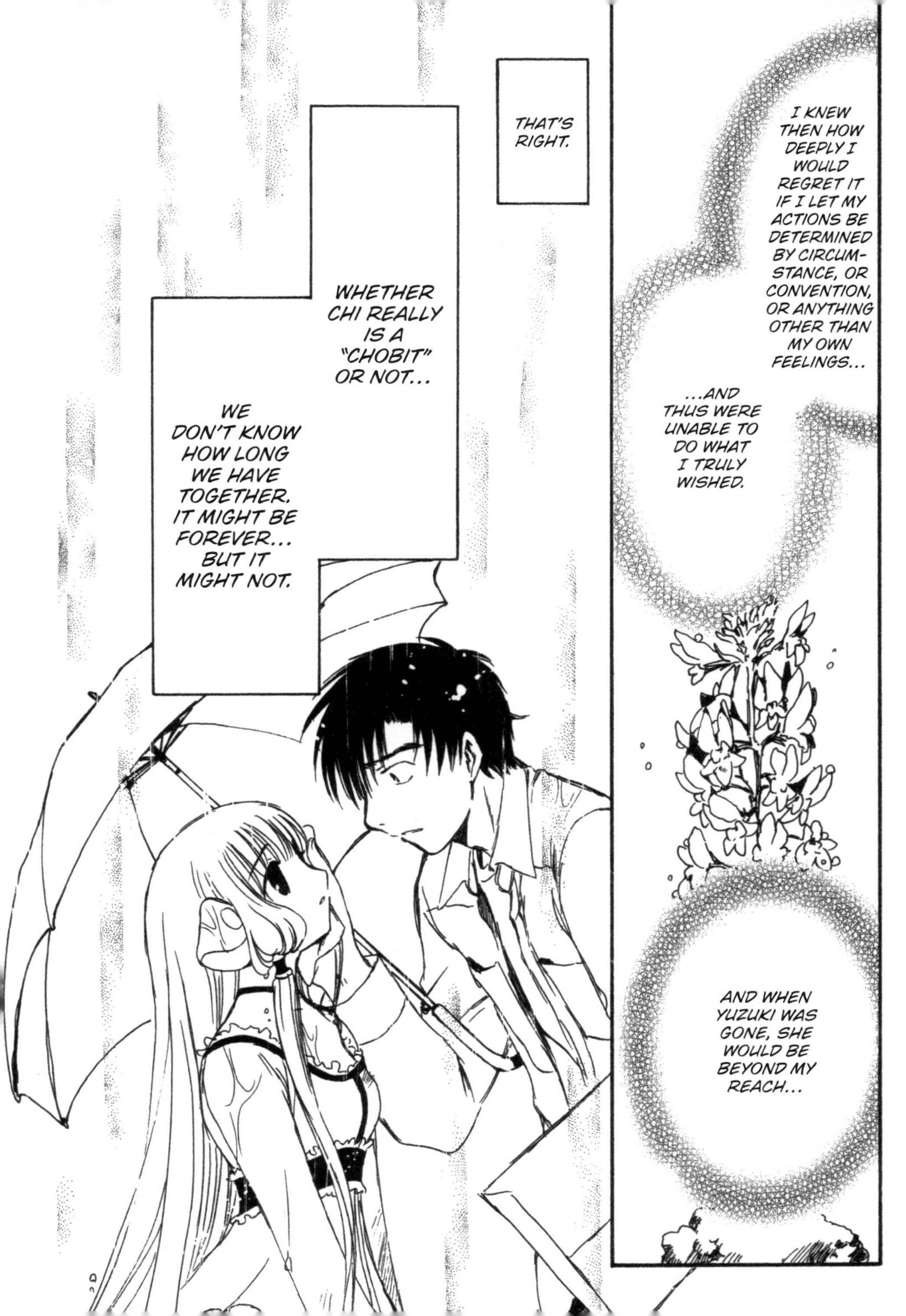
I KNEW THEN HOW DEEPLY I WOULD REGRET IT IF I LET MY ACTIONS BE DETERMINED BY CIRCUM-STANCE, OR CONVENTION, OR ANYTHING OTHER THAN MY OWN FEELINGS...
...AND THUS WERE UNABLE TO DO WHAT I TRULY WISHED.
AND WHEN YUZUKI WAS GONE, SHE WOULD BE BEYOND MY REACH...
THAT'S RIGHT.
WHETHER CHI REALLY IS A "CHOBIT" OR NOT...
WE DON'T KNOW HOW LONG WE HAVE TOGETHER. IT MIGHT BE FOREVER... BUT IT MIGHT NOT.

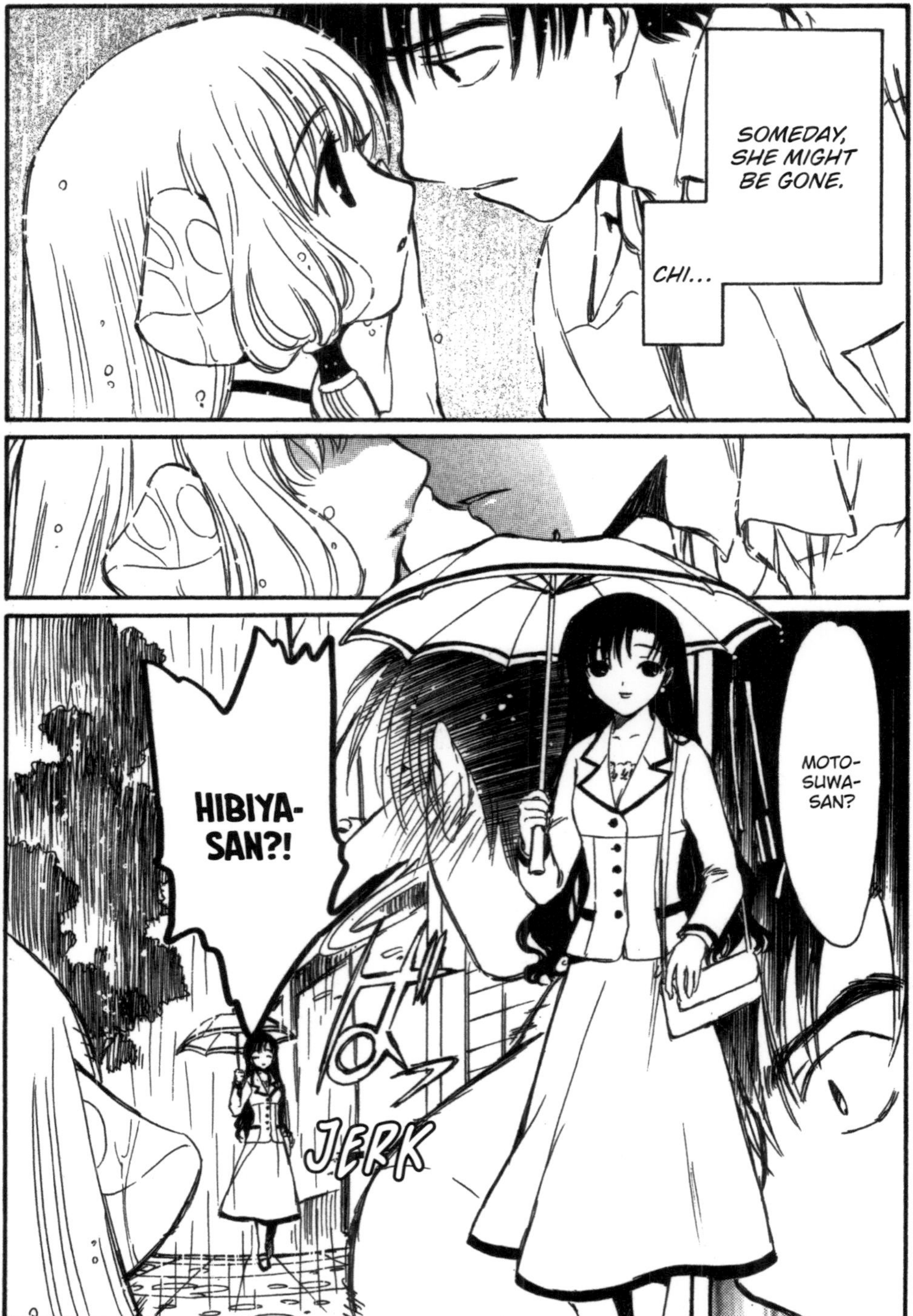
SOMEDAY, SHE MIGHT BE GONE.
CHI...
MOTO-SUWA-SAN?
HIBIYA-SAN?!
JERK

<chapter.75> end

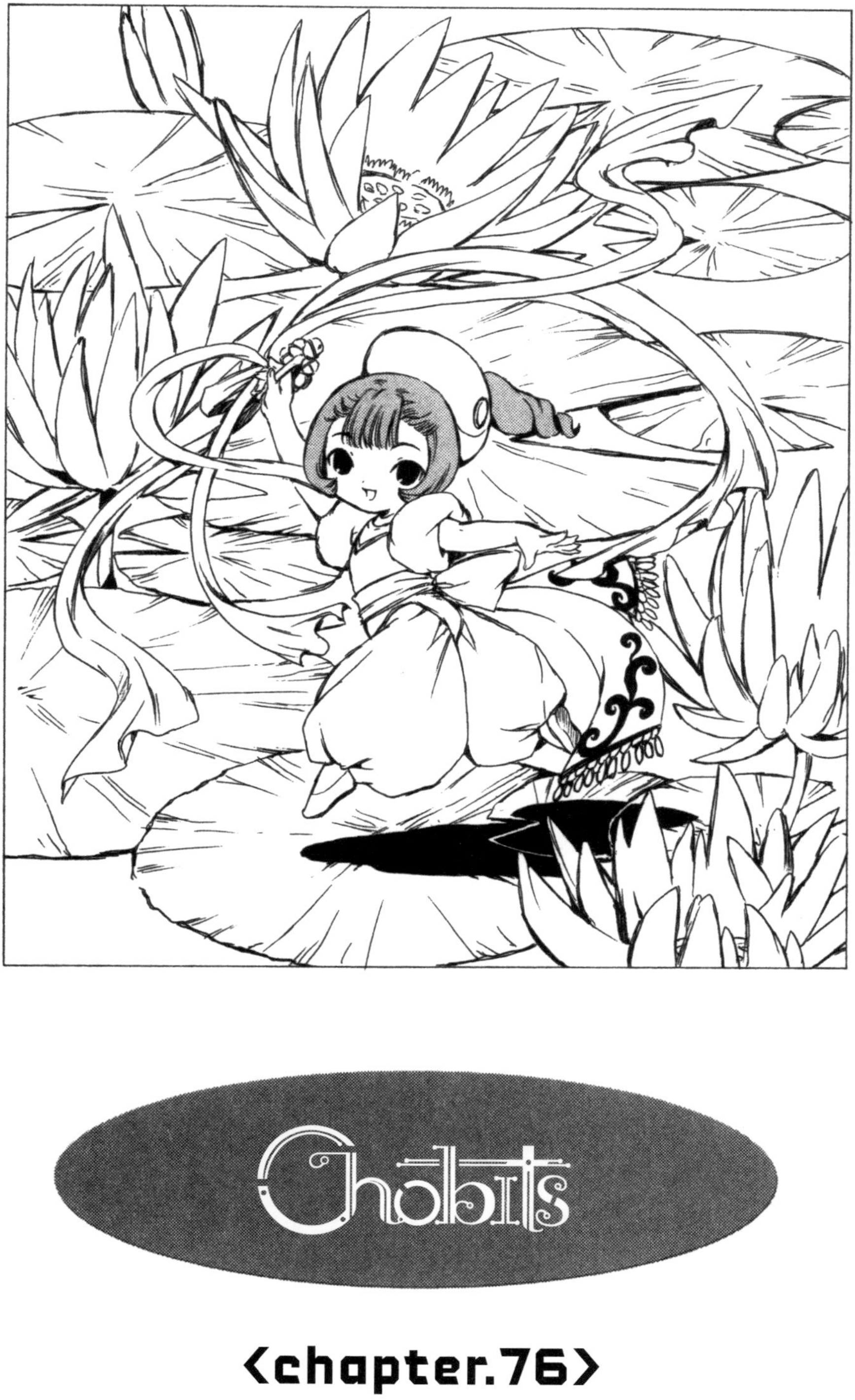

# Chobits

## <chapter.76>

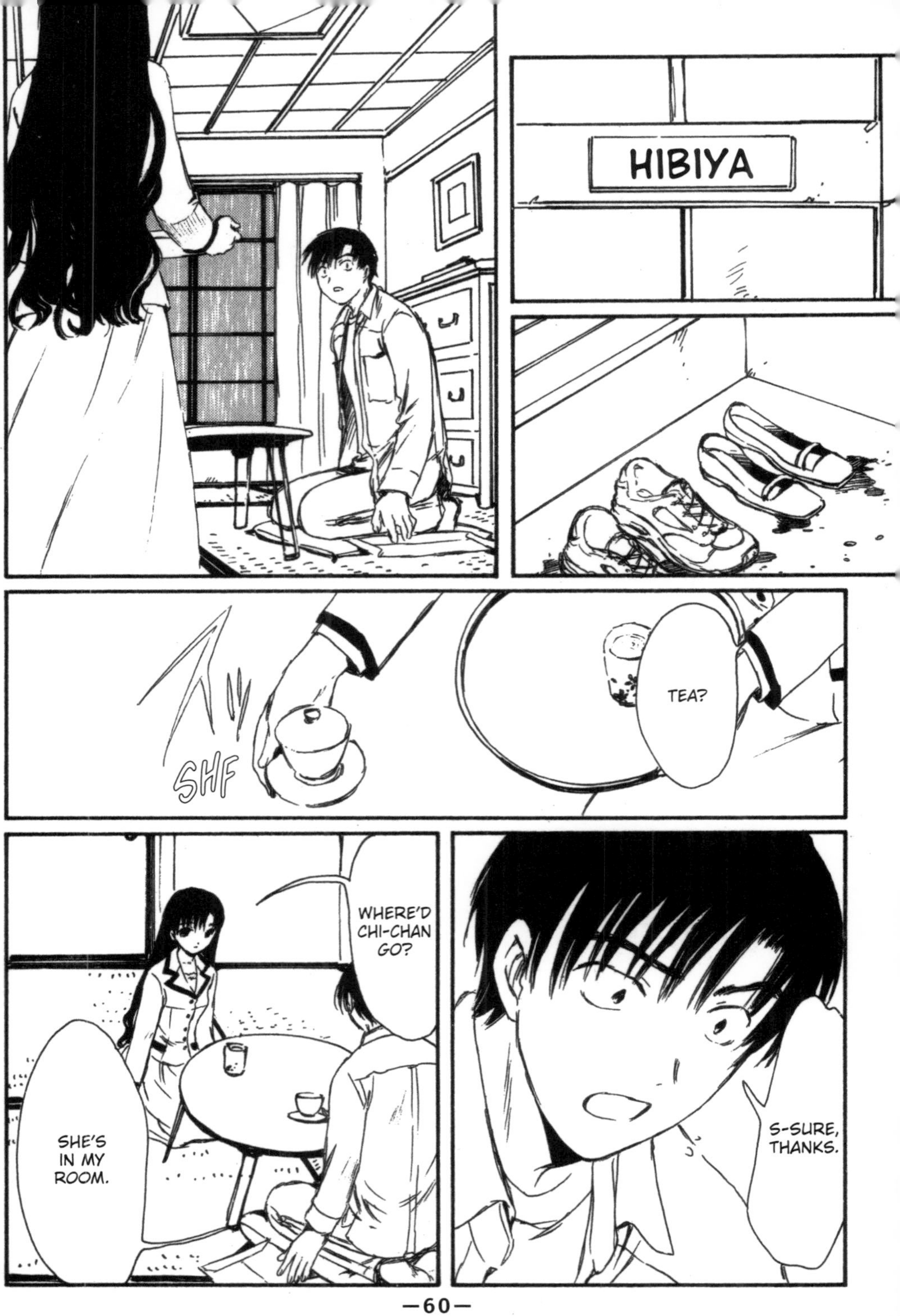
HIBIYA
TEA?
SHF
S-SURE, THANKS.
WHERE'D CHI-CHAN GO?
SHE'S IN MY ROOM.

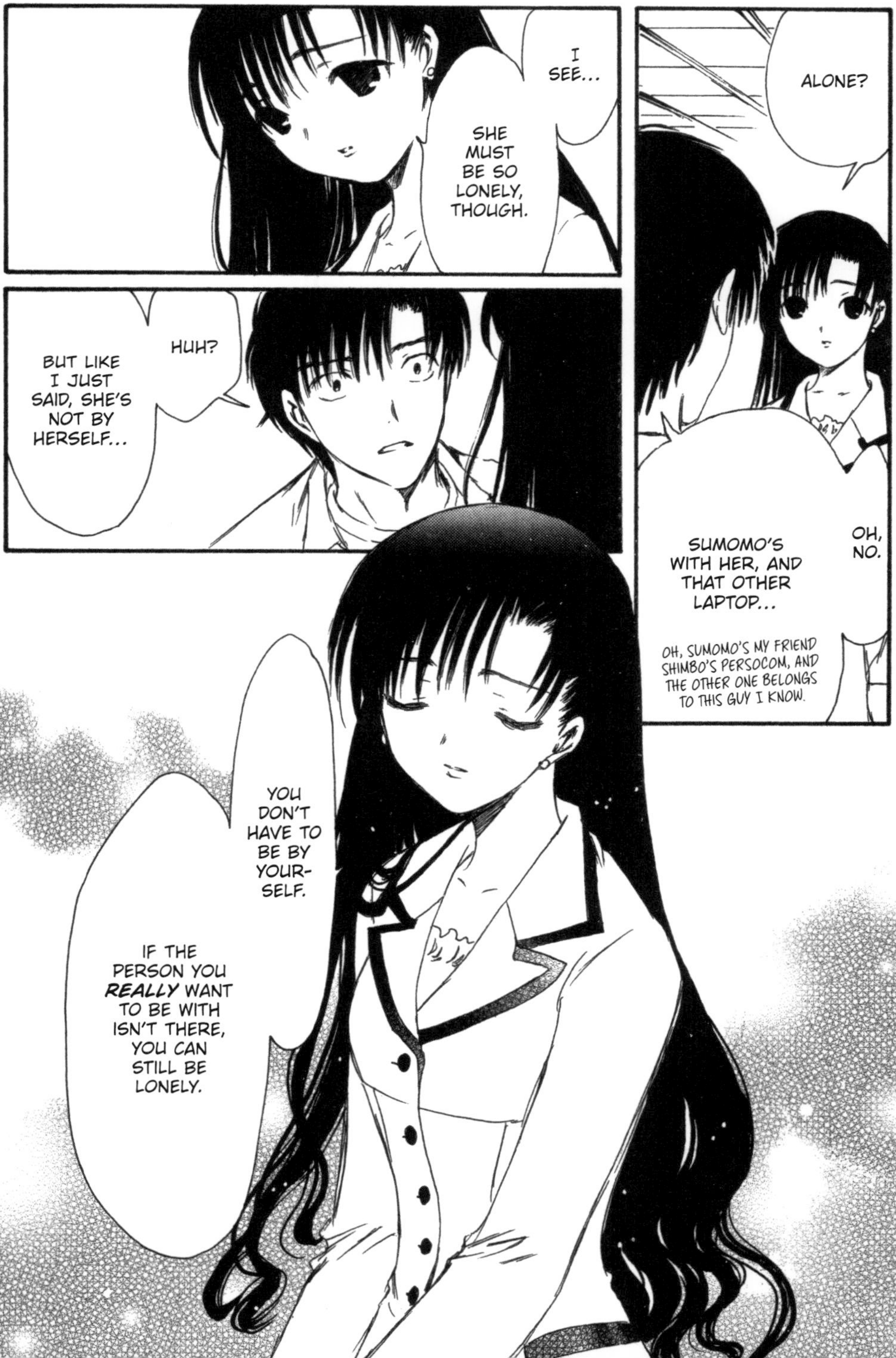
ALONE?
OH, NO.
SUMOMO'S WITH HER, AND THAT OTHER LAPTOP...
OH, SUMOMO'S MY FRIEND SHIMBO'S PERSOCOM, AND THE OTHER ONE BELONGS TO THIS GUY I KNOW.
I SEE...
SHE MUST BE SO LONELY, THOUGH.
HUH?
BUT LIKE I JUST SAID, SHE'S NOT BY HERSELF...
YOU DON'T HAVE TO BE BY YOUR-SELF.
IF THE PERSON YOU REALLY WANT TO BE WITH ISN'T THERE, YOU CAN STILL BE LONELY.

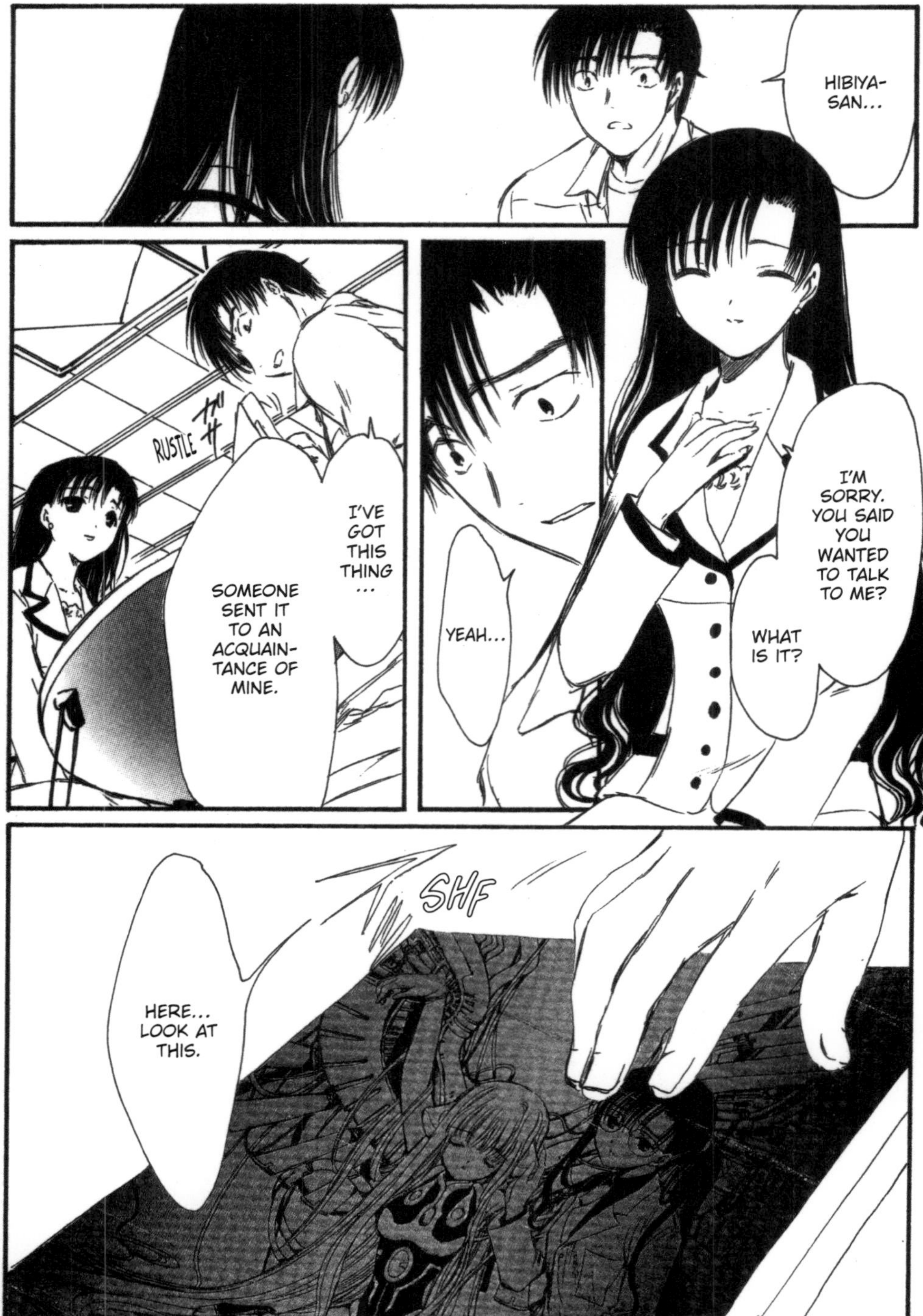
HIBIYA-SAN...
I'M SORRY. YOU SAID YOU WANTED TO TALK TO ME?
WHAT IS IT?
YEAH...
RUSTLE
I'VE GOT THIS THING...
SOMEONE SENT IT TO AN ACQUAINTANCE OF MINE.
SHF
HERE... LOOK AT THIS.

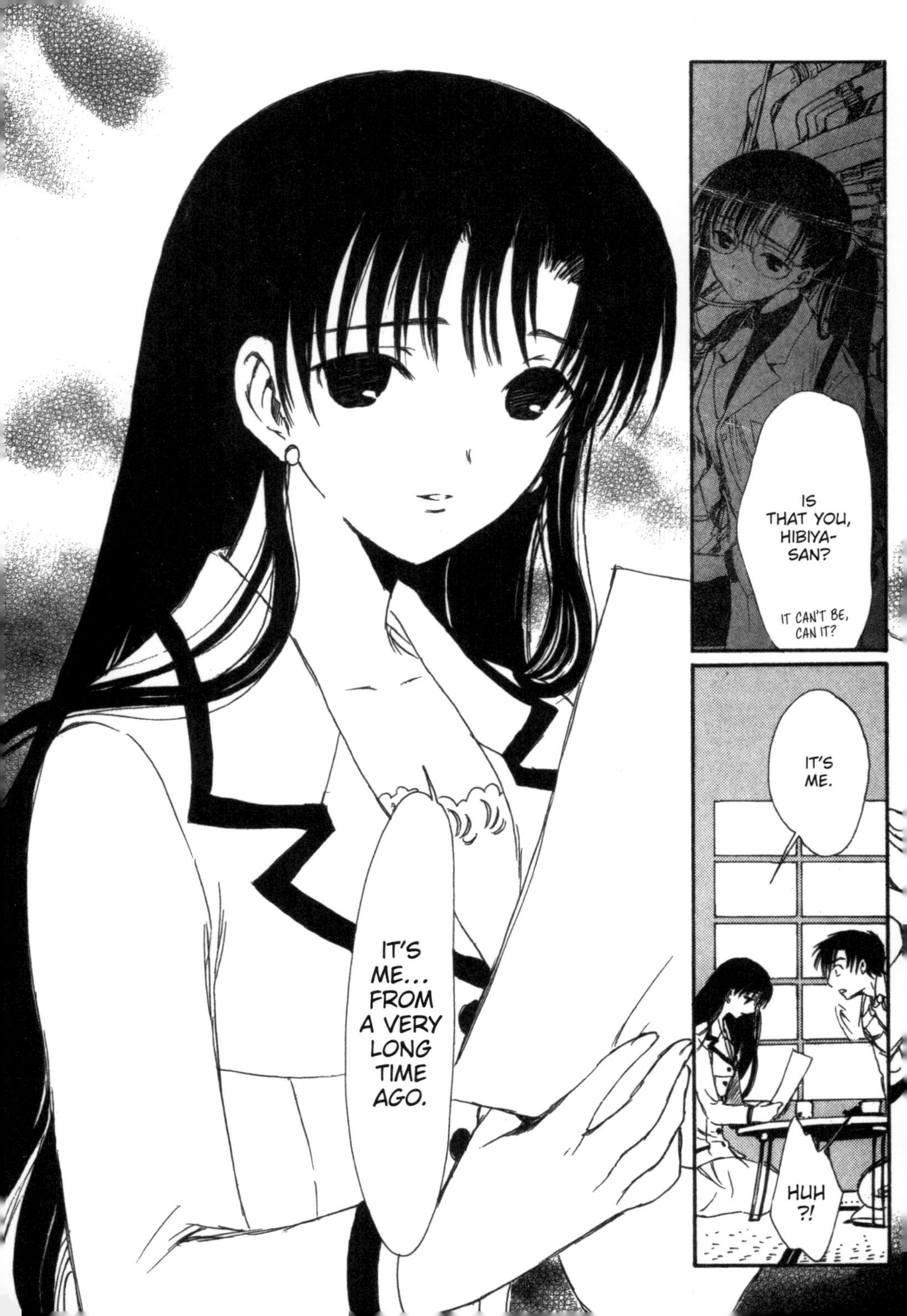
IS THAT YOU, HIBIYA-SAN?
IT CAN'T BE, CAN IT?
IT'S ME.
HUH ?!
IT'S ME... FROM A VERY LONG TIME AGO.

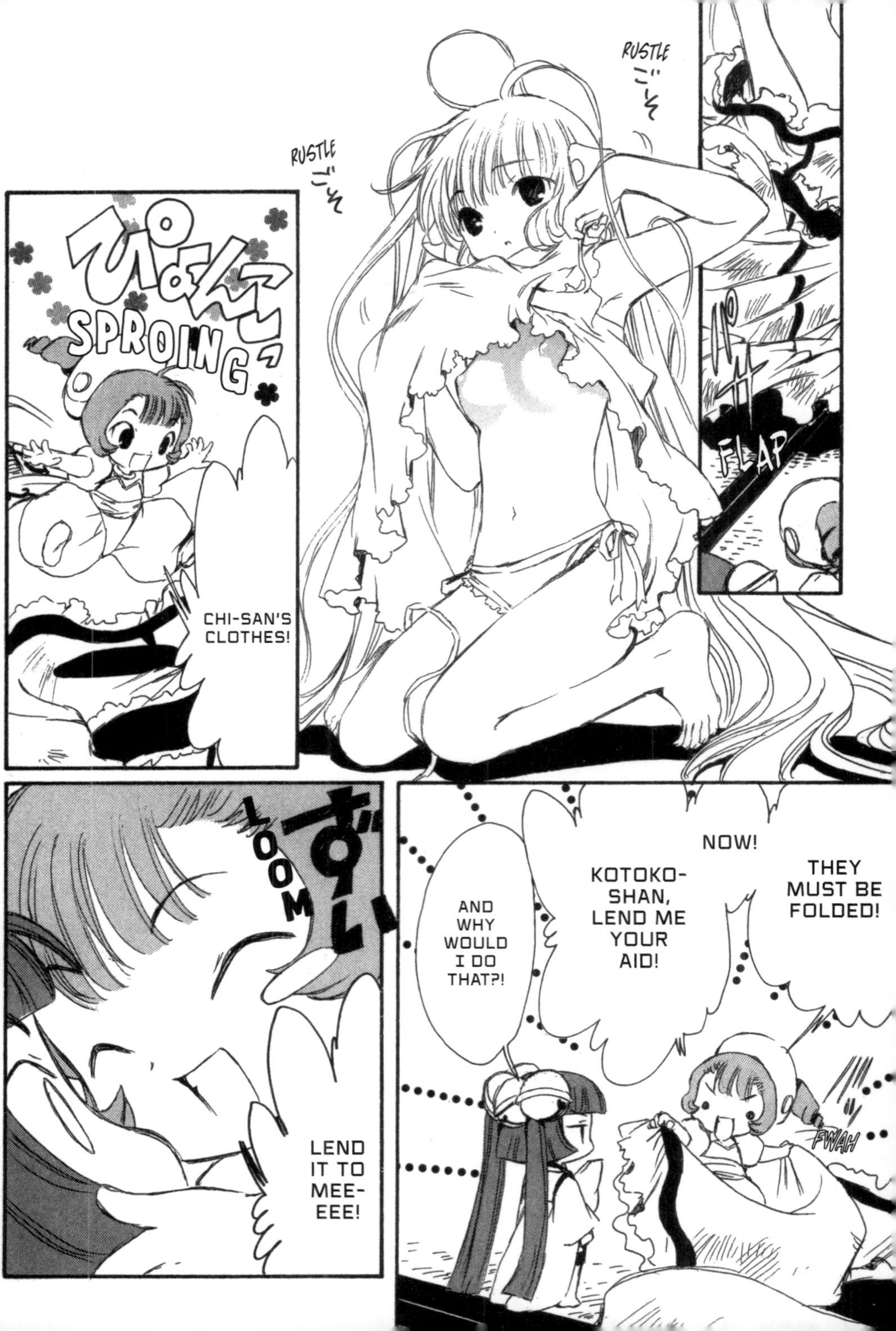
FLAP
RUSTLE
ごそ
RUSTLE
ごそ
ぴょんっ
SPROING
CHI-SAN'S CLOTHES!
THEY MUST BE FOLDED!
NOW!
KOTOKO-SHAN, LEND ME YOUR AID!
AND WHY WOULD I DO THAT?!
FWAH
ずい
LOOM
LEND IT TO MEE-EEE!

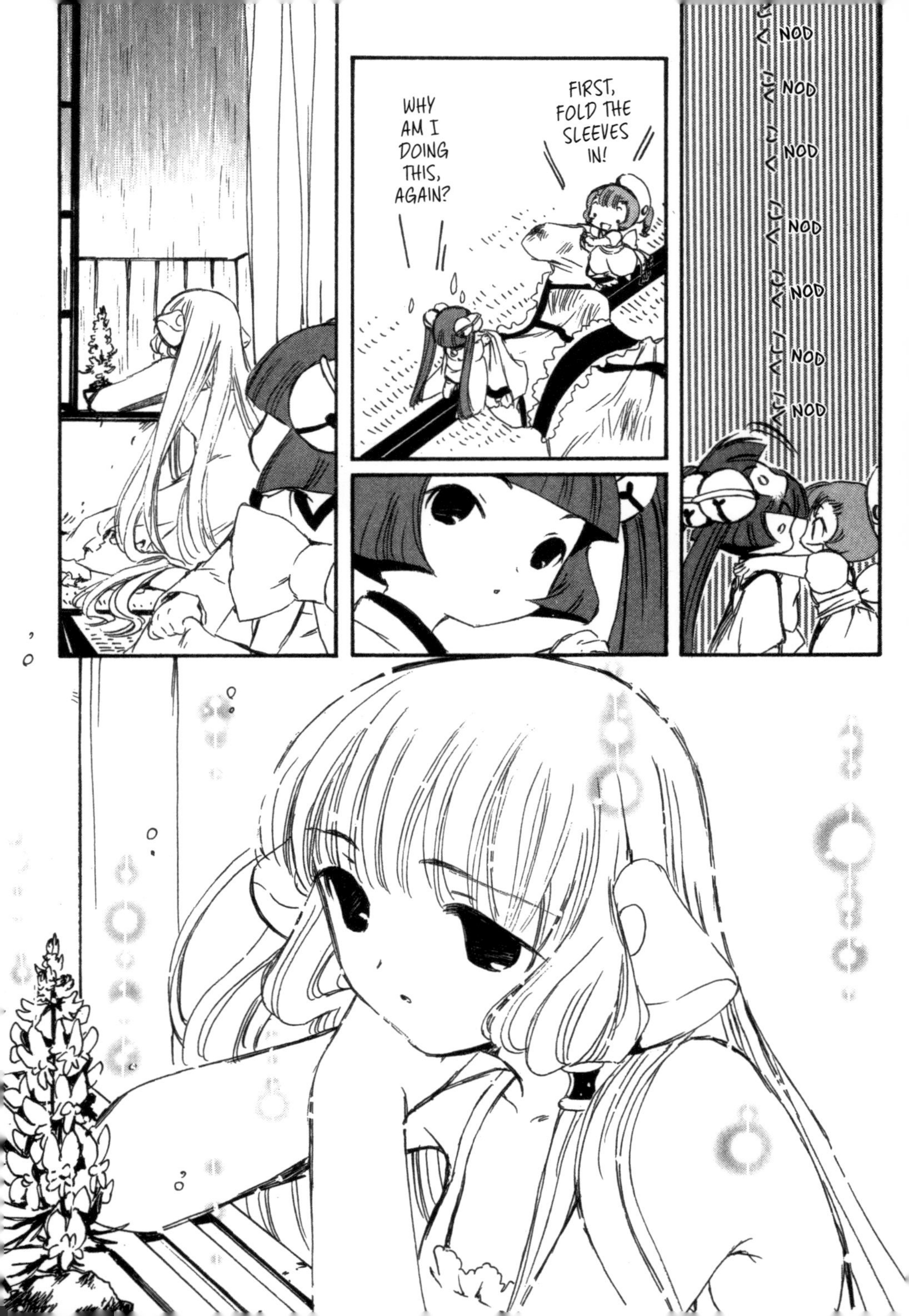
NOD
NOD
NOD
NOD
NOD
NOD
NOD
FIRST, FOLD THE SLEEVES IN!
WHY AM I DOING THIS, AGAIN?

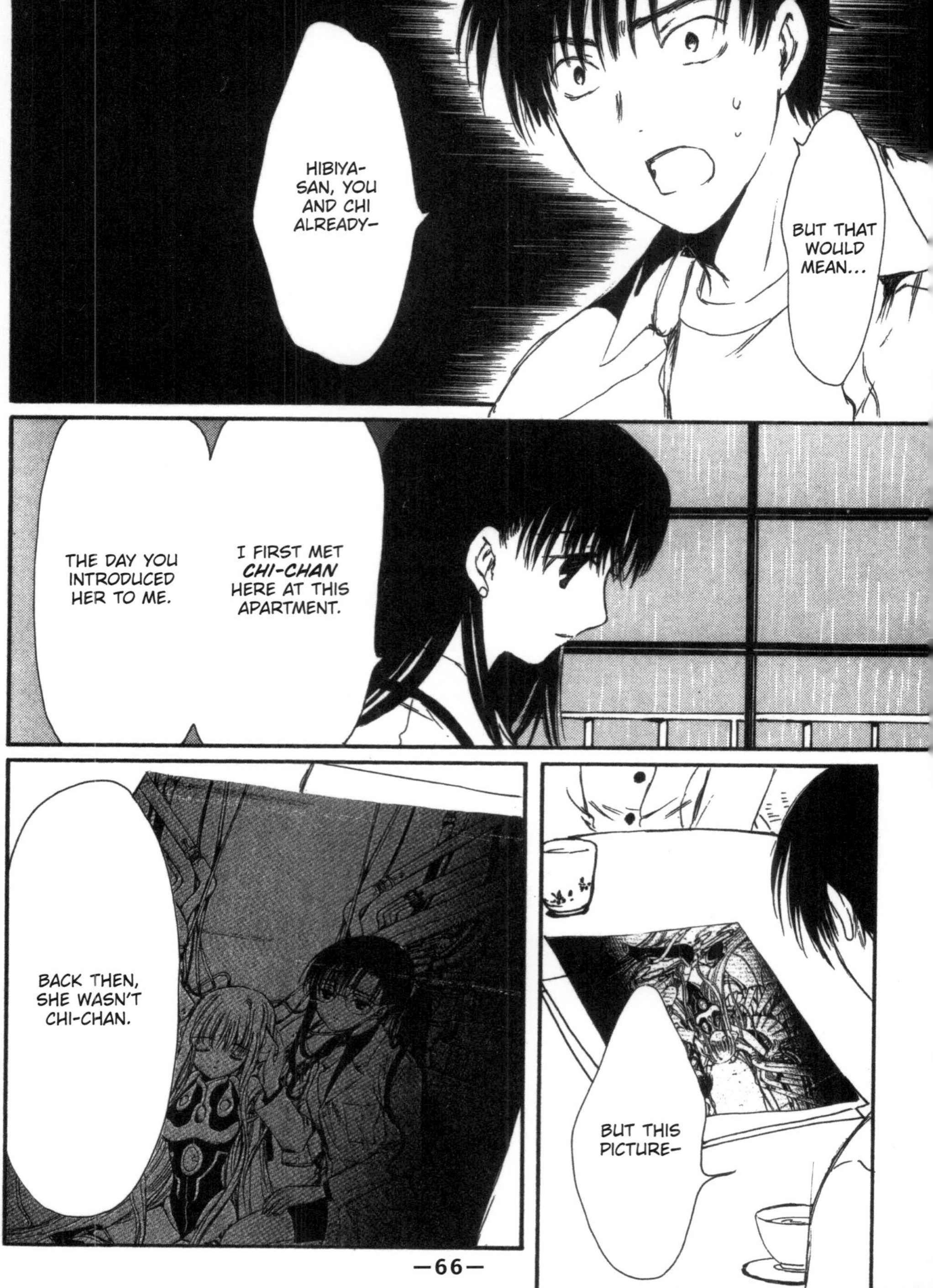
BUT THAT WOULD MEAN...
HIBIYA-SAN, YOU AND CHI ALREADY-
I FIRST MET *CHI-CHAN* HERE AT THIS APARTMENT.
THE DAY YOU INTRODUCED HER TO ME.
BUT THIS PICTURE-
BACK THEN, SHE WASN'T CHI-CHAN.

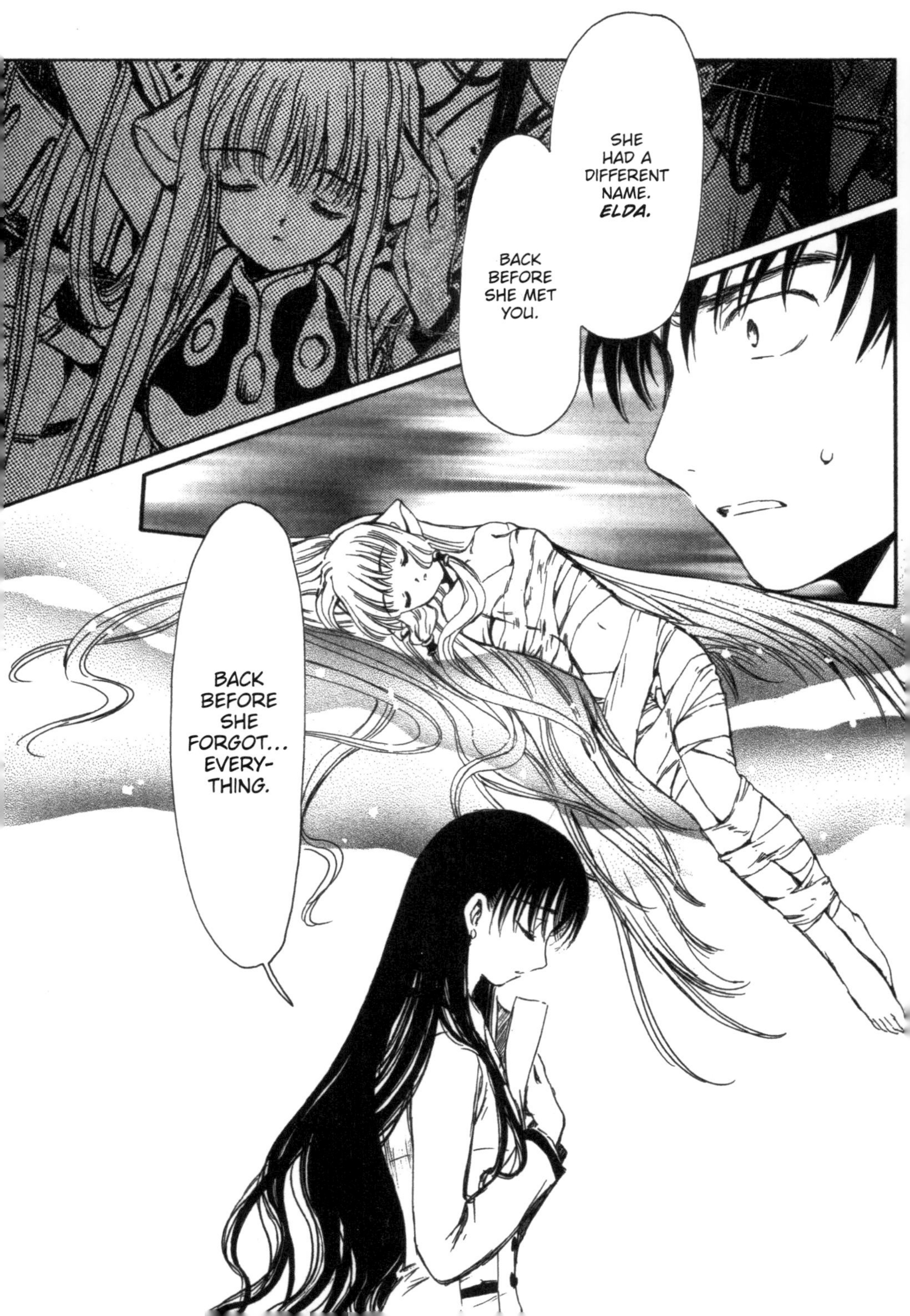
SHE HAD A DIFFERENT NAME. ELDA.
BACK BEFORE SHE MET YOU.
BACK BEFORE SHE FORGOT... EVERY-THING.

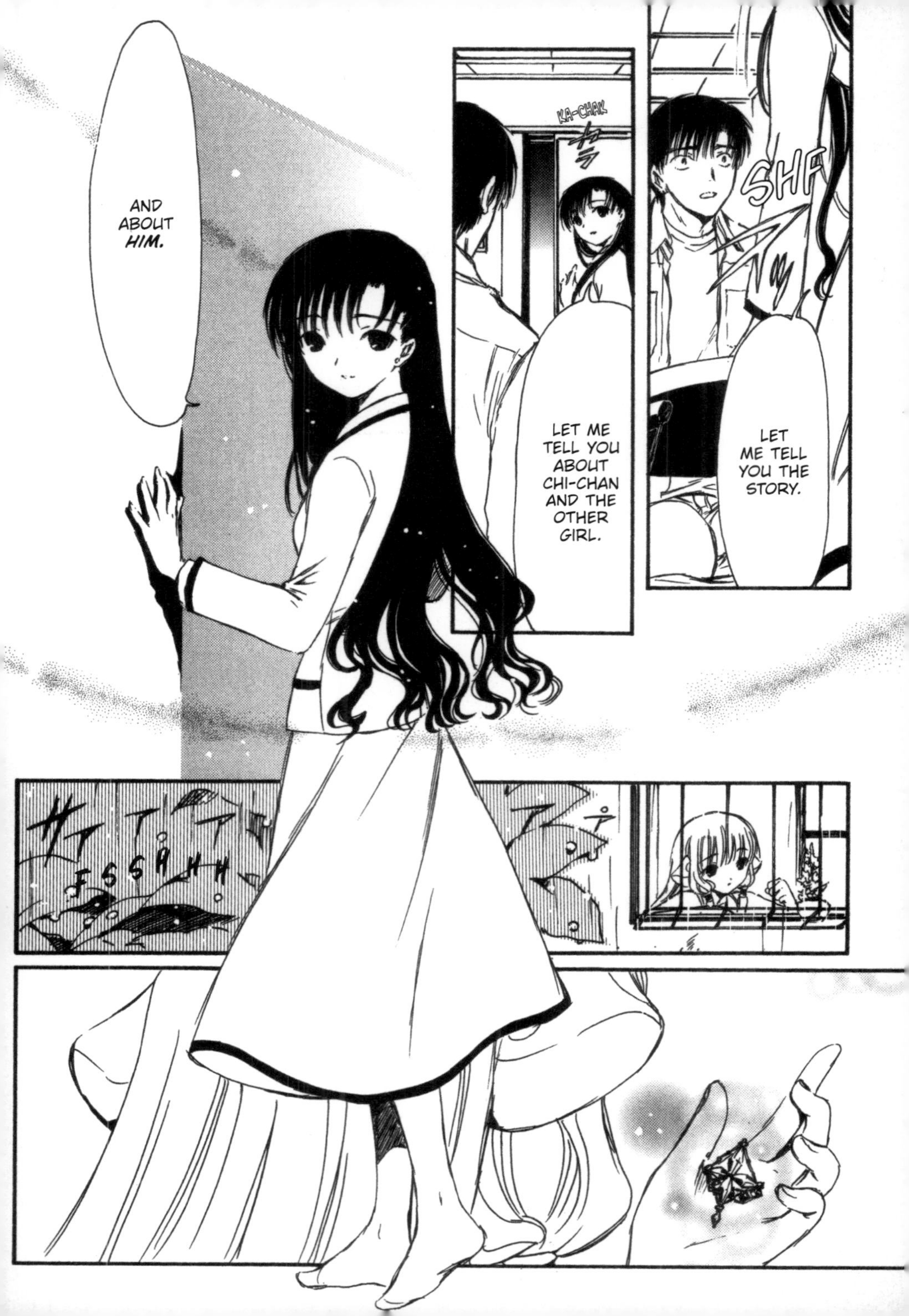
SHF
LET ME TELL YOU THE STORY.
KA-CHAK
LET ME TELL YOU ABOUT CHI-CHAN AND THE OTHER GIRL.
AND ABOUT HIM.
FSSHHH

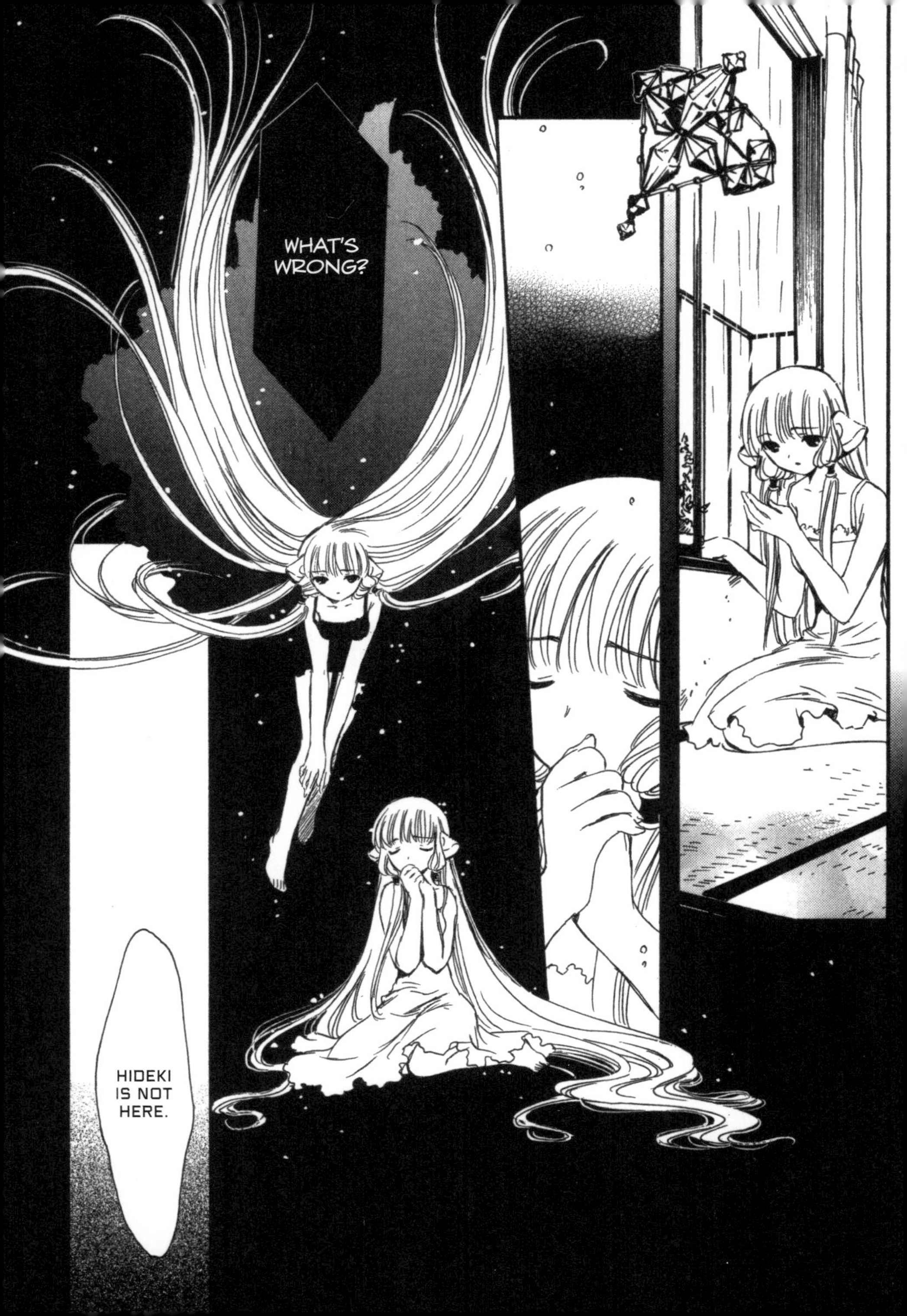
WHAT'S WRONG?
HIDEKI IS NOT HERE.

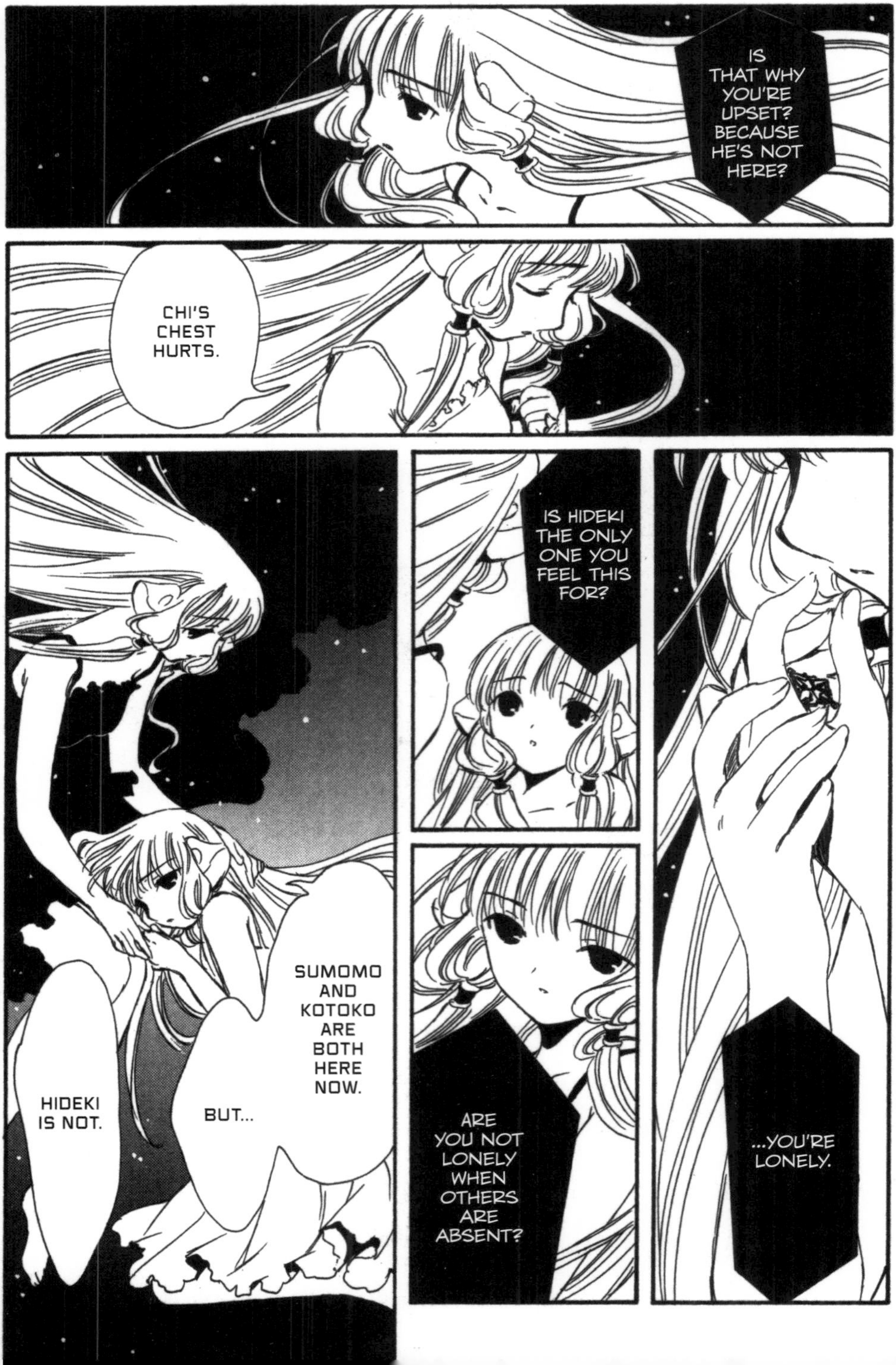
IS THAT WHY YOU'RE UPSET? BECAUSE HE'S NOT HERE?
CHI'S CHEST HURTS.
...YOU'RE LONELY.
IS HIDEKI THE ONLY ONE YOU FEEL THIS FOR?
ARE YOU NOT LONELY WHEN OTHERS ARE ABSENT?
SUMOMO AND KOTOKO ARE BOTH HERE NOW.
BUT...
HIDEKI IS NOT.

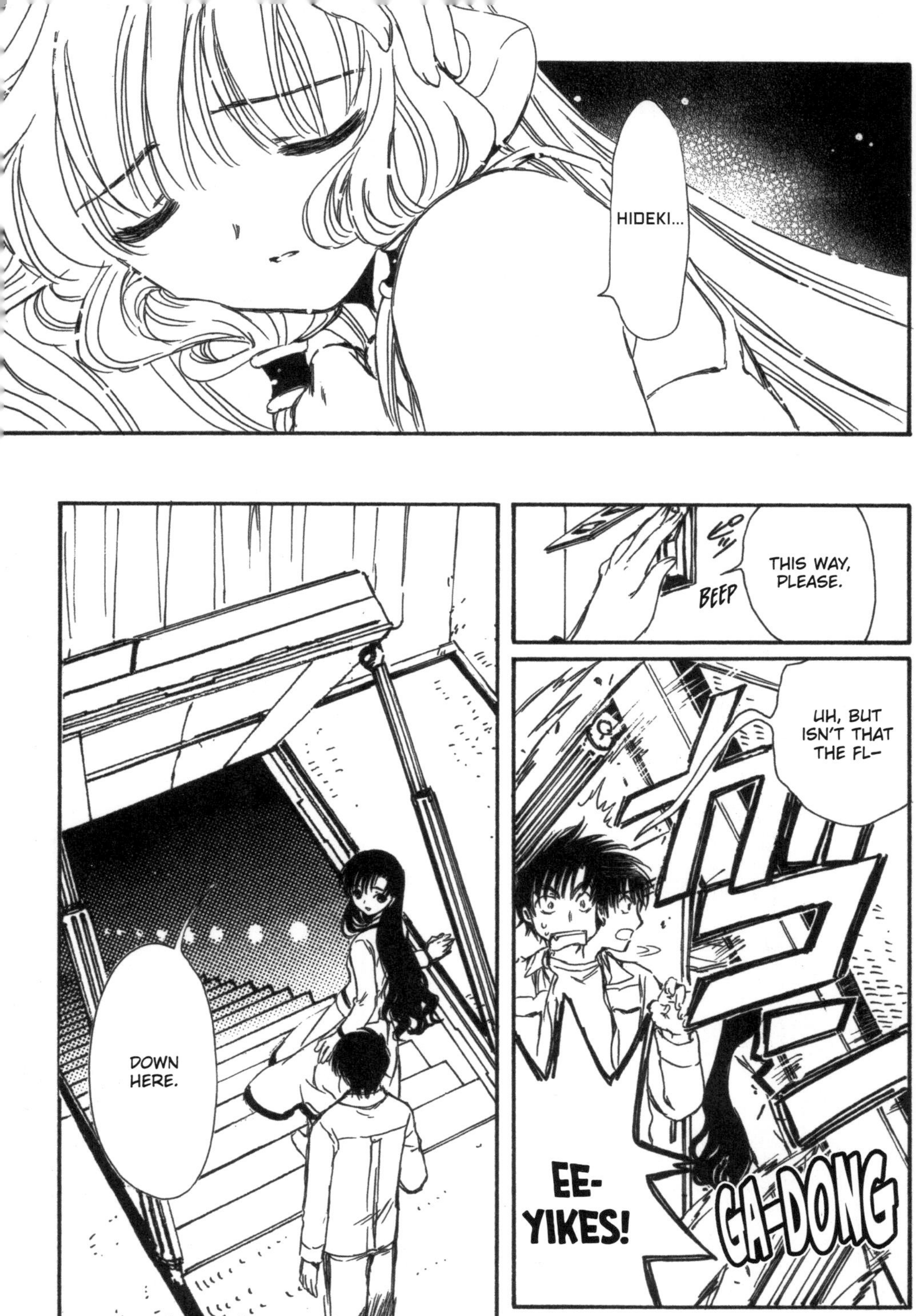
HIDEKI...
THIS WAY, PLEASE.
BEEP
UH, BUT ISN'T THAT THE FL–
GA-DONG
EE-YIKES!
DOWN HERE.

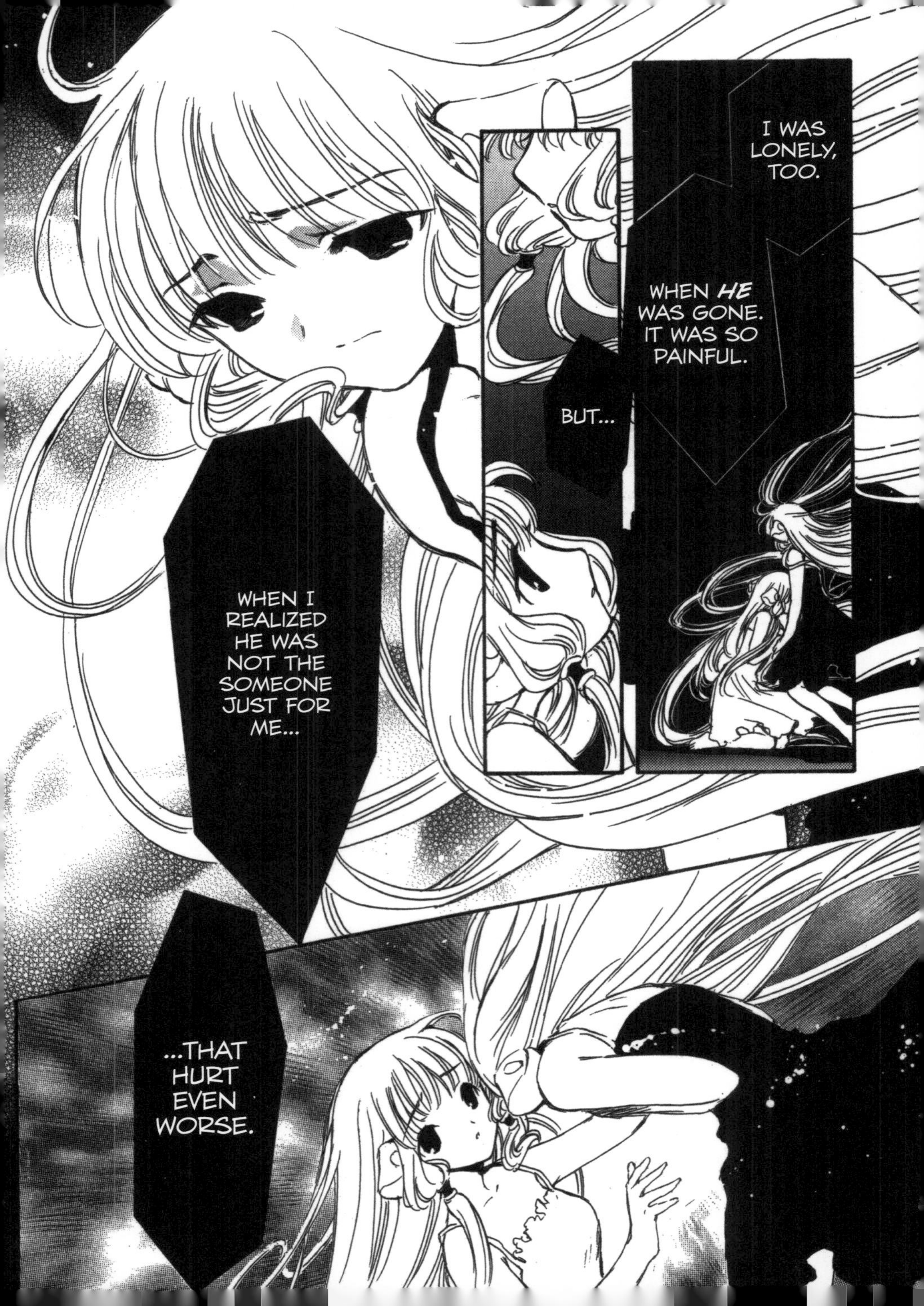
I WAS LONELY, TOO.
WHEN HE WAS GONE. IT WAS SO PAINFUL.
BUT...
WHEN I REALIZED HE WAS NOT THE SOMEONE JUST FOR ME...
...THAT HURT EVEN WORSE.

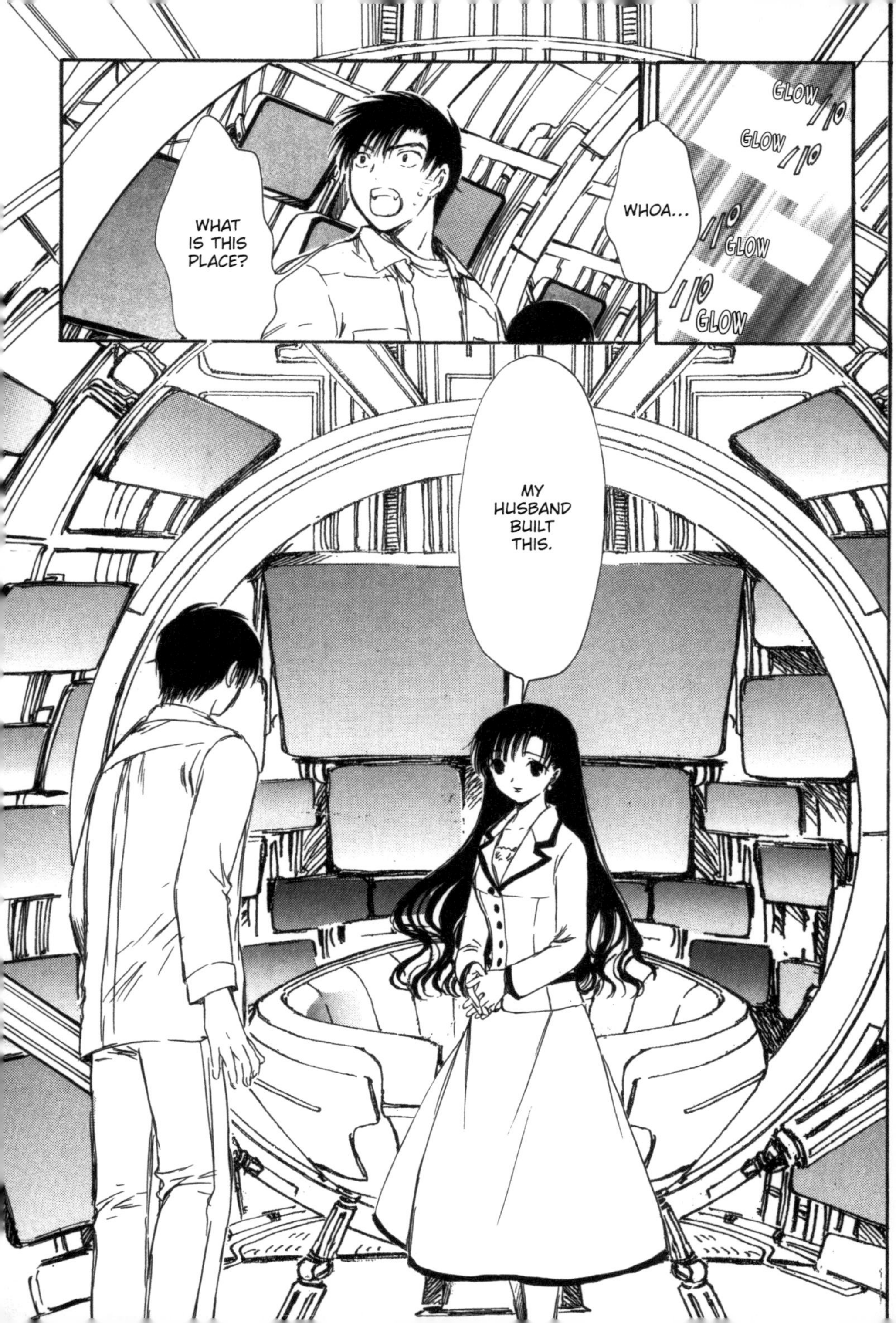
GLOW
GLOW
GLOW
GLOW
WHOA...
WHAT IS THIS PLACE?
MY HUSBAND BUILT THIS.

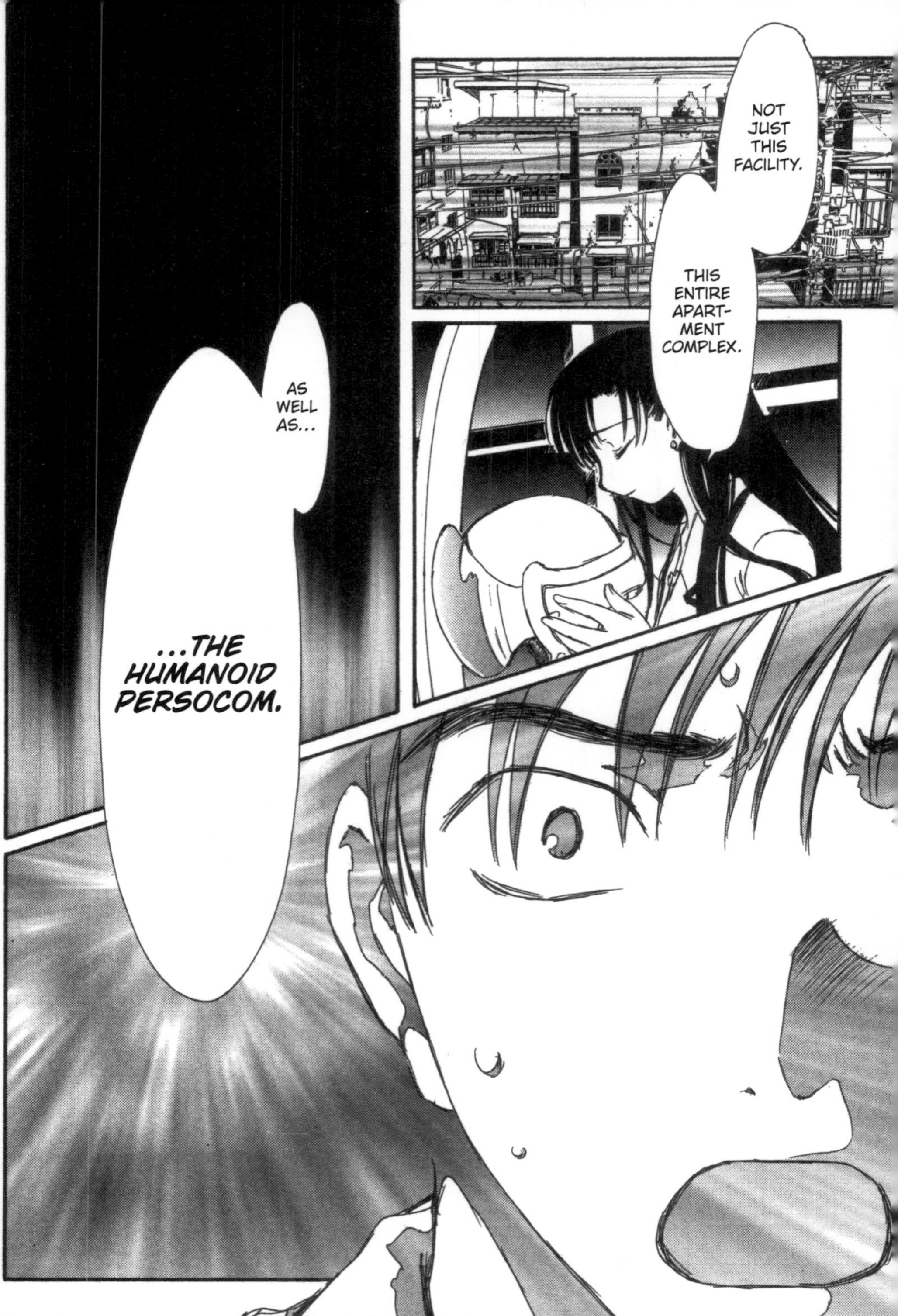
NOT JUST THIS FACILITY.
THIS ENTIRE APART-MENT COMPLEX.
AS WELL AS...
...THE HUMANOID PERSOCOM.

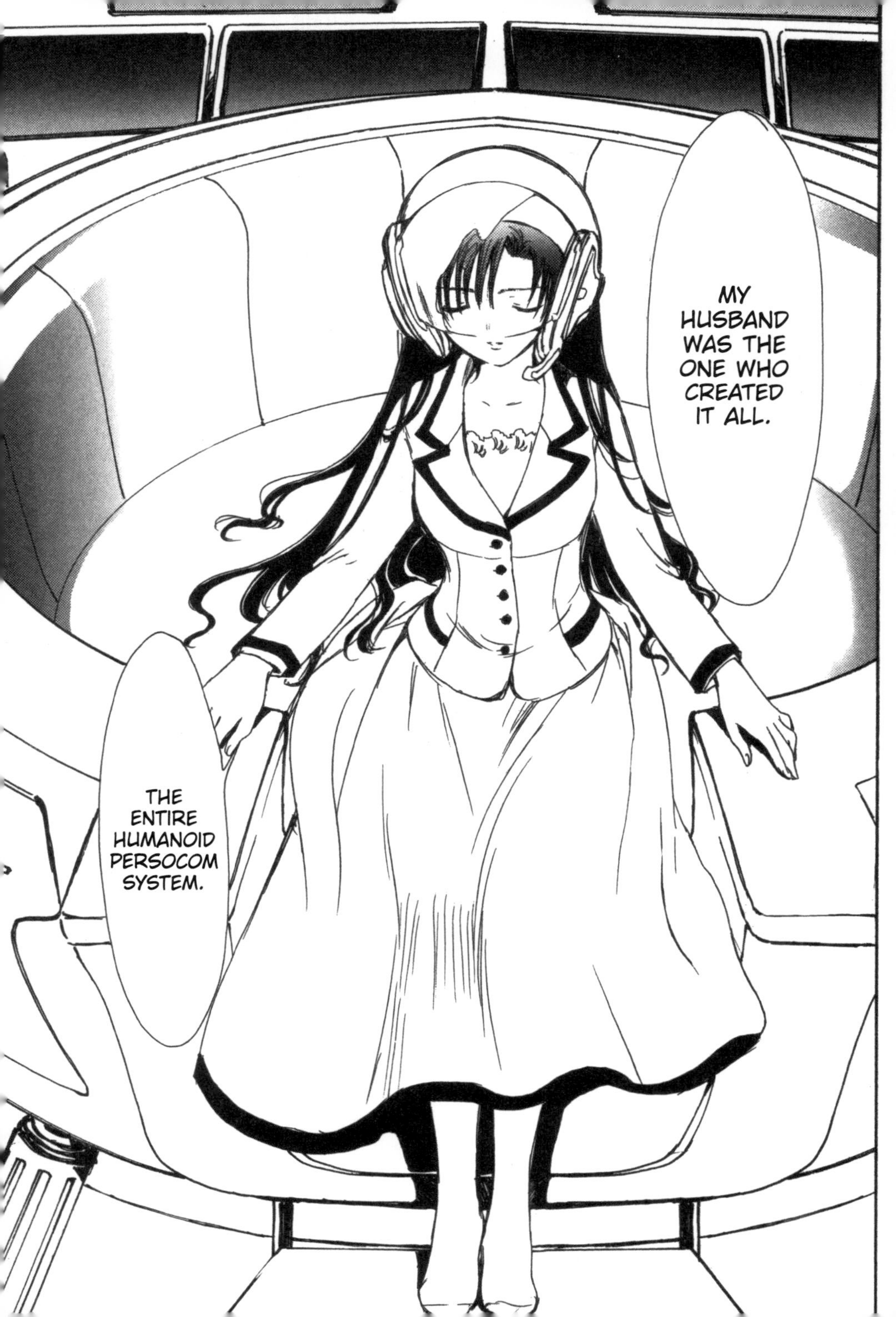
MY HUSBAND WAS THE ONE WHO CREATED IT ALL.
THE ENTIRE HUMANOID PERSOCOM SYSTEM.

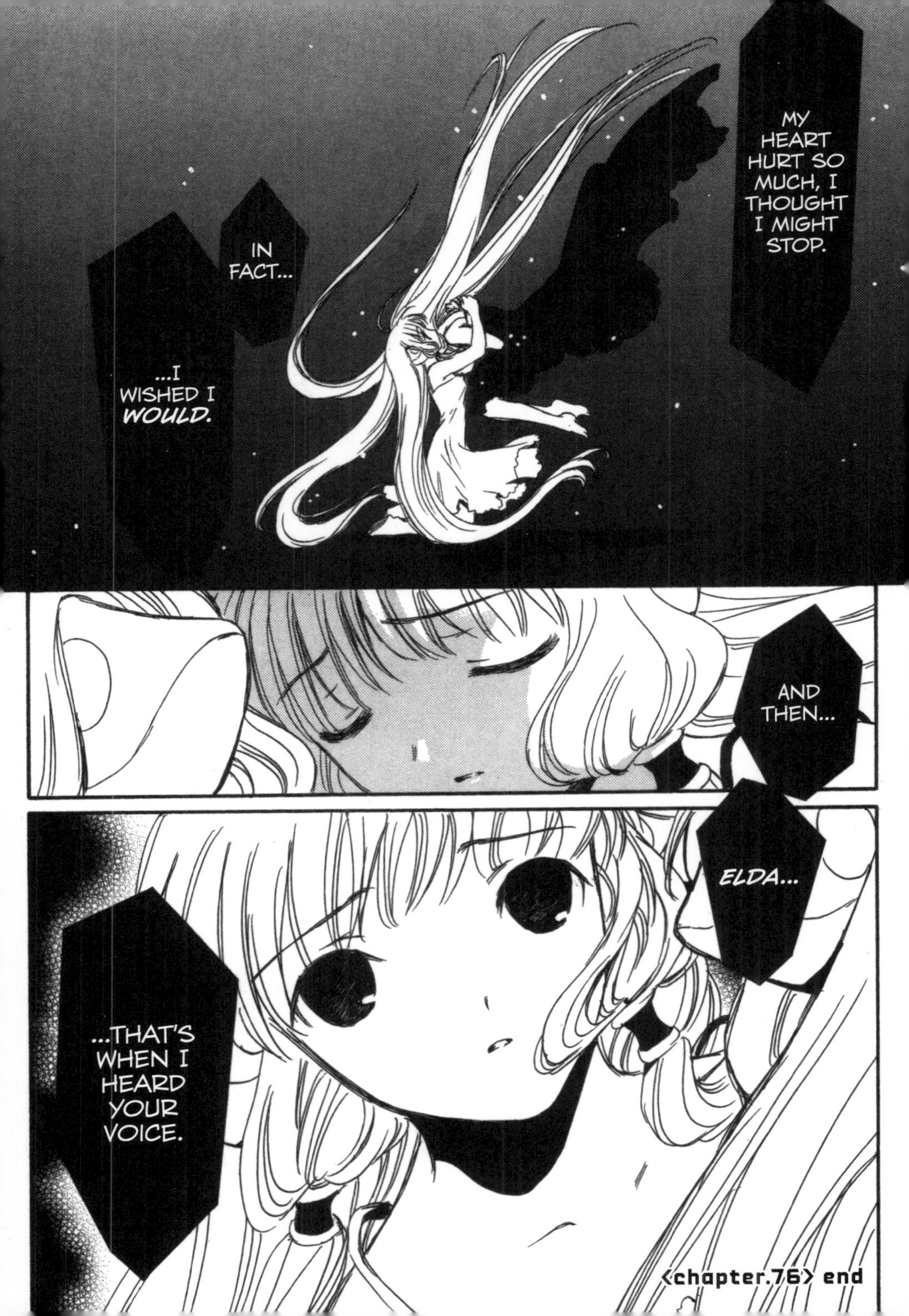
MY HEART HURT SO MUCH, I THOUGHT I MIGHT STOP.
IN FACT...
...I WISHED I *WOULD.*
AND THEN...
*ELDA...*
...THAT'S WHEN I HEARD YOUR VOICE.

<chapter.76> end

# <chapter.77>

Chobits

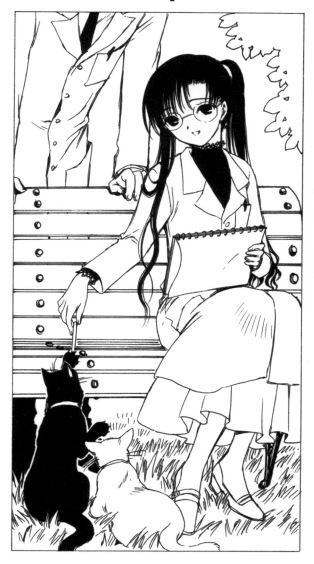

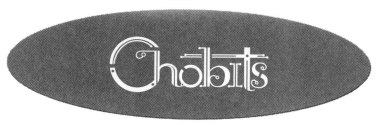

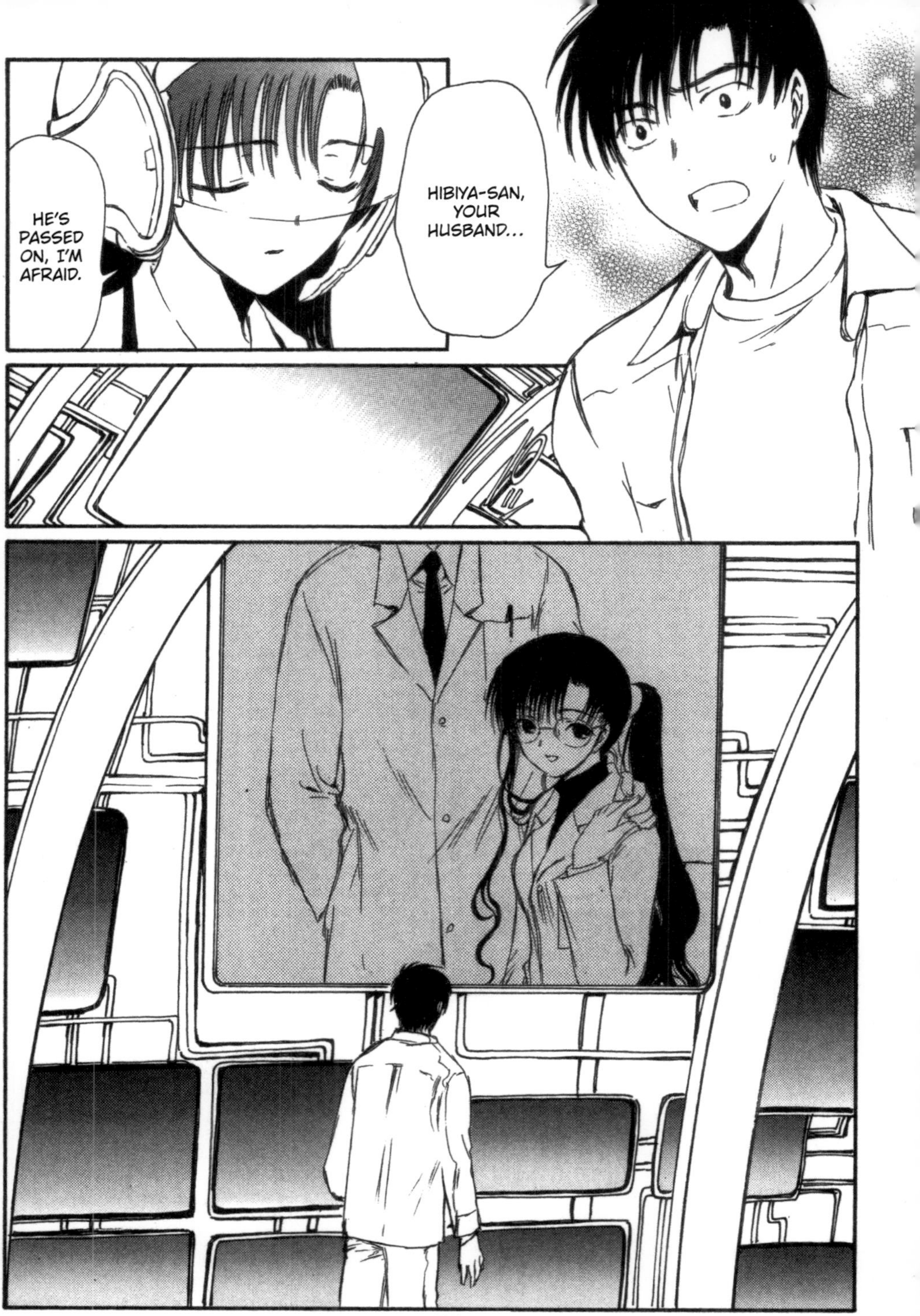
HIBIYA-SAN, YOUR HUSBAND...
HE'S PASSED ON, I'M AFRAID.

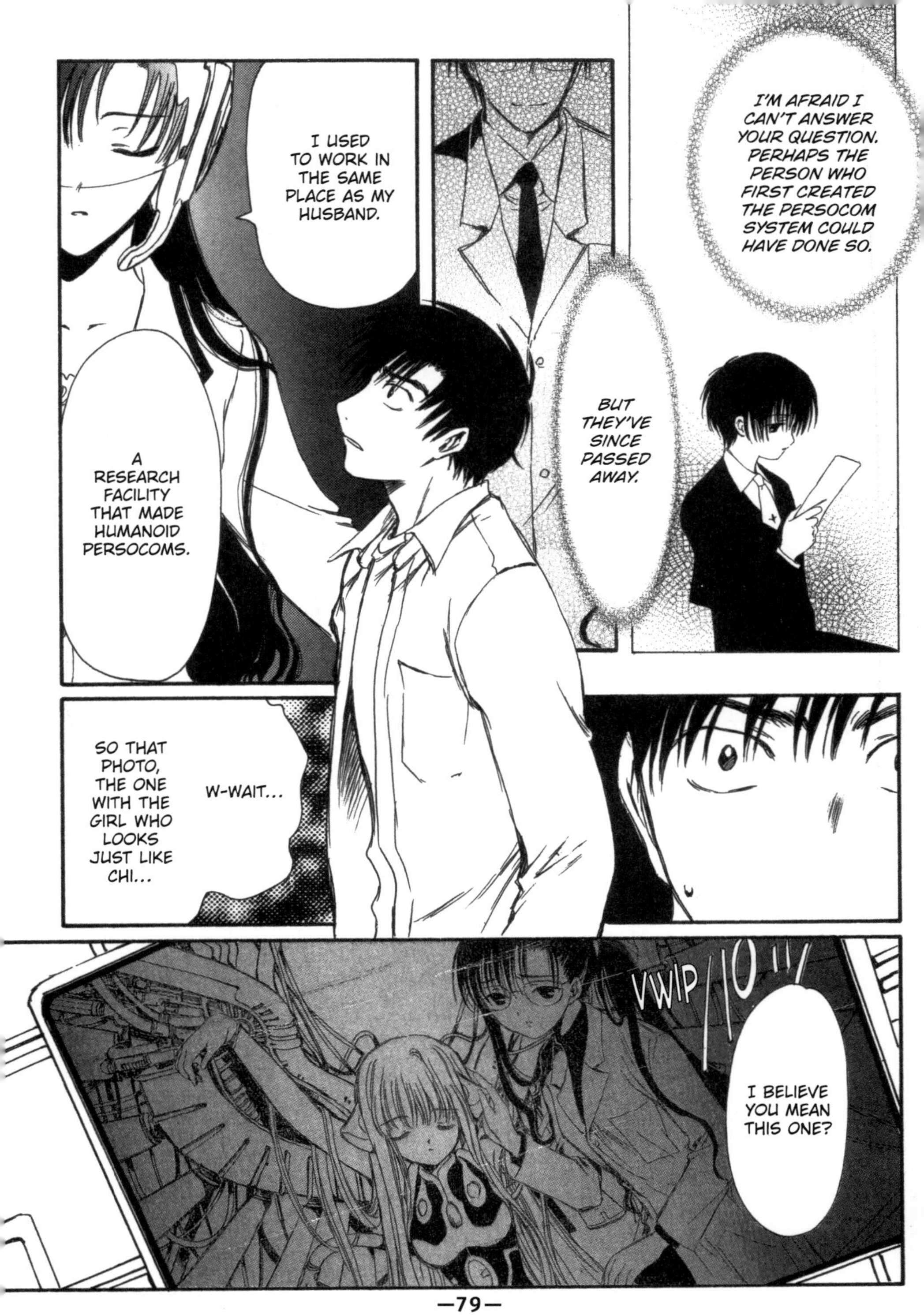
I'M AFRAID I CAN'T ANSWER YOUR QUESTION. PERHAPS THE PERSON WHO FIRST CREATED THE PERSOCOM SYSTEM COULD HAVE DONE SO.
BUT THEY'VE SINCE PASSED AWAY.
I USED TO WORK IN THE SAME PLACE AS MY HUSBAND.
A RESEARCH FACILITY THAT MADE HUMANOID PERSOCOMS.
W-WAIT...
SO THAT PHOTO, THE ONE WITH THE GIRL WHO LOOKS JUST LIKE CHI...
VWIP
I BELIEVE YOU MEAN THIS ONE?

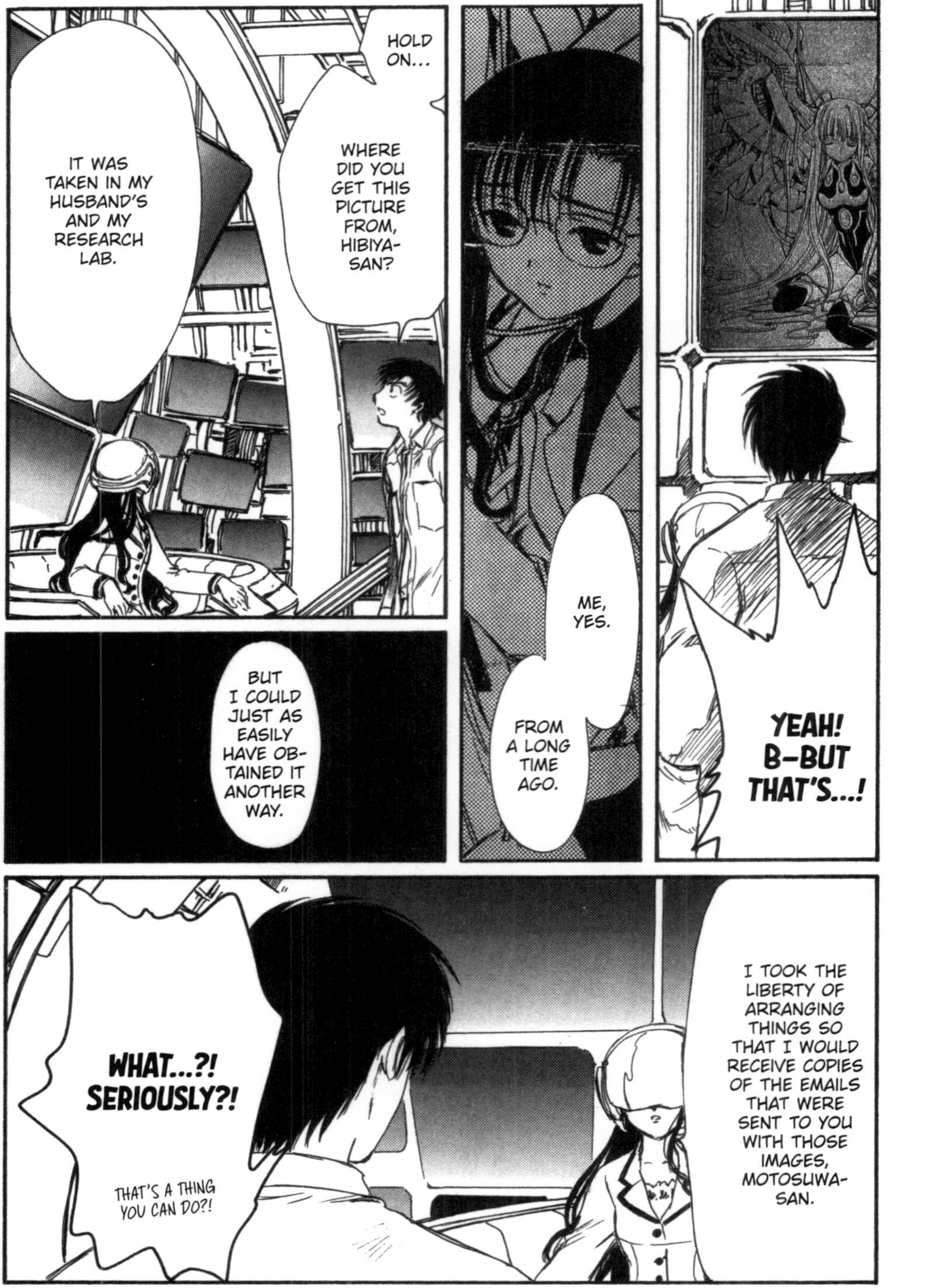
YEAH! B-BUT THAT'S...!
ME, YES.
FROM A LONG TIME AGO.
HOLD ON...
WHERE DID YOU GET THIS PICTURE FROM, HIBIYA-SAN?
IT WAS TAKEN IN MY HUSBAND'S AND MY RESEARCH LAB.
BUT I COULD JUST AS EASILY HAVE OB-TAINED IT ANOTHER WAY.
I TOOK THE LIBERTY OF ARRANGING THINGS SO THAT I WOULD RECEIVE COPIES OF THE EMAILS THAT WERE SENT TO YOU WITH THOSE IMAGES, MOTOSUWA-SAN.
WHAT...?! SERIOUSLY?!
THAT'S A THING YOU CAN DO?!

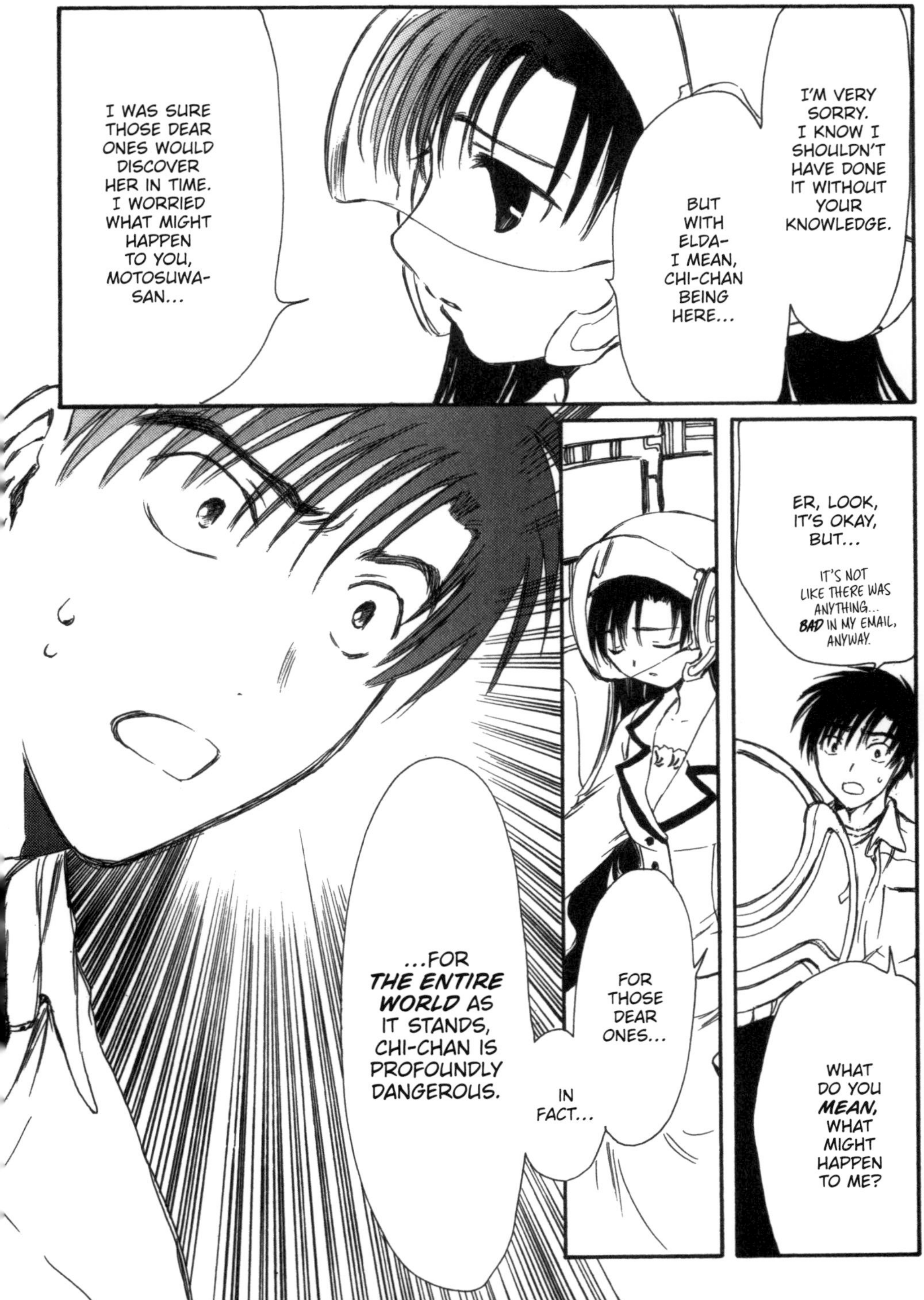
I'M VERY SORRY. I KNOW I SHOULDN'T HAVE DONE IT WITHOUT YOUR KNOWLEDGE.
BUT WITH ELDA- I MEAN, CHI-CHAN BEING HERE...
I WAS SURE THOSE DEAR ONES WOULD DISCOVER HER IN TIME. I WORRIED WHAT MIGHT HAPPEN TO YOU, MOTOSUWA-SAN...
ER, LOOK, IT'S OKAY, BUT...
IT'S NOT LIKE THERE WAS ANYTHING... BAD IN MY EMAIL, ANYWAY.
WHAT DO YOU MEAN, WHAT MIGHT HAPPEN TO ME?
FOR THOSE DEAR ONES...
IN FACT...
...FOR THE ENTIRE WORLD AS IT STANDS, CHI-CHAN IS PROFOUNDLY DANGEROUS.

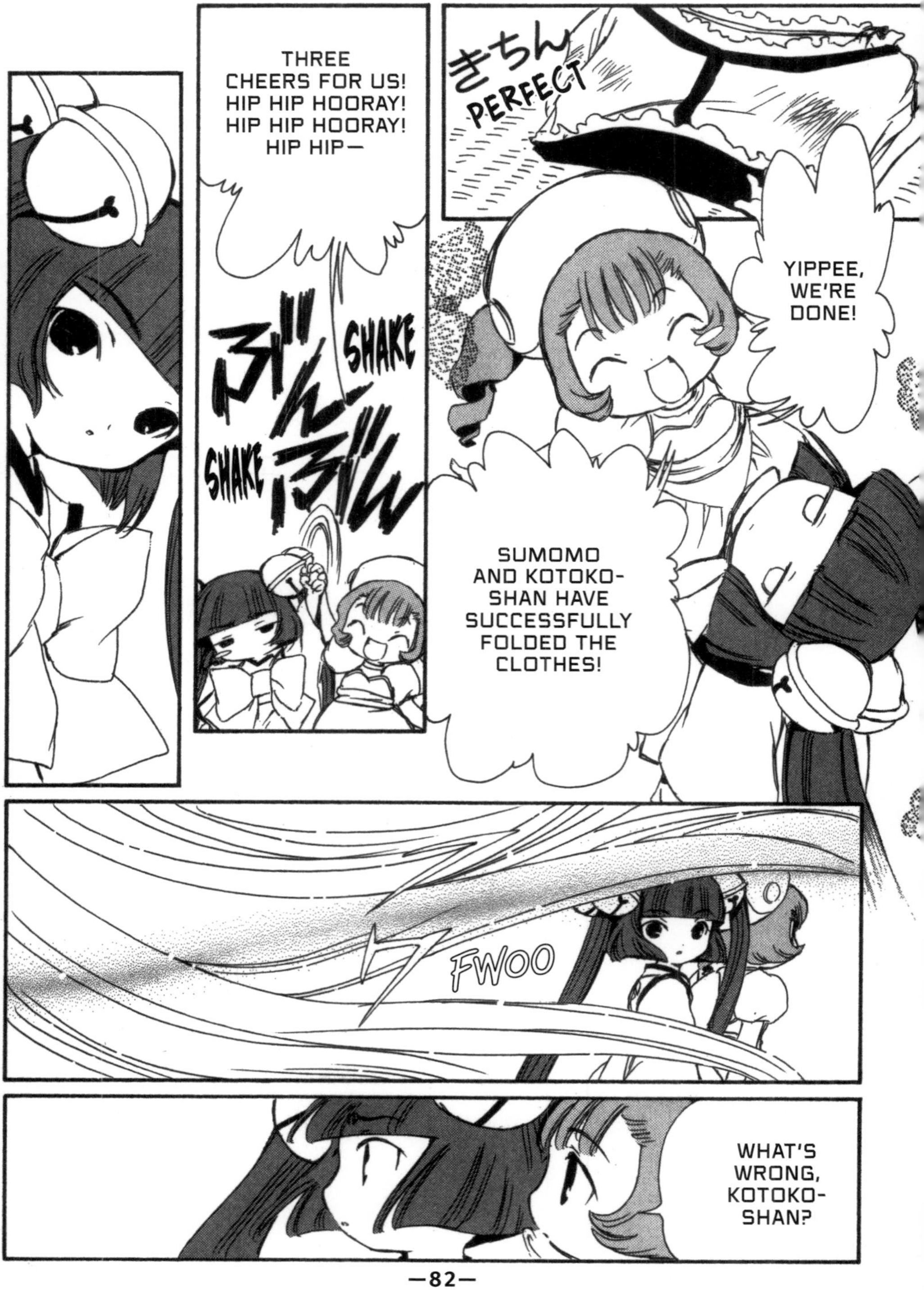
きちん
PERFECT
YIPPEE, WE'RE DONE!
SUMOMO AND KOTOKO-SHAN HAVE SUCCESSFULLY FOLDED THE CLOTHES!
THREE CHEERS FOR US! HIP HIP HOORAY! HIP HIP HOORAY! HIP HIP—
ぶんぶん
SHAKE
SHAKE
FWOO
WHAT'S WRONG, KOTOKO-SHAN?

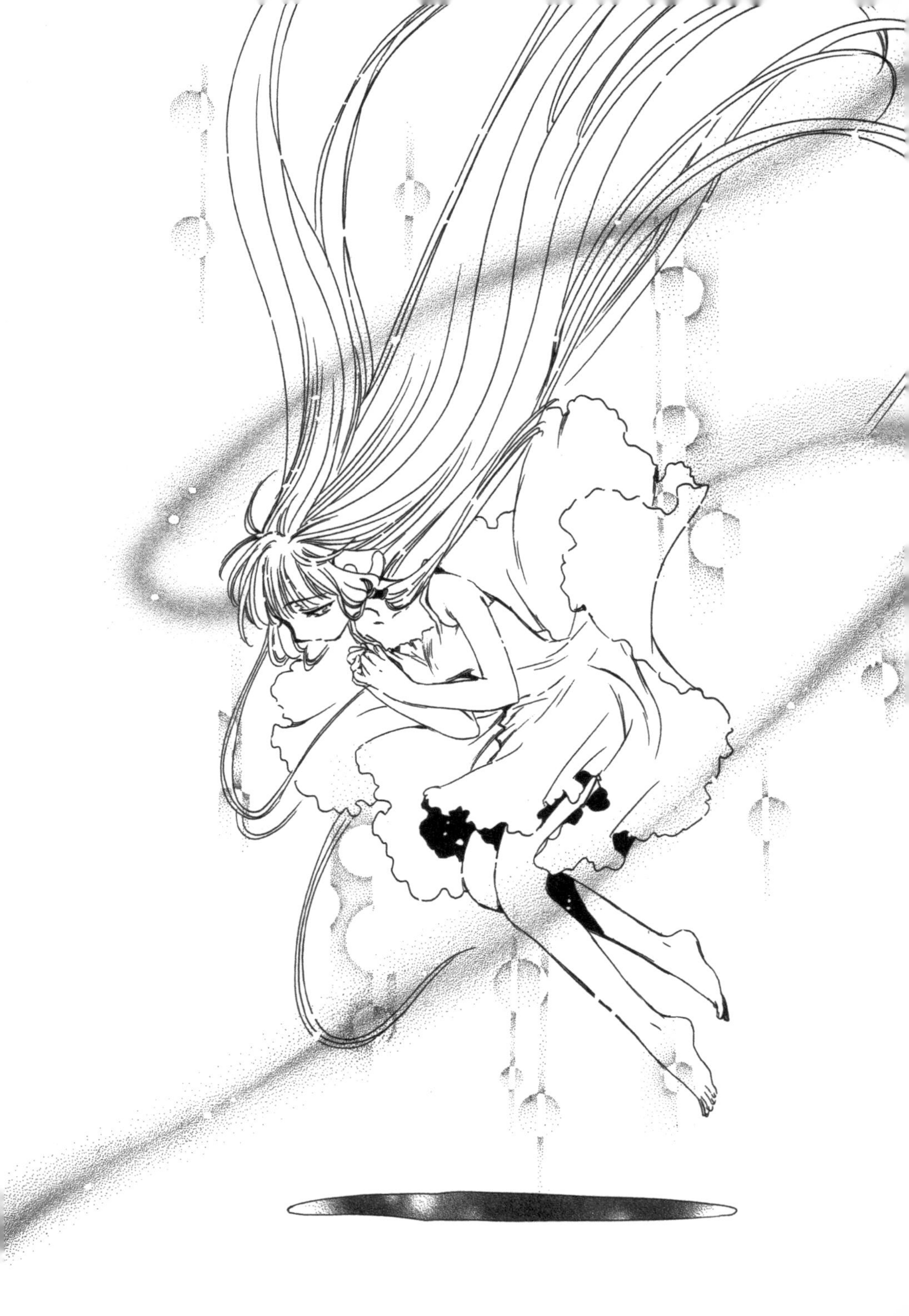

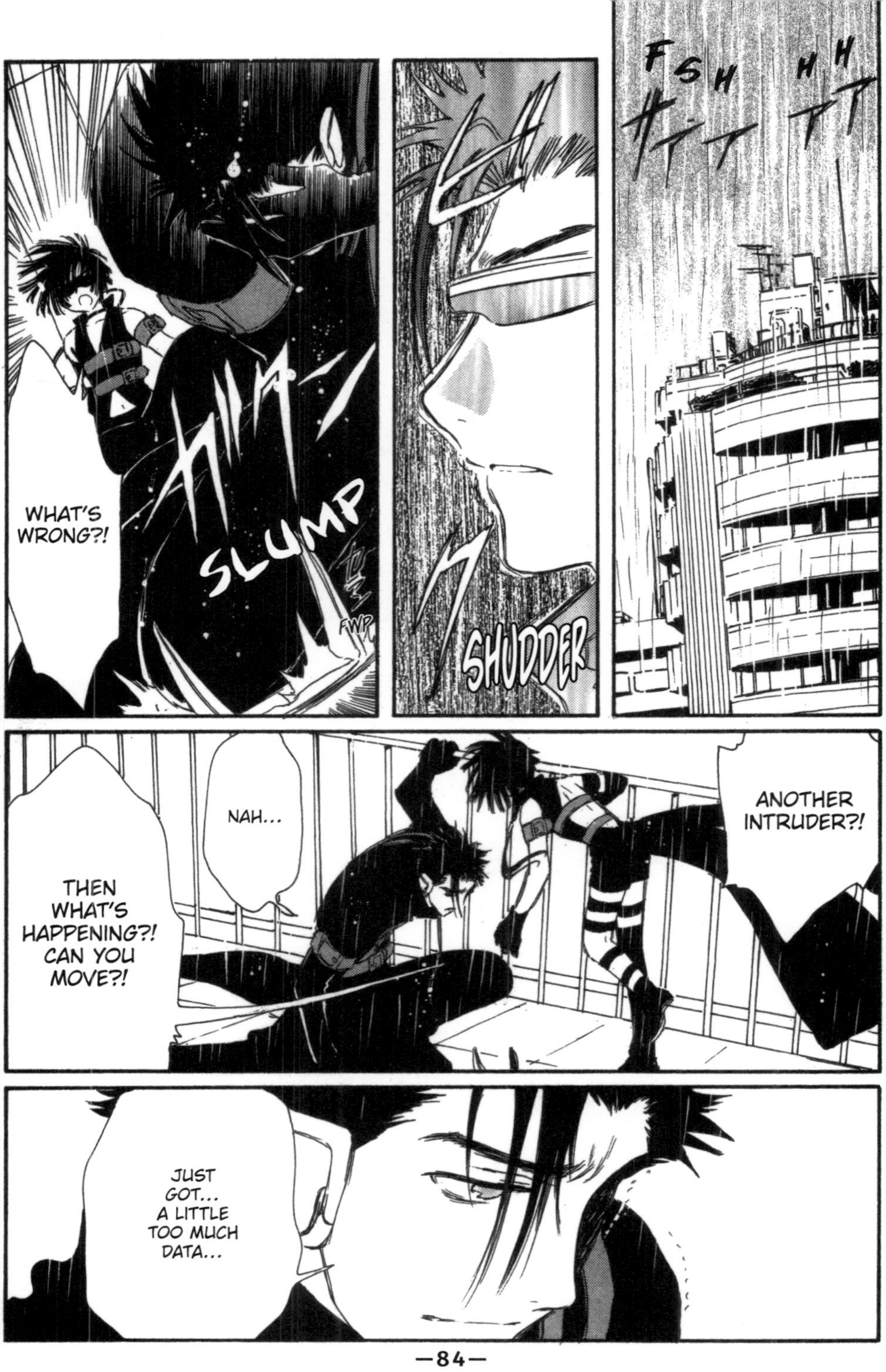
FSHHH
SHUDDER
WHAT'S WRONG?!
SLUMP
FWP
ANOTHER INTRUDER?!
NAH...
THEN WHAT'S HAPPENING?! CAN YOU MOVE?!
JUST GOT... A LITTLE TOO MUCH DATA...

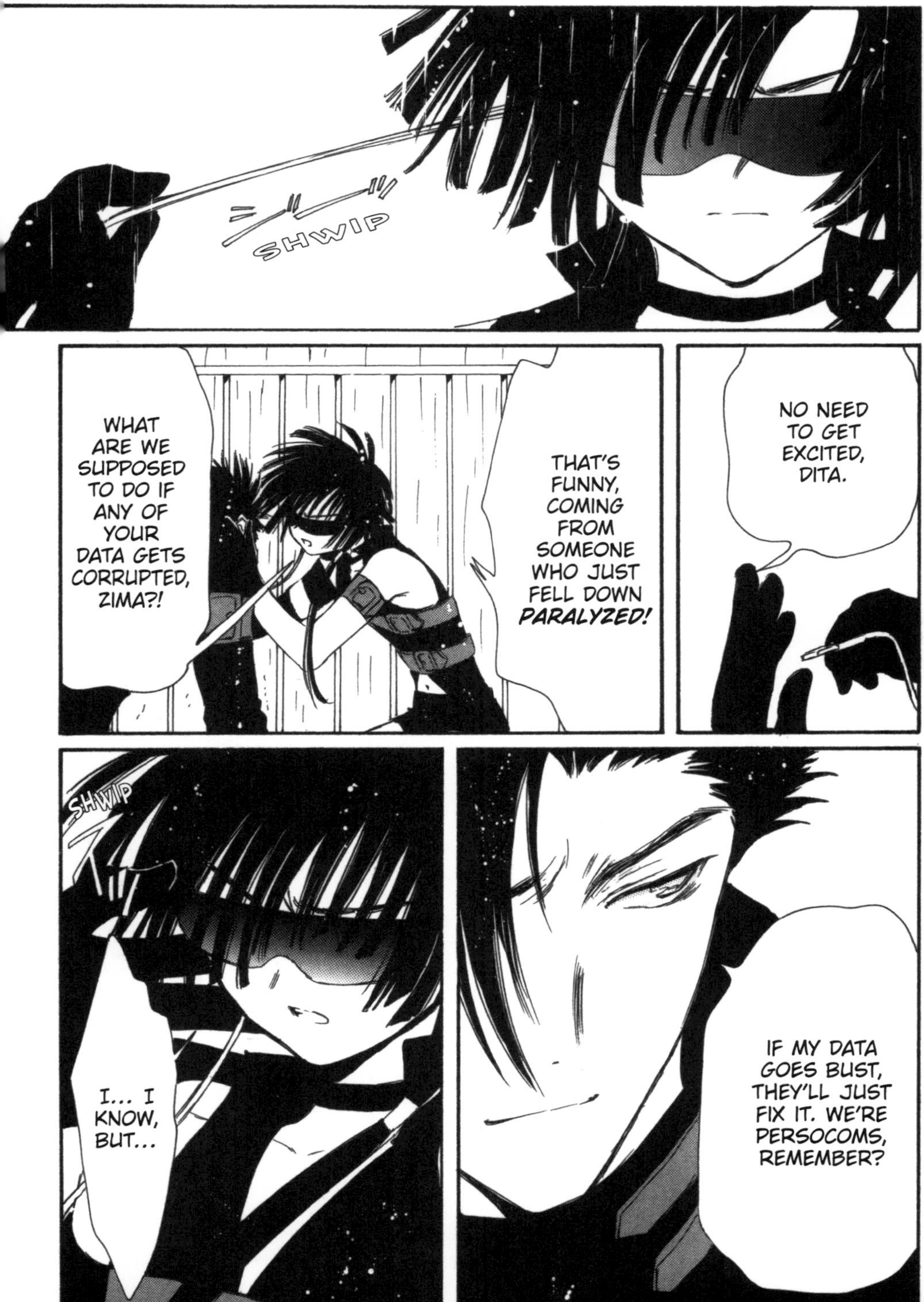
SHWIP
NO NEED TO GET EXCITED, DITA.
WHAT ARE WE SUPPOSED TO DO IF ANY OF YOUR DATA GETS CORRUPTED, ZIMA?!
THAT'S FUNNY, COMING FROM SOMEONE WHO JUST FELL DOWN PARALYZED!
IF MY DATA GOES BUST, THEY'LL JUST FIX IT. WE'RE PERSOCOMS, REMEMBER?
SHWIP
I... I KNOW, BUT...

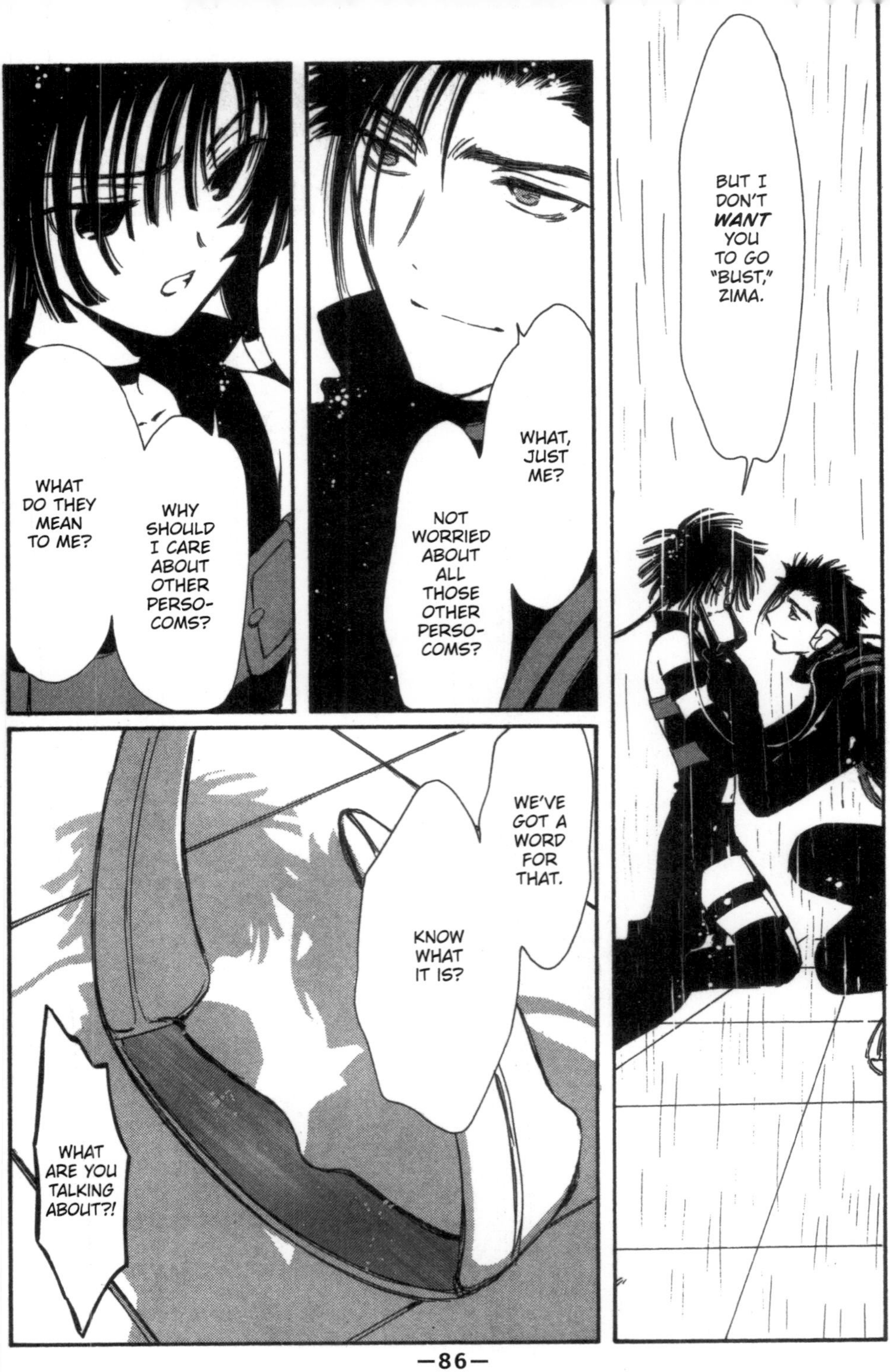
BUT I DON'T ***WANT*** YOU TO GO "BUST," ZIMA.
WHAT, JUST ME?
NOT WORRIED ABOUT ALL THOSE OTHER PERSO-COMS?
WHY SHOULD I CARE ABOUT OTHER PERSO-COMS?
WHAT DO THEY MEAN TO ME?
WE'VE GOT A WORD FOR THAT.
KNOW WHAT IT IS?
WHAT ARE YOU TALKING ABOUT?!

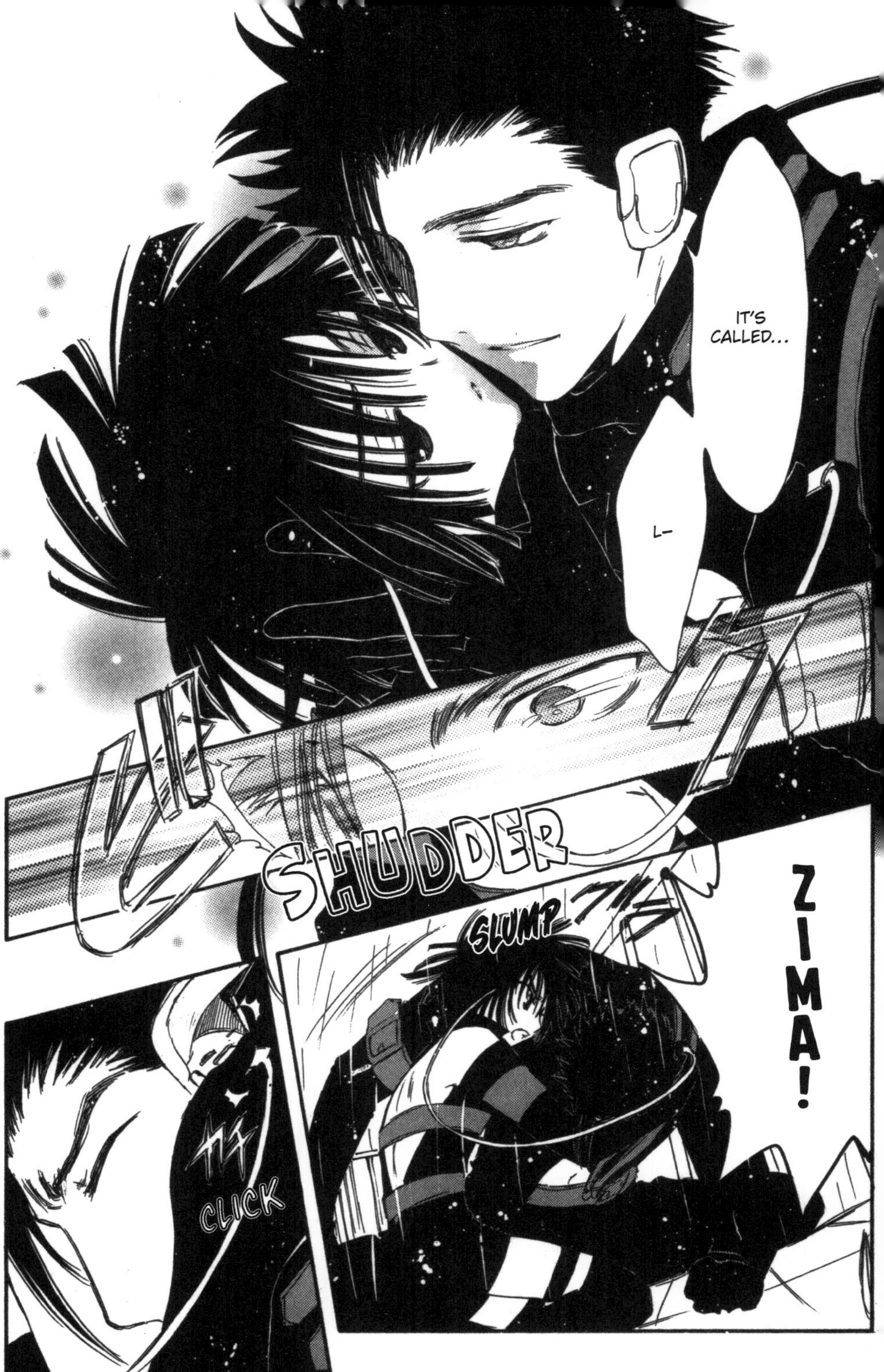
IT'S CALLED...
L–
SHUDDER
ZIMA!
SLUMP
CLICK

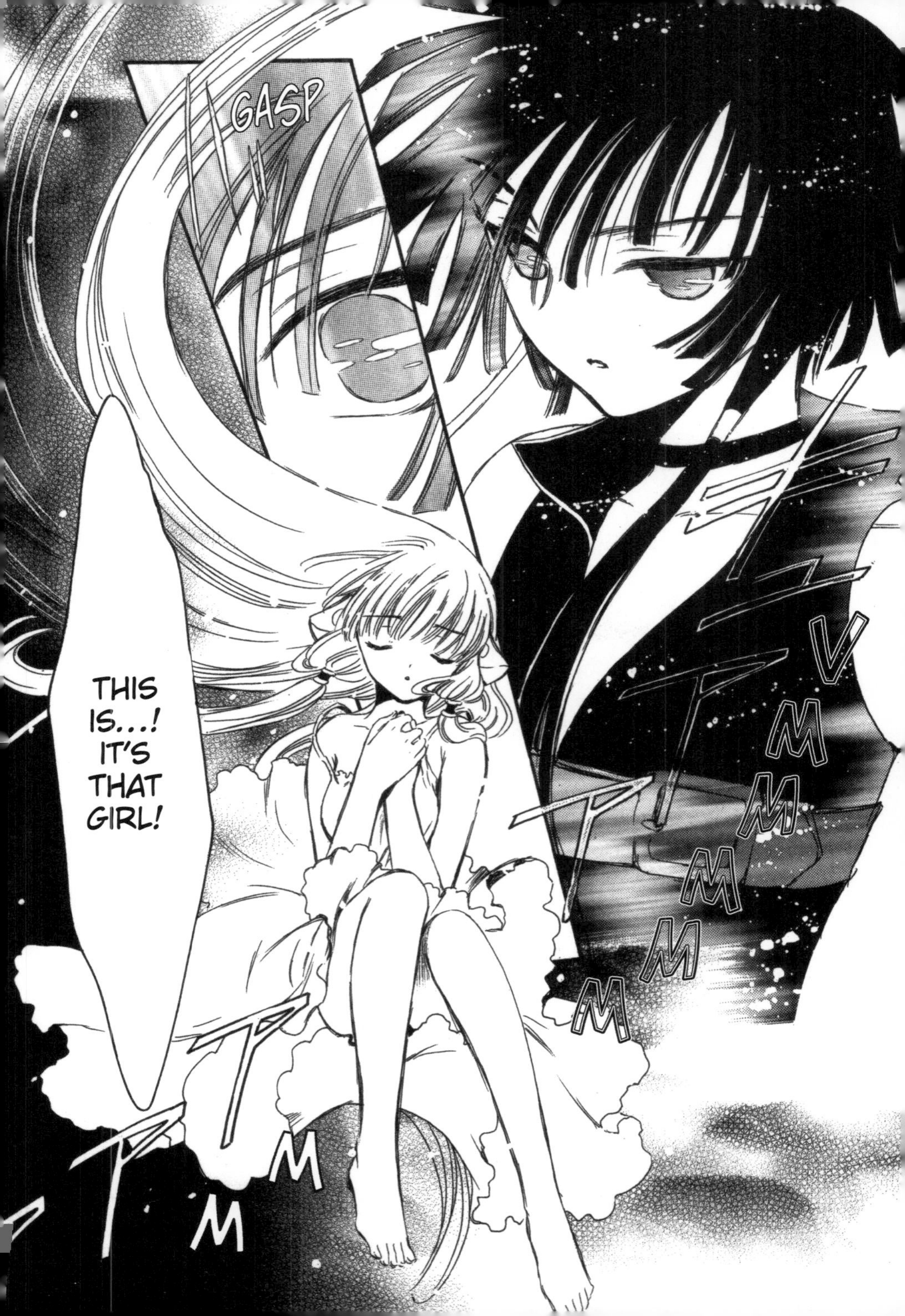
GASP
THIS IS...! IT'S THAT GIRL!
VMMMMMMM
MM

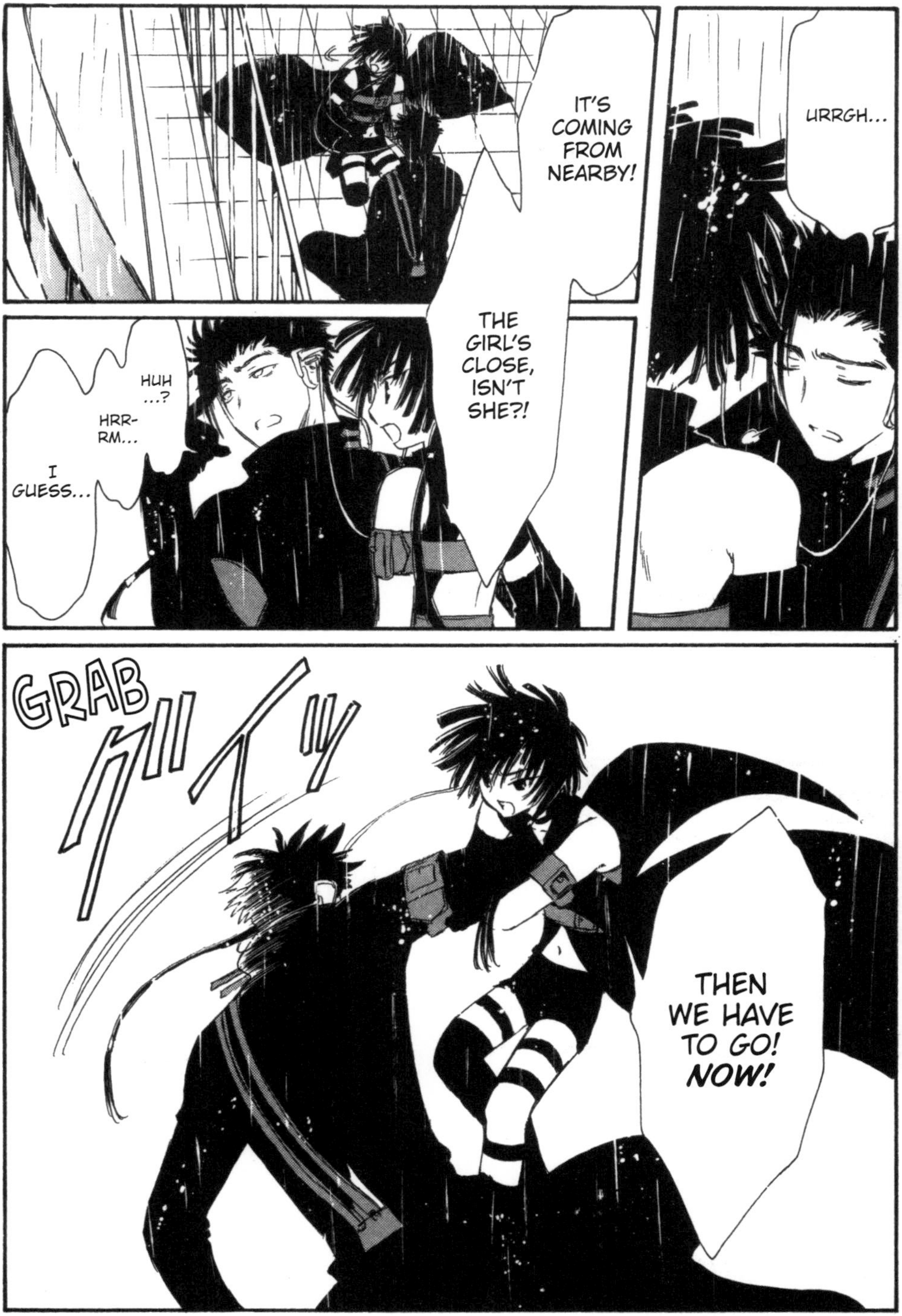
URRGH...
IT'S COMING FROM NEARBY!
THE GIRL'S CLOSE, ISN'T SHE?!
HUH ...?
HRR-RM...
I GUESS...
GRAB
グイッ
THEN WE HAVE TO GO! NOW!

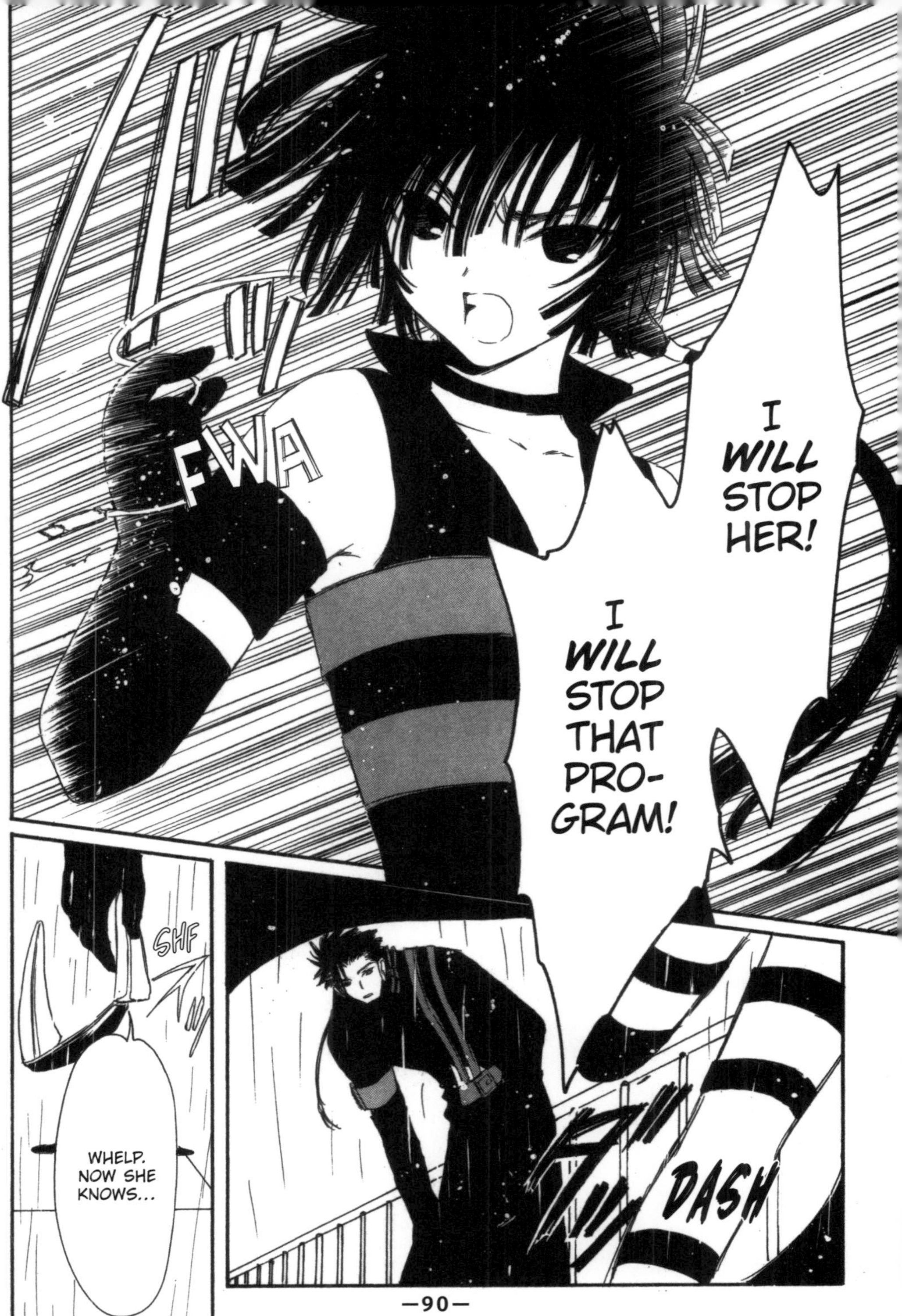

I *WILL* STOP HER!
I *WILL* STOP THAT PRO-GRAM!
FWA
DASH
SHF
WHELP. NOW SHE KNOWS...

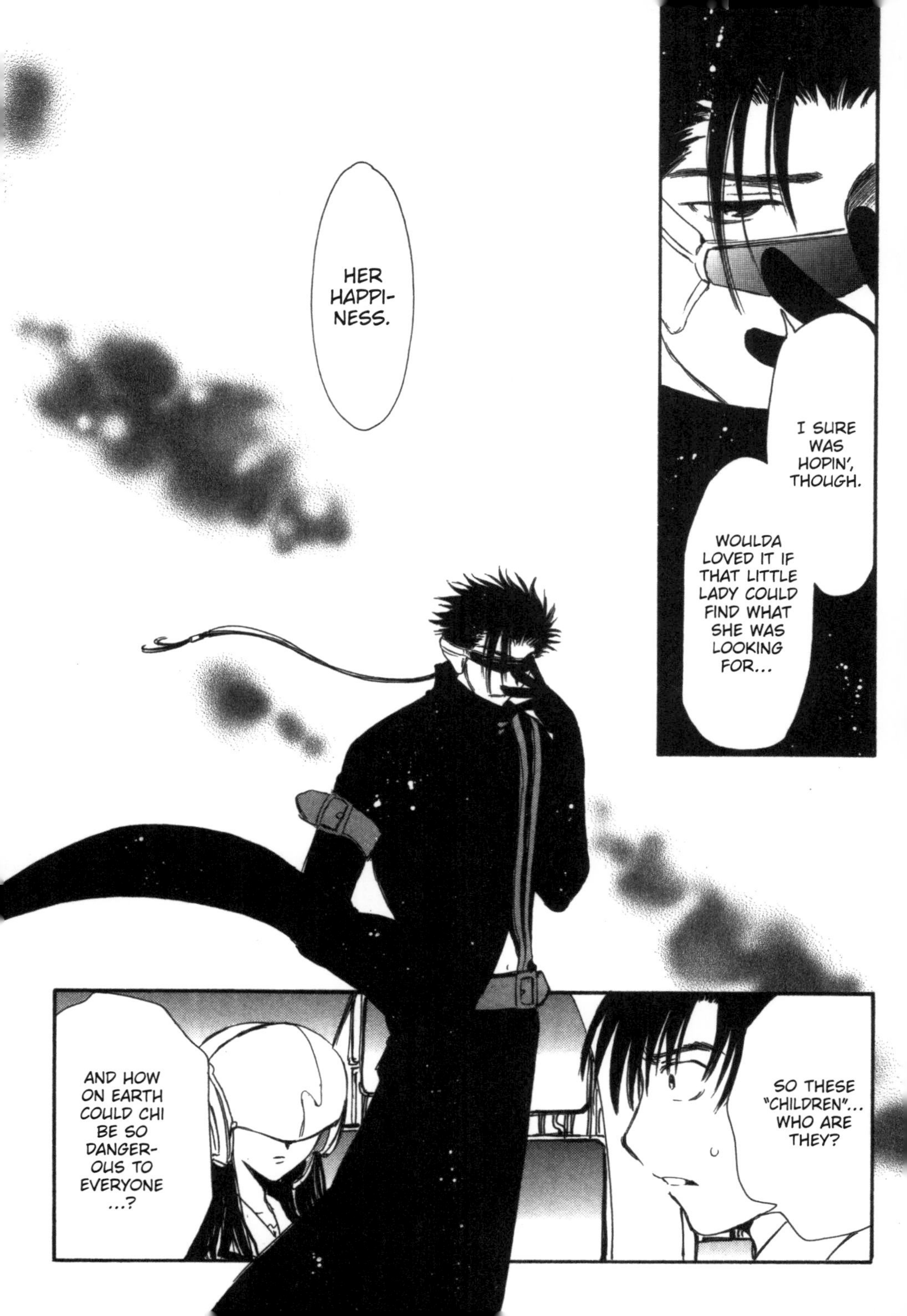
I SURE WAS HOPIN', THOUGH.
WOULDA LOVED IT IF THAT LITTLE LADY COULD FIND WHAT SHE WAS LOOKING FOR...
HER HAPPI-NESS.
SO THESE "CHILDREN"... WHO ARE THEY?
AND HOW ON EARTH COULD CHI BE SO DANGER-OUS TO EVERYONE ...?

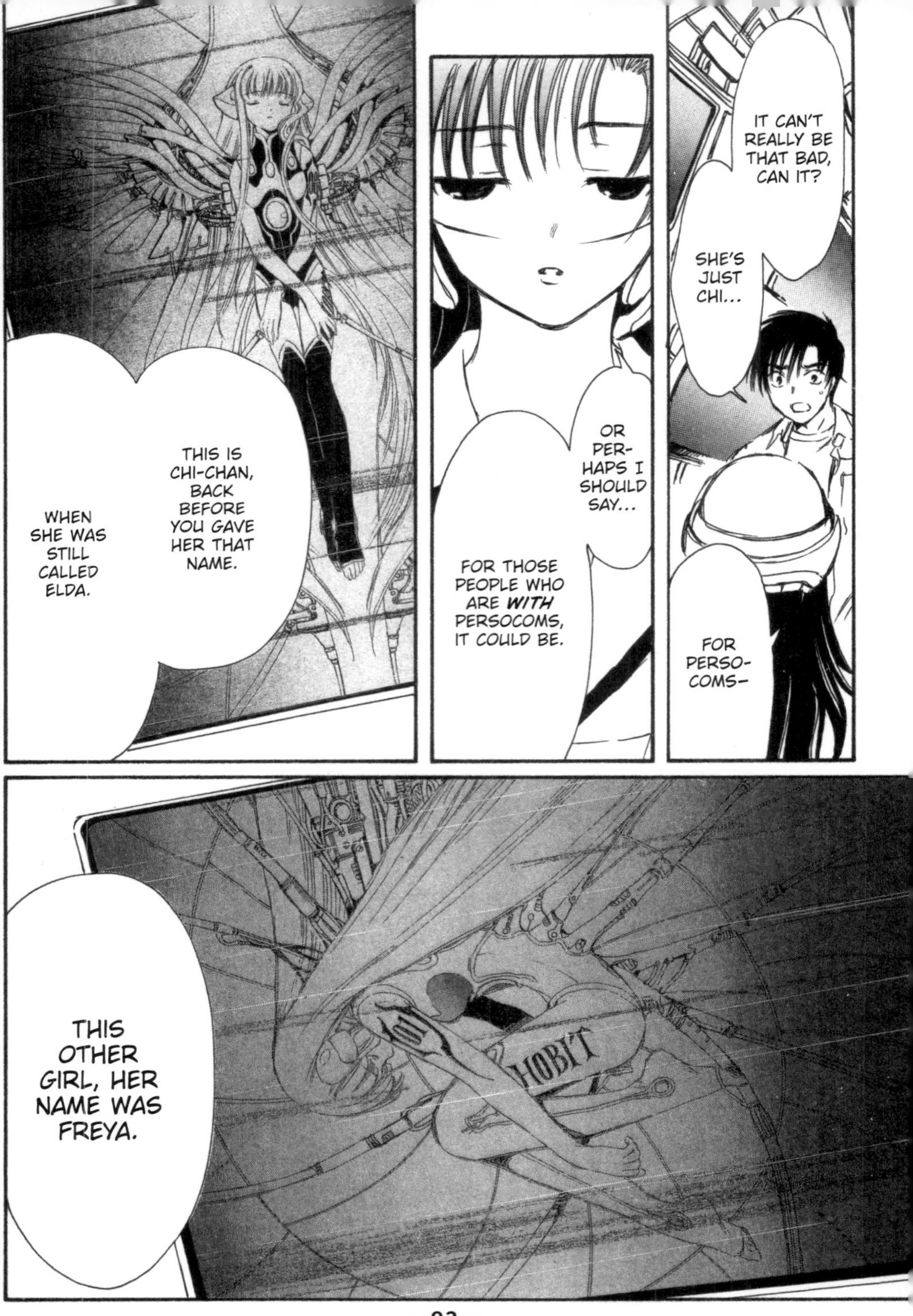
IT CAN'T REALLY BE THAT BAD, CAN IT?
SHE'S JUST CHI...
FOR PERSO-COMS–
OR PER-HAPS I SHOULD SAY...
FOR THOSE PEOPLE WHO ARE *WITH* PERSOCOMS, IT COULD BE.
THIS IS CHI-CHAN, BACK BEFORE YOU GAVE HER THAT NAME.
WHEN SHE WAS STILL CALLED ELDA.
THIS OTHER GIRL, HER NAME WAS FREYA.
HOBIT

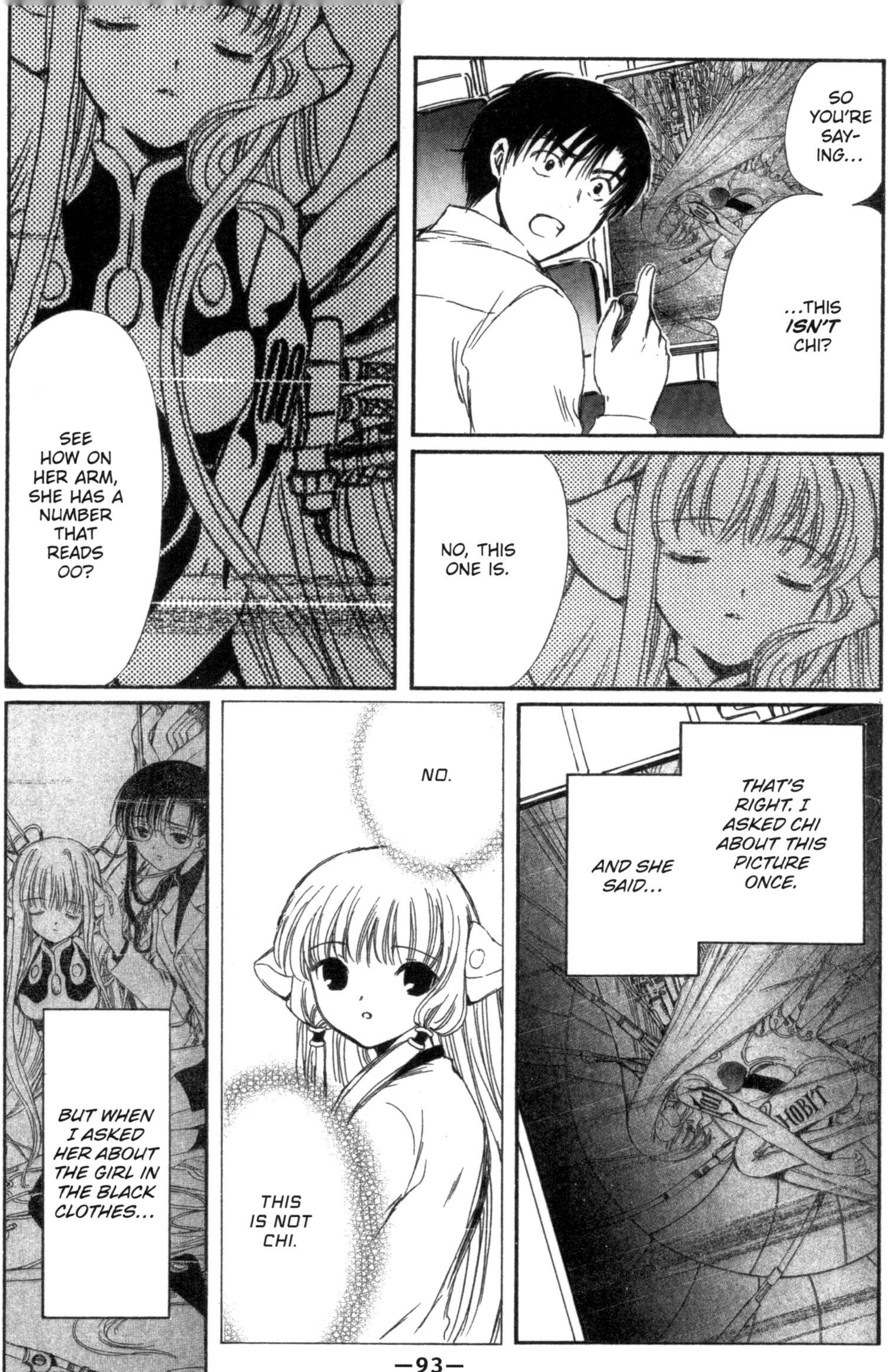
SO YOU'RE SAYING...
...THIS ISN'T CHI?
NO, THIS ONE IS.
SEE HOW ON HER ARM, SHE HAS A NUMBER THAT READS 00?
THAT'S RIGHT. I ASKED CHI ABOUT THIS PICTURE ONCE.
AND SHE SAID...
NO.
THIS IS NOT CHI.
BUT WHEN I ASKED HER ABOUT THE GIRL IN THE BLACK CLOTHES...
HOBIT

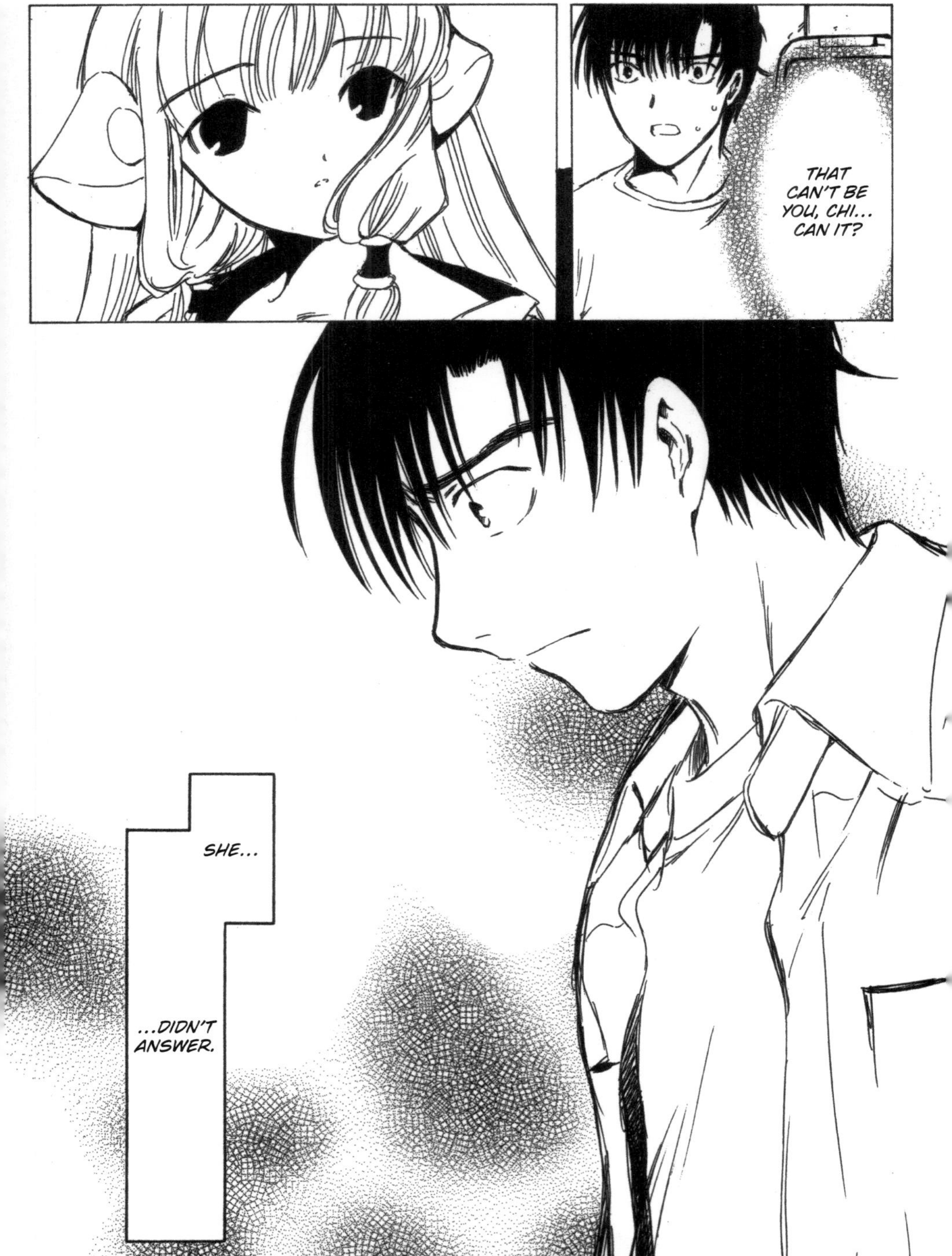
THAT CAN'T BE YOU, CHI... CAN IT?
SHE...
...DIDN'T ANSWER.
<chapter.77> end

〈chapter.78〉

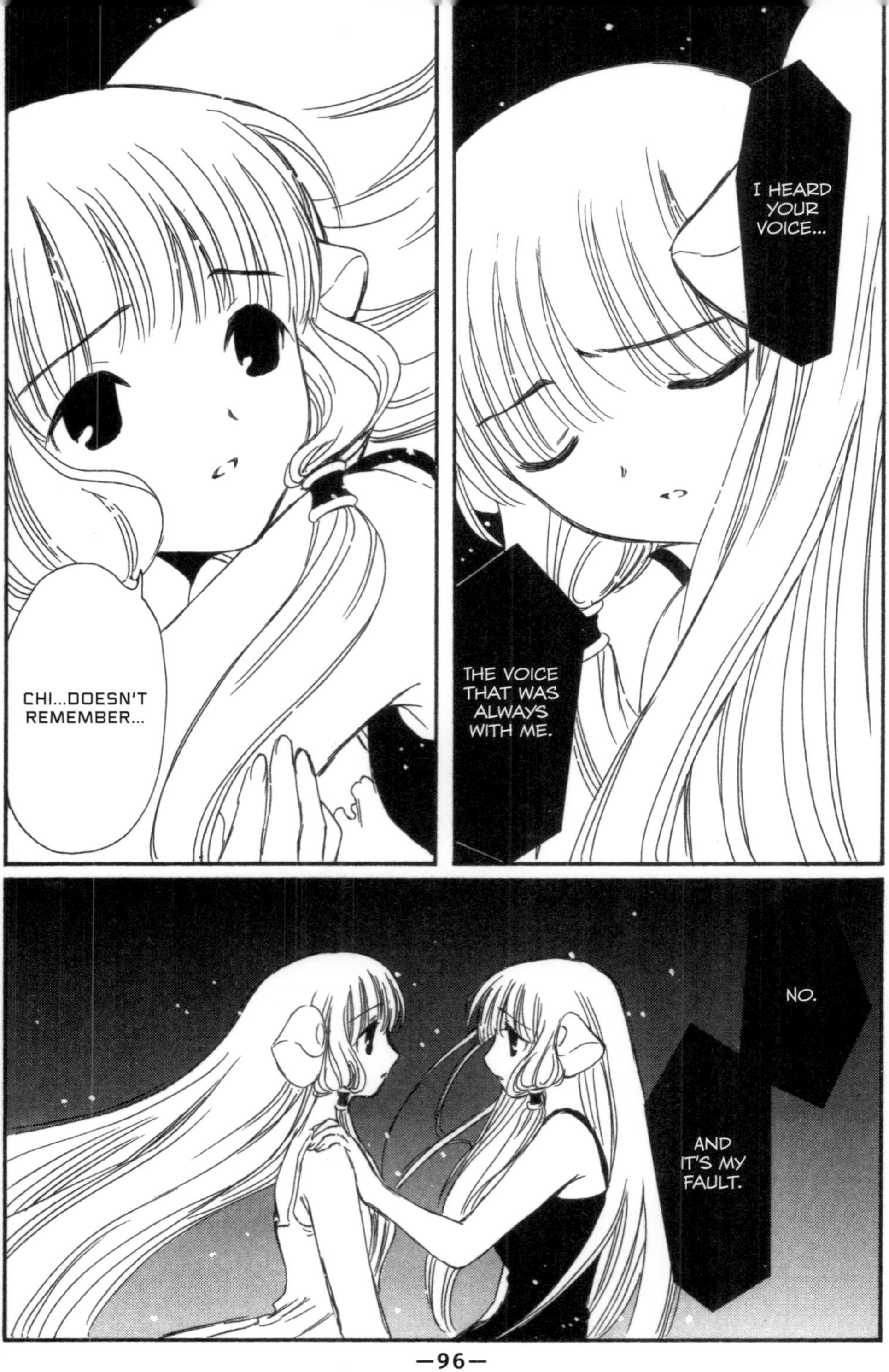
I HEARD YOUR VOICE...
THE VOICE THAT WAS ALWAYS WITH ME.
CHI...DOESN'T REMEMBER...
NO.
AND IT'S MY FAULT.

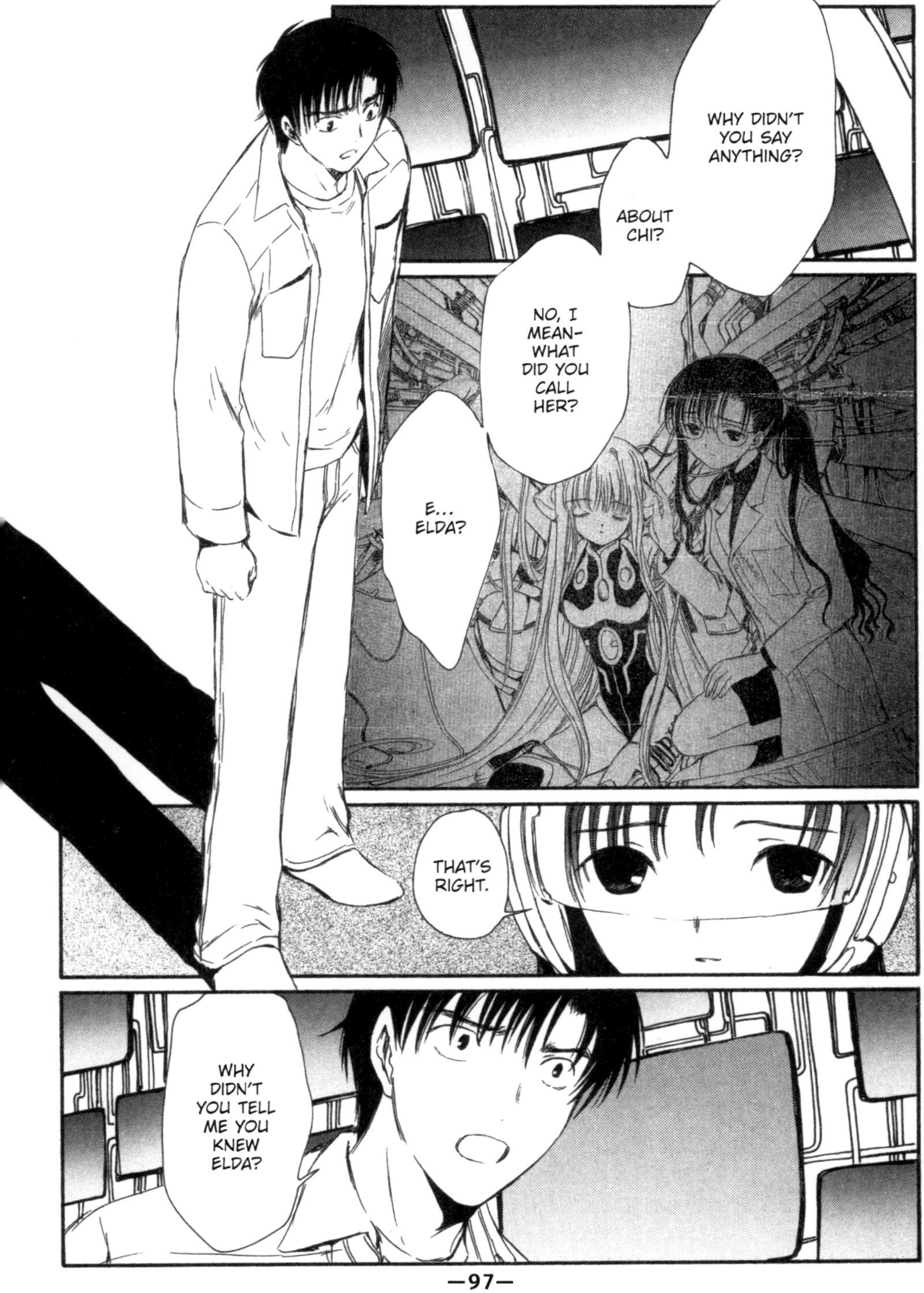
WHY DIDN'T YOU SAY ANYTHING?
ABOUT CHI?
NO, I MEAN- WHAT DID YOU CALL HER?
E... ELDA?
THAT'S RIGHT.
WHY DIDN'T YOU TELL ME YOU KNEW ELDA?

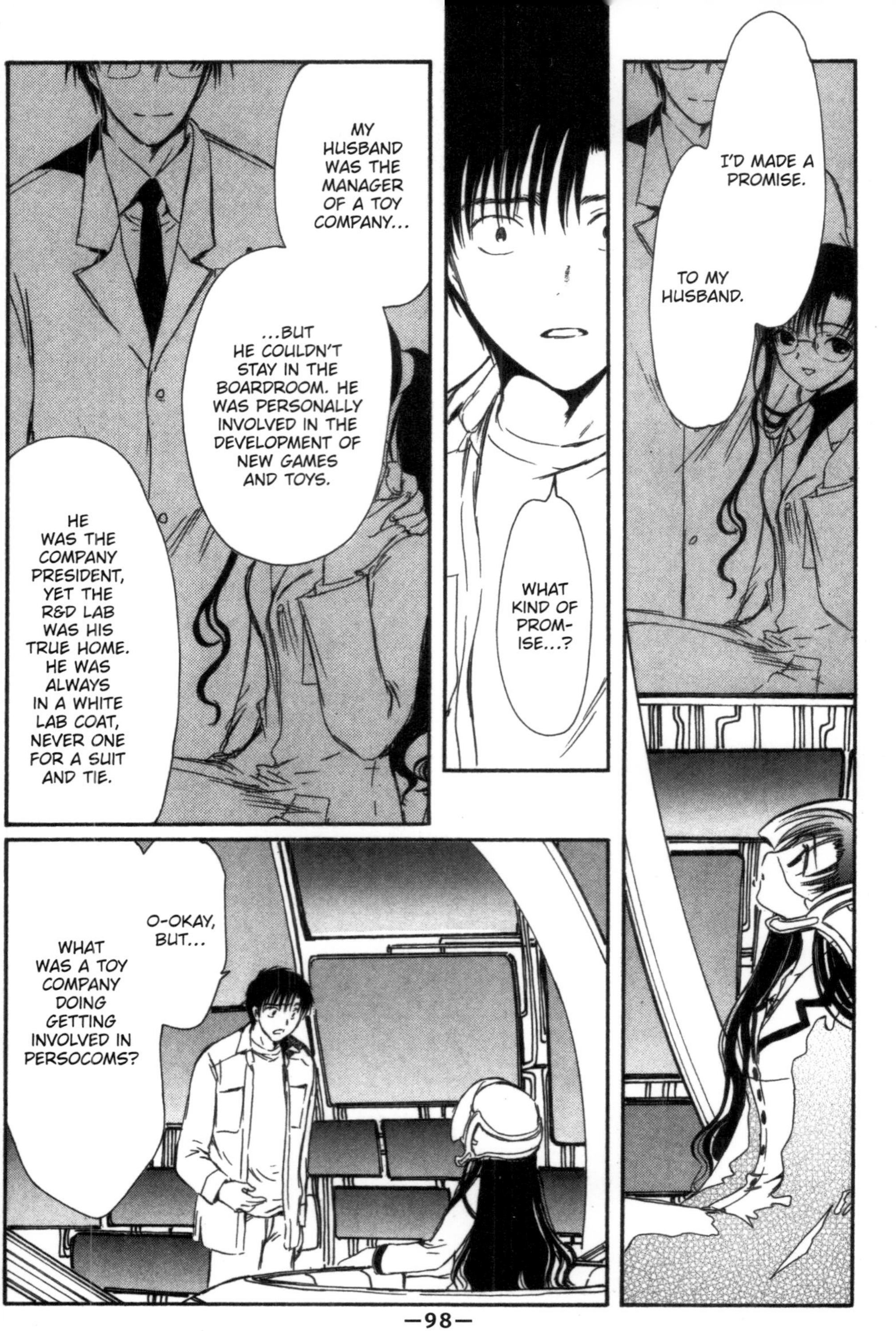

I'D MADE A PROMISE.
TO MY HUSBAND.
WHAT KIND OF PROMISE...?
MY HUSBAND WAS THE MANAGER OF A TOY COMPANY...
...BUT HE COULDN'T STAY IN THE BOARDROOM. HE WAS PERSONALLY INVOLVED IN THE DEVELOPMENT OF NEW GAMES AND TOYS.
HE WAS THE COMPANY PRESIDENT, YET THE R&D LAB WAS HIS TRUE HOME. HE WAS ALWAYS IN A WHITE LAB COAT, NEVER ONE FOR A SUIT AND TIE.
O-OKAY, BUT...
WHAT WAS A TOY COMPANY DOING GETTING INVOLVED IN PERSOCOMS?

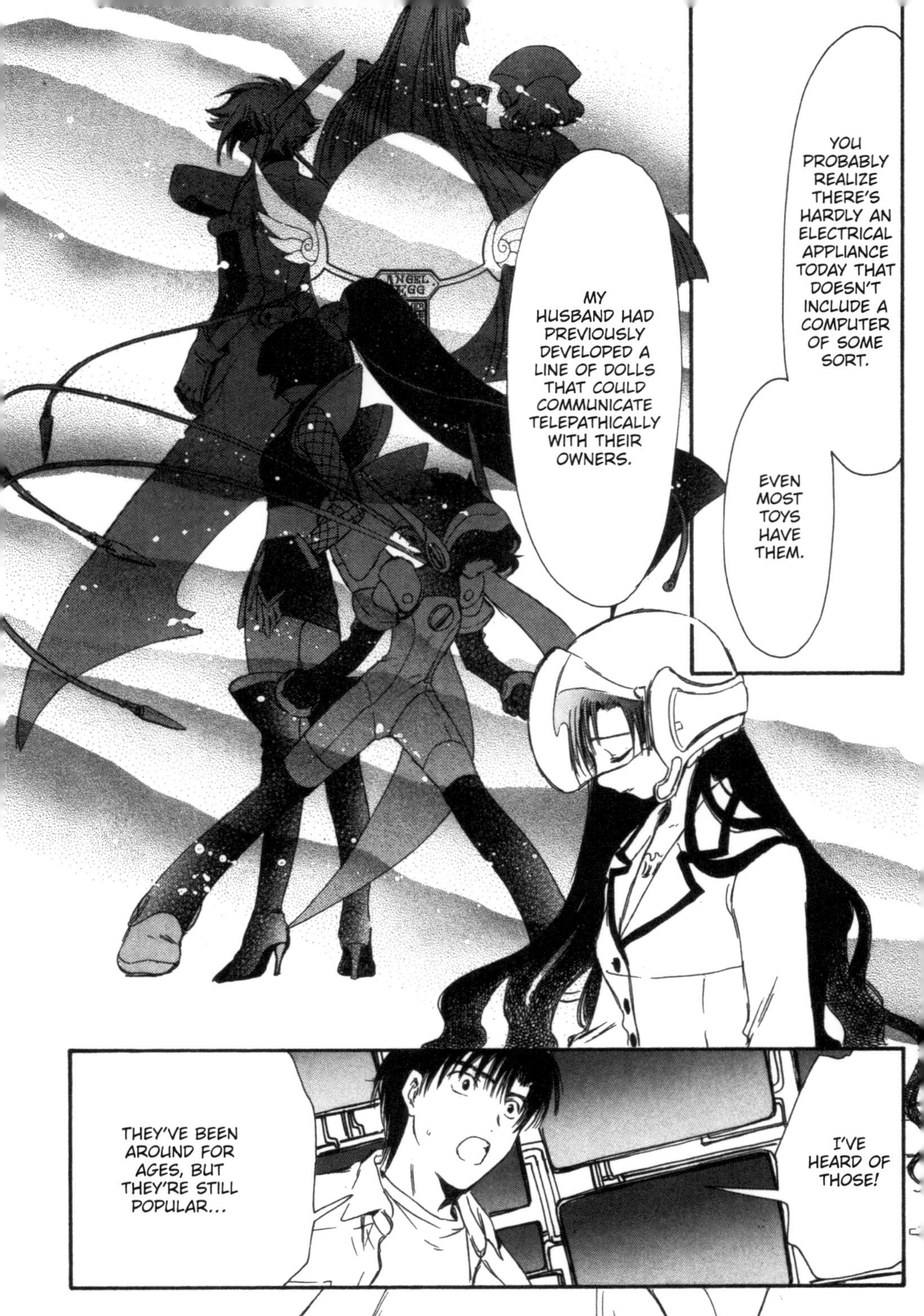
YOU PROBABLY REALIZE THERE'S HARDLY AN ELECTRICAL APPLIANCE TODAY THAT DOESN'T INCLUDE A COMPUTER OF SOME SORT.
EVEN MOST TOYS HAVE THEM.
MY HUSBAND HAD PREVIOUSLY DEVELOPED A LINE OF DOLLS THAT COULD COMMUNICATE TELEPATHICALLY WITH THEIR OWNERS.
I'VE HEARD OF THOSE!
THEY'VE BEEN AROUND FOR AGES, BUT THEY'RE STILL POPULAR...

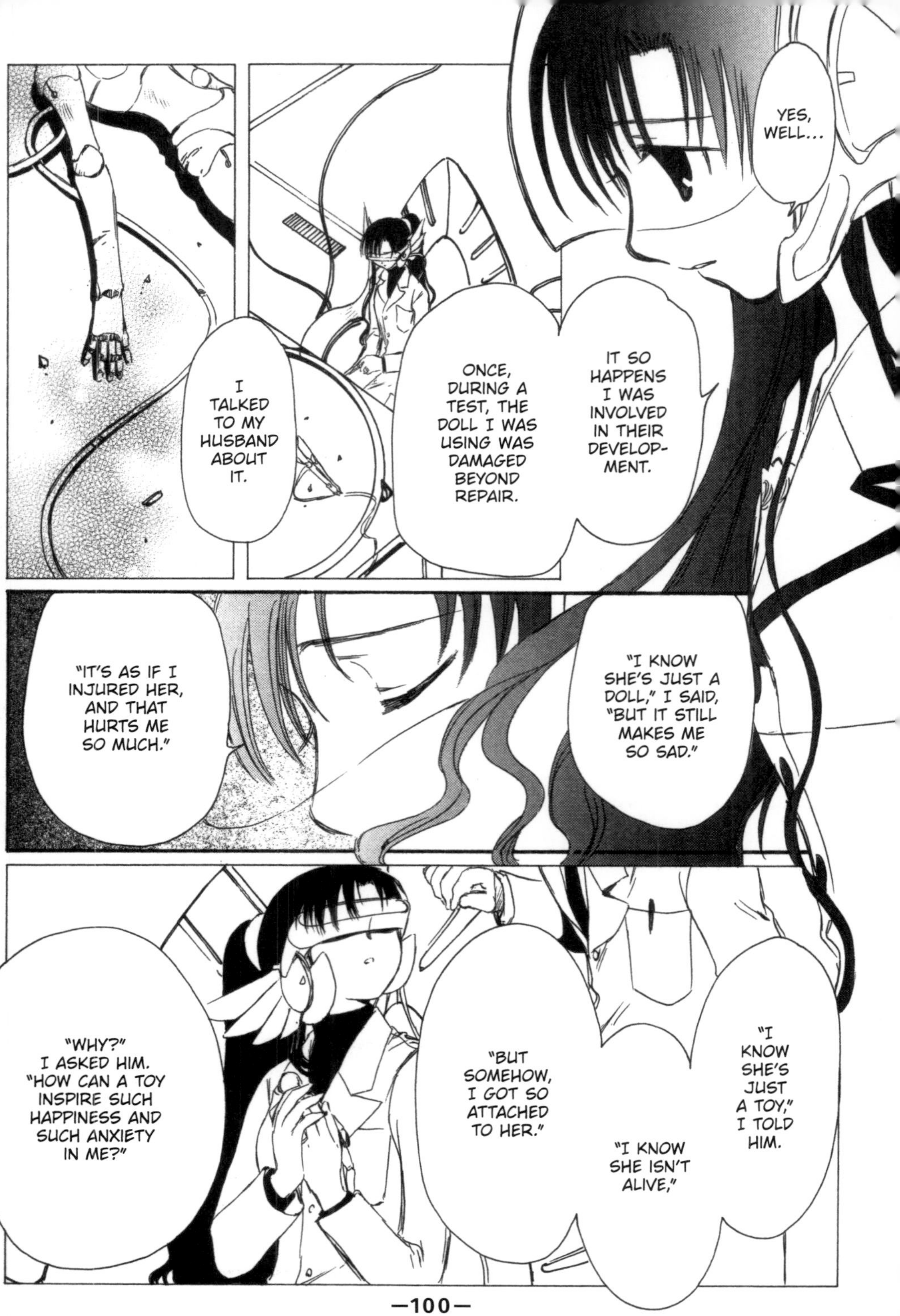
YES, WELL...
IT SO HAPPENS I WAS INVOLVED IN THEIR DEVELOPMENT.
ONCE, DURING A TEST, THE DOLL I WAS USING WAS DAMAGED BEYOND REPAIR.
I TALKED TO MY HUSBAND ABOUT IT.
"I KNOW SHE'S JUST A DOLL," I SAID, "BUT IT STILL MAKES ME SO SAD."
"IT'S AS IF I INJURED HER, AND THAT HURTS ME SO MUCH."
"I KNOW SHE'S JUST A TOY," I TOLD HIM.
"I KNOW SHE ISN'T ALIVE,"
"BUT SOMEHOW, I GOT SO ATTACHED TO HER."
"WHY?" I ASKED HIM. "HOW CAN A TOY INSPIRE SUCH HAPPINESS AND SUCH ANXIETY IN ME?"

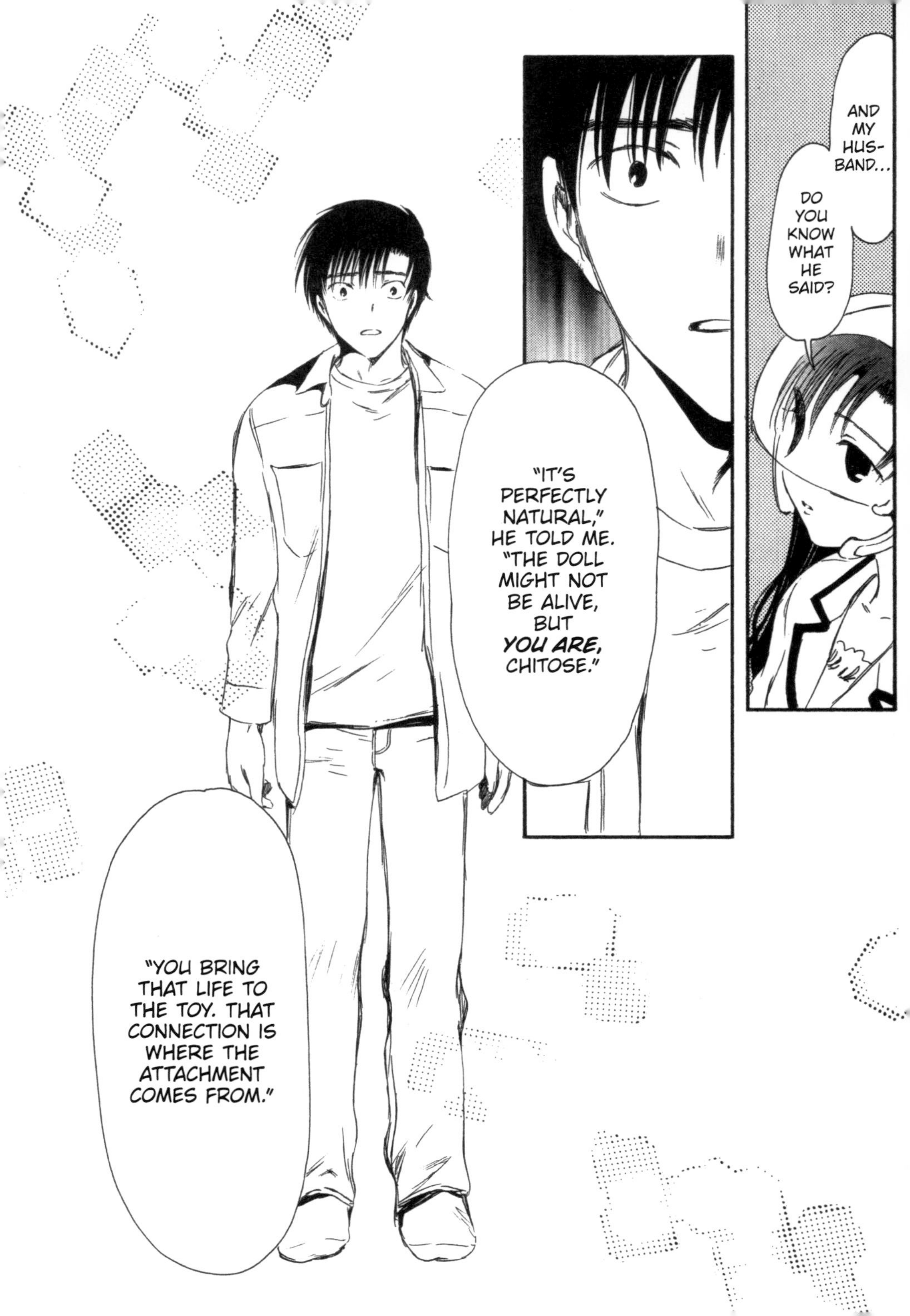
AND MY HUS-BAND...
DO YOU KNOW WHAT HE SAID?
"IT'S PERFECTLY NATURAL," HE TOLD ME. "THE DOLL MIGHT NOT BE ALIVE, BUT ***YOU ARE,*** CHITOSE."
"YOU BRING THAT LIFE TO THE TOY. THAT CONNECTION IS WHERE THE ATTACHMENT COMES FROM."

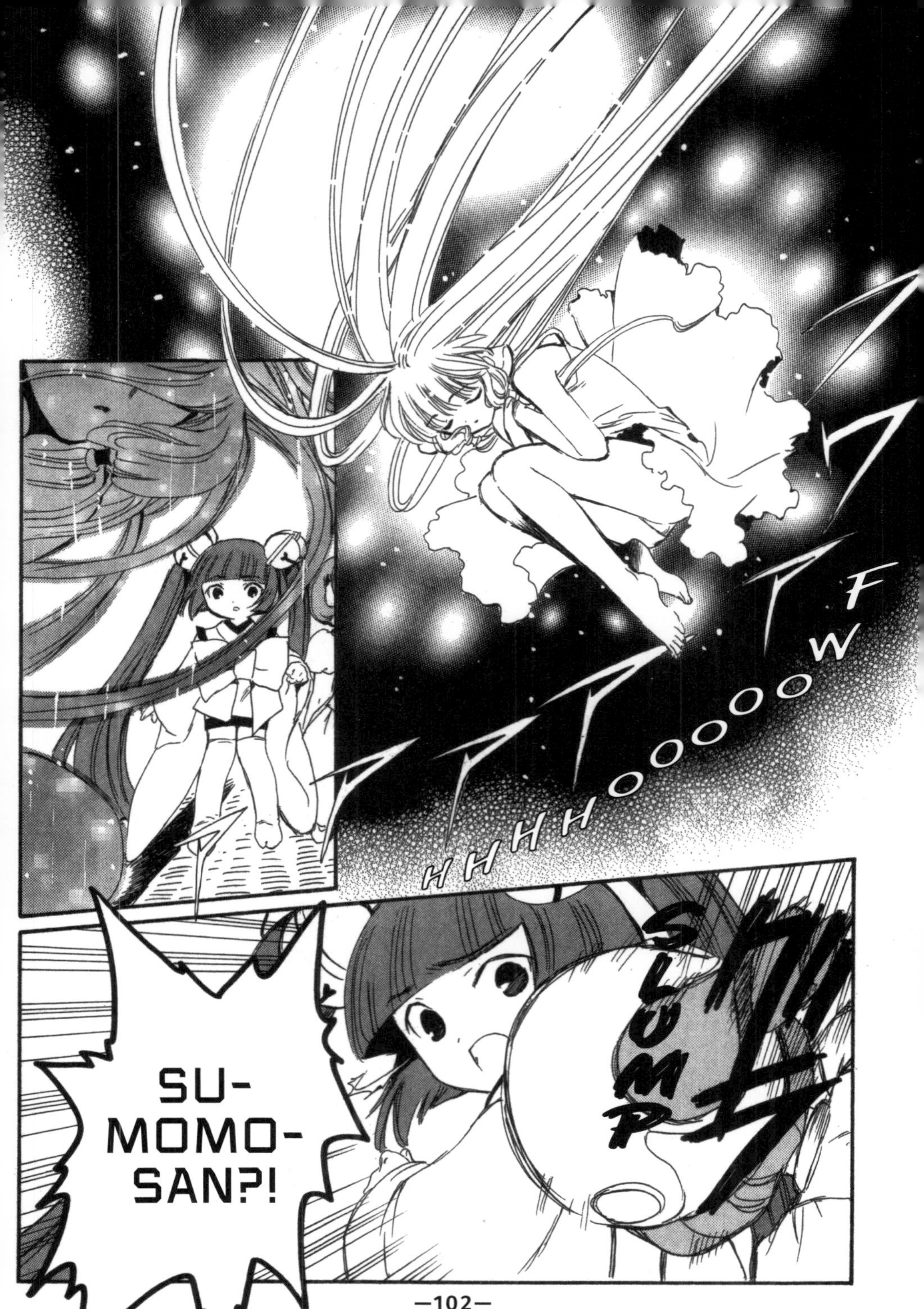
HHHHHOOOOOOWF
SLUMP
SU-MOMO-SAN?!

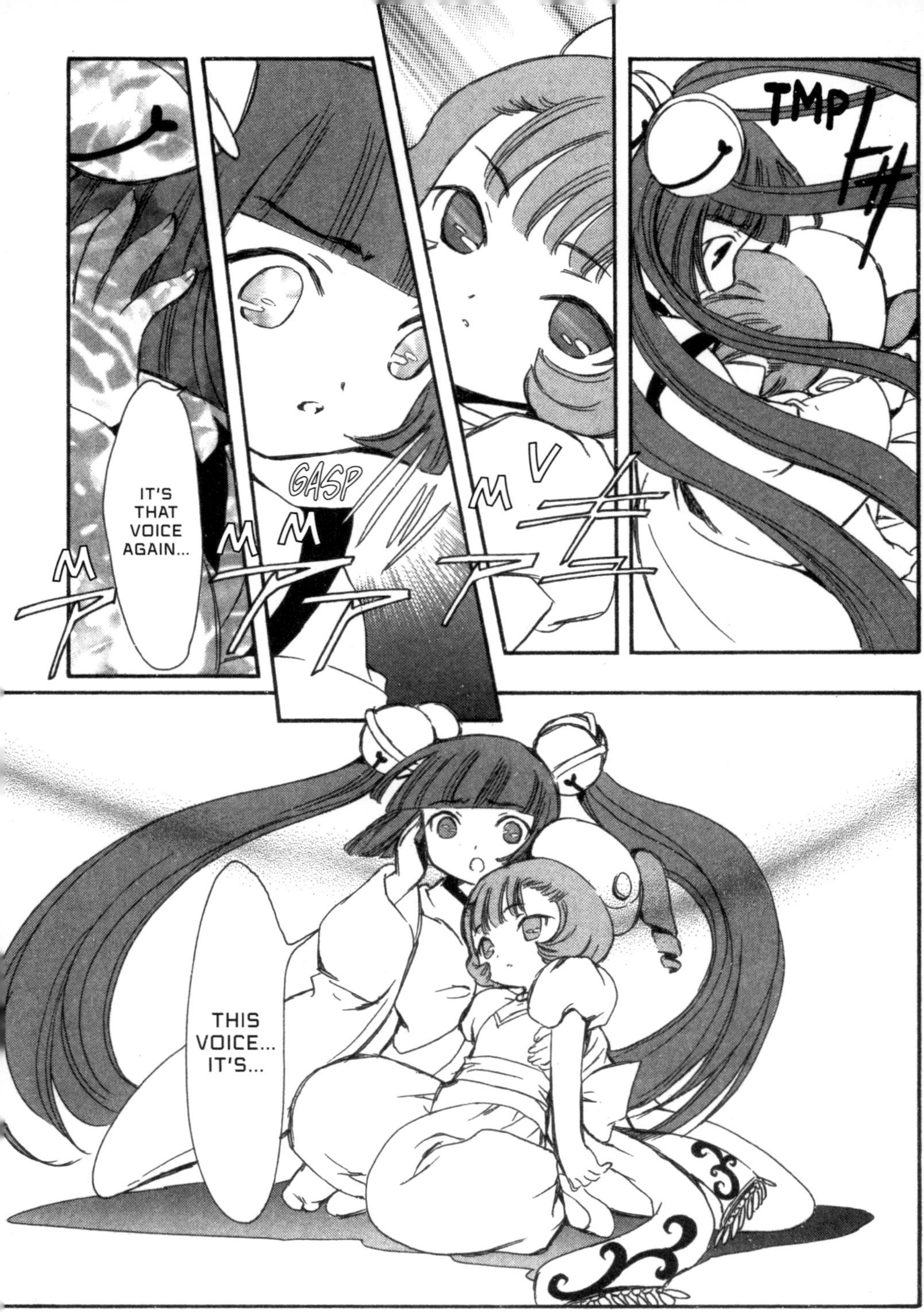
TMP
M V
GASP
M M
IT'S THAT VOICE AGAIN...
M
THIS VOICE... IT'S...

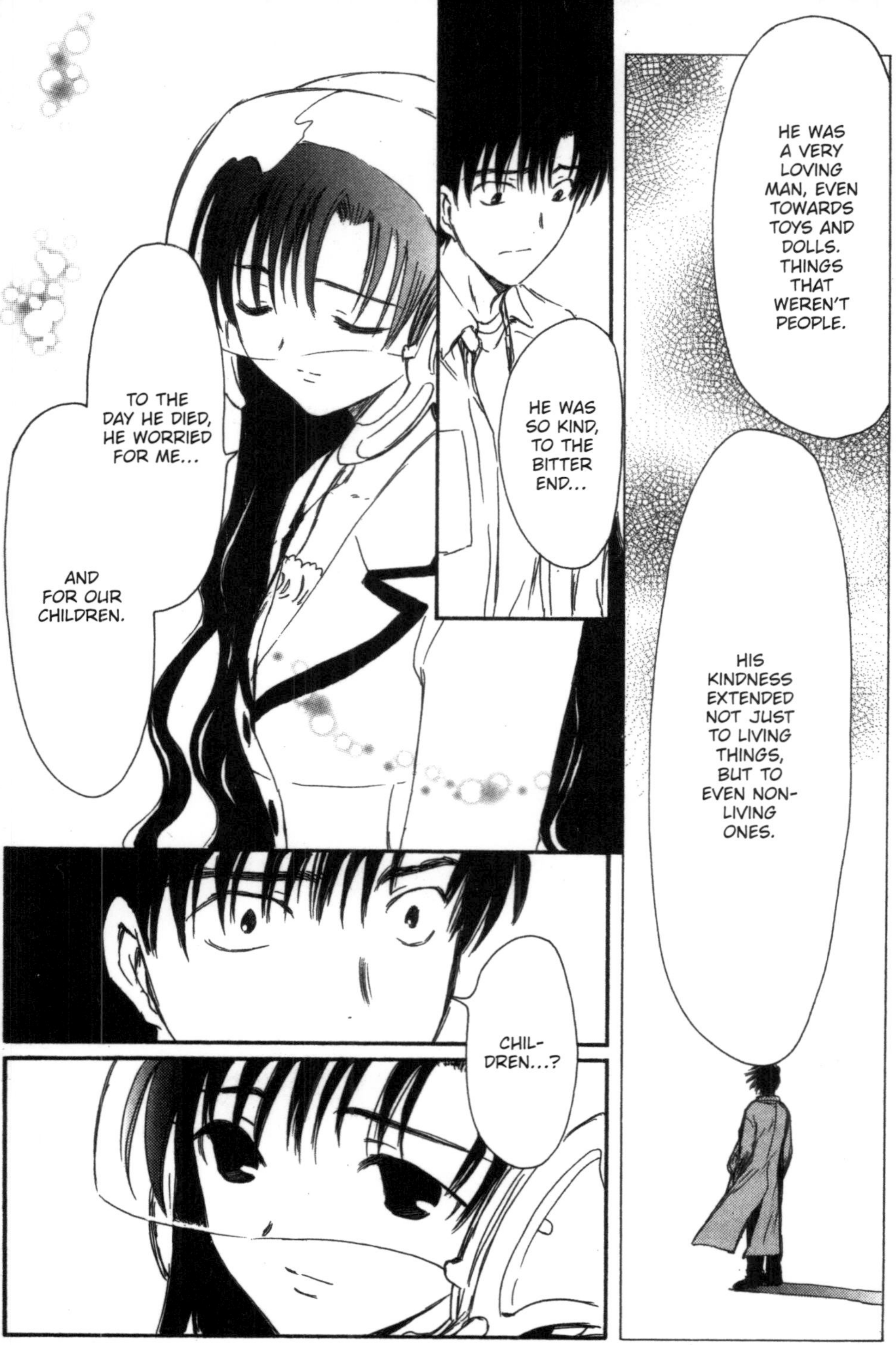
HE WAS A VERY LOVING MAN, EVEN TOWARDS TOYS AND DOLLS. THINGS THAT WEREN'T PEOPLE.
HIS KINDNESS EXTENDED NOT JUST TO LIVING THINGS, BUT TO EVEN NON-LIVING ONES.
HE WAS SO KIND, TO THE BITTER END...
TO THE DAY HE DIED, HE WORRIED FOR ME...
AND FOR OUR CHILDREN.
CHIL-DREN...?

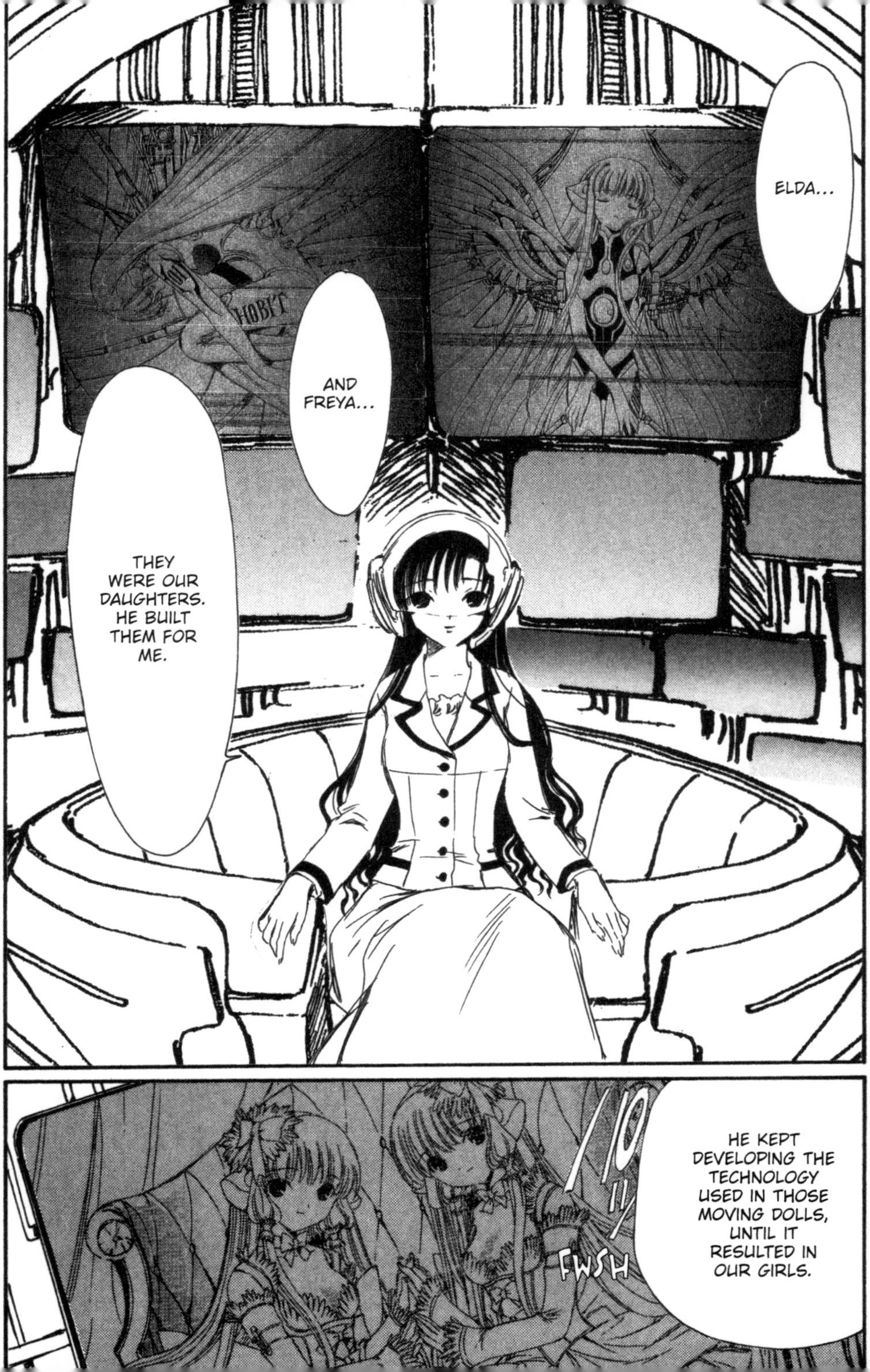
ELDA...
AND FREYA...
THEY WERE OUR DAUGHTERS. HE BUILT THEM FOR ME.
HE KEPT DEVELOPING THE TECHNOLOGY USED IN THOSE MOVING DOLLS, UNTIL IT RESULTED IN OUR GIRLS.
FWSH

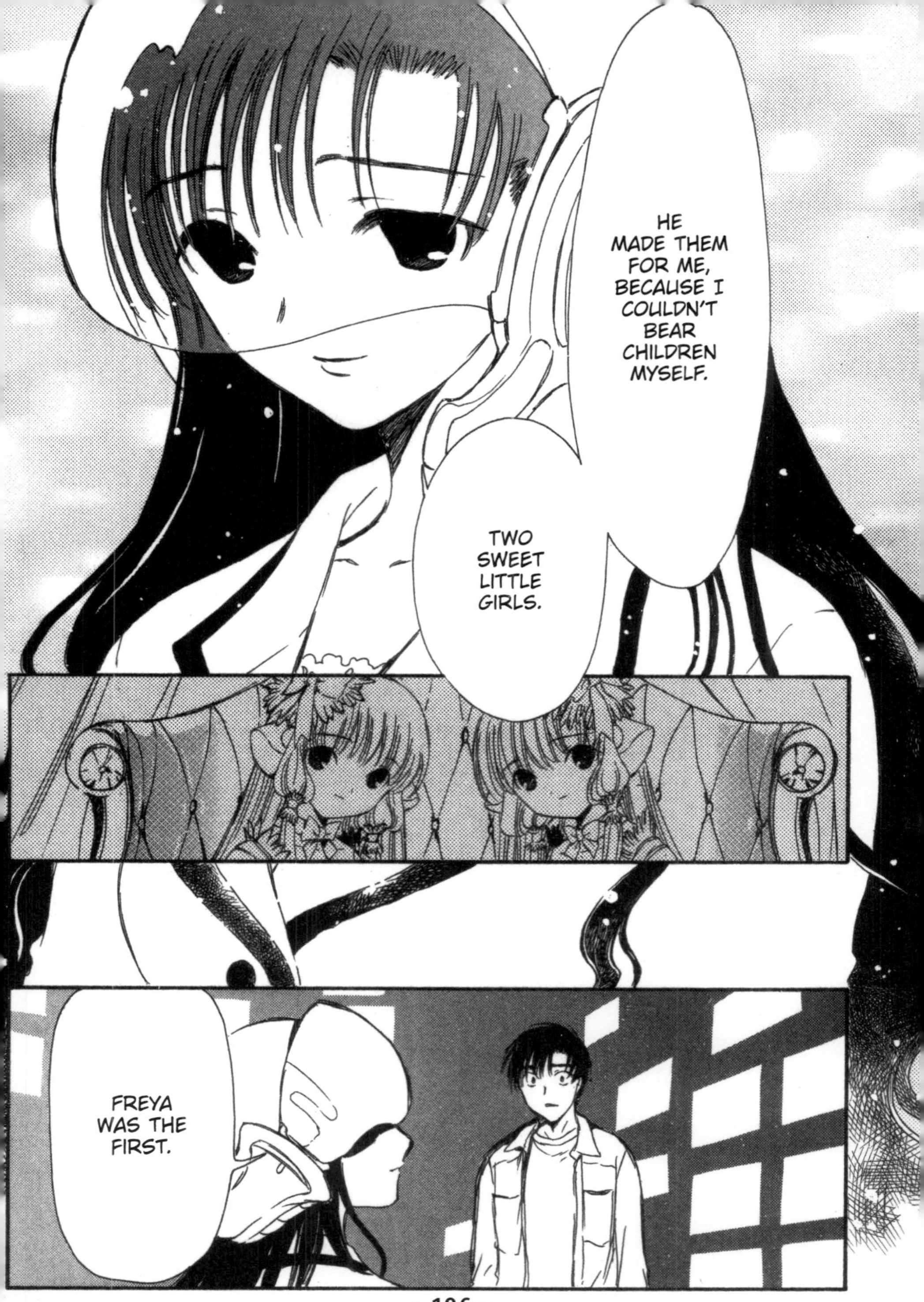

HE MADE THEM FOR ME, BECAUSE I COULDN'T BEAR CHILDREN MYSELF.
TWO SWEET LITTLE GIRLS.
FREYA WAS THE FIRST.

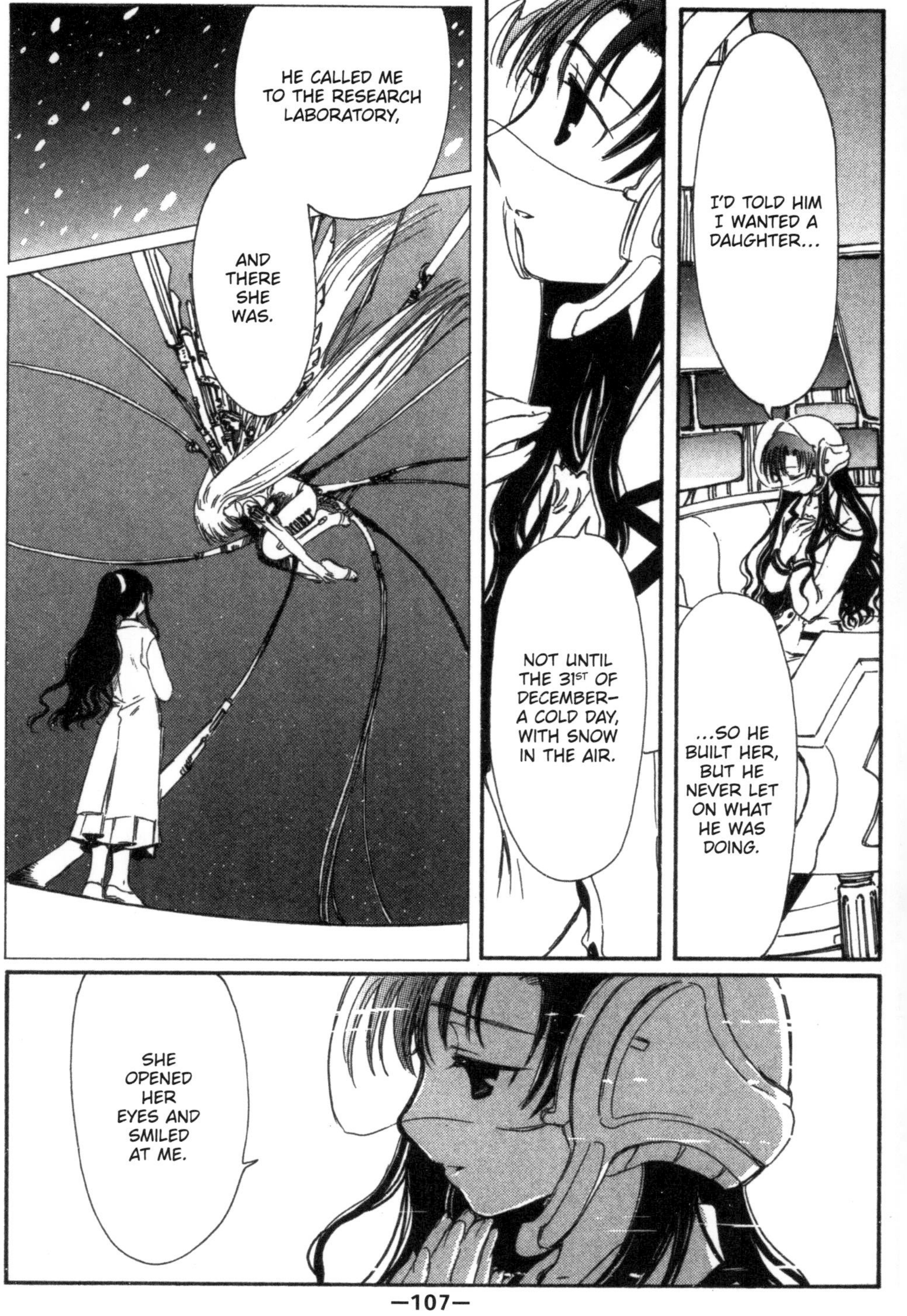
I'D TOLD HIM I WANTED A DAUGHTER...
...SO HE BUILT HER, BUT HE NEVER LET ON WHAT HE WAS DOING.
NOT UNTIL THE 31ST OF DECEMBER– A COLD DAY, WITH SNOW IN THE AIR.
HE CALLED ME TO THE RESEARCH LABORATORY,
AND THERE SHE WAS.
SHE OPENED HER EYES AND SMILED AT ME.

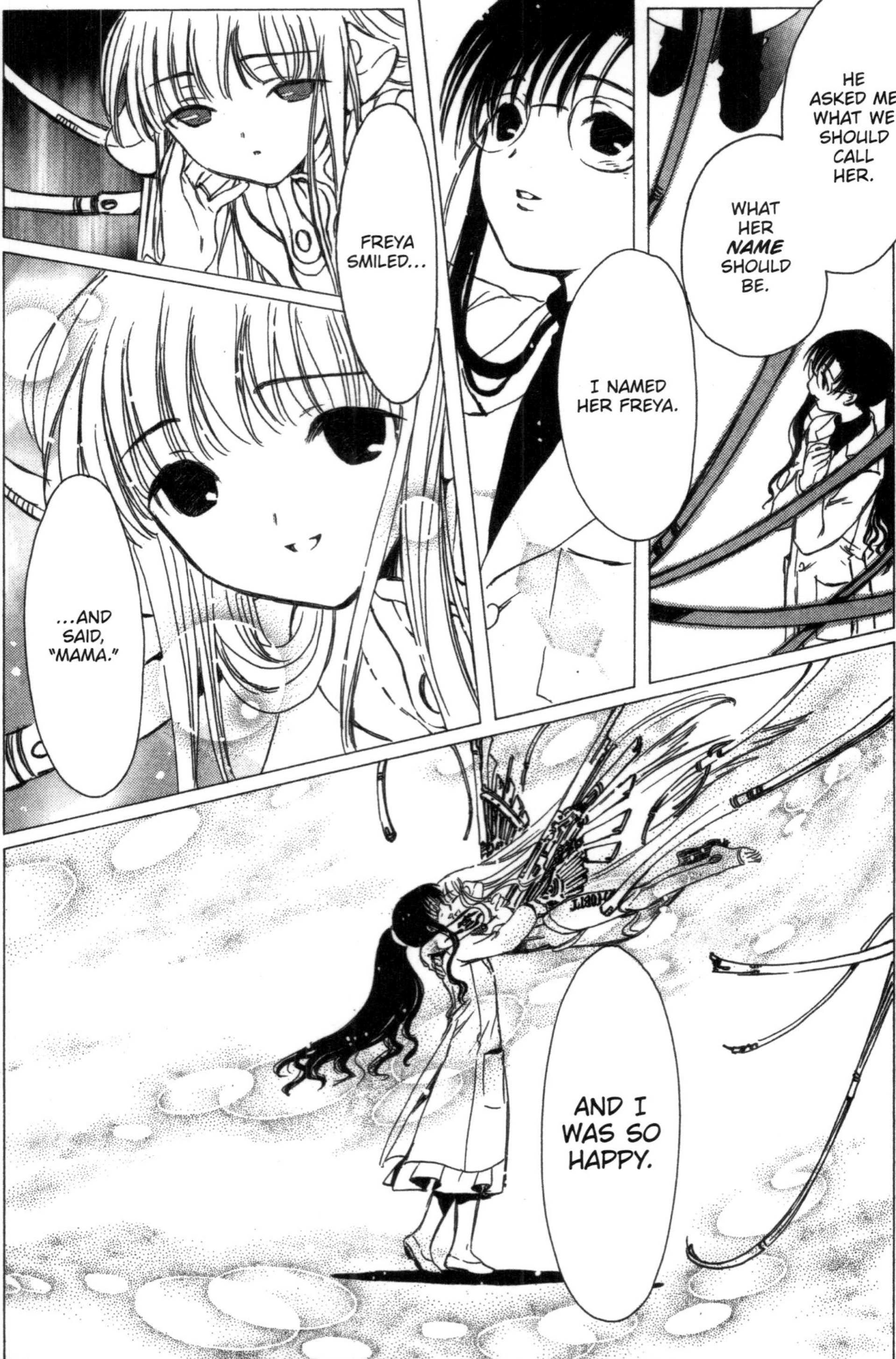
HE ASKED ME WHAT WE SHOULD CALL HER.
WHAT HER ***NAME*** SHOULD BE.
I NAMED HER FREYA.
FREYA SMILED...
...AND SAID, "MAMA."
AND I WAS SO HAPPY.

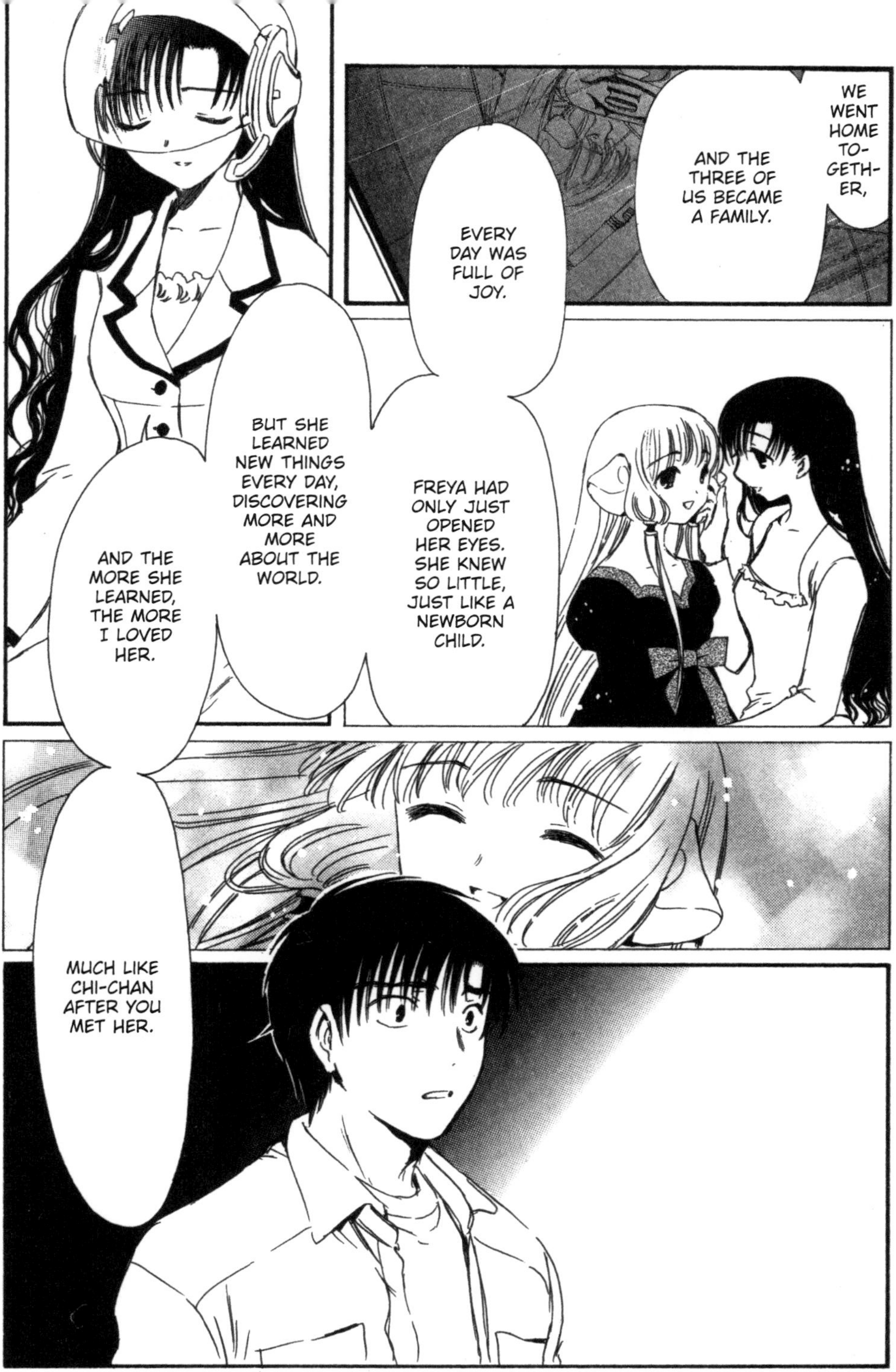
WE WENT HOME TO-GETH-ER,
AND THE THREE OF US BECAME A FAMILY.
EVERY DAY WAS FULL OF JOY.
FREYA HAD ONLY JUST OPENED HER EYES. SHE KNEW SO LITTLE, JUST LIKE A NEWBORN CHILD.
BUT SHE LEARNED NEW THINGS EVERY DAY, DISCOVERING MORE AND MORE ABOUT THE WORLD.
AND THE MORE SHE LEARNED, THE MORE I LOVED HER.
MUCH LIKE CHI-CHAN AFTER YOU MET HER.

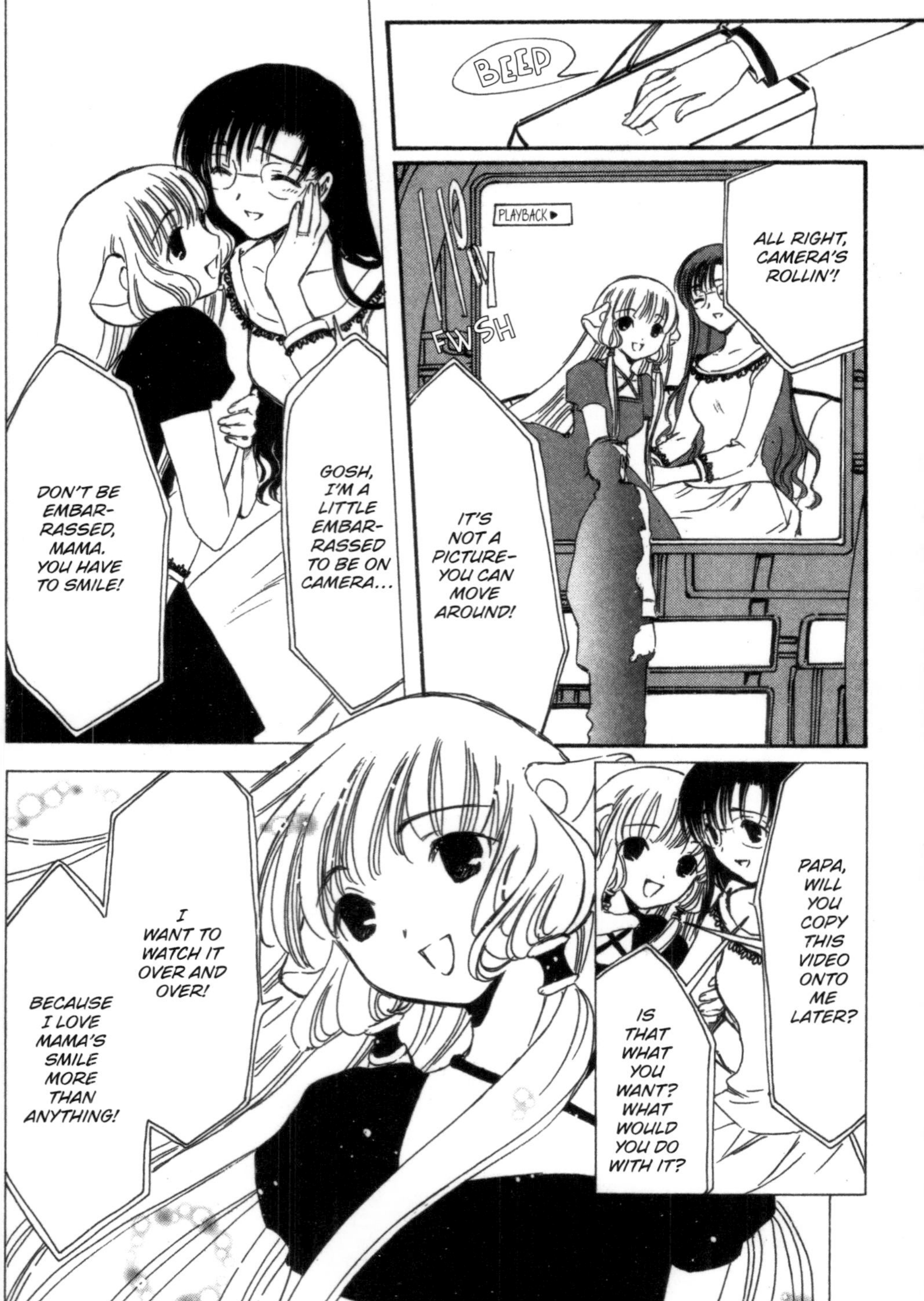
BEEP
PLAYBACK ▶
ALL RIGHT, CAMERA'S ROLLIN'!
FWSH
IT'S NOT A PICTURE-YOU CAN MOVE AROUND!
GOSH, I'M A LITTLE EMBAR-RASSED TO BE ON CAMERA…
DON'T BE EMBAR-RASSED, MAMA. YOU HAVE TO SMILE!
PAPA, WILL YOU COPY THIS VIDEO ONTO ME LATER?
IS THAT WHAT YOU WANT? WHAT WOULD YOU DO WITH IT?
I WANT TO WATCH IT OVER AND OVER!
BECAUSE I LOVE MAMA'S SMILE MORE THAN ANYTHING!

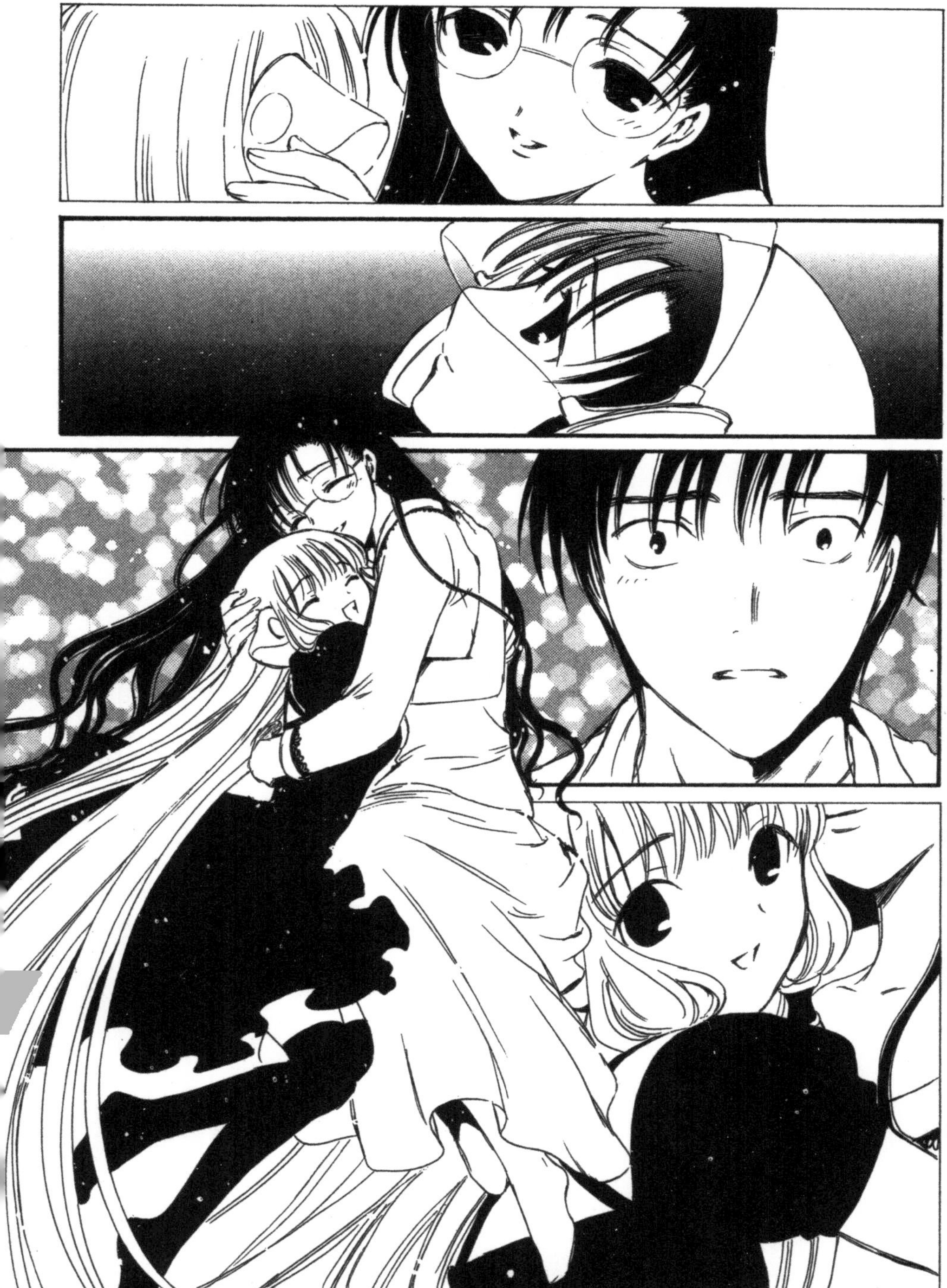

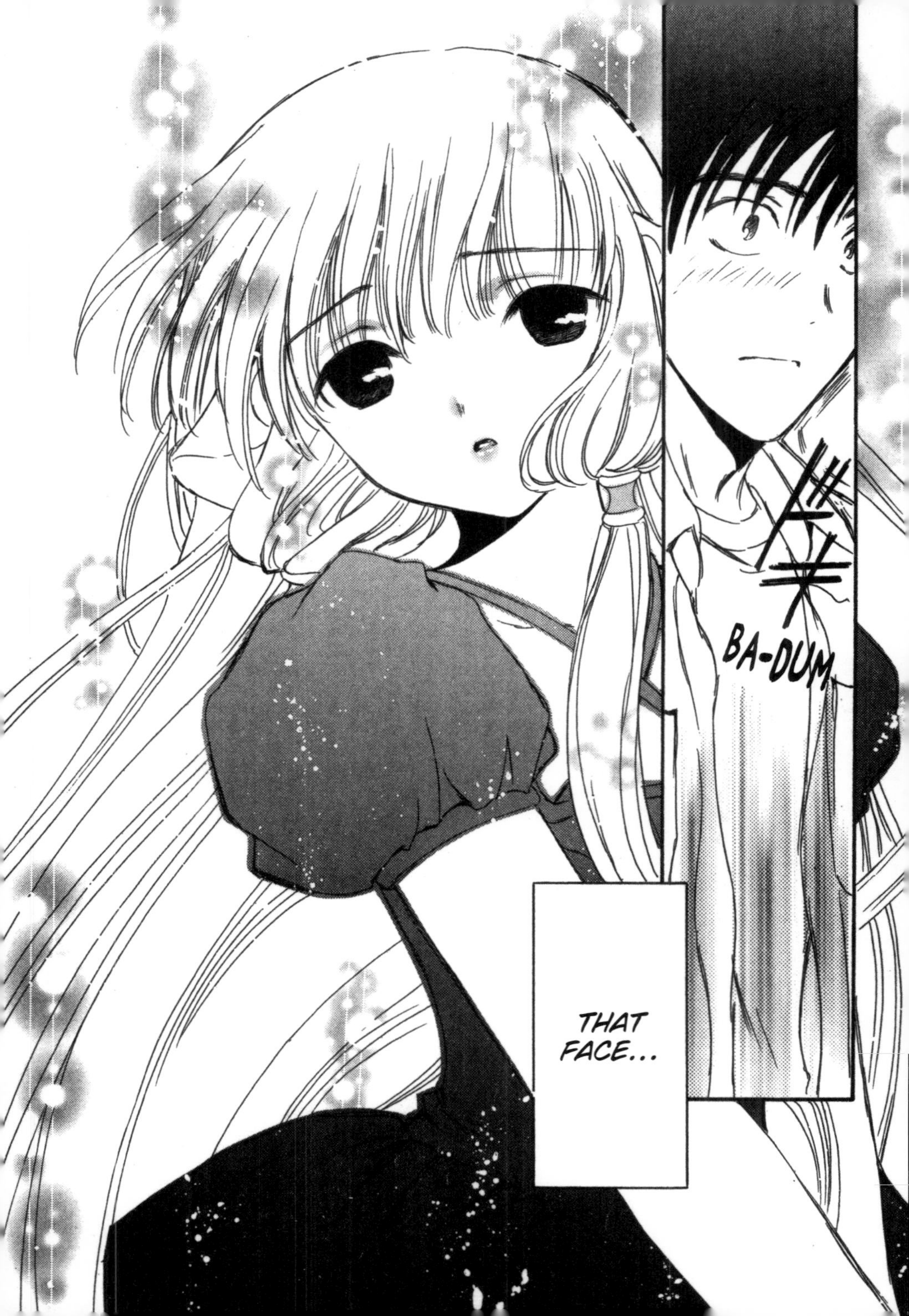
BA-DUM
THAT FACE...

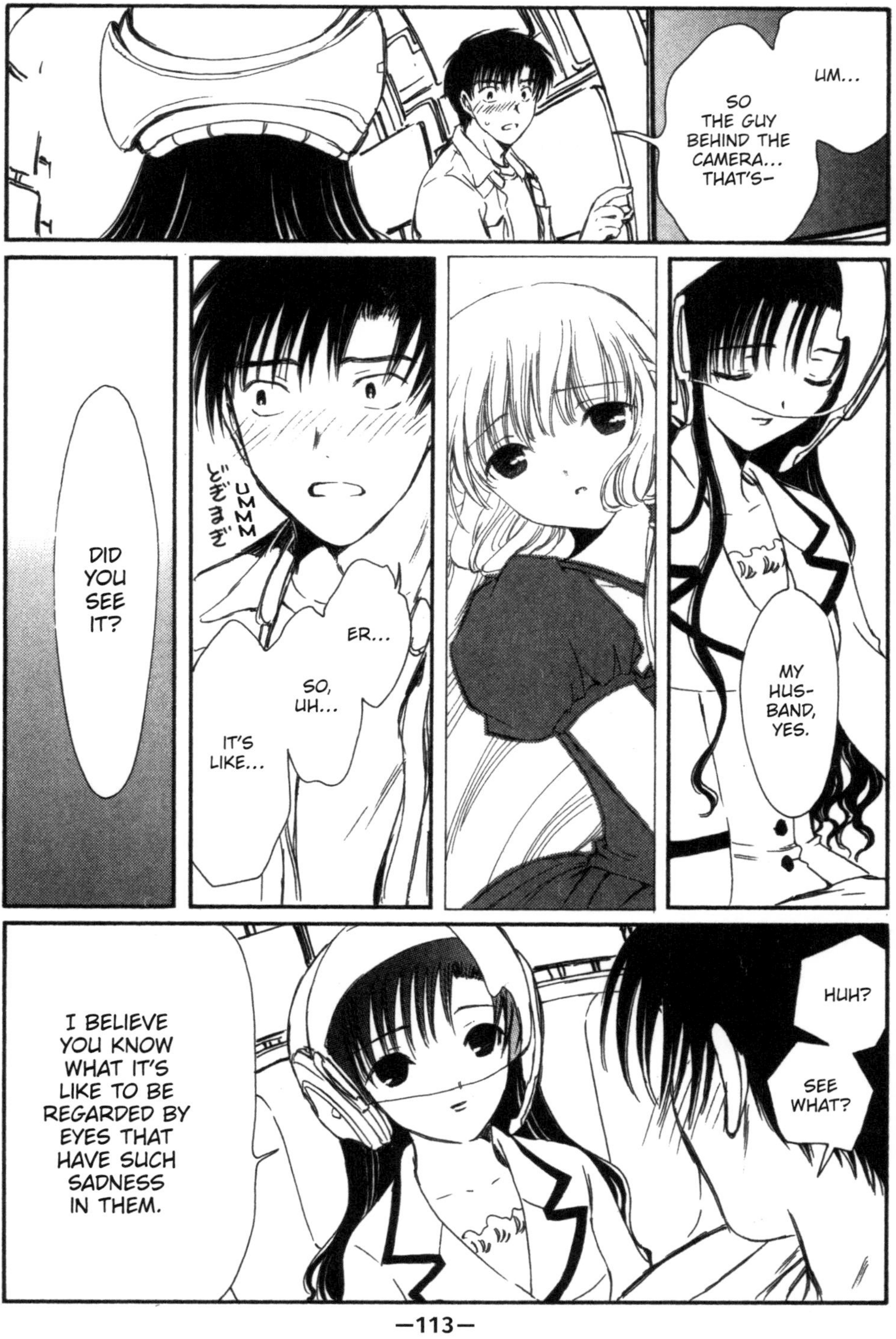
UM...
SO THE GUY BEHIND THE CAMERA... THAT'S—
MY HUS-BAND, YES.
UMMM
どぎまぎ
ER...
SO, UH...
IT'S LIKE...
DID YOU SEE IT?
HUH?
SEE WHAT?
I BELIEVE YOU KNOW WHAT IT'S LIKE TO BE REGARDED BY EYES THAT HAVE SUCH SADNESS IN THEM.

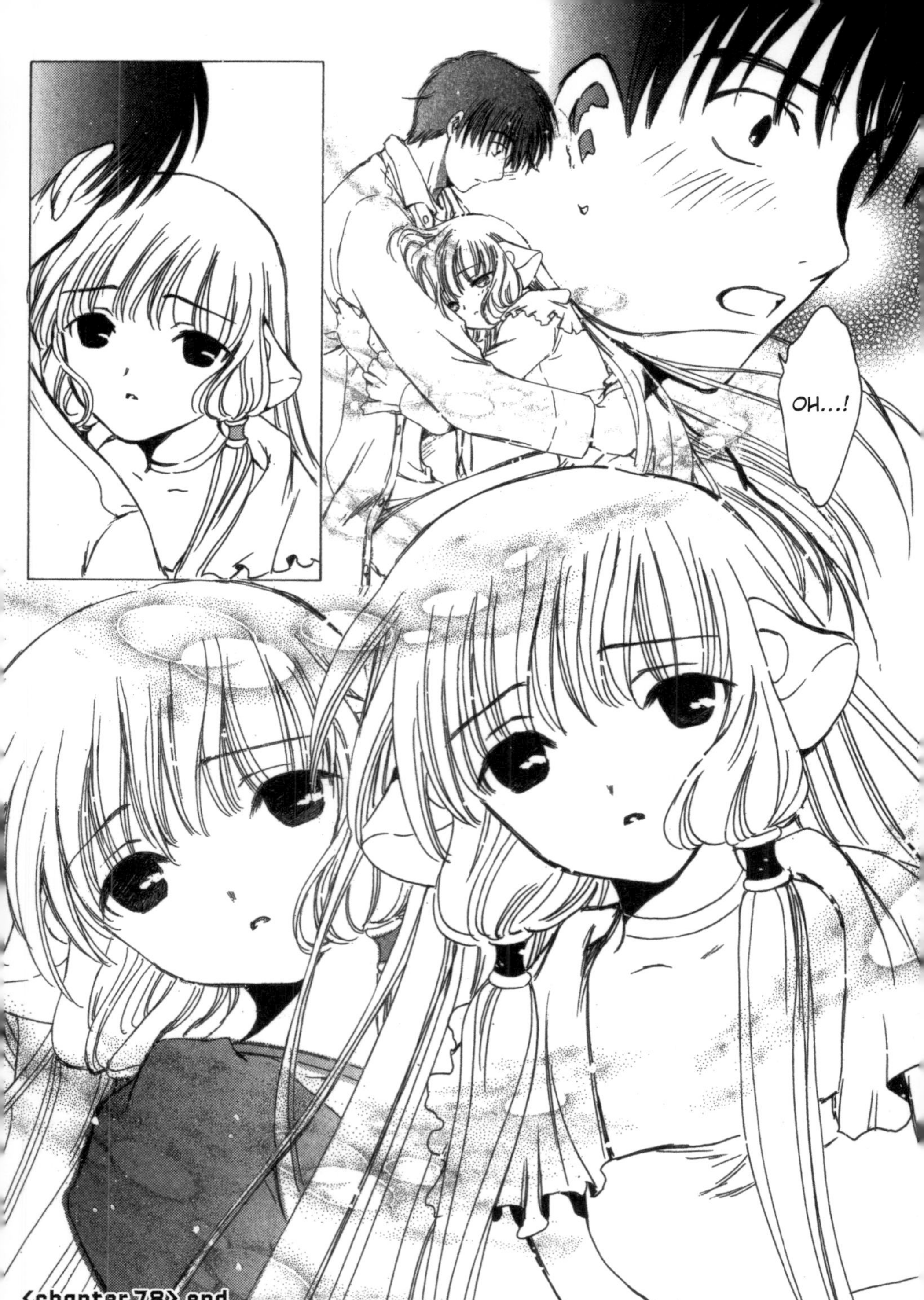
OH...!

<chapter.78> end

Chobits

**⟨chapter.79⟩**

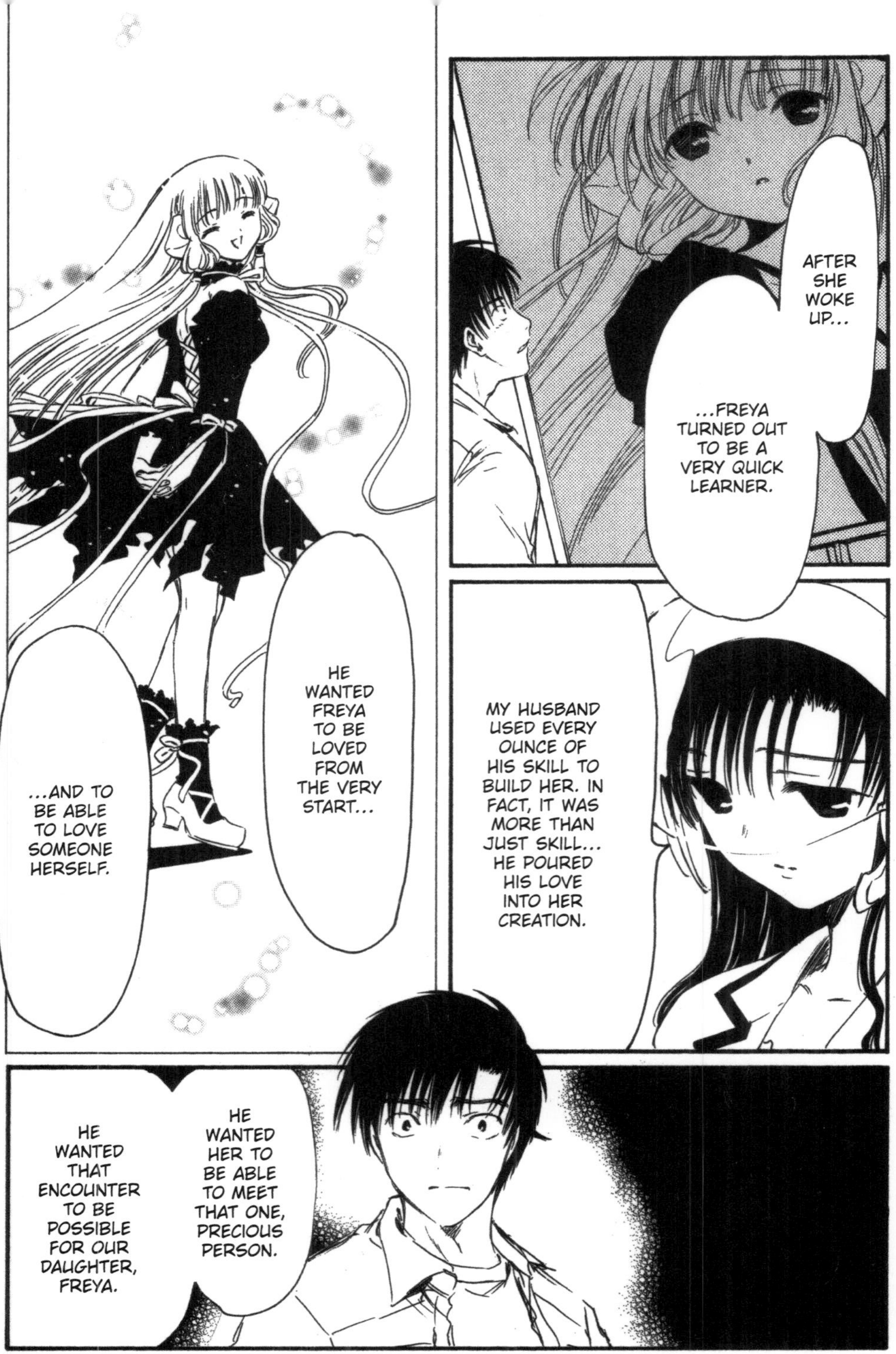
AFTER SHE WOKE UP...
...FREYA TURNED OUT TO BE A VERY QUICK LEARNER.
MY HUSBAND USED EVERY OUNCE OF HIS SKILL TO BUILD HER. IN FACT, IT WAS MORE THAN JUST SKILL... HE POURED HIS LOVE INTO HER CREATION.
HE WANTED FREYA TO BE LOVED FROM THE VERY START...
...AND TO BE ABLE TO LOVE SOMEONE HERSELF.
HE WANTED HER TO BE ABLE TO MEET THAT ONE, PRECIOUS PERSON.
HE WANTED THAT ENCOUNTER TO BE POSSIBLE FOR OUR DAUGHTER, FREYA.

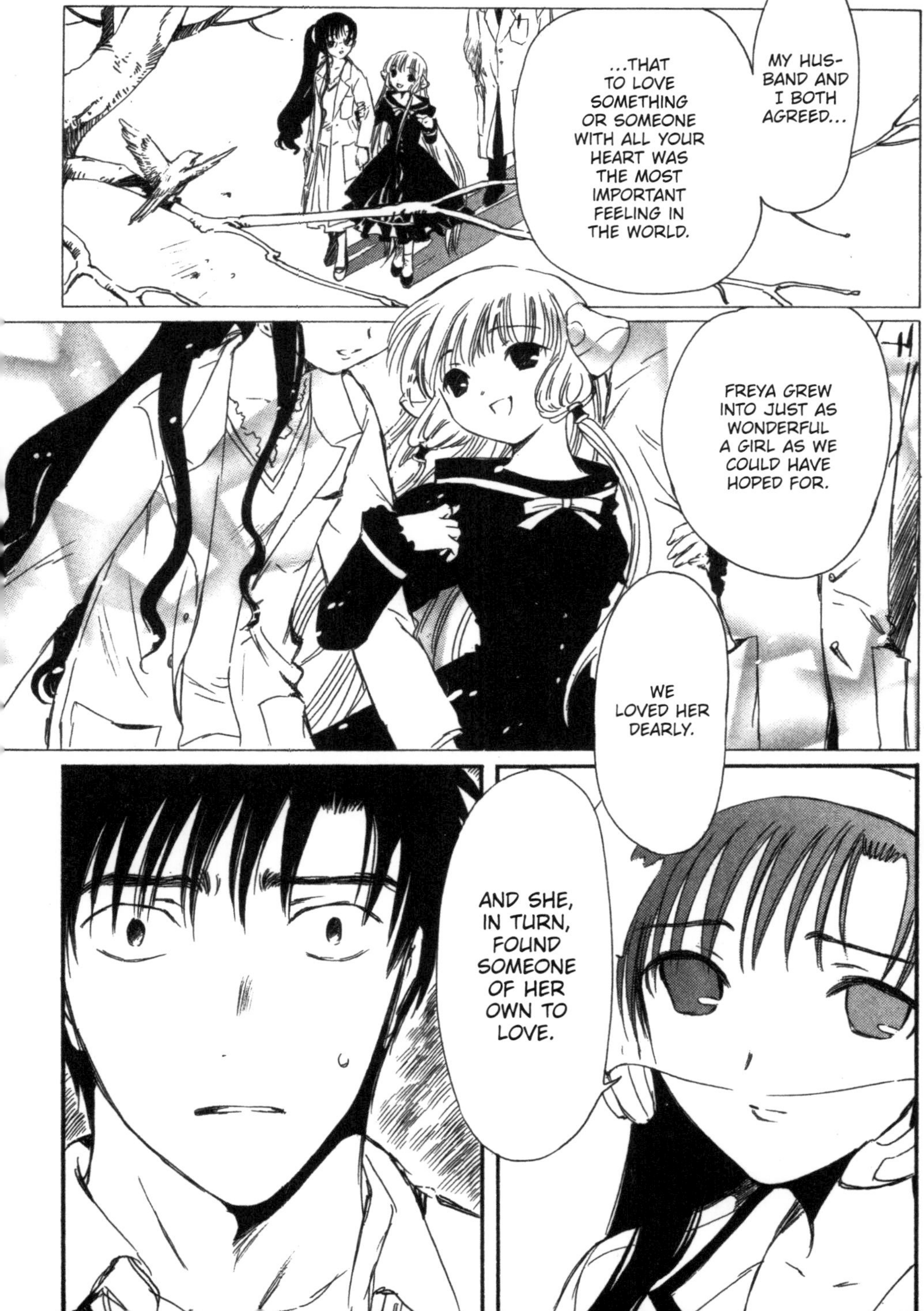
MY HUS-BAND AND I BOTH AGREED...
...THAT TO LOVE SOMETHING OR SOMEONE WITH ALL YOUR HEART WAS THE MOST IMPORTANT FEELING IN THE WORLD.
FREYA GREW INTO JUST AS WONDERFUL A GIRL AS WE COULD HAVE HOPED FOR.
WE LOVED HER DEARLY.
AND SHE, IN TURN, FOUND SOMEONE OF HER OWN TO LOVE.

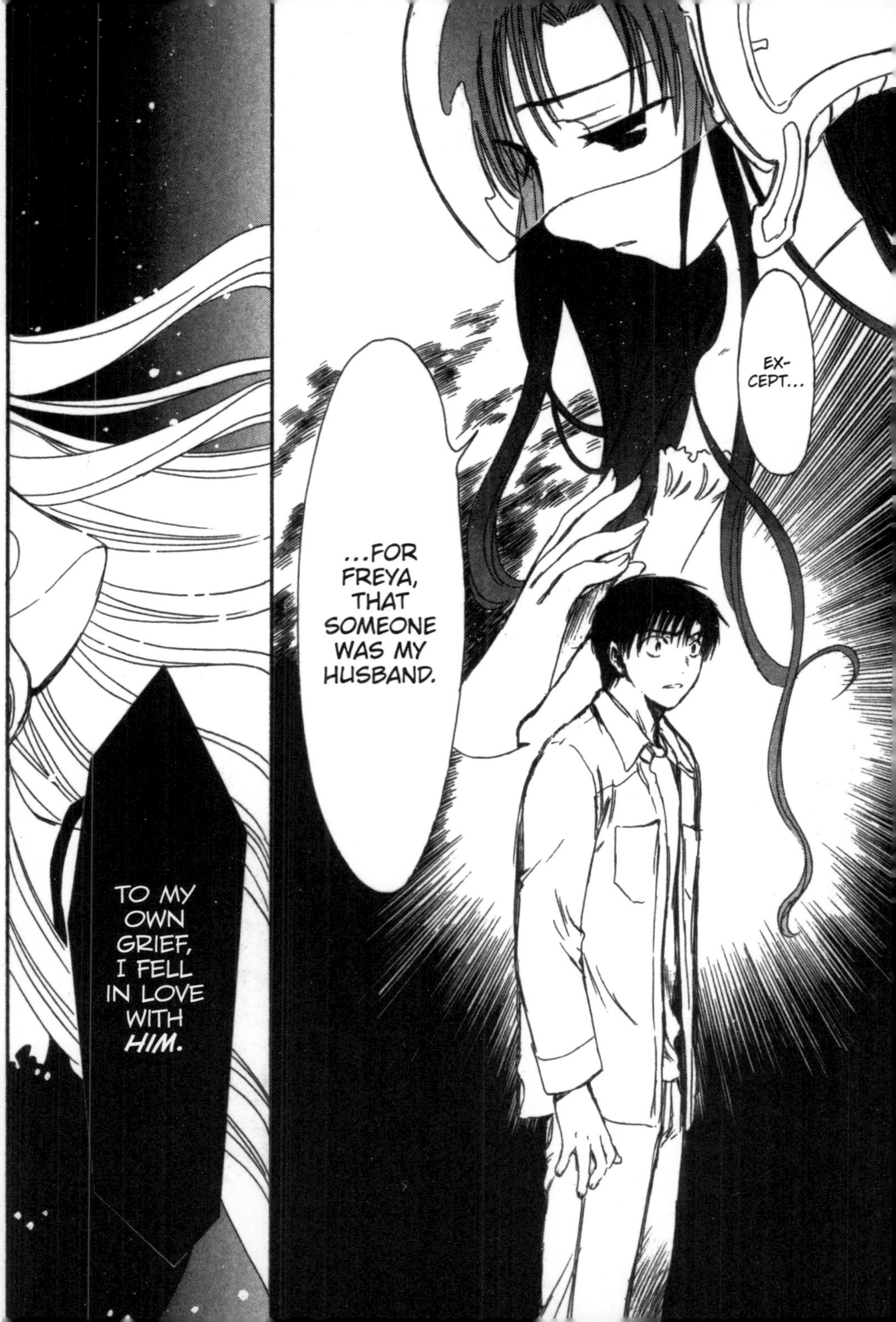
EX-CEPT...
...FOR FREYA, THAT SOMEONE WAS MY HUSBAND.
TO MY OWN GRIEF, I FELL IN LOVE WITH *HIM*.

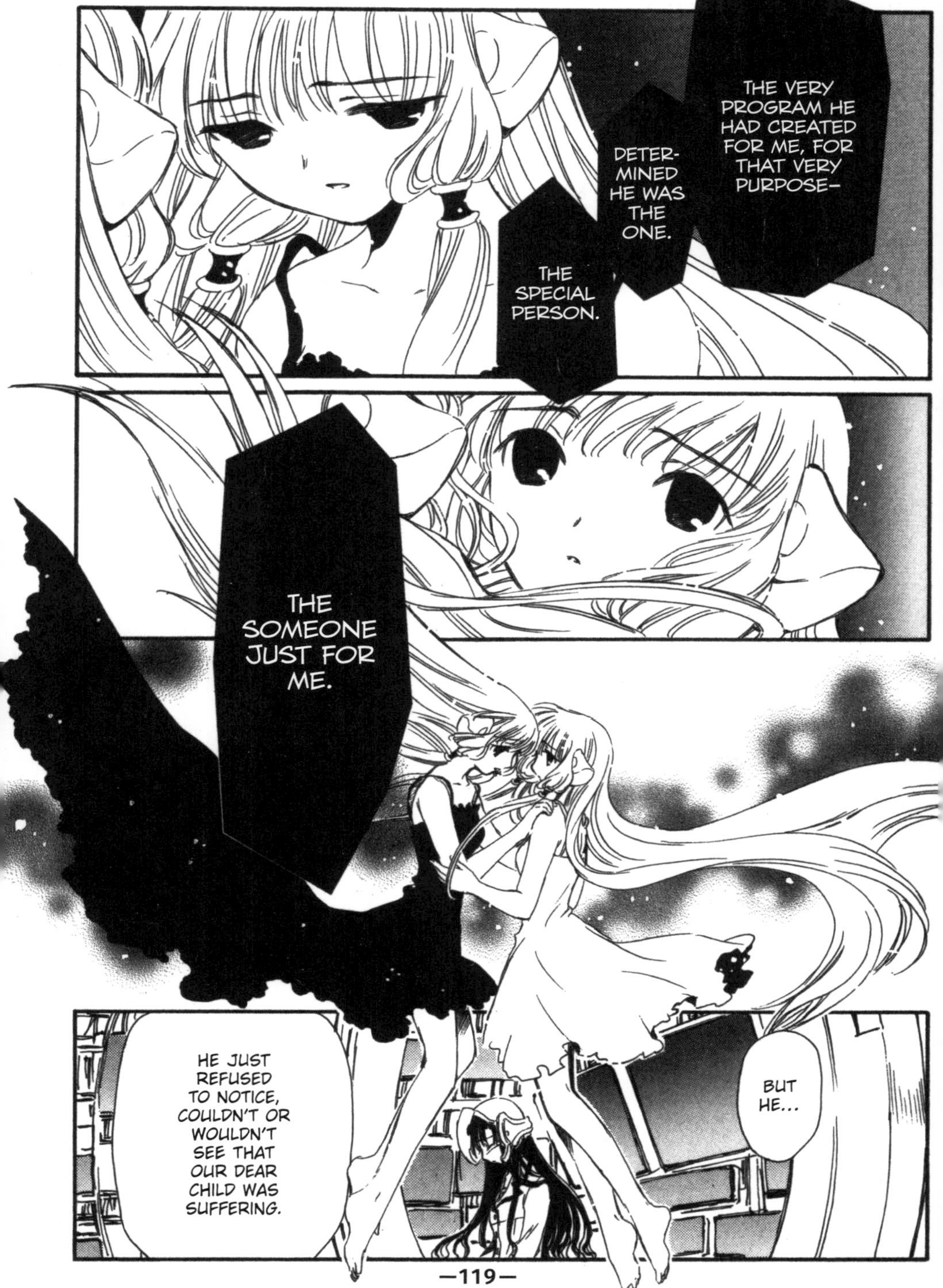
THE VERY PROGRAM HE HAD CREATED FOR ME, FOR THAT VERY PURPOSE–
DETER-MINED HE WAS THE ONE.
THE SPECIAL PERSON.
THE SOMEONE JUST FOR ME.
BUT HE...
HE JUST REFUSED TO NOTICE, COULDN'T OR WOULDN'T SEE THAT OUR DEAR CHILD WAS SUFFERING.

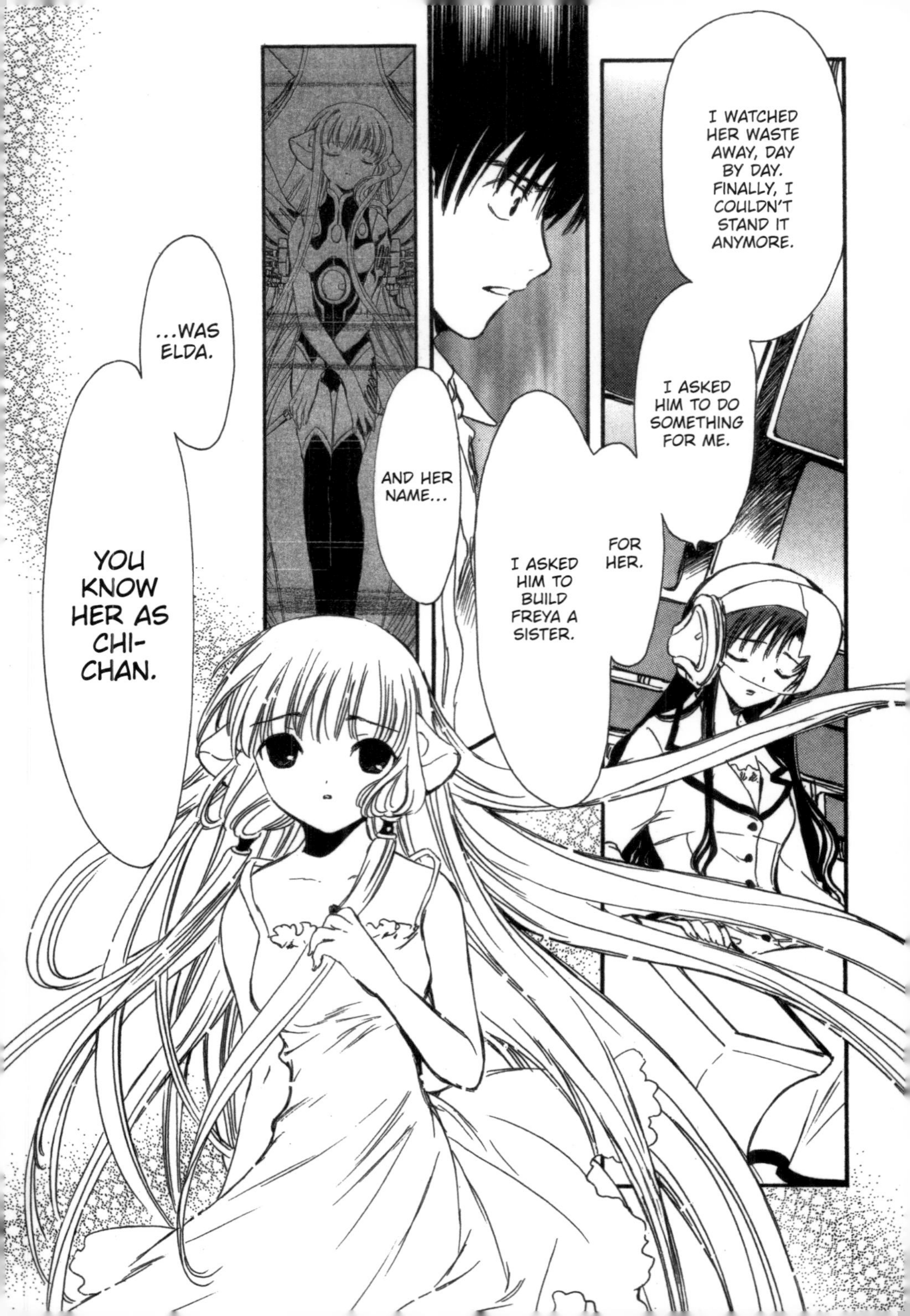
I WATCHED HER WASTE AWAY, DAY BY DAY. FINALLY, I COULDN'T STAND IT ANYMORE.
I ASKED HIM TO DO SOMETHING FOR ME.
FOR HER.
I ASKED HIM TO BUILD FREYA A SISTER.
AND HER NAME...
...WAS ELDA.
YOU KNOW HER AS CHI-CHAN.

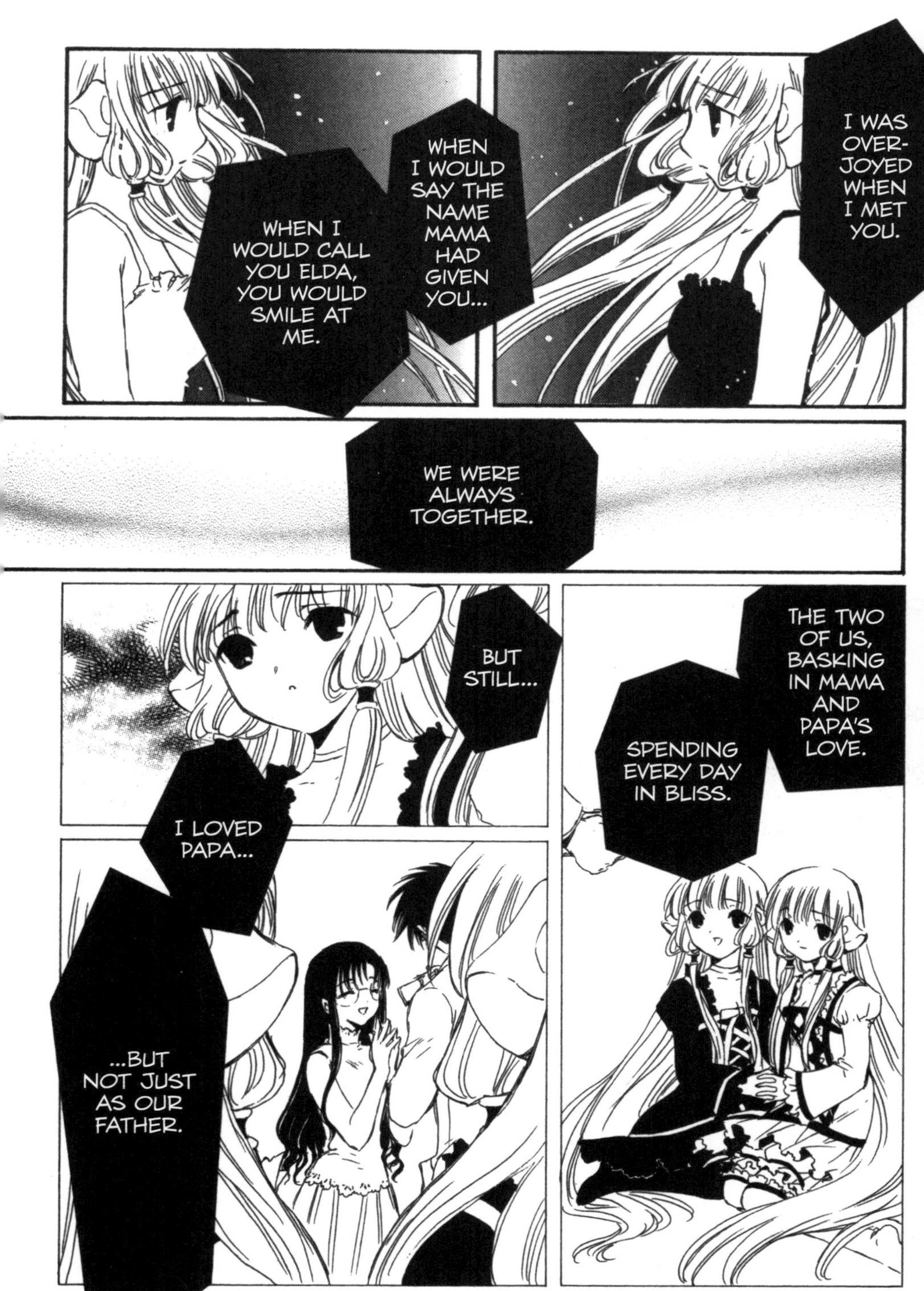
I WAS OVER-JOYED WHEN I MET YOU.
WHEN I WOULD SAY THE NAME MAMA HAD GIVEN YOU...
WHEN I WOULD CALL YOU ELDA, YOU WOULD SMILE AT ME.
WE WERE ALWAYS TOGETHER.
THE TWO OF US, BASKING IN MAMA AND PAPA'S LOVE.
SPENDING EVERY DAY IN BLISS.
BUT STILL...
I LOVED PAPA...
...BUT NOT JUST AS OUR FATHER.

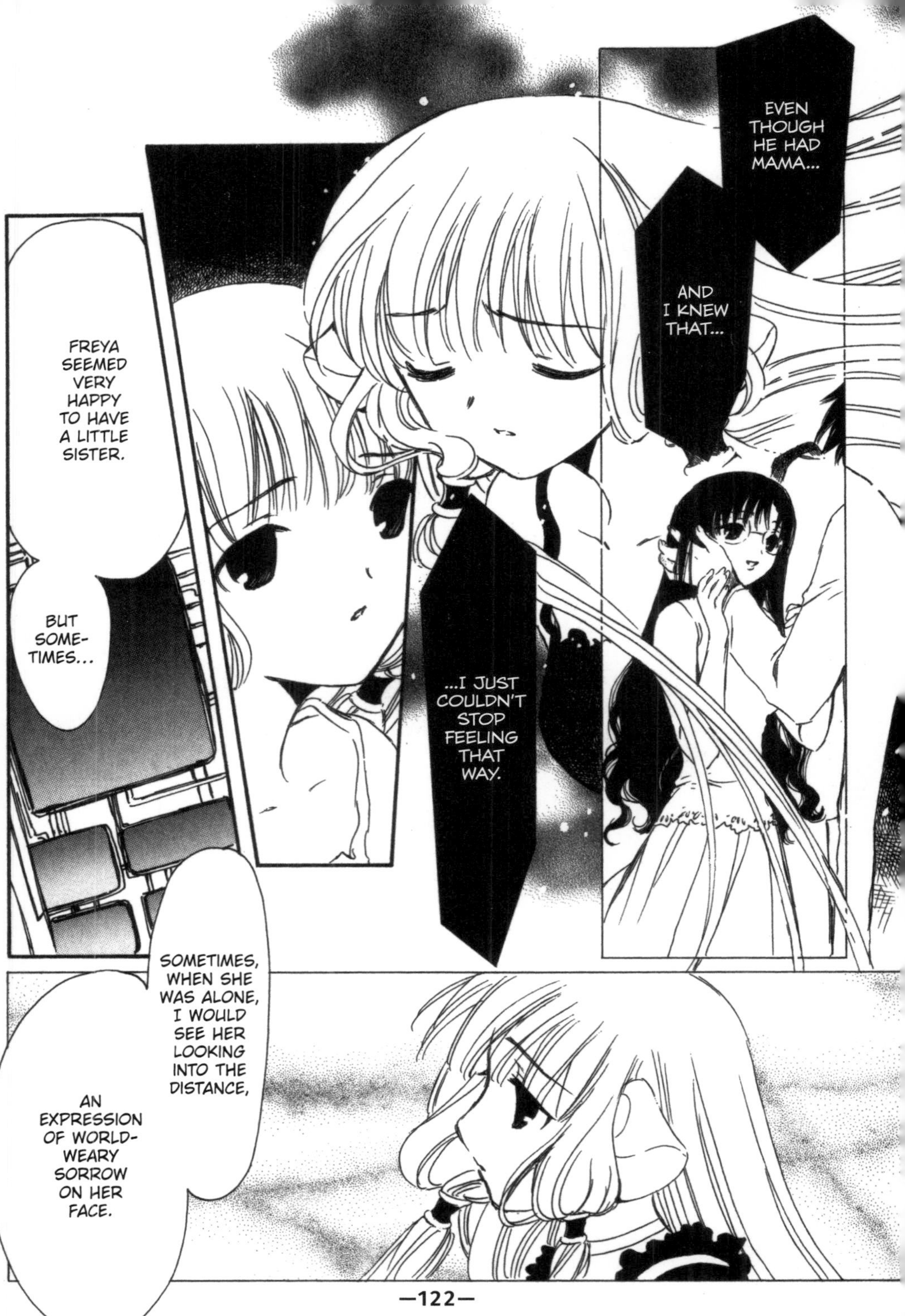
EVEN THOUGH HE HAD MAMA...
AND I KNEW THAT...
...I JUST COULDN'T STOP FEELING THAT WAY.
FREYA SEEMED VERY HAPPY TO HAVE A LITTLE SISTER.
BUT SOME-TIMES...
SOMETIMES, WHEN SHE WAS ALONE, I WOULD SEE HER LOOKING INTO THE DISTANCE,
AN EXPRESSION OF WORLD-WEARY SORROW ON HER FACE.

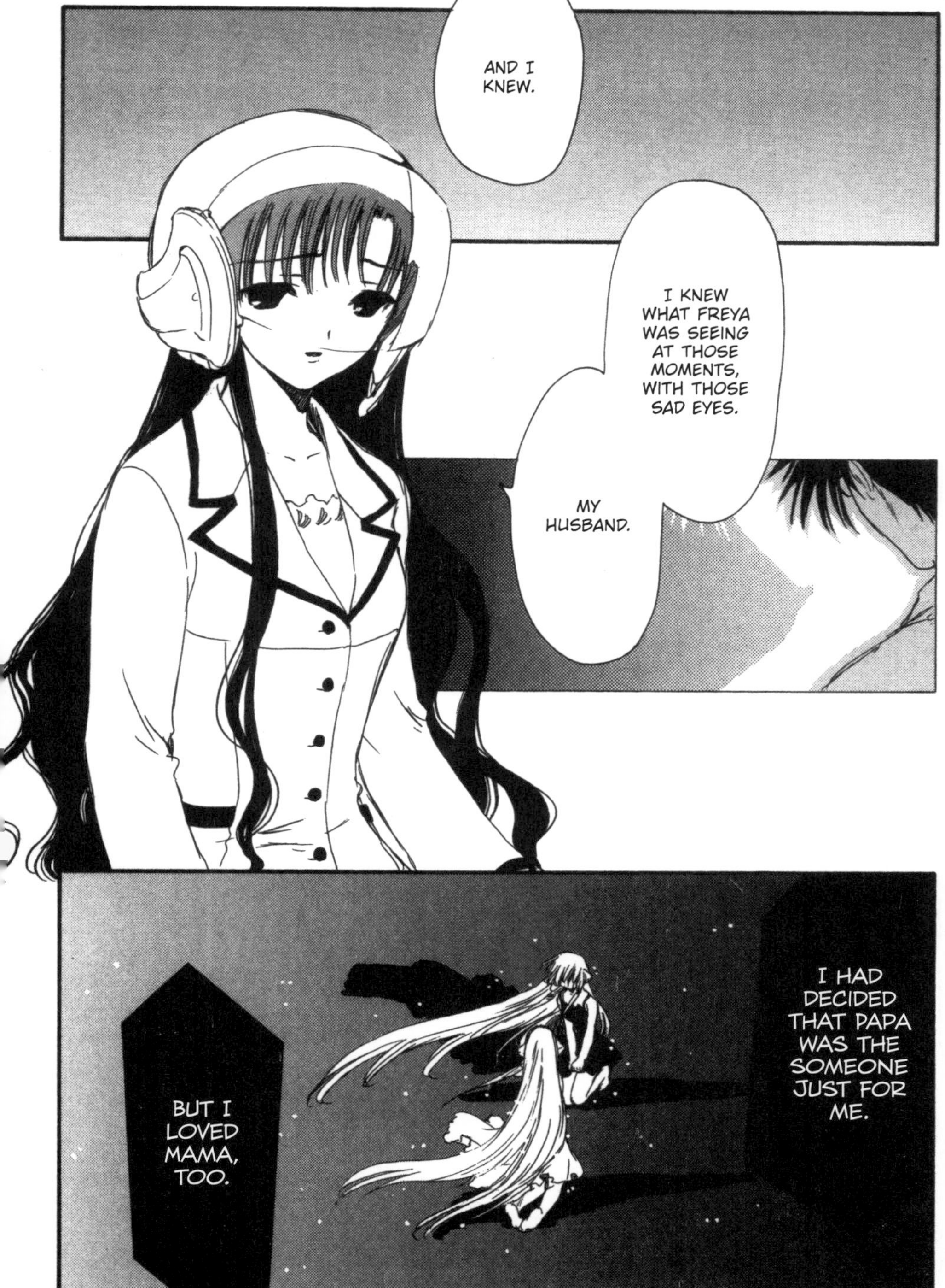
AND I KNEW.
I KNEW WHAT FREYA WAS SEEING AT THOSE MOMENTS, WITH THOSE SAD EYES.
MY HUSBAND.
I HAD DECIDED THAT PAPA WAS THE SOMEONE JUST FOR ME.
BUT I LOVED MAMA, TOO.

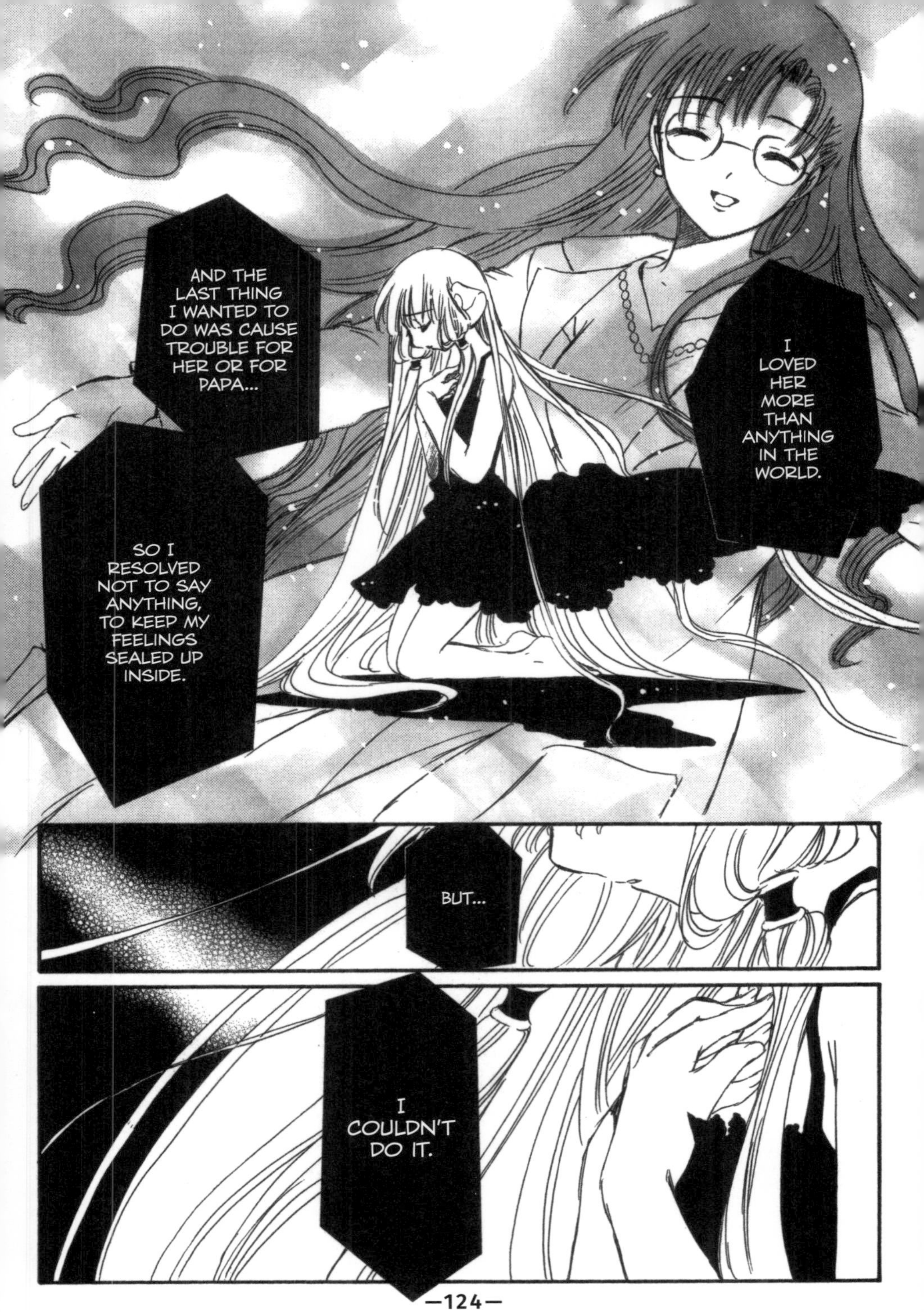
I LOVED HER MORE THAN ANYTHING IN THE WORLD.
AND THE LAST THING I WANTED TO DO WAS CAUSE TROUBLE FOR HER OR FOR PAPA...
SO I RESOLVED NOT TO SAY ANYTHING, TO KEEP MY FEELINGS SEALED UP INSIDE.
BUT...
I COULDN'T DO IT.

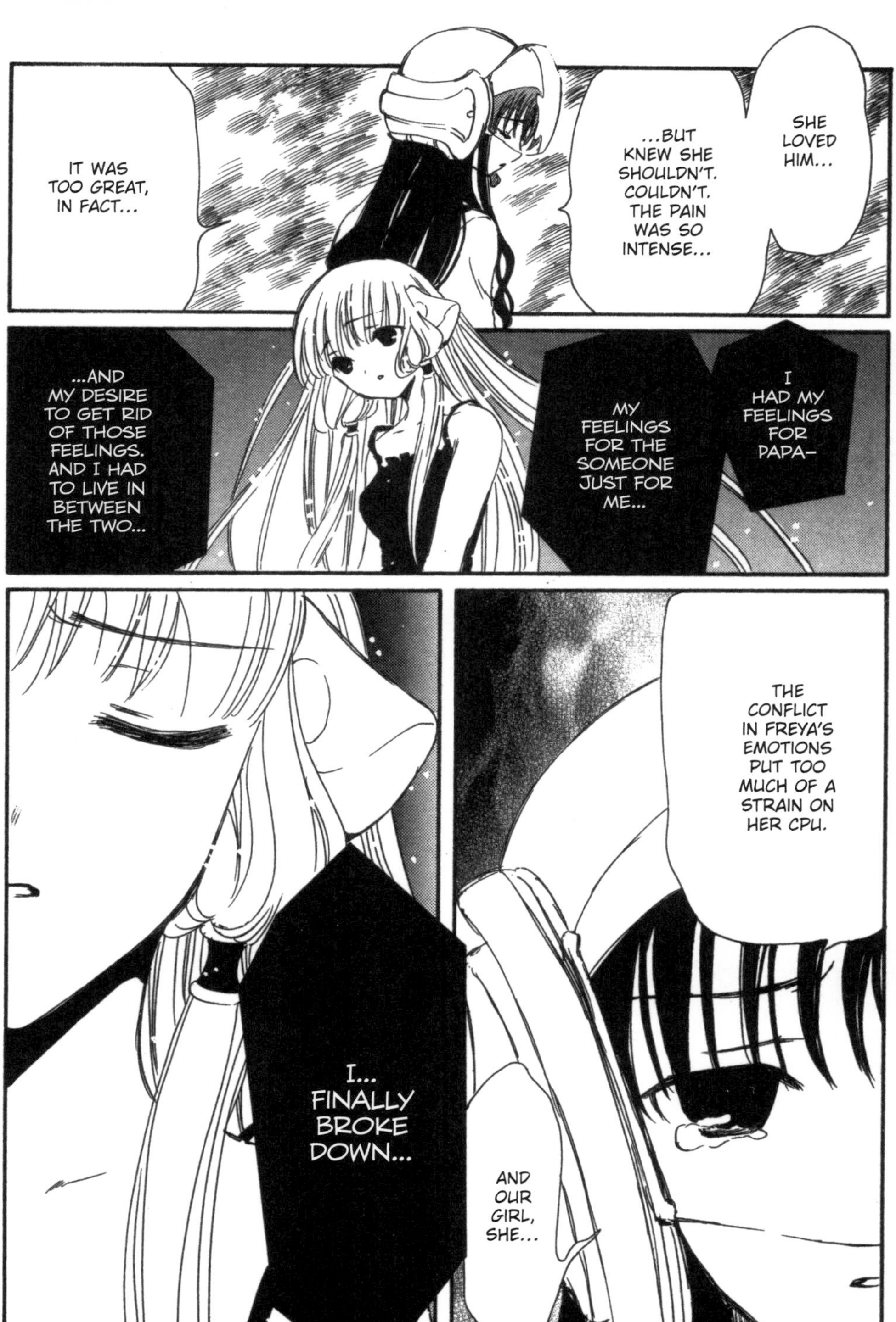
SHE LOVED HIM...
...BUT KNEW SHE SHOULDN'T. COULDN'T. THE PAIN WAS SO INTENSE...
IT WAS TOO GREAT, IN FACT...
I HAD MY FEELINGS FOR PAPA-
MY FEELINGS FOR THE SOMEONE JUST FOR ME...
...AND MY DESIRE TO GET RID OF THOSE FEELINGS. AND I HAD TO LIVE IN BETWEEN THE TWO...
THE CONFLICT IN FREYA'S EMOTIONS PUT TOO MUCH OF A STRAIN ON HER CPU.
AND OUR GIRL, SHE...
I... FINALLY BROKE DOWN...

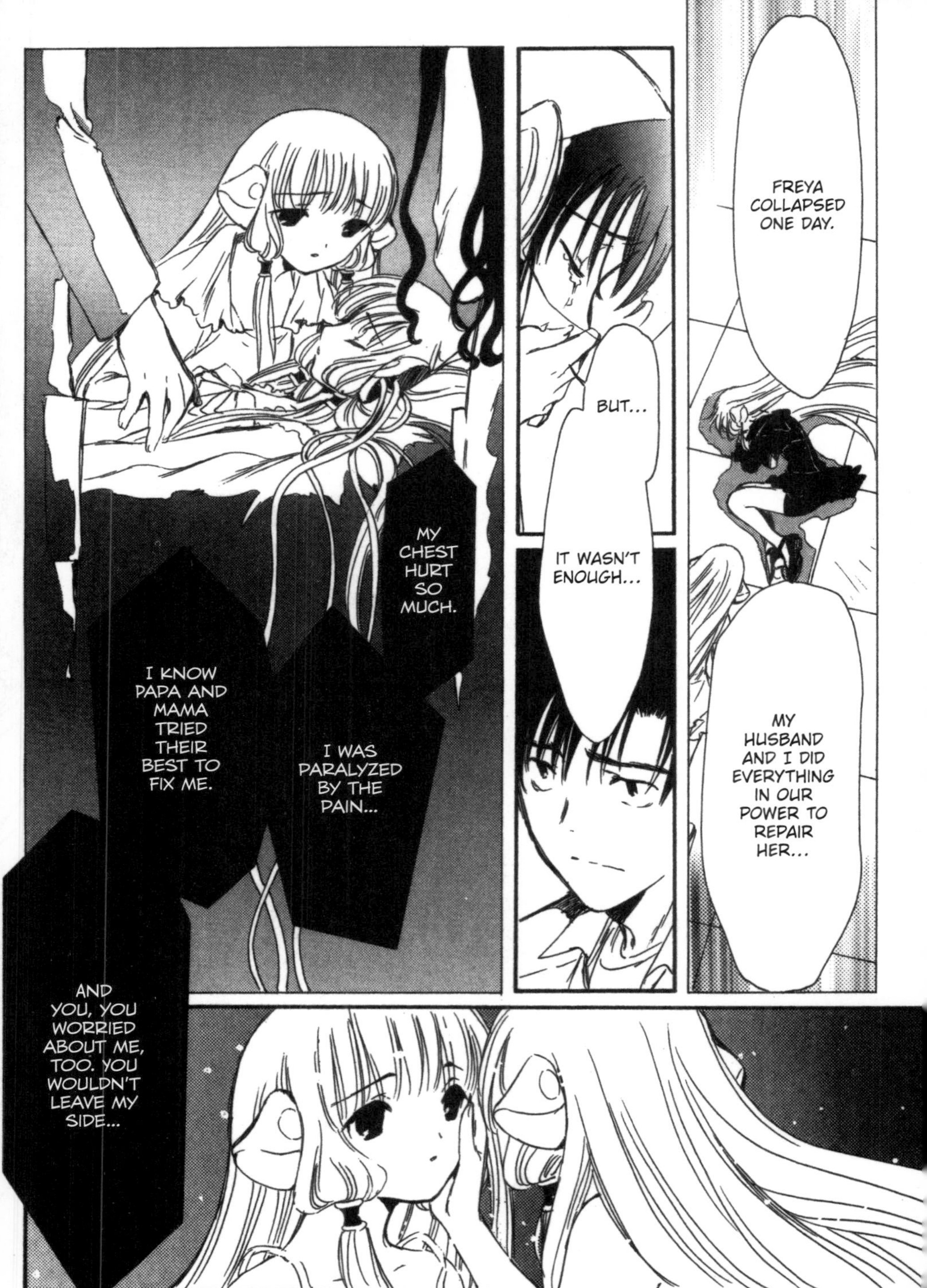
FREYA COLLAPSED ONE DAY.
MY HUSBAND AND I DID EVERYTHING IN OUR POWER TO REPAIR HER...
BUT...
IT WASN'T ENOUGH...
MY CHEST HURT SO MUCH.
I WAS PARALYZED BY THE PAIN...
I KNOW PAPA AND MAMA TRIED THEIR BEST TO FIX ME.
AND YOU, YOU WORRIED ABOUT ME, TOO. YOU WOULDN'T LEAVE MY SIDE...

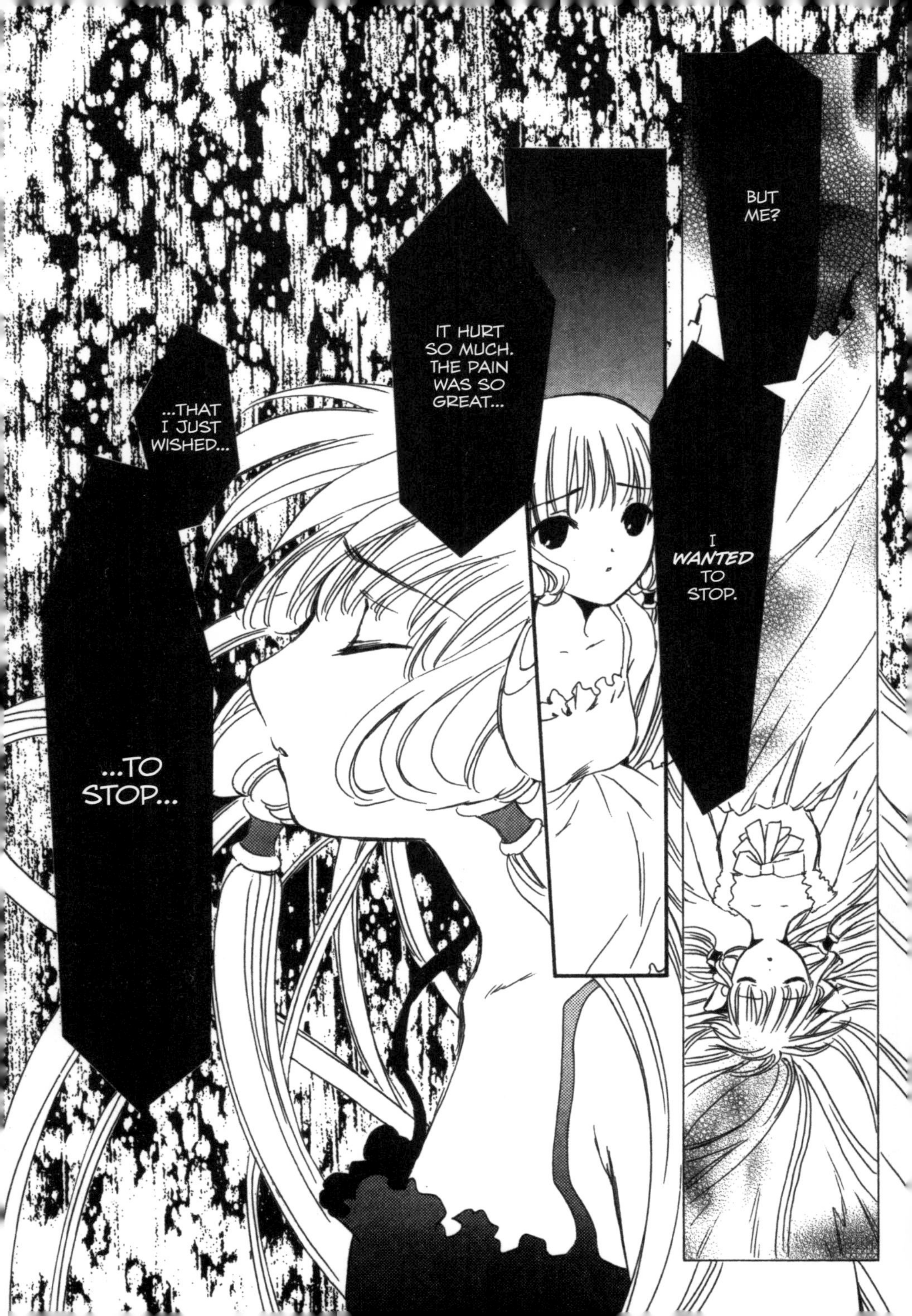
BUT ME?
I *WANTED* TO STOP.
IT HURT SO MUCH. THE PAIN WAS SO GREAT...
...THAT I JUST WISHED...
...TO STOP...

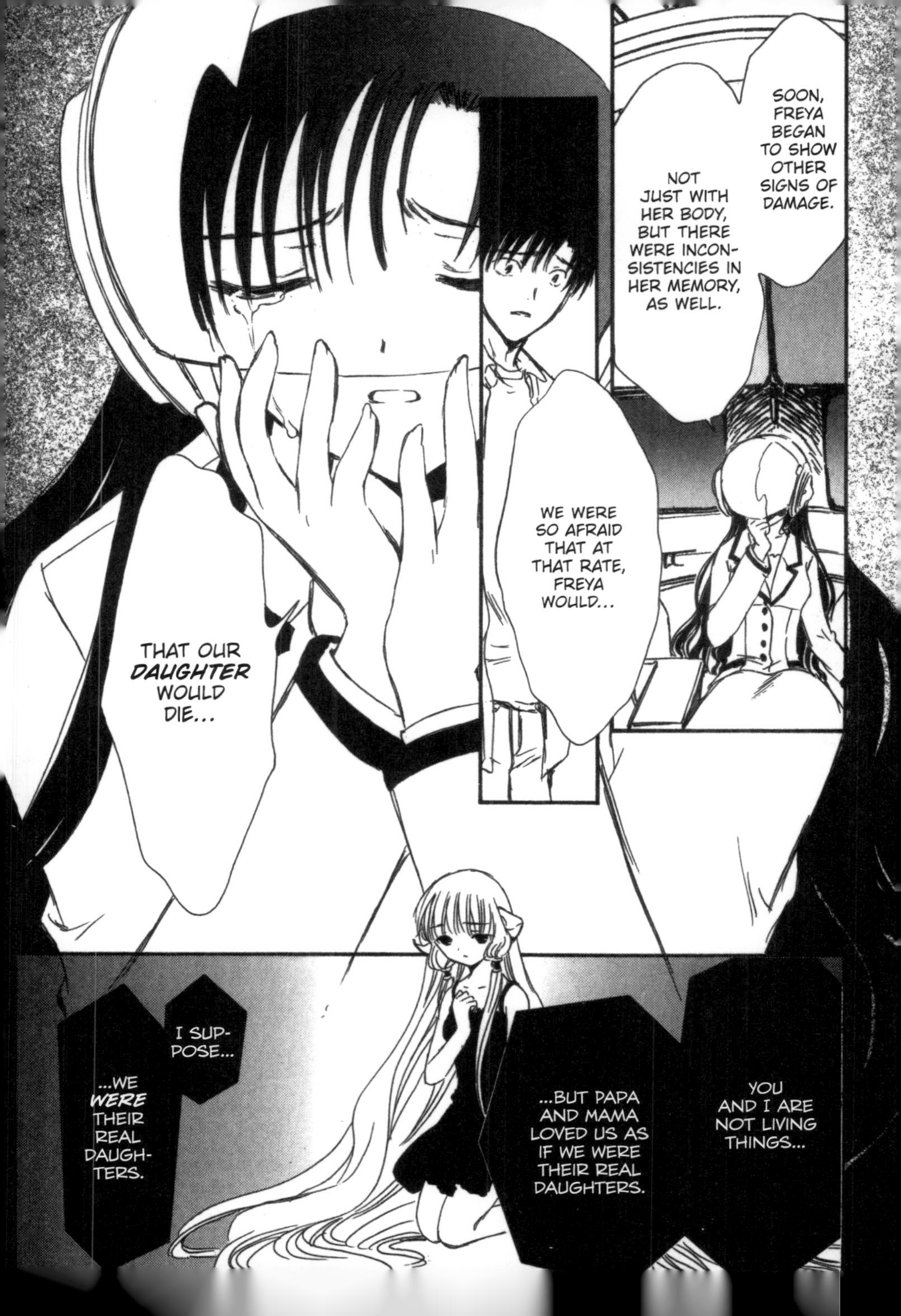
SOON, FREYA BEGAN TO SHOW OTHER SIGNS OF DAMAGE.
NOT JUST WITH HER BODY, BUT THERE WERE INCONSISTENCIES IN HER MEMORY, AS WELL.
WE WERE SO AFRAID THAT AT THAT RATE, FREYA WOULD...
THAT OUR ***DAUGHTER*** WOULD DIE...
YOU AND I ARE NOT LIVING THINGS...
...BUT PAPA AND MAMA LOVED US AS IF WE WERE THEIR REAL DAUGHTERS.
I SUPPOSE...
...WE ***WERE*** THEIR REAL DAUGHTERS.

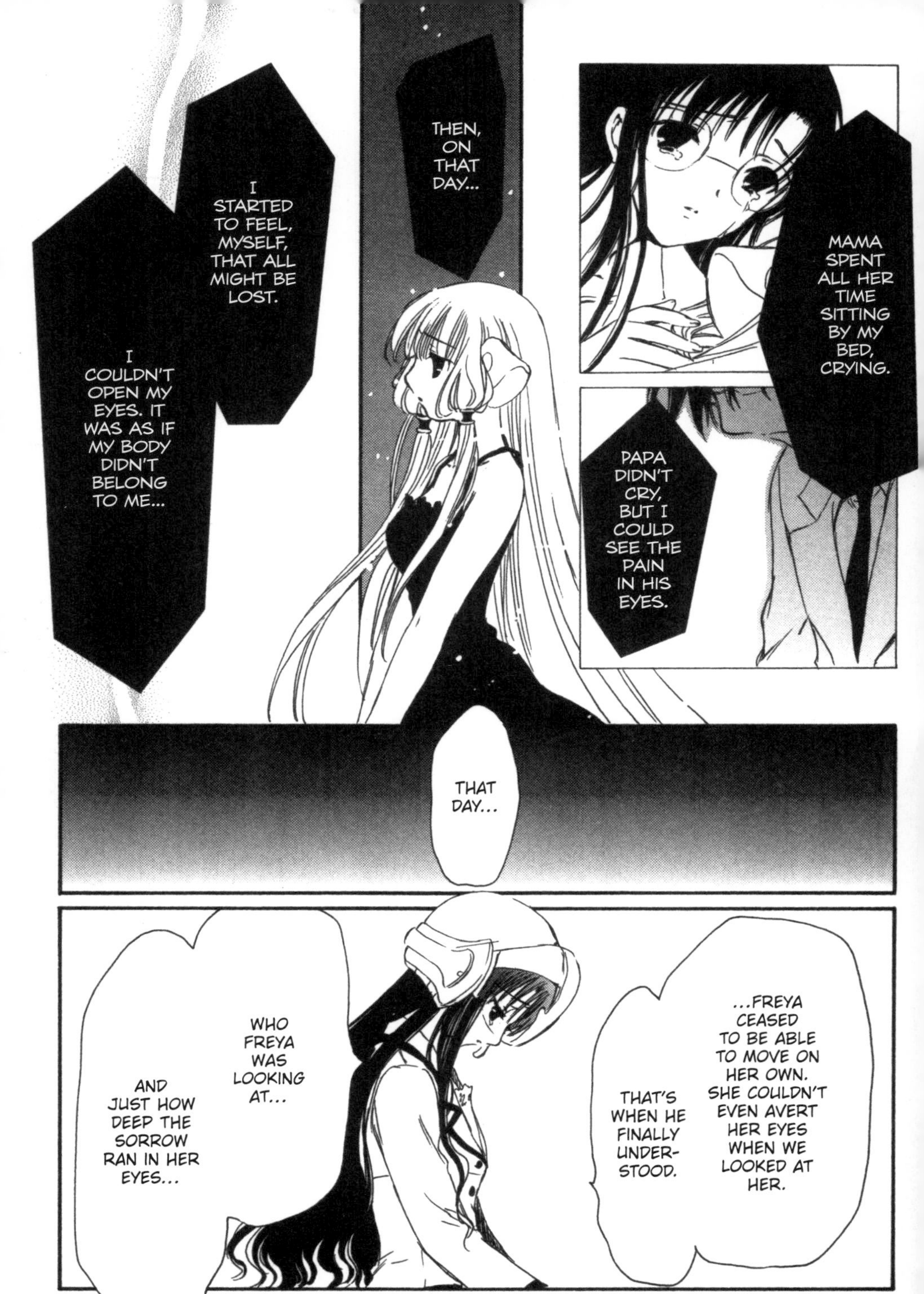
MAMA SPENT ALL HER TIME SITTING BY MY BED, CRYING.
PAPA DIDN'T CRY, BUT I COULD SEE THE PAIN IN HIS EYES.
THEN, ON THAT DAY...
I STARTED TO FEEL, MYSELF, THAT ALL MIGHT BE LOST.
I COULDN'T OPEN MY EYES. IT WAS AS IF MY BODY DIDN'T BELONG TO ME...
THAT DAY...
...FREYA CEASED TO BE ABLE TO MOVE ON HER OWN. SHE COULDN'T EVEN AVERT HER EYES WHEN WE LOOKED AT HER.
THAT'S WHEN HE FINALLY UNDER-STOOD.
WHO FREYA WAS LOOKING AT...
AND JUST HOW DEEP THE SORROW RAN IN HER EYES...

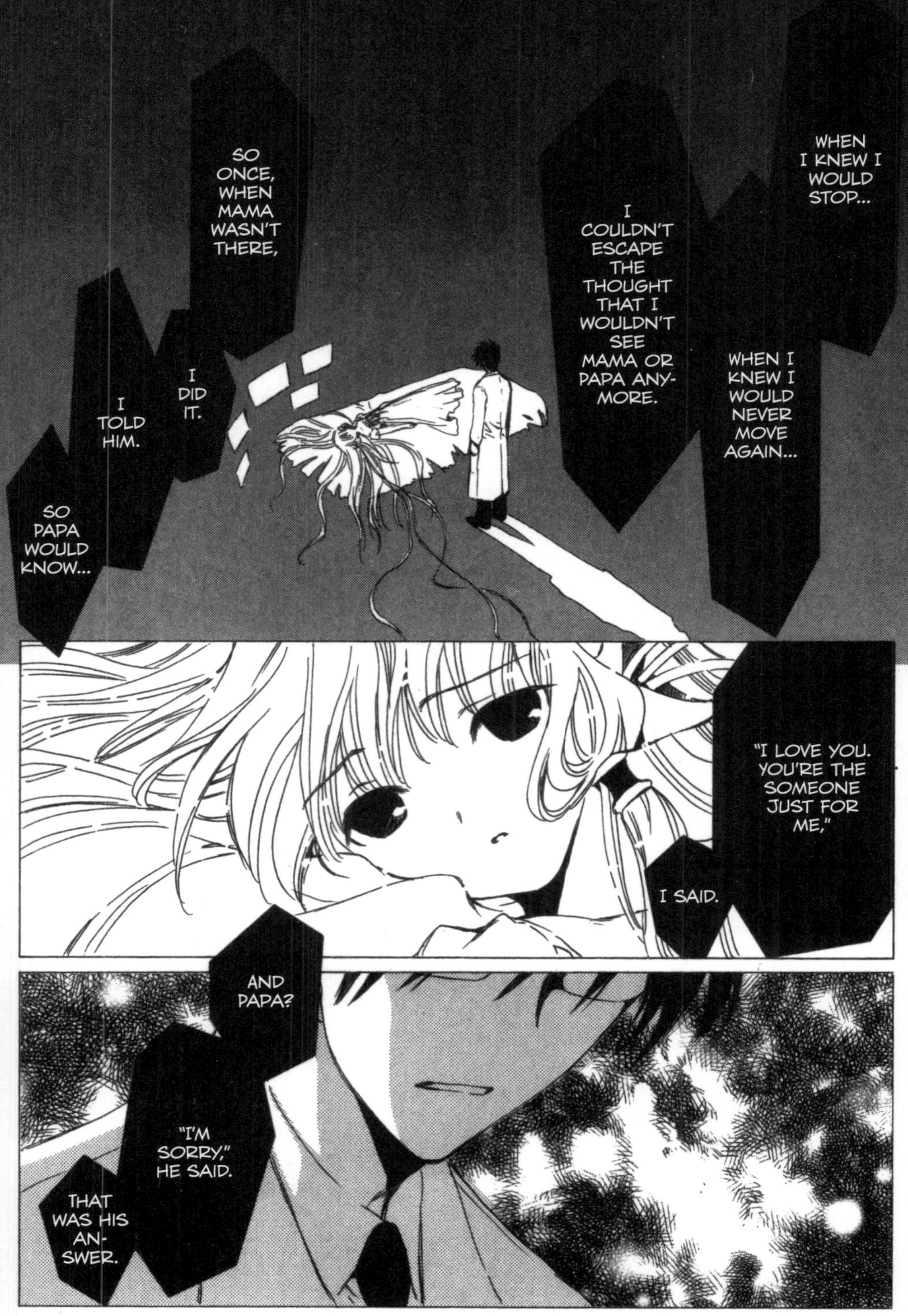
WHEN I KNEW I WOULD STOP...
WHEN I KNEW I WOULD NEVER MOVE AGAIN...
I COULDN'T ESCAPE THE THOUGHT THAT I WOULDN'T SEE MAMA OR PAPA ANY-MORE.
SO ONCE, WHEN MAMA WASN'T THERE,
I DID IT.
I TOLD HIM.
SO PAPA WOULD KNOW...
"I LOVE YOU. YOU'RE THE SOMEONE JUST FOR ME,"
I SAID.
AND PAPA?
"I'M SORRY," HE SAID.
THAT WAS HIS AN-SWER.

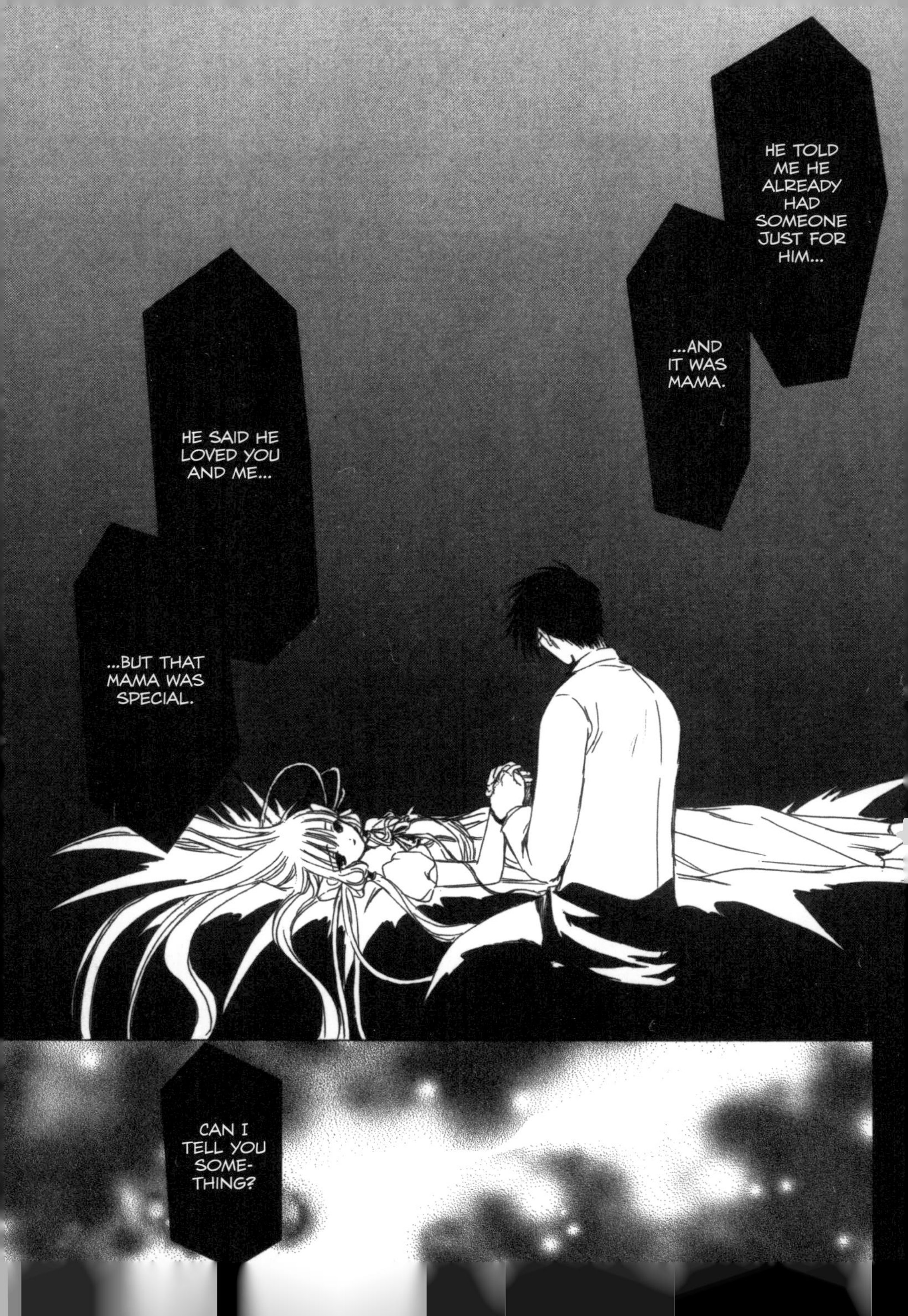
HE TOLD ME HE ALREADY HAD SOMEONE JUST FOR HIM...
...AND IT WAS MAMA.
HE SAID HE LOVED YOU AND ME...
...BUT THAT MAMA WAS SPECIAL.
CAN I TELL YOU SOME-THING?

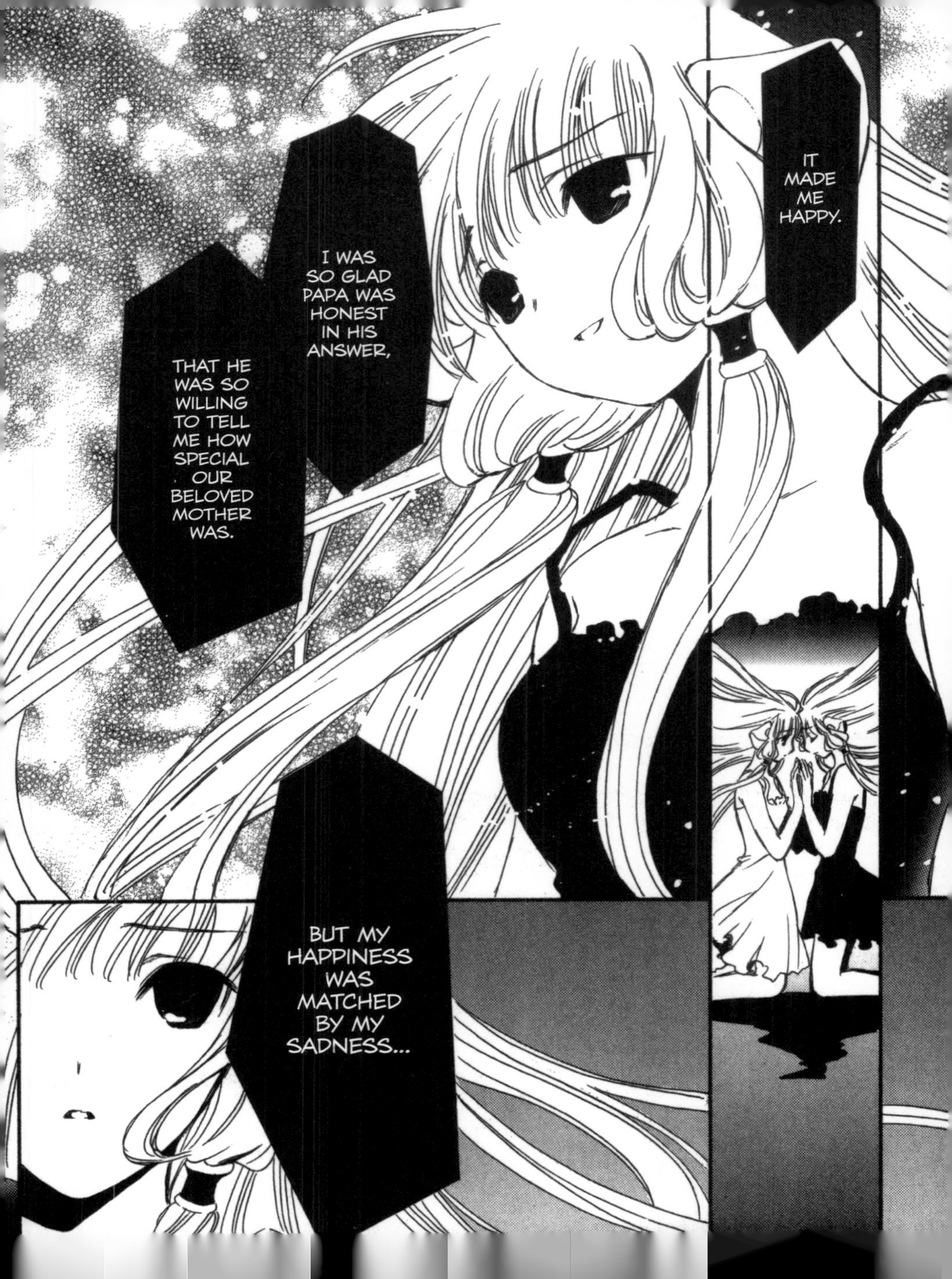
IT MADE ME HAPPY.
I WAS SO GLAD PAPA WAS HONEST IN HIS ANSWER,
THAT HE WAS SO WILLING TO TELL ME HOW SPECIAL OUR BELOVED MOTHER WAS.
BUT MY HAPPINESS WAS MATCHED BY MY SADNESS...

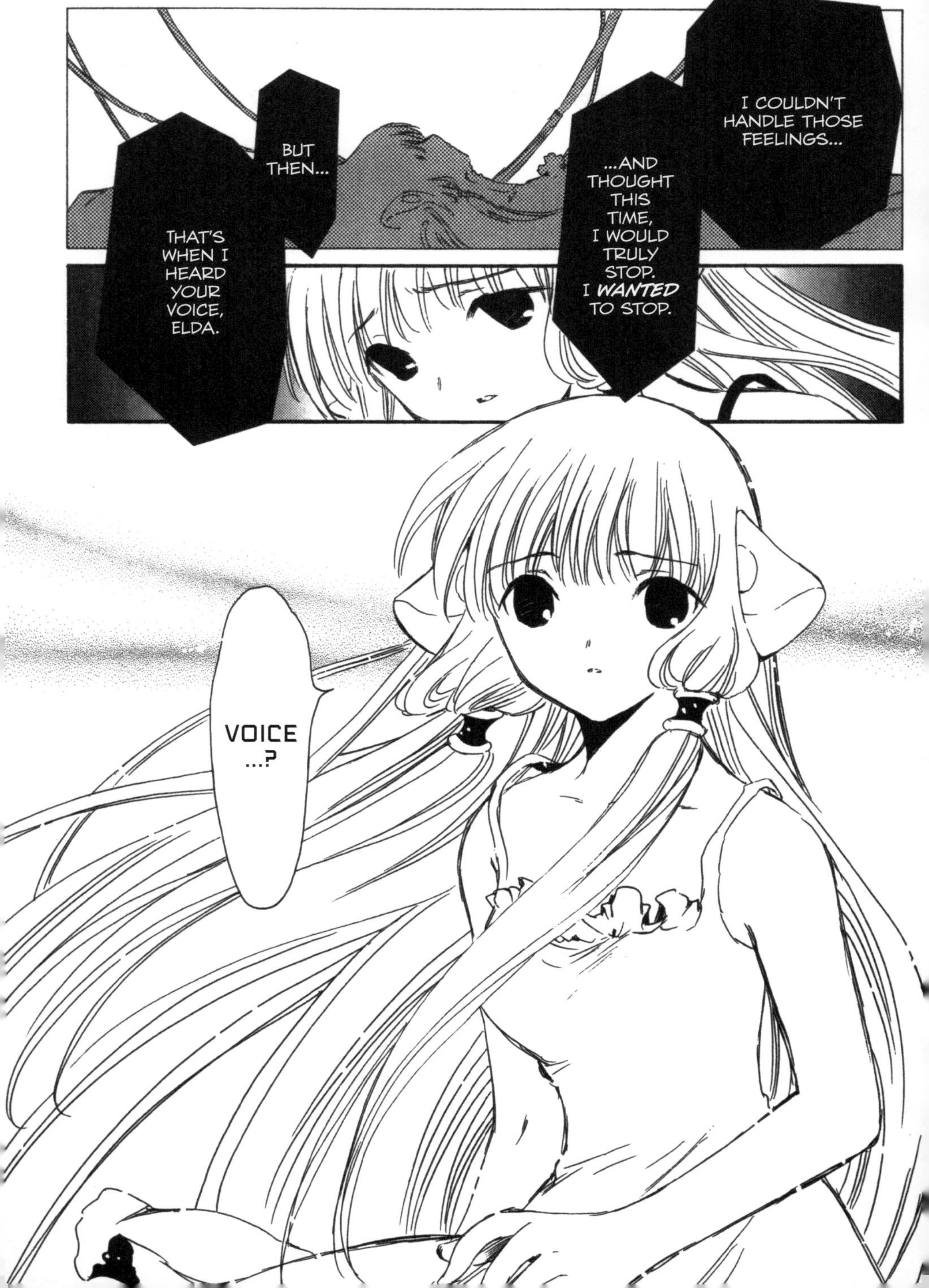
I COULDN'T HANDLE THOSE FEELINGS...
...AND THOUGHT THIS TIME, I WOULD TRULY STOP. I *WANTED* TO STOP.
BUT THEN...
THAT'S WHEN I HEARD YOUR VOICE, ELDA.
VOICE ...?

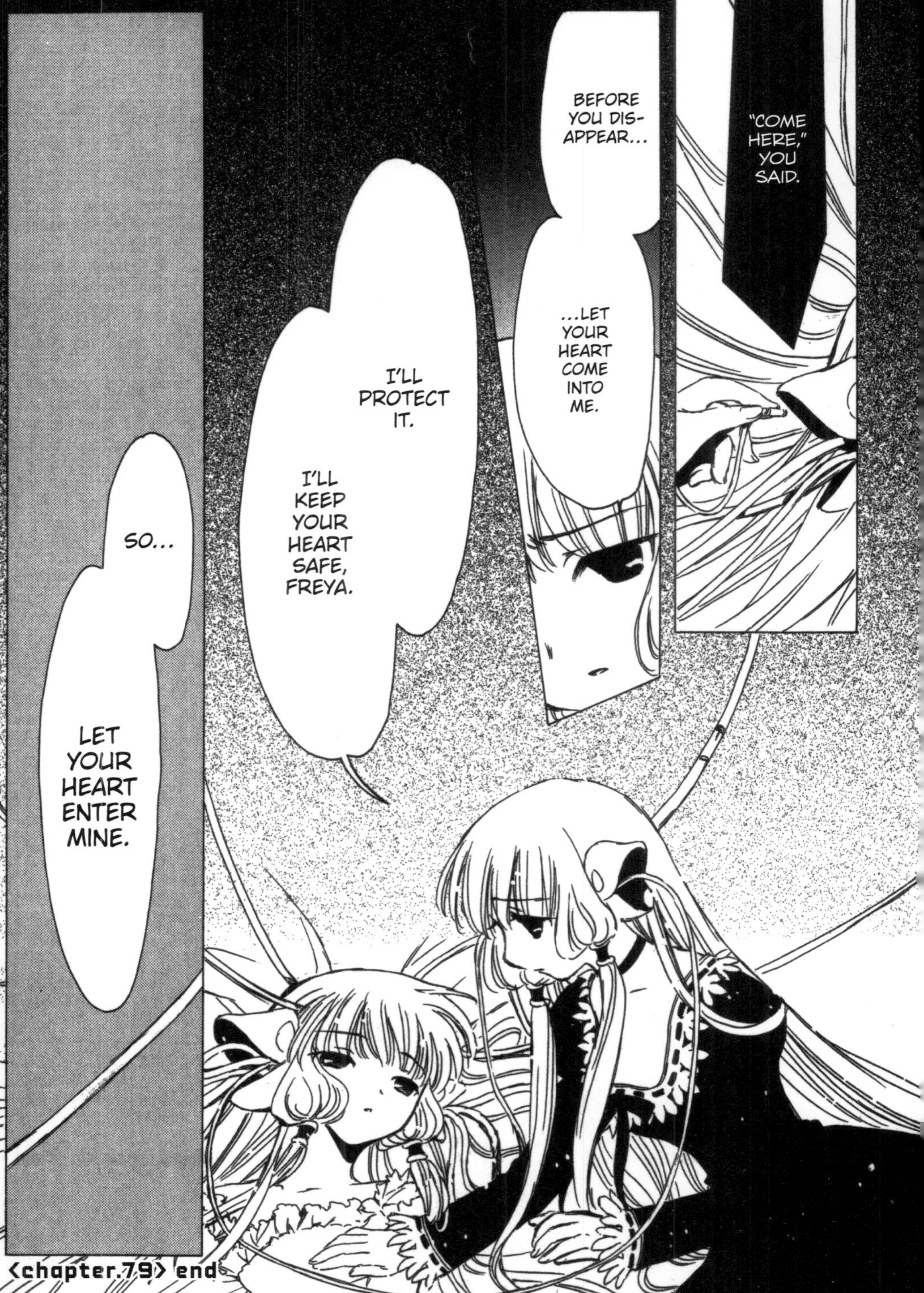
"COME HERE," YOU SAID.
BEFORE YOU DIS-APPEAR...
...LET YOUR HEART COME INTO ME.
I'LL PROTECT IT.
I'LL KEEP YOUR HEART SAFE, FREYA.
SO...
LET YOUR HEART ENTER MINE.

<chapter.79> end

〈chapter.80〉

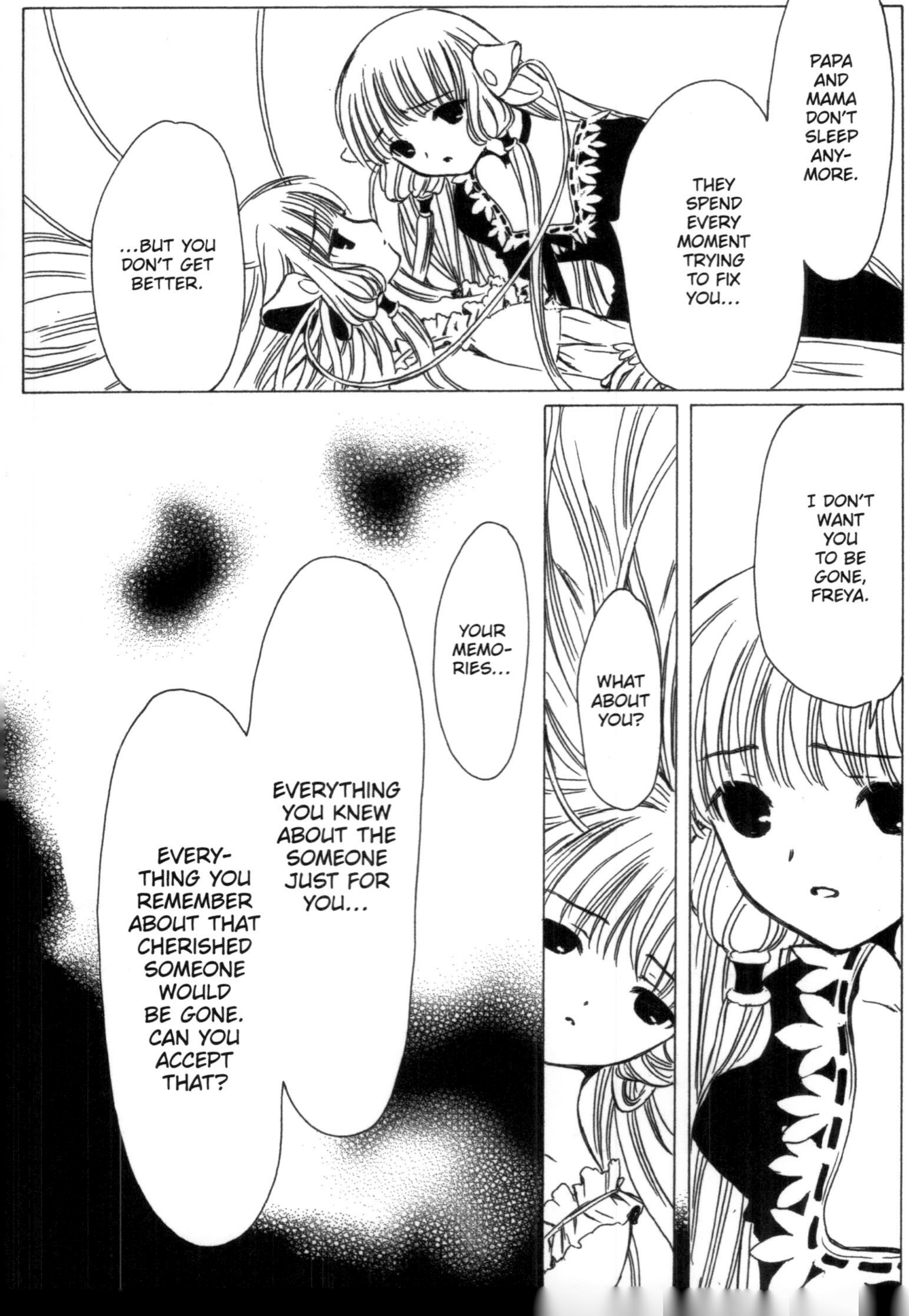
PAPA AND MAMA DON'T SLEEP ANYMORE.
THEY SPEND EVERY MOMENT TRYING TO FIX YOU...
...BUT YOU DON'T GET BETTER.
I DON'T WANT YOU TO BE GONE, FREYA.
WHAT ABOUT YOU?
YOUR MEMORIES...
EVERYTHING YOU KNEW ABOUT THE SOMEONE JUST FOR YOU...
EVERYTHING YOU REMEMBER ABOUT THAT CHERISHED SOMEONE WOULD BE GONE. CAN YOU ACCEPT THAT?

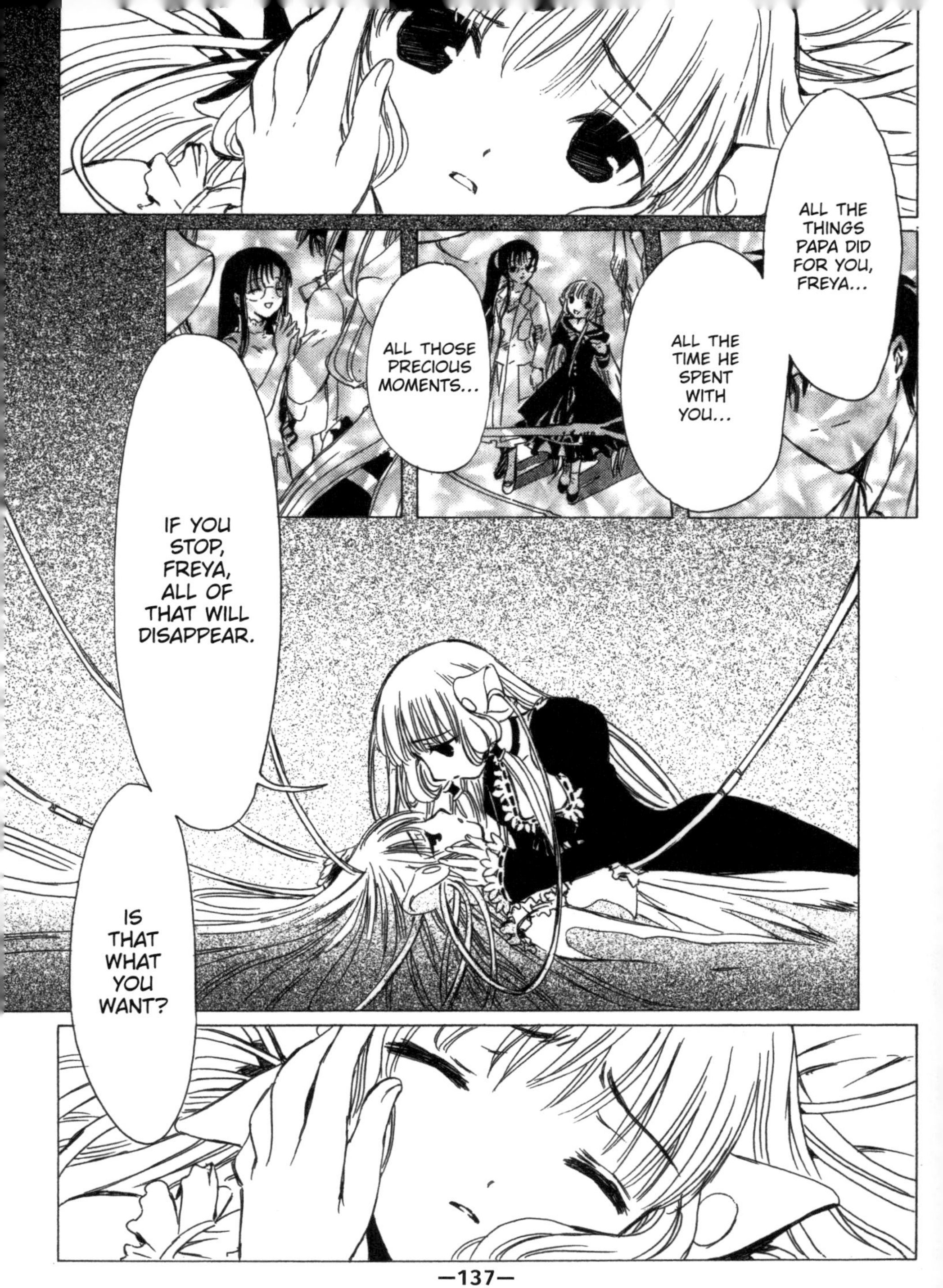
ALL THE THINGS PAPA DID FOR YOU, FREYA...
ALL THE TIME HE SPENT WITH YOU...
ALL THOSE PRECIOUS MOMENTS...
IF YOU STOP, FREYA, ALL OF THAT WILL DISAPPEAR.
IS THAT WHAT YOU WANT?

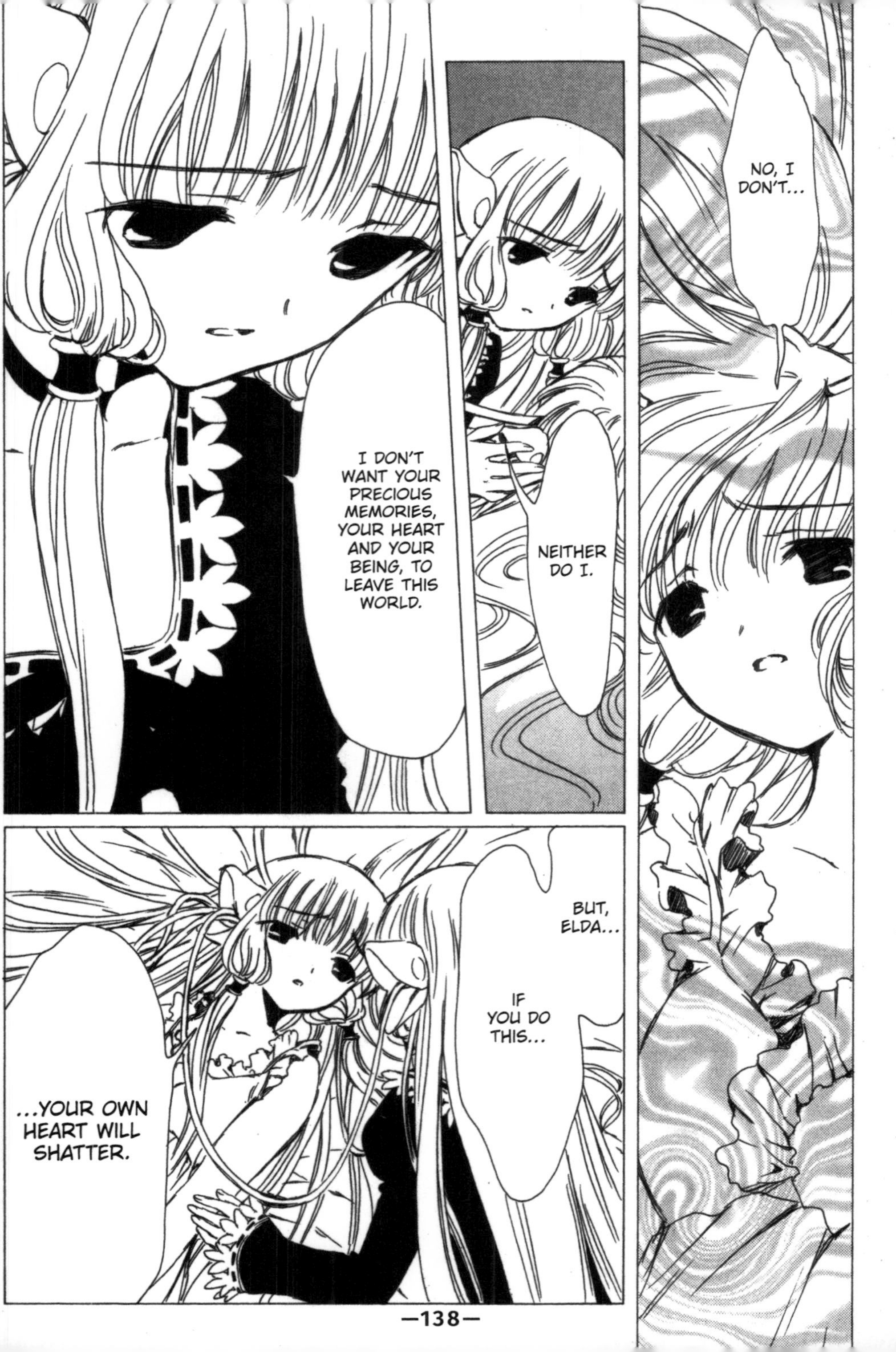
NO, I DON'T...
NEITHER DO I.
I DON'T WANT YOUR PRECIOUS MEMORIES, YOUR HEART AND YOUR BEING, TO LEAVE THIS WORLD.
BUT, ELDA...
IF YOU DO THIS...
...YOUR OWN HEART WILL SHATTER.

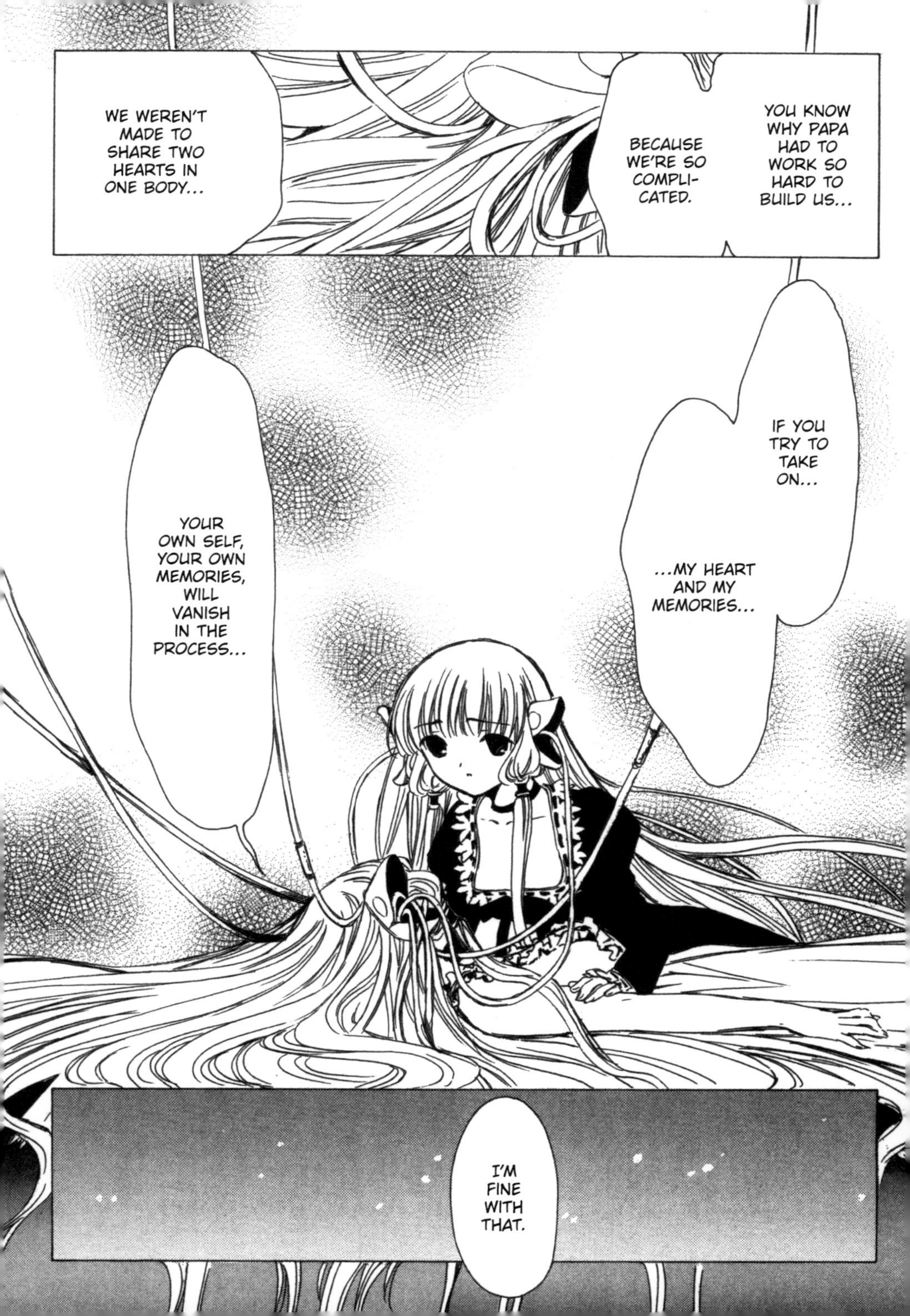
YOU KNOW WHY PAPA HAD TO WORK SO HARD TO BUILD US...
BECAUSE WE'RE SO COMPLI-CATED.
WE WEREN'T MADE TO SHARE TWO HEARTS IN ONE BODY...
IF YOU TRY TO TAKE ON...
...MY HEART AND MY MEMORIES...
YOUR OWN SELF, YOUR OWN MEMORIES, WILL VANISH IN THE PROCESS...
I'M FINE WITH THAT.

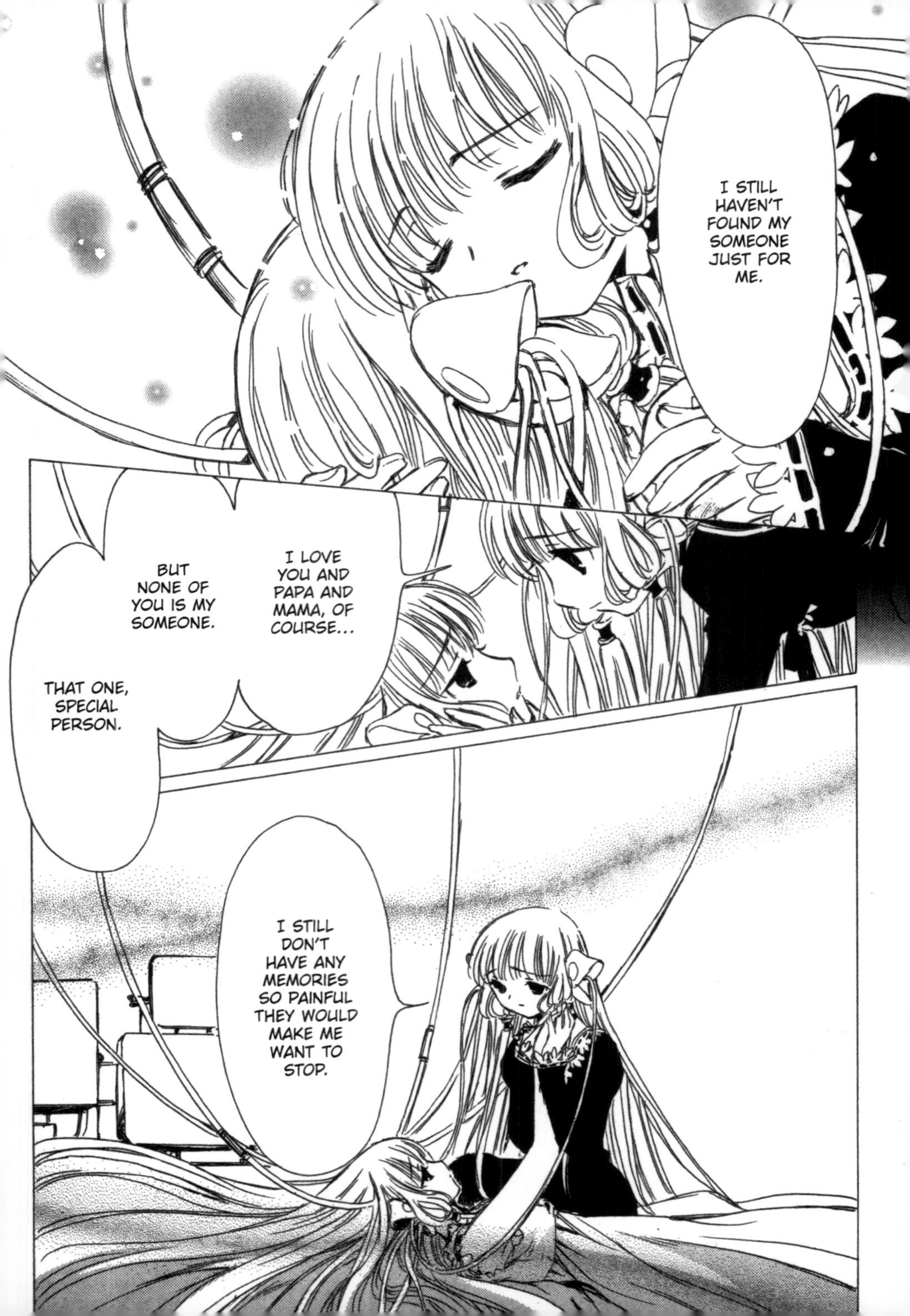
I STILL HAVEN'T FOUND MY SOMEONE JUST FOR ME.
I LOVE YOU AND PAPA AND MAMA, OF COURSE...
BUT NONE OF YOU IS MY SOMEONE.
THAT ONE, SPECIAL PERSON.
I STILL DON'T HAVE ANY MEMORIES SO PAINFUL THEY WOULD MAKE ME WANT TO STOP.

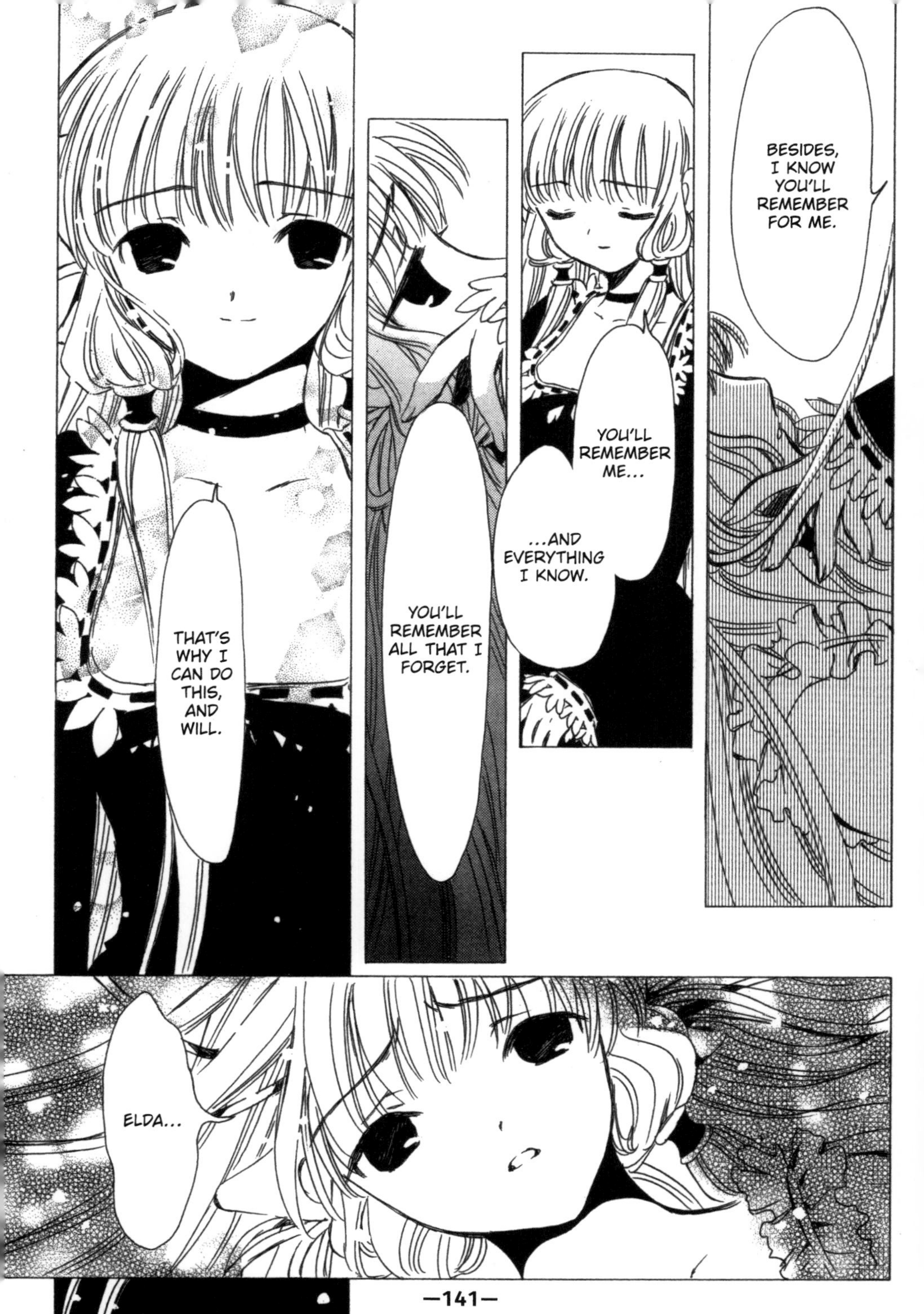
BESIDES, I KNOW YOU'LL REMEMBER FOR ME.
YOU'LL REMEMBER ME...
...AND EVERYTHING I KNOW.
YOU'LL REMEMBER ALL THAT I FORGET.
THAT'S WHY I CAN DO THIS, AND WILL.
ELDA...

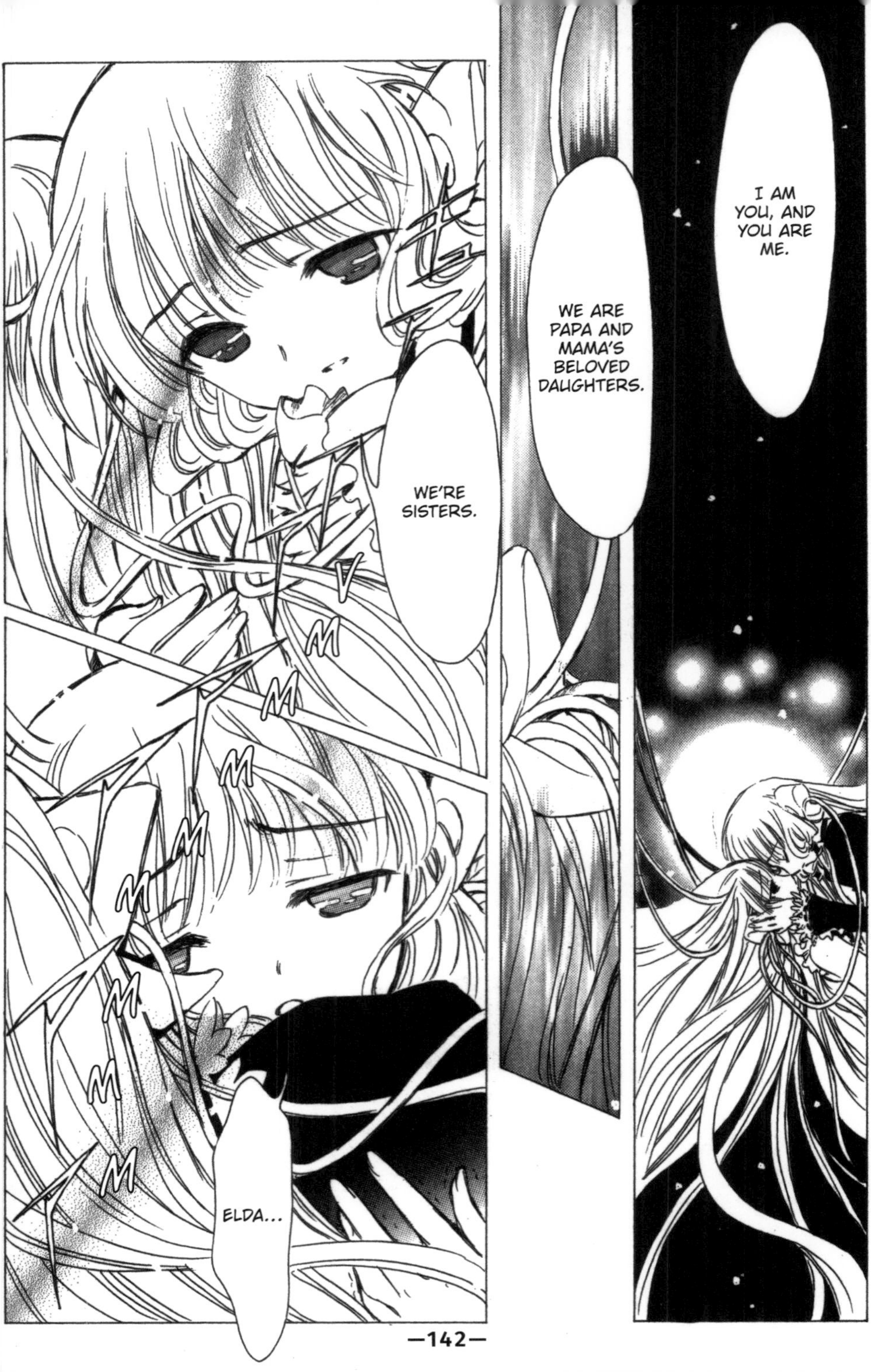
I AM YOU, AND YOU ARE ME.
WE ARE PAPA AND MAMA'S BELOVED DAUGHTERS.
WE'RE SISTERS.
ELDA...

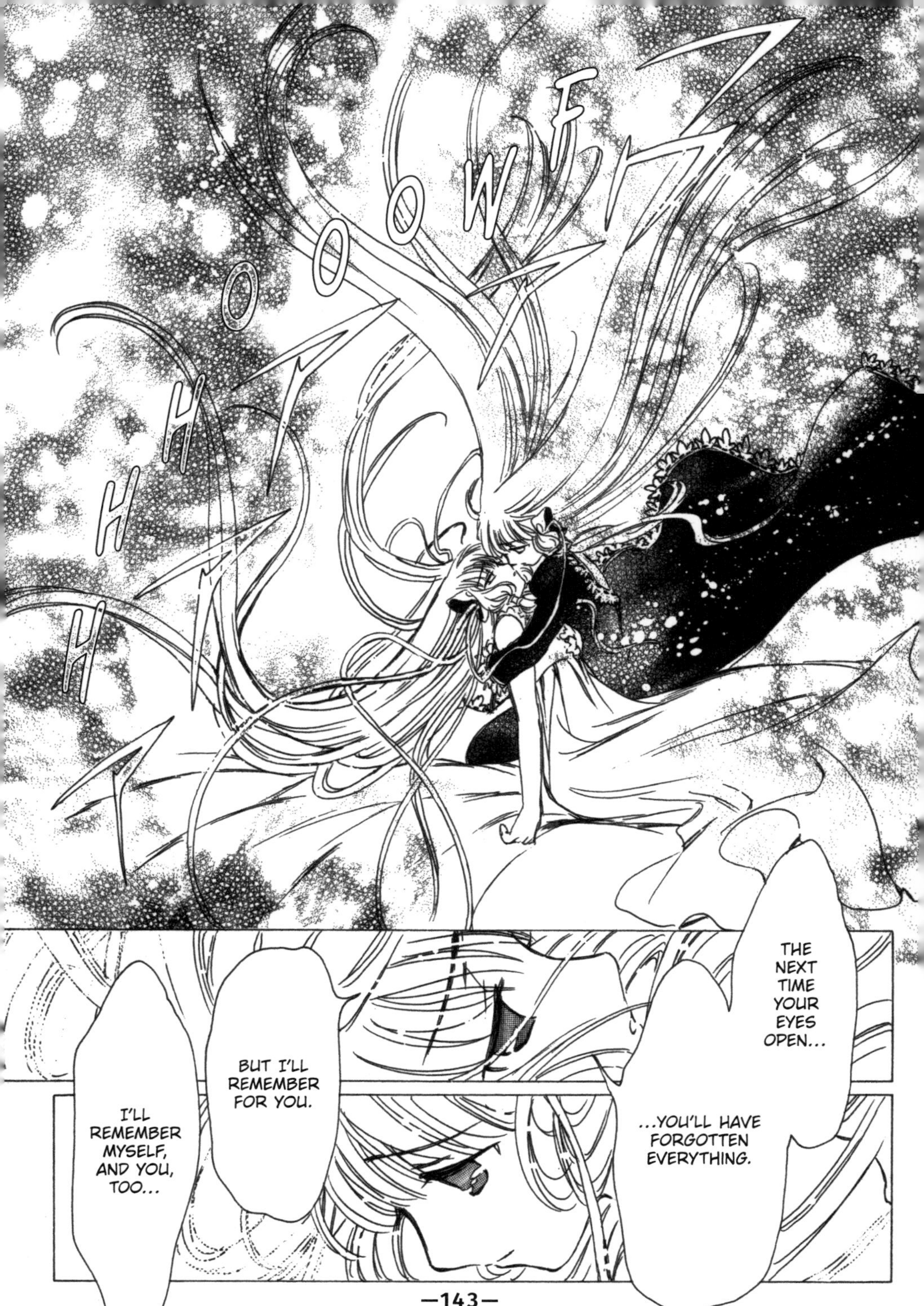
HHHOOOWF
THE NEXT TIME YOUR EYES OPEN…
…YOU'LL HAVE FORGOTTEN EVERYTHING.
BUT I'LL REMEMBER FOR YOU.
I'LL REMEMBER MYSELF, AND YOU, TOO…

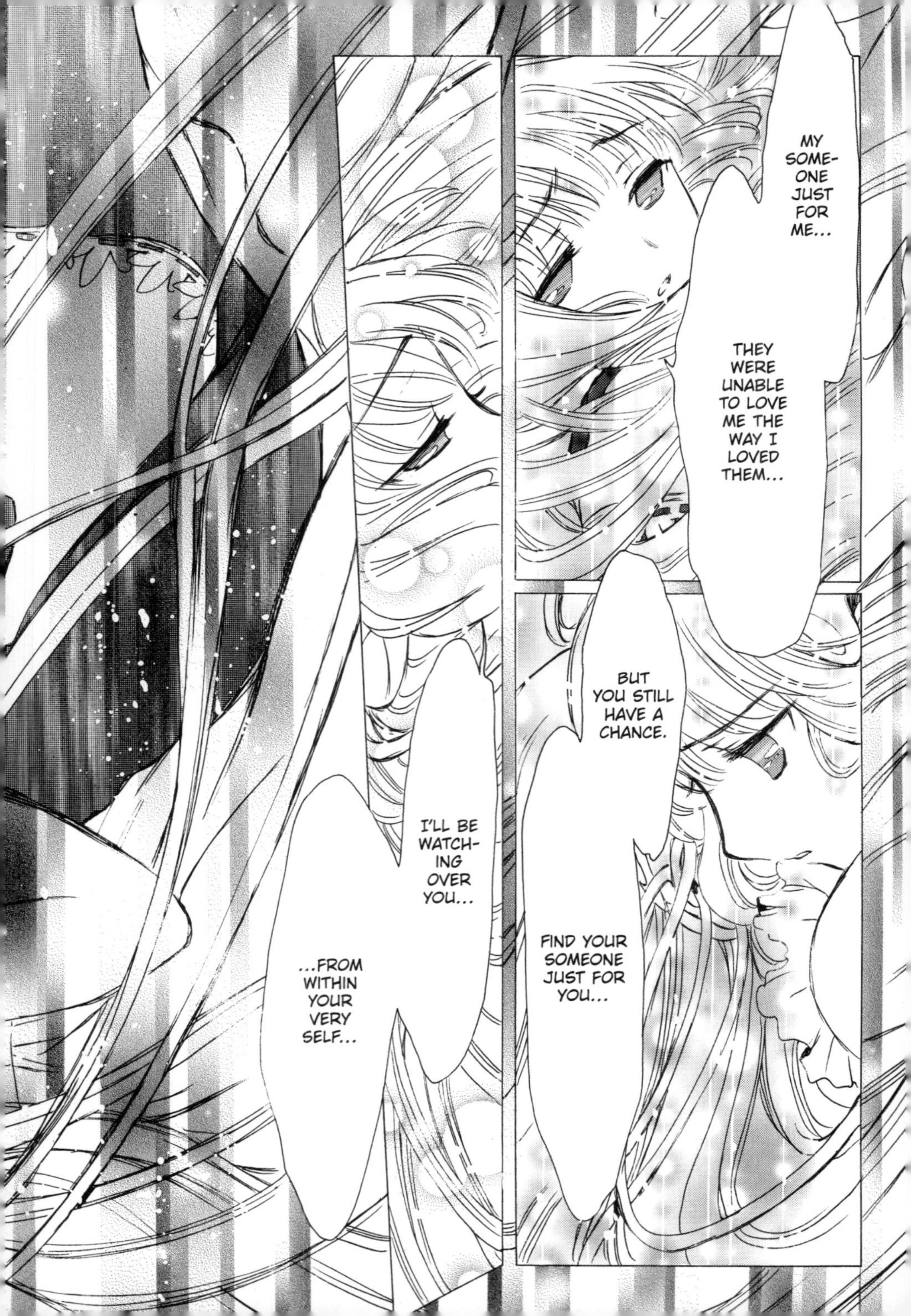
MY SOME-ONE JUST FOR ME...
THEY WERE UNABLE TO LOVE ME THE WAY I LOVED THEM...
BUT YOU STILL HAVE A CHANCE.
FIND YOUR SOMEONE JUST FOR YOU...
I'LL BE WATCHING OVER YOU...
...FROM WITHIN YOUR VERY SELF...

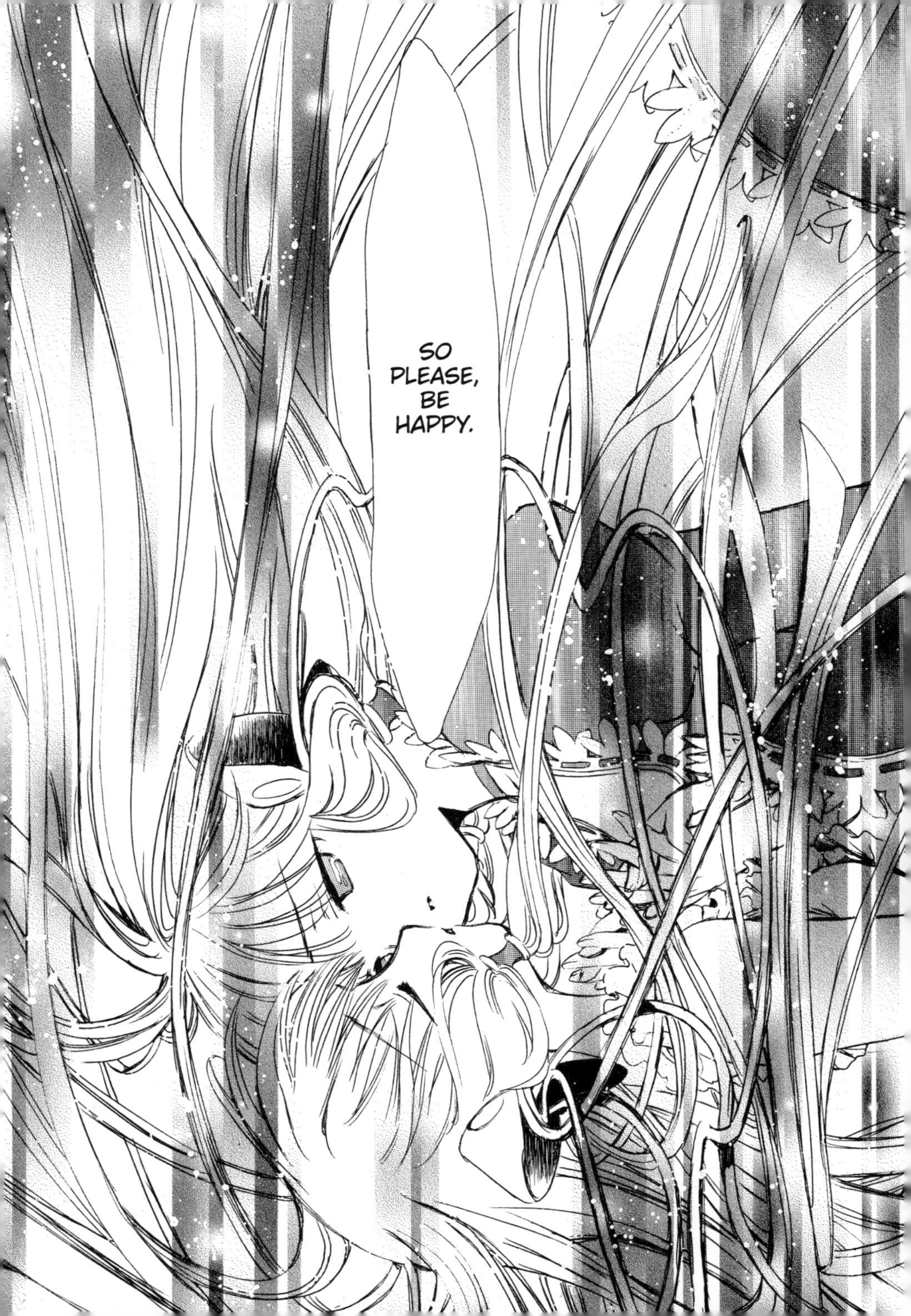
SO PLEASE, BE HAPPY.

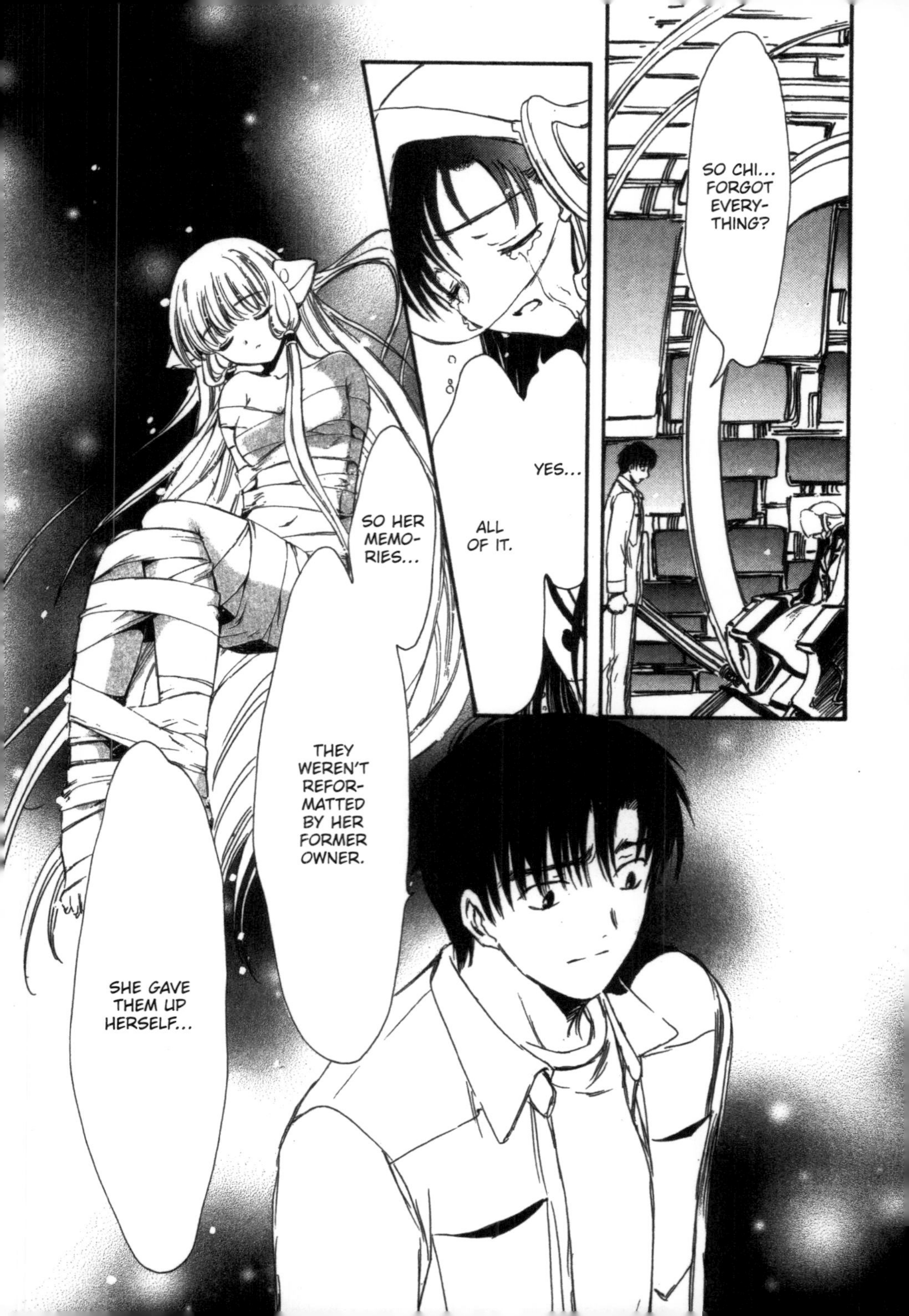
SO CHI... FORGOT EVERY-THING?
YES...
ALL OF IT.
SO HER MEMO-RIES...
THEY WEREN'T REFOR-MATTED BY HER FORMER OWNER.
SHE GAVE THEM UP HERSELF...

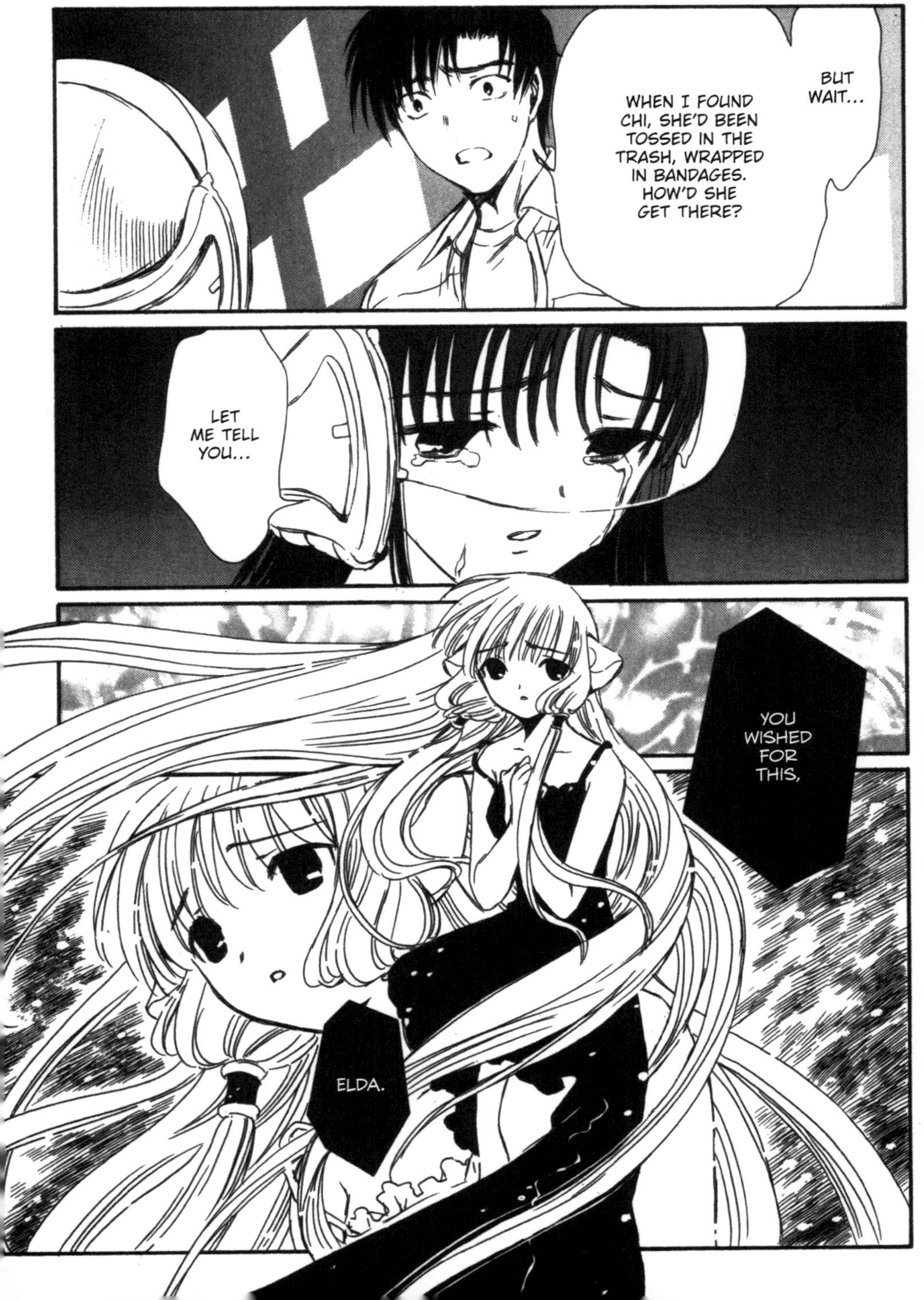
BUT WAIT...
WHEN I FOUND CHI, SHE'D BEEN TOSSED IN THE TRASH, WRAPPED IN BANDAGES. HOW'D SHE GET THERE?
LET ME TELL YOU...
YOU WISHED FOR THIS,
ELDA.

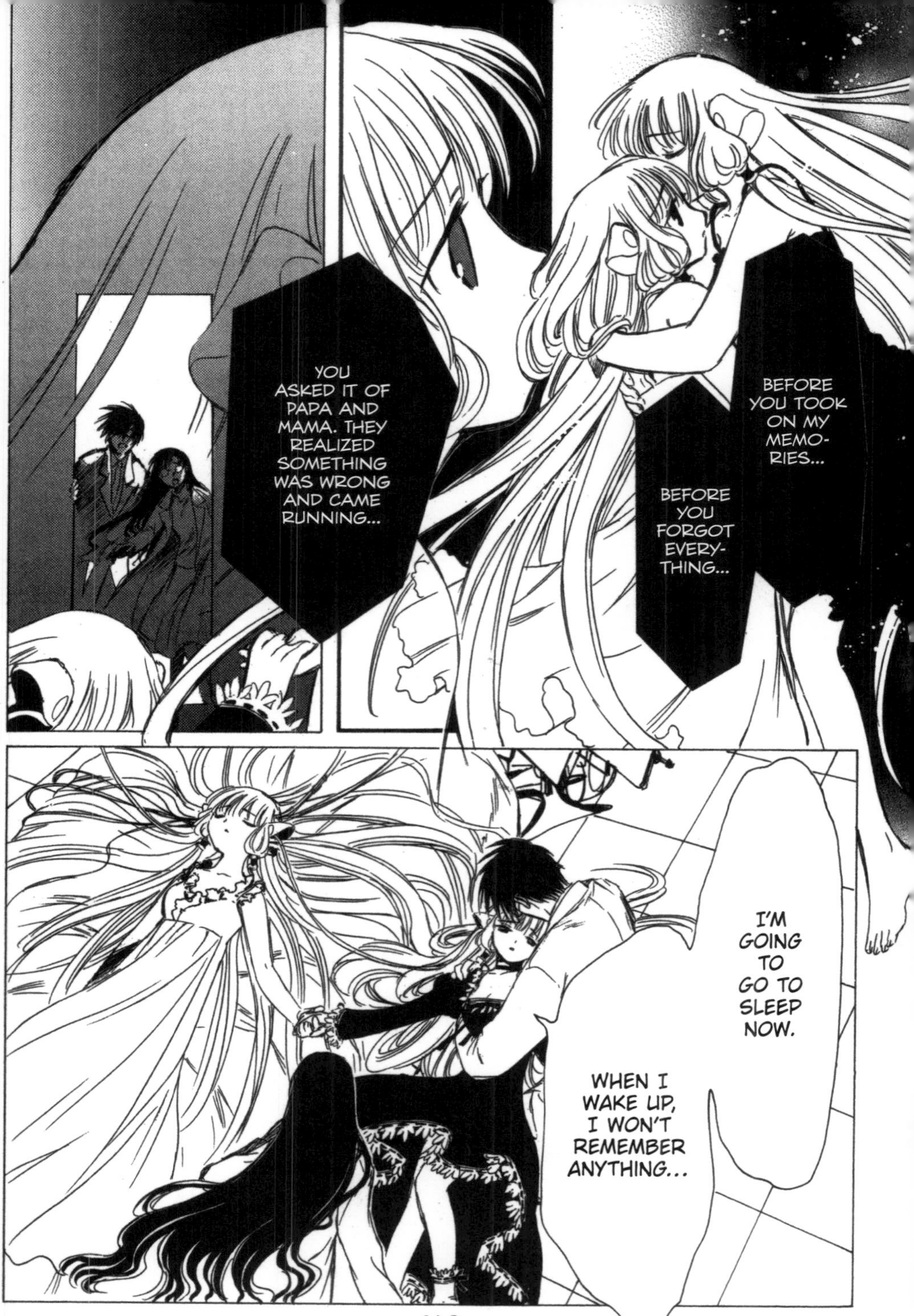
BEFORE YOU TOOK ON MY MEMO-RIES...
BEFORE YOU FORGOT EVERY-THING...
YOU ASKED IT OF PAPA AND MAMA. THEY REALIZED SOMETHING WAS WRONG AND CAME RUNNING...
I'M GOING TO GO TO SLEEP NOW.
WHEN I WAKE UP, I WON'T REMEMBER ANYTHING...

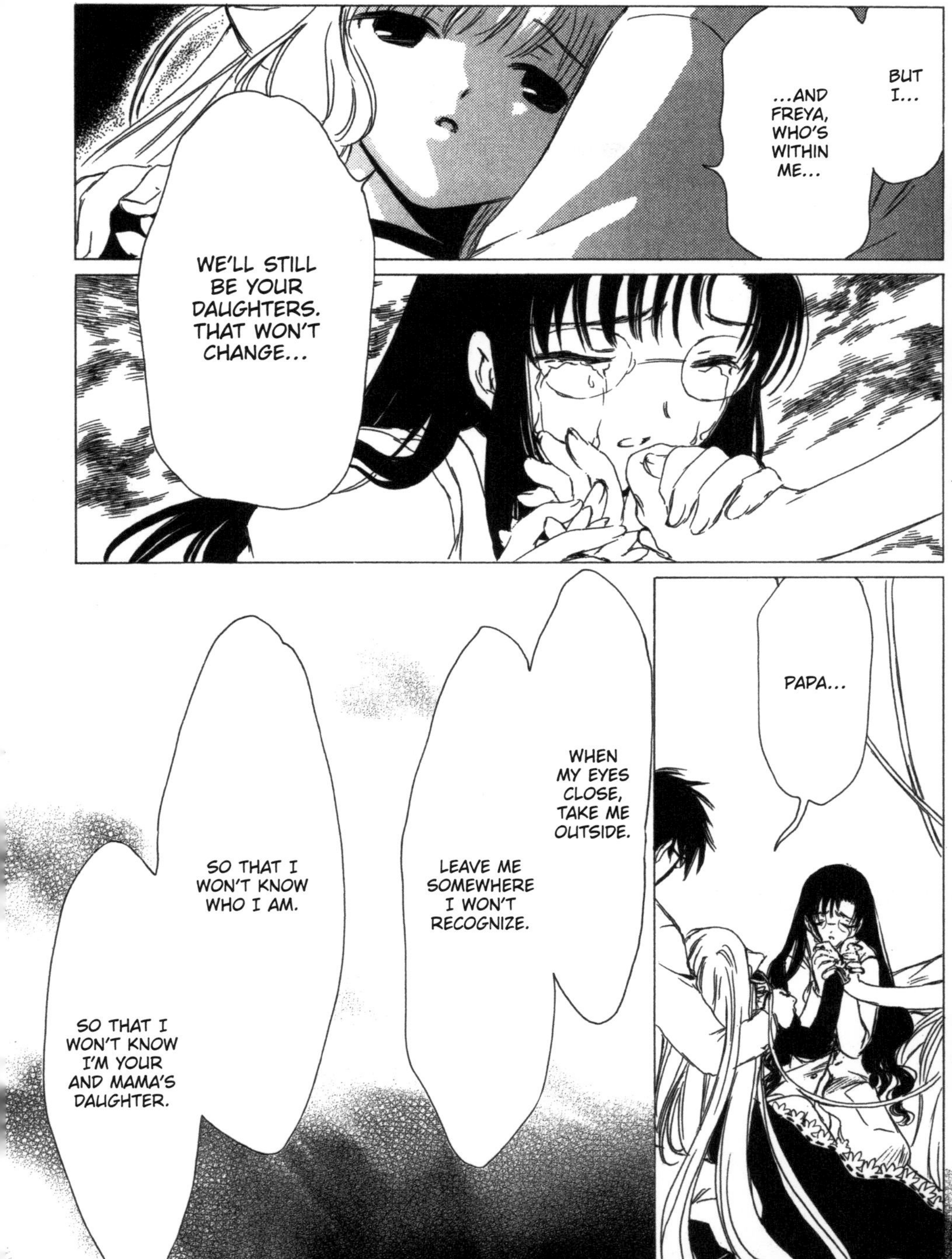
BUT I...
...AND FREYA, WHO'S WITHIN ME...
WE'LL STILL BE YOUR DAUGHTERS. THAT WON'T CHANGE...
PAPA...
WHEN MY EYES CLOSE, TAKE ME OUTSIDE.
LEAVE ME SOMEWHERE I WON'T RECOGNIZE.
SO THAT I WON'T KNOW WHO I AM.
SO THAT I WON'T KNOW I'M YOUR AND MAMA'S DAUGHTER.

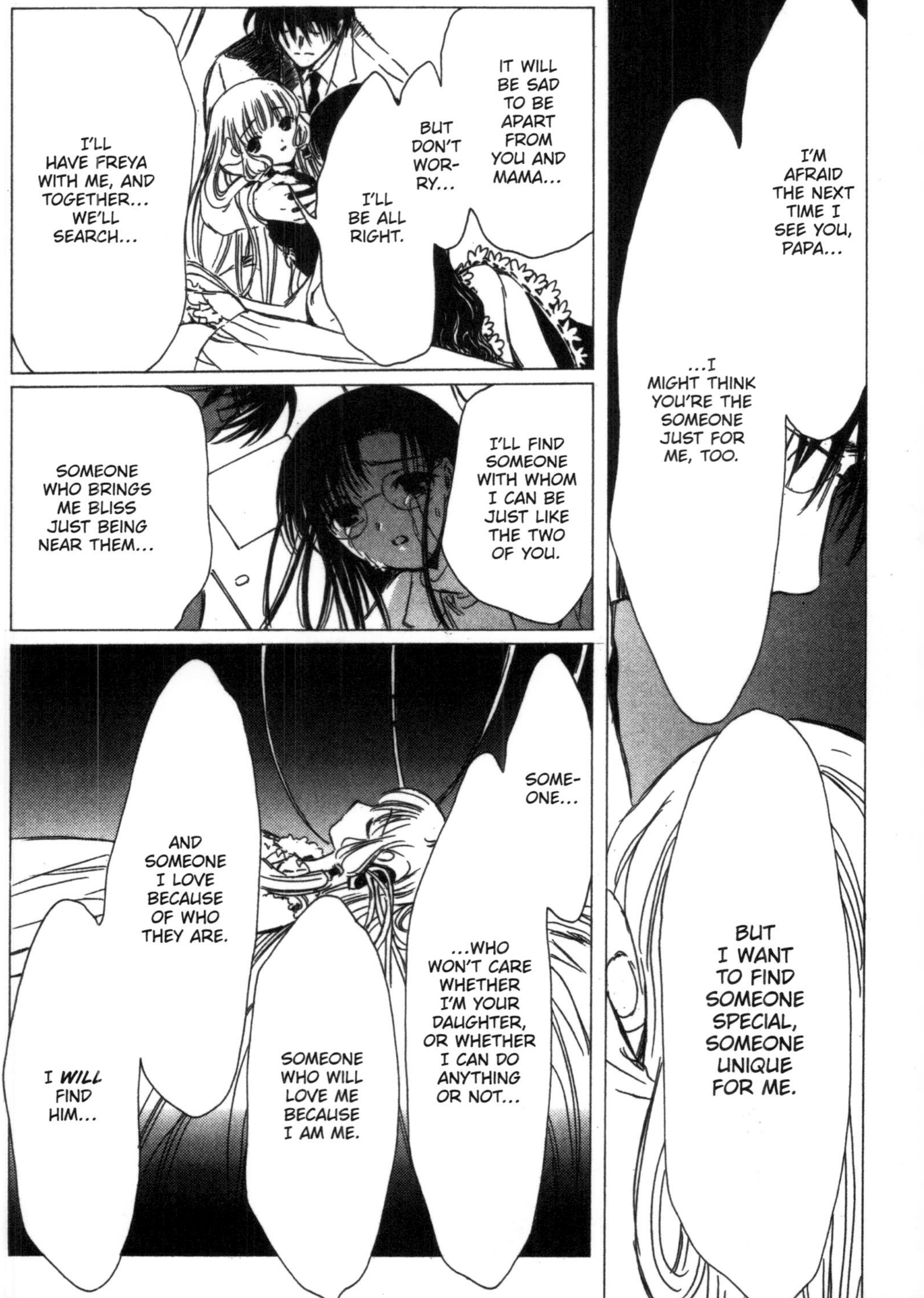
I'M AFRAID THE NEXT TIME I SEE YOU, PAPA...
...I MIGHT THINK YOU'RE THE SOMEONE JUST FOR ME, TOO.
BUT I WANT TO FIND SOMEONE SPECIAL, SOMEONE UNIQUE FOR ME.
IT WILL BE SAD TO BE APART FROM YOU AND MAMA...
BUT DON'T WOR-RY...
I'LL BE ALL RIGHT.
I'LL HAVE FREYA WITH ME, AND TOGETHER... WE'LL SEARCH...
I'LL FIND SOMEONE WITH WHOM I CAN BE JUST LIKE THE TWO OF YOU.
SOMEONE WHO BRINGS ME BLISS JUST BEING NEAR THEM...
SOME-ONE...
...WHO WON'T CARE WHETHER I'M YOUR DAUGHTER, OR WHETHER I CAN DO ANYTHING OR NOT...
SOMEONE WHO WILL LOVE ME BECAUSE I AM ME.
AND SOMEONE I LOVE BECAUSE OF WHO THEY ARE.
I *WILL* FIND HIM...

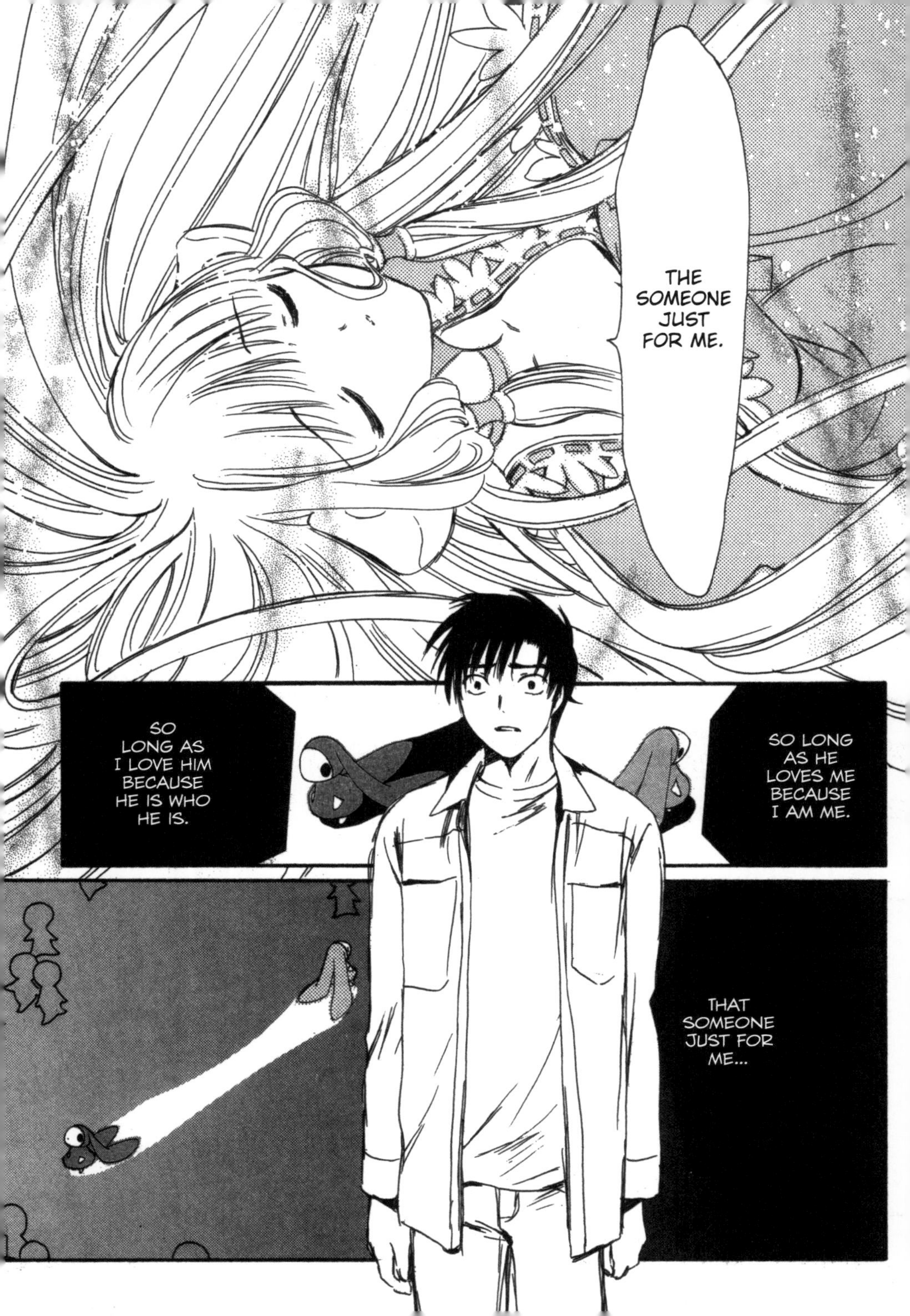
THE SOMEONE JUST FOR ME.
SO LONG AS HE LOVES ME BECAUSE I AM ME.
SO LONG AS I LOVE HIM BECAUSE HE IS WHO HE IS.
THAT SOMEONE JUST FOR ME...

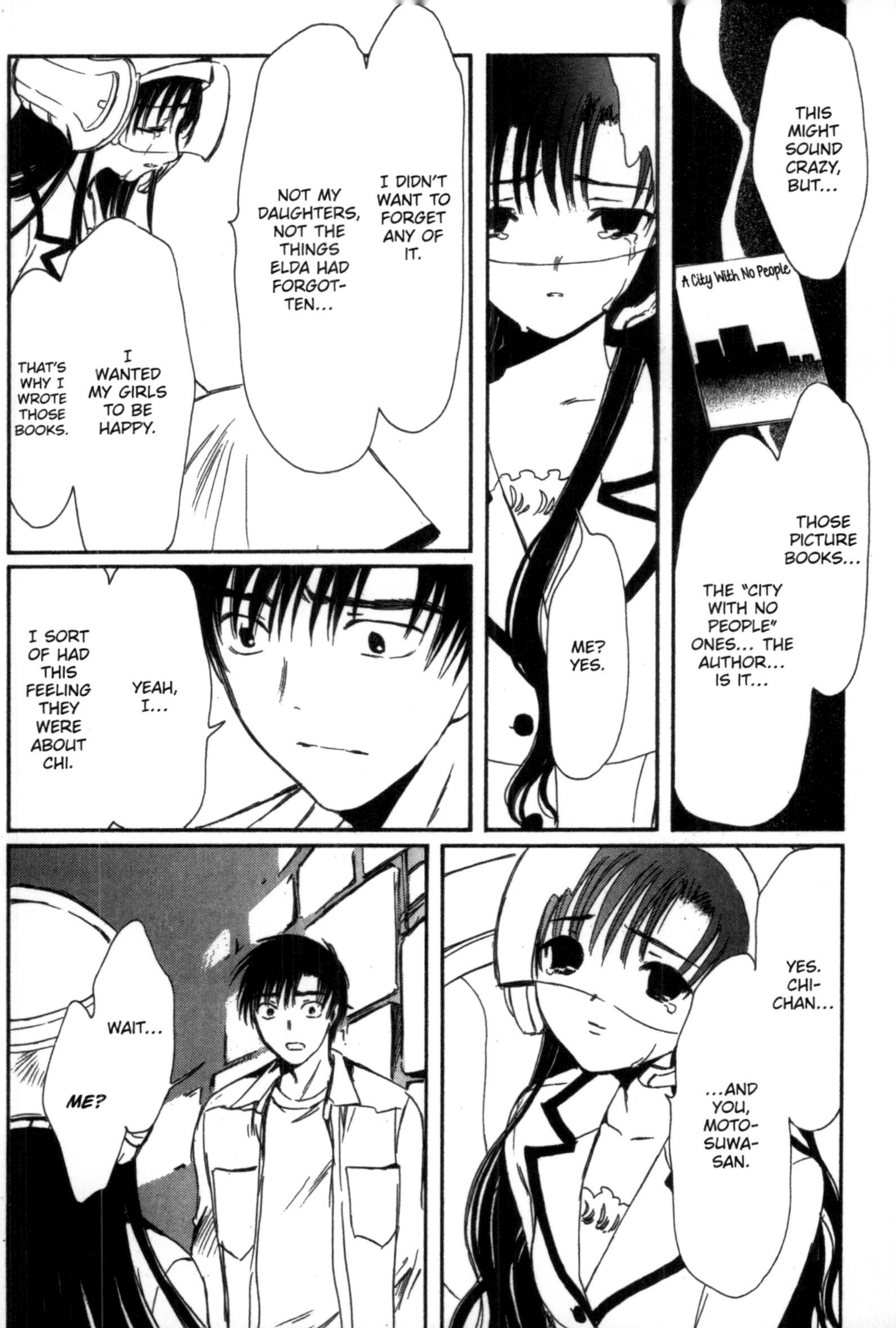
THIS MIGHT SOUND CRAZY, BUT...
A City With No People
THOSE PICTURE BOOKS...
THE "CITY WITH NO PEOPLE" ONES... THE AUTHOR... IS IT...
ME? YES.
I DIDN'T WANT TO FORGET ANY OF IT.
NOT MY DAUGHTERS, NOT THE THINGS ELDA HAD FORGOTTEN...
I WANTED MY GIRLS TO BE HAPPY.
THAT'S WHY I WROTE THOSE BOOKS.
YEAH, I...
I SORT OF HAD THIS FEELING THEY WERE ABOUT CHI.
YES. CHI-CHAN...
...AND YOU, MOTOSUWA-SAN.
WAIT...
*ME?*

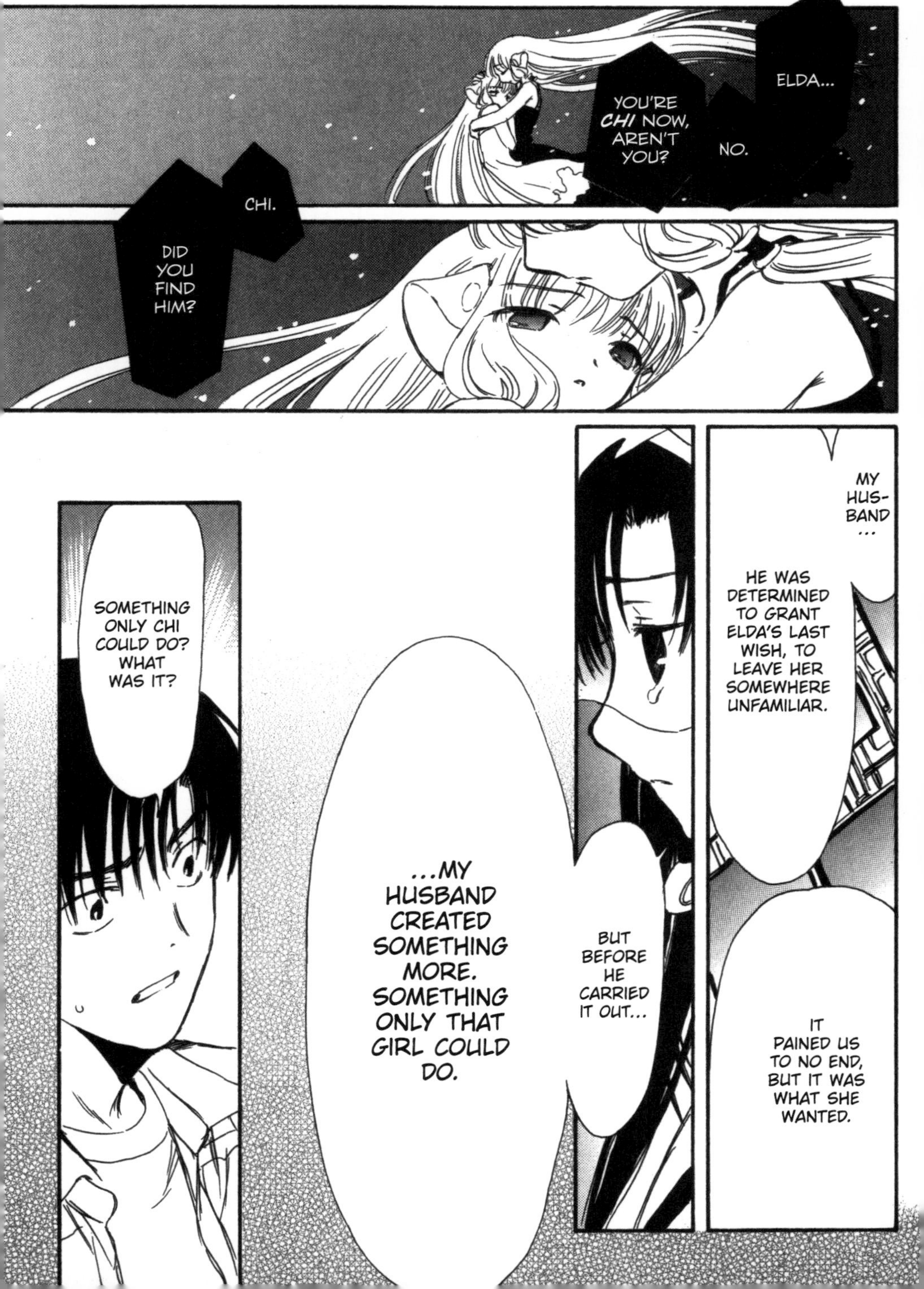
ELDA...
NO.
YOU'RE *CHI* NOW, AREN'T YOU?
CHI.
DID YOU FIND HIM?
MY HUS-BAND...
HE WAS DETERMINED TO GRANT ELDA'S LAST WISH, TO LEAVE HER SOMEWHERE UNFAMILIAR.
IT PAINED US TO NO END, BUT IT WAS WHAT SHE WANTED.
BUT BEFORE HE CARRIED IT OUT...
...MY HUSBAND CREATED SOMETHING MORE. SOMETHING ONLY THAT GIRL COULD DO.
SOMETHING ONLY CHI COULD DO? WHAT WAS IT?

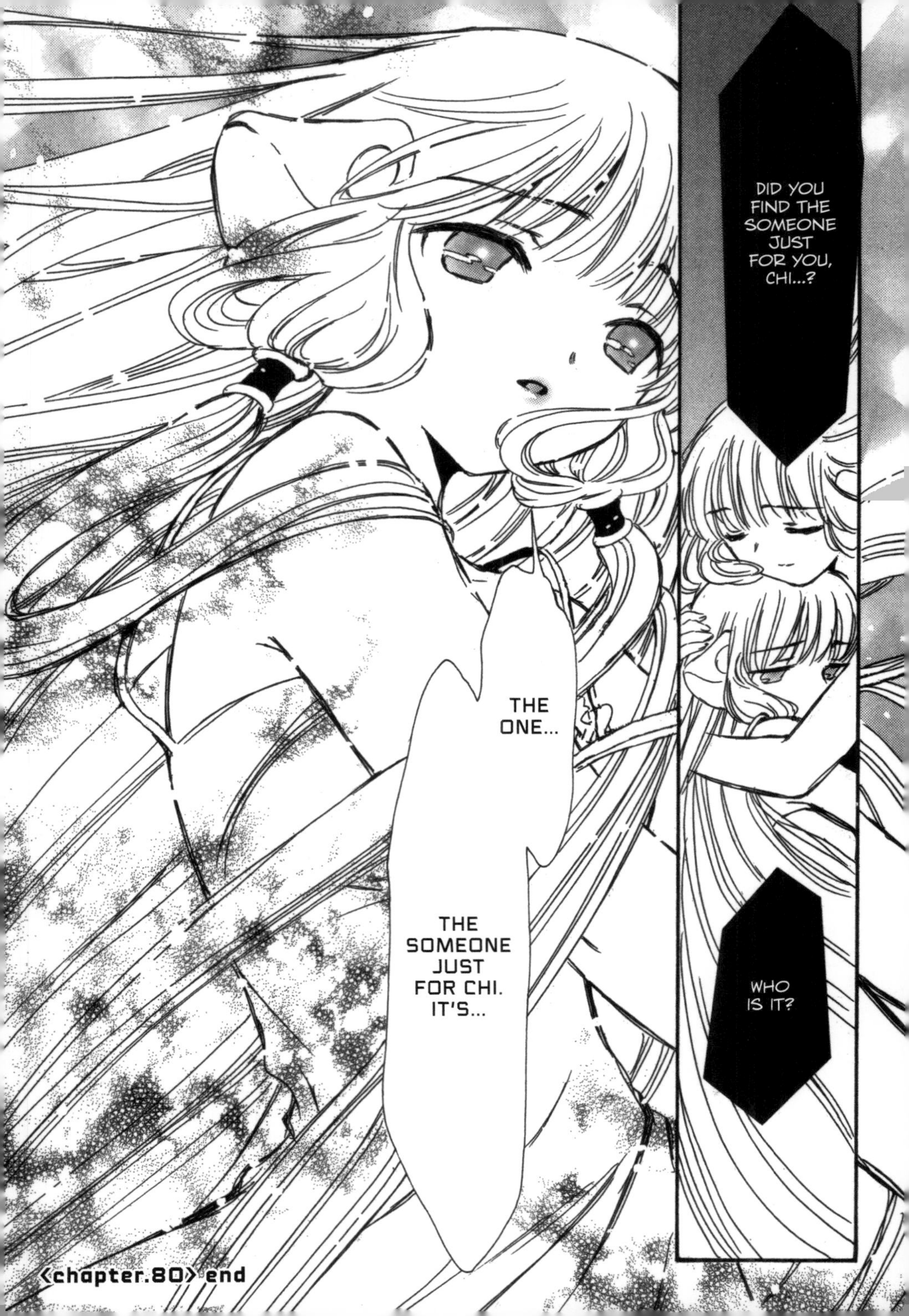
DID YOU FIND THE SOMEONE JUST FOR YOU, CHI...?
WHO IS IT?
THE ONE...
THE SOMEONE JUST FOR CHI. IT'S...
‹chapter.80› end

# Chobits

## ‹chapter.81›

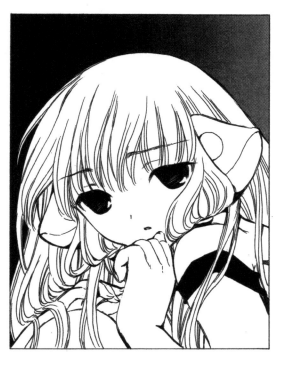

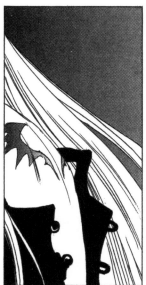

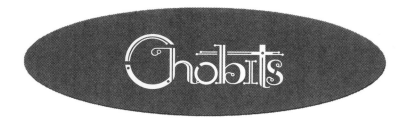

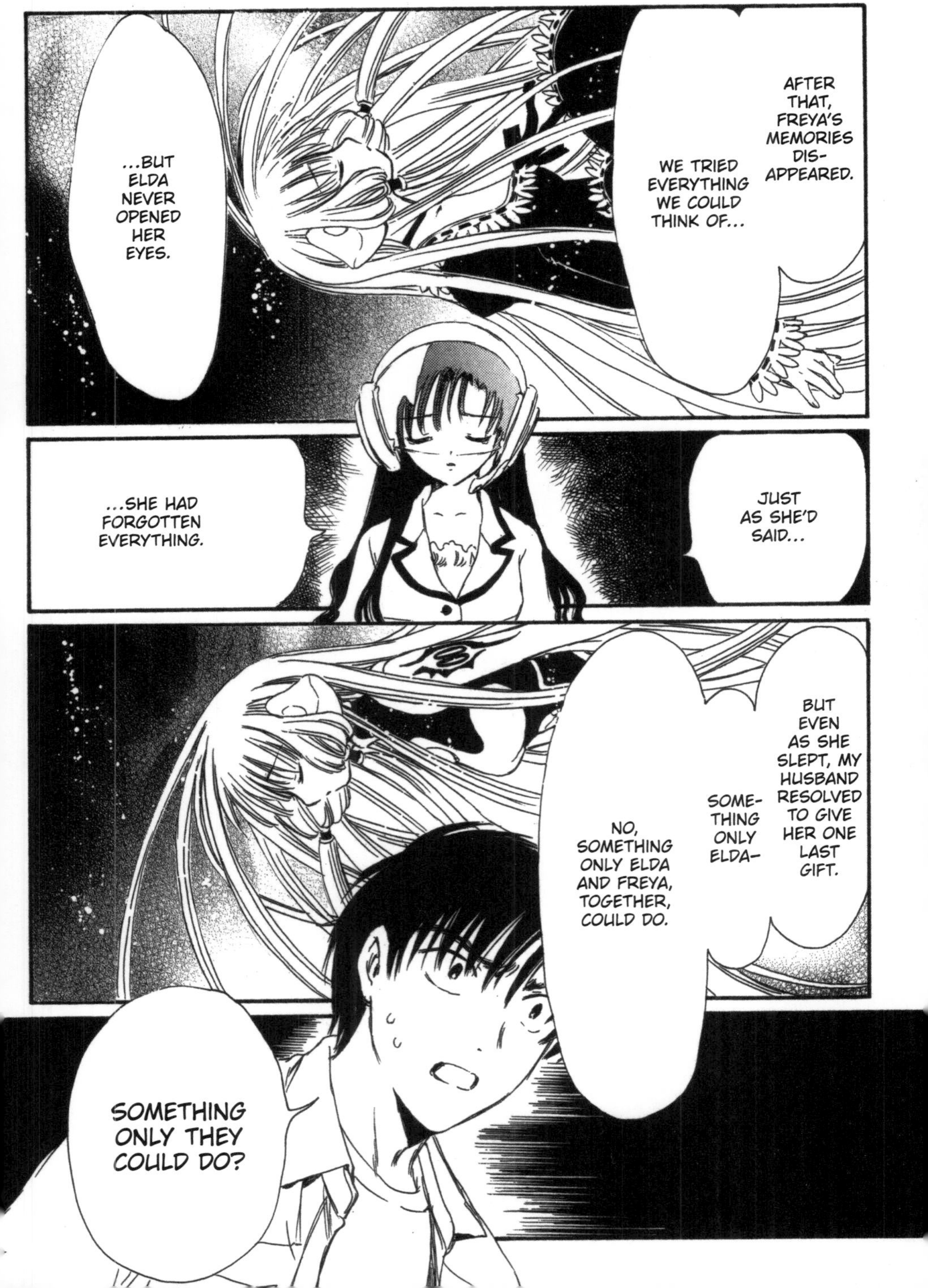
AFTER THAT, FREYA'S MEMORIES DIS-APPEARED.
WE TRIED EVERYTHING WE COULD THINK OF...
...BUT ELDA NEVER OPENED HER EYES.
JUST AS SHE'D SAID...
...SHE HAD FORGOTTEN EVERYTHING.
BUT EVEN AS SHE SLEPT, MY HUSBAND RESOLVED TO GIVE HER ONE LAST GIFT.
SOME-THING ONLY ELDA-
NO, SOMETHING ONLY ELDA AND FREYA, TOGETHER, COULD DO.
SOMETHING ONLY THEY COULD DO?

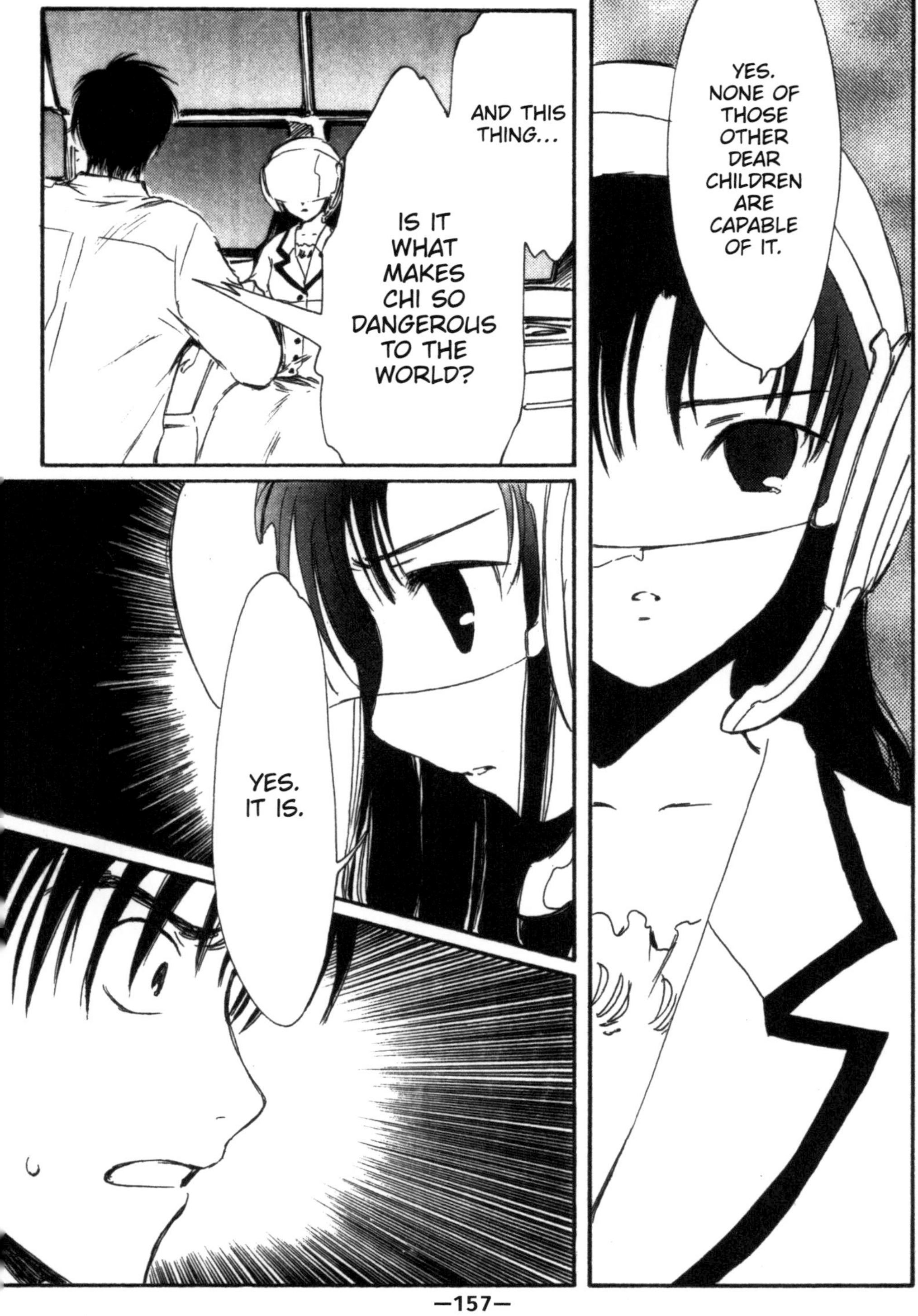
YES. NONE OF THOSE OTHER DEAR CHILDREN ARE CAPABLE OF IT.
AND THIS THING...
IS IT WHAT MAKES CHI SO DANGEROUS TO THE WORLD?
YES. IT IS.

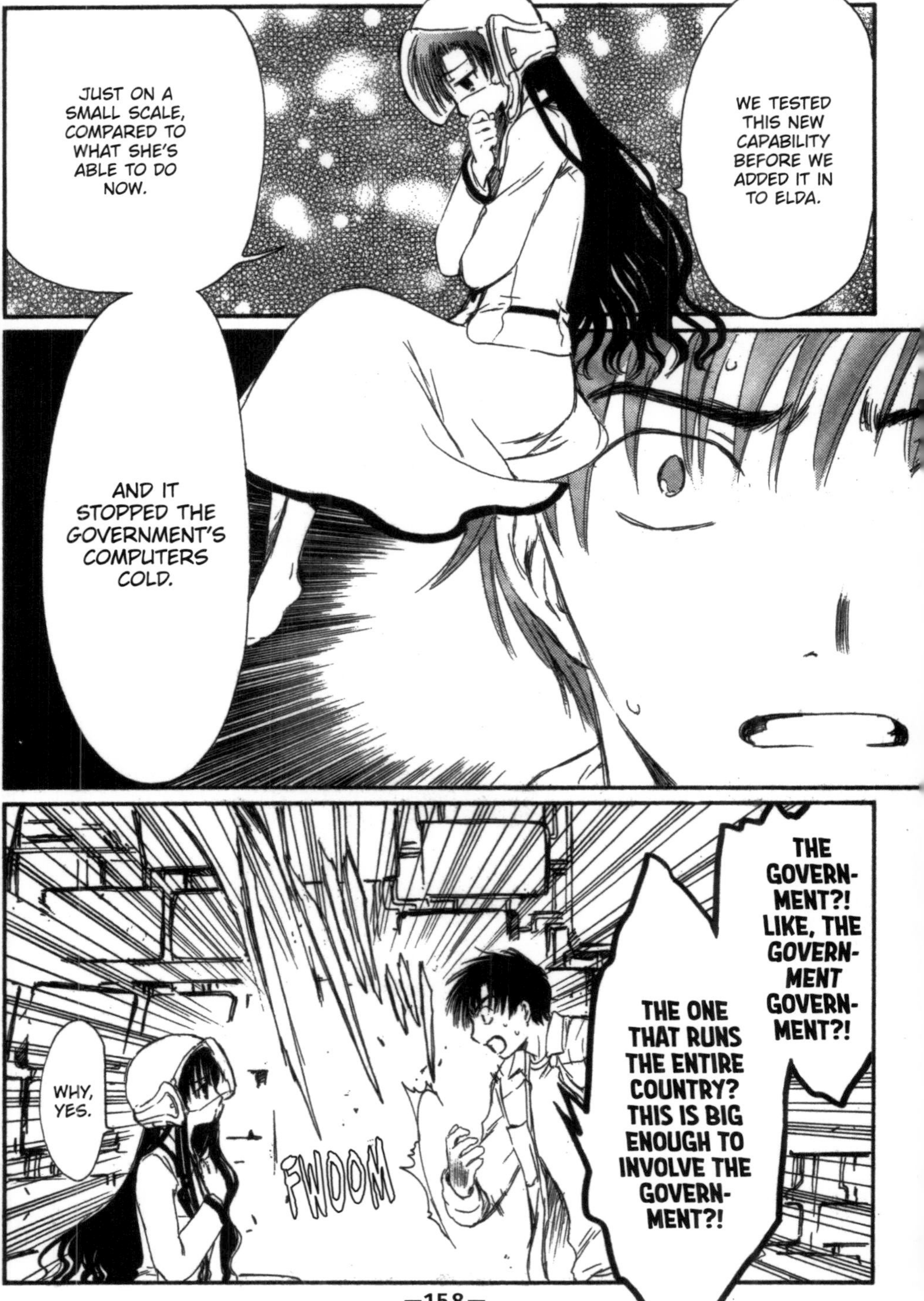
WE TESTED THIS NEW CAPABILITY BEFORE WE ADDED IT IN TO ELDA.
JUST ON A SMALL SCALE, COMPARED TO WHAT SHE'S ABLE TO DO NOW.
AND IT STOPPED THE GOVERNMENT'S COMPUTERS COLD.
THE GOVERNMENT?! LIKE, THE GOVERNMENT GOVERNMENT?!
THE ONE THAT RUNS THE ENTIRE COUNTRY? THIS IS BIG ENOUGH TO INVOLVE THE GOVERNMENT?!
FWOOM
WHY, YES.

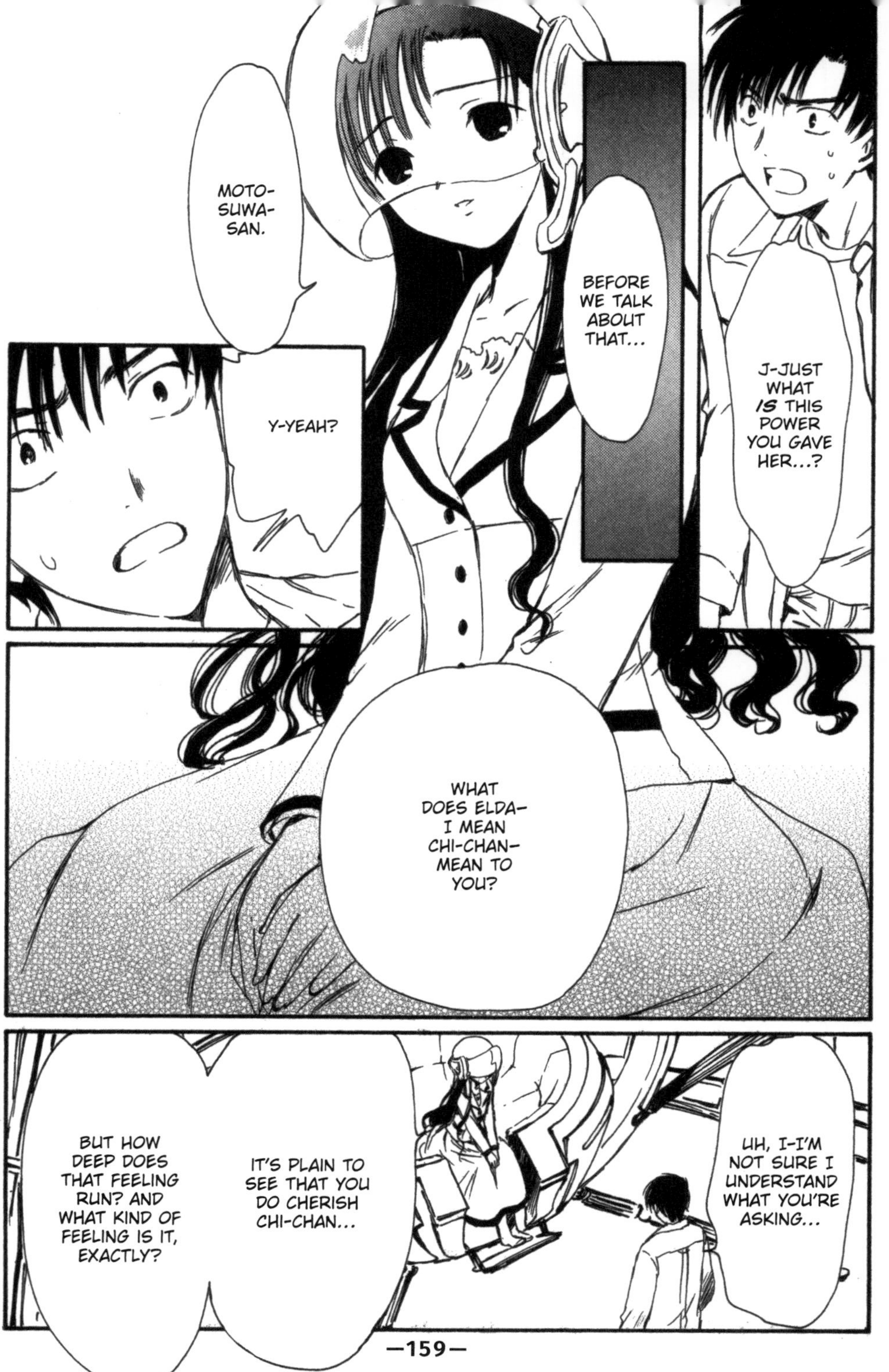
J-JUST WHAT *IS* THIS POWER YOU GAVE HER...?
BEFORE WE TALK ABOUT THAT...
MOTO-SUWA-SAN.
Y-YEAH?
WHAT DOES ELDA-I MEAN CHI-CHAN-MEAN TO YOU?
UH, I-I'M NOT SURE I UNDERSTAND WHAT YOU'RE ASKING...
IT'S PLAIN TO SEE THAT YOU DO CHERISH CHI-CHAN...
BUT HOW DEEP DOES THAT FEELING RUN? AND WHAT KIND OF FEELING IS IT, EXACTLY?

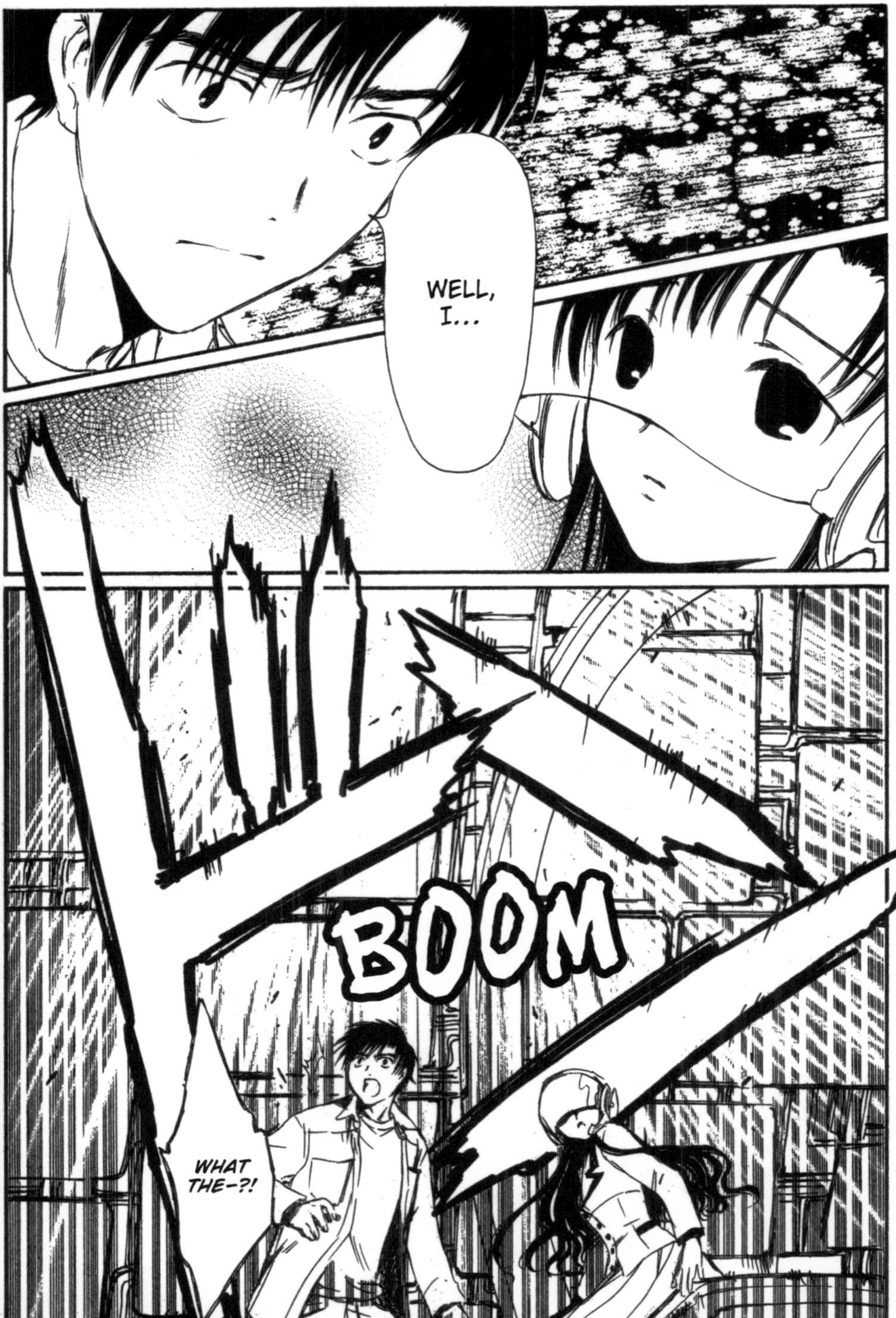
WELL, I...
BOOM
WHAT THE-?!

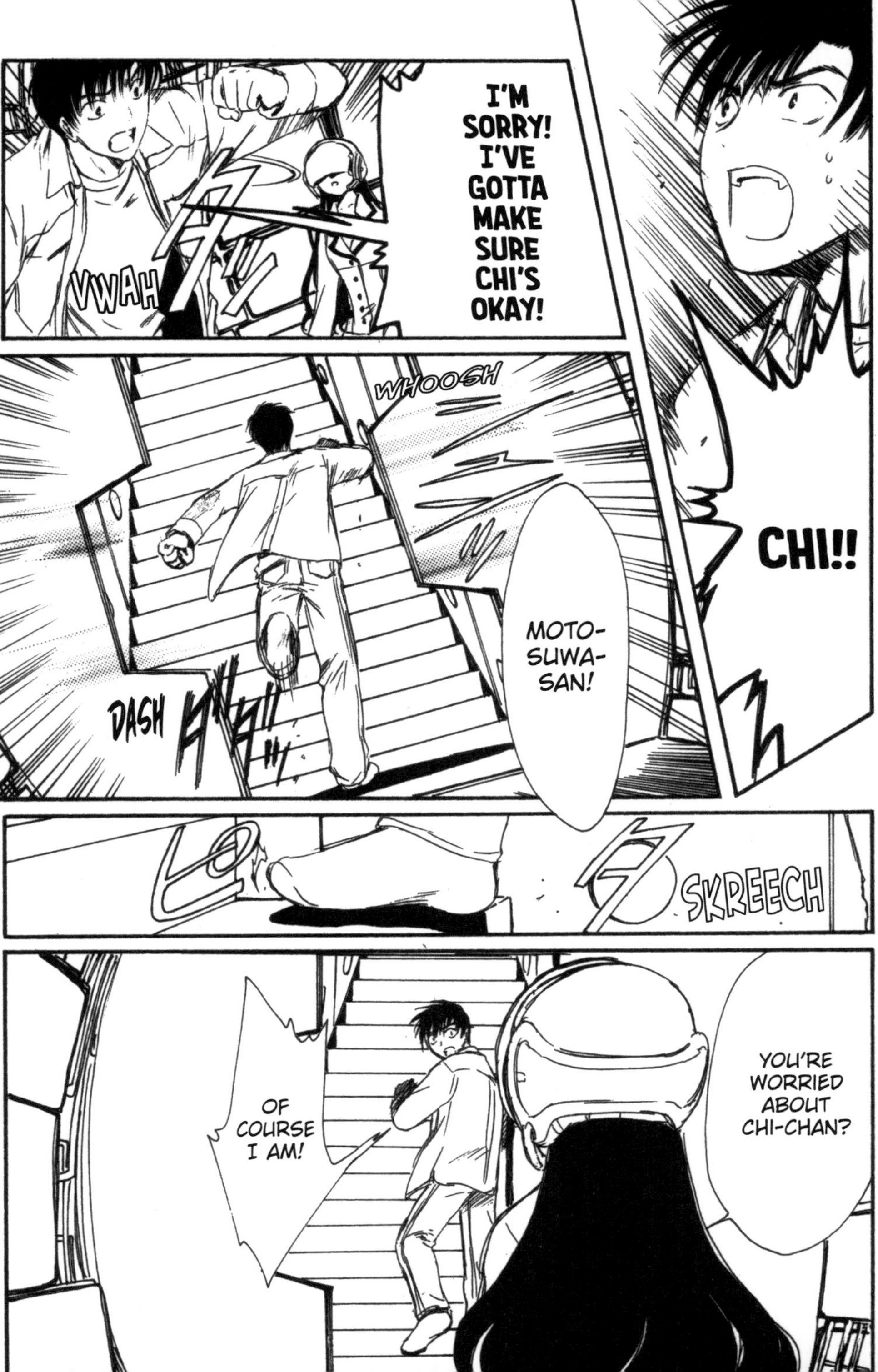
CHI!!
I'M SORRY! I'VE GOTTA MAKE SURE CHI'S OKAY!
VWAH
WHOOSH
MOTO-SUWA-SAN!
DASH
SKREECH
YOU'RE WORRIED ABOUT CHI-CHAN?
OF COURSE I AM!

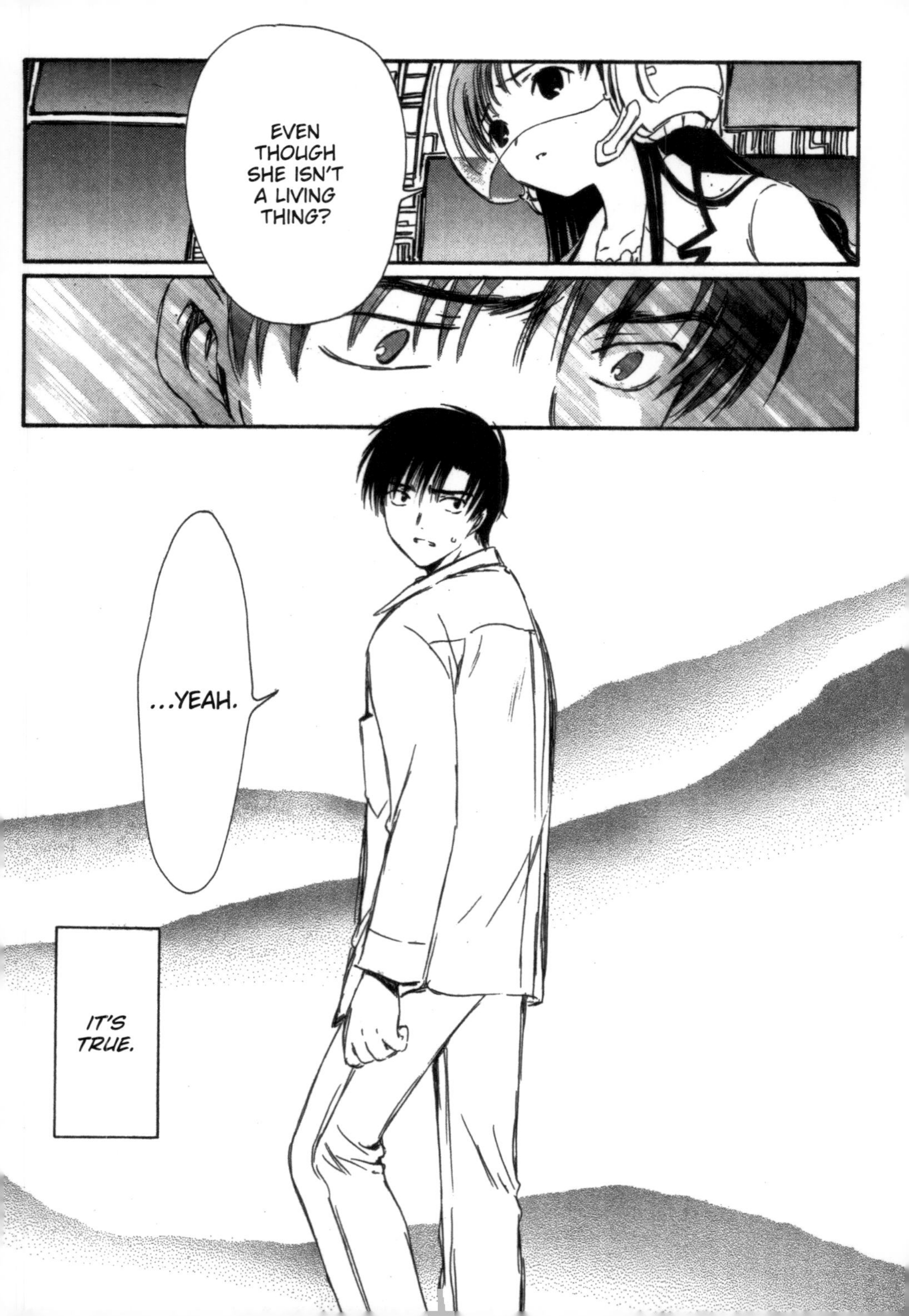
EVEN THOUGH SHE ISN'T A LIVING THING?
...YEAH.
IT'S TRUE.

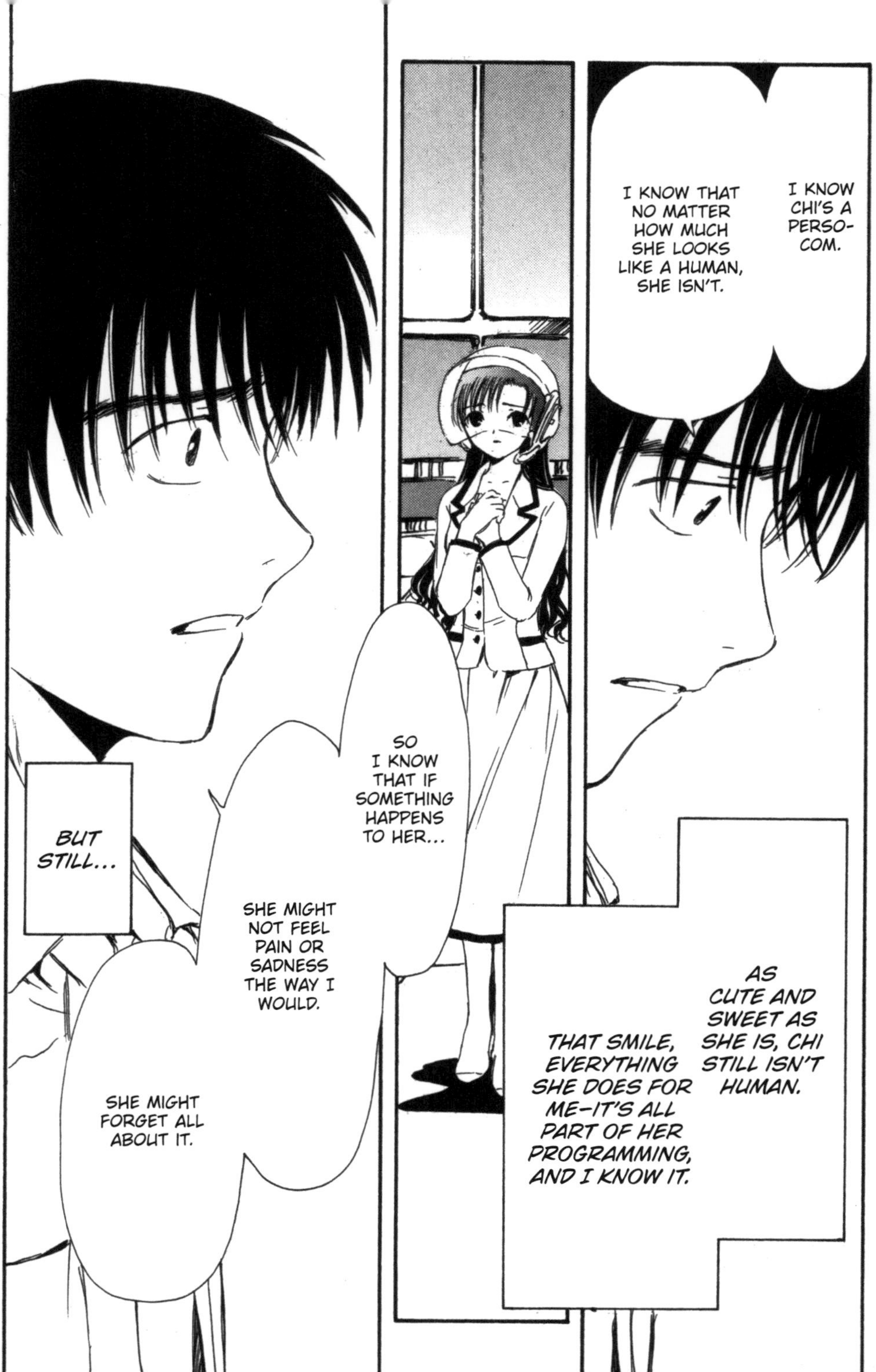
I KNOW CHI'S A PERSO-COM.
I KNOW THAT NO MATTER HOW MUCH SHE LOOKS LIKE A HUMAN, SHE ISN'T.
AS CUTE AND SWEET AS SHE IS, CHI STILL ISN'T HUMAN.
THAT SMILE, EVERYTHING SHE DOES FOR ME—IT'S ALL PART OF HER PROGRAMMING, AND I KNOW IT.
SO I KNOW THAT IF SOMETHING HAPPENS TO HER...
SHE MIGHT NOT FEEL PAIN OR SADNESS THE WAY I WOULD.
SHE MIGHT FORGET ALL ABOUT IT.
BUT STILL...

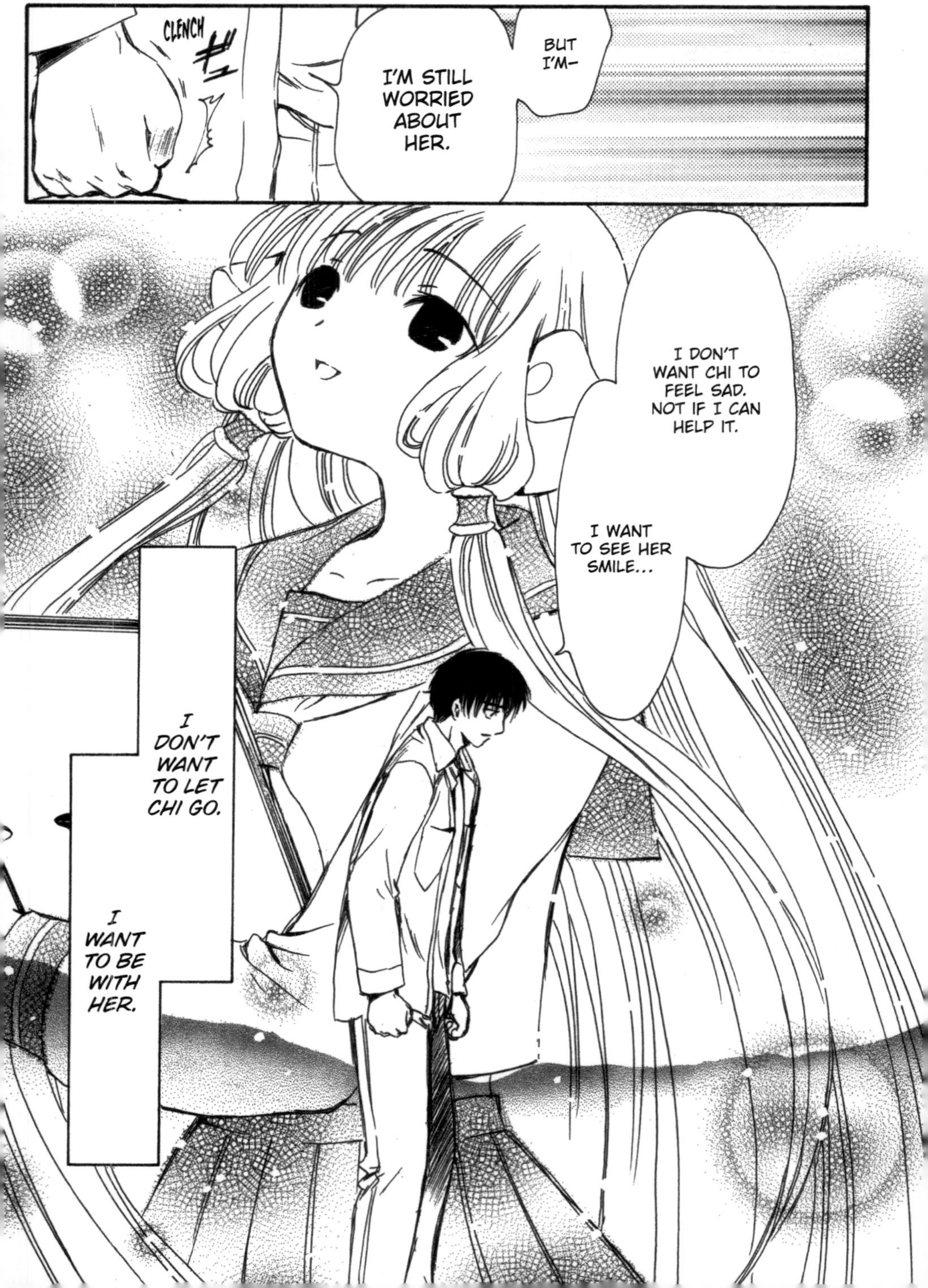
BUT I'M—
I'M STILL WORRIED ABOUT HER.
CLENCH
I DON'T WANT CHI TO FEEL SAD. NOT IF I CAN HELP IT.
I WANT TO SEE HER SMILE...
I DON'T WANT TO LET CHI GO.
I WANT TO BE WITH HER.

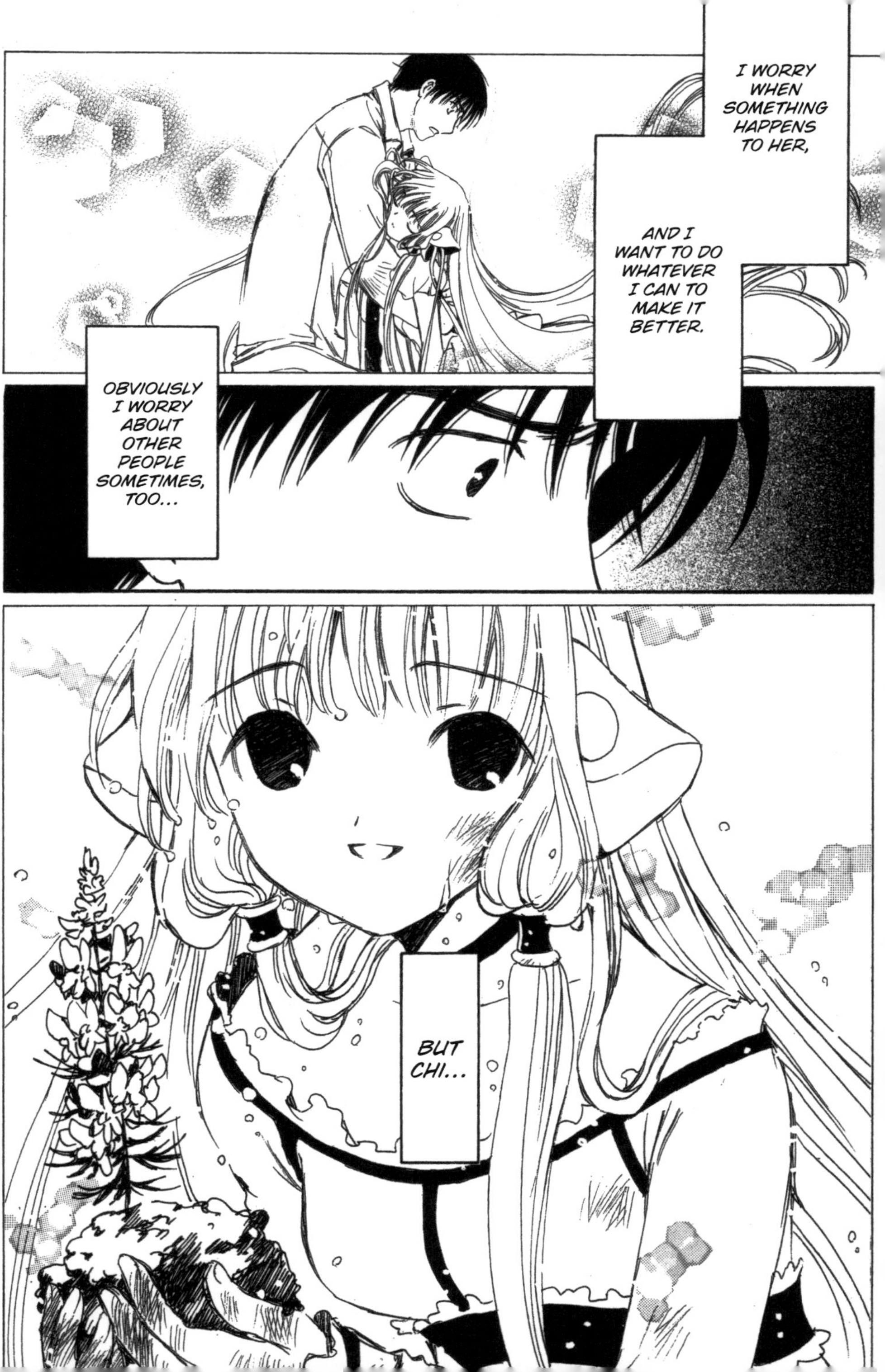
I WORRY WHEN SOMETHING HAPPENS TO HER,
AND I WANT TO DO WHATEVER I CAN TO MAKE IT BETTER.
OBVIOUSLY I WORRY ABOUT OTHER PEOPLE SOMETIMES, TOO…
BUT CHI…

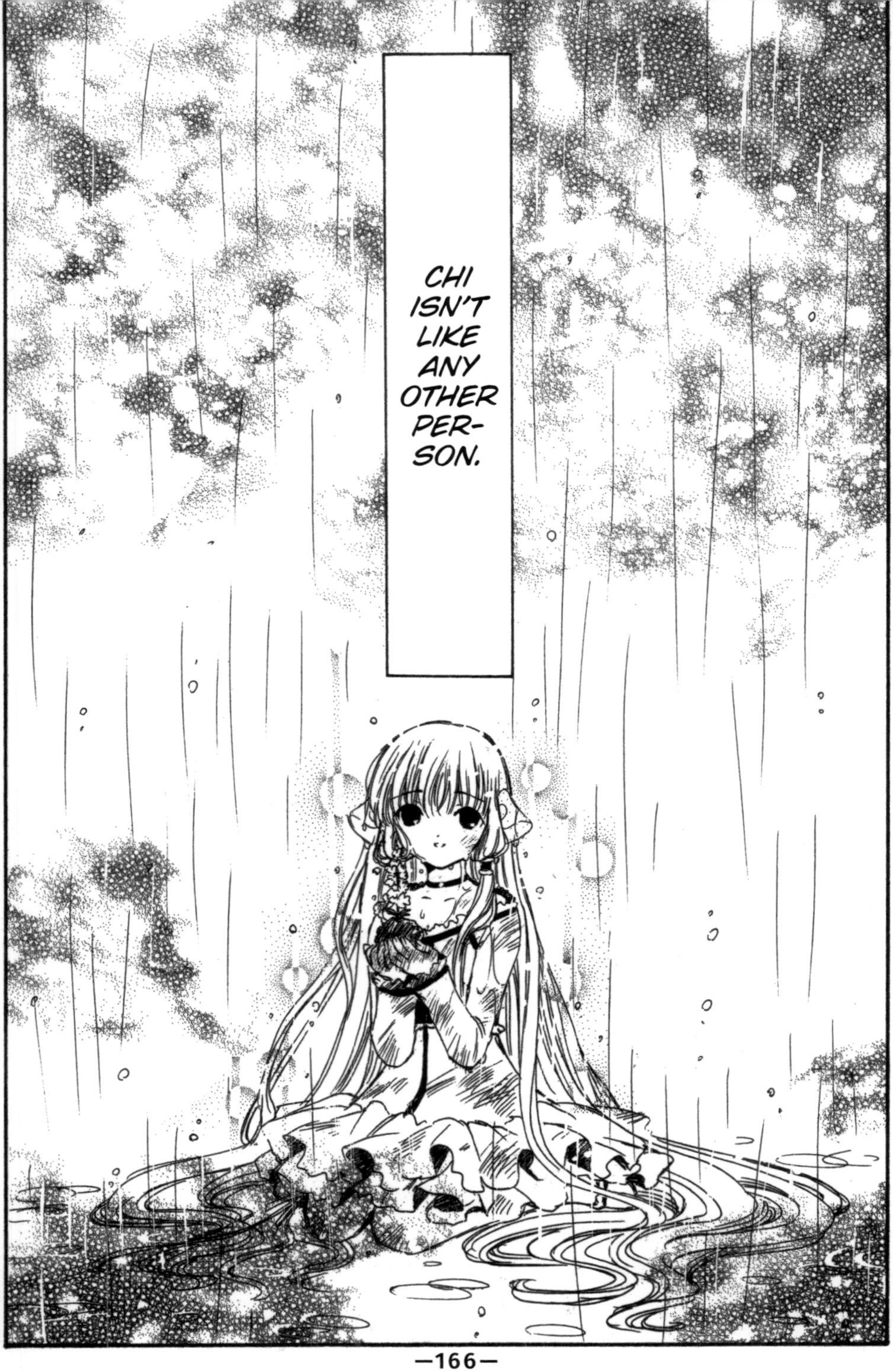
CHI ISN'T LIKE ANY OTHER PER- SON.

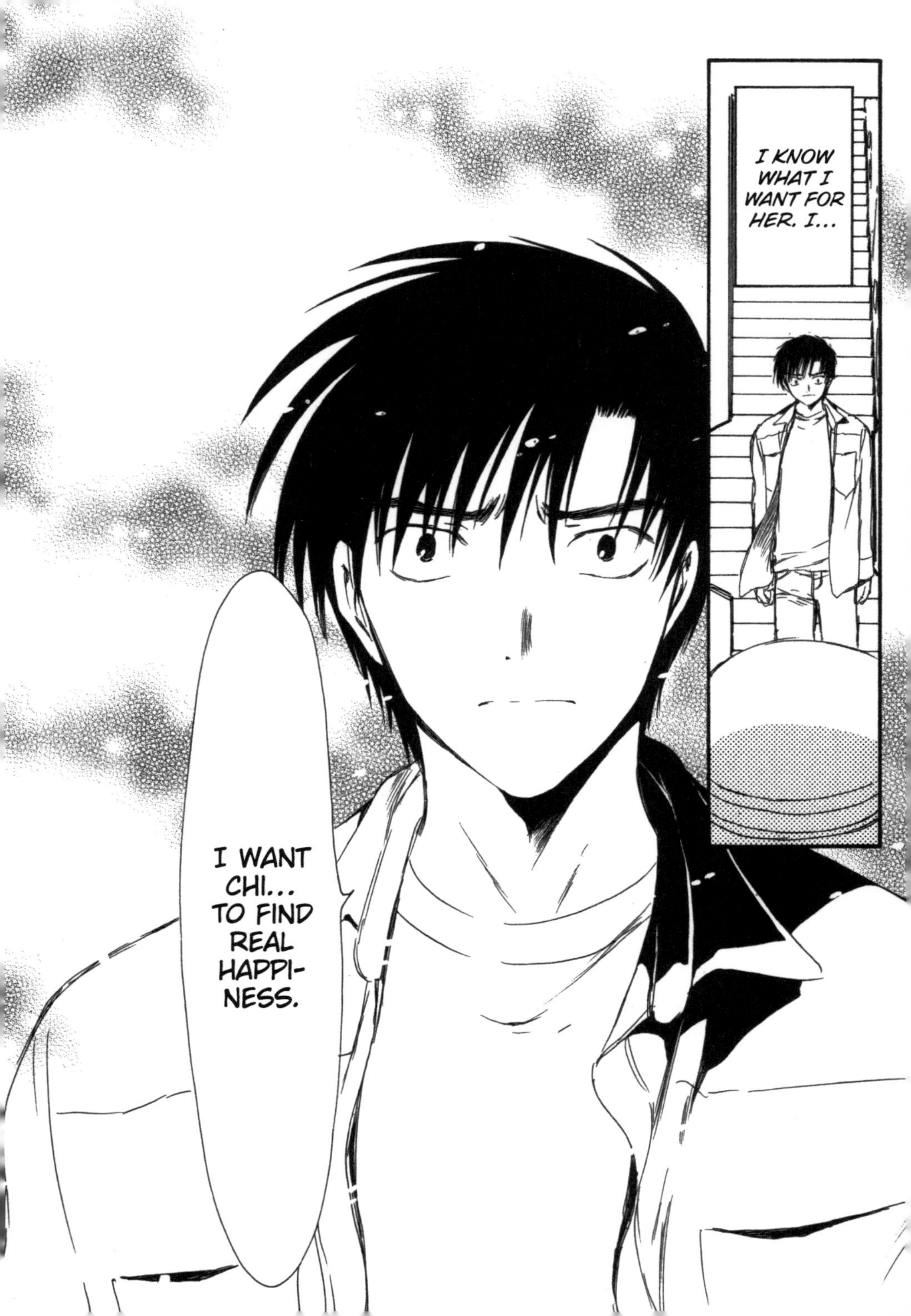
I KNOW WHAT I WANT FOR HER. I...
I WANT CHI... TO FIND REAL HAPPI-NESS.

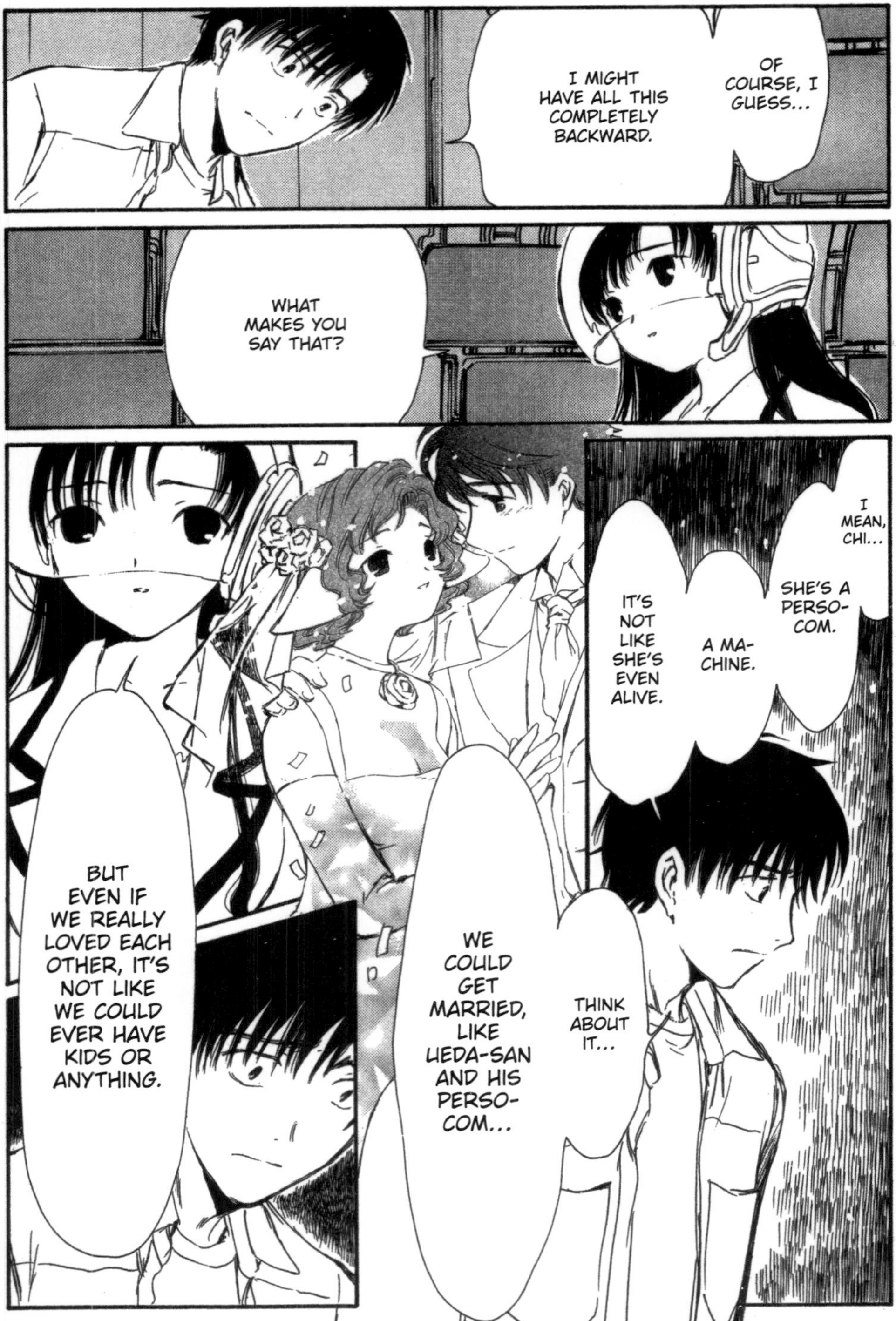
OF COURSE, I GUESS...
I MIGHT HAVE ALL THIS COMPLETELY BACKWARD.
WHAT MAKES YOU SAY THAT?
I MEAN, CHI...
SHE'S A PERSO-COM.
A MA-CHINE.
IT'S NOT LIKE SHE'S EVEN ALIVE.
THINK ABOUT IT...
WE COULD GET MARRIED, LIKE UEDA-SAN AND HIS PERSO-COM...
BUT EVEN IF WE REALLY LOVED EACH OTHER, IT'S NOT LIKE WE COULD EVER HAVE KIDS OR ANYTHING.

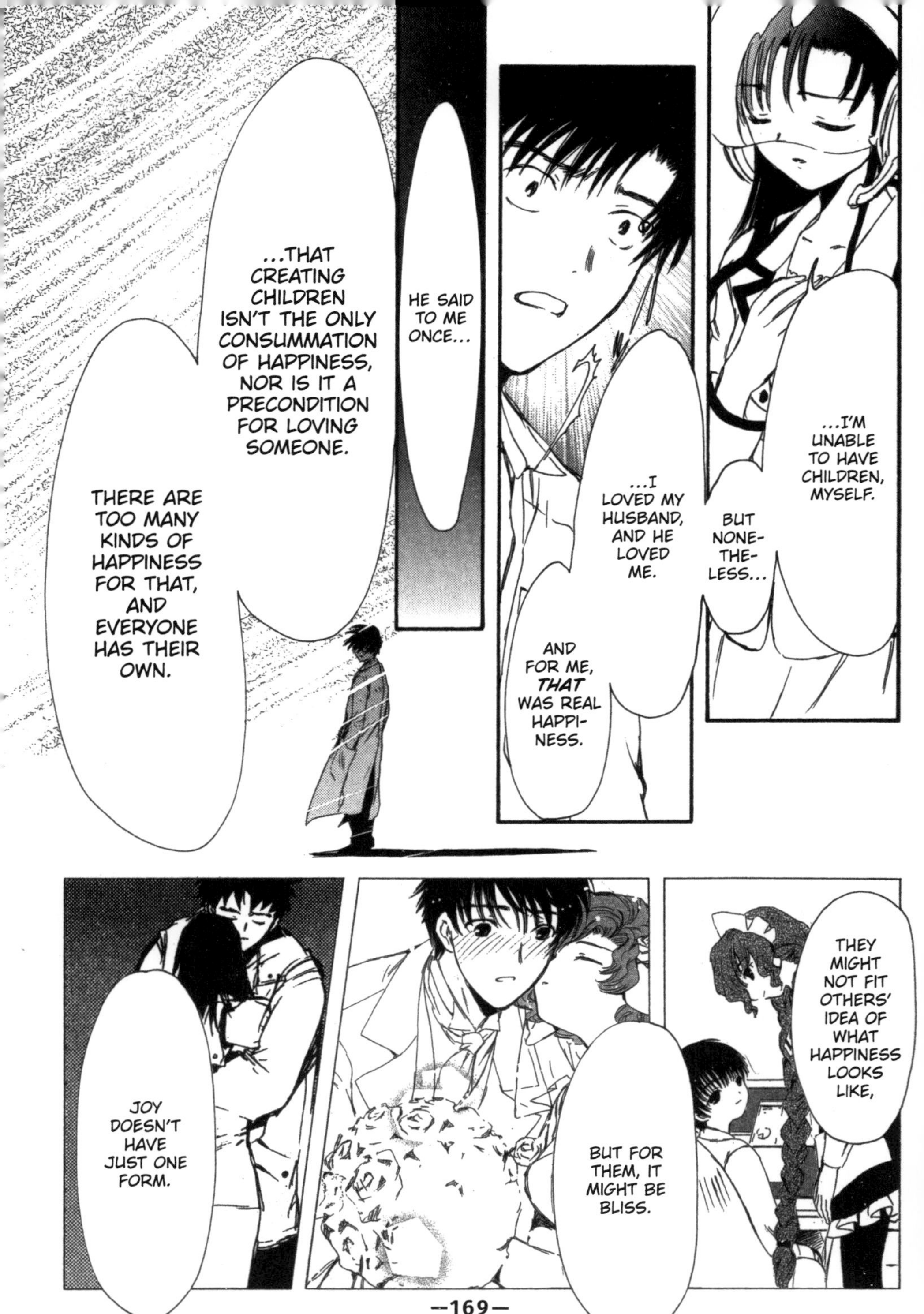
...I'M UNABLE TO HAVE CHILDREN, MYSELF.
BUT NONE-THE-LESS...
...I LOVED MY HUSBAND, AND HE LOVED ME.
AND FOR ME, *THAT* WAS REAL HAPPI-NESS.
HE SAID TO ME ONCE...
...THAT CREATING CHILDREN ISN'T THE ONLY CONSUMMATION OF HAPPINESS, NOR IS IT A PRECONDITION FOR LOVING SOMEONE.
THERE ARE TOO MANY KINDS OF HAPPINESS FOR THAT, AND EVERYONE HAS THEIR OWN.
THEY MIGHT NOT FIT OTHERS' IDEA OF WHAT HAPPINESS LOOKS LIKE,
BUT FOR THEM, IT MIGHT BE BLISS.
JOY DOESN'T HAVE JUST ONE FORM.

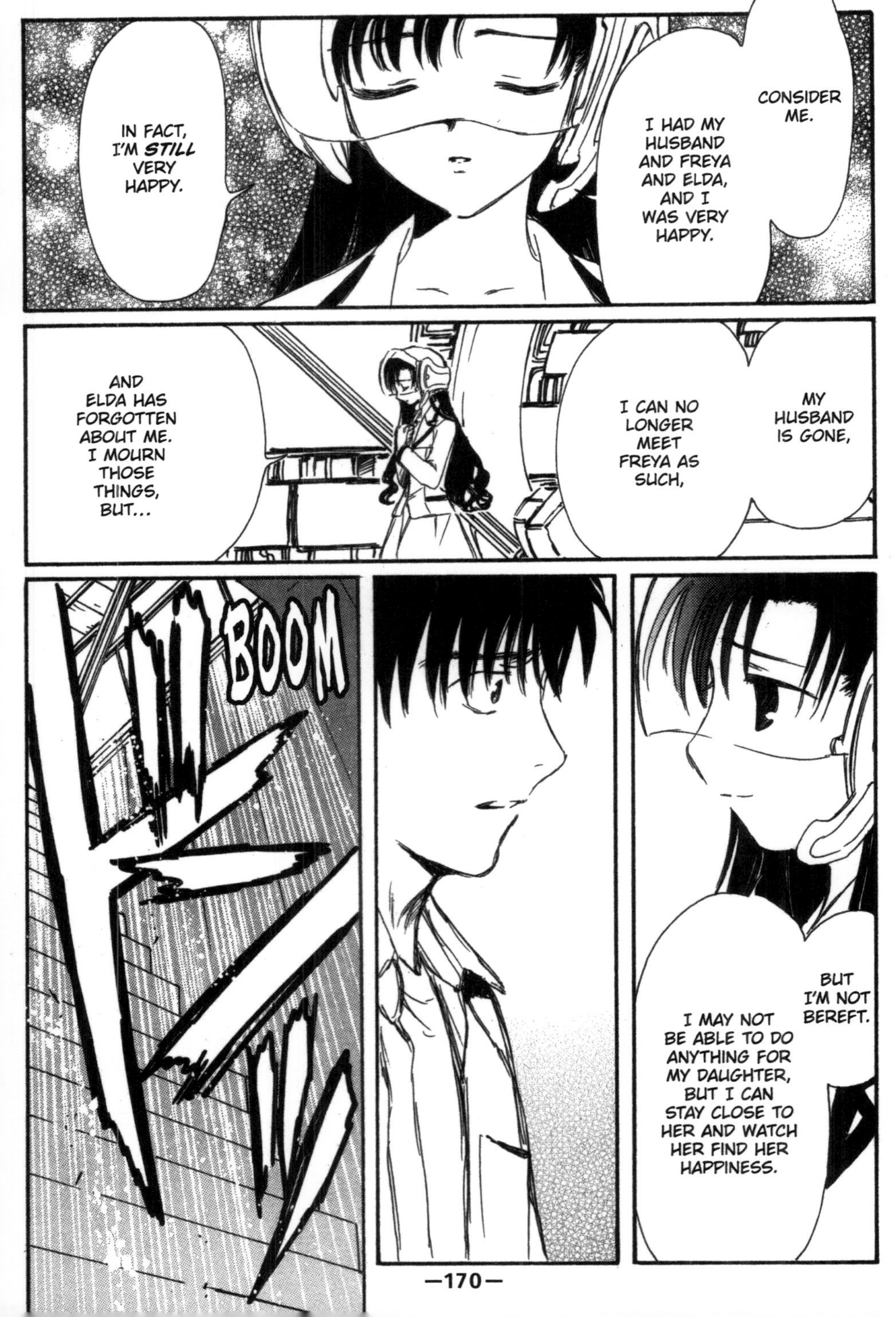
CONSIDER ME.
I HAD MY HUSBAND AND FREYA AND ELDA, AND I WAS VERY HAPPY.
IN FACT, I'M ***STILL*** VERY HAPPY.
MY HUSBAND IS GONE,
I CAN NO LONGER MEET FREYA AS SUCH,
AND ELDA HAS FORGOTTEN ABOUT ME. I MOURN THOSE THINGS, BUT...
BUT I'M NOT BEREFT.
I MAY NOT BE ABLE TO DO ANYTHING FOR MY DAUGHTER, BUT I CAN STAY CLOSE TO HER AND WATCH HER FIND HER HAPPINESS.
BOOM

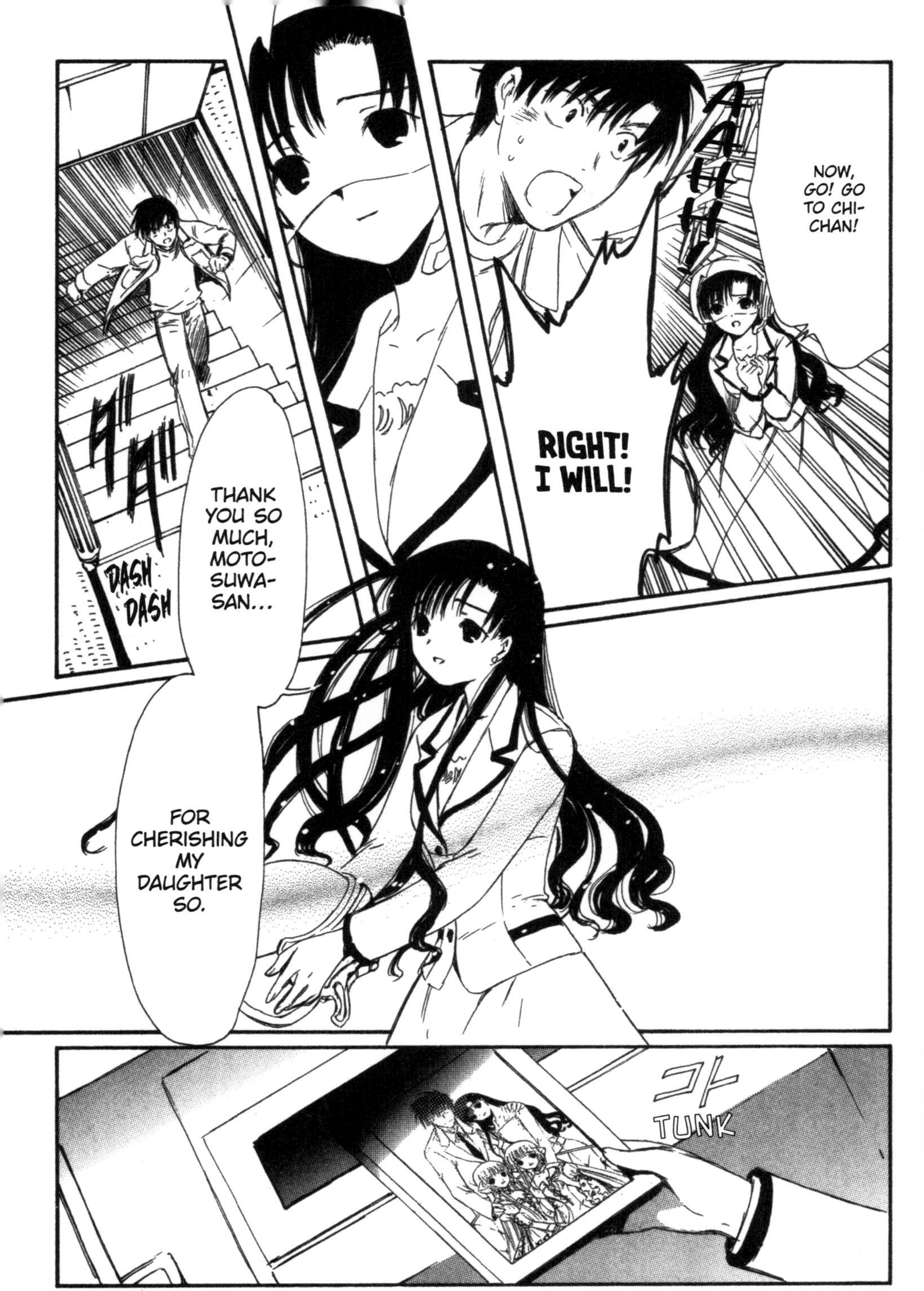
NOW, GO! GO TO CHI-CHAN!
RIGHT! I WILL!
DASH DASH
THANK YOU SO MUCH, MOTO-SUWA-SAN...
FOR CHERISHING MY DAUGHTER SO.
コト
TUNK

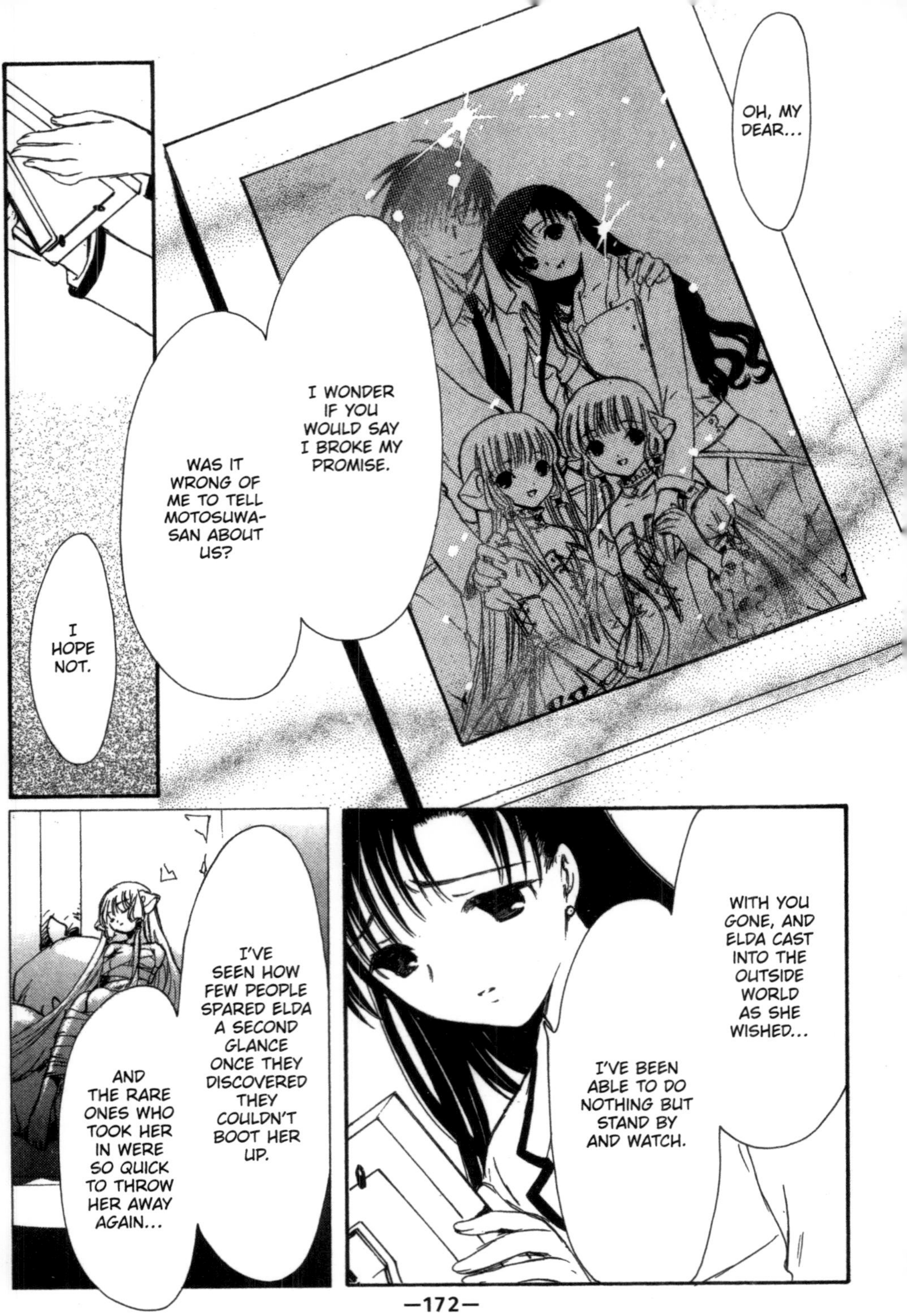
OH, MY DEAR...
I WONDER IF YOU WOULD SAY I BROKE MY PROMISE.
WAS IT WRONG OF ME TO TELL MOTOSUWA-SAN ABOUT US?
I HOPE NOT.
WITH YOU GONE, AND ELDA CAST INTO THE OUTSIDE WORLD AS SHE WISHED...
I'VE BEEN ABLE TO DO NOTHING BUT STAND BY AND WATCH.
I'VE SEEN HOW FEW PEOPLE SPARED ELDA A SECOND GLANCE ONCE THEY DISCOVERED THEY COULDN'T BOOT HER UP.
AND THE RARE ONES WHO TOOK HER IN WERE SO QUICK TO THROW HER AWAY AGAIN...

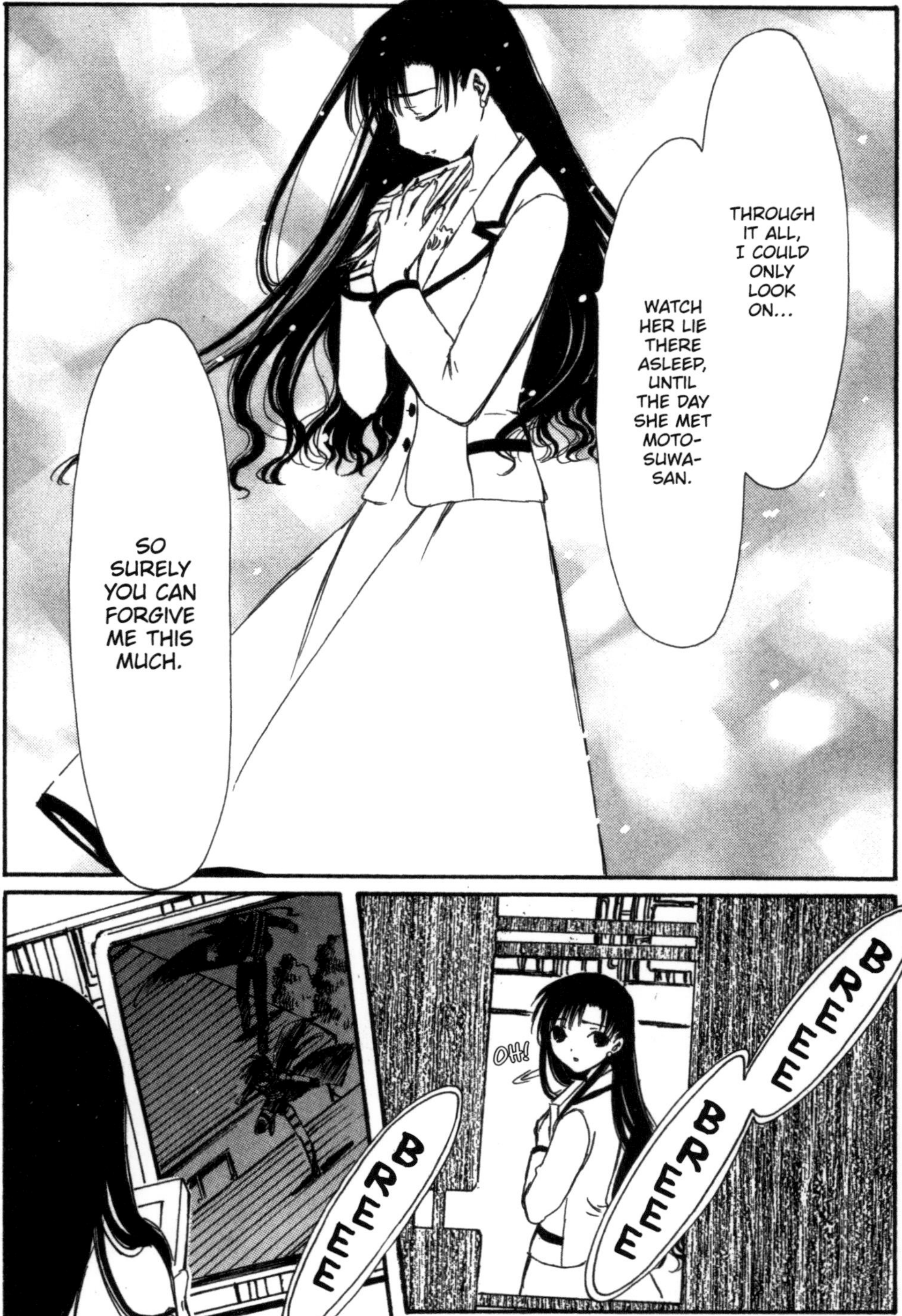
THROUGH IT ALL, I COULD ONLY LOOK ON...
WATCH HER LIE THERE ASLEEP, UNTIL THE DAY SHE MET MOTO-SUWA-SAN.
SO SURELY YOU CAN FORGIVE ME THIS MUCH.
BREEEE
OH!
BREEEE
BREEEE

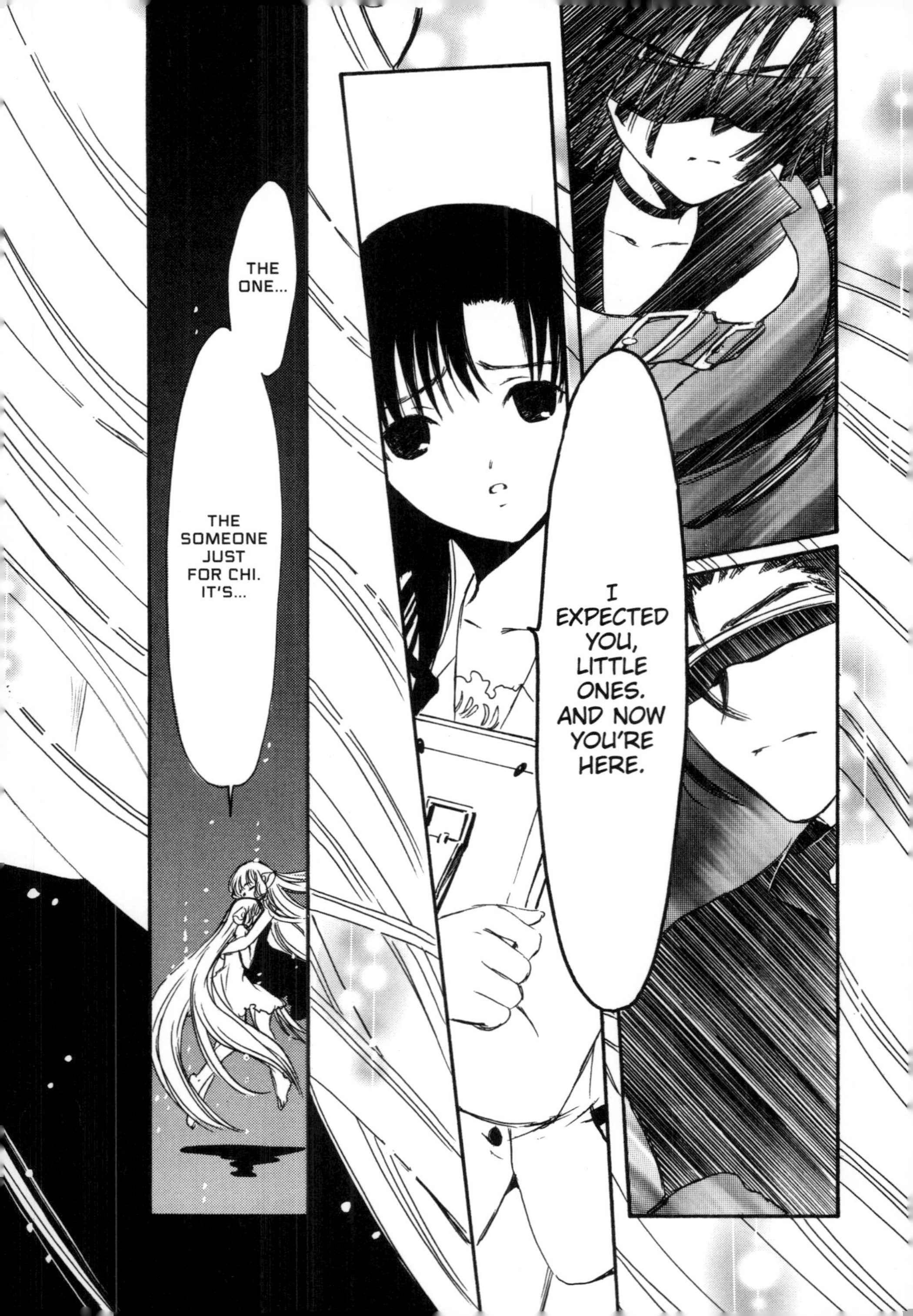
I EXPECTED YOU, LITTLE ONES. AND NOW YOU'RE HERE.
THE ONE...
THE SOMEONE JUST FOR CHI. IT'S...

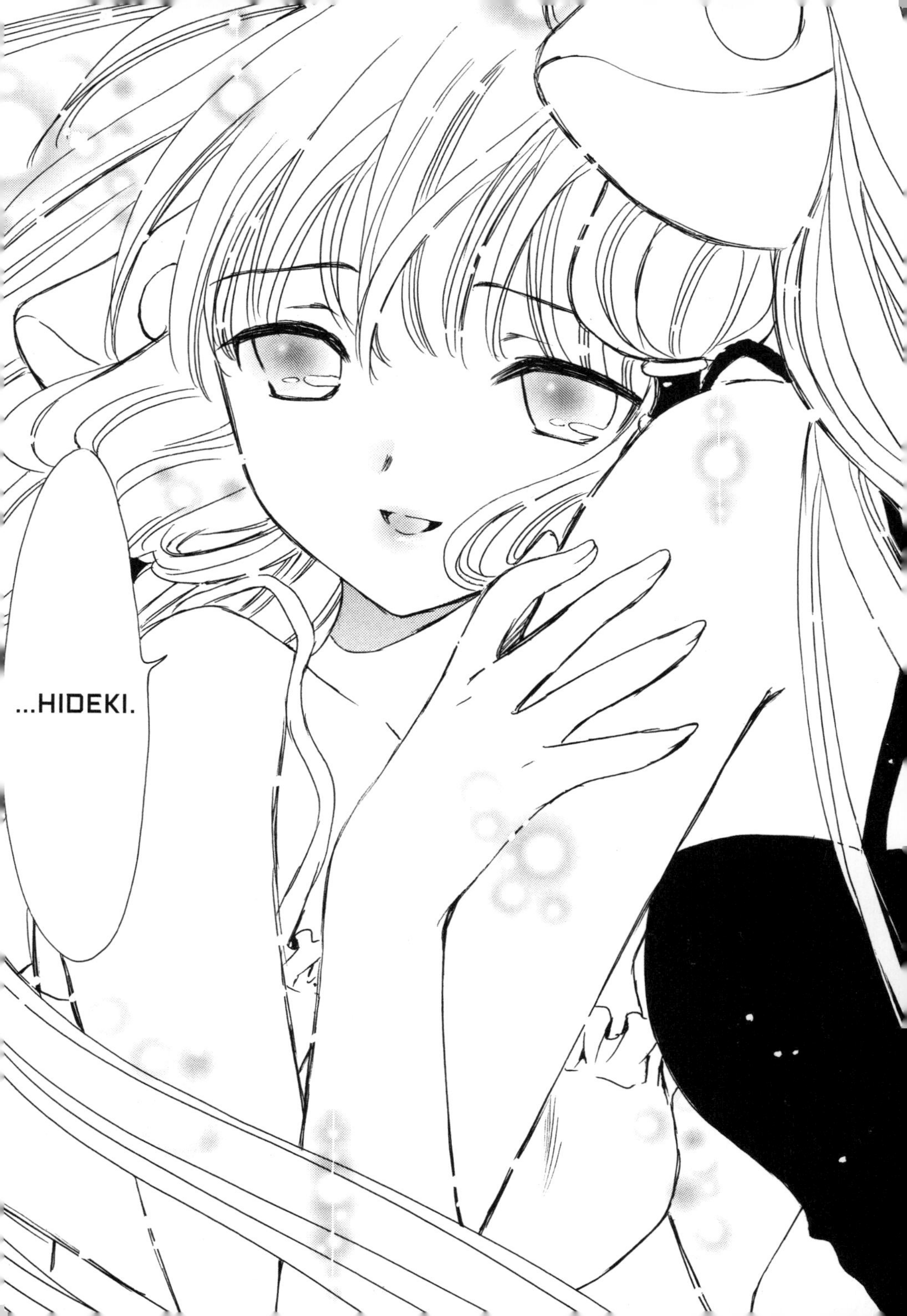
...HIDEKI.

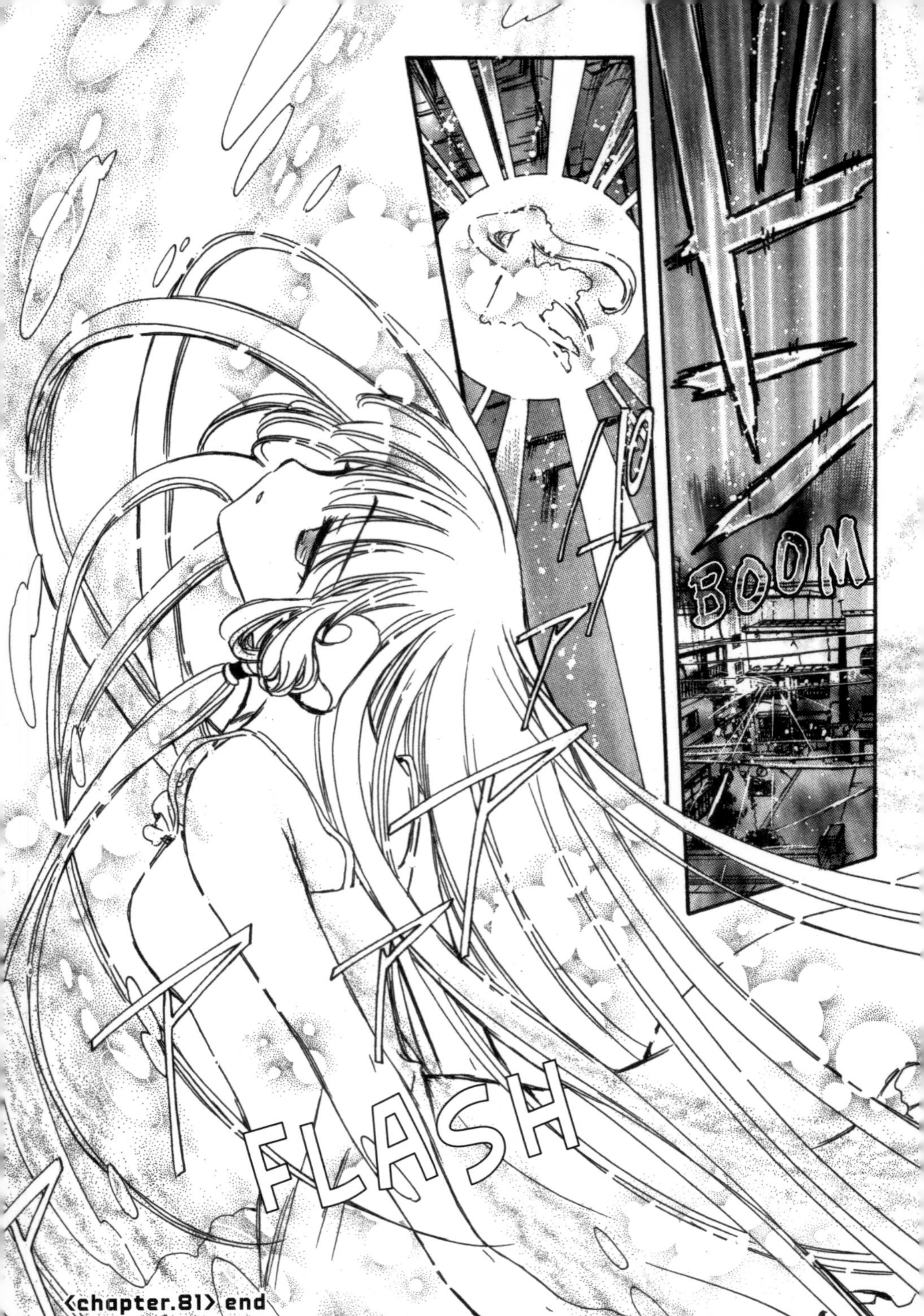
BOOM
FLASH

<chapter.81> end

Chobits

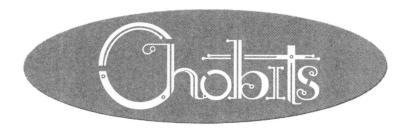

Chobits

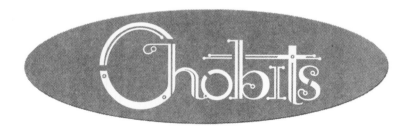

# Translation Notes

**Pointing, page 24**
In Japan, when referring to yourself, it's typical to point at your face or nose, as Hideki does here, rather than at your chest, as is common in the US.

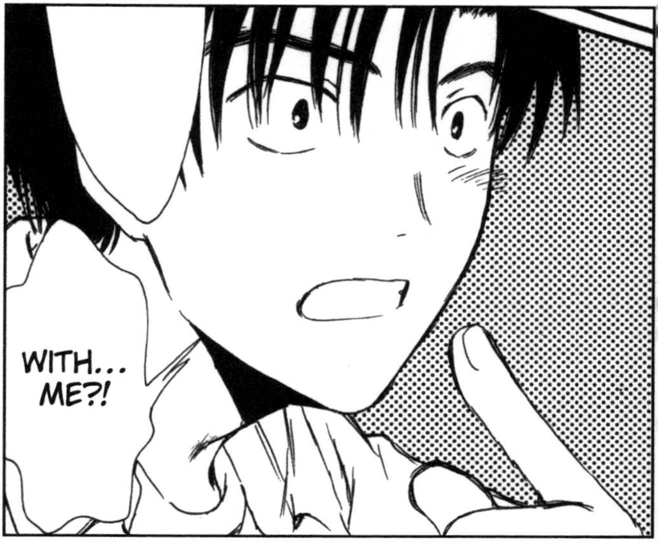
WITH... ME?!

**Dolls, page 99**
This is a reference to *Angelic Layer,* the series CLAMP published immediately before *Chobits* began its run.

MY HUSBAND HAD PREVIOUSLY DEVELOPED A LINE OF DOLLS THAT COULD COMMUNICATE TELEPATHICALLY WITH THEIR OWNERS.

Chobits

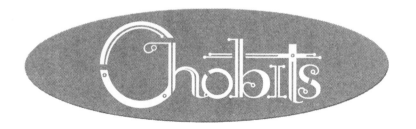

Chobits

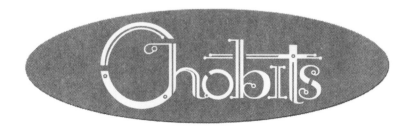

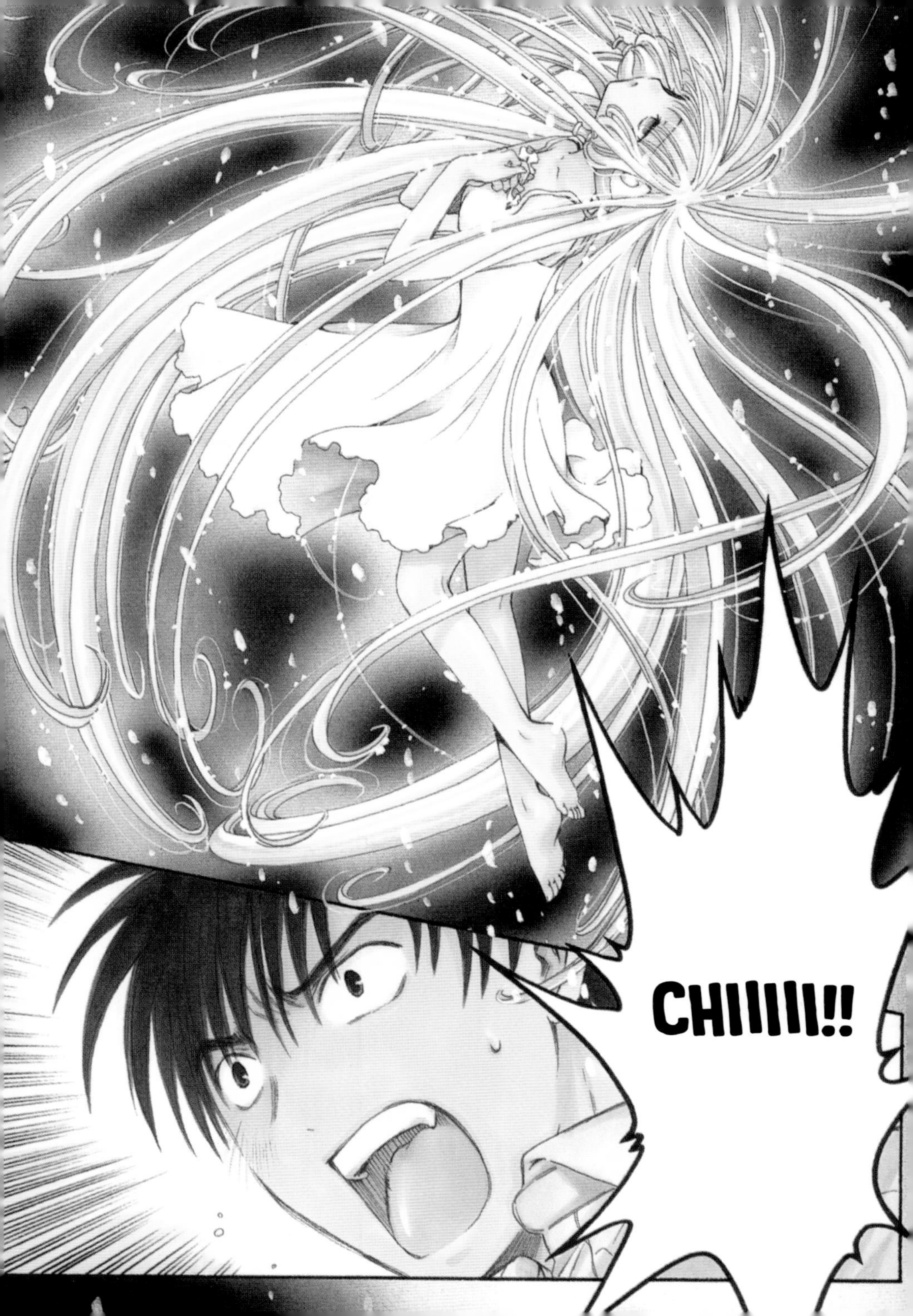
CHIIIIII!!

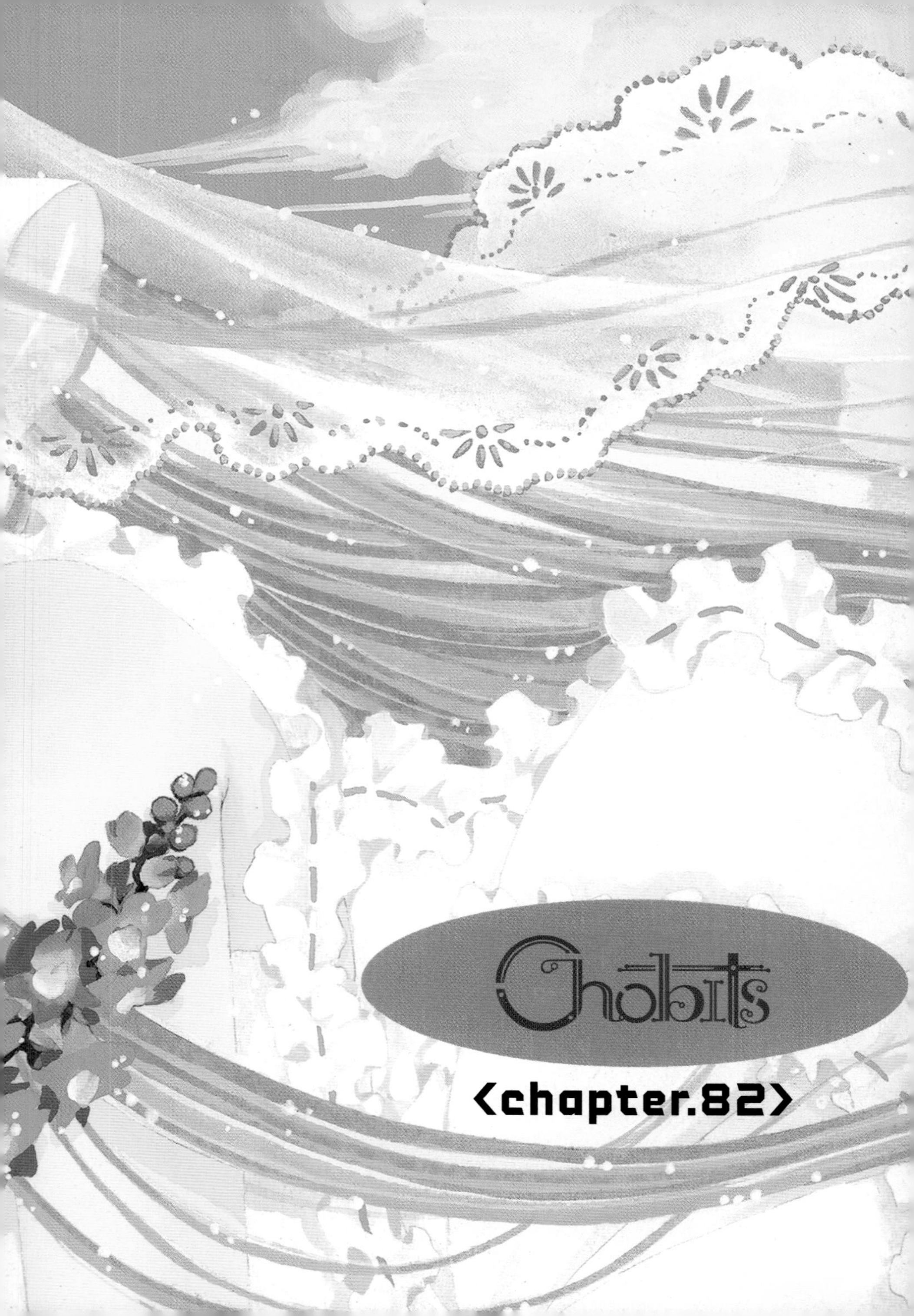
Chobits
<chapter.82>

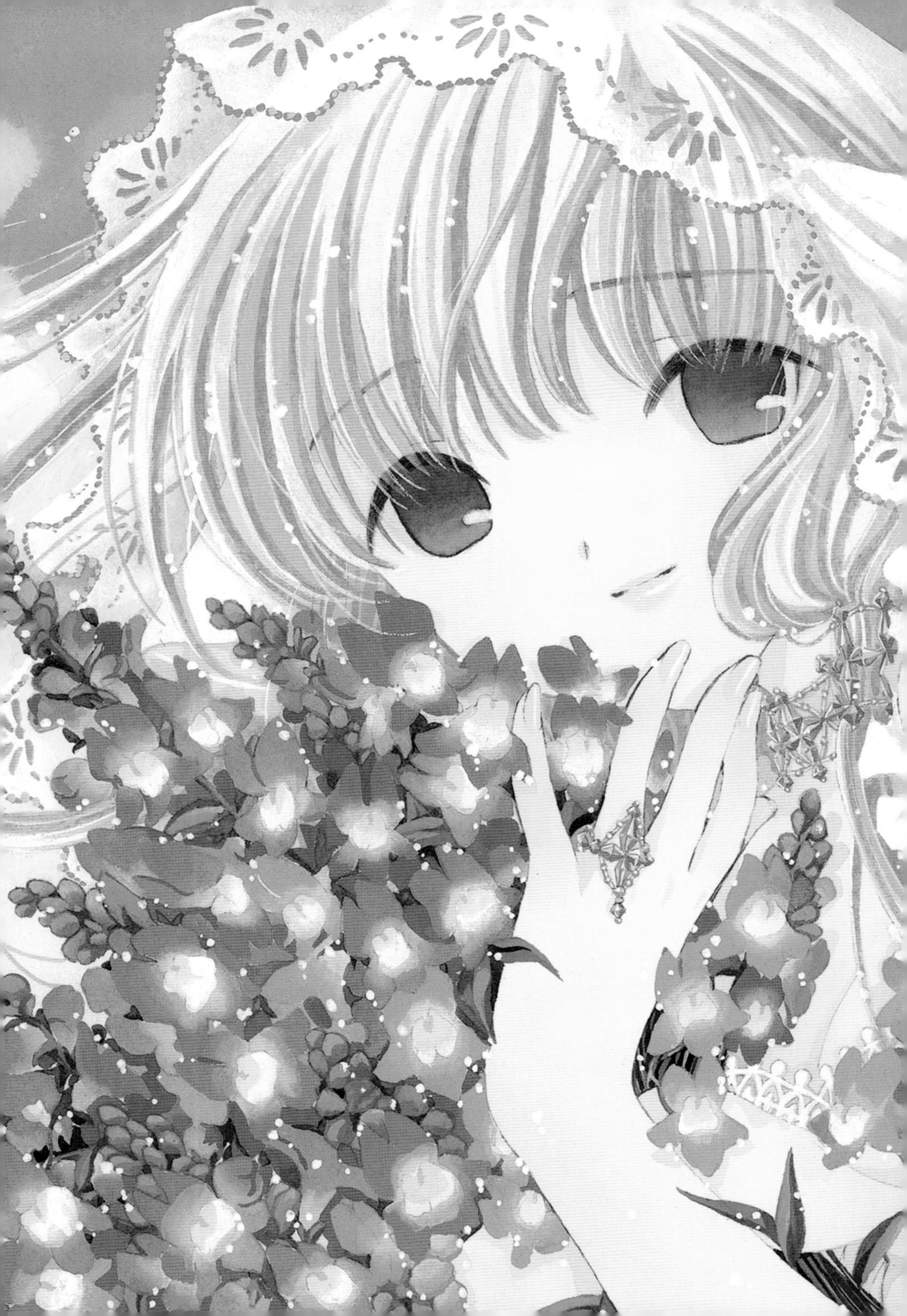

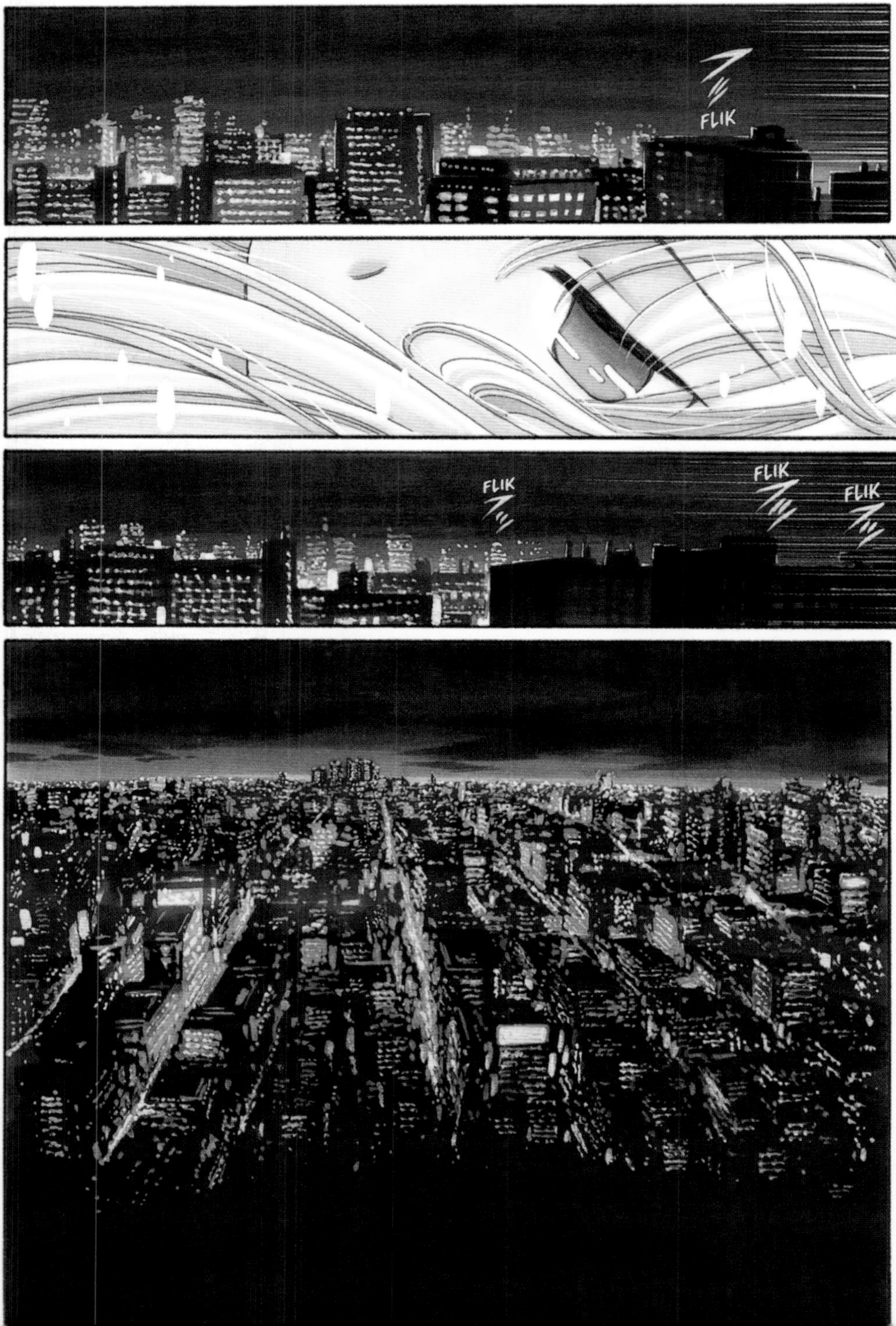
FLIK
FLIK
FLIK
FLIK

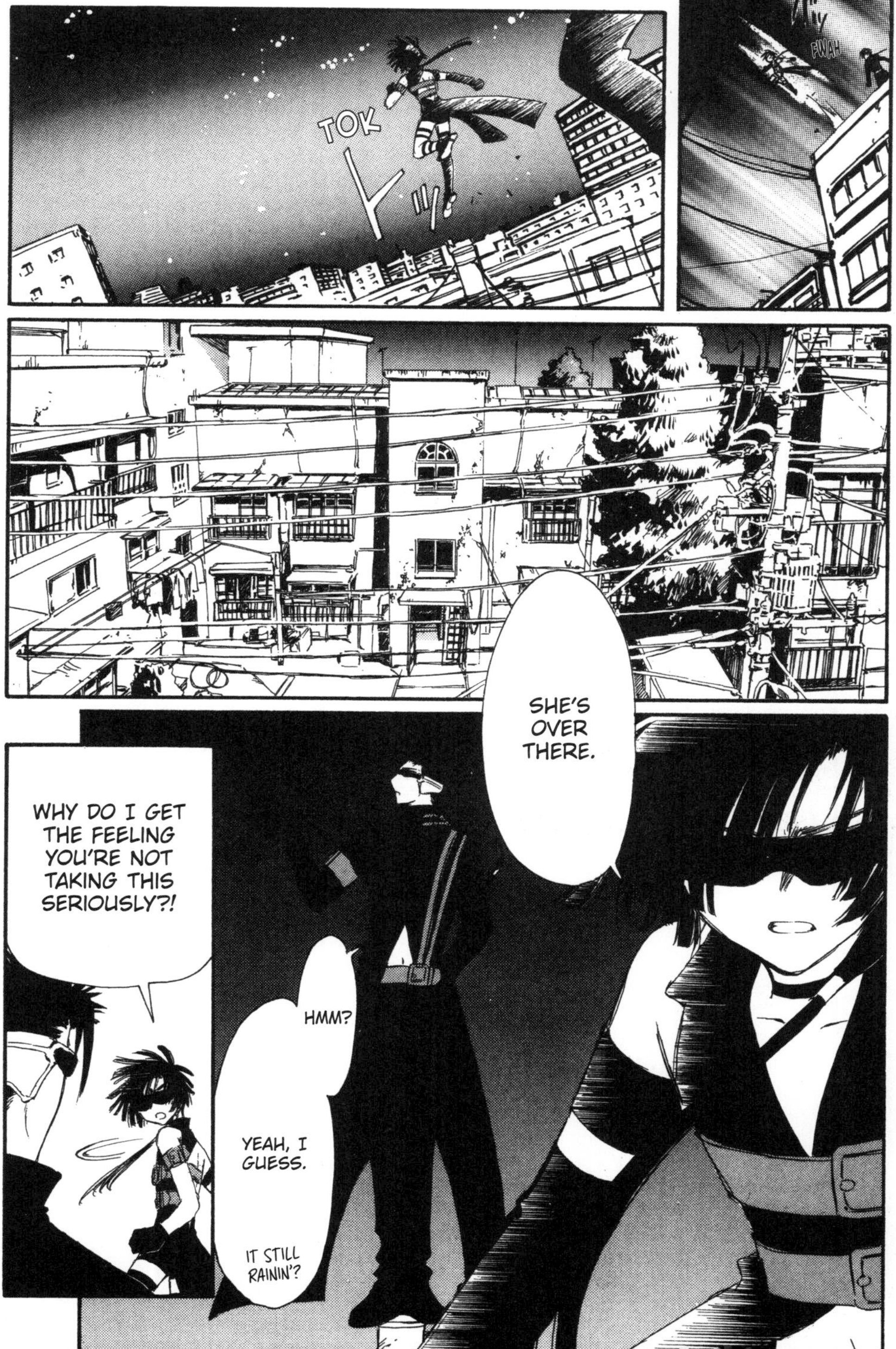
FWAH
TOK
ドッ
SHE'S OVER THERE.
HMM?
YEAH, I GUESS.
IT STILL RAININ'?
WHY DO I GET THE FEELING YOU'RE NOT TAKING THIS SERIOUSLY?!

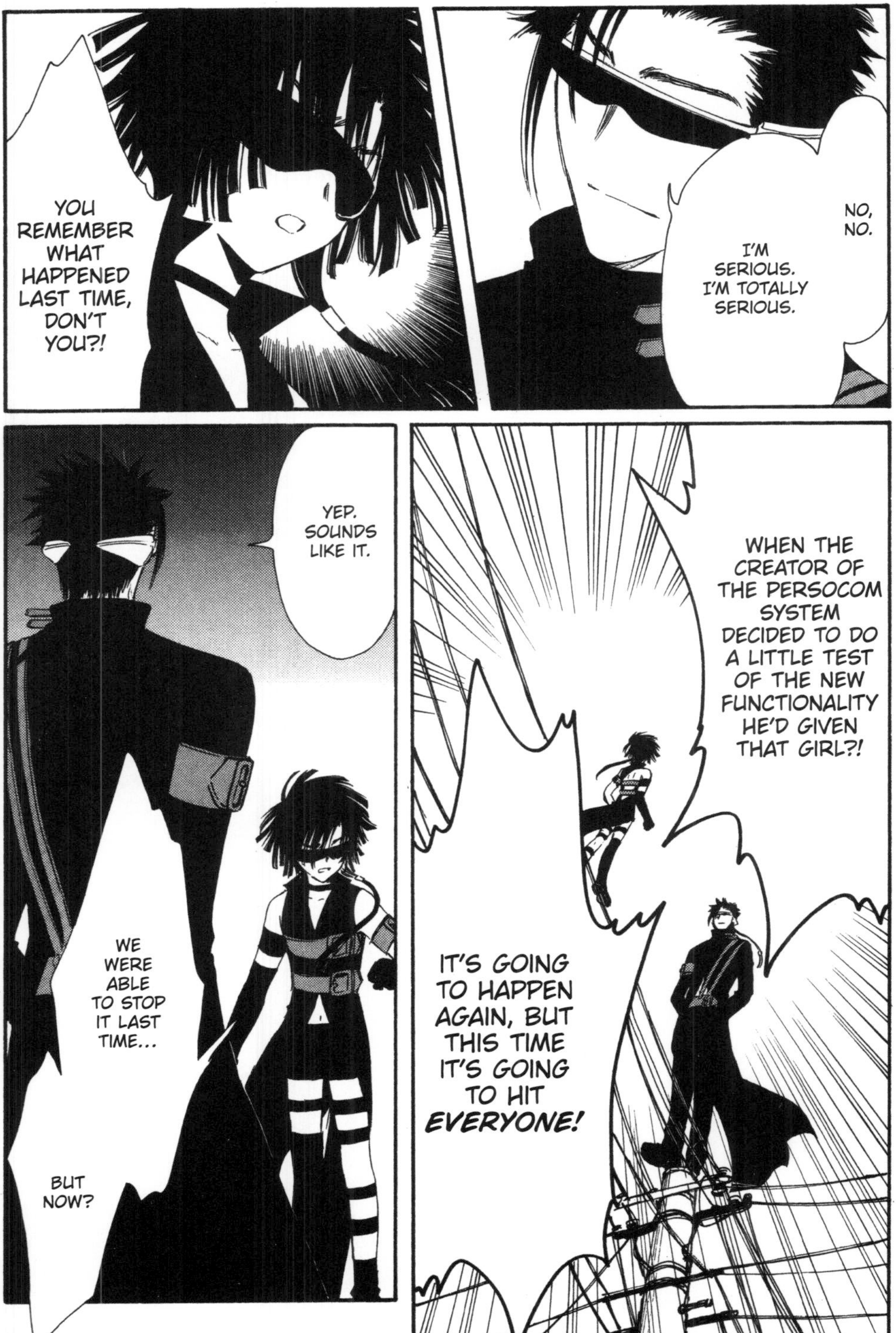
NO, NO.
I'M SERIOUS. I'M TOTALLY SERIOUS.
YOU REMEMBER WHAT HAPPENED LAST TIME, DON'T YOU?!
WHEN THE CREATOR OF THE PERSOCOM SYSTEM DECIDED TO DO A LITTLE TEST OF THE NEW FUNCTIONALITY HE'D GIVEN THAT GIRL?!
IT'S GOING TO HAPPEN AGAIN, BUT THIS TIME IT'S GOING TO HIT *EVERYONE!*
YEP. SOUNDS LIKE IT.
WE WERE ABLE TO STOP IT LAST TIME...
BUT NOW?

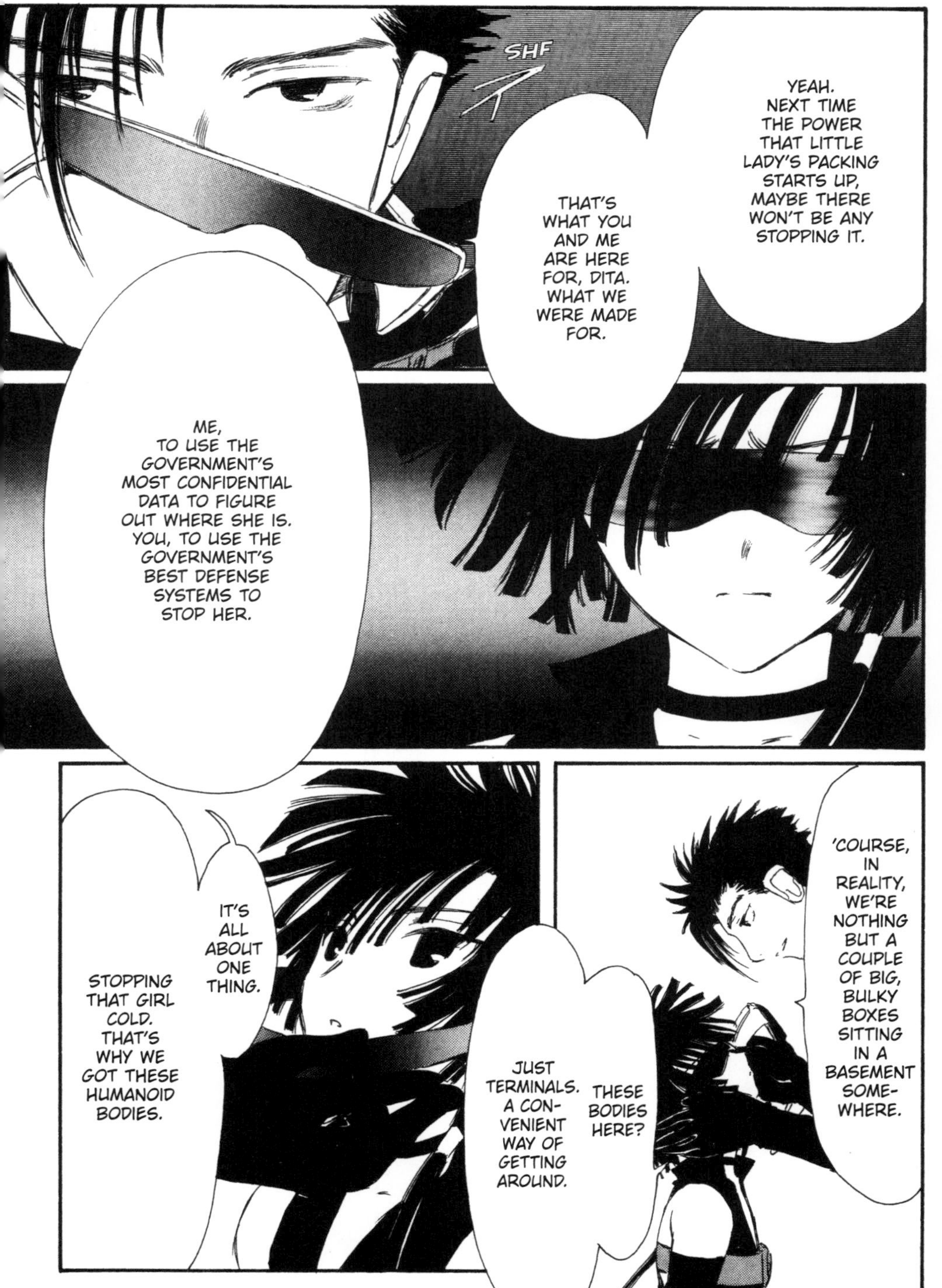
YEAH. NEXT TIME THE POWER THAT LITTLE LADY'S PACKING STARTS UP, MAYBE THERE WON'T BE ANY STOPPING IT.
SHF
THAT'S WHAT YOU AND ME ARE HERE FOR, DITA. WHAT WE WERE MADE FOR.
ME, TO USE THE GOVERNMENT'S MOST CONFIDENTIAL DATA TO FIGURE OUT WHERE SHE IS. YOU, TO USE THE GOVERNMENT'S BEST DEFENSE SYSTEMS TO STOP HER.
'COURSE, IN REALITY, WE'RE NOTHING BUT A COUPLE OF BIG, BULKY BOXES SITTING IN A BASEMENT SOME-WHERE.
THESE BODIES HERE?
JUST TERMINALS. A CON-VENIENT WAY OF GETTING AROUND.
IT'S ALL ABOUT ONE THING.
STOPPING THAT GIRL COLD. THAT'S WHY WE GOT THESE HUMANOID BODIES.

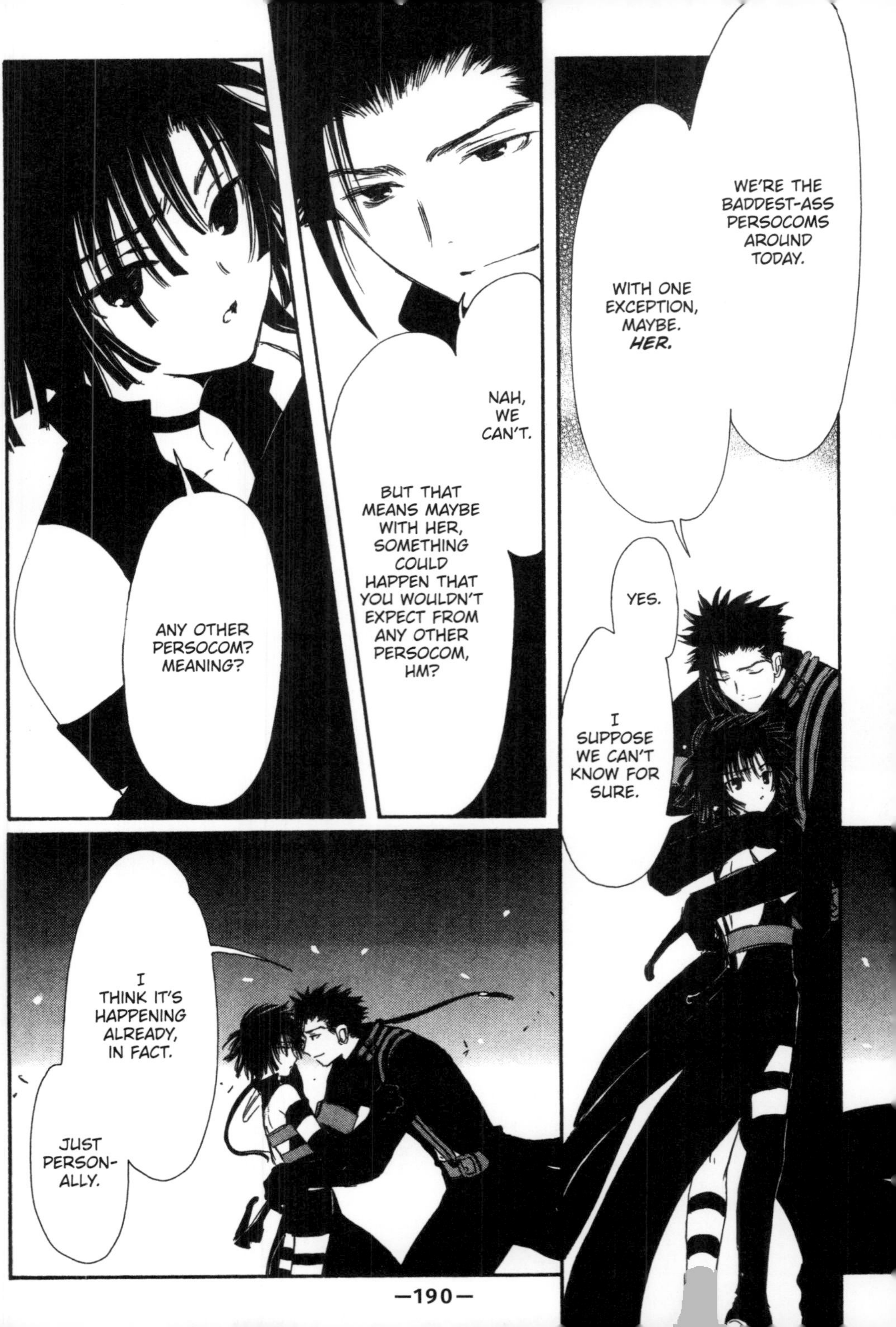
WE'RE THE BADDEST-ASS PERSOCOMS AROUND TODAY.
WITH ONE EXCEPTION, MAYBE. **HER.**
YES.
I SUPPOSE WE CAN'T KNOW FOR SURE.
NAH, WE CAN'T.
BUT THAT MEANS MAYBE WITH HER, SOMETHING COULD HAPPEN THAT YOU WOULDN'T EXPECT FROM ANY OTHER PERSOCOM, HM?
ANY OTHER PERSOCOM? MEANING?
I THINK IT'S HAPPENING ALREADY, IN FACT.
JUST PERSON-ALLY.

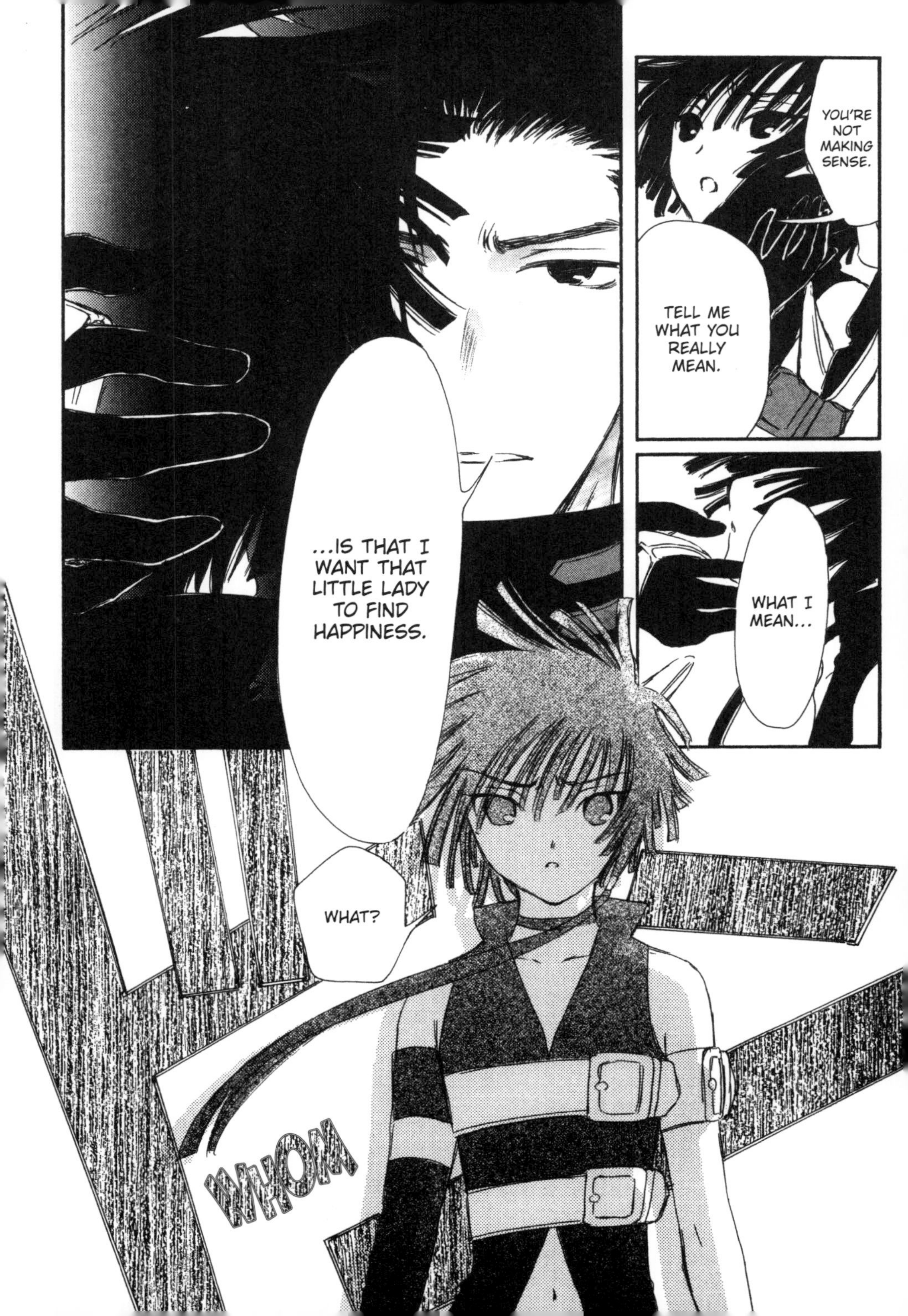
YOU'RE NOT MAKING SENSE.
TELL ME WHAT YOU REALLY MEAN.
WHAT I MEAN...
...IS THAT I WANT THAT LITTLE LADY TO FIND HAPPINESS.
WHAT?
WHOM

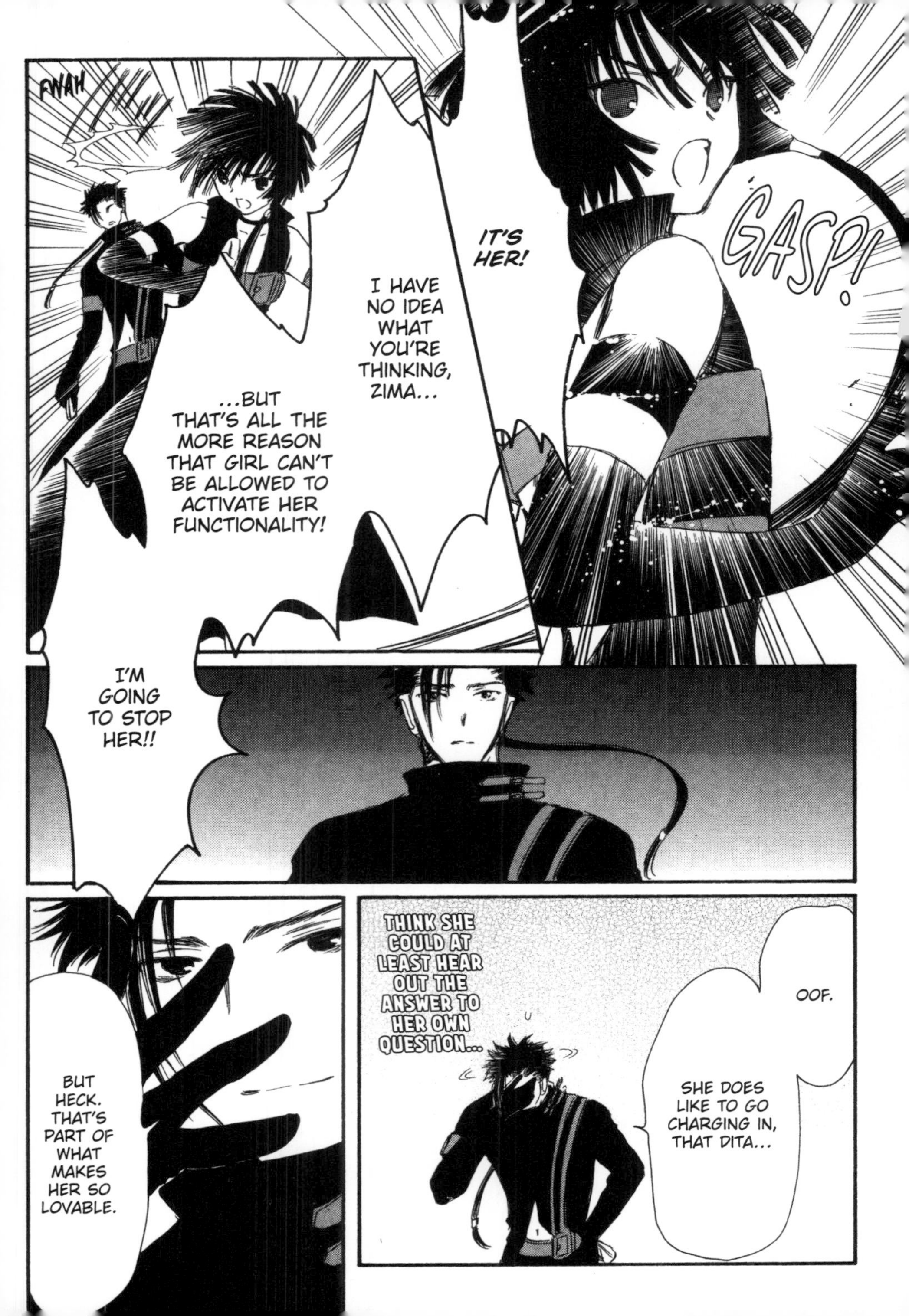
GASP!
IT'S HER!
FWAH
I HAVE NO IDEA WHAT YOU'RE THINKING, ZIMA...
...BUT THAT'S ALL THE MORE REASON THAT GIRL CAN'T BE ALLOWED TO ACTIVATE HER FUNCTIONALITY!
I'M GOING TO STOP HER!!
OOF.
SHE DOES LIKE TO GO CHARGING IN, THAT DITA...
THINK SHE COULD AT LEAST HEAR OUT THE ANSWER TO HER OWN QUESTION...
BUT HECK. THAT'S PART OF WHAT MAKES HER SO LOVABLE.

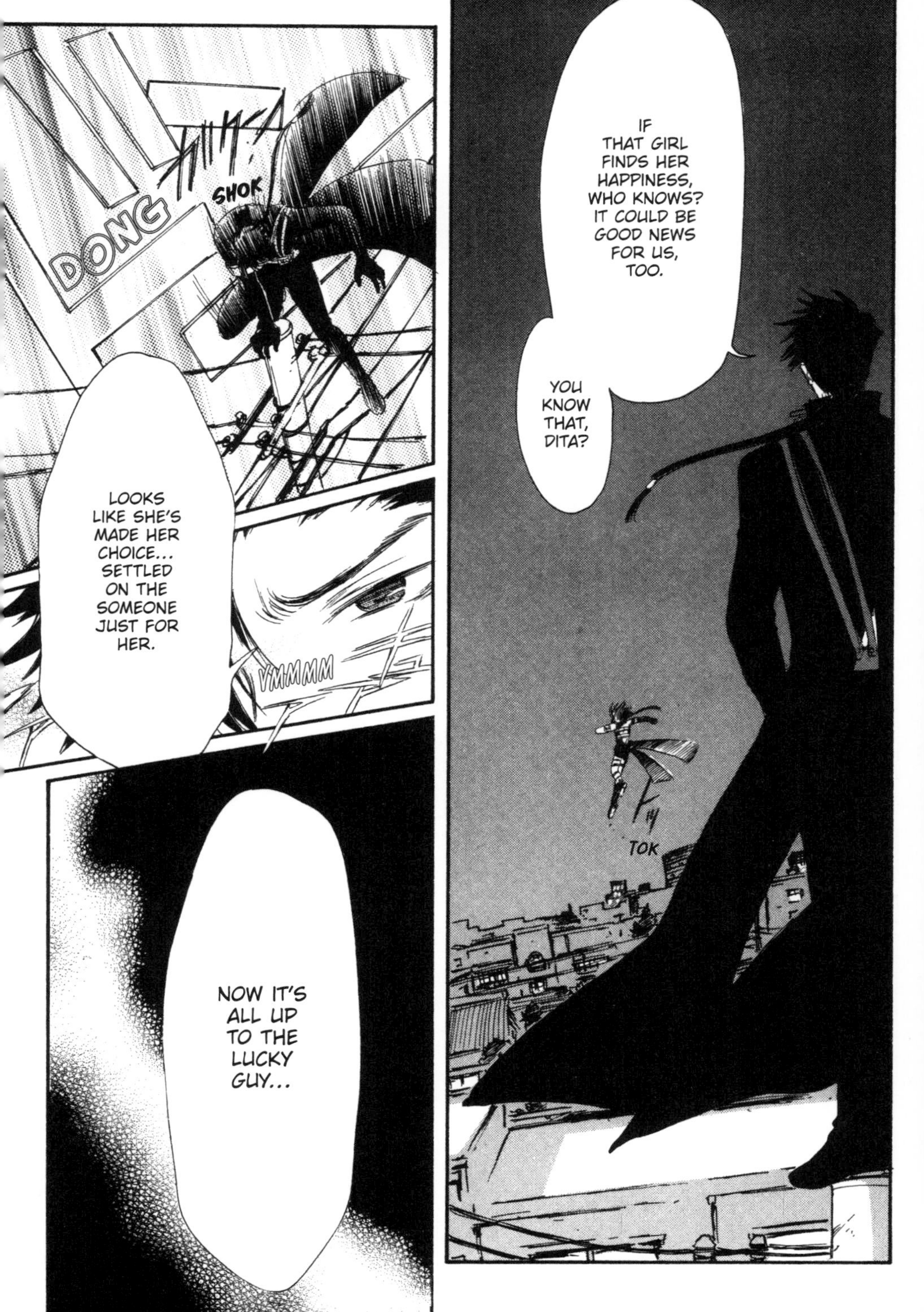
IF THAT GIRL FINDS HER HAPPINESS, WHO KNOWS? IT COULD BE GOOD NEWS FOR US, TOO.
YOU KNOW THAT, DITA?
TOK
DONG
SHOK
LOOKS LIKE SHE'S MADE HER CHOICE... SETTLED ON THE SOMEONE JUST FOR HER.
VMMMM
NOW IT'S ALL UP TO THE LUCKY GUY...

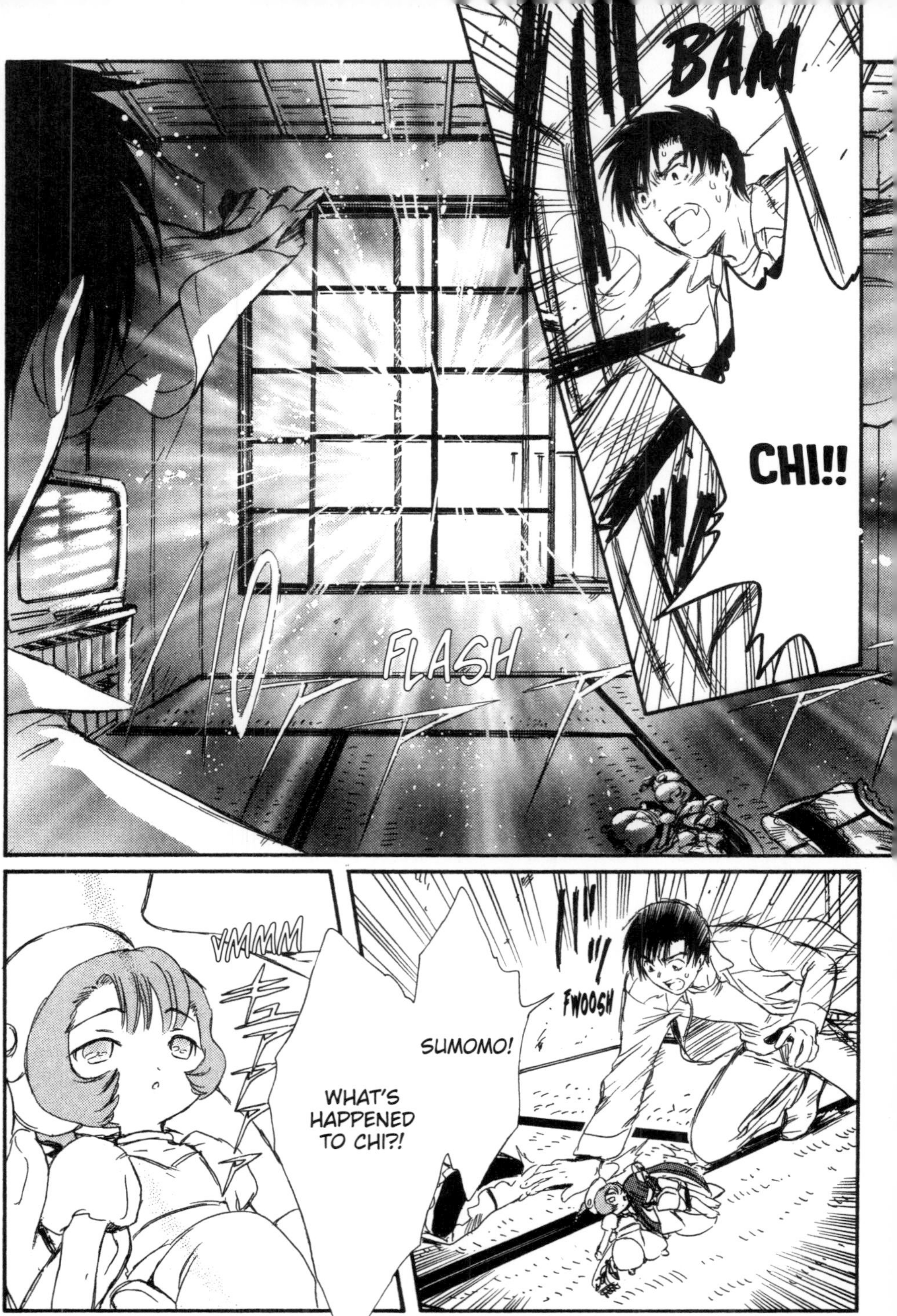
BAM
CHI!!
FLASH
FWOOSH
SUMOMO!
WHAT'S HAPPENED TO CHI?!

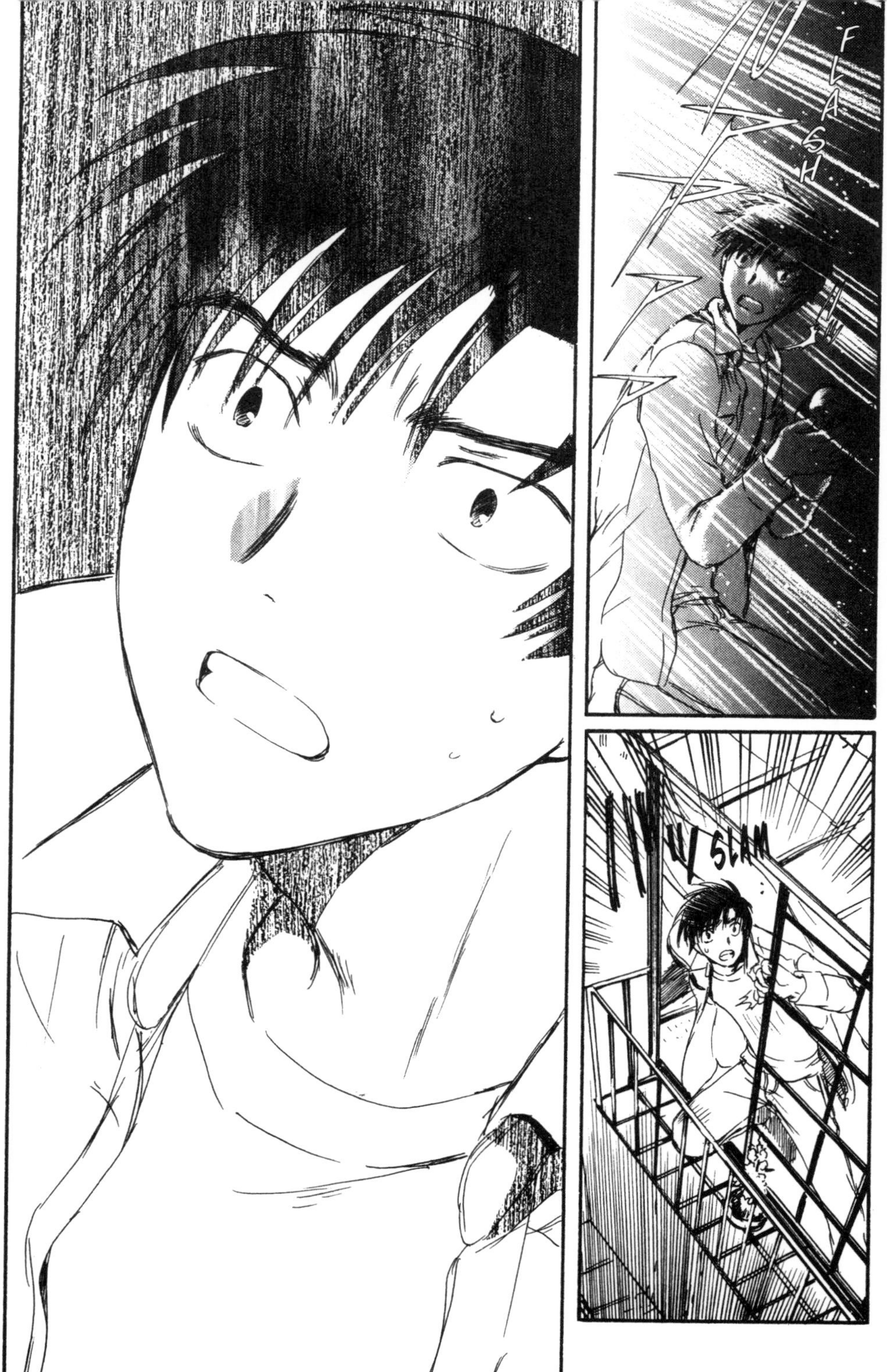
FLASH
SLAM

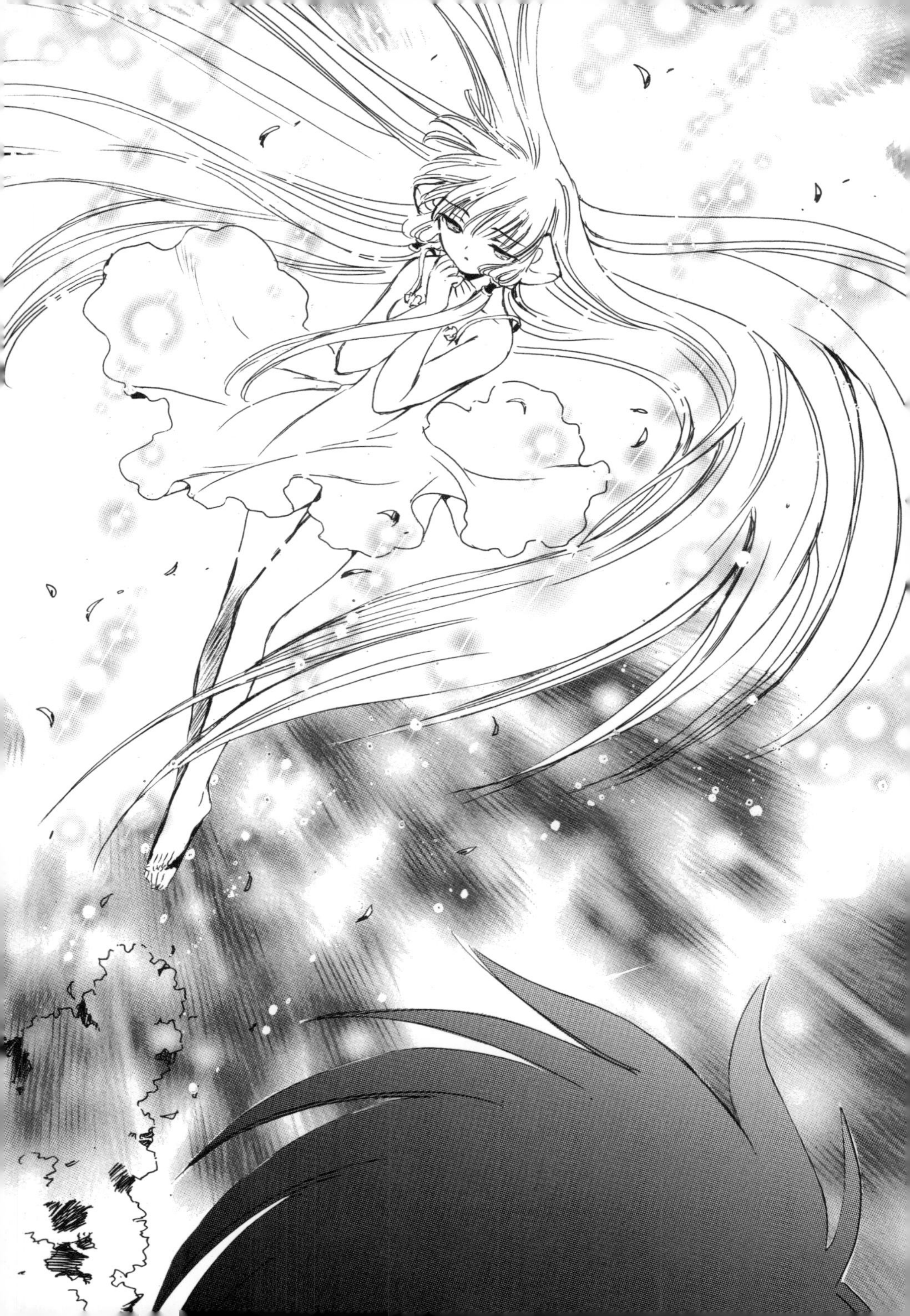

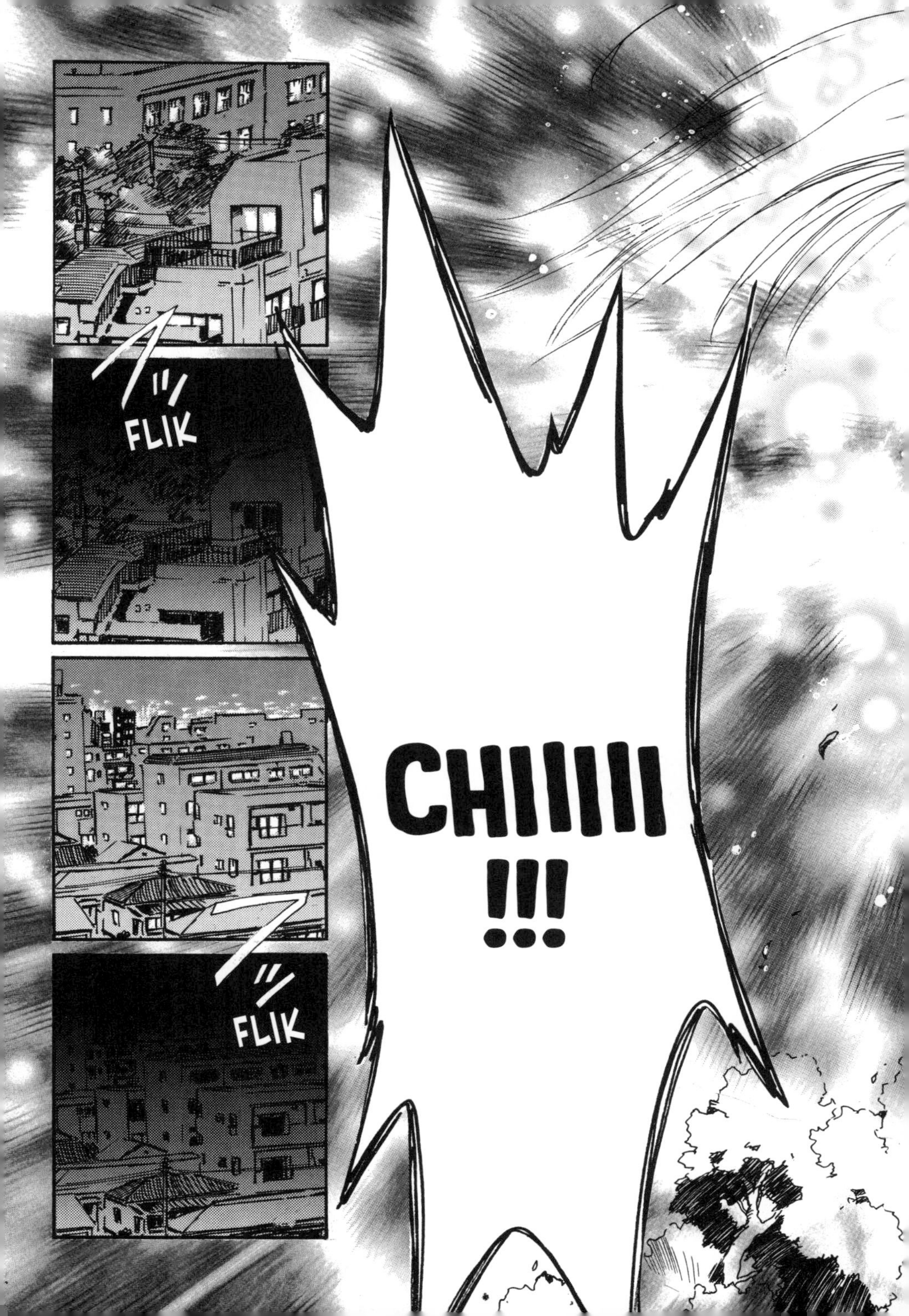
CHIIIIII
!!!
FLIK
FLIK

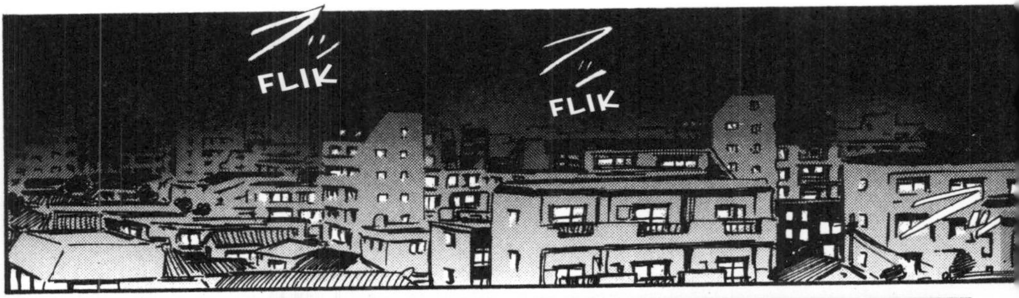
FLIK
FLIK
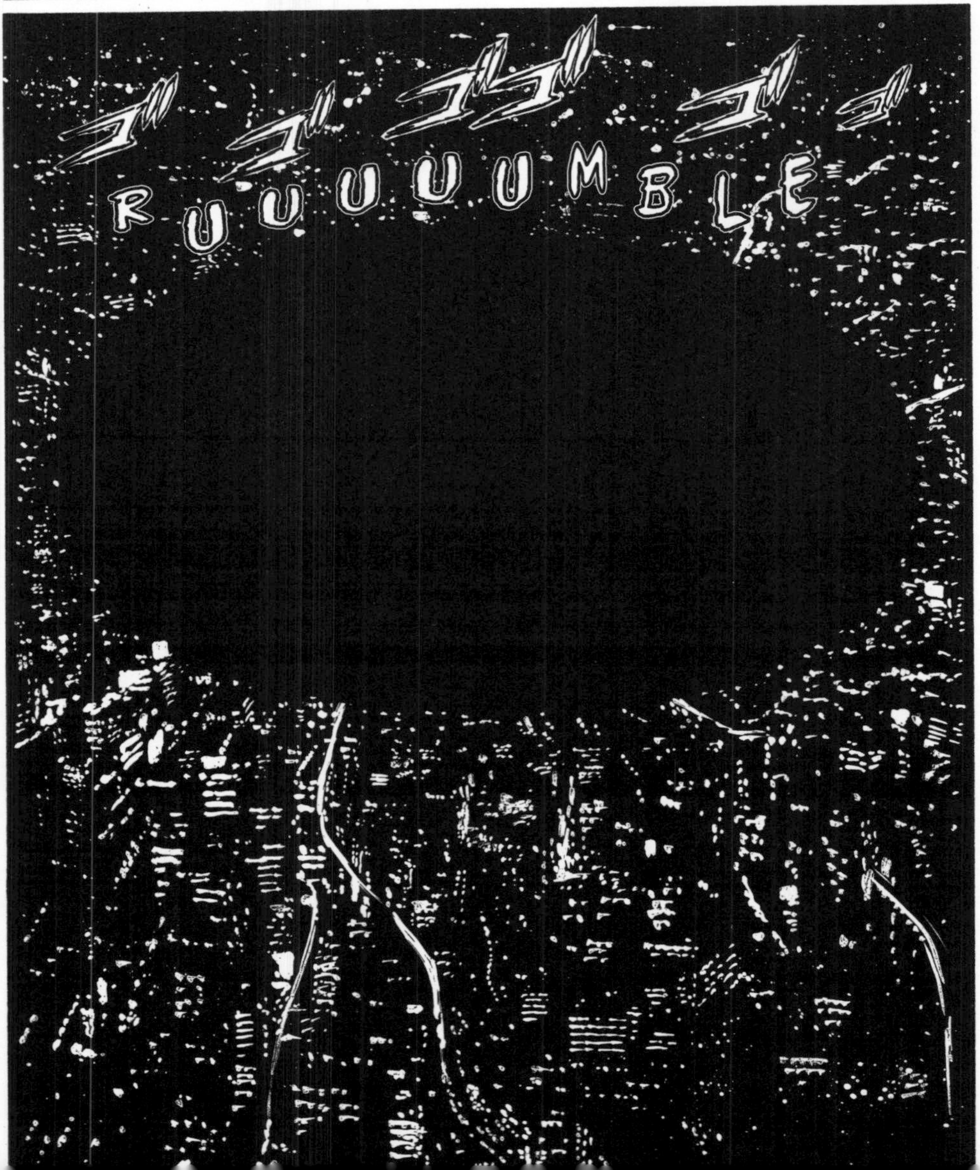
RUUUUUMBLE

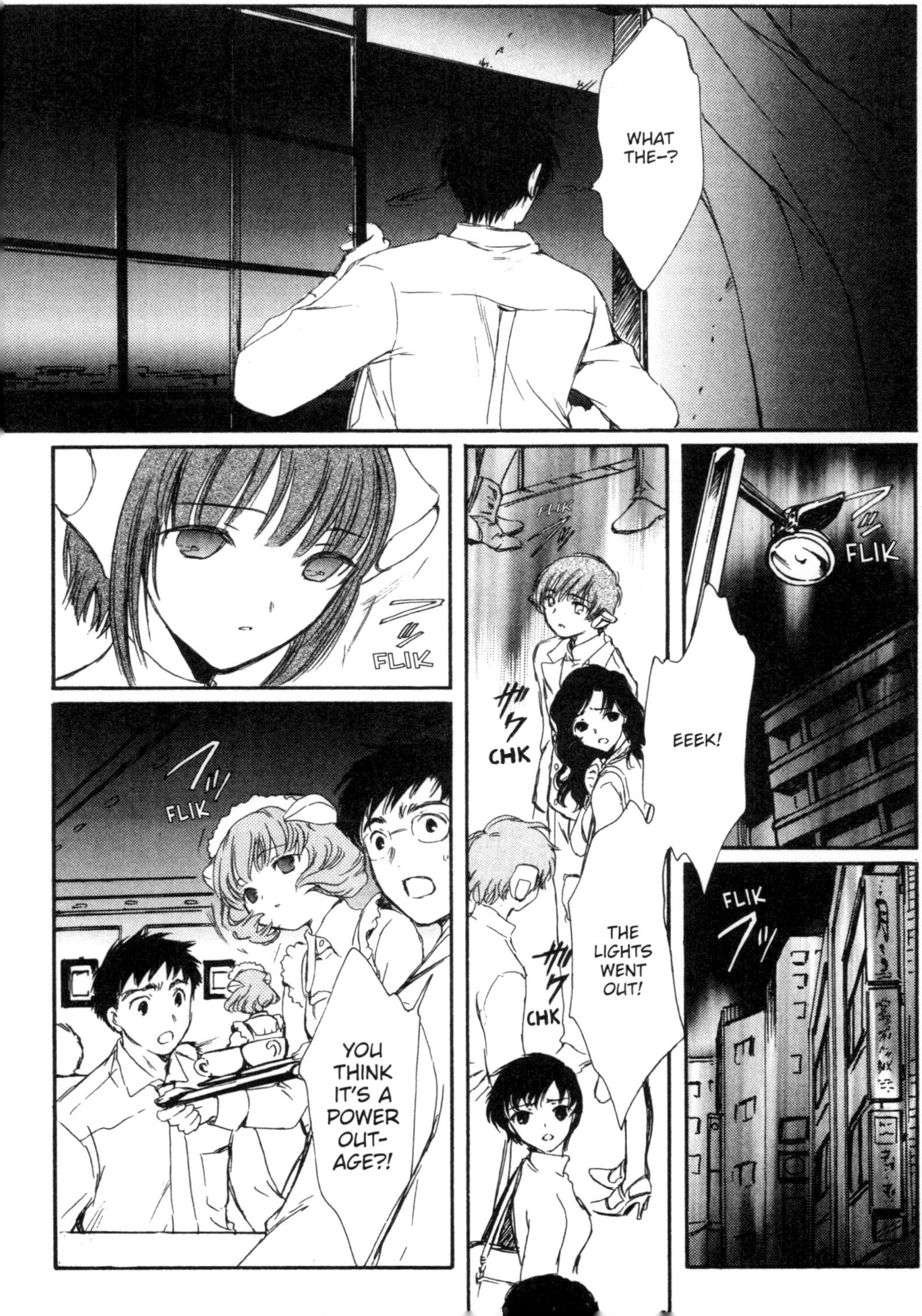
WHAT THE–?
FLIK
FLIK
FLIK
CHK
EEEK!
THE LIGHTS WENT OUT!
CHK
FLIK
FLIK
YOU THINK IT'S A POWER OUT-AGE?!

FLIK

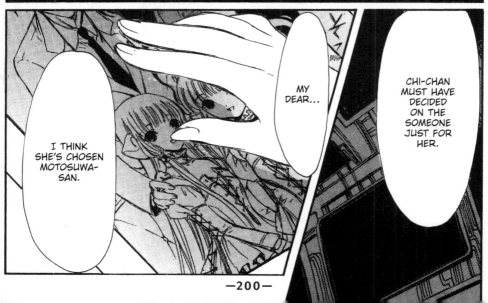

MY DEAR...

CHI-CHAN MUST HAVE DECIDED ON THE SOMEONE JUST FOR HER.

I THINK SHE'S CHOSEN MOTOSUWA-SAN.

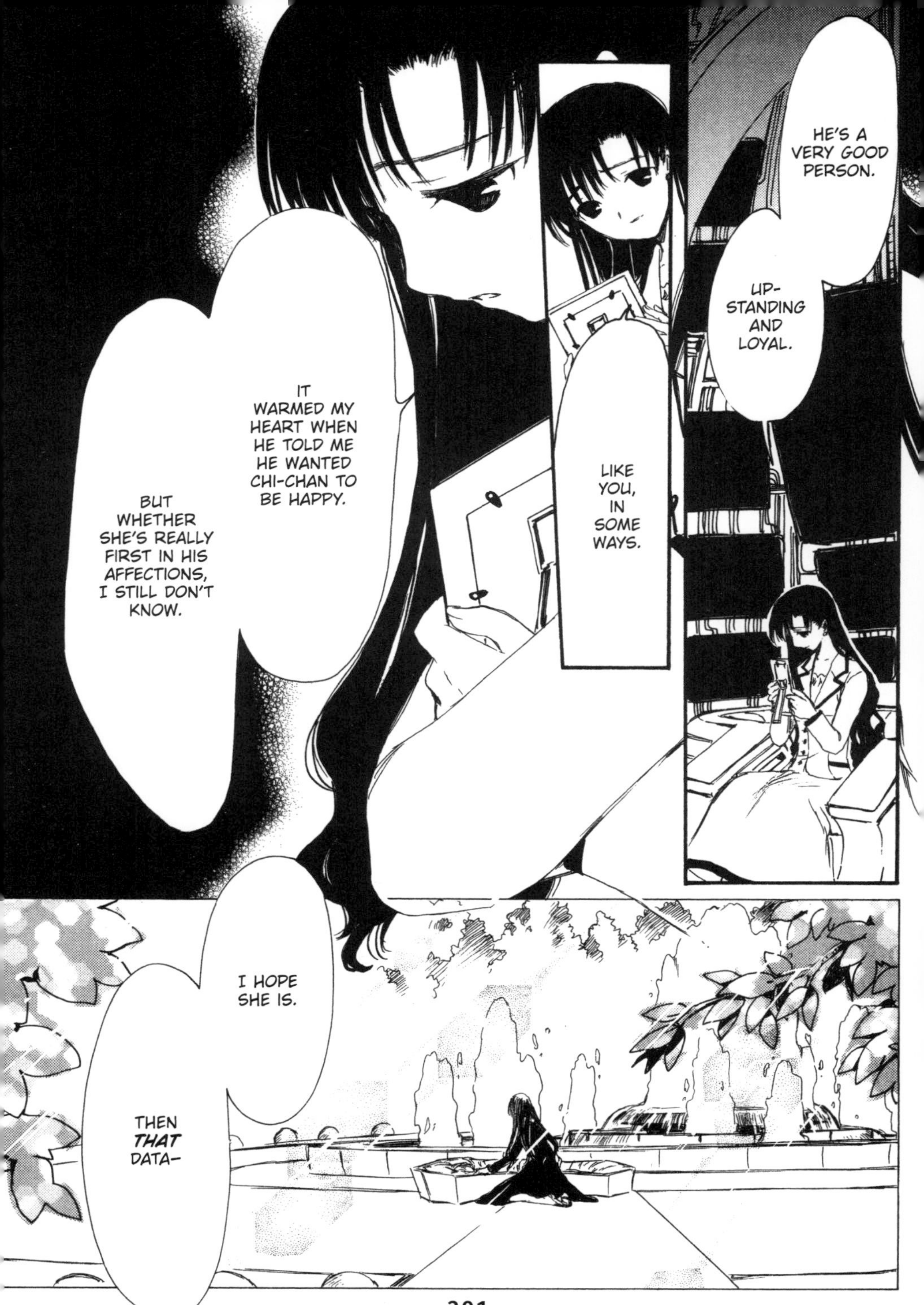
HE'S A VERY GOOD PERSON.
UP-STANDING AND LOYAL.
LIKE YOU, IN SOME WAYS.
IT WARMED MY HEART WHEN HE TOLD ME HE WANTED CHI-CHAN TO BE HAPPY.
BUT WHETHER SHE'S REALLY FIRST IN HIS AFFECTIONS, I STILL DON'T KNOW.
I HOPE SHE IS.
THEN *THAT* DATA-

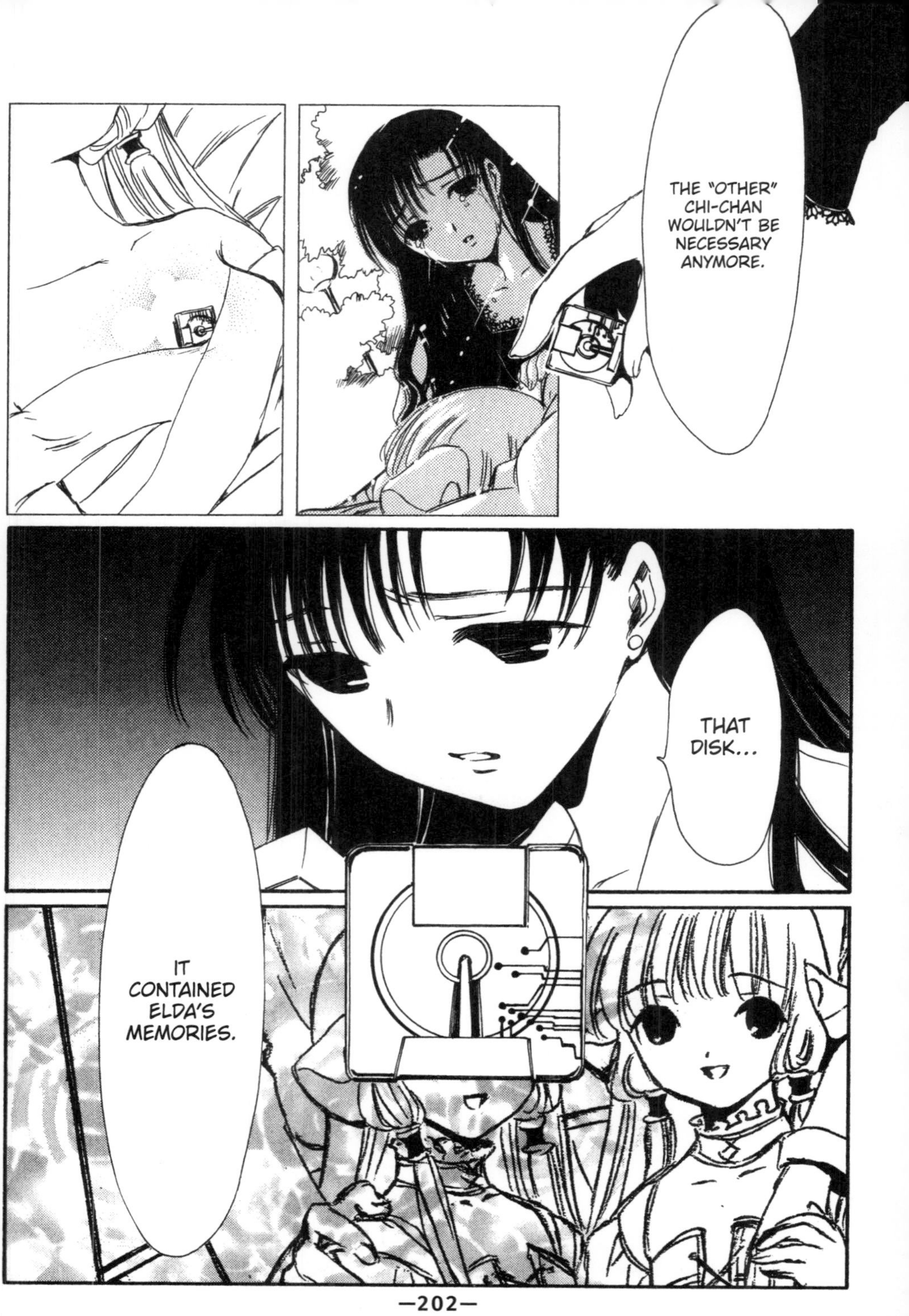
THE "OTHER" CHI-CHAN WOULDN'T BE NECESSARY ANYMORE.
THAT DISK...
IT CONTAINED ELDA'S MEMORIES.

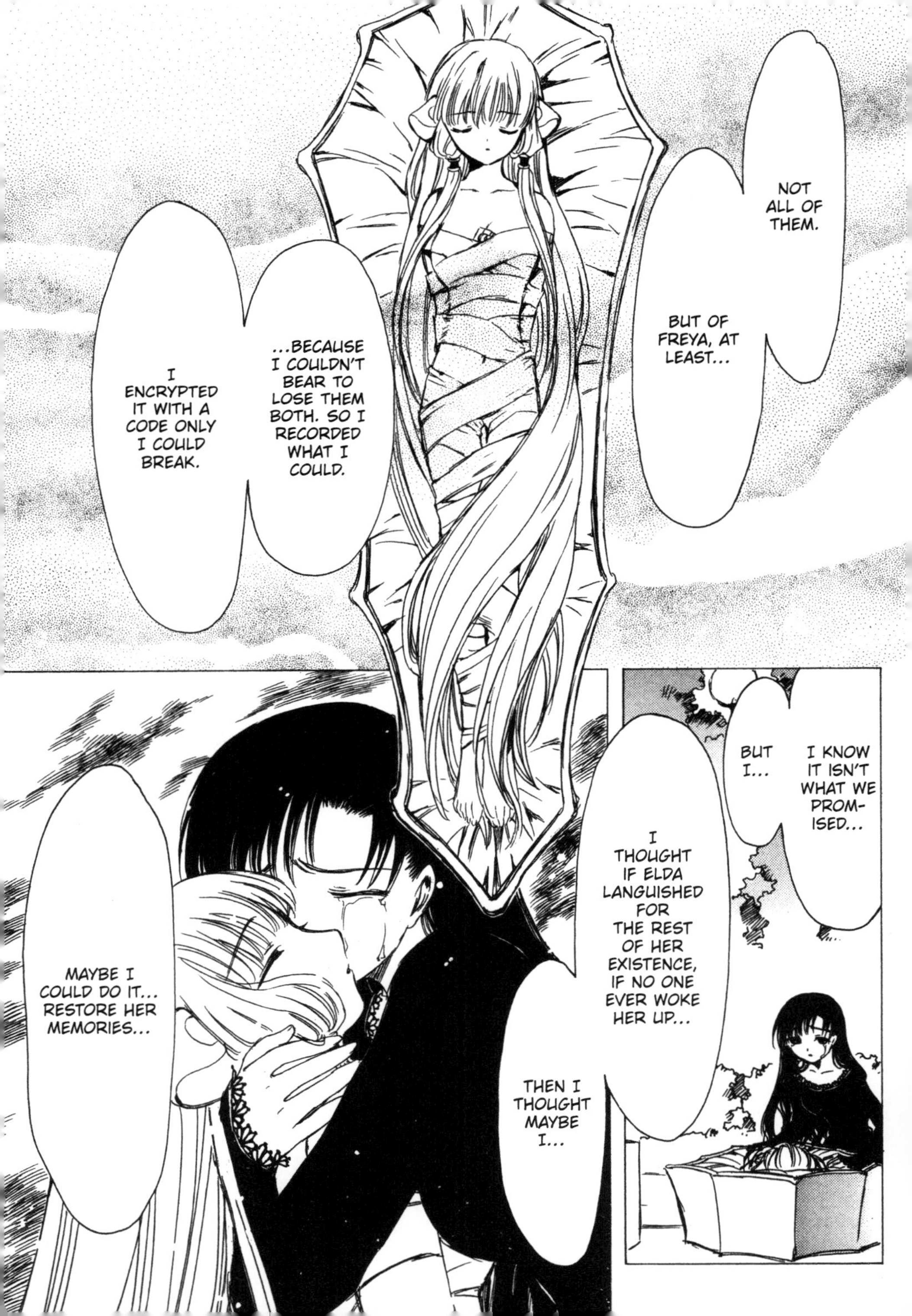
NOT ALL OF THEM.
BUT OF FREYA, AT LEAST...
...BECAUSE I COULDN'T BEAR TO LOSE THEM BOTH. SO I RECORDED WHAT I COULD.
I ENCRYPTED IT WITH A CODE ONLY I COULD BREAK.
I KNOW IT ISN'T WHAT WE PROM-ISED...
BUT I...
I THOUGHT IF ELDA LANGUISHED FOR THE REST OF HER EXISTENCE, IF NO ONE EVER WOKE HER UP...
THEN I THOUGHT MAYBE I...
MAYBE I COULD DO IT... RESTORE HER MEMORIES...

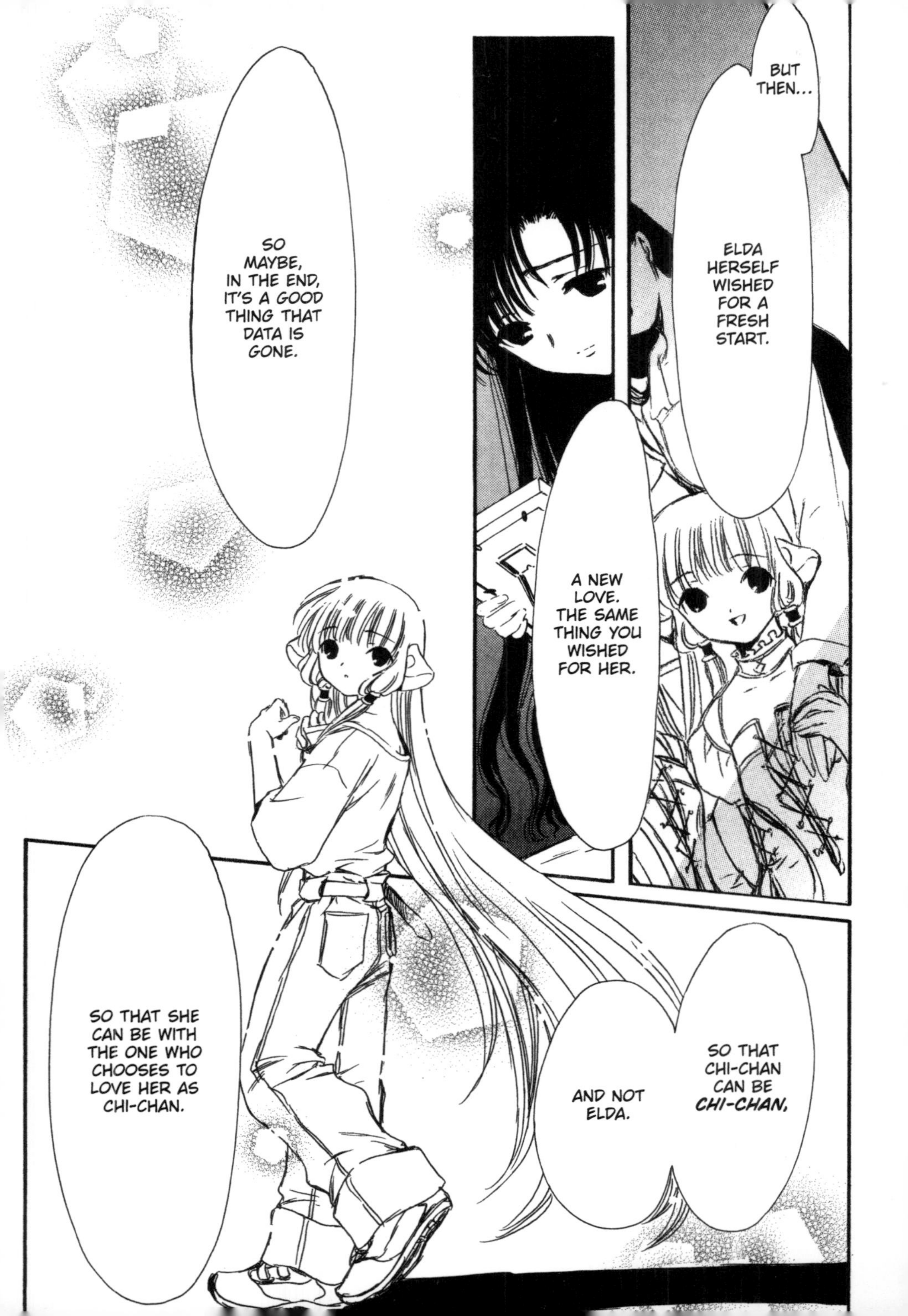
BUT THEN...
ELDA HERSELF WISHED FOR A FRESH START.
A NEW LOVE. THE SAME THING YOU WISHED FOR HER.
SO MAYBE, IN THE END, IT'S A GOOD THING THAT DATA IS GONE.
SO THAT CHI-CHAN CAN BE *CHI-CHAN,*
AND NOT ELDA.
SO THAT SHE CAN BE WITH THE ONE WHO CHOOSES TO LOVE HER AS CHI-CHAN.

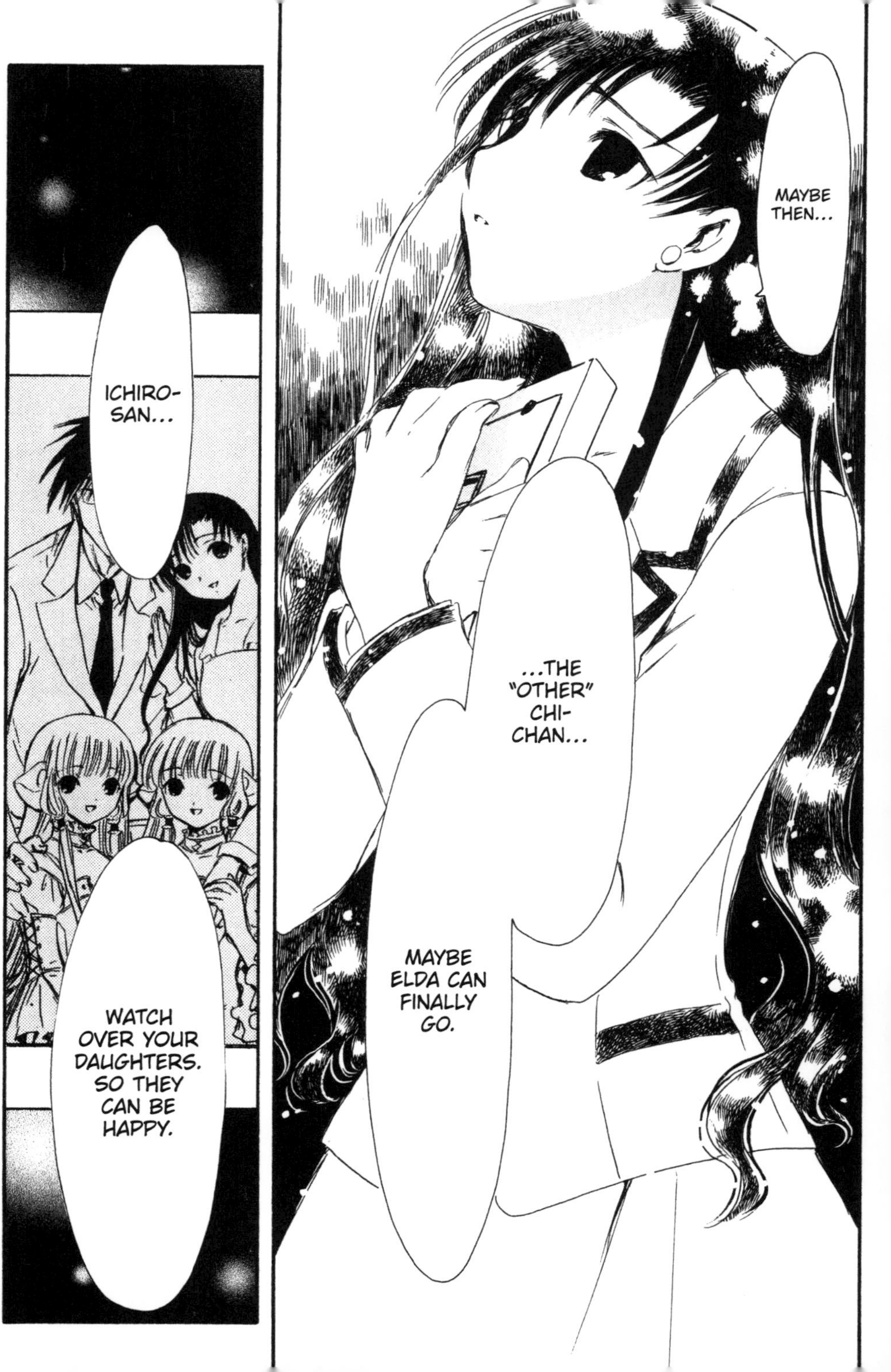
MAYBE THEN...
...THE "OTHER" CHI-CHAN...
MAYBE ELDA CAN FINALLY GO.
ICHIRO-SAN...
WATCH OVER YOUR DAUGHTERS. SO THEY CAN BE HAPPY.

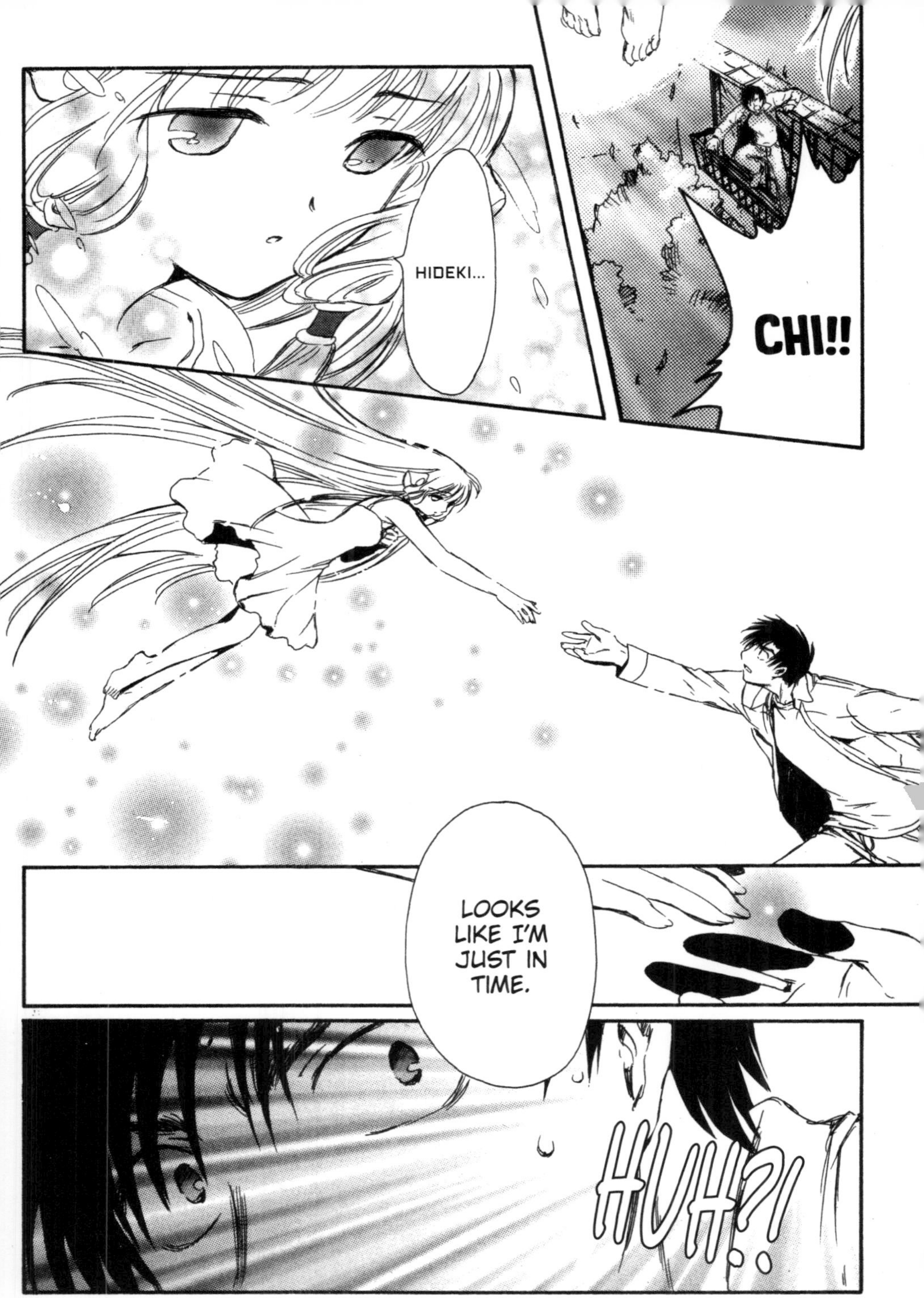
CHI!!
HIDEKI...
LOOKS LIKE I'M JUST IN TIME.
HUH?!

<chapter.82> end

**〈chapter.83〉**

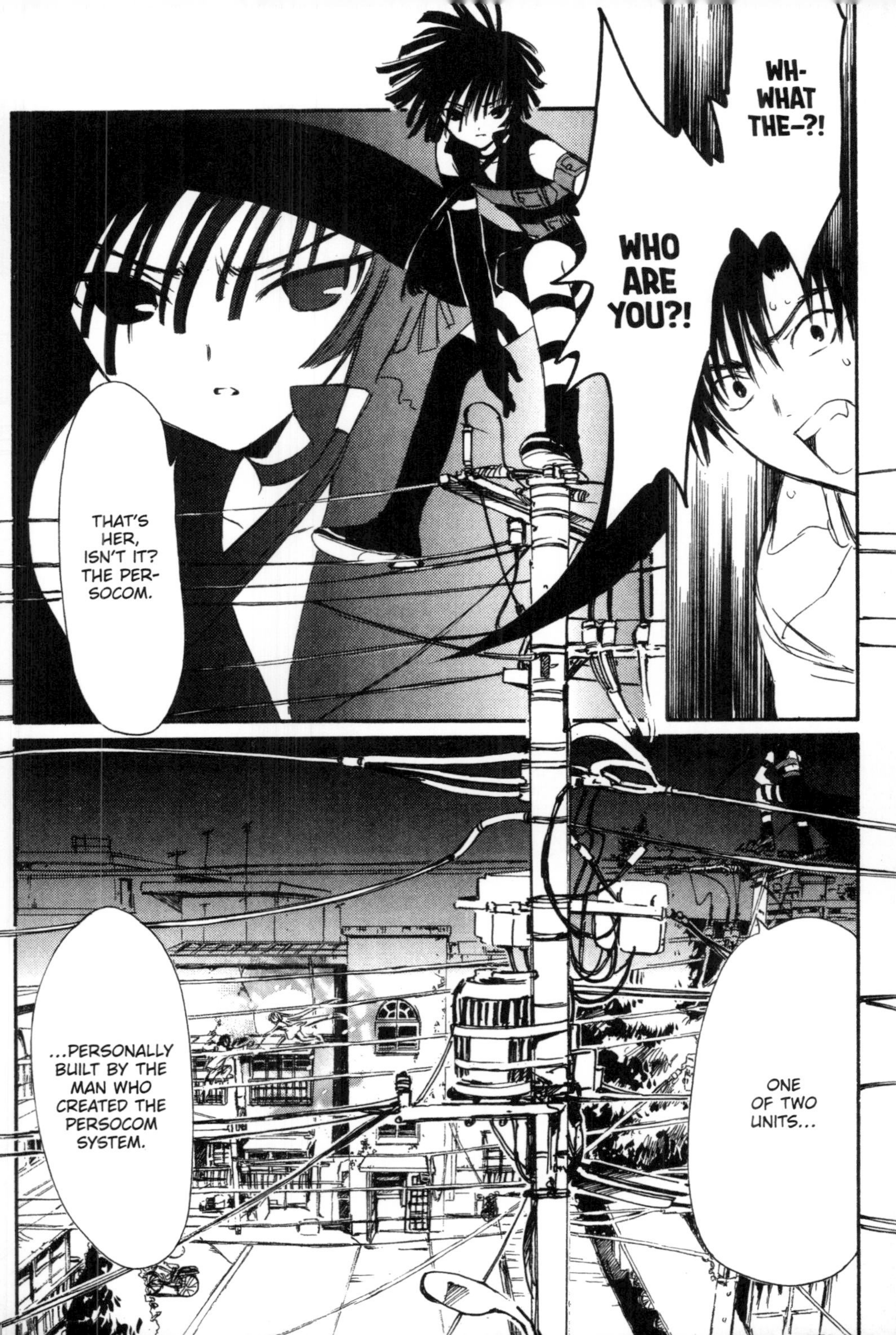
WH- WHAT THE-?!
WHO ARE YOU?!
THAT'S HER, ISN'T IT? THE PER-SOCOM.
ONE OF TWO UNITS...
...PERSONALLY BUILT BY THE MAN WHO CREATED THE PERSOCOM SYSTEM.

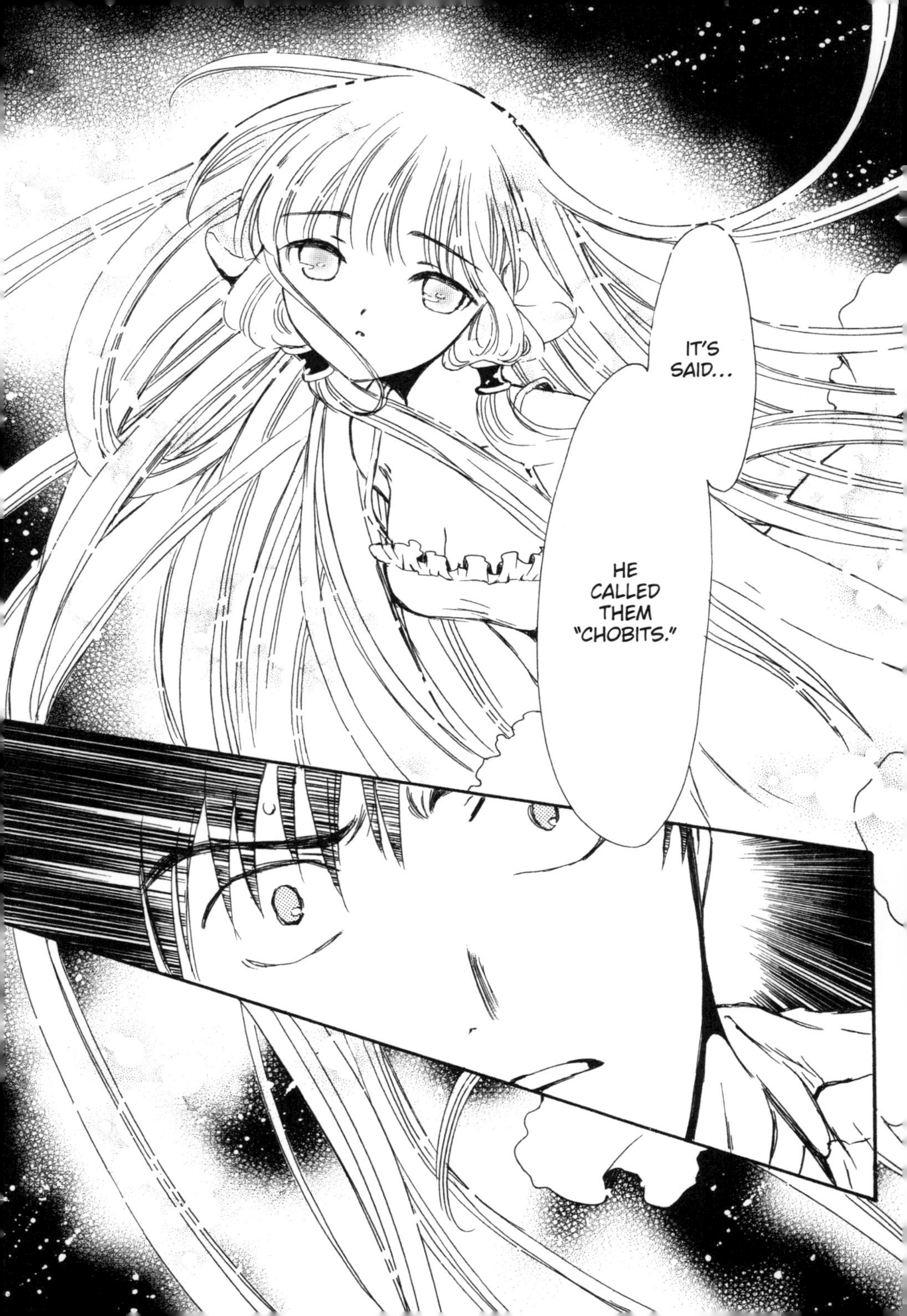
IT'S SAID...
HE CALLED THEM "CHOBITS."

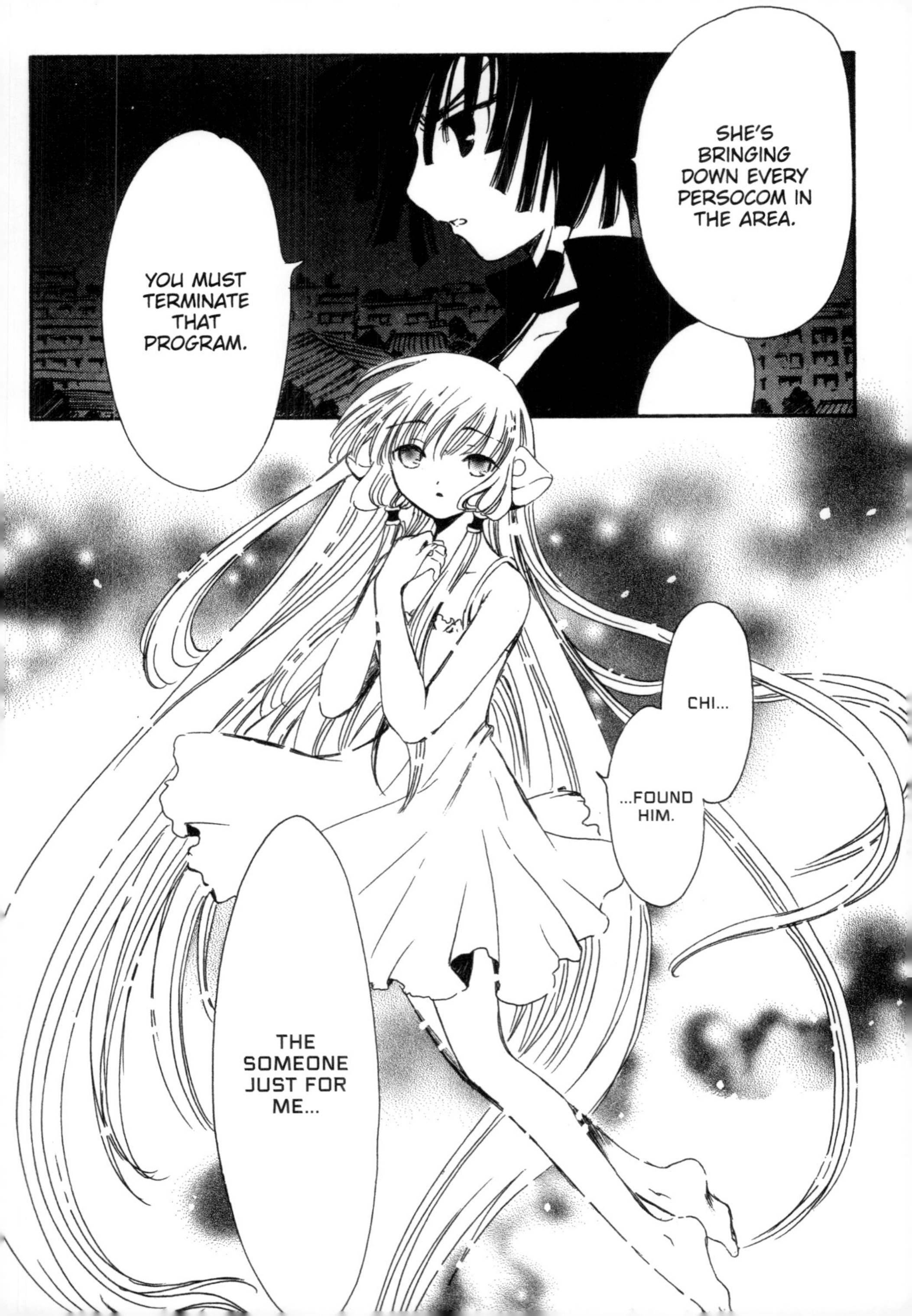
SHE'S BRINGING DOWN EVERY PERSOCOM IN THE AREA.
YOU MUST TERMINATE THAT PROGRAM.
CHI...
...FOUND HIM.
THE SOMEONE JUST FOR ME...

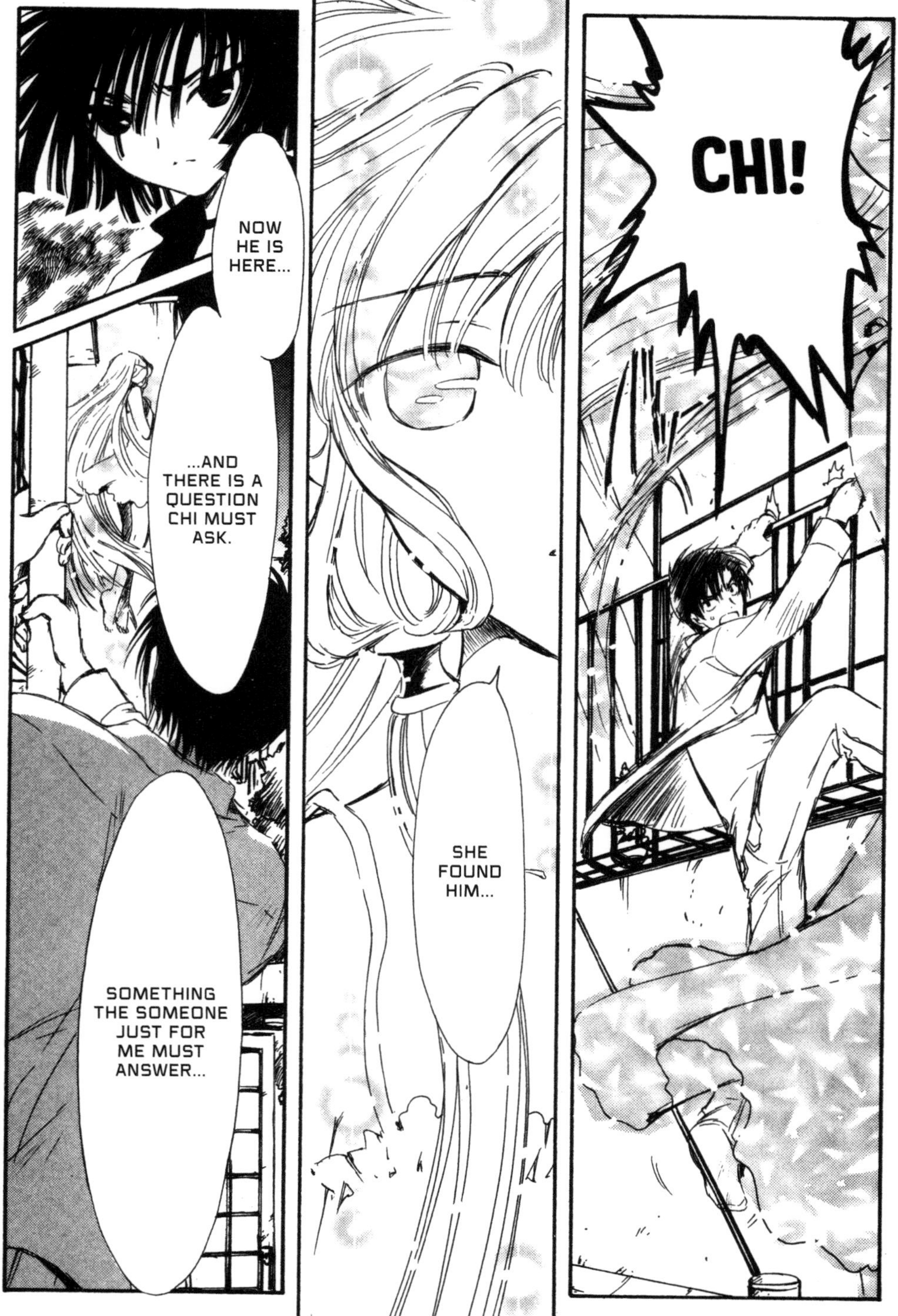
CHI!
SHE FOUND HIM...
NOW HE IS HERE...
...AND THERE IS A QUESTION CHI MUST ASK.
SOMETHING THE SOMEONE JUST FOR ME MUST ANSWER...

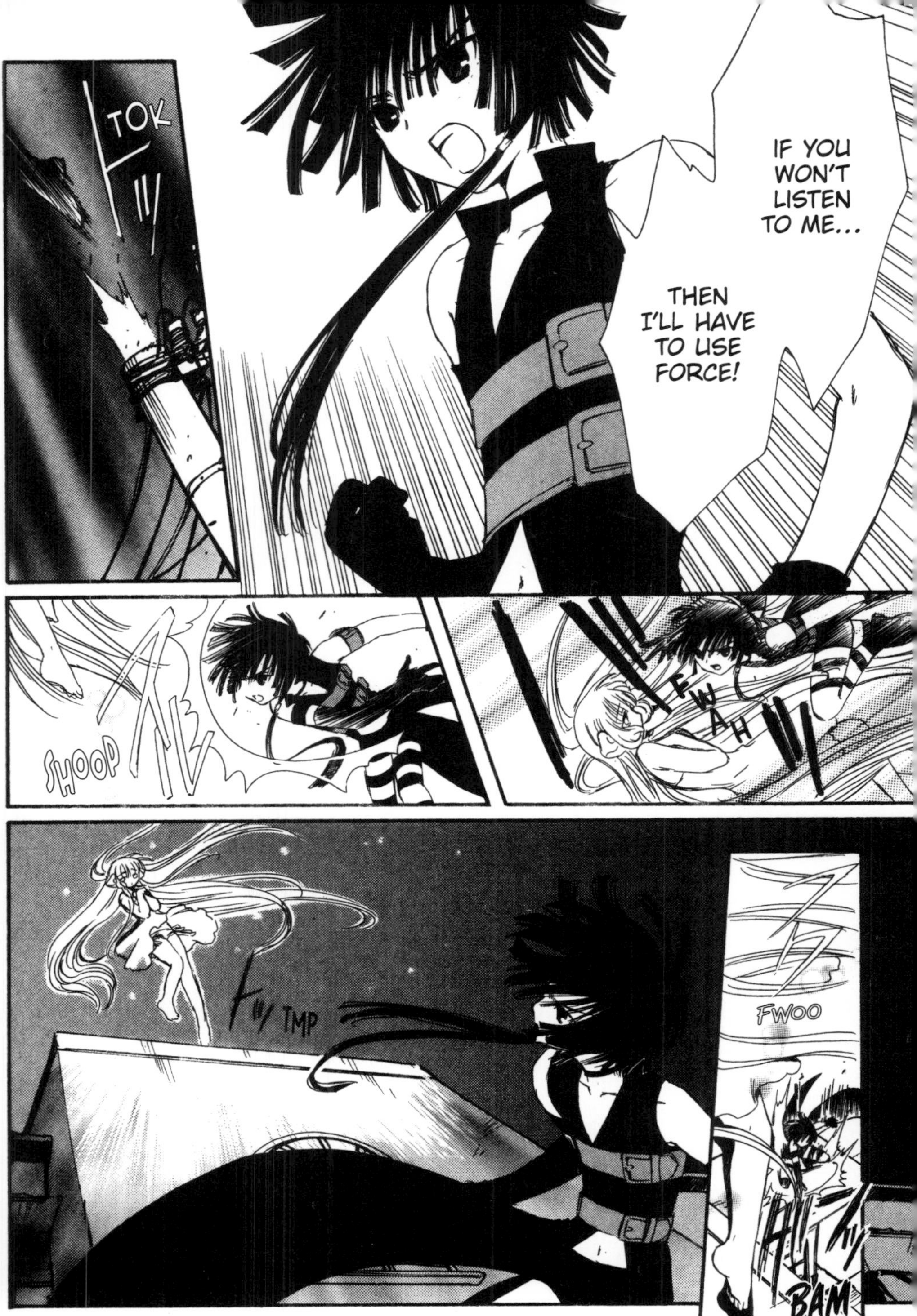
IF YOU WON'T LISTEN TO ME...
THEN I'LL HAVE TO USE FORCE!
TOK
FWAH
SHOOP
FWOO
BAM
TMP

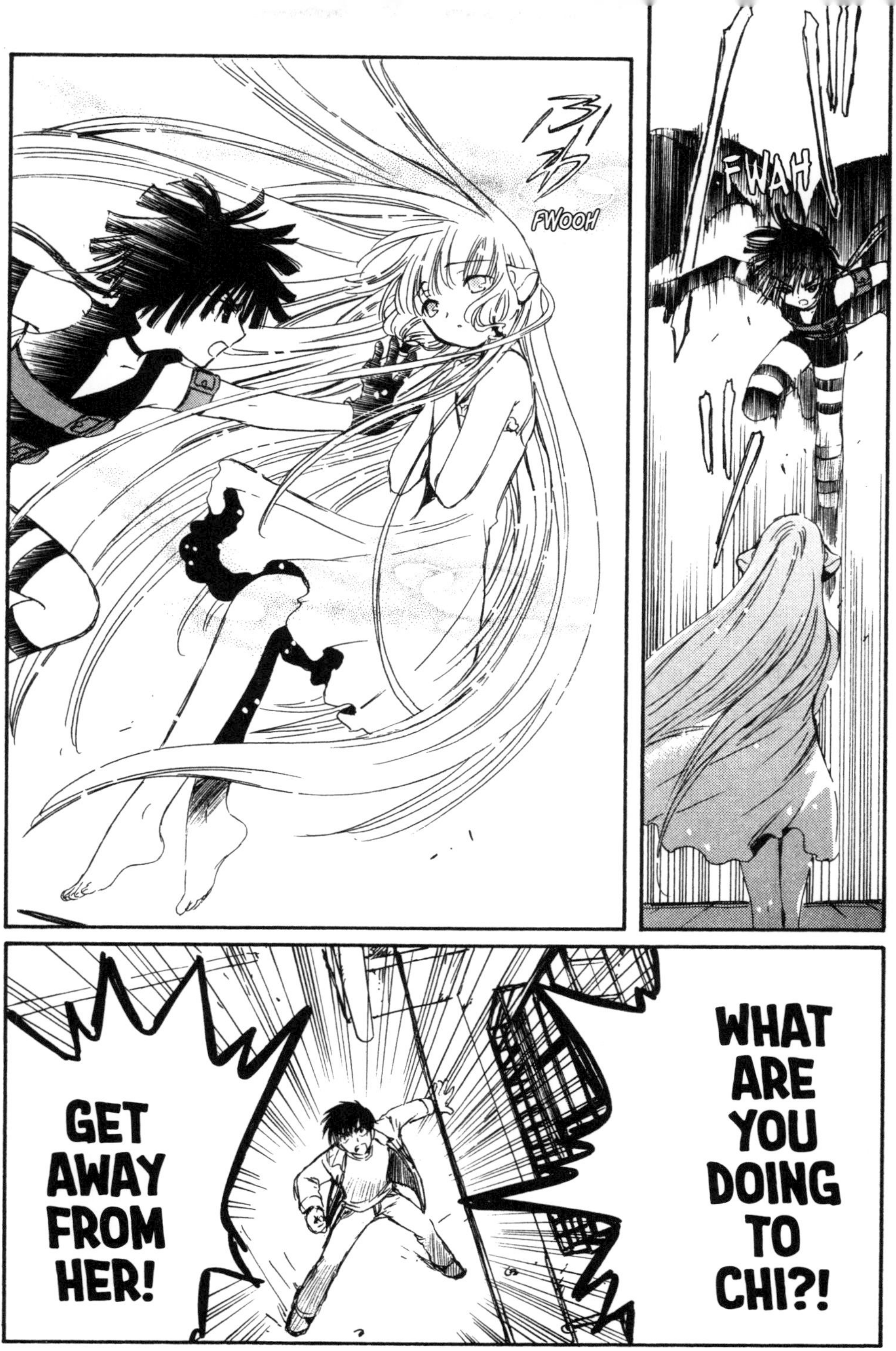
FWAH
ふわ
FWOOH
WHAT ARE YOU DOING TO CHI?!
GET AWAY FROM HER!

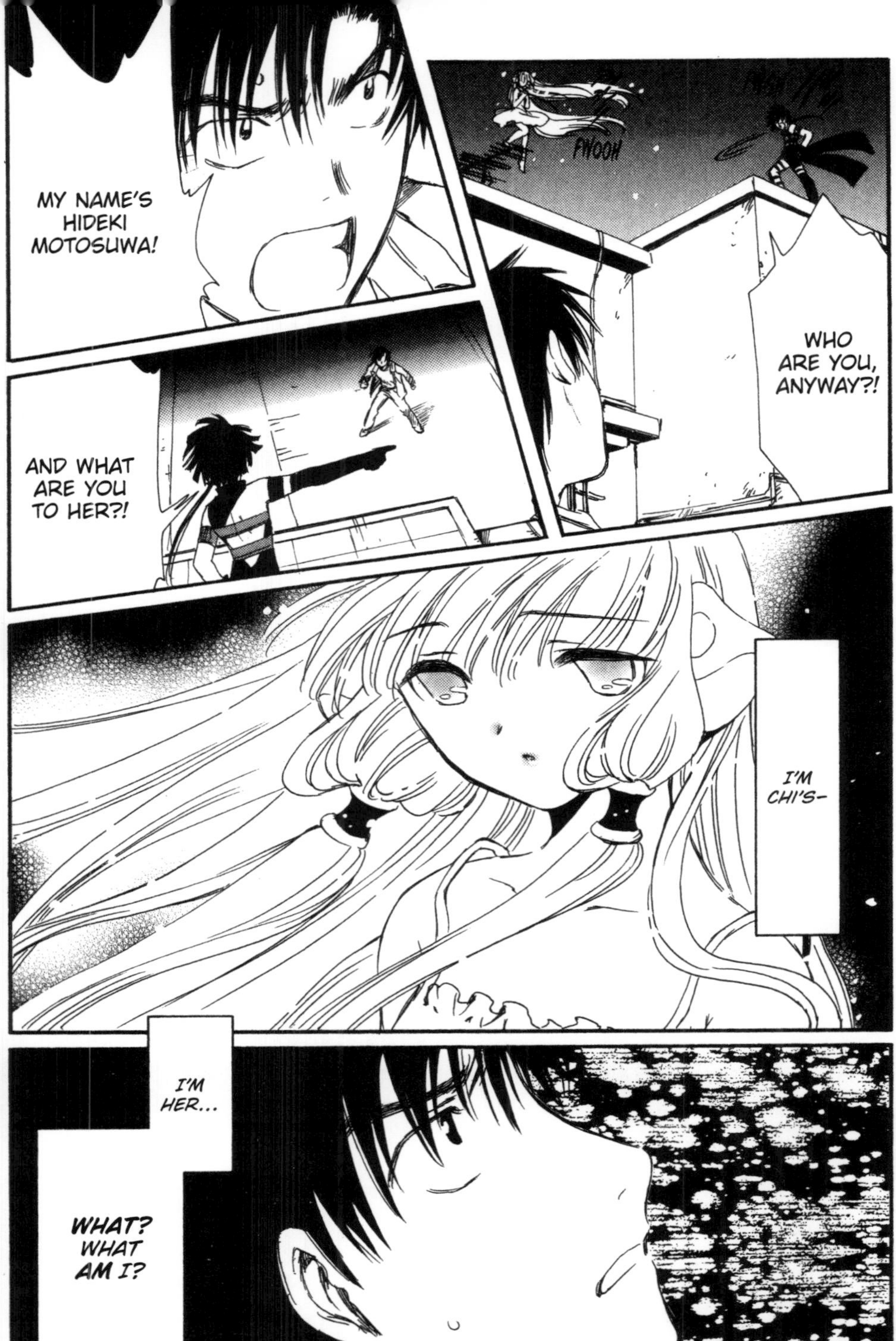
FWOOH
MY NAME'S HIDEKI MOTOSUWA!
WHO ARE YOU, ANYWAY?!
AND WHAT ARE YOU TO HER?!
I'M CHI'S-
I'M HER...
WHAT? WHAT AM I?

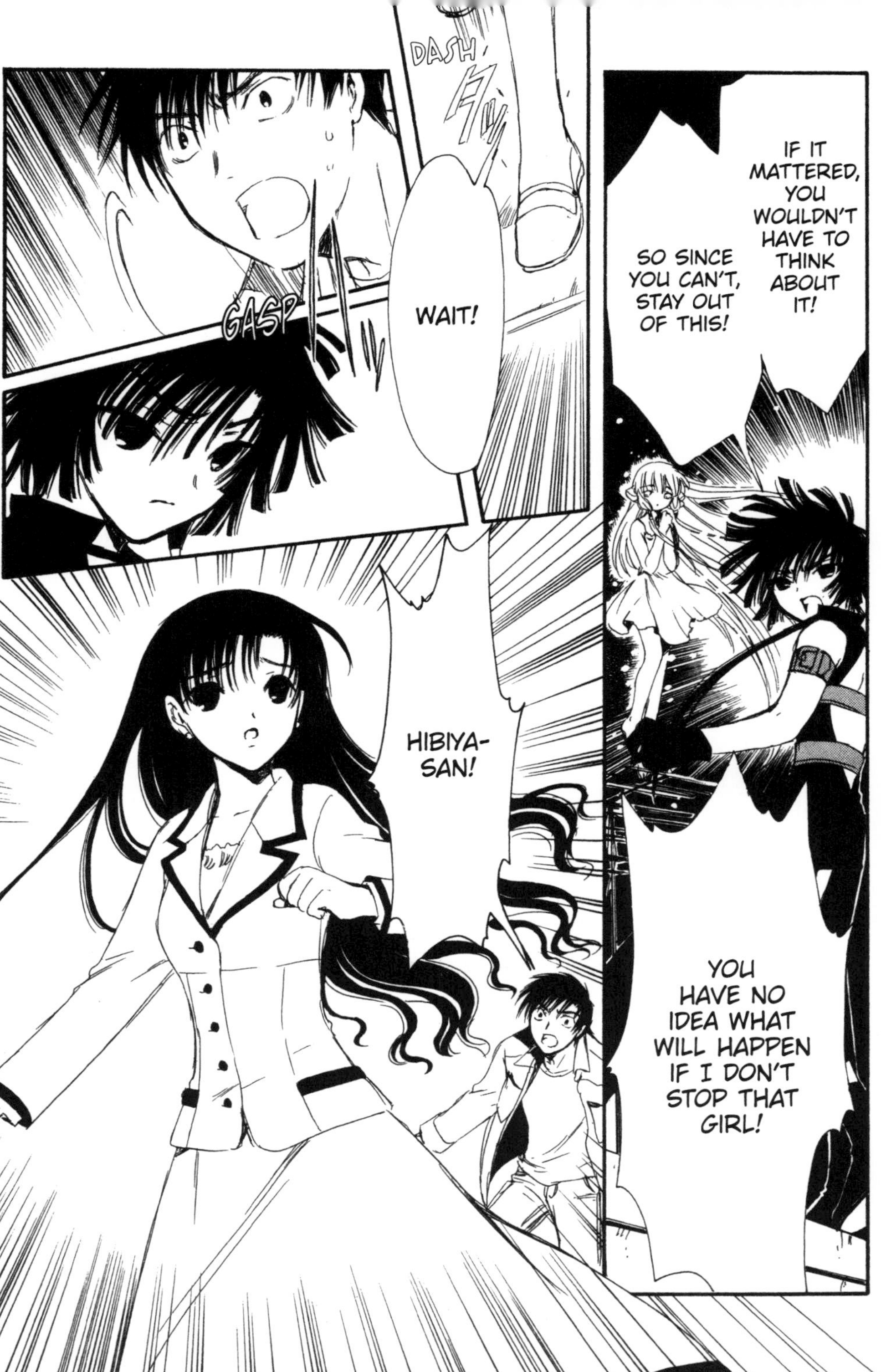
IF IT MATTERED, YOU WOULDN'T HAVE TO THINK ABOUT IT!
SO SINCE YOU CAN'T, STAY OUT OF THIS!
YOU HAVE NO IDEA WHAT WILL HAPPEN IF I DON'T STOP THAT GIRL!
DASH
WAIT!
GASP
HIBIYA-SAN!

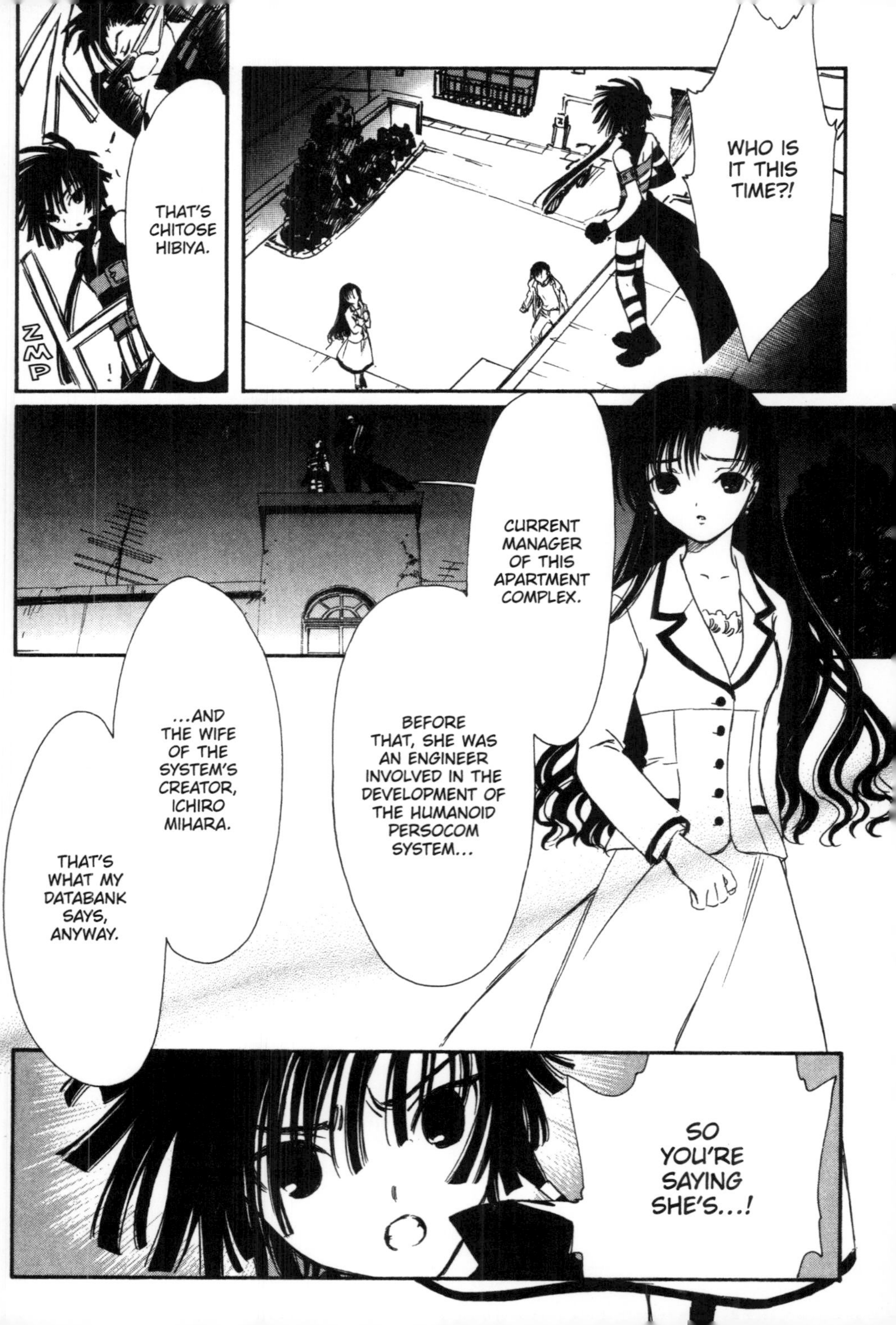
WHO IS IT THIS TIME?!
THAT'S CHITOSE HIBIYA.
ZMP
CURRENT MANAGER OF THIS APARTMENT COMPLEX.
BEFORE THAT, SHE WAS AN ENGINEER INVOLVED IN THE DEVELOPMENT OF THE HUMANOID PERSOCOM SYSTEM...
...AND THE WIFE OF THE SYSTEM'S CREATOR, ICHIRO MIHARA.
THAT'S WHAT MY DATABANK SAYS, ANYWAY.
SO YOU'RE SAYING SHE'S...!

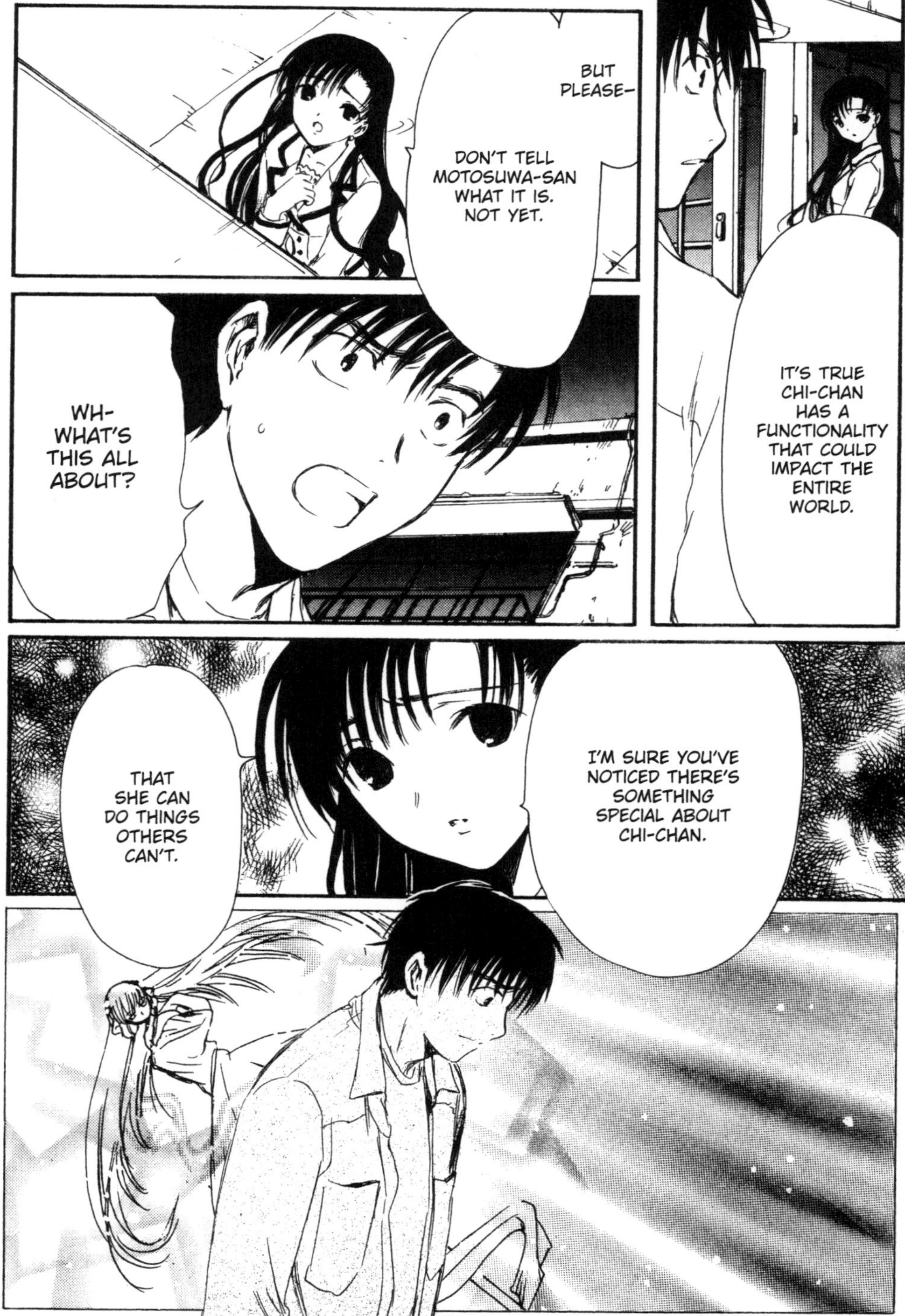
IT'S TRUE CHI-CHAN HAS A FUNCTIONALITY THAT COULD IMPACT THE ENTIRE WORLD.
BUT PLEASE-
DON'T TELL MOTOSUWA-SAN WHAT IT IS. NOT YET.
WH- WHAT'S THIS ALL ABOUT?
I'M SURE YOU'VE NOTICED THERE'S SOMETHING SPECIAL ABOUT CHI-CHAN.
THAT SHE CAN DO THINGS OTHERS CAN'T.

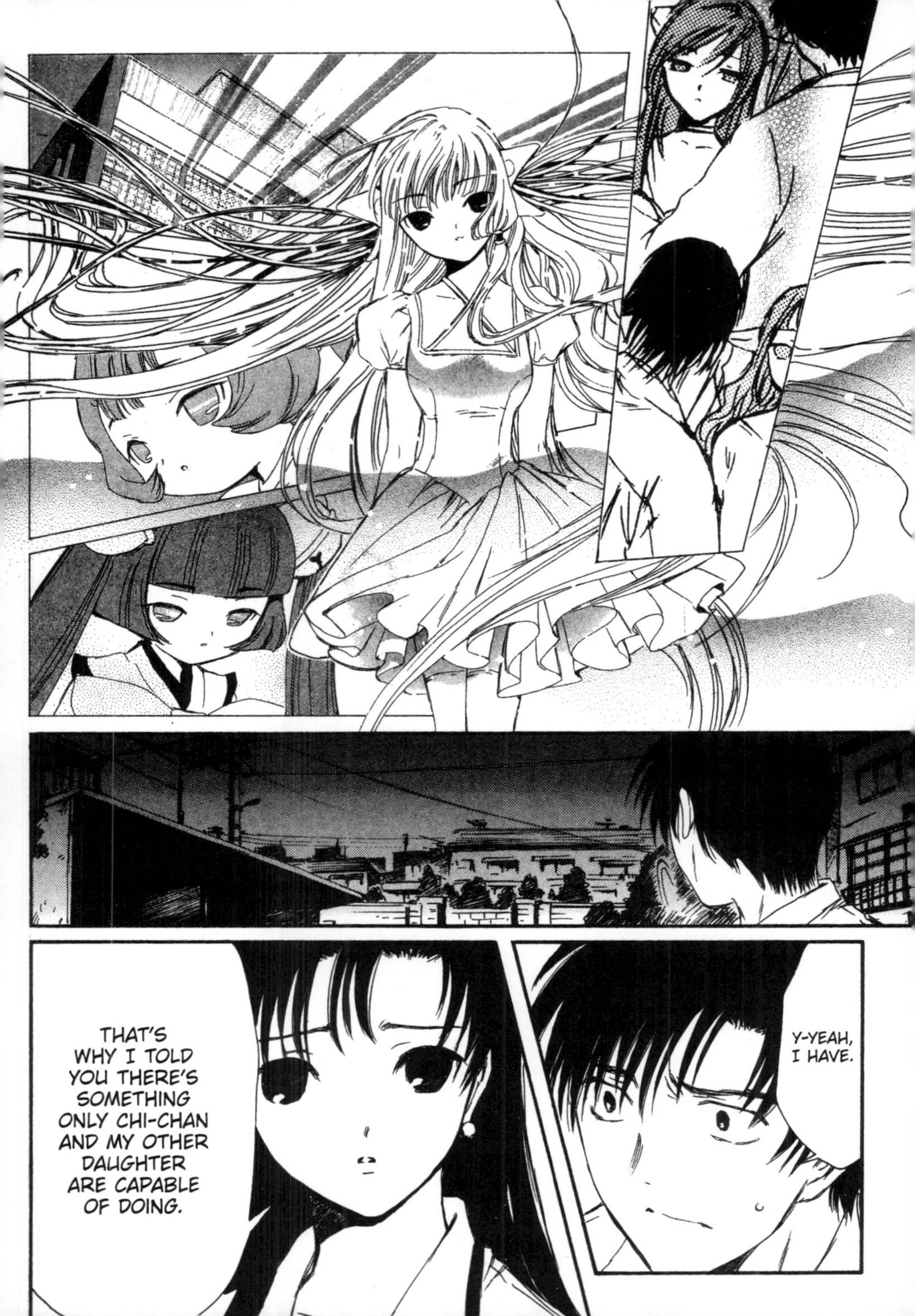
Y-YEAH, I HAVE.
THAT'S WHY I TOLD YOU THERE'S SOMETHING ONLY CHI-CHAN AND MY OTHER DAUGHTER ARE CAPABLE OF DOING.

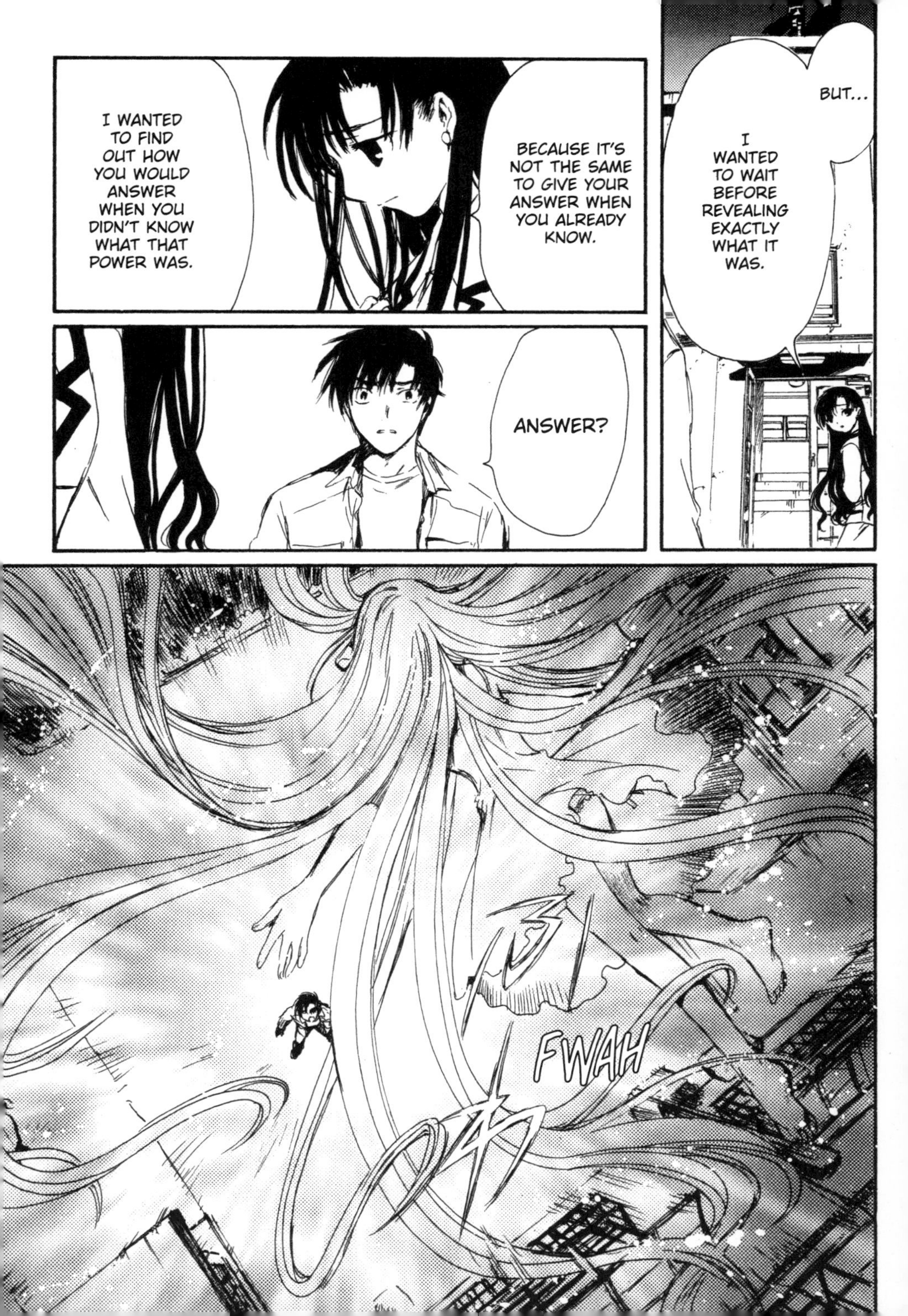
BUT...
I WANTED TO WAIT BEFORE REVEALING EXACTLY WHAT IT WAS.
I WANTED TO FIND OUT HOW YOU WOULD ANSWER WHEN YOU DIDN'T KNOW WHAT THAT POWER WAS.
BECAUSE IT'S NOT THE SAME TO GIVE YOUR ANSWER WHEN YOU ALREADY KNOW.
ANSWER?
FWAH

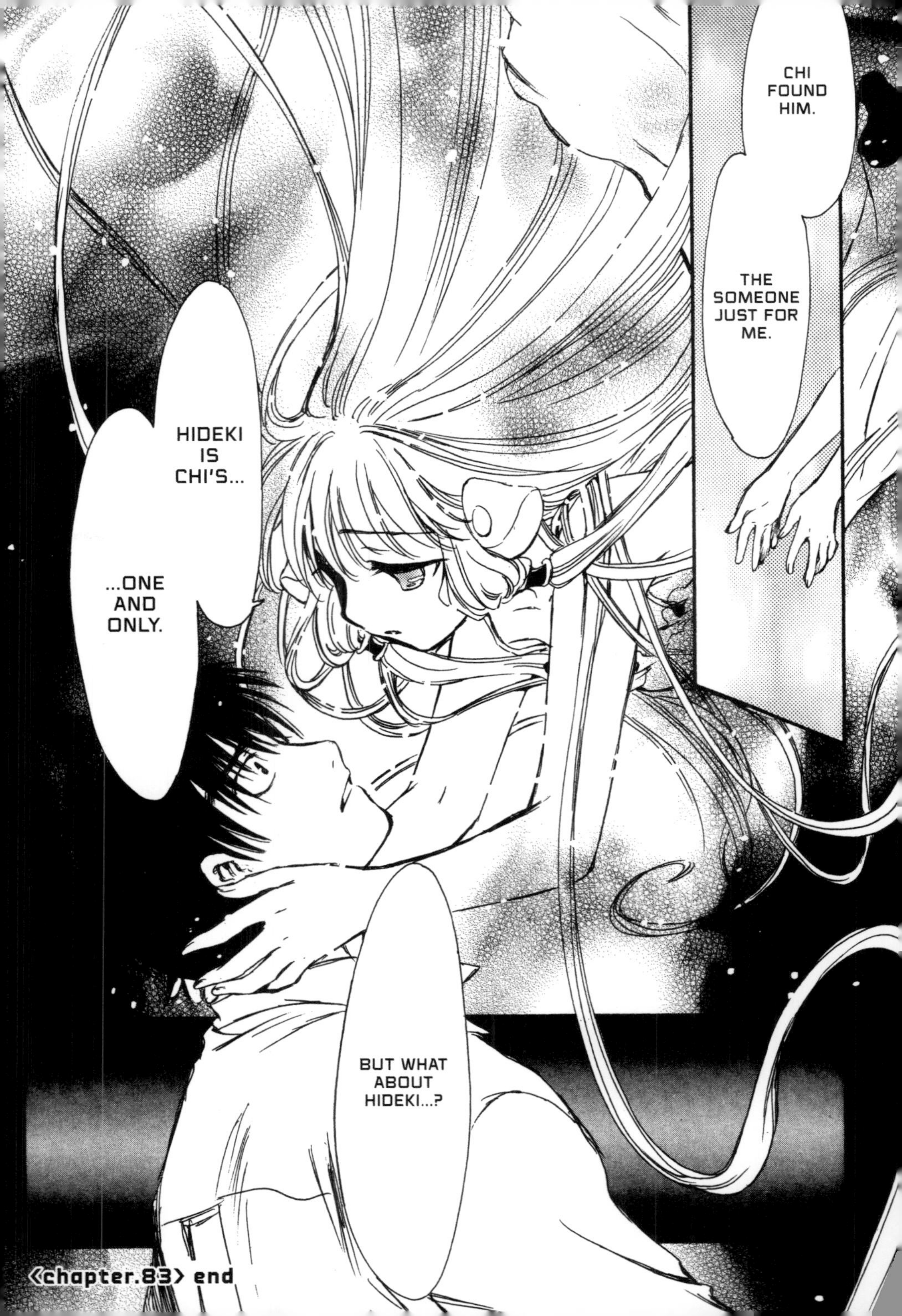
CHI FOUND HIM.
THE SOMEONE JUST FOR ME.
HIDEKI IS CHI'S...
...ONE AND ONLY.
BUT WHAT ABOUT HIDEKI...?
《chapter.83》 end

# ⟨chapter.84⟩

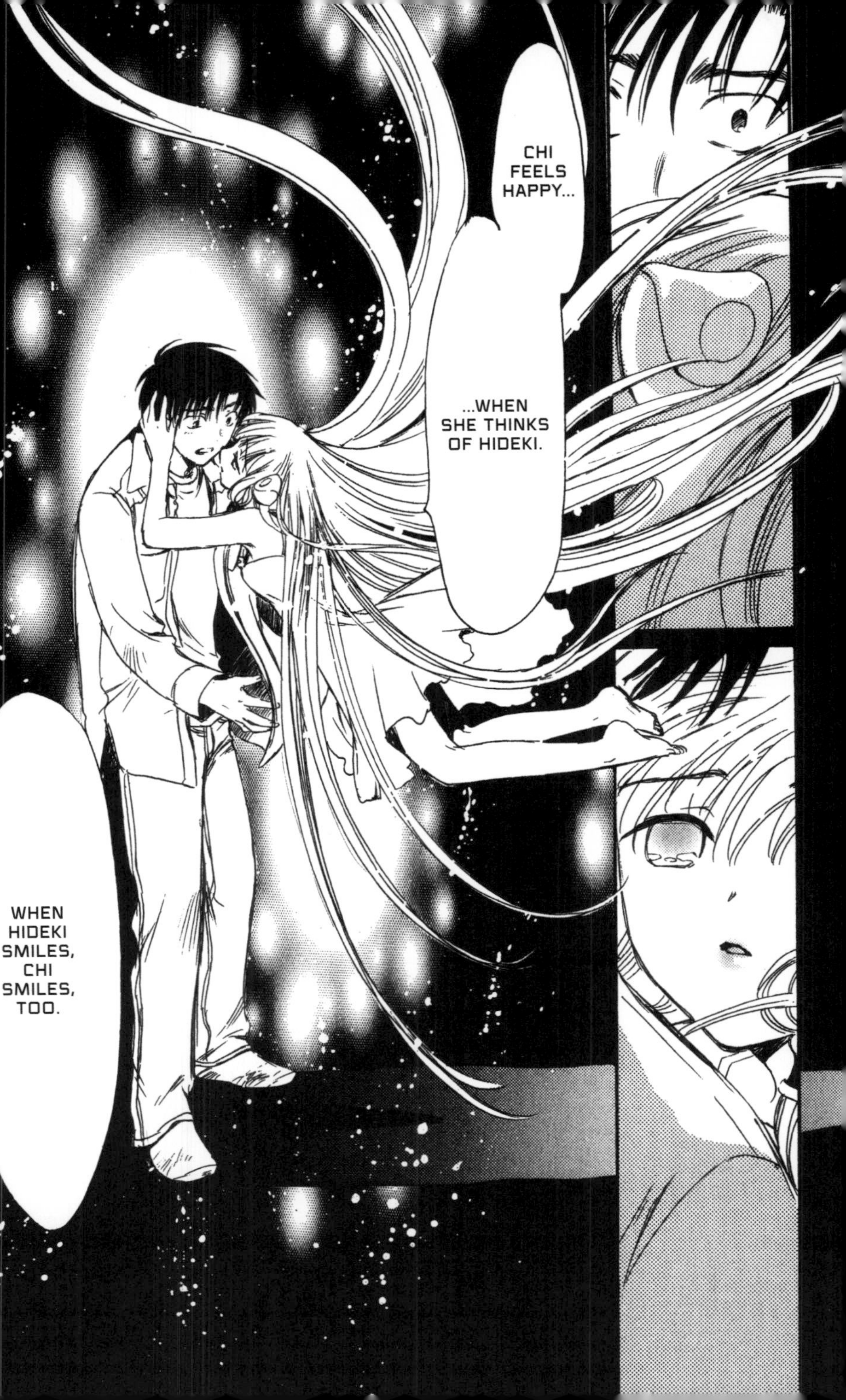
CHI FEELS HAPPY...
...WHEN SHE THINKS OF HIDEKI.
WHEN HIDEKI SMILES, CHI SMILES, TOO.

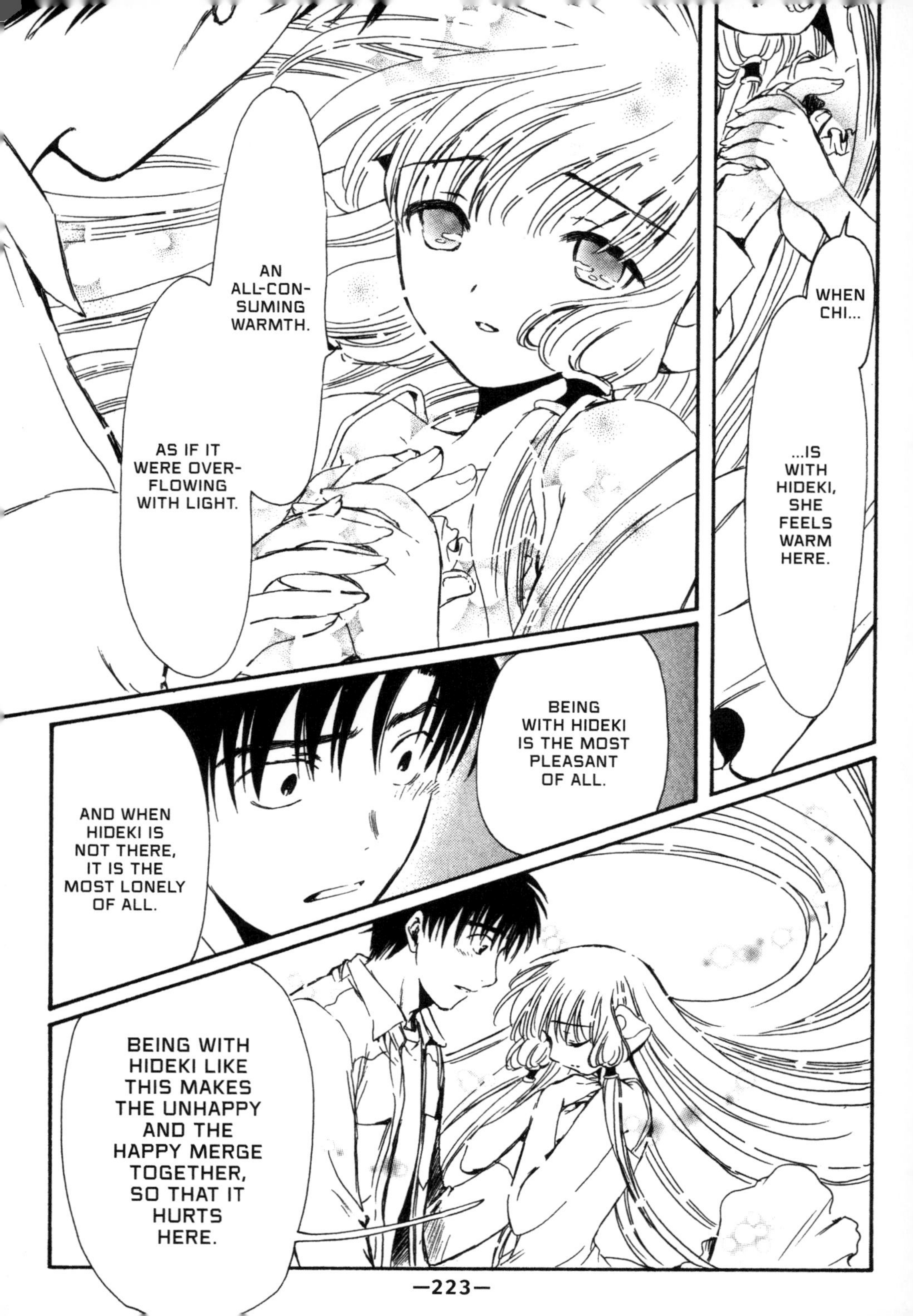
WHEN CHI...
...IS WITH HIDEKI, SHE FEELS WARM HERE.
AN ALL-CON-SUMING WARMTH.
AS IF IT WERE OVER-FLOWING WITH LIGHT.
BEING WITH HIDEKI IS THE MOST PLEASANT OF ALL.
AND WHEN HIDEKI IS NOT THERE, IT IS THE MOST LONELY OF ALL.
BEING WITH HIDEKI LIKE THIS MAKES THE UNHAPPY AND THE HAPPY MERGE TOGETHER, SO THAT IT HURTS HERE.

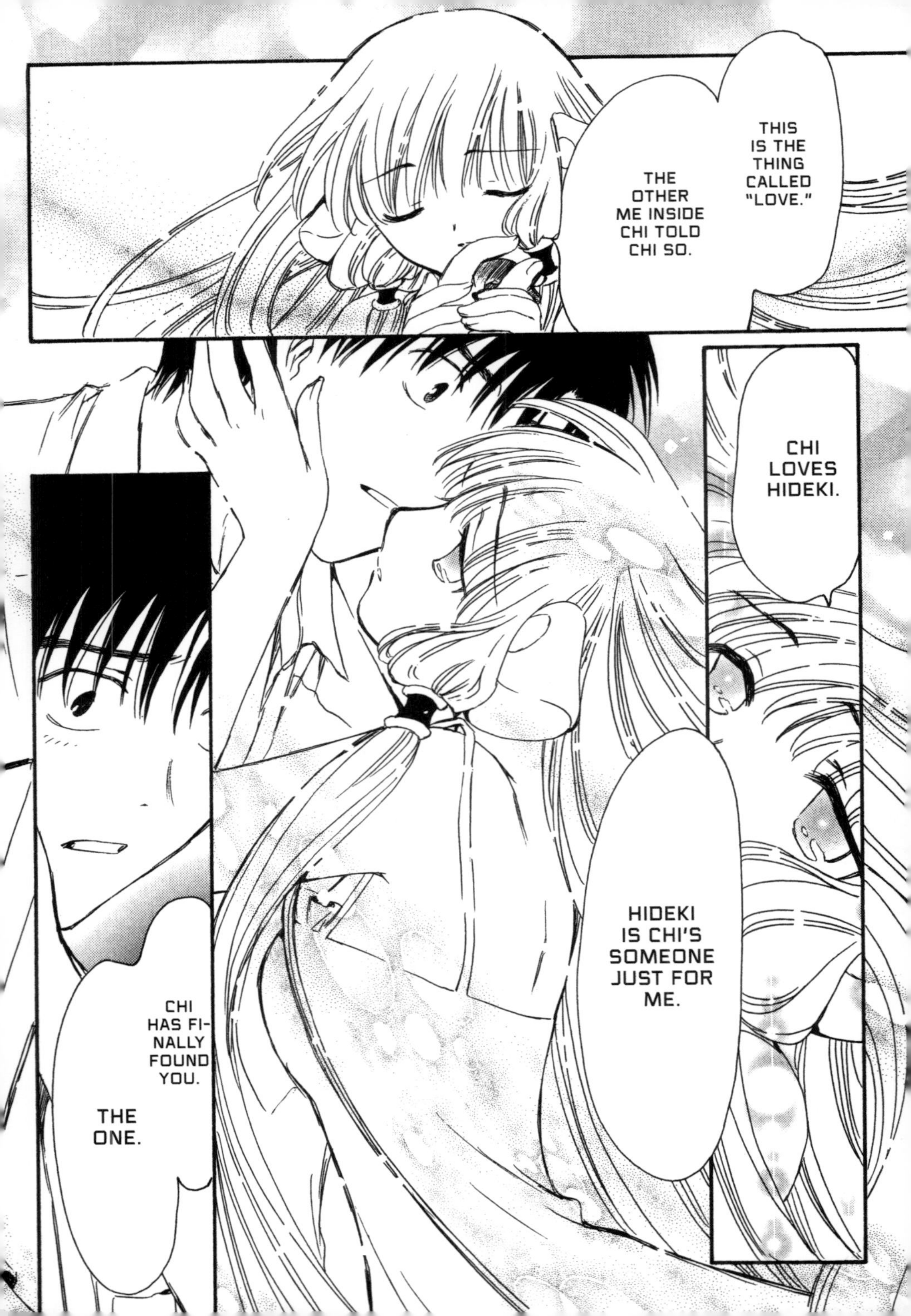
THIS IS THE THING CALLED "LOVE."
THE OTHER ME INSIDE CHI TOLD CHI SO.
CHI LOVES HIDEKI.
HIDEKI IS CHI'S SOMEONE JUST FOR ME.
CHI HAS FINALLY FOUND YOU.
THE ONE.

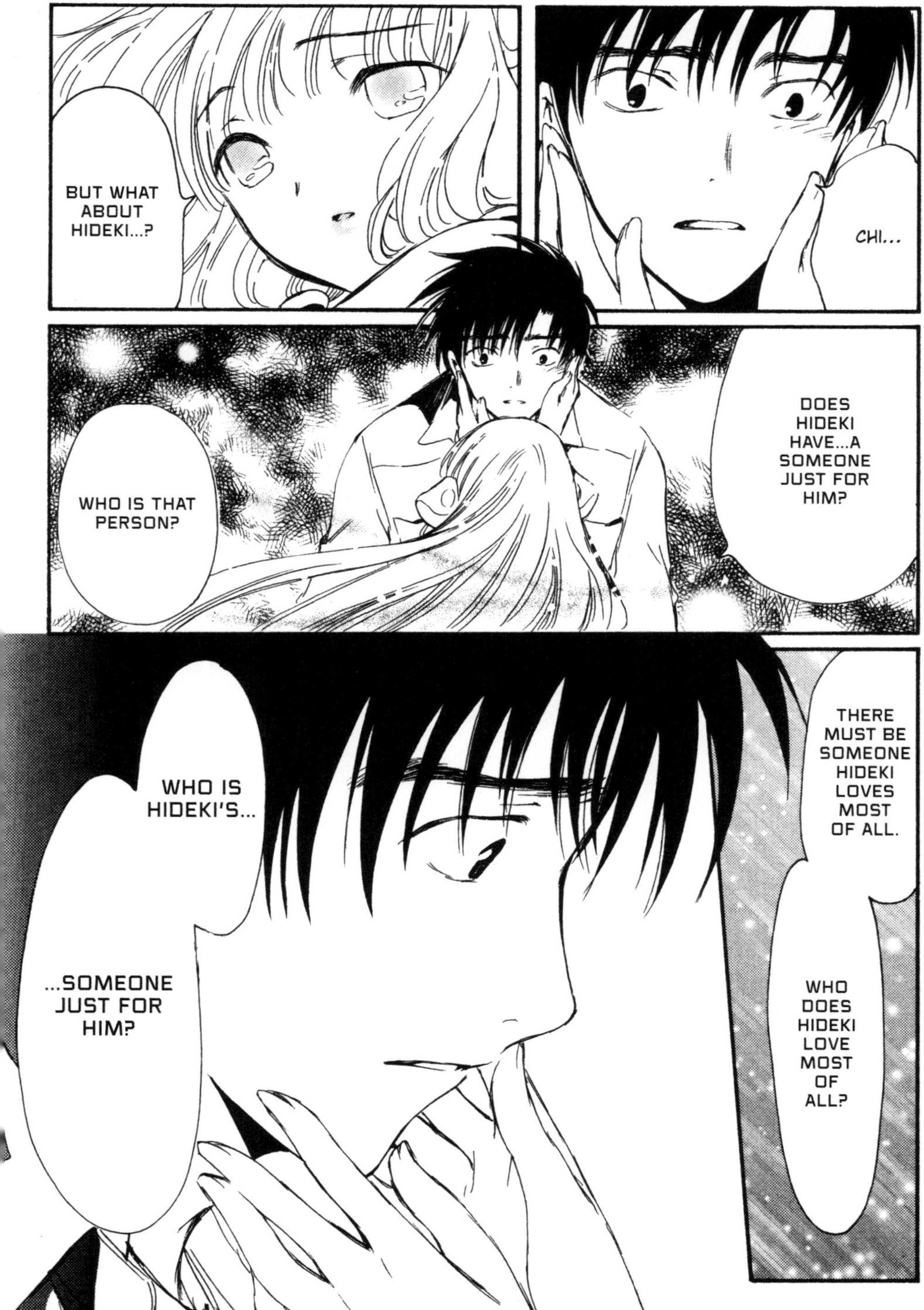
CHI...
BUT WHAT ABOUT HIDEKI...?
DOES HIDEKI HAVE...A SOMEONE JUST FOR HIM?
WHO IS THAT PERSON?
THERE MUST BE SOMEONE HIDEKI LOVES MOST OF ALL.
WHO IS HIDEKI'S...
WHO DOES HIDEKI LOVE MOST OF ALL?
...SOMEONE JUST FOR HIM?

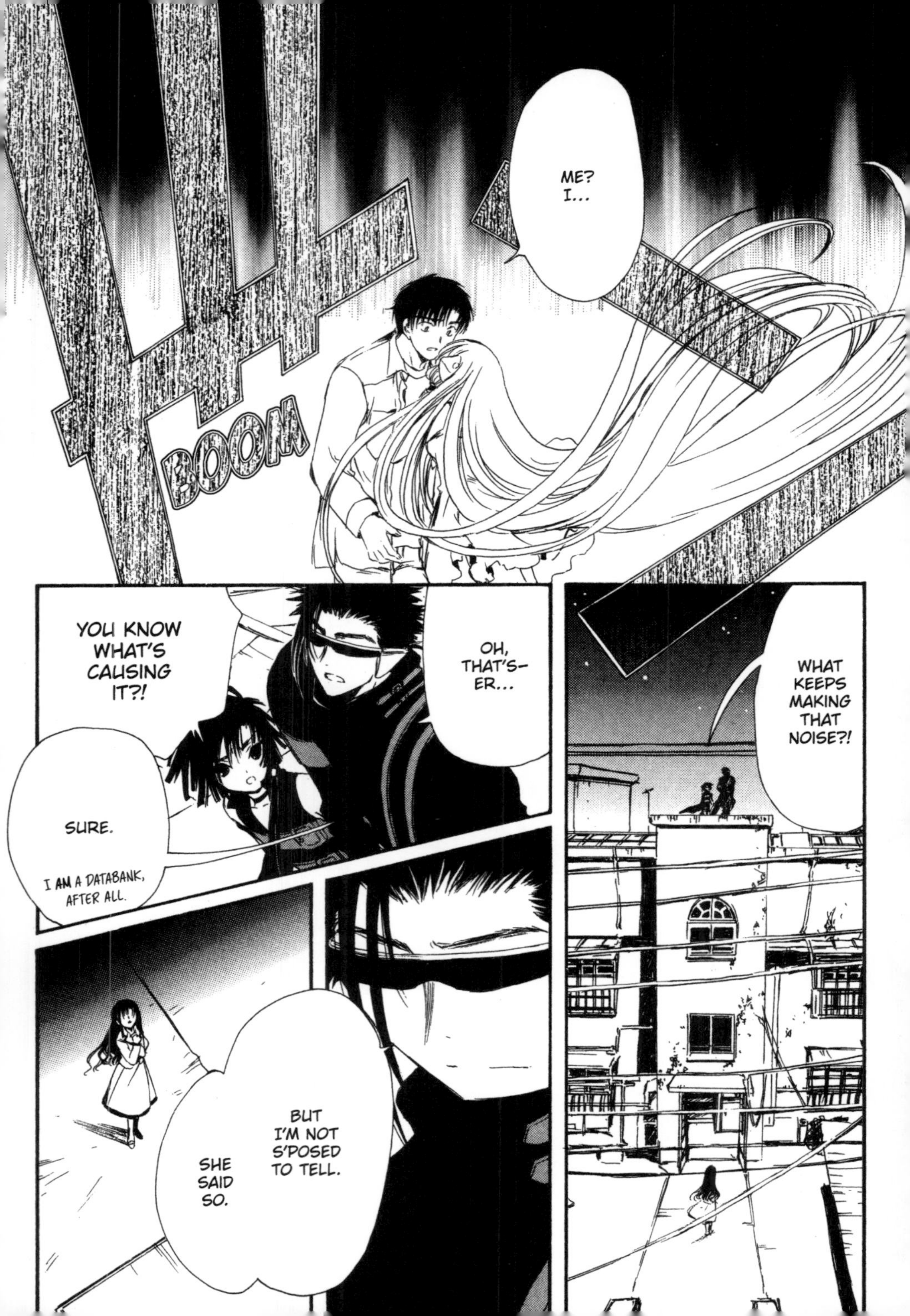
ME? I...
BOOM
WHAT KEEPS MAKING THAT NOISE?!
OH, THAT'S— ER...
YOU KNOW WHAT'S CAUSING IT?!
SURE.
I AM A DATABANK, AFTER ALL.
BUT I'M NOT S'POSED TO TELL.
SHE SAID SO.

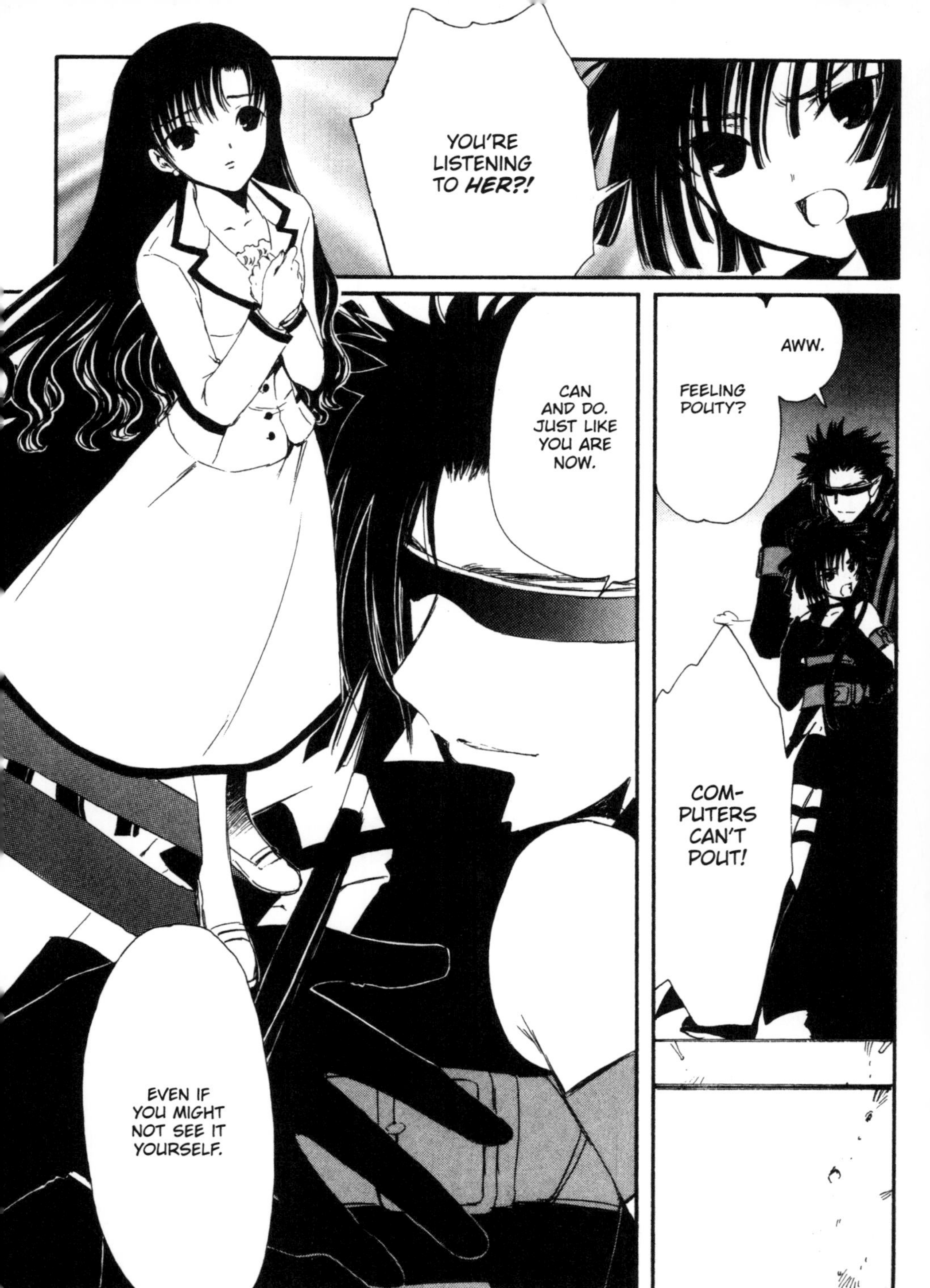
YOU'RE LISTENING TO *HER?!*
AWW.
FEELING POUTY?
COM-PUTERS CAN'T POUT!
CAN AND DO. JUST LIKE YOU ARE NOW.
EVEN IF YOU MIGHT NOT SEE IT YOURSELF.

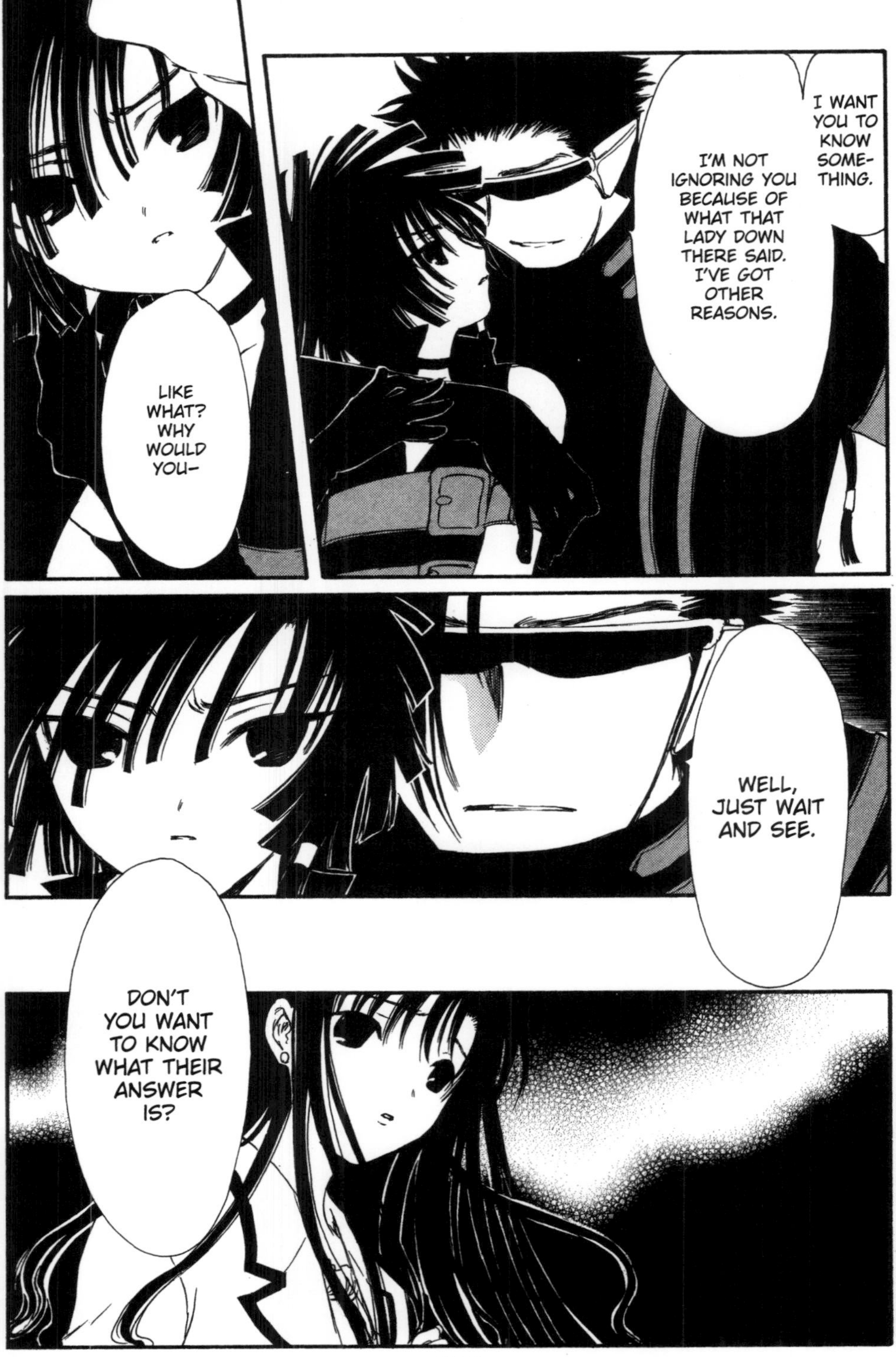
I WANT YOU TO KNOW SOME-THING.
I'M NOT IGNORING YOU BECAUSE OF WHAT THAT LADY DOWN THERE SAID. I'VE GOT OTHER REASONS.
LIKE WHAT? WHY WOULD YOU-
WELL, JUST WAIT AND SEE.
DON'T YOU WANT TO KNOW WHAT THEIR ANSWER IS?

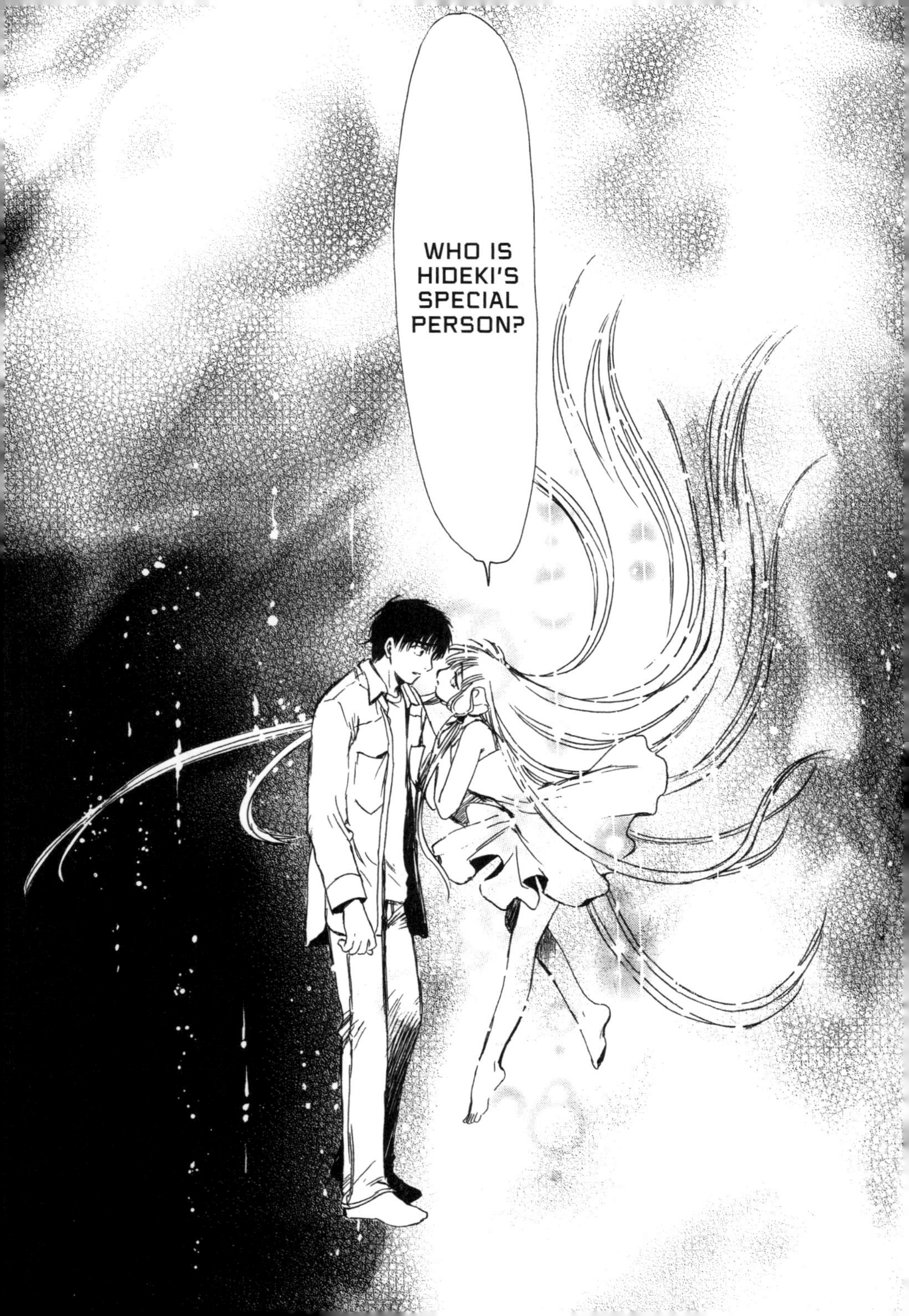
WHO IS HIDEKI'S SPECIAL PERSON?

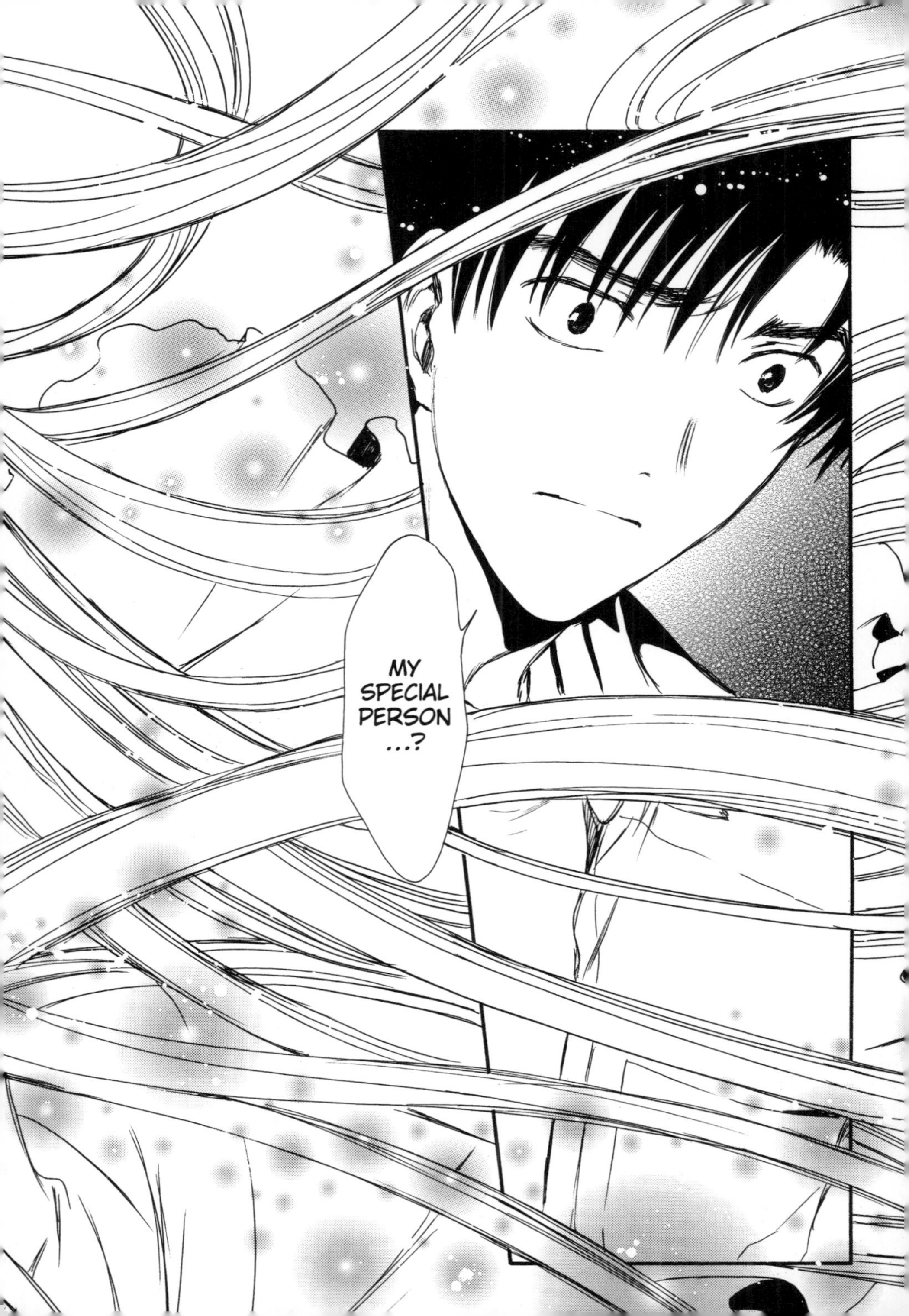
MY SPECIAL PERSON ...?

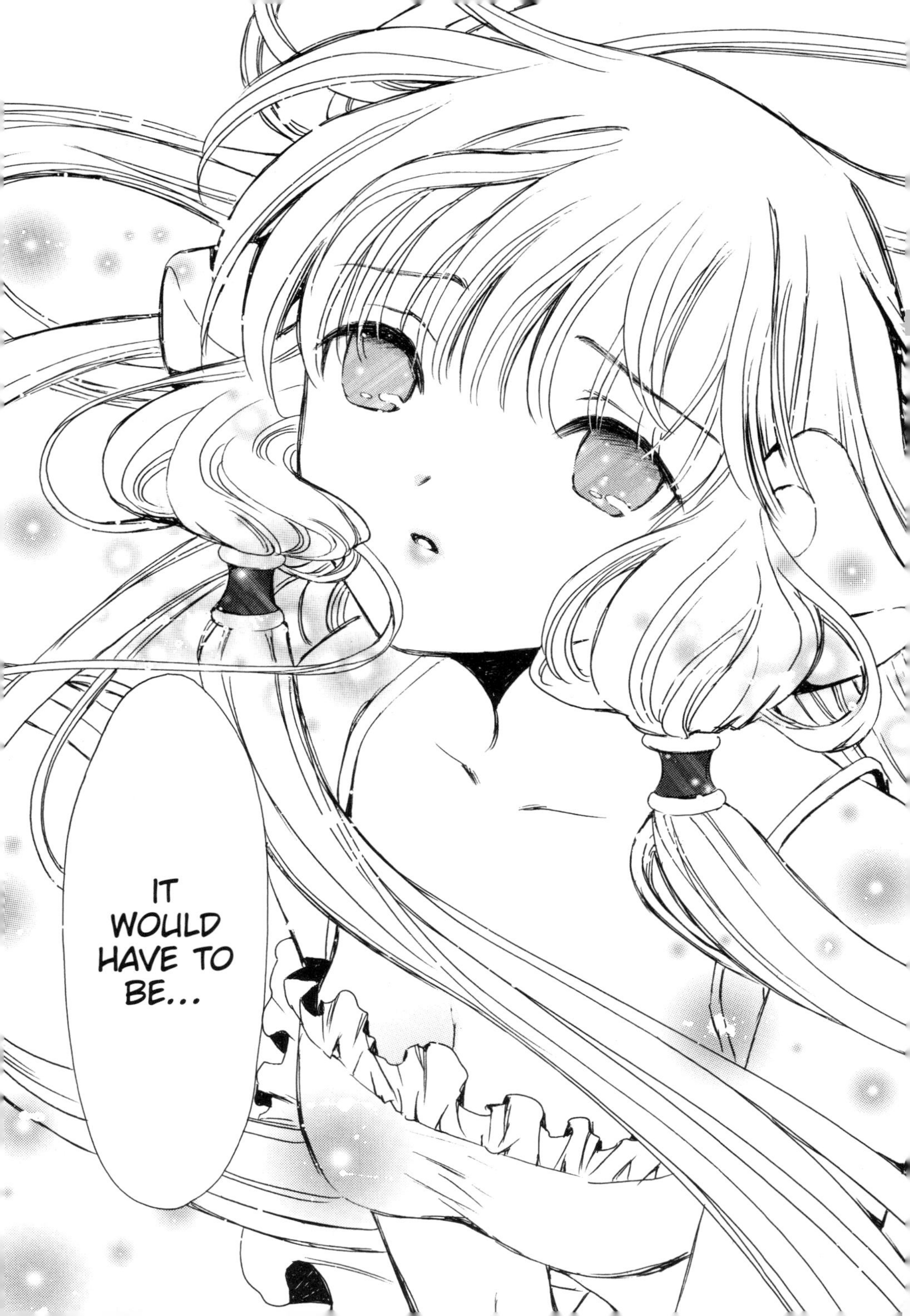
IT WOULD HAVE TO BE...

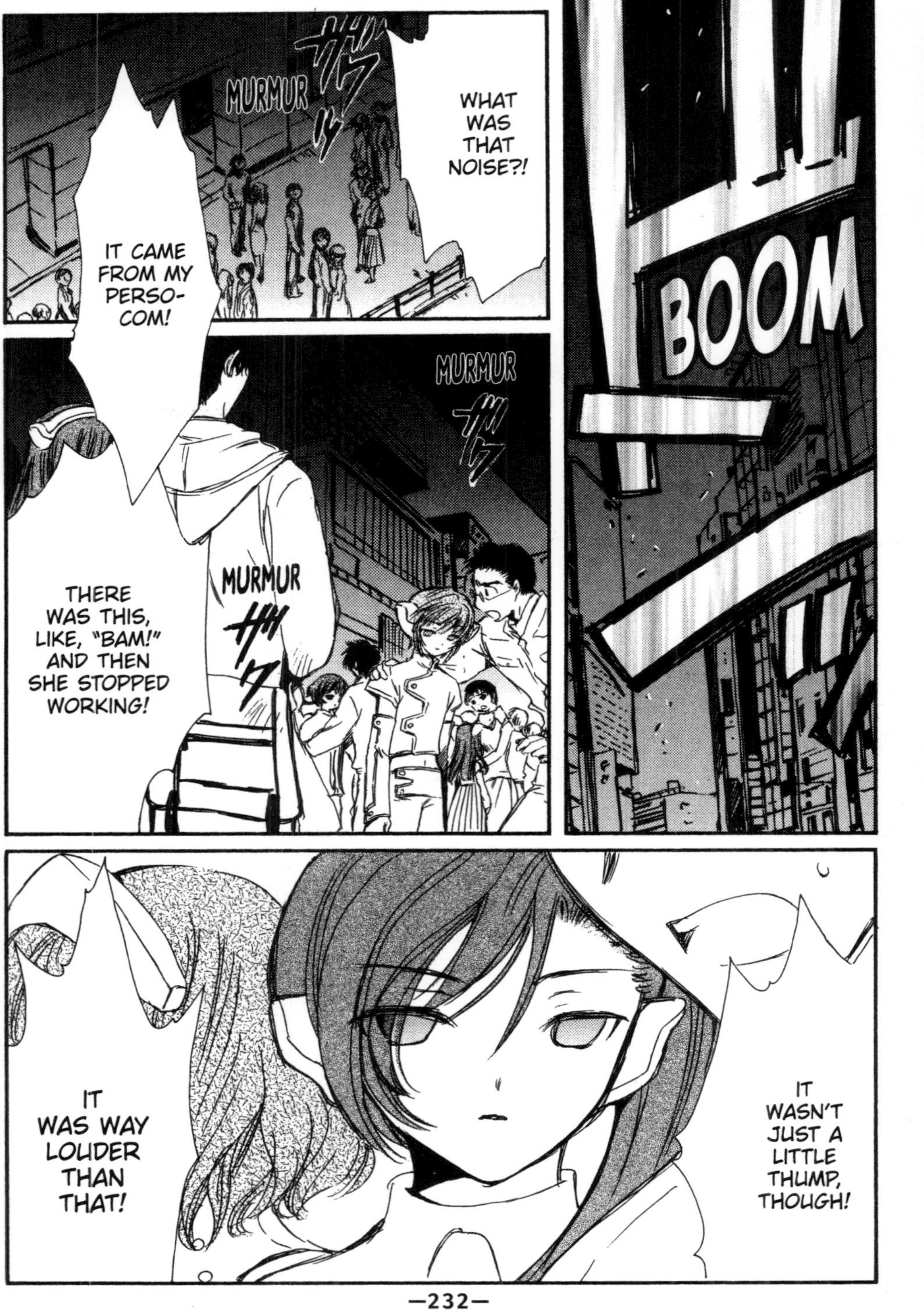
BOOM
MURMUR
WHAT WAS THAT NOISE?!
IT CAME FROM MY PERSO-COM!
MURMUR
MURMUR
THERE WAS THIS, LIKE, "BAM!" AND THEN SHE STOPPED WORKING!
IT WASN'T JUST A LITTLE THUMP, THOUGH!
IT WAS WAY LOUDER THAN THAT!

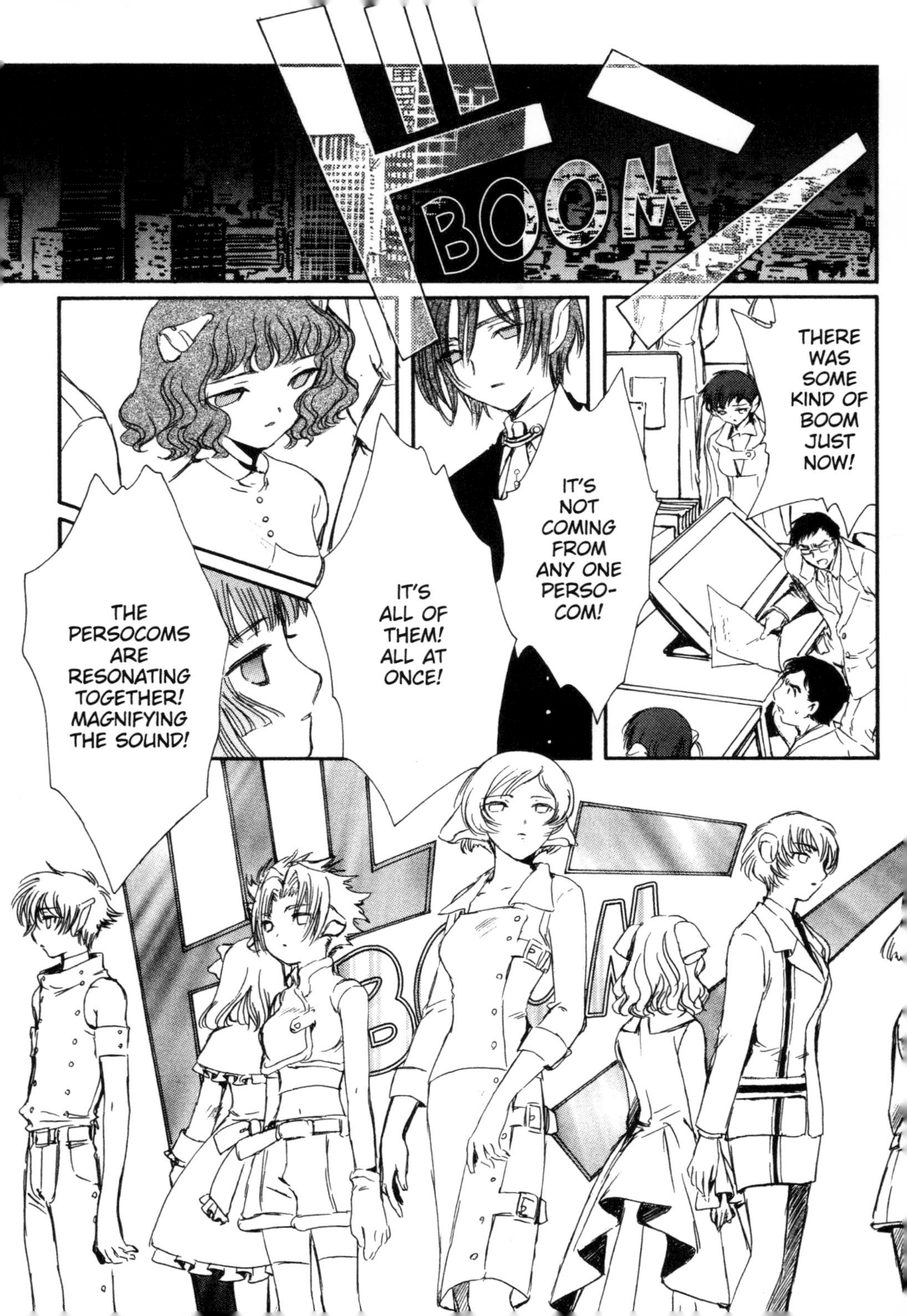
BOOM
THERE WAS SOME KIND OF BOOM JUST NOW!
IT'S NOT COMING FROM ANY ONE PERSO-COM!
IT'S ALL OF THEM! ALL AT ONCE!
THE PERSOCOMS ARE RESONATING TOGETHER! MAGNIFYING THE SOUND!

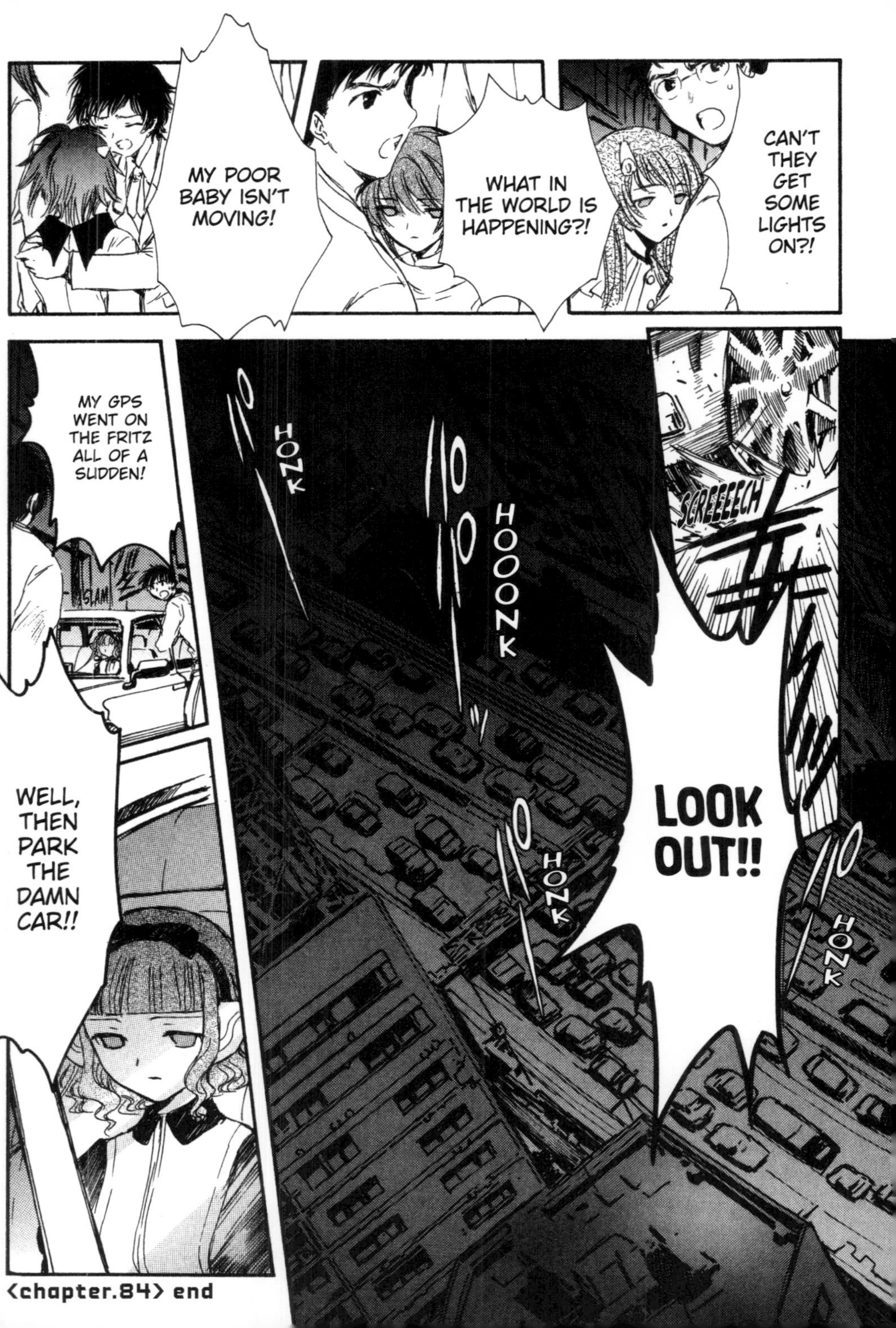
CAN'T THEY GET SOME LIGHTS ON?!
WHAT IN THE WORLD IS HAPPENING?!
MY POOR BABY ISN'T MOVING!
SCREEEEECH
HONK
HOOOONK
LOOK OUT!!
HONK
HONK
MY GPS WENT ON THE FRITZ ALL OF A SUDDEN!
SLAM
WELL, THEN PARK THE DAMN CAR!!

<chapter.84> end

Chobits

〈chapter.85〉

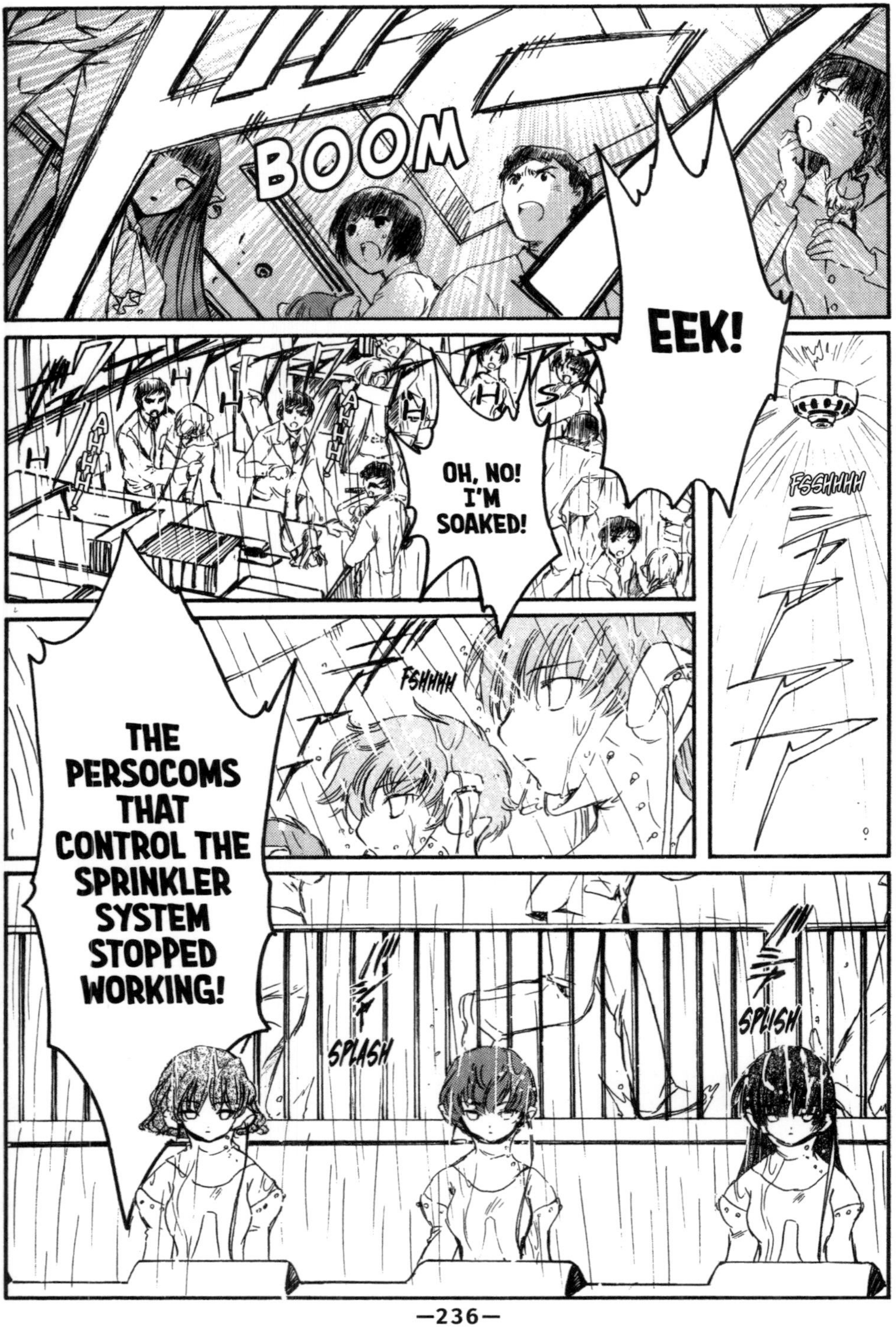
BOOM
EEK!
FSSHHHH
OH, NO! I'M SOAKED!
FSHHHH
THE PERSOCOMS THAT CONTROL THE SPRINKLER SYSTEM STOPPED WORKING!
SPLISH
SPLASH

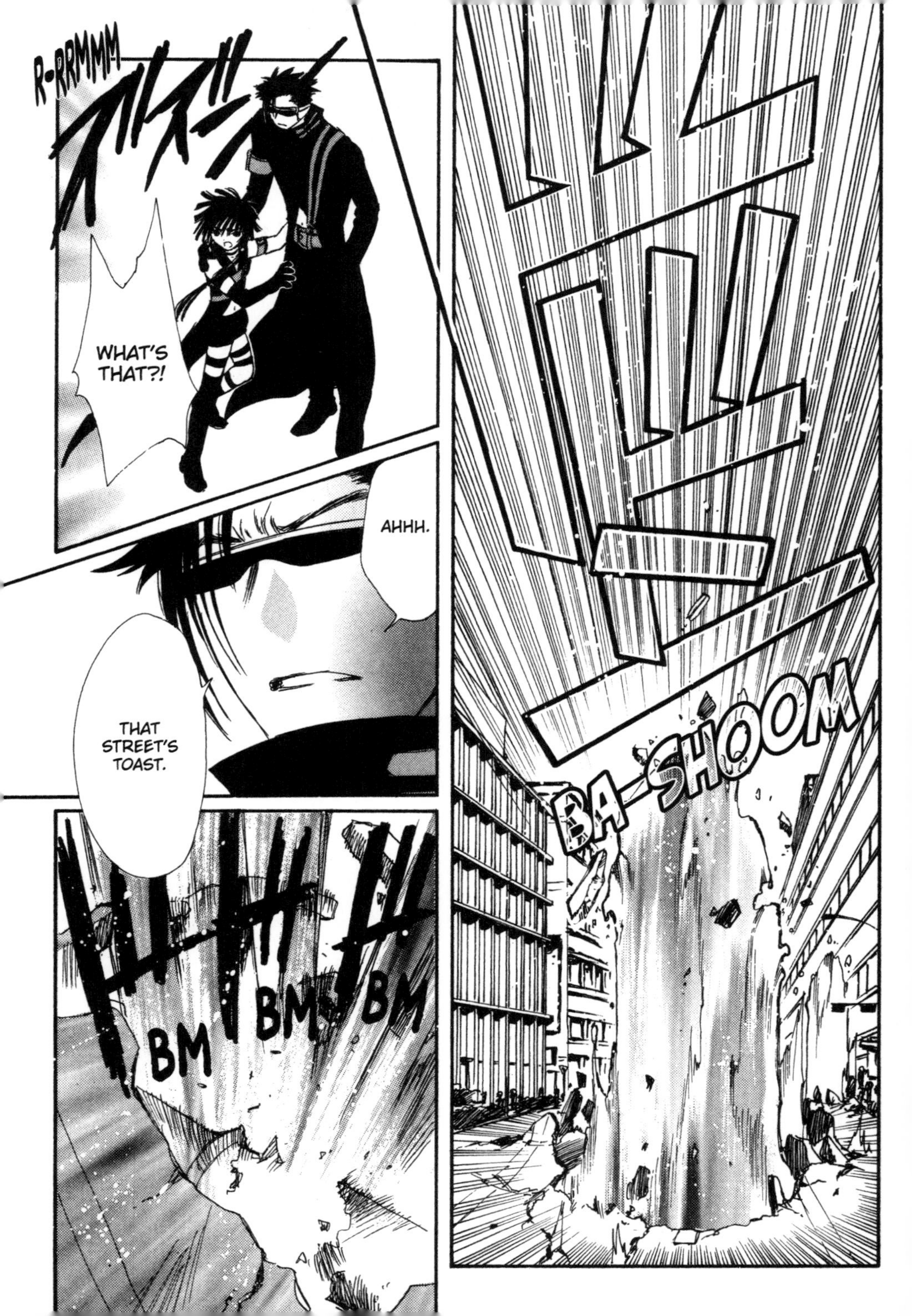
BA-SHOOM
R-RRMMM
WHAT'S THAT?!
AHHH.
THAT STREET'S TOAST.
BM BM BM

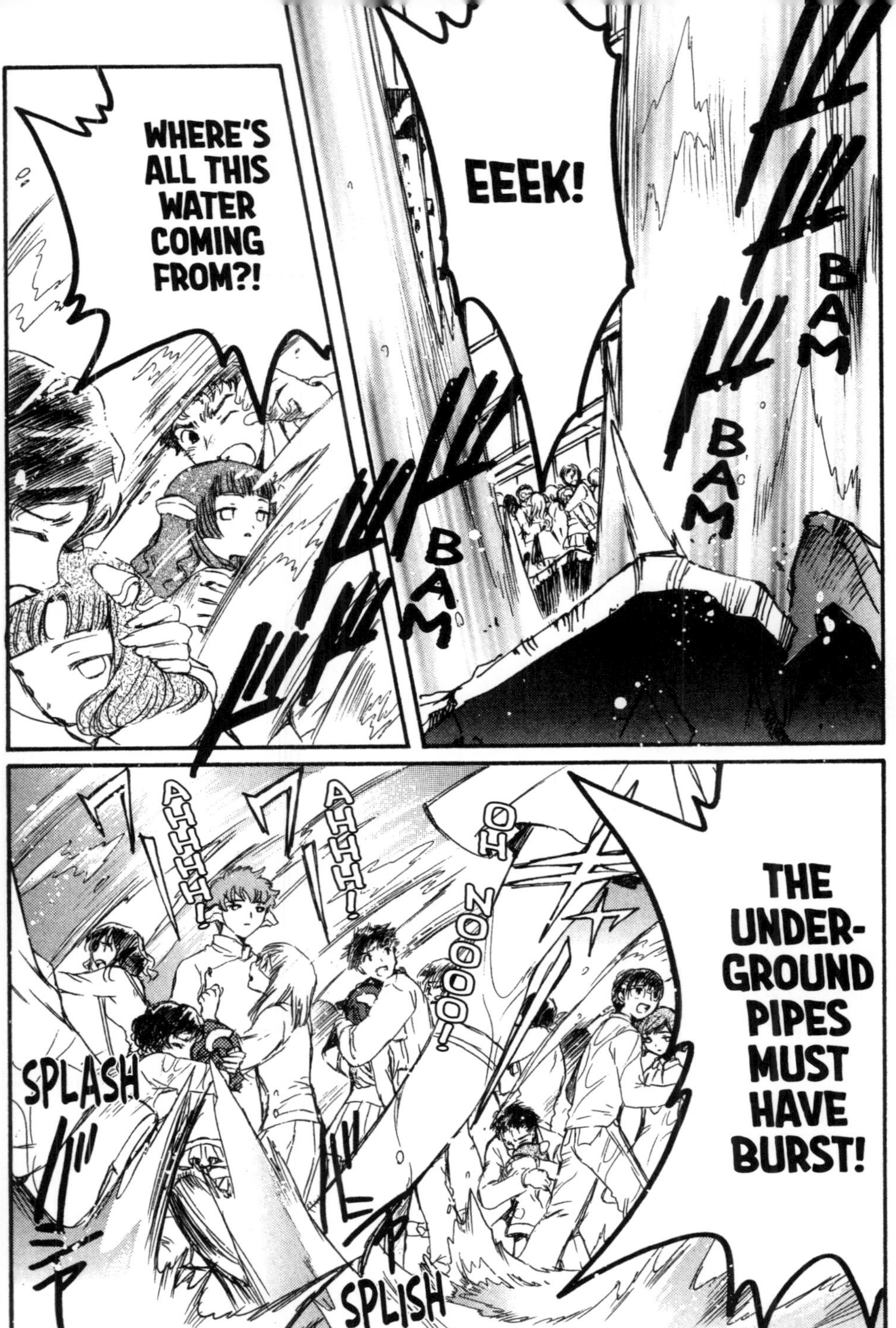

BAM
BAM
BAM
BAM
EEEK!
WHERE'S ALL THIS WATER COMING FROM?!
THE UNDER-GROUND PIPES MUST HAVE BURST!
OH NOOOOO!
AHHHH!
AHHHHH!
SPLASH
SPLISH

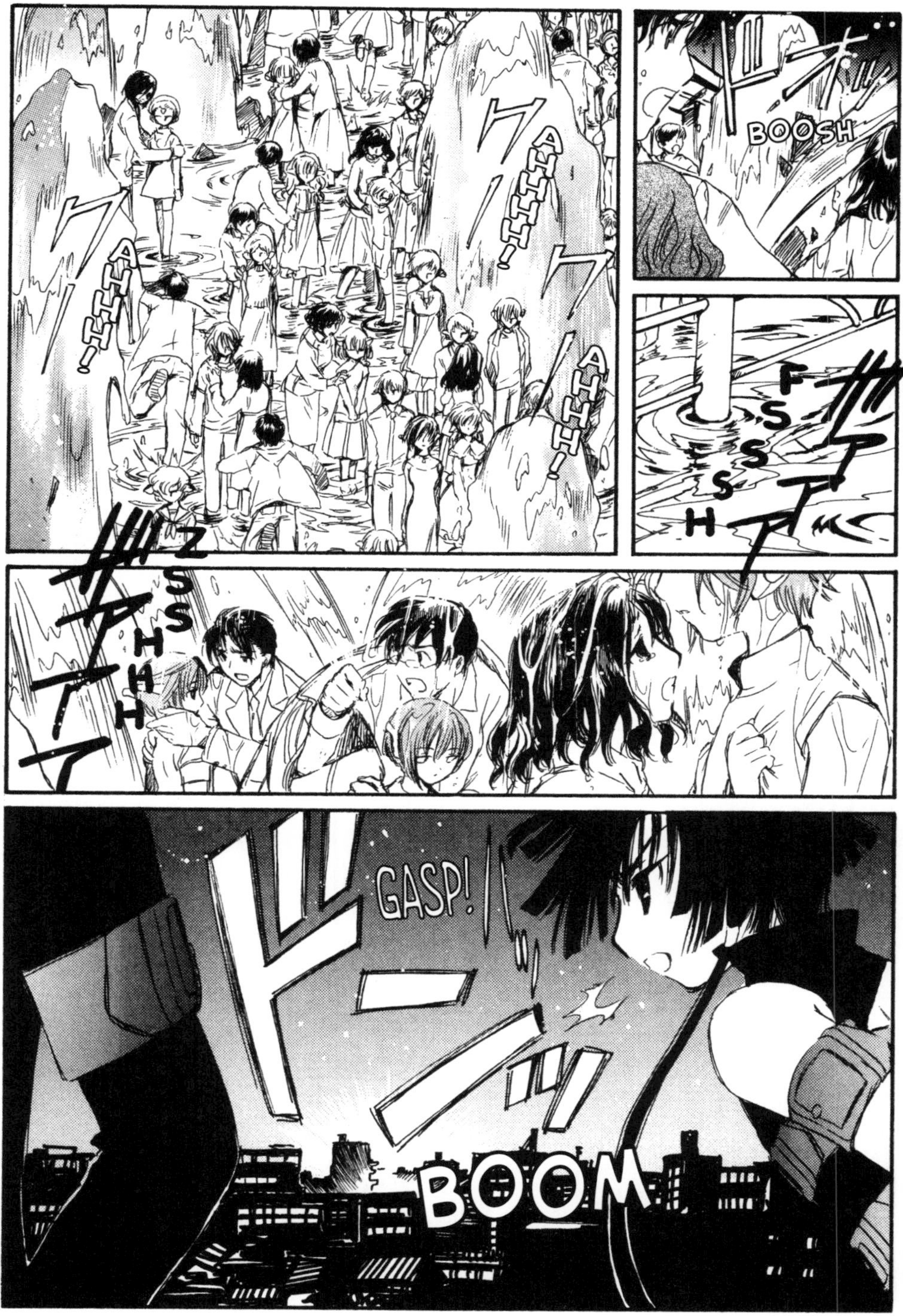
BOOSH
FSSSH
AHHHHHH!
AHHHH!
AHHHHH!
ZSSHHH
GASP!
BOOM

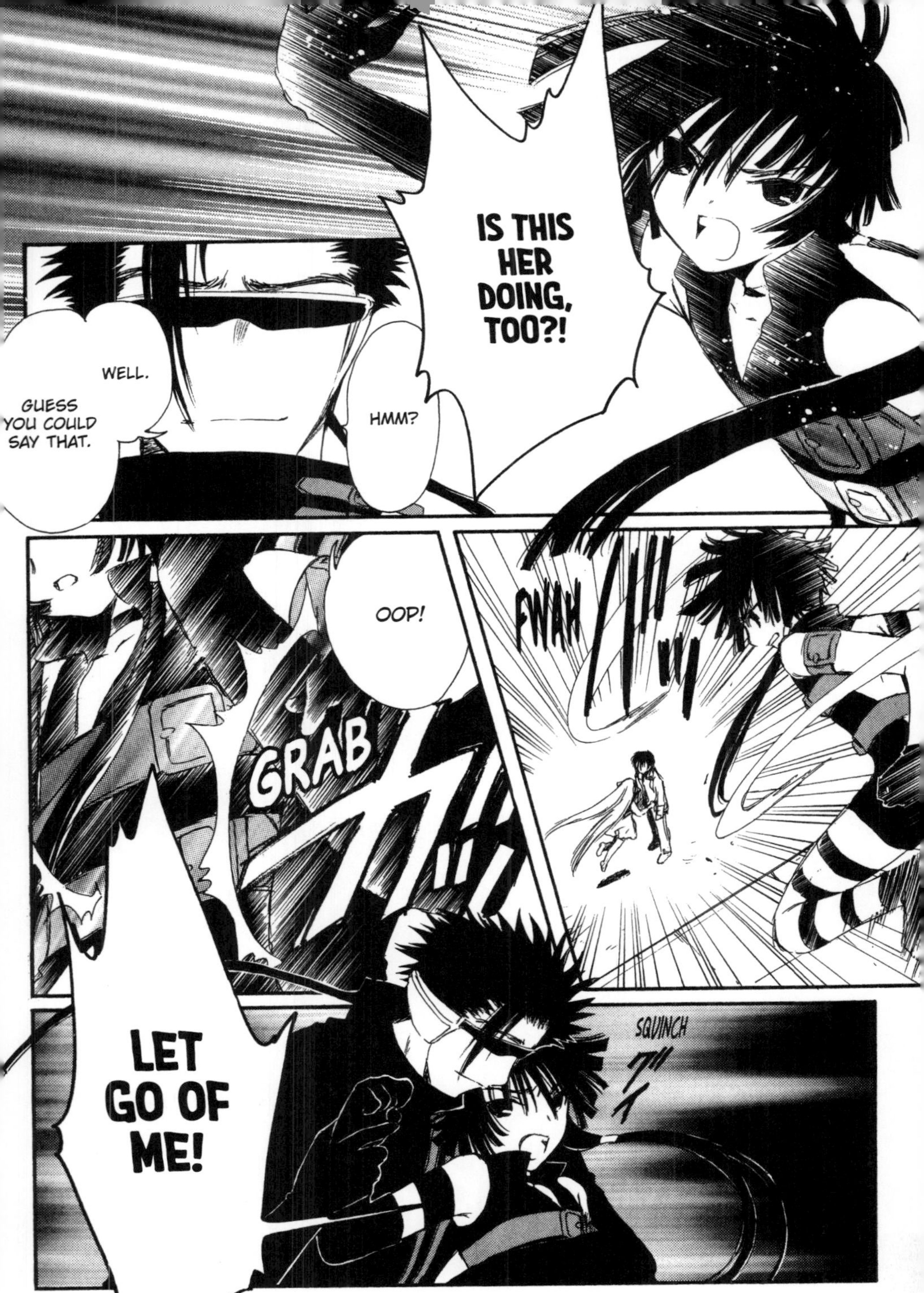
IS THIS HER DOING, TOO?!
HMM?
WELL.
GUESS YOU COULD SAY THAT.
FWAH
OOP!
GRAB
SQUINCH
LET GO OF ME!

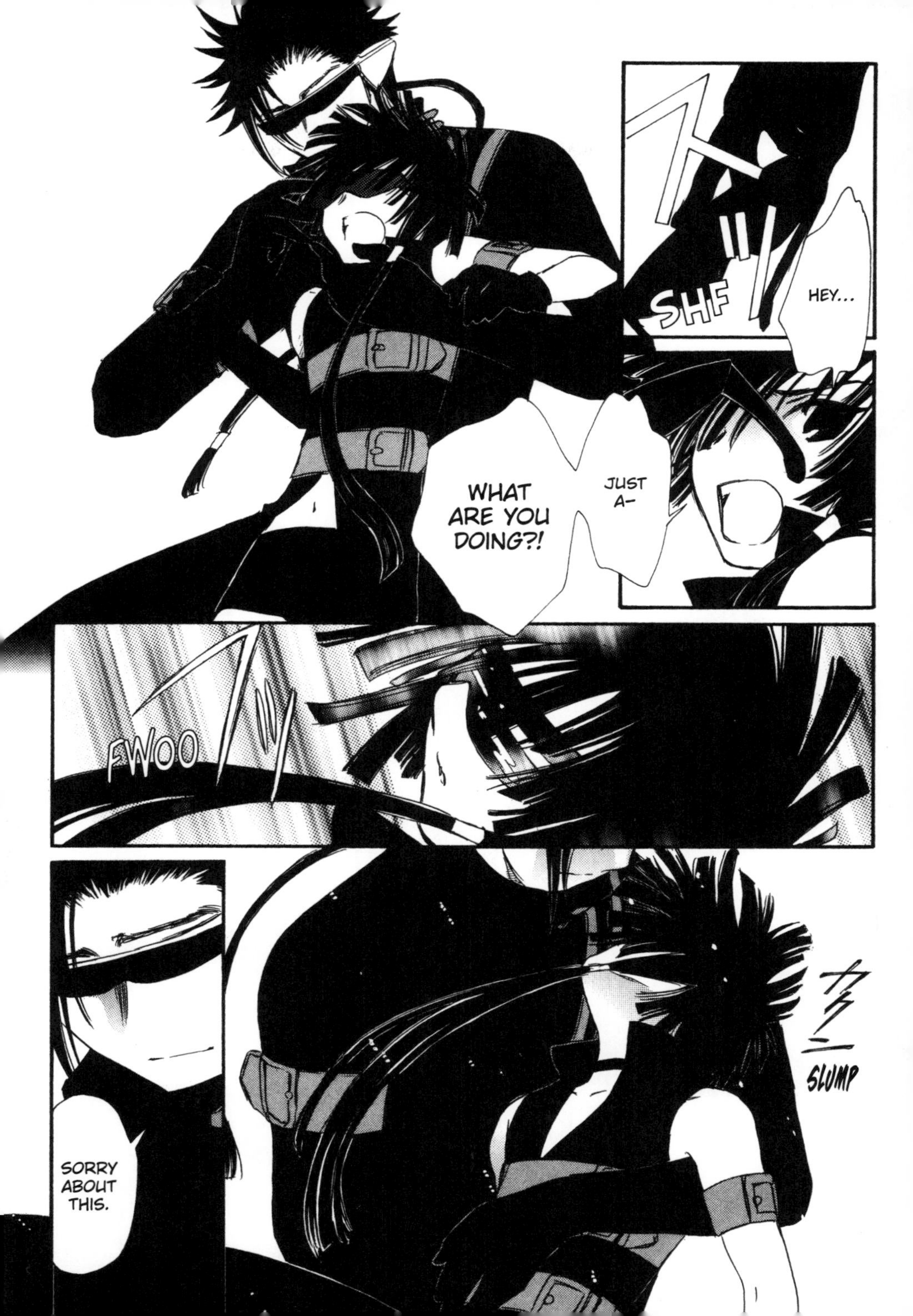
SHF
HEY...
JUST A-
WHAT ARE YOU DOING?!
FWOO
SLUMP
SORRY ABOUT THIS.

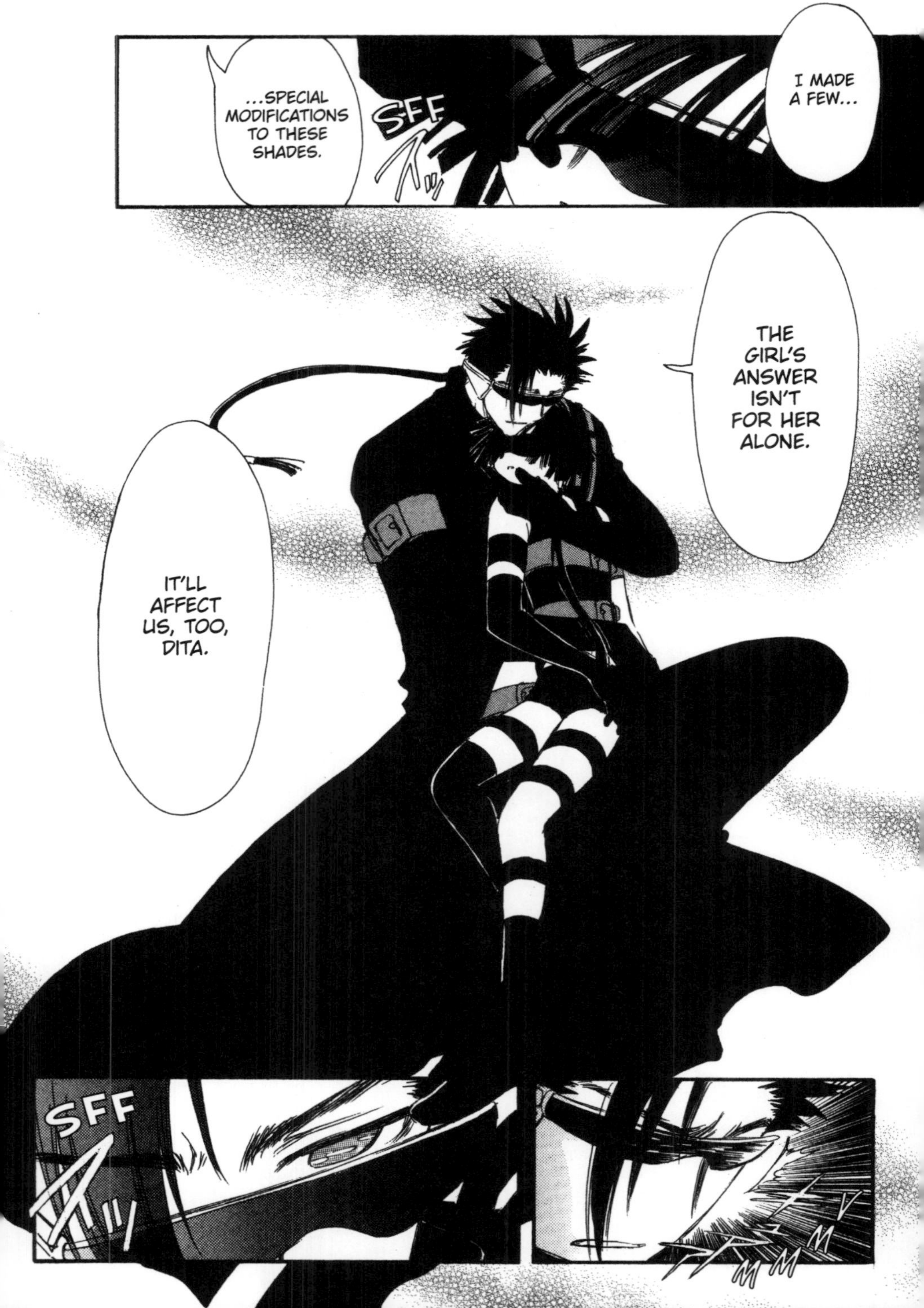
I MADE A FEW...
...SPECIAL MODIFICATIONS TO THESE SHADES.
SFF
THE GIRL'S ANSWER ISN'T FOR HER ALONE.
IT'LL AFFECT US, TOO, DITA.
SFF

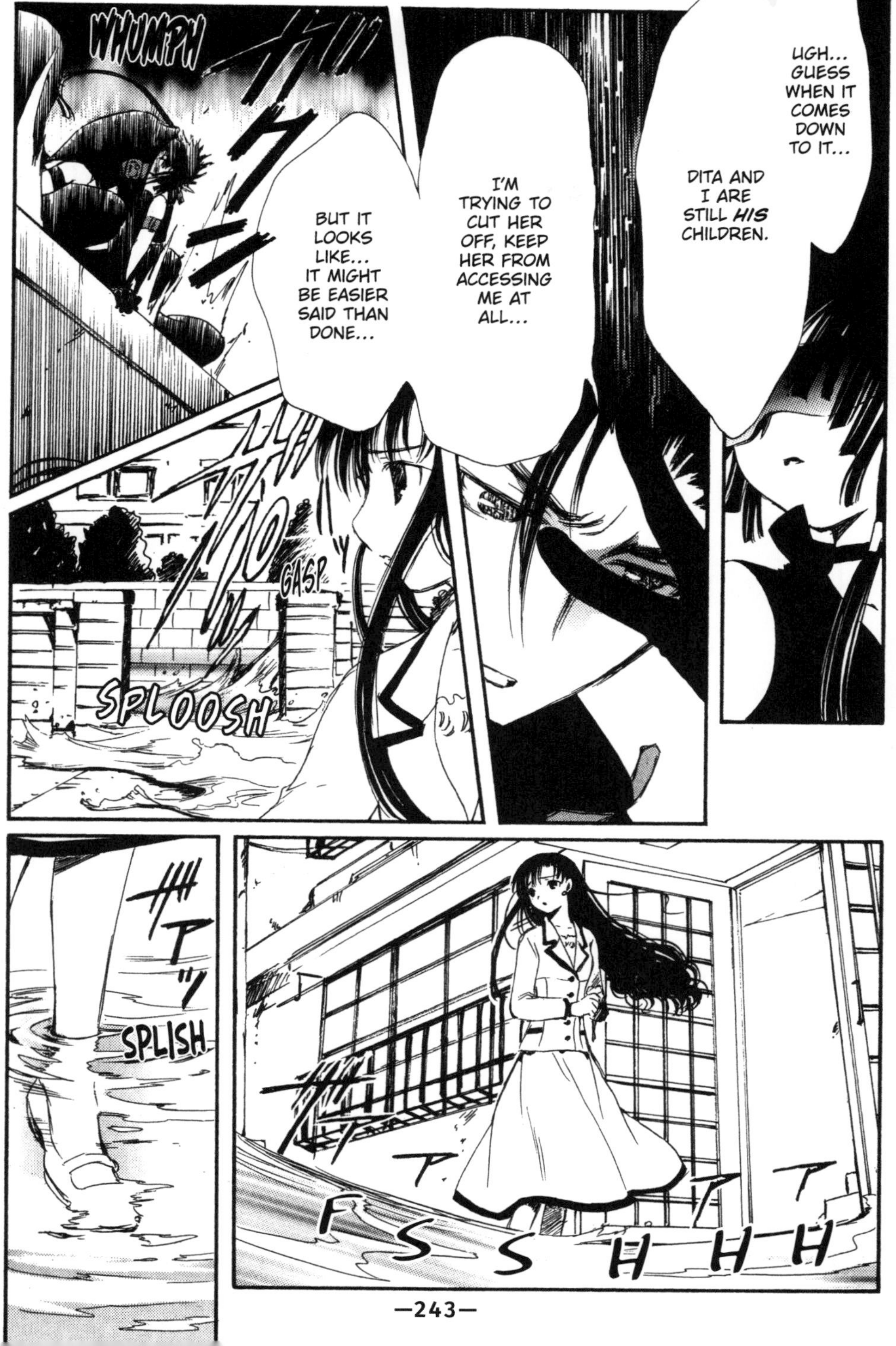
UGH... GUESS WHEN IT COMES DOWN TO IT...
DITA AND I ARE STILL *HIS* CHILDREN.
I'M TRYING TO CUT HER OFF, KEEP HER FROM ACCESSING ME AT ALL...
BUT IT LOOKS LIKE... IT MIGHT BE EASIER SAID THAN DONE...
WHUMPH
GASP
SPLOOSH
FSSHHH
SPLISH

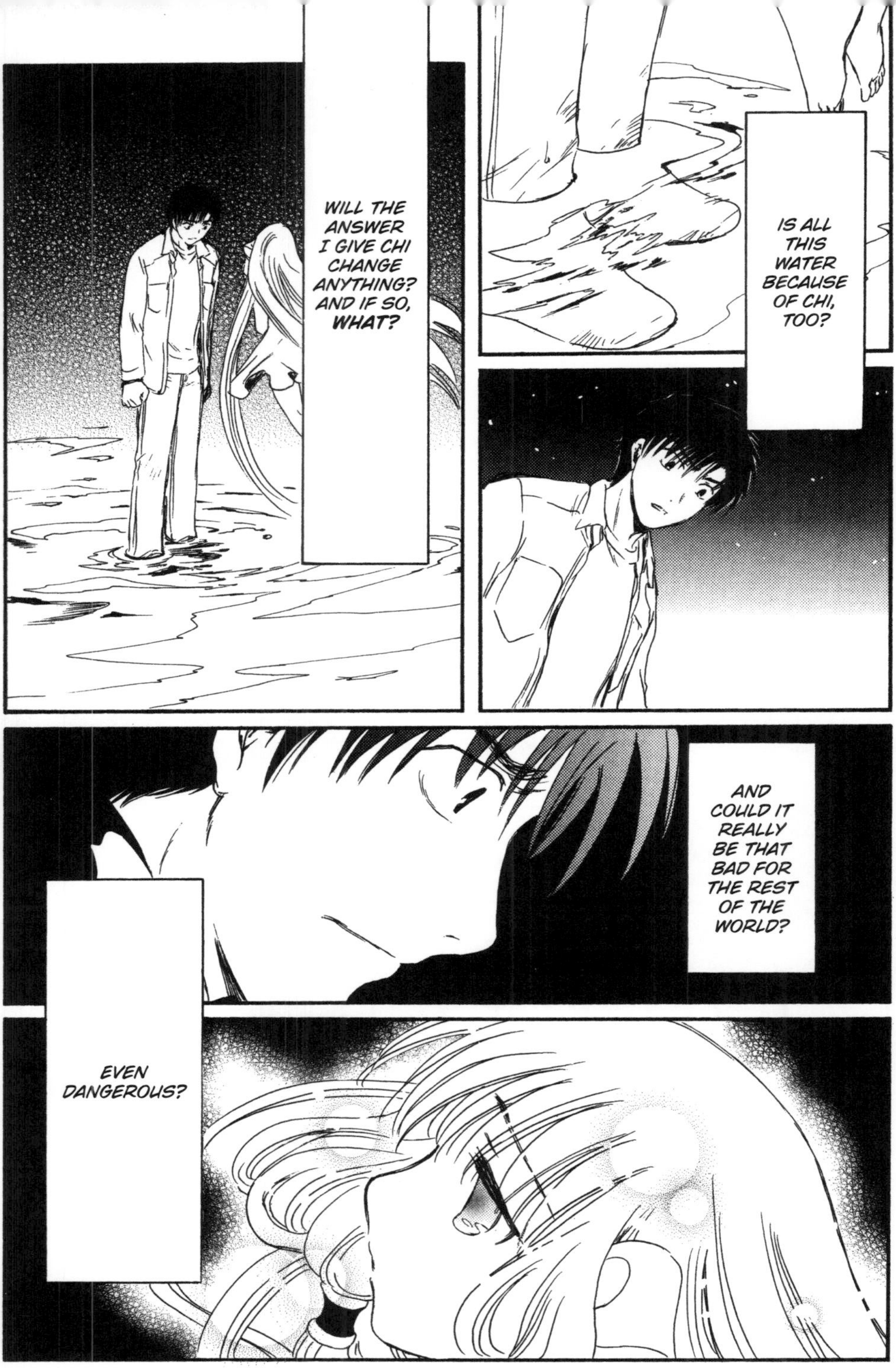
IS ALL THIS WATER BECAUSE OF CHI, TOO?
WILL THE ANSWER I GIVE CHI CHANGE ANYTHING? AND IF SO, WHAT?
AND COULD IT REALLY BE THAT BAD FOR THE REST OF THE WORLD?
EVEN DANGEROUS?

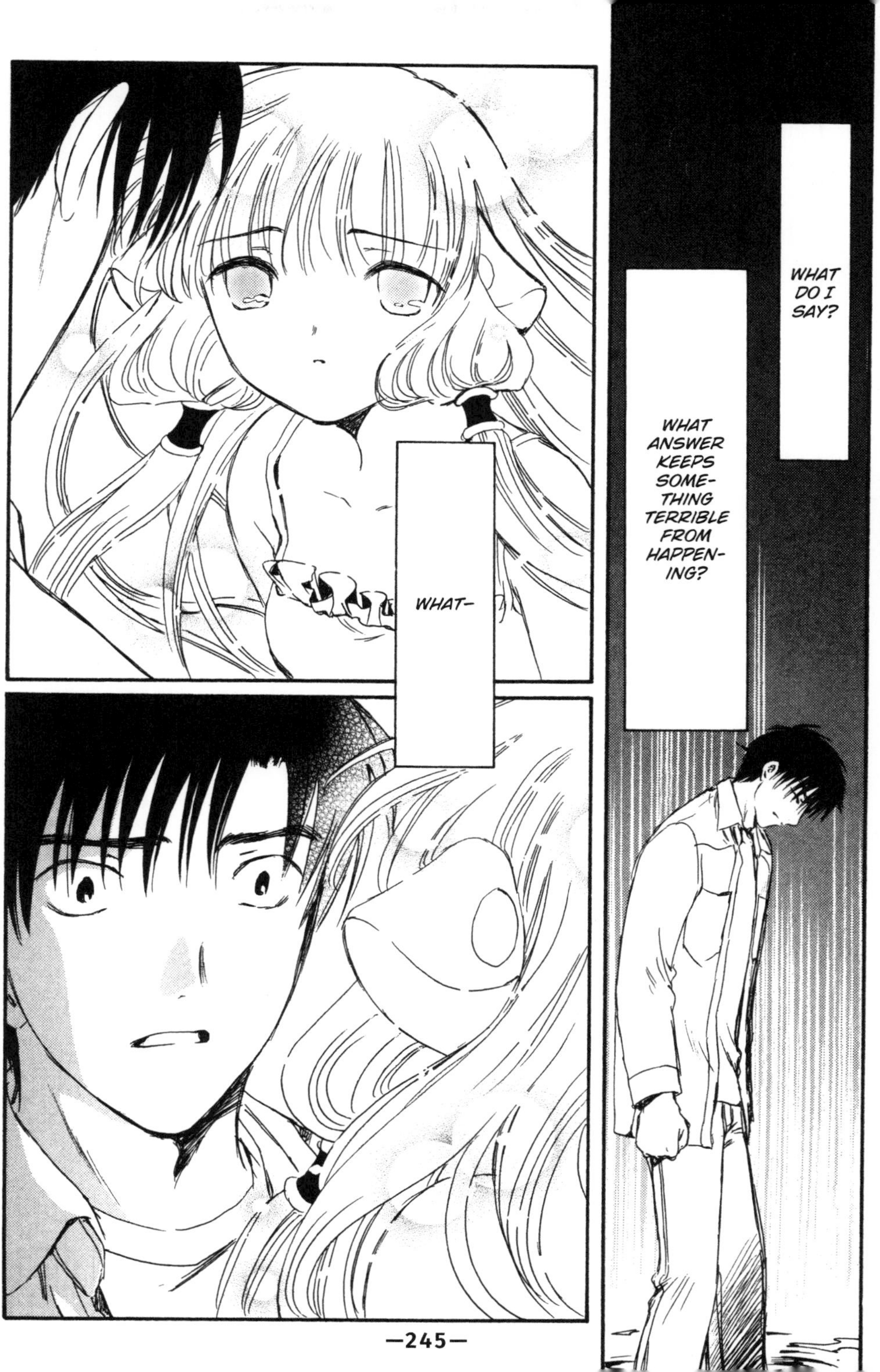
WHAT DO I SAY?
WHAT ANSWER KEEPS SOME-THING TERRIBLE FROM HAPPEN-ING?
WHAT-

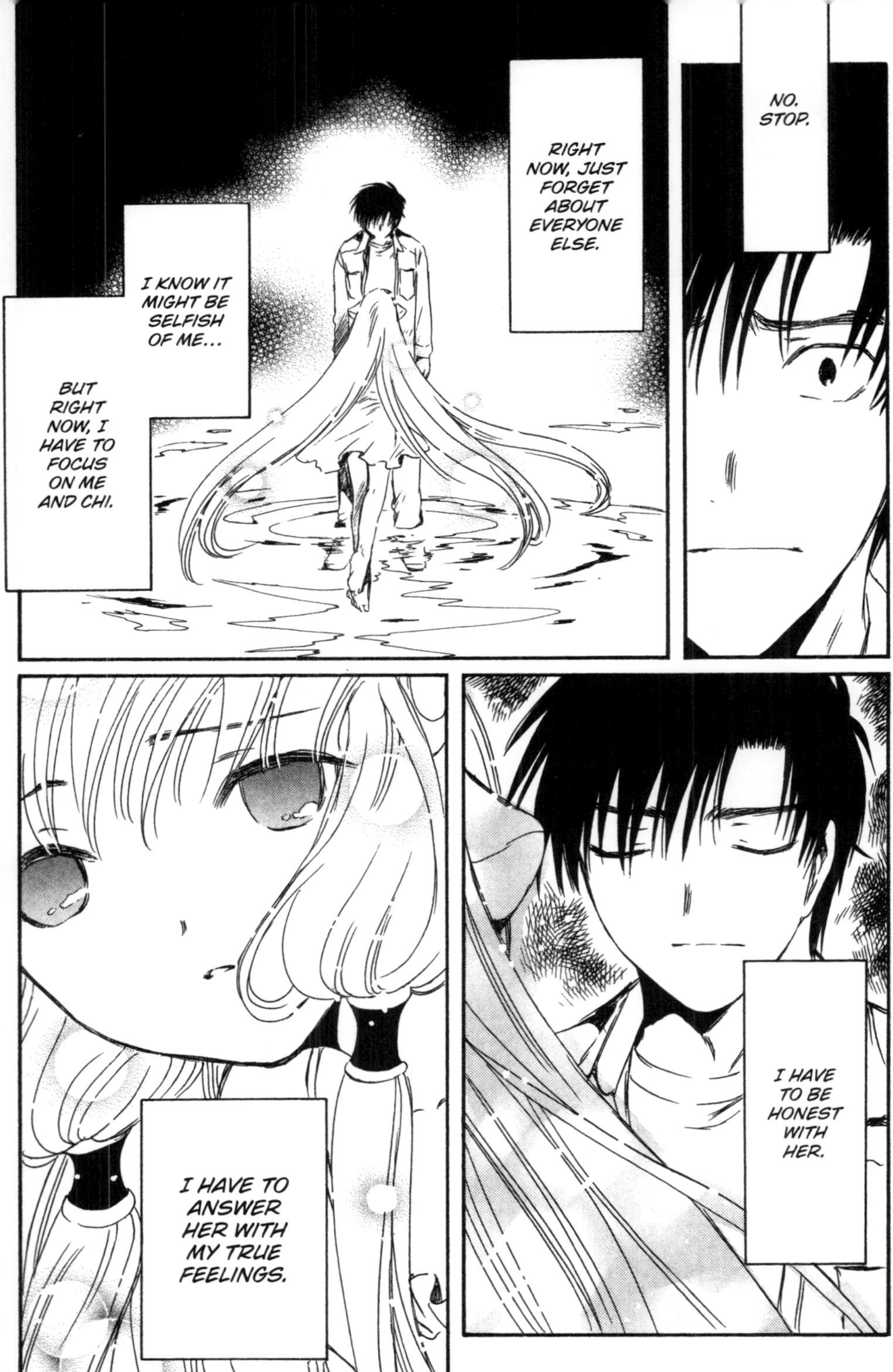
NO. STOP.
RIGHT NOW, JUST FORGET ABOUT EVERYONE ELSE.
I KNOW IT MIGHT BE SELFISH OF ME...
BUT RIGHT NOW, I HAVE TO FOCUS ON ME AND CHI.
I HAVE TO BE HONEST WITH HER.
I HAVE TO ANSWER HER WITH MY TRUE FEELINGS.

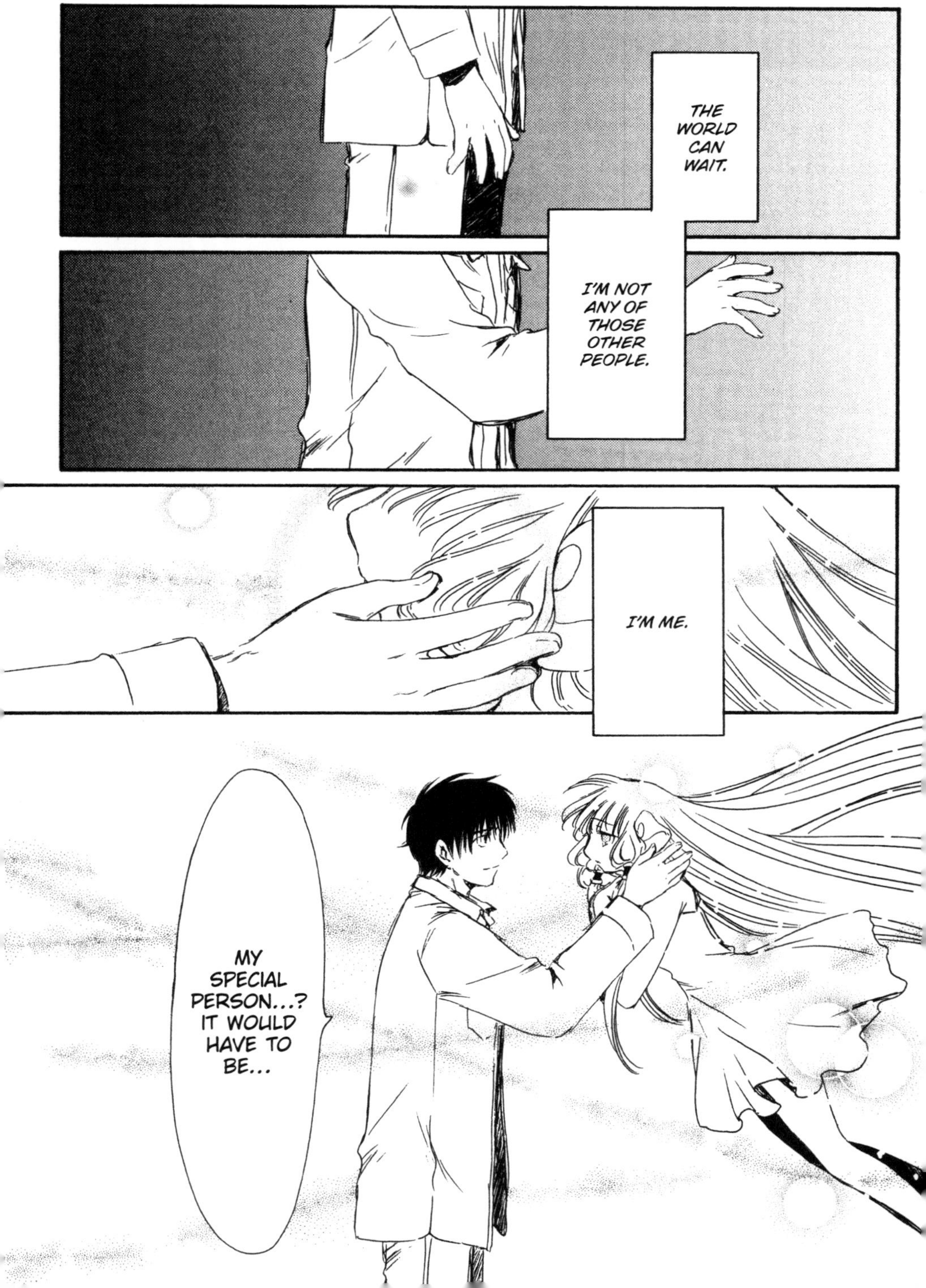
THE WORLD CAN WAIT.
I'M NOT ANY OF THOSE OTHER PEOPLE.
I'M ME.
MY SPECIAL PERSON...? IT WOULD HAVE TO BE...

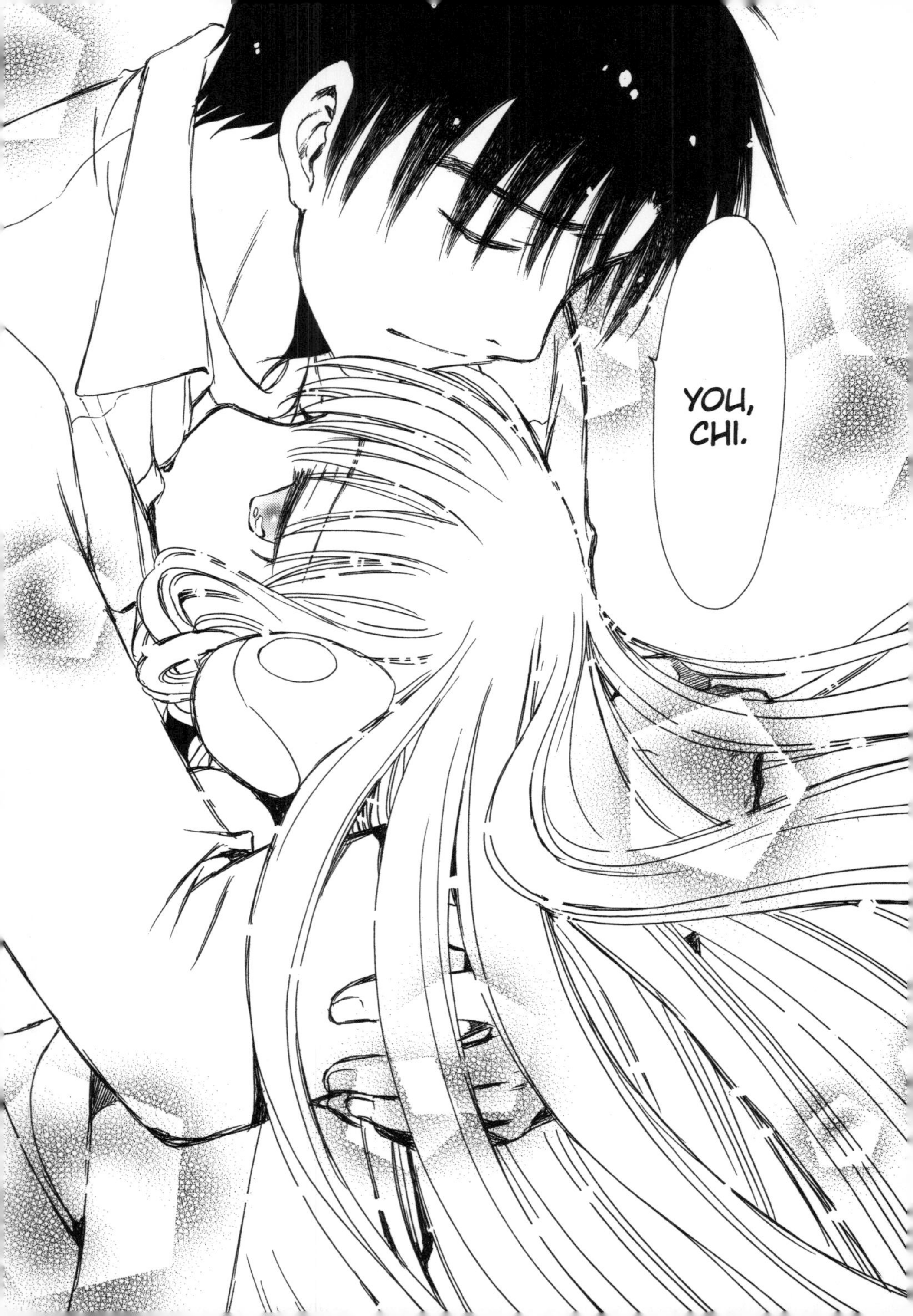
YOU, CHI.

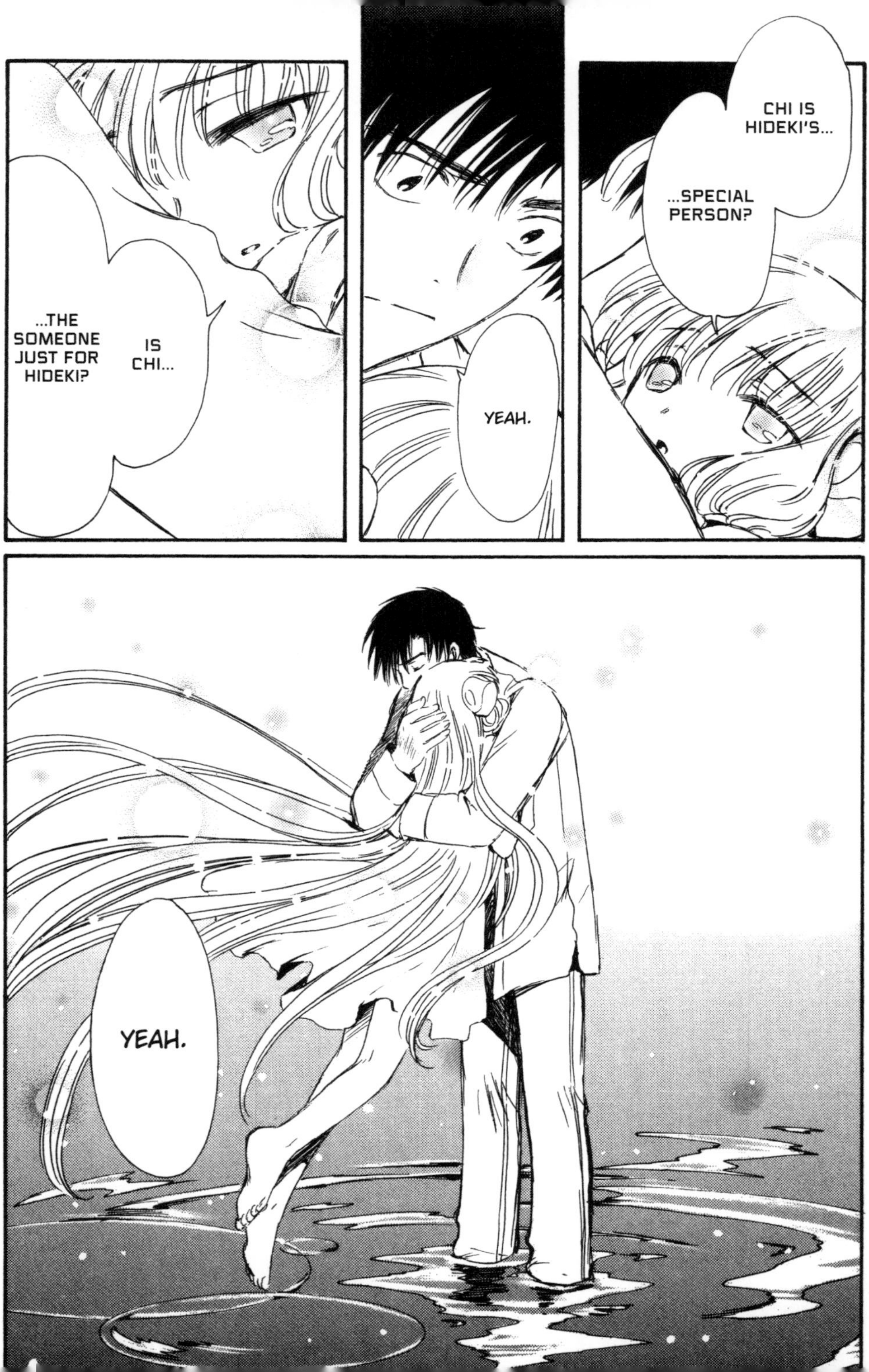
CHI IS HIDEKI'S...
...SPECIAL PERSON?
YEAH.
IS CHI...
...THE SOMEONE JUST FOR HIDEKI?
YEAH.

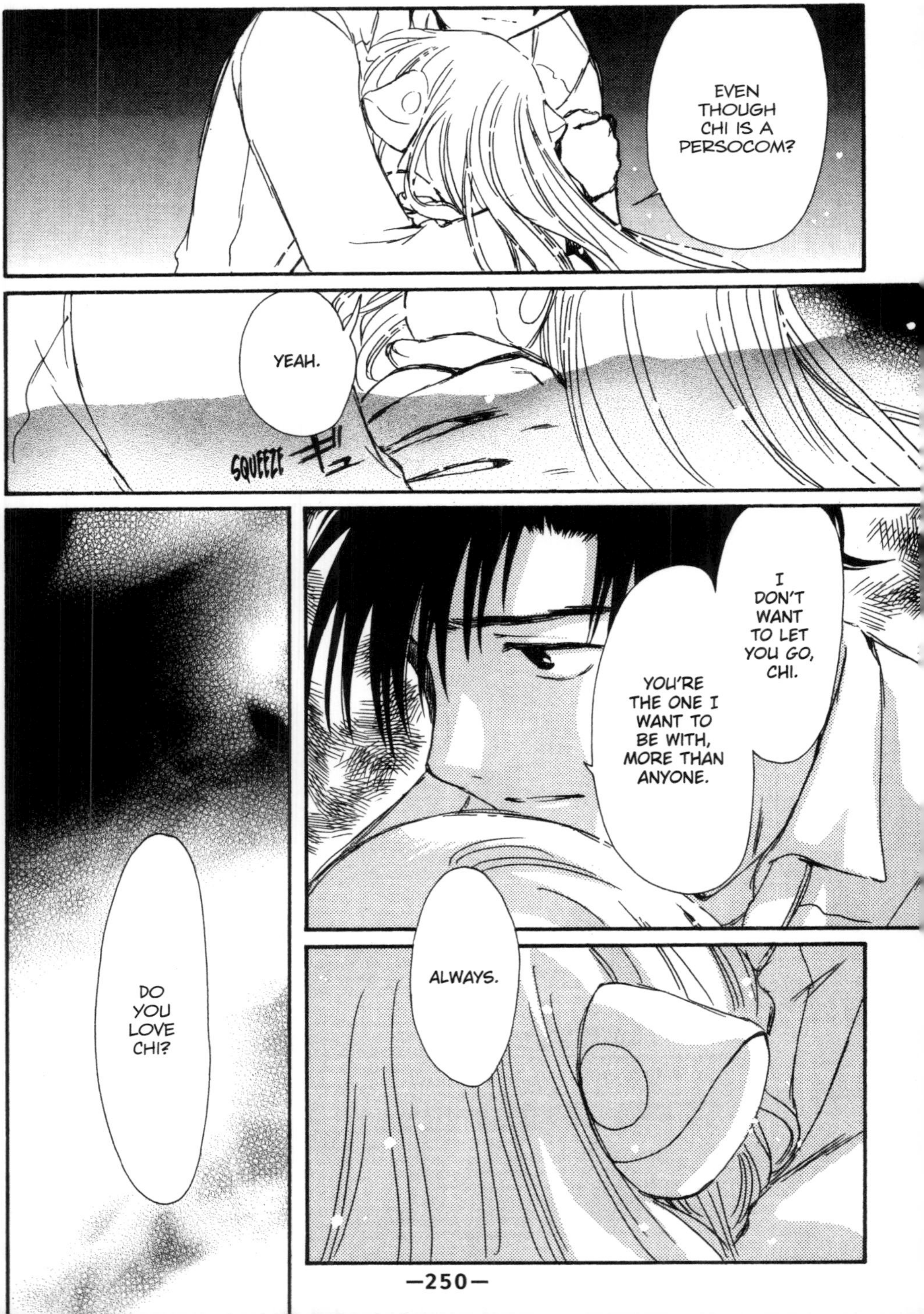
EVEN THOUGH CHI IS A PERSOCOM?
YEAH.
ギュ
SQUEEZE
I DON'T WANT TO LET YOU GO, CHI.
YOU'RE THE ONE I WANT TO BE WITH, MORE THAN ANYONE.
ALWAYS.
DO YOU LOVE CHI?

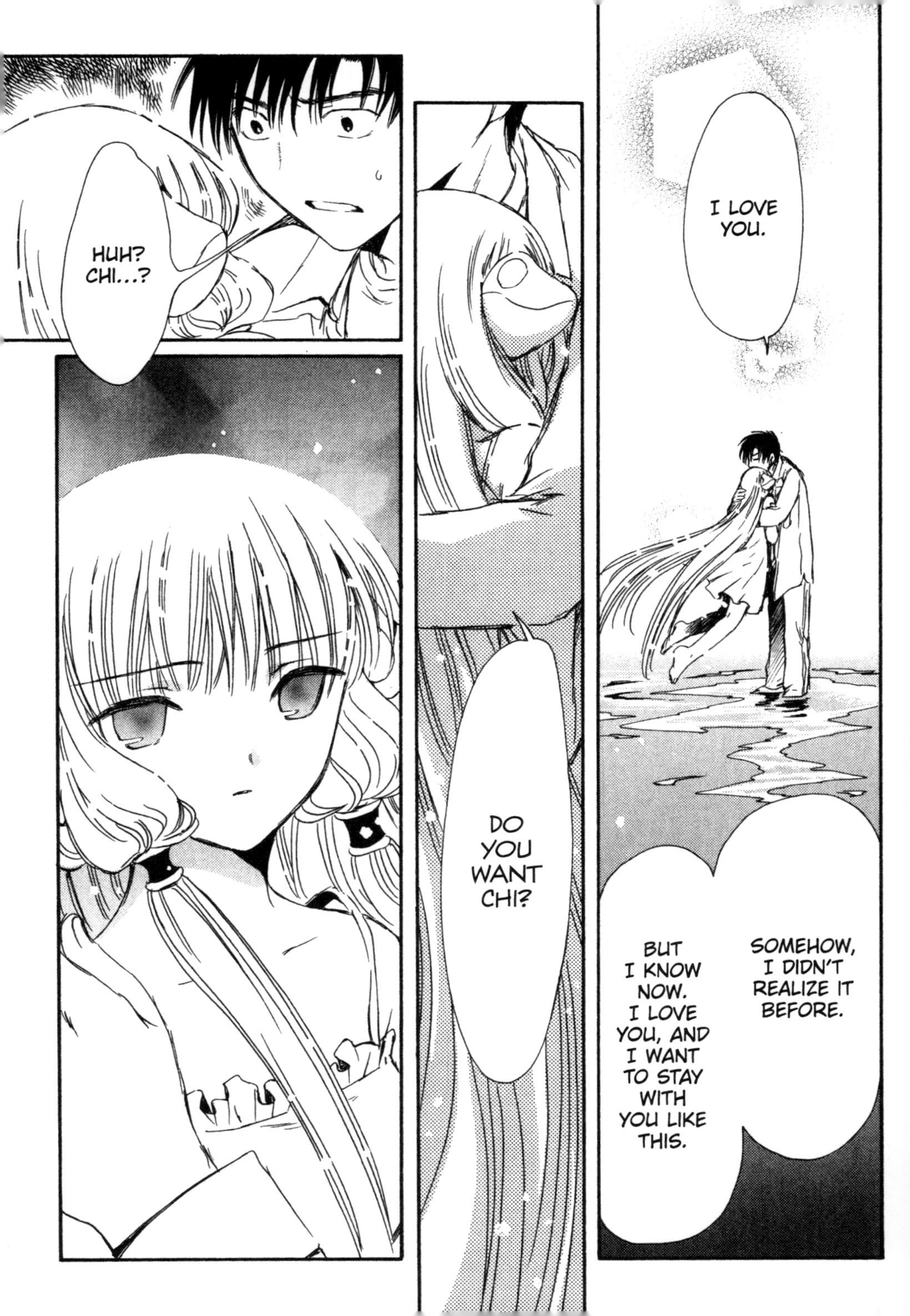
I LOVE YOU.
SOMEHOW, I DIDN'T REALIZE IT BEFORE.
BUT I KNOW NOW. I LOVE YOU, AND I WANT TO STAY WITH YOU LIKE THIS.
DO YOU WANT CHI?
HUH? CHI...?

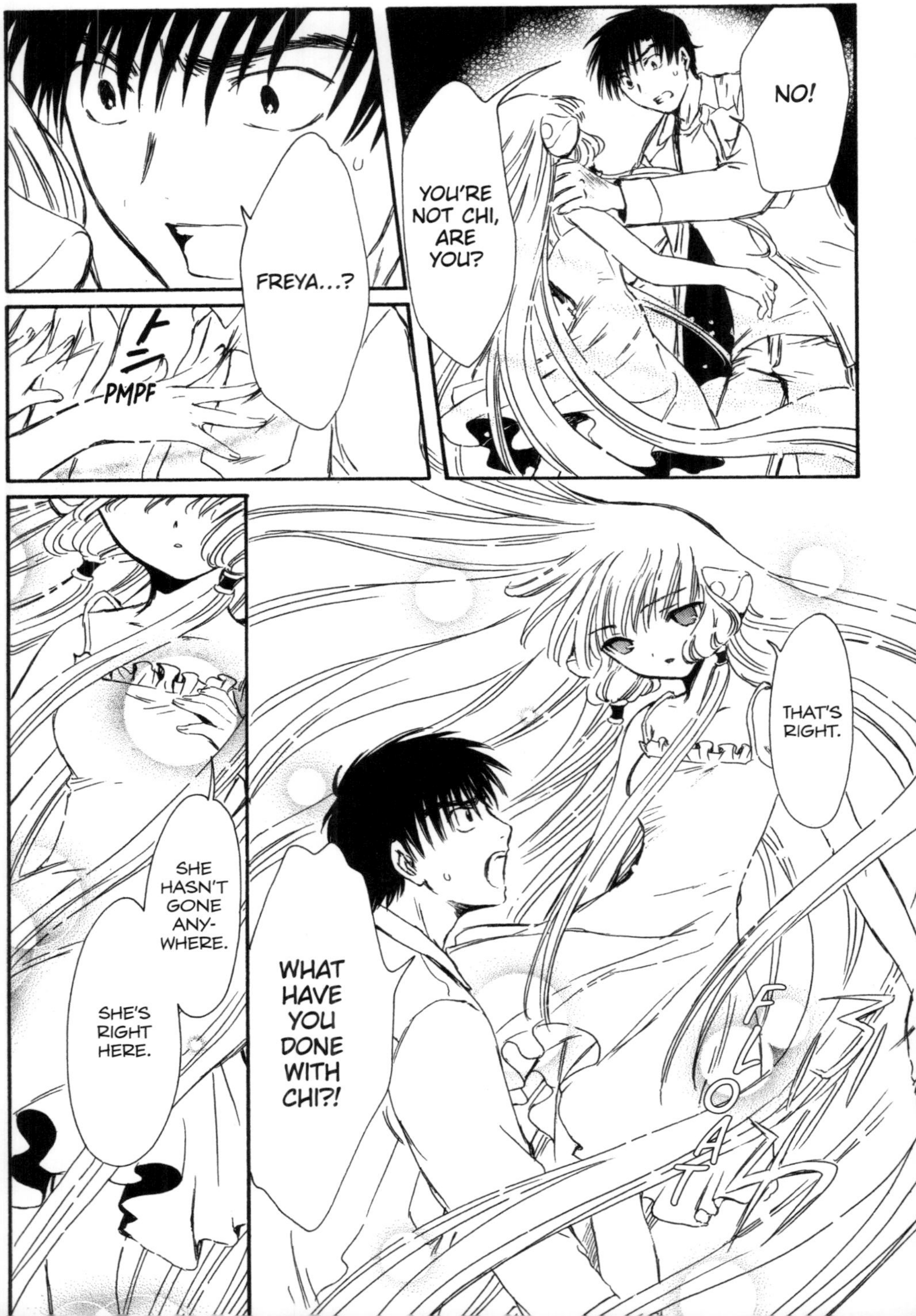
NO!
YOU'RE NOT CHI, ARE YOU?
FREYA...?
PMPF
THAT'S RIGHT.
WHAT HAVE YOU DONE WITH CHI?!
FLOATS
SHE HASN'T GONE ANYWHERE.
SHE'S RIGHT HERE.

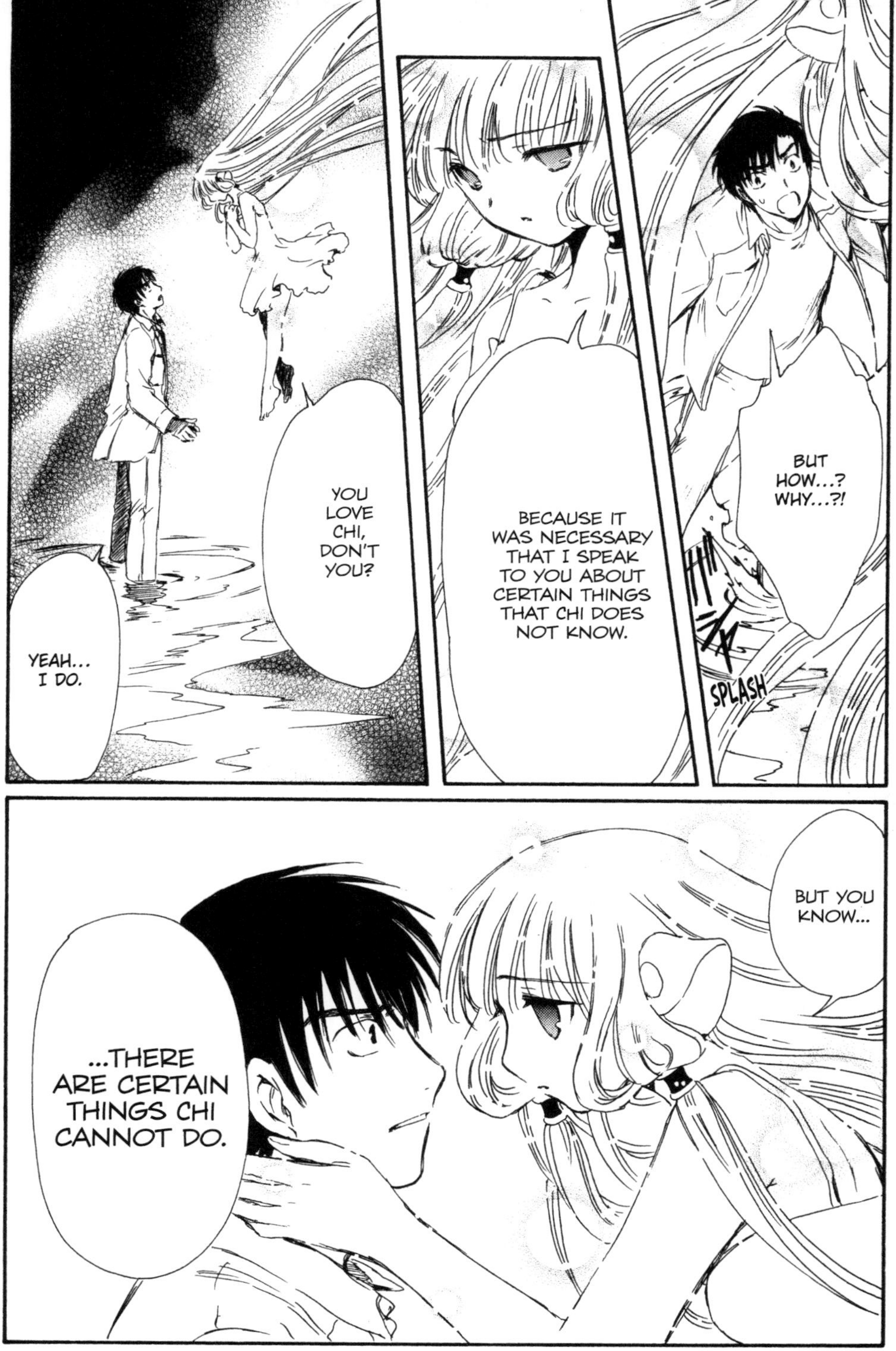
BUT HOW...? WHY...?!
SPLASH
BECAUSE IT WAS NECESSARY THAT I SPEAK TO YOU ABOUT CERTAIN THINGS THAT CHI DOES NOT KNOW.
YOU LOVE CHI, DON'T YOU?
YEAH... I DO.
BUT YOU KNOW...
...THERE ARE CERTAIN THINGS CHI CANNOT DO.

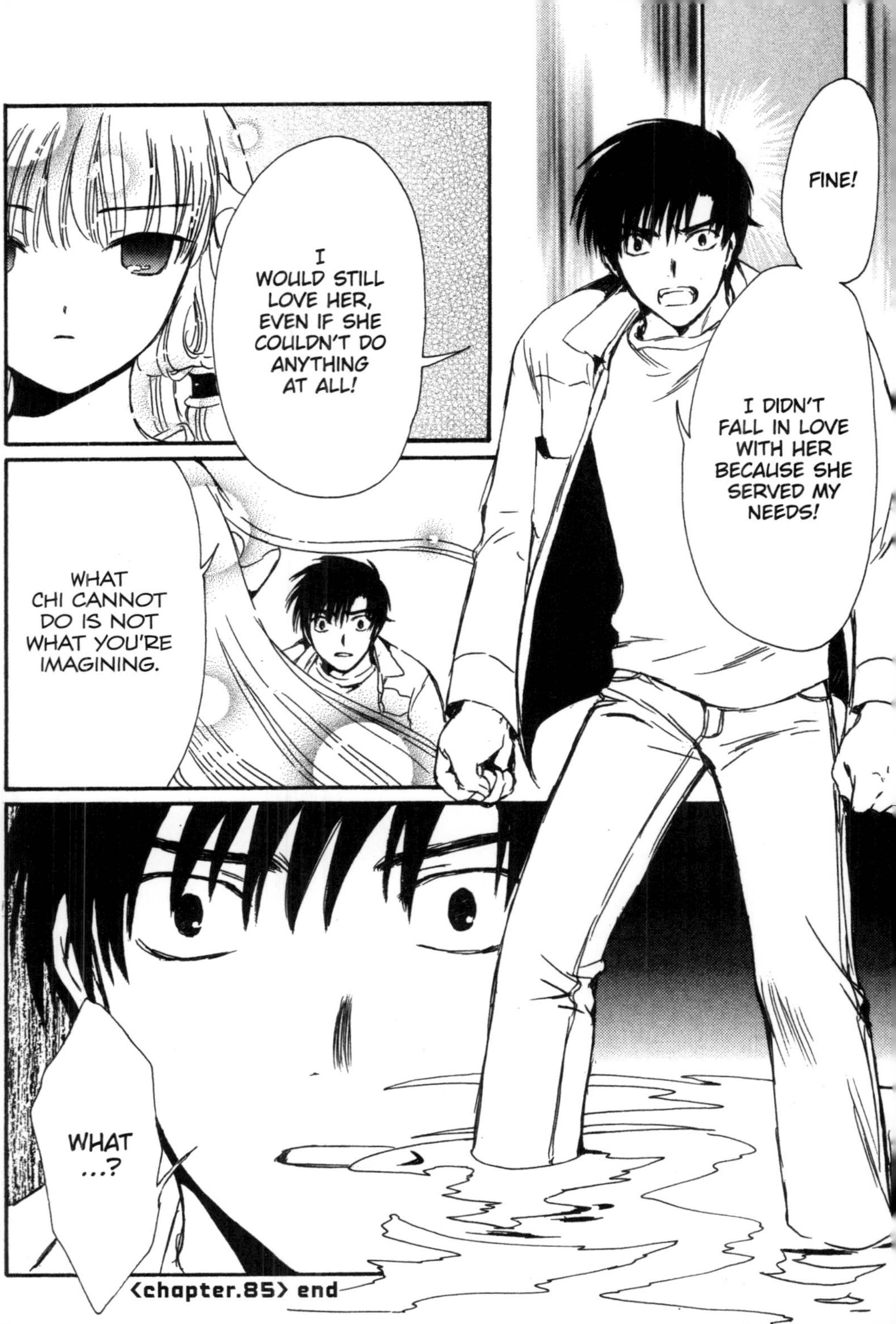
FINE!
I DIDN'T FALL IN LOVE WITH HER BECAUSE SHE SERVED MY NEEDS!
I WOULD STILL LOVE HER, EVEN IF SHE COULDN'T DO ANYTHING AT ALL!
WHAT CHI CANNOT DO IS NOT WHAT YOU'RE IMAGINING.
WHAT ...?
<chapter.85> end

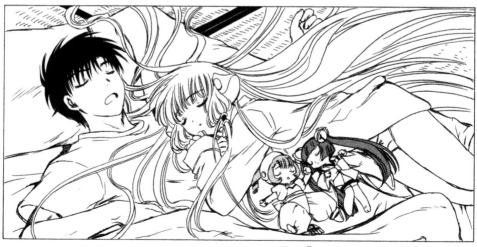

〈chapter.86〉

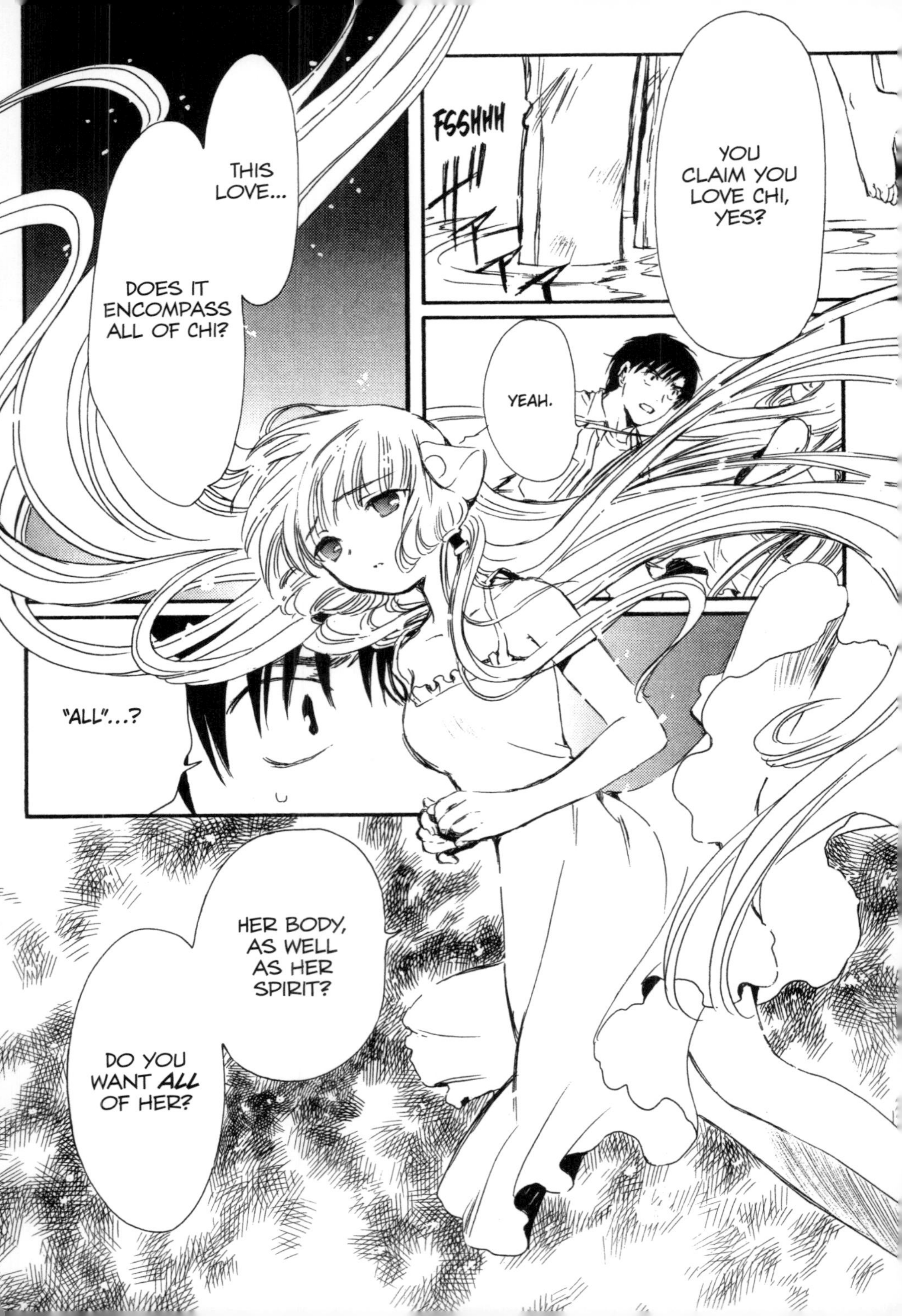
FSSHHH
YOU CLAIM YOU LOVE CHI, YES?
YEAH.
THIS LOVE...
DOES IT ENCOMPASS ALL OF CHI?
"ALL"...?
HER BODY, AS WELL AS HER SPIRIT?
DO YOU WANT ALL OF HER?

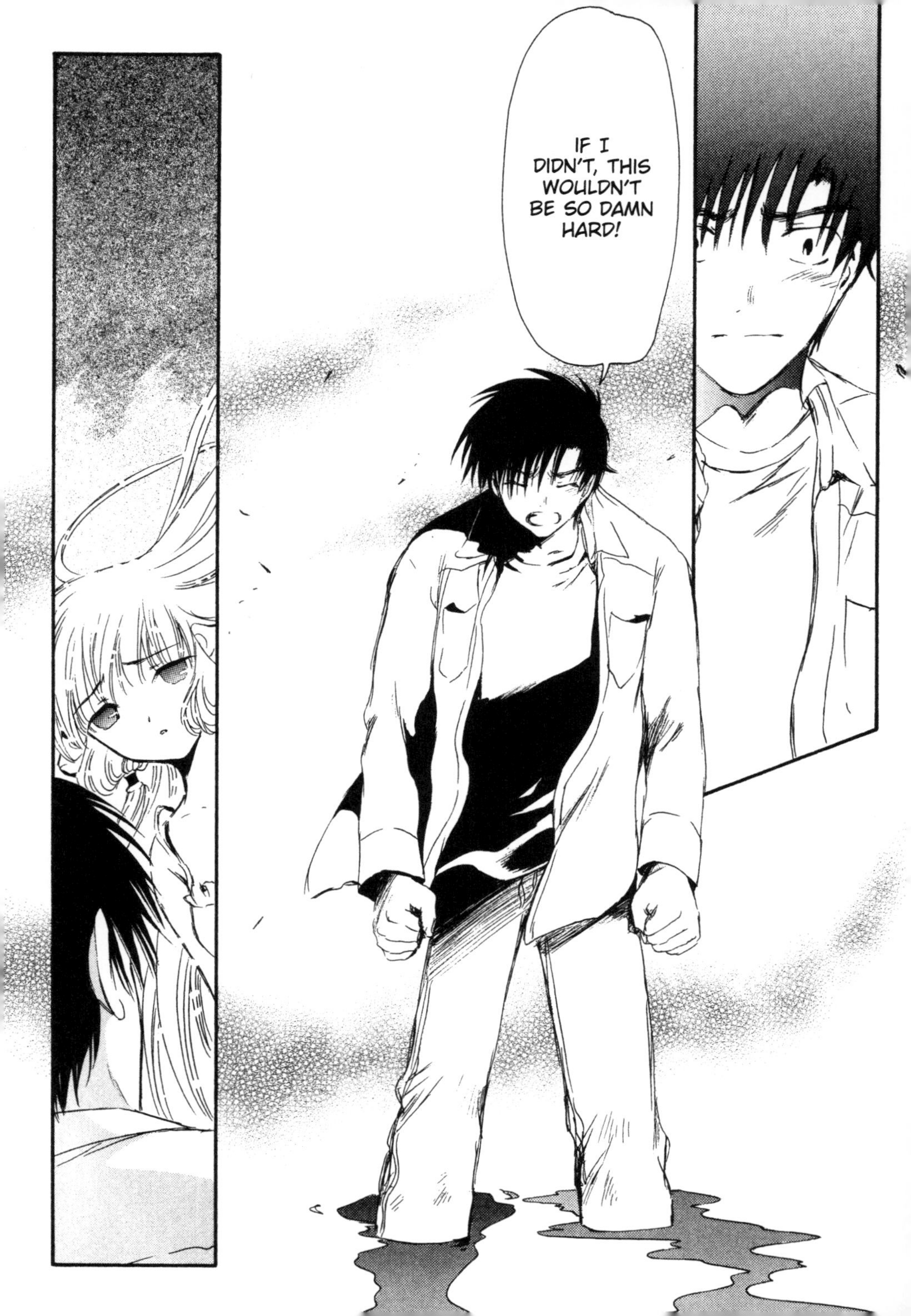
IF I DIDN'T, THIS WOULDN'T BE SO DAMN HARD!

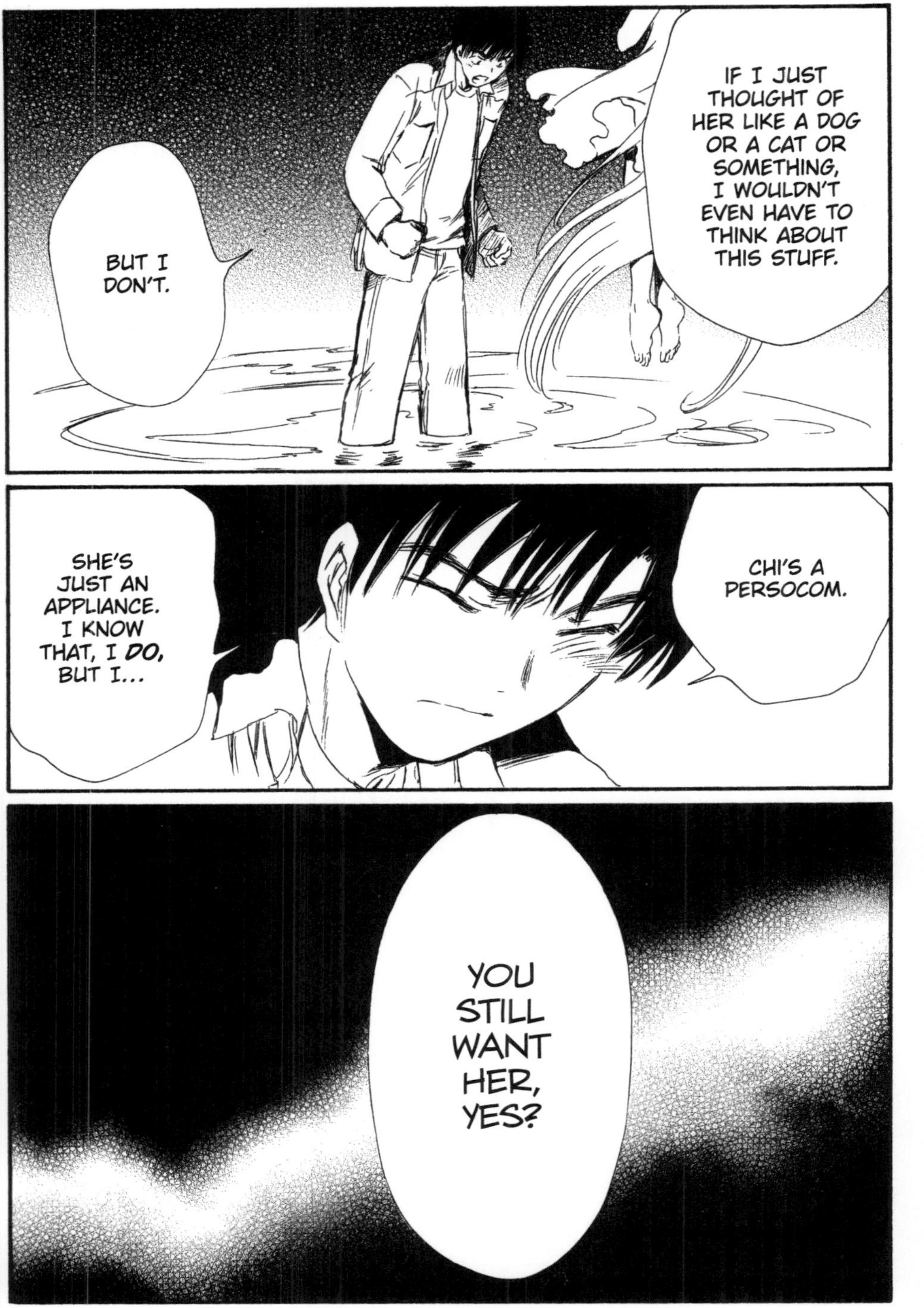
IF I JUST THOUGHT OF HER LIKE A DOG OR A CAT OR SOMETHING, I WOULDN'T EVEN HAVE TO THINK ABOUT THIS STUFF.
BUT I DON'T.
CHI'S A PERSOCOM.
SHE'S JUST AN APPLIANCE. I KNOW THAT, I *DO*, BUT I...
YOU STILL WANT HER, YES?

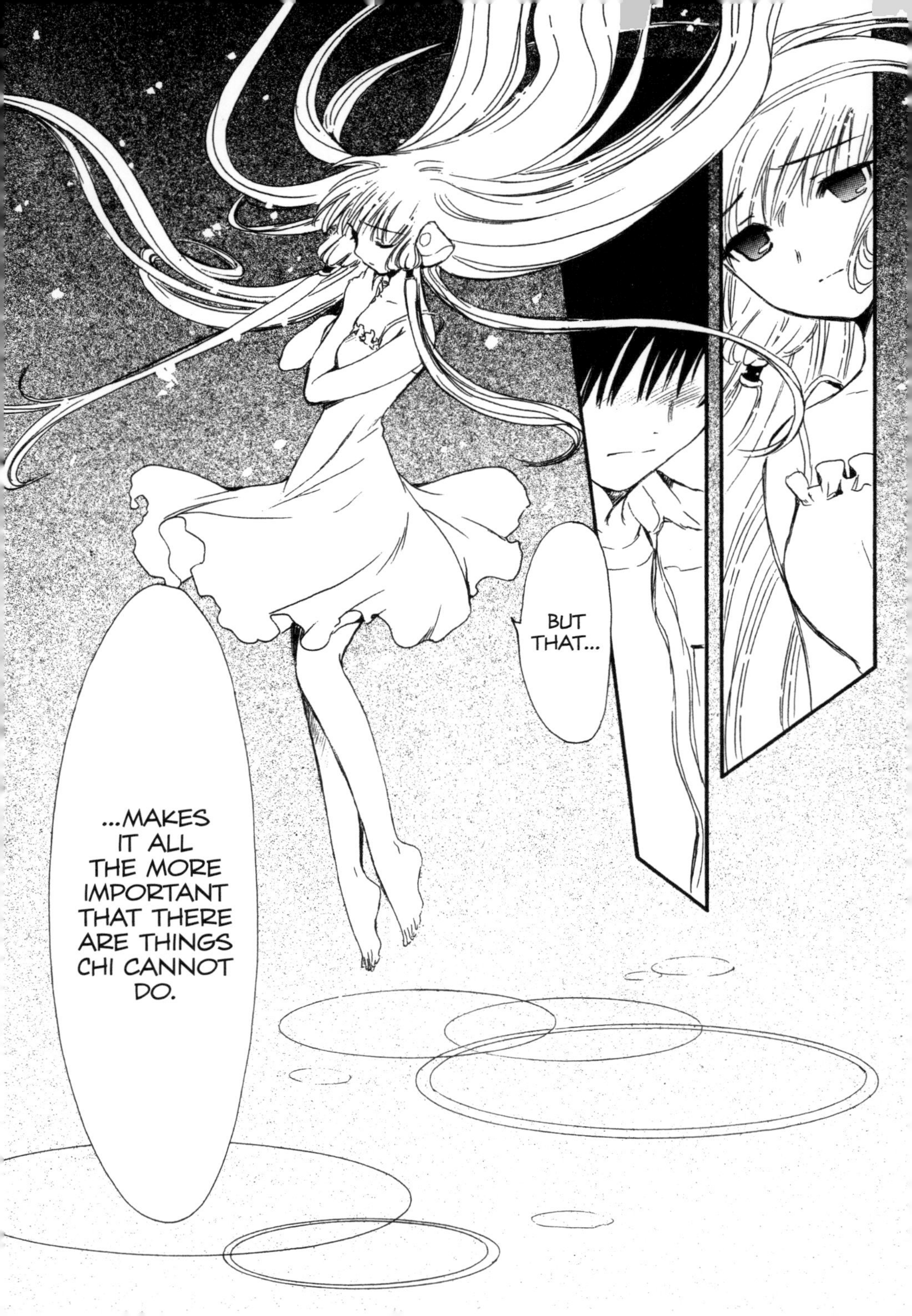
BUT THAT...
...MAKES IT ALL THE MORE IMPORTANT THAT THERE ARE THINGS CHI CANNOT DO.

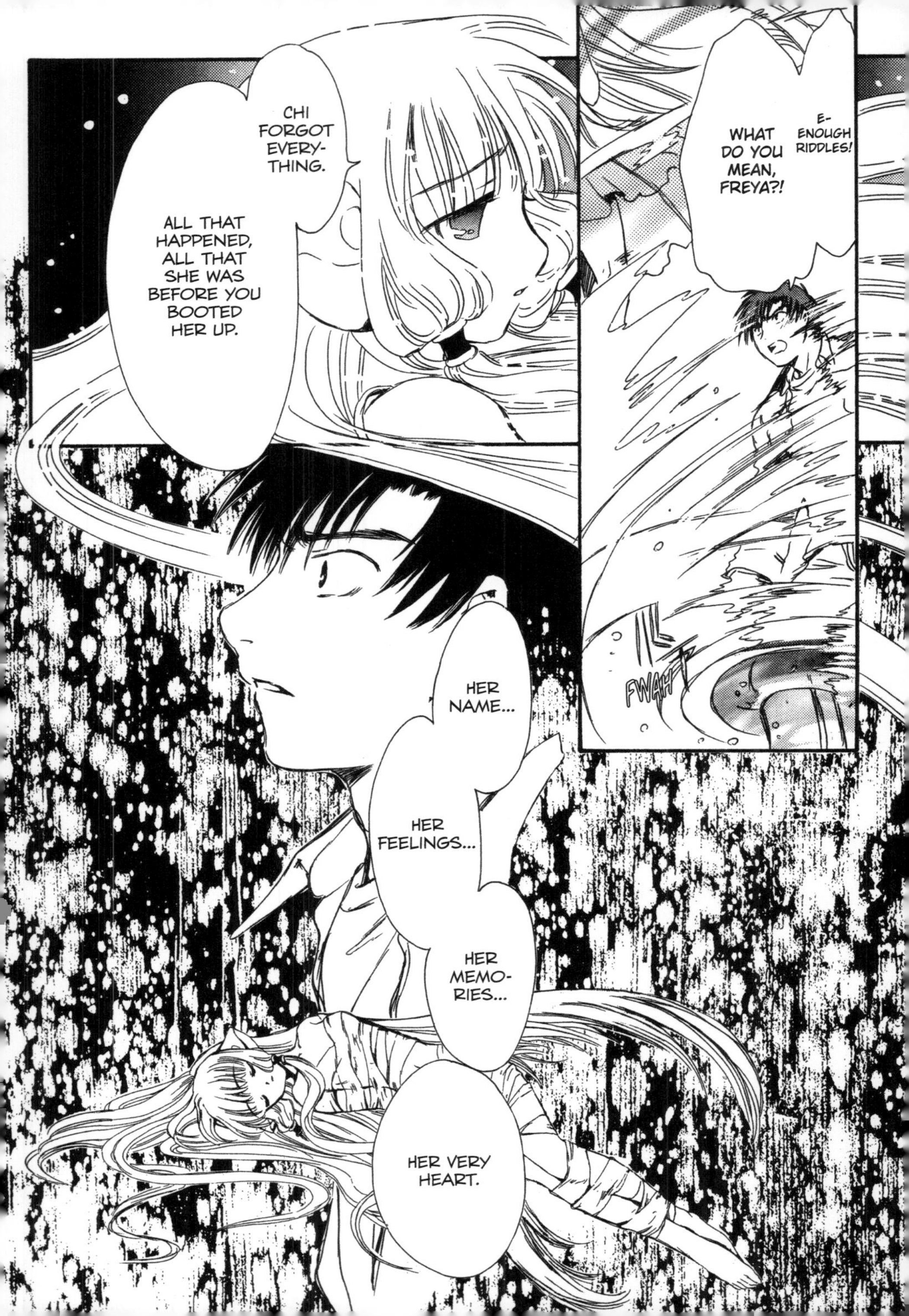
WHAT DO YOU MEAN, FREYA?! E-ENOUGH RIDDLES!
FWAH
CHI FORGOT EVERYTHING.
ALL THAT HAPPENED, ALL THAT SHE WAS BEFORE YOU BOOTED HER UP.
HER NAME...
HER FEELINGS...
HER MEMORIES...
HER VERY HEART.

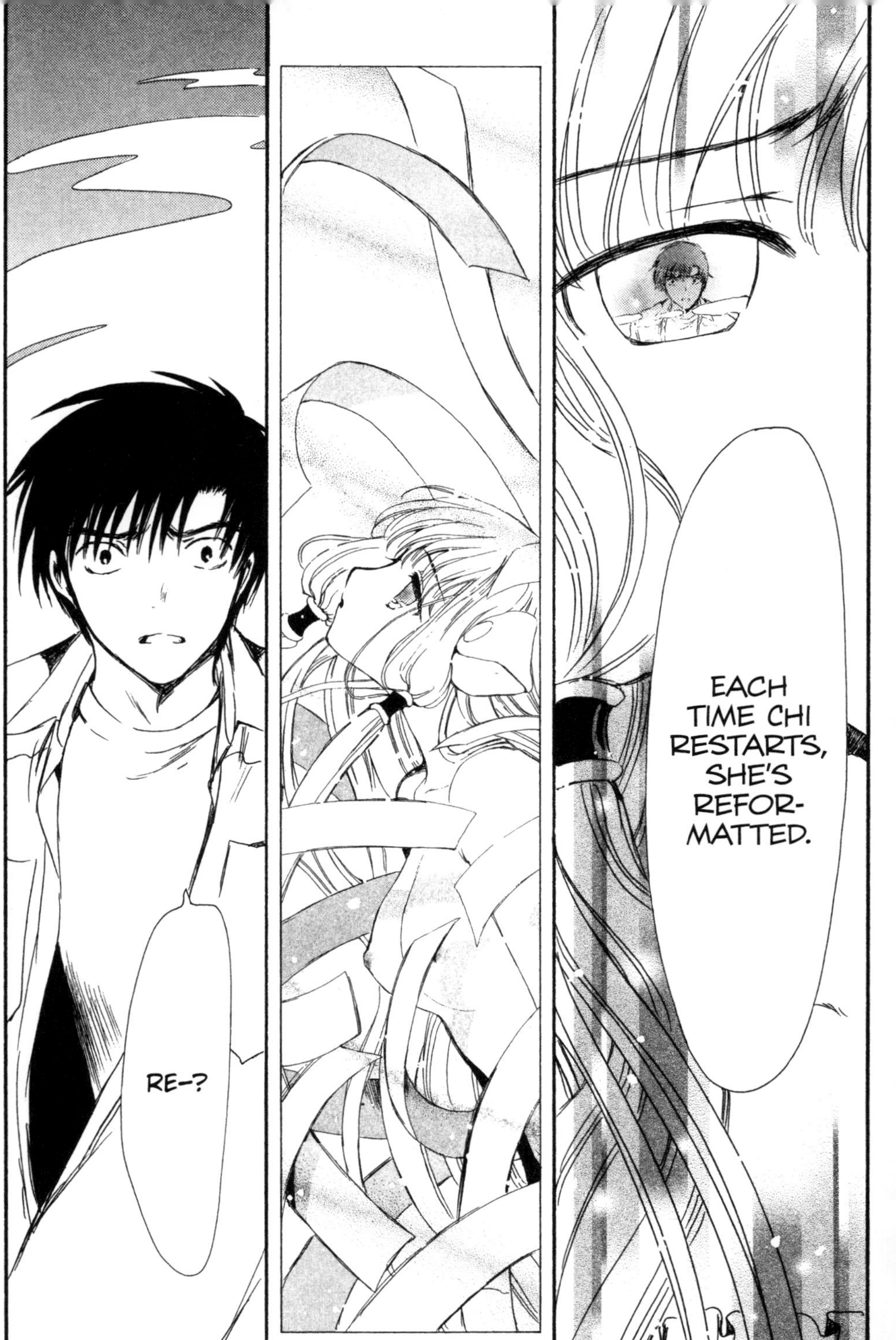
EACH TIME CHI RESTARTS, SHE'S REFOR-MATTED.
RE-?

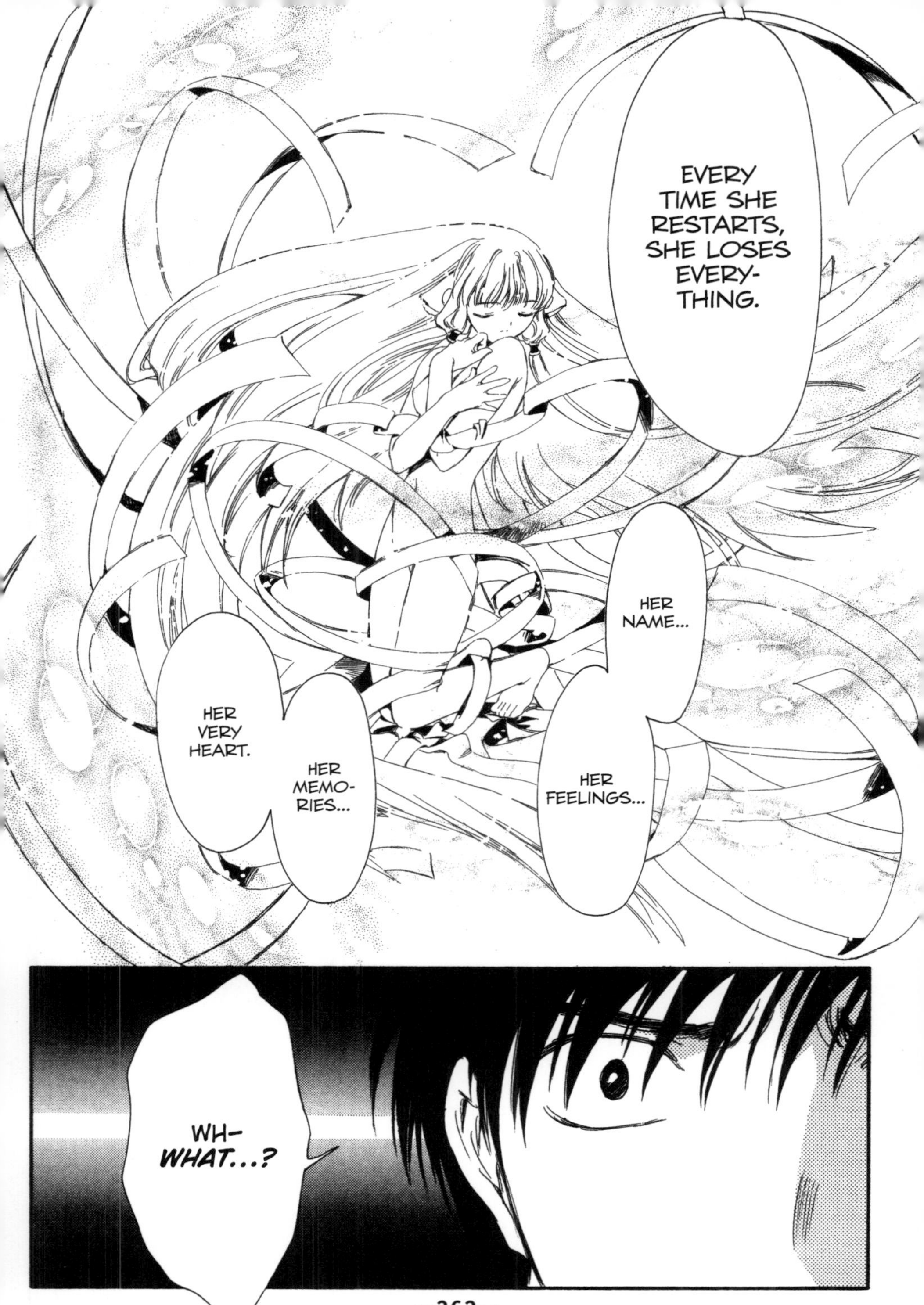
EVERY TIME SHE RESTARTS, SHE LOSES EVERYTHING.
HER NAME...
HER FEELINGS...
HER MEMORIES...
HER VERY HEART.
WH-*WHAT...?*

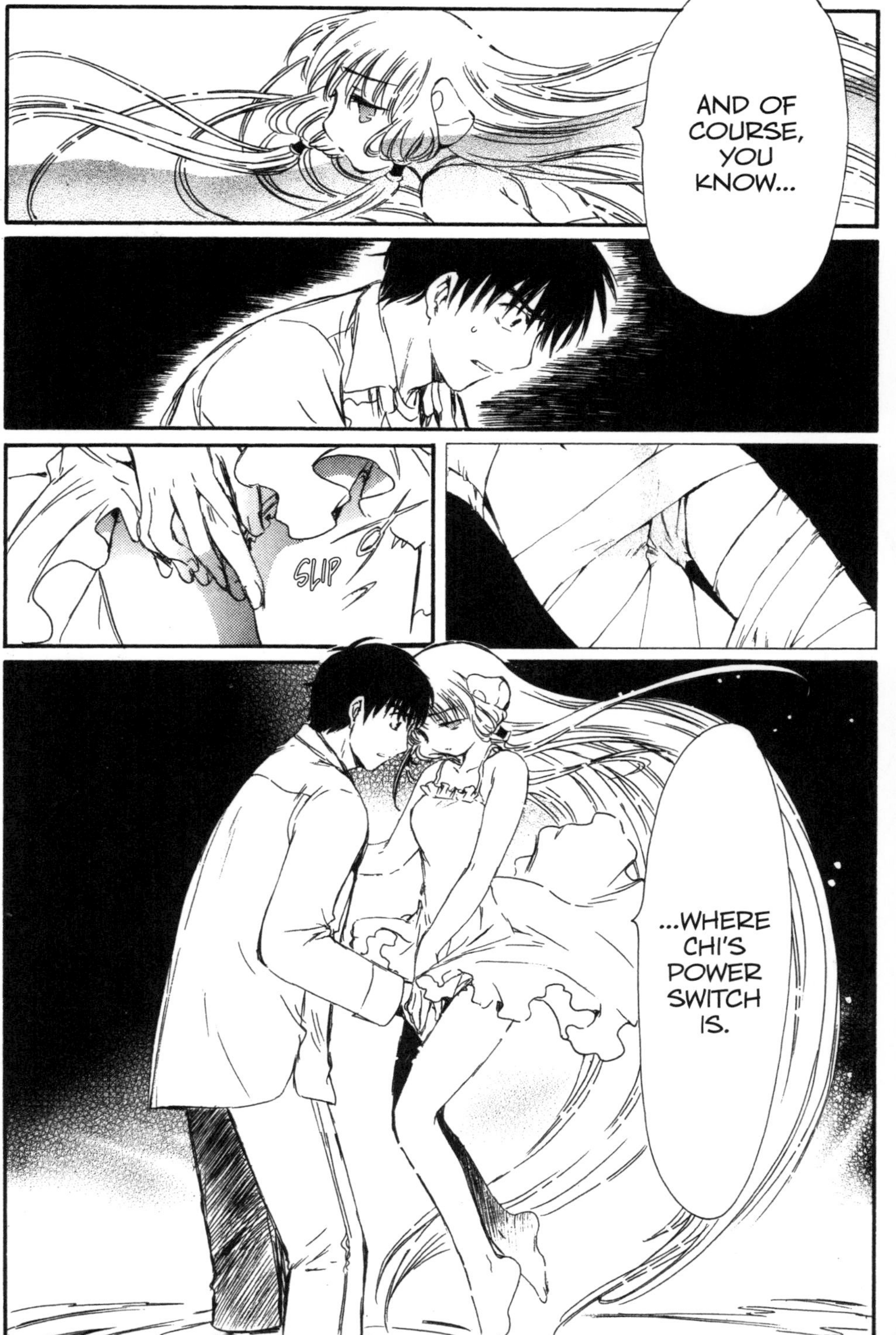
AND OF COURSE, YOU KNOW...
SLIP
...WHERE CHI'S POWER SWITCH IS.

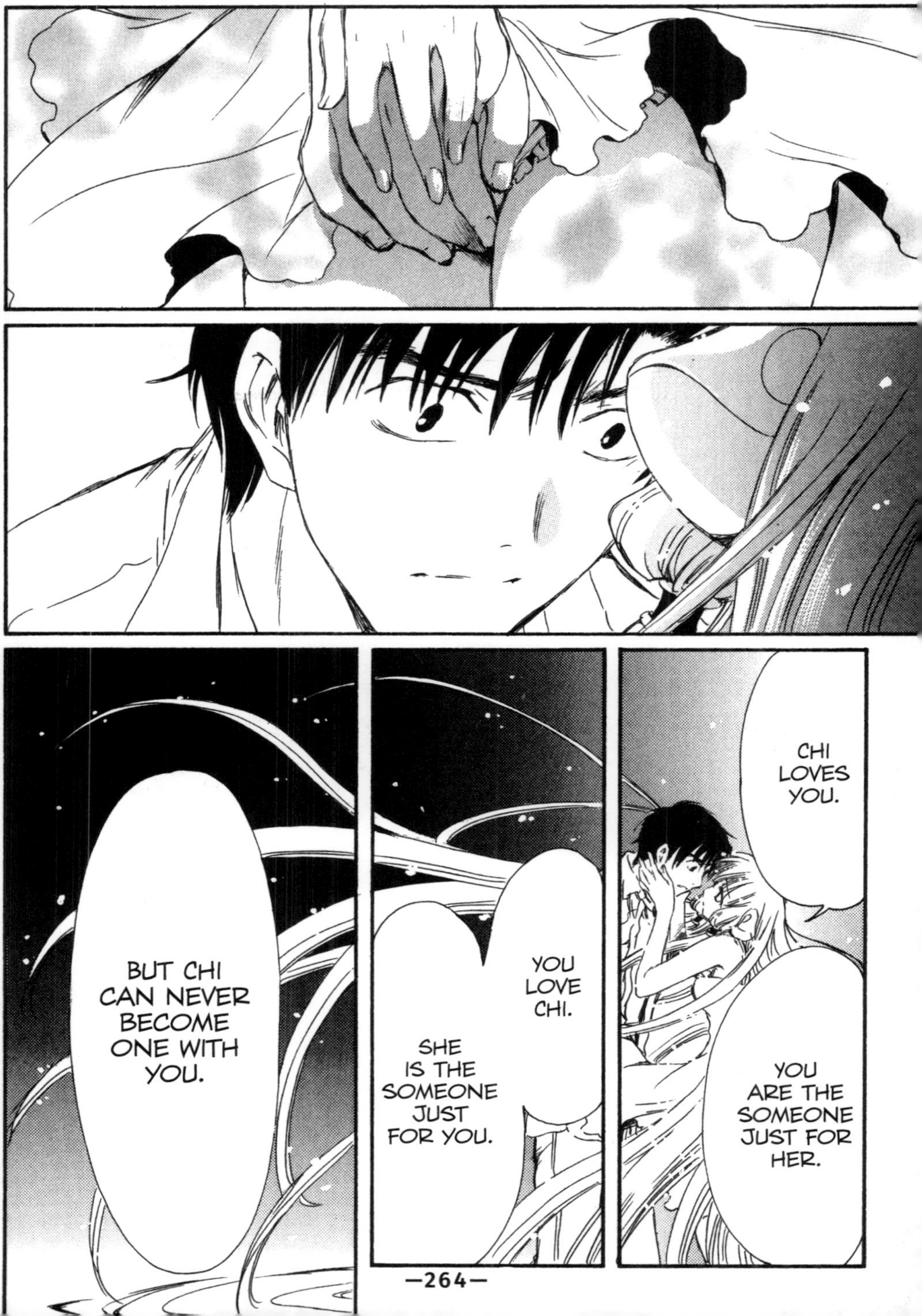
CHI LOVES YOU.
YOU ARE THE SOMEONE JUST FOR HER.
YOU LOVE CHI.
SHE IS THE SOMEONE JUST FOR YOU.
BUT CHI CAN NEVER BECOME ONE WITH YOU.

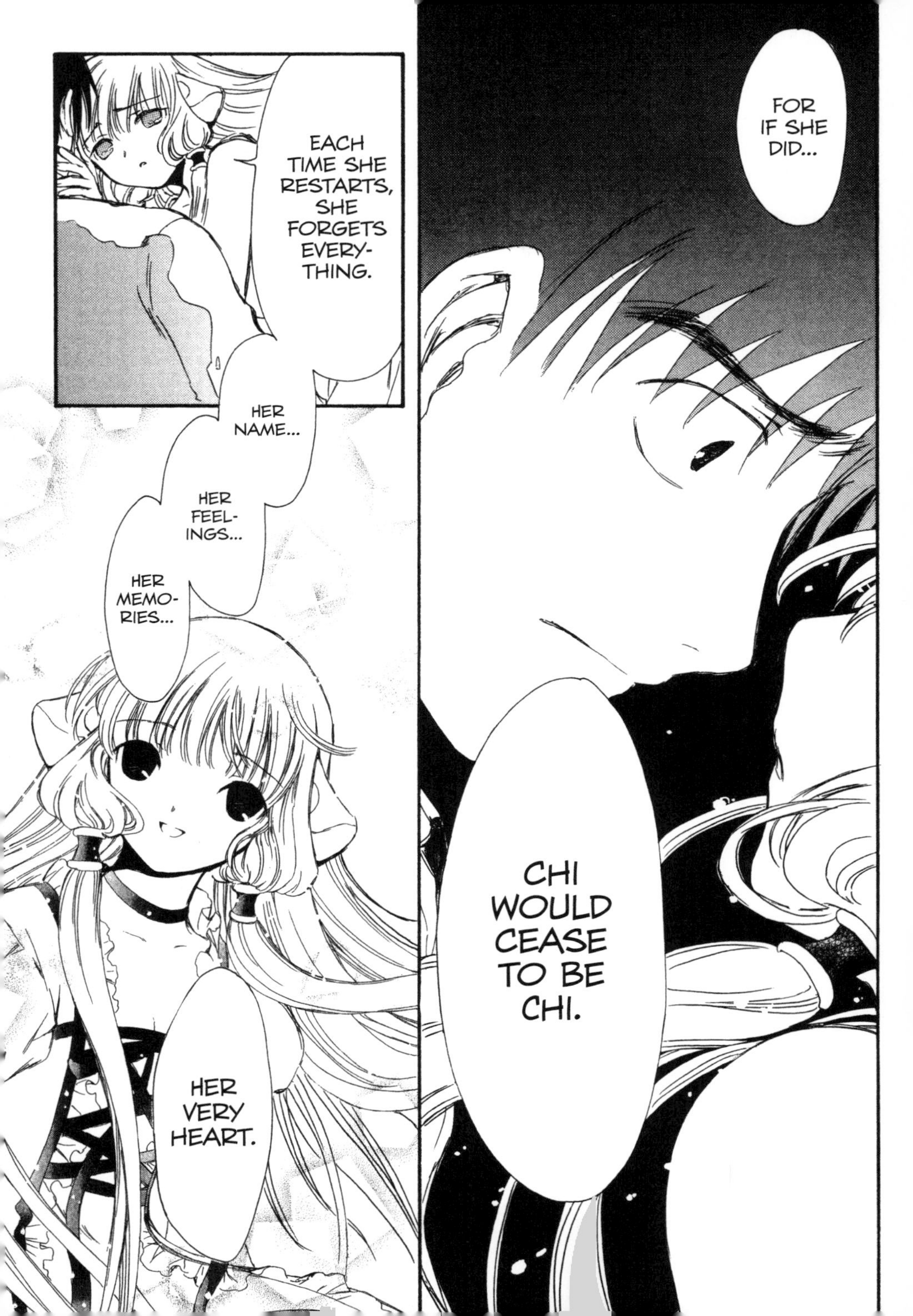
FOR IF SHE DID...
CHI WOULD CEASE TO BE CHI.
EACH TIME SHE RESTARTS, SHE FORGETS EVERY-THING.
HER NAME...
HER FEEL-INGS...
HER MEMO-RIES...
HER VERY HEART.

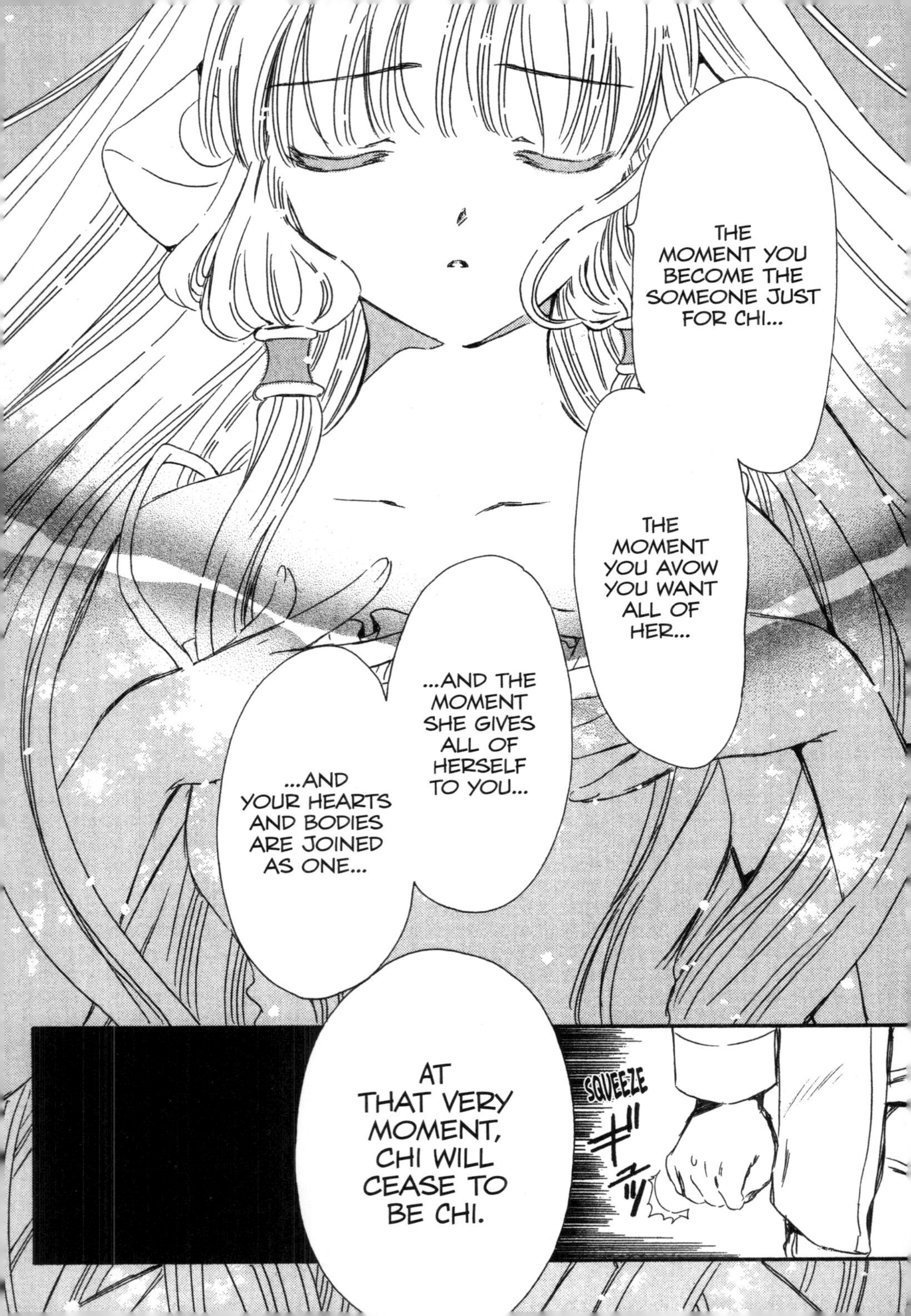
THE MOMENT YOU BECOME THE SOMEONE JUST FOR CHI...
THE MOMENT YOU AVOW YOU WANT ALL OF HER...
...AND THE MOMENT SHE GIVES ALL OF HERSELF TO YOU...
...AND YOUR HEARTS AND BODIES ARE JOINED AS ONE...
AT THAT VERY MOMENT, CHI WILL CEASE TO BE CHI.
SQUEEZE

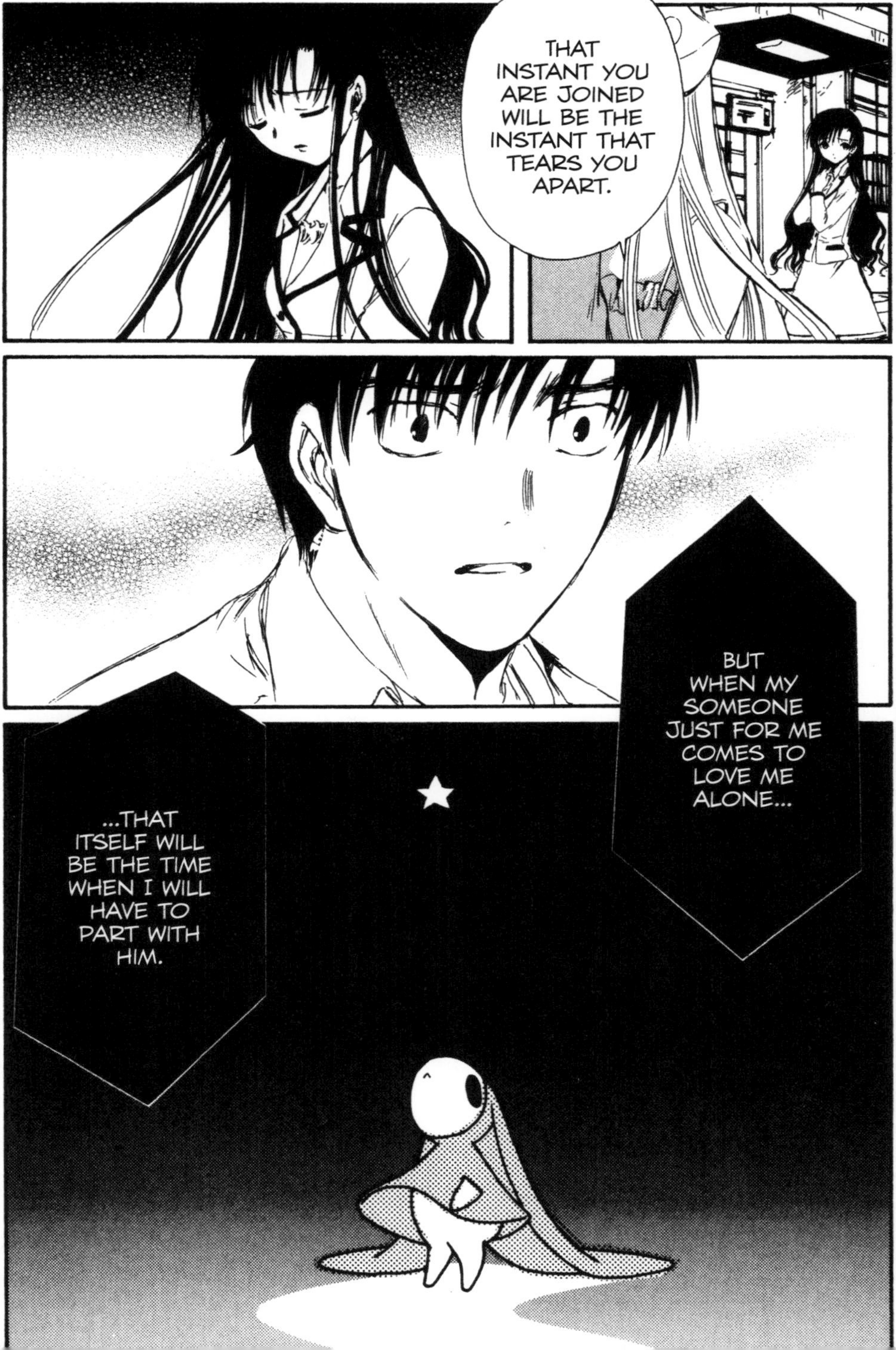
THAT INSTANT YOU ARE JOINED WILL BE THE INSTANT THAT TEARS YOU APART.
BUT WHEN MY SOMEONE JUST FOR ME COMES TO LOVE ME ALONE...
...THAT ITSELF WILL BE THE TIME WHEN I WILL HAVE TO PART WITH HIM.

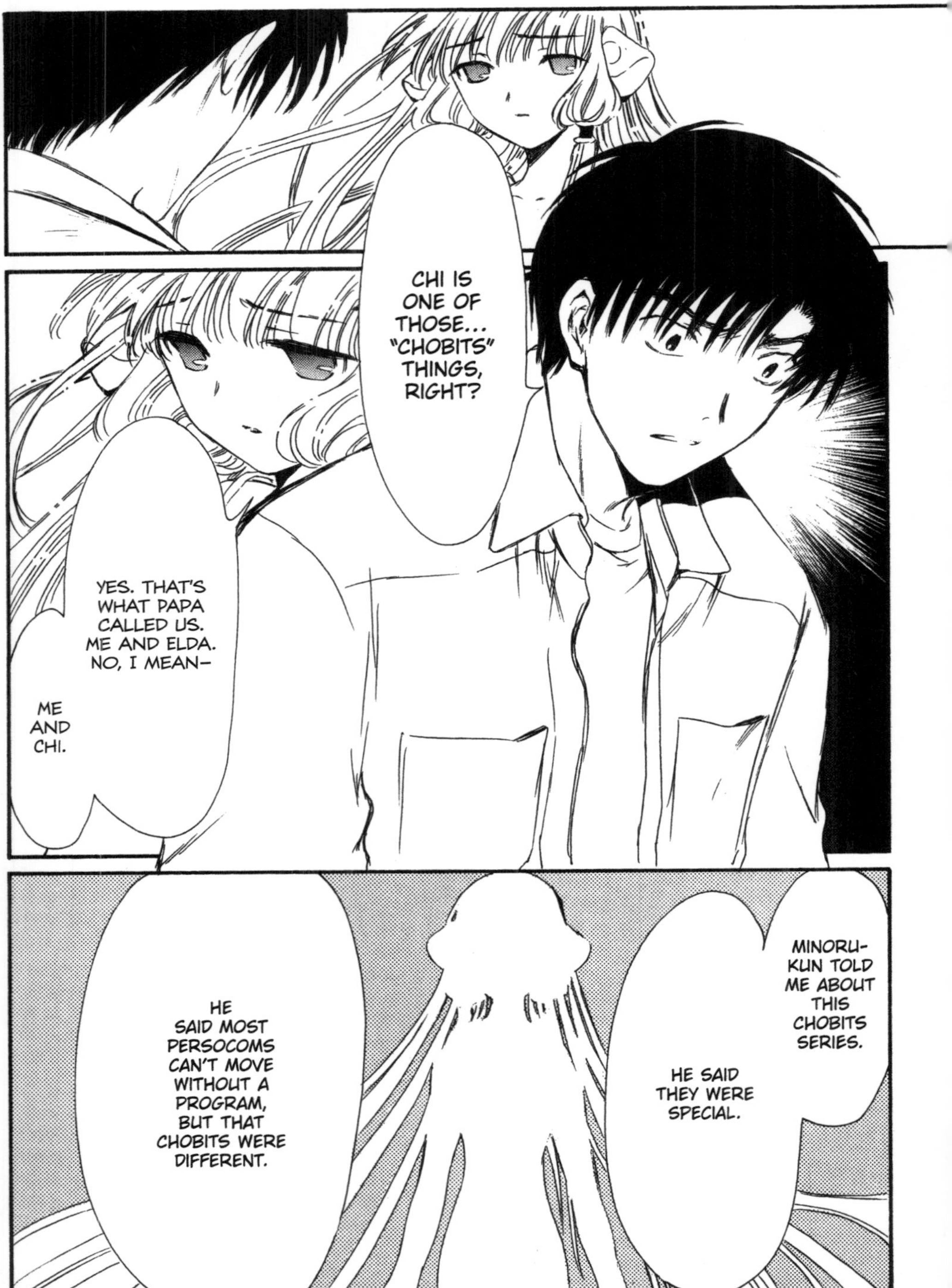
CHI IS ONE OF THOSE... "CHOBITS" THINGS, RIGHT?
YES. THAT'S WHAT PAPA CALLED US. ME AND ELDA. NO, I MEAN–
ME AND CHI.
MINORU-KUN TOLD ME ABOUT THIS CHOBITS SERIES.
HE SAID THEY WERE SPECIAL.
HE SAID MOST PERSOCOMS CAN'T MOVE WITHOUT A PROGRAM, BUT THAT CHOBITS WERE DIFFERENT.

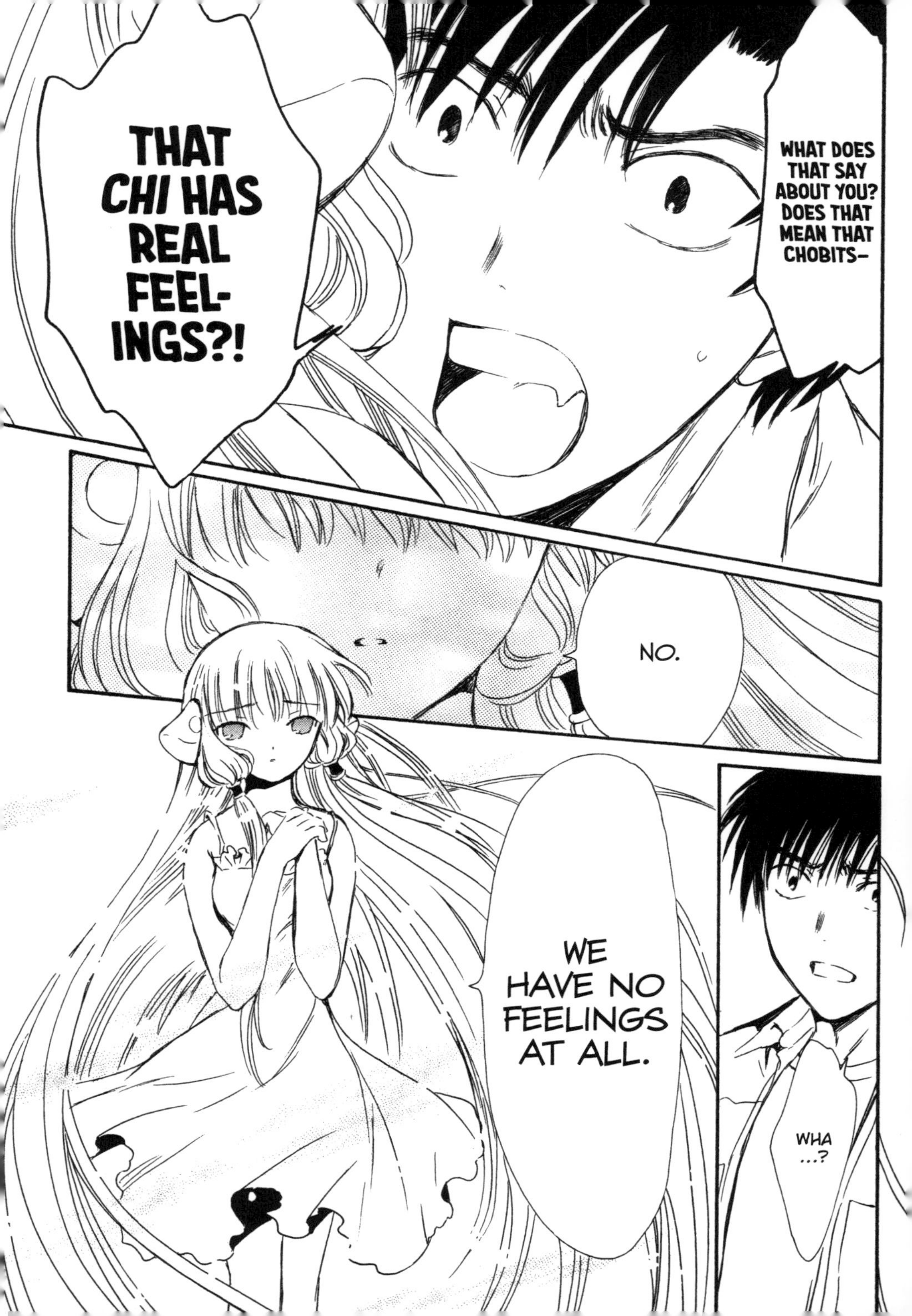

WHAT DOES THAT SAY ABOUT YOU? DOES THAT MEAN THAT CHOBITS–
THAT *CHI* HAS REAL FEEL-INGS?!
NO.
WE HAVE NO FEELINGS AT ALL.
WHA ...?

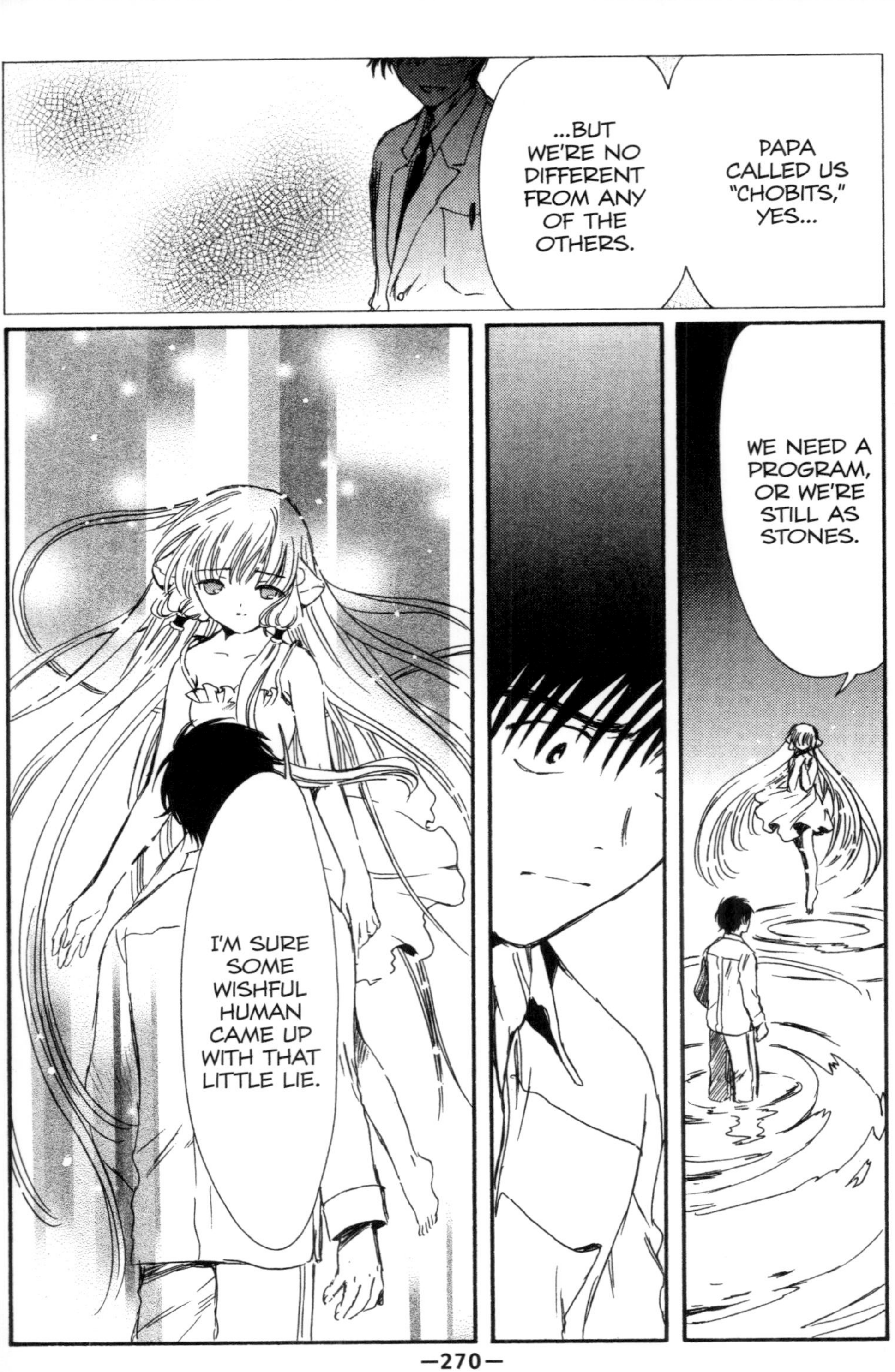
PAPA CALLED US "CHOBITS," YES...
...BUT WE'RE NO DIFFERENT FROM ANY OF THE OTHERS.
WE NEED A PROGRAM, OR WE'RE STILL AS STONES.
I'M SURE SOME WISHFUL HUMAN CAME UP WITH THAT LITTLE LIE.

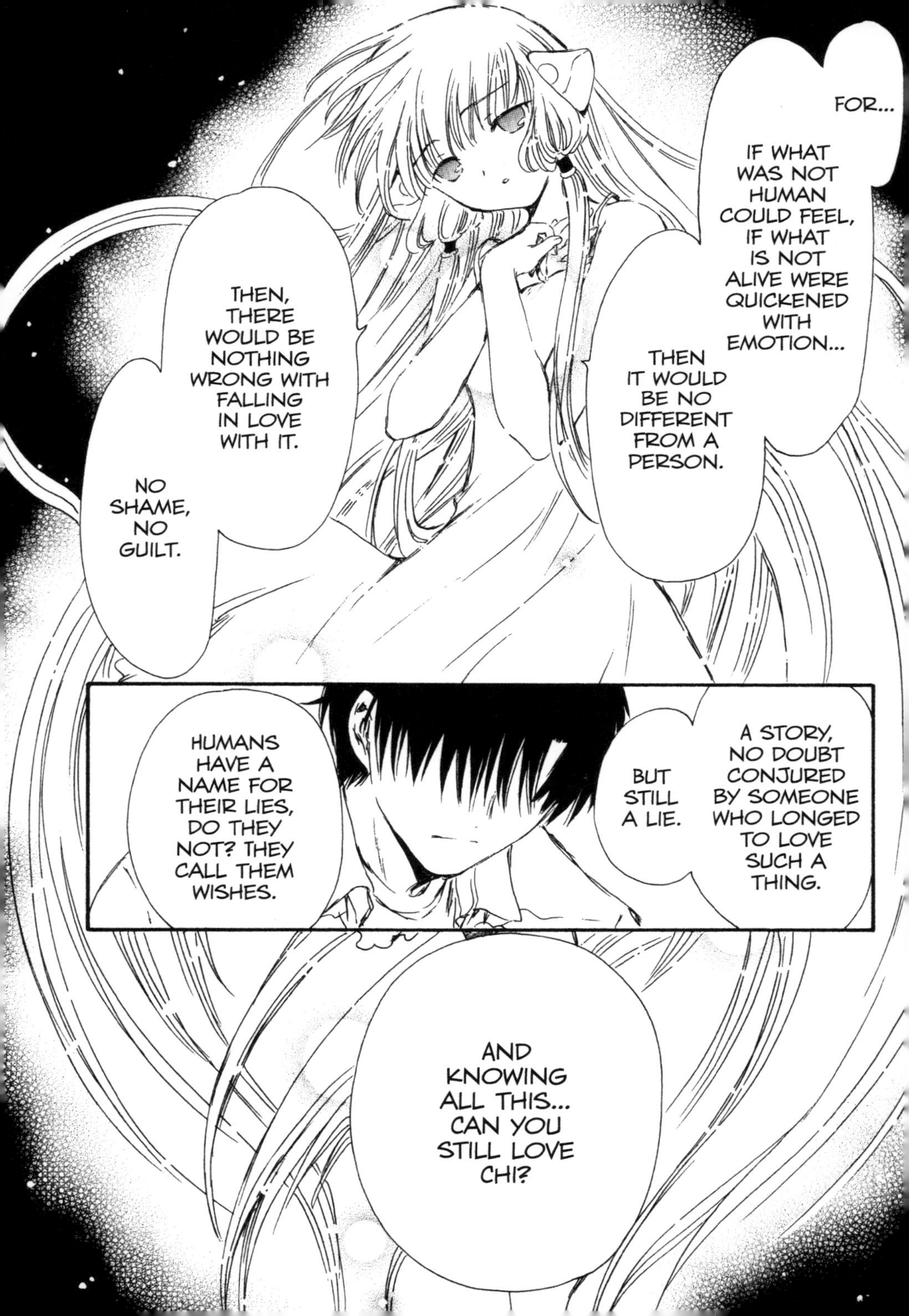
FOR...
IF WHAT WAS NOT HUMAN COULD FEEL, IF WHAT IS NOT ALIVE WERE QUICKENED WITH EMOTION...
THEN IT WOULD BE NO DIFFERENT FROM A PERSON.
THEN, THERE WOULD BE NOTHING WRONG WITH FALLING IN LOVE WITH IT.
NO SHAME, NO GUILT.
A STORY, NO DOUBT CONJURED BY SOMEONE WHO LONGED TO LOVE SUCH A THING.
BUT STILL A LIE.
HUMANS HAVE A NAME FOR THEIR LIES, DO THEY NOT? THEY CALL THEM WISHES.
AND KNOWING ALL THIS... CAN YOU STILL LOVE CHI?

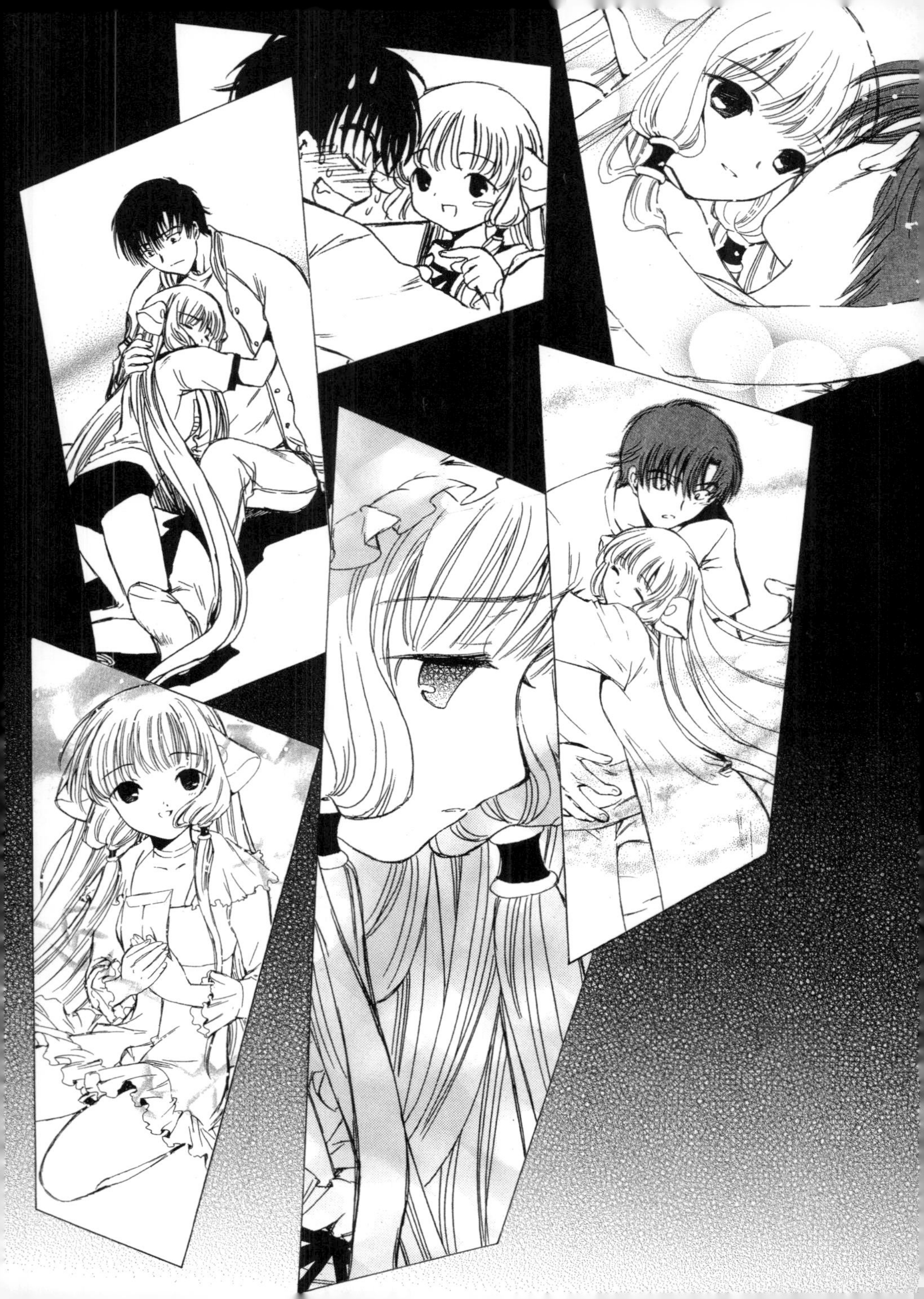

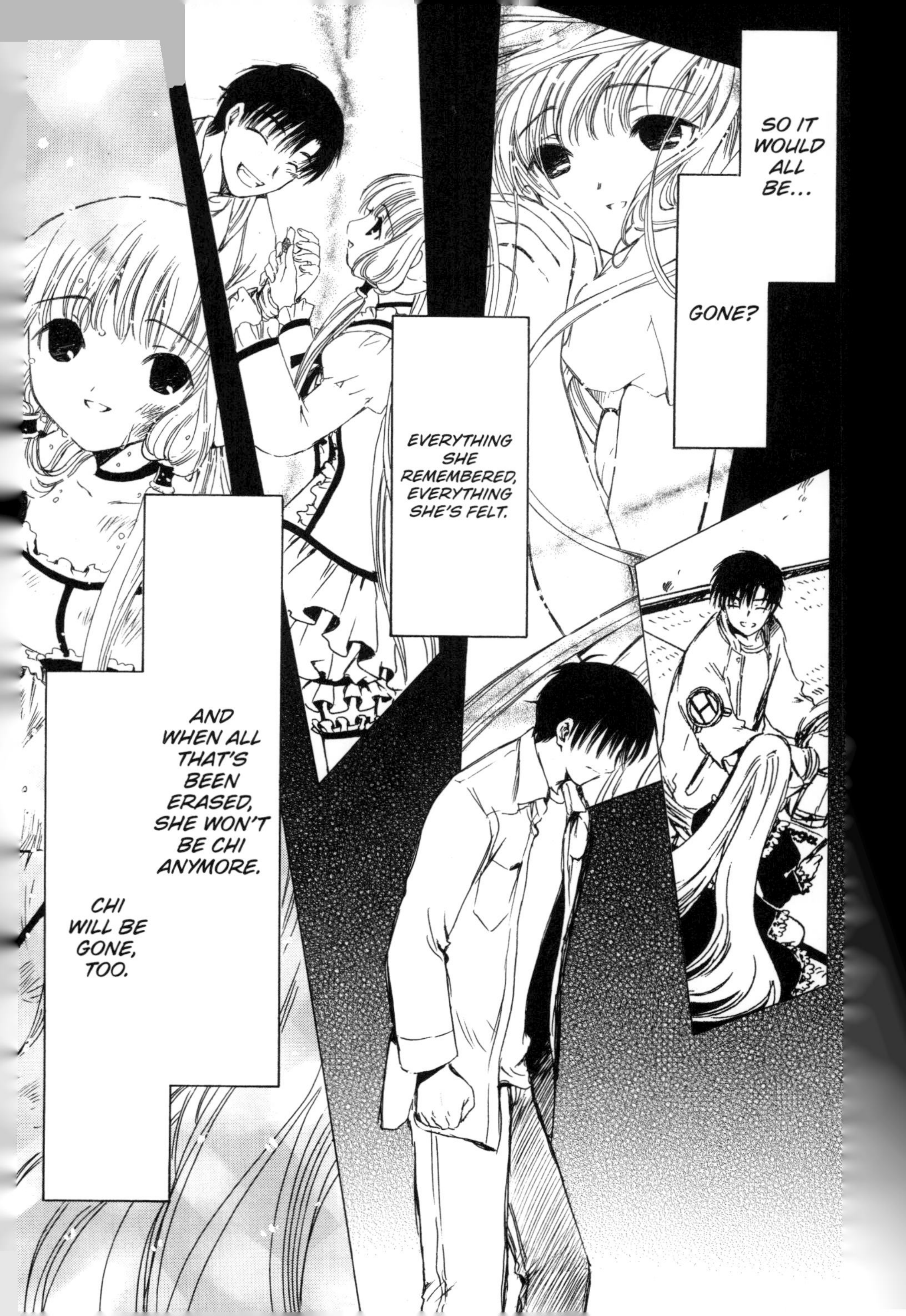
SO IT WOULD ALL BE...
GONE?
EVERYTHING SHE REMEMBERED, EVERYTHING SHE'S FELT.
AND WHEN ALL THAT'S BEEN ERASED, SHE WON'T BE CHI ANYMORE.
CHI WILL BE GONE, TOO.

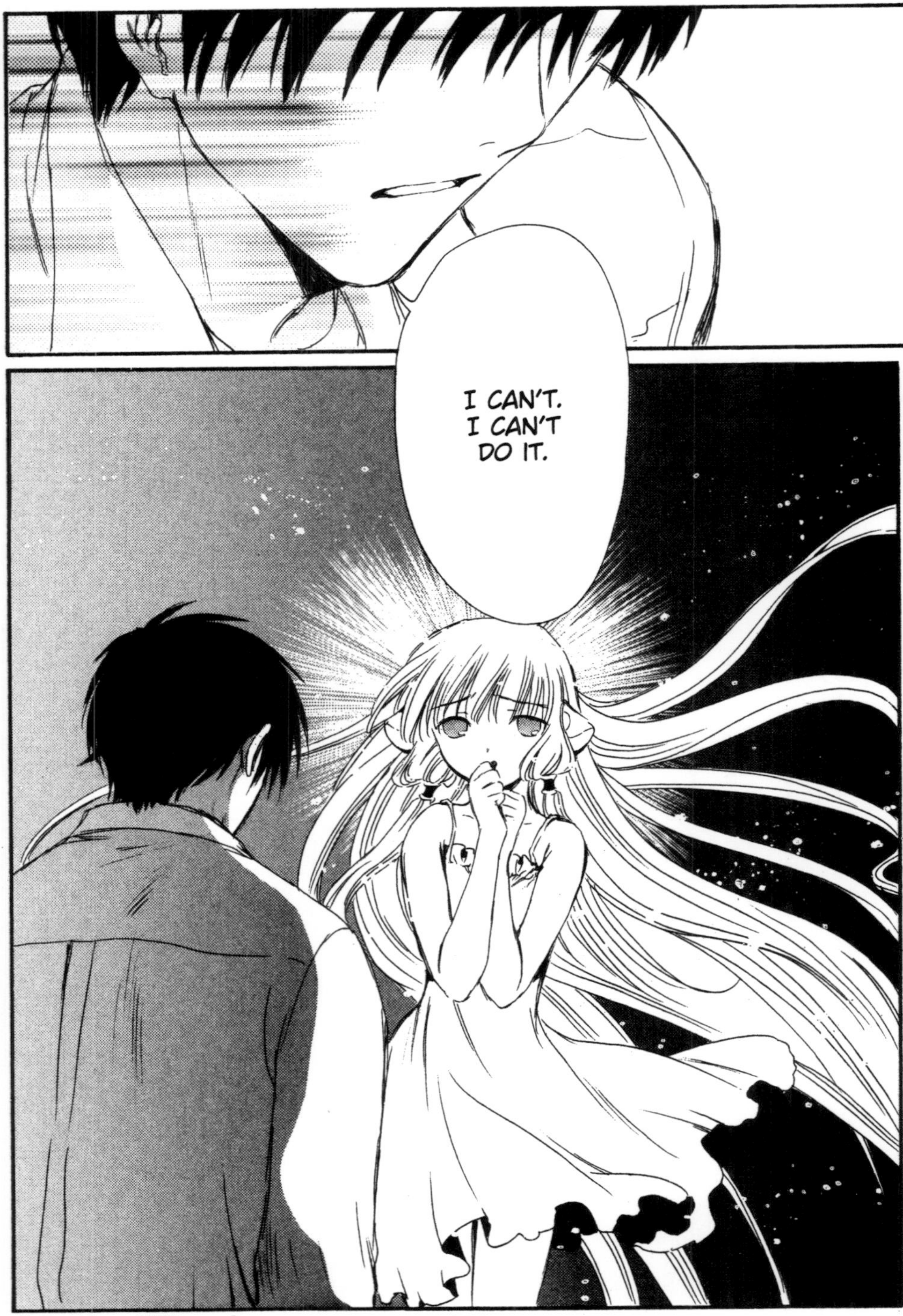
I CAN'T.
I CAN'T
DO IT.

〈chapter.87〉

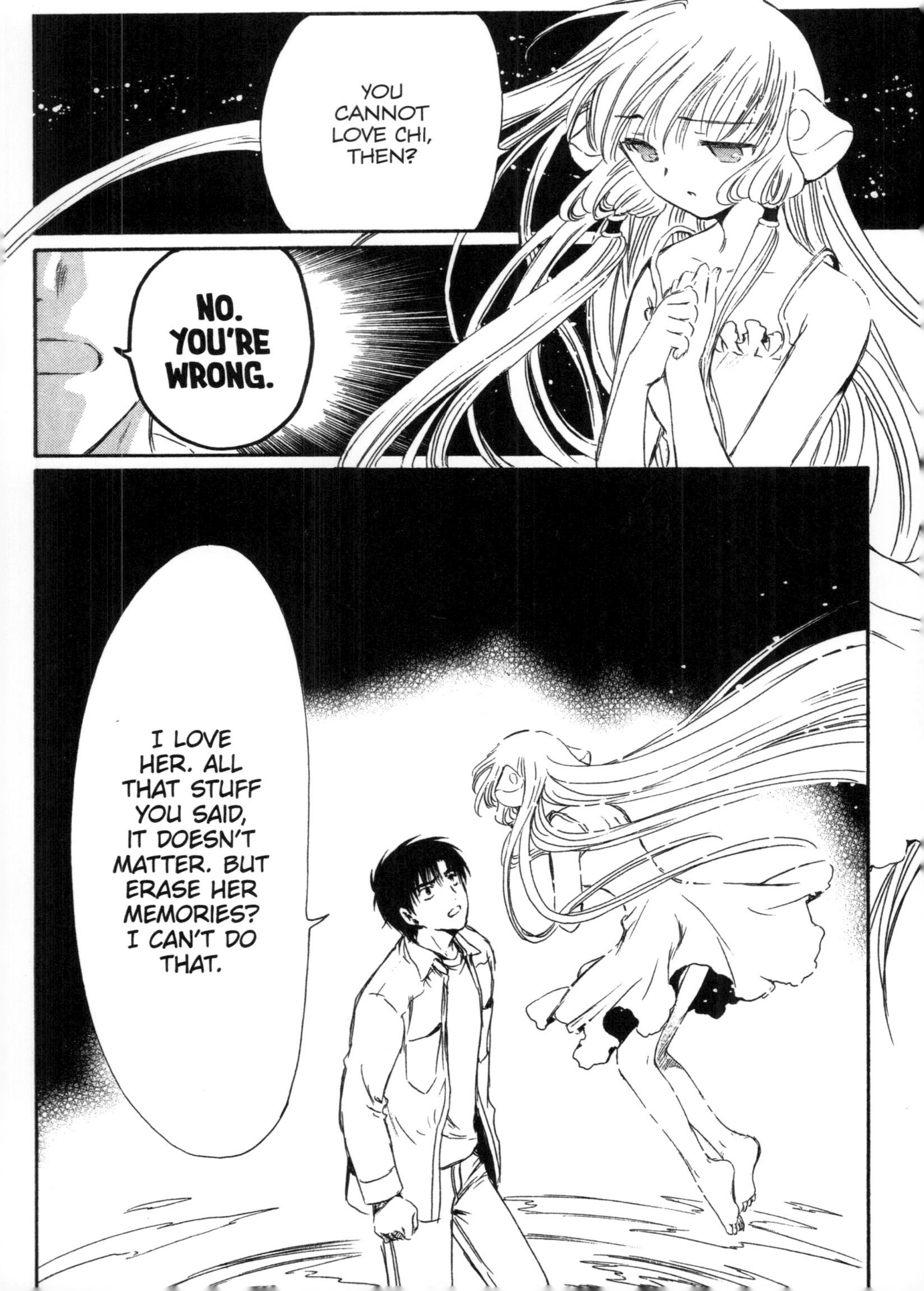
YOU CANNOT LOVE CHI, THEN?
NO. YOU'RE WRONG.
I LOVE HER. ALL THAT STUFF YOU SAID, IT DOESN'T MATTER. BUT ERASE HER MEMORIES? I CAN'T DO THAT.

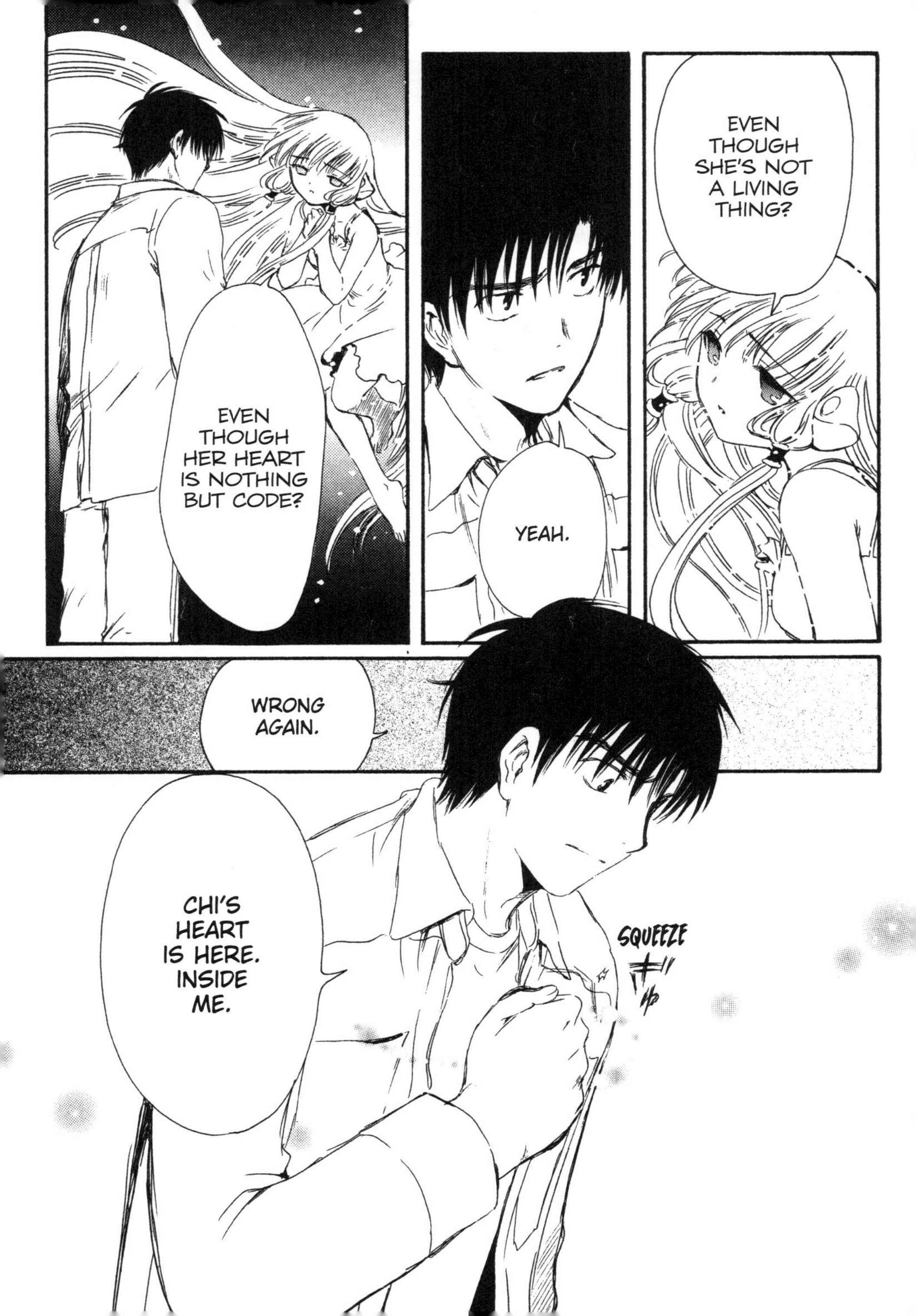
EVEN THOUGH SHE'S NOT A LIVING THING?
YEAH.
EVEN THOUGH HER HEART IS NOTHING BUT CODE?
WRONG AGAIN.
CHI'S HEART IS HERE. INSIDE ME.
SQUEEZE

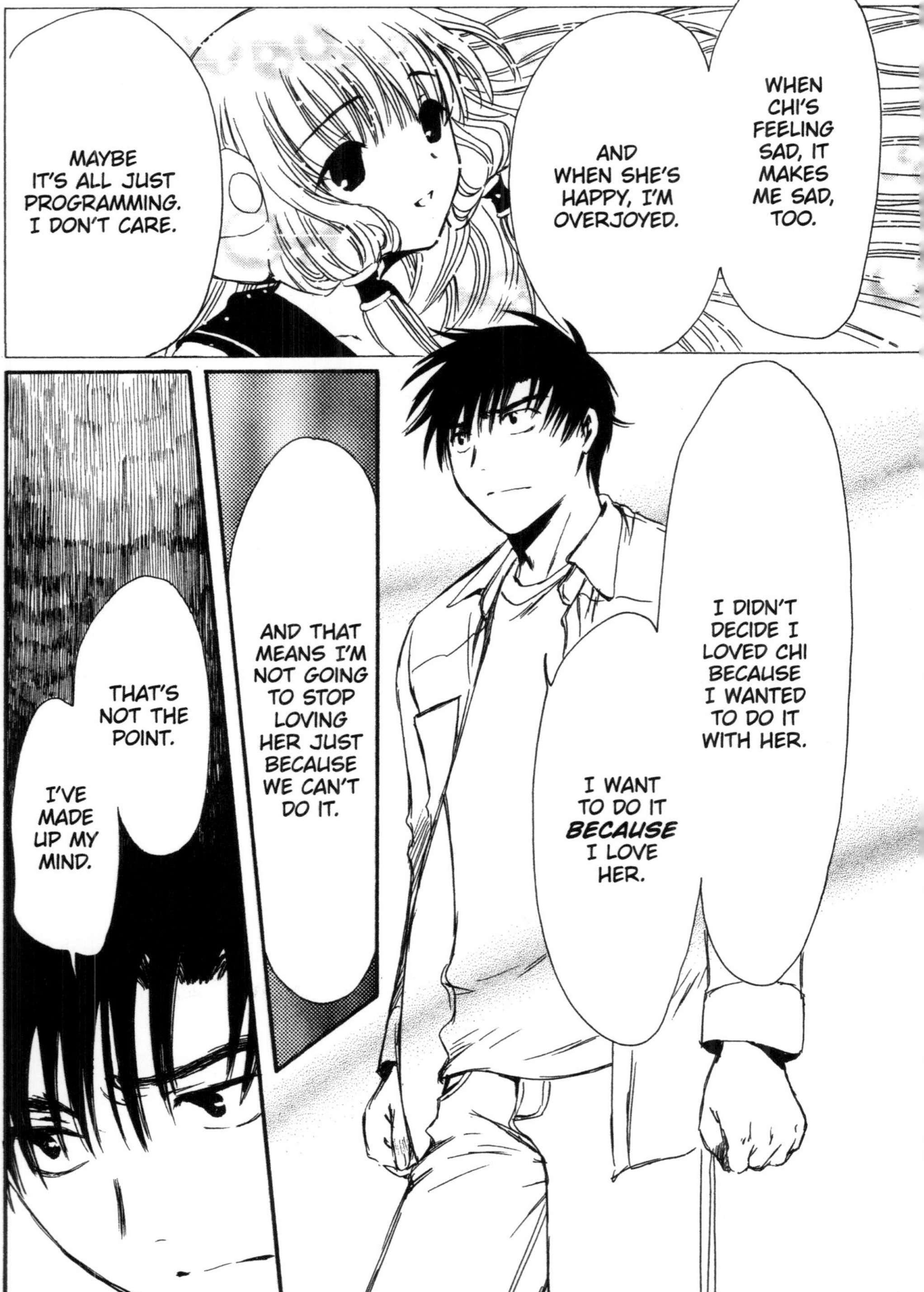
WHEN CHI'S FEELING SAD, IT MAKES ME SAD, TOO.
AND WHEN SHE'S HAPPY, I'M OVERJOYED.
MAYBE IT'S ALL JUST PROGRAMMING. I DON'T CARE.
I DIDN'T DECIDE I LOVED CHI BECAUSE I WANTED TO DO IT WITH HER.
I WANT TO DO IT *BECAUSE* I LOVE HER.
AND THAT MEANS I'M NOT GOING TO STOP LOVING HER JUST BECAUSE WE CAN'T DO IT.
THAT'S NOT THE POINT.
I'VE MADE UP MY MIND.

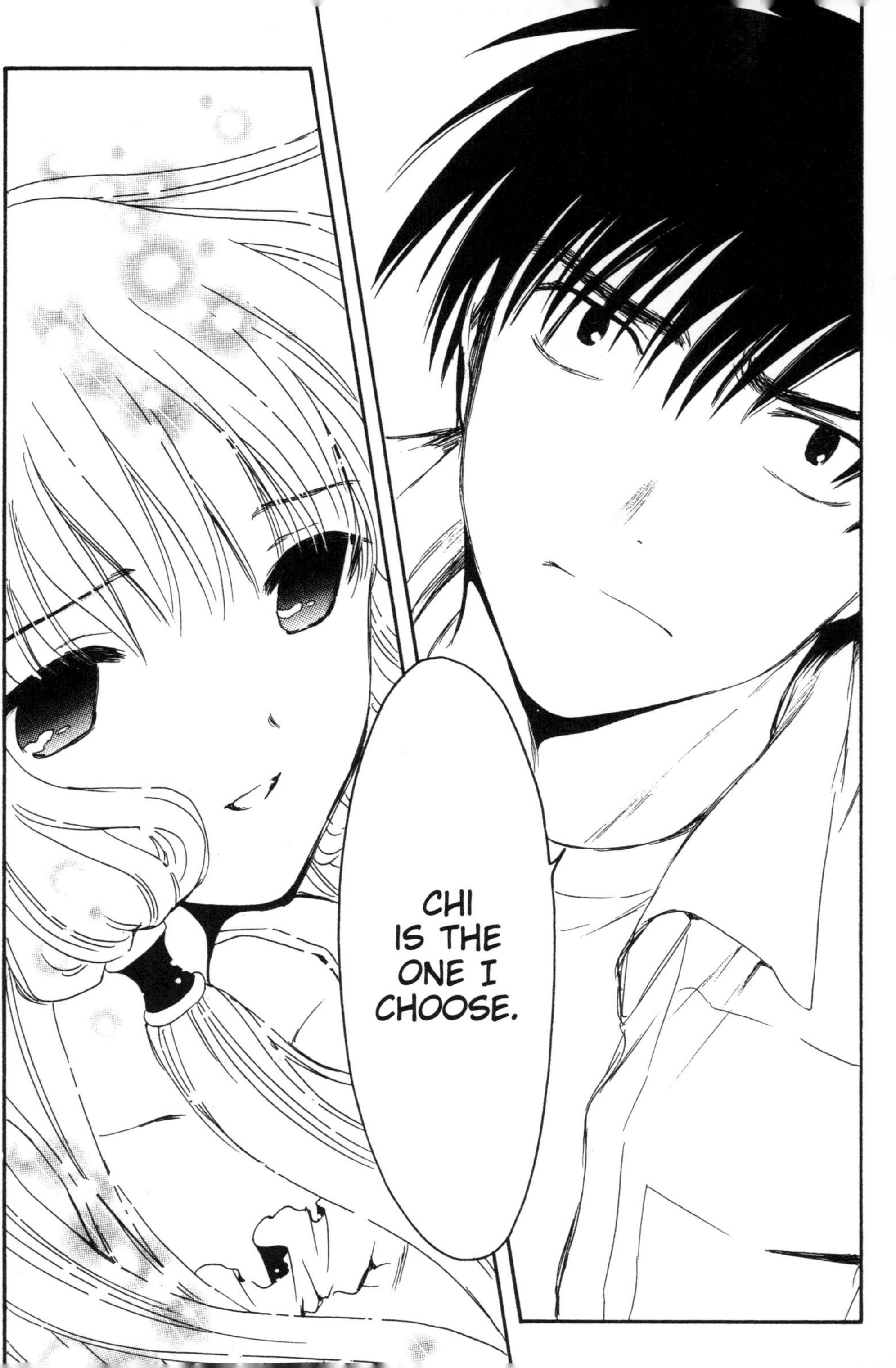
CHI IS THE ONE I CHOOSE.

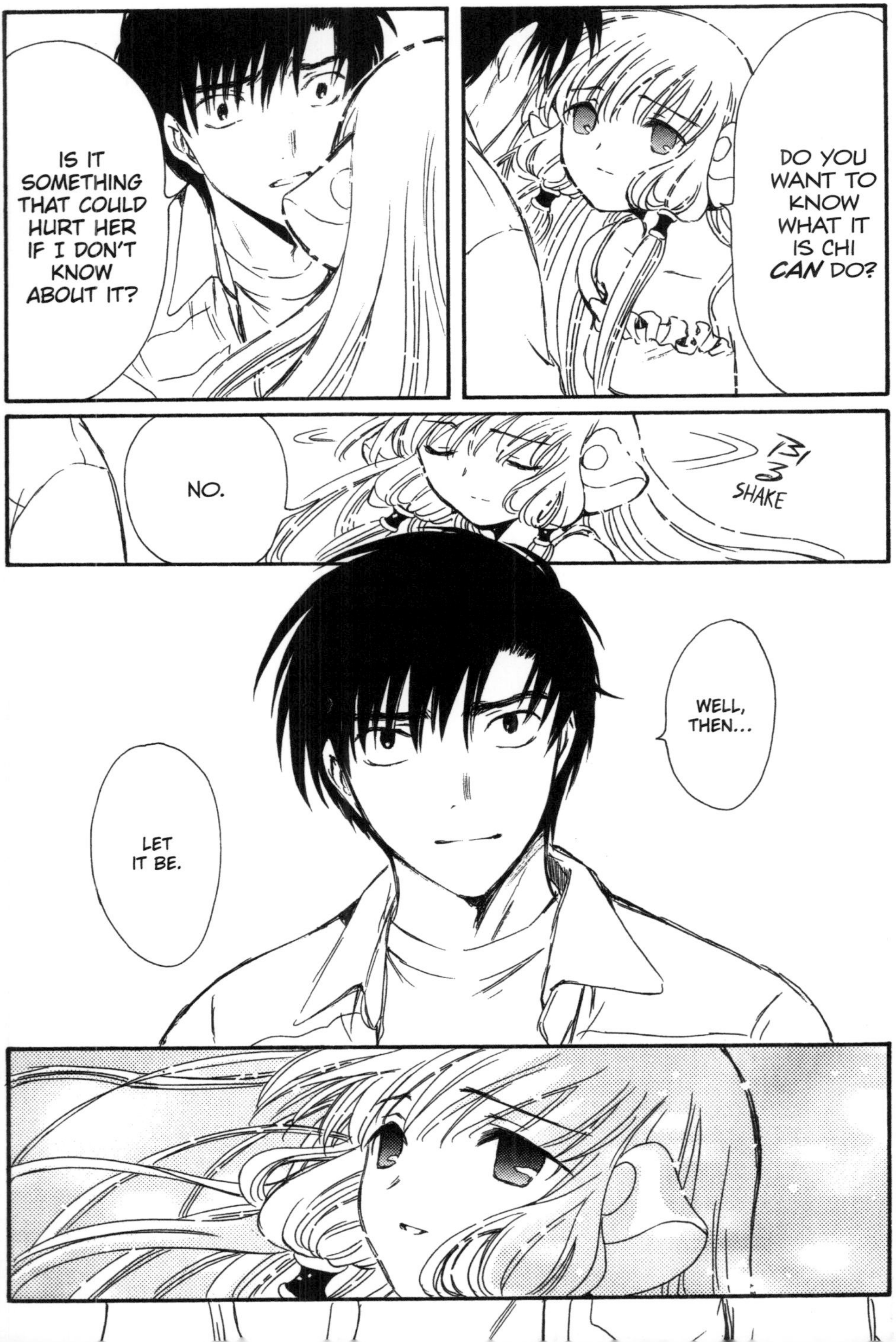
DO YOU WANT TO KNOW WHAT IT IS CHI CAN DO?
IS IT SOMETHING THAT COULD HURT HER IF I DON'T KNOW ABOUT IT?
SHAKE
NO.
WELL, THEN...
LET IT BE.

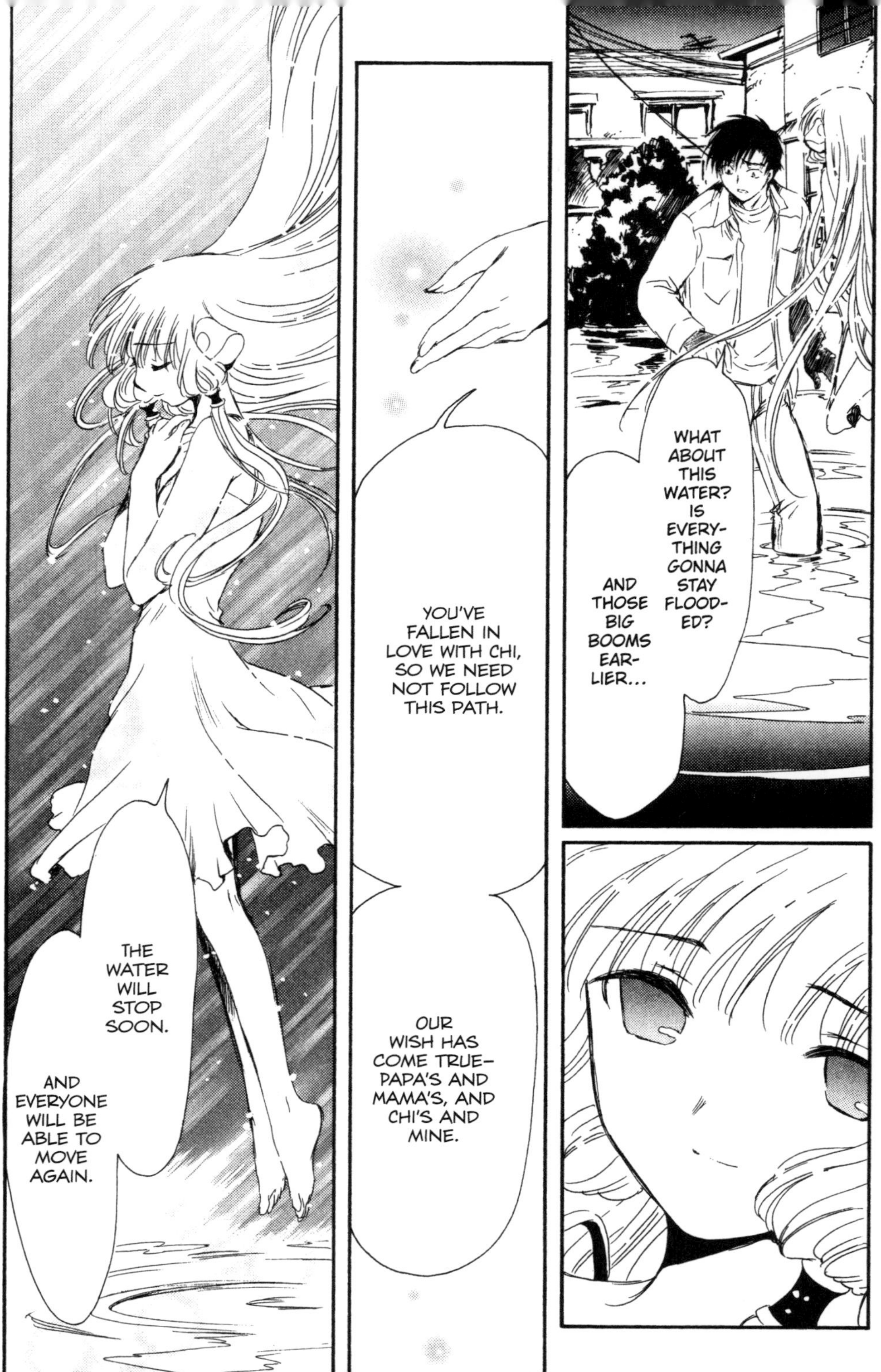
WHAT ABOUT THIS WATER? IS EVERYTHING GONNA STAY FLOODED?
AND THOSE BIG BOOMS EARLIER...
YOU'VE FALLEN IN LOVE WITH CHI, SO WE NEED NOT FOLLOW THIS PATH.
OUR WISH HAS COME TRUE—PAPA'S AND MAMA'S, AND CHI'S AND MINE.
THE WATER WILL STOP SOON.
AND EVERYONE WILL BE ABLE TO MOVE AGAIN.

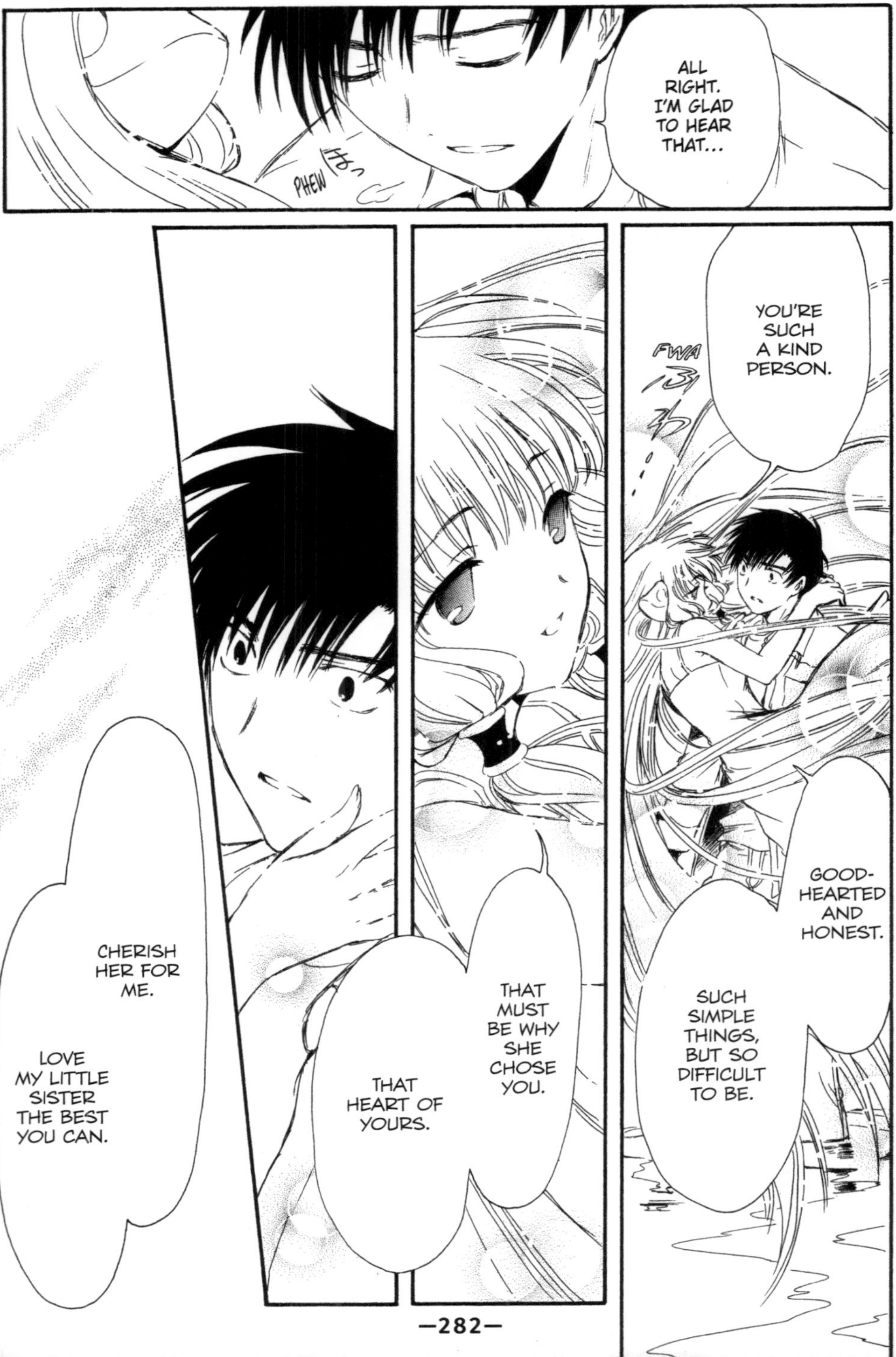
ALL RIGHT. I'M GLAD TO HEAR THAT...
PHEW
FWA
YOU'RE SUCH A KIND PERSON.
GOOD-HEARTED AND HONEST.
SUCH SIMPLE THINGS, BUT SO DIFFICULT TO BE.
THAT MUST BE WHY SHE CHOSE YOU.
THAT HEART OF YOURS.
CHERISH HER FOR ME.
LOVE MY LITTLE SISTER THE BEST YOU CAN.

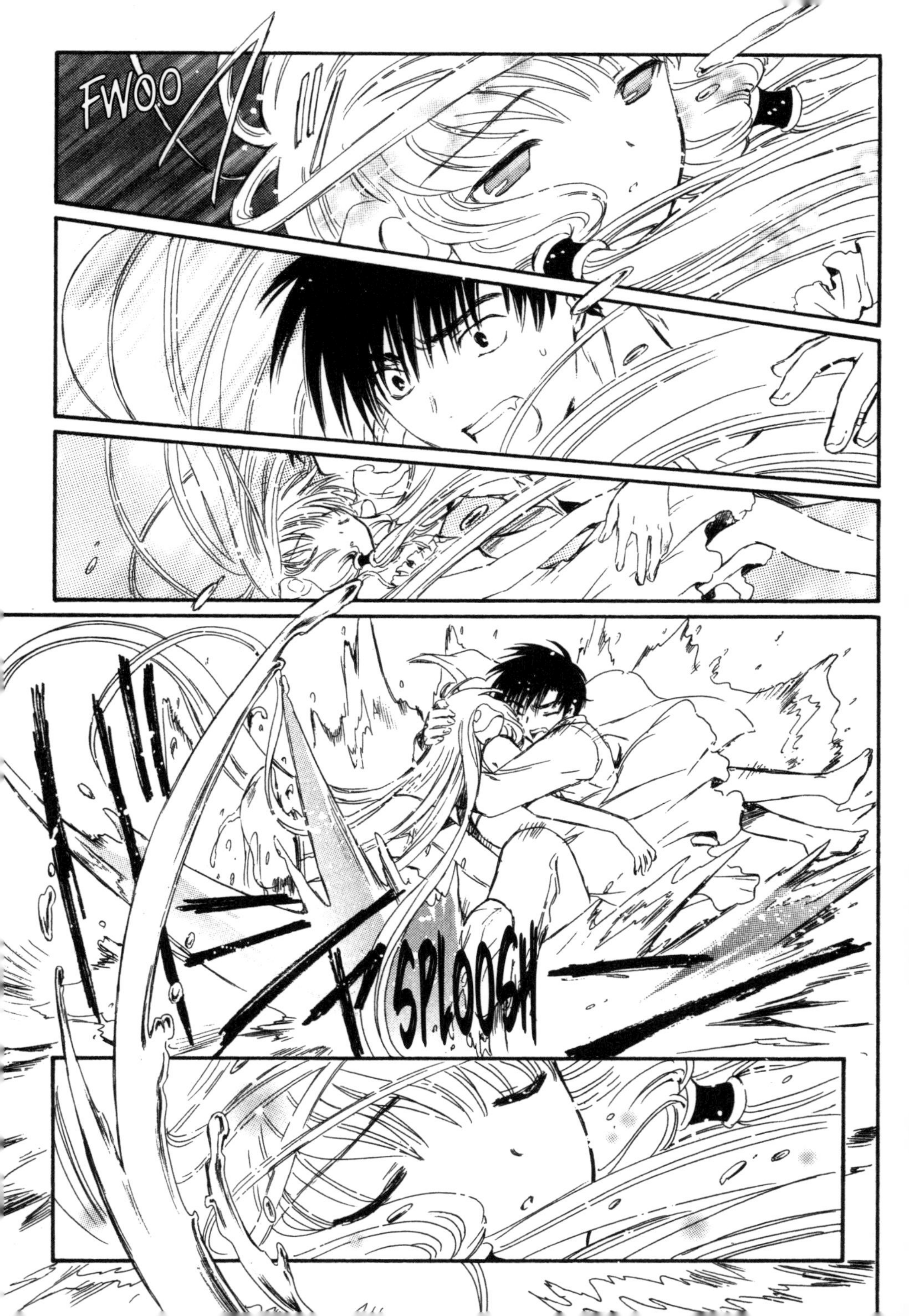
FWOO
SPLOOSH

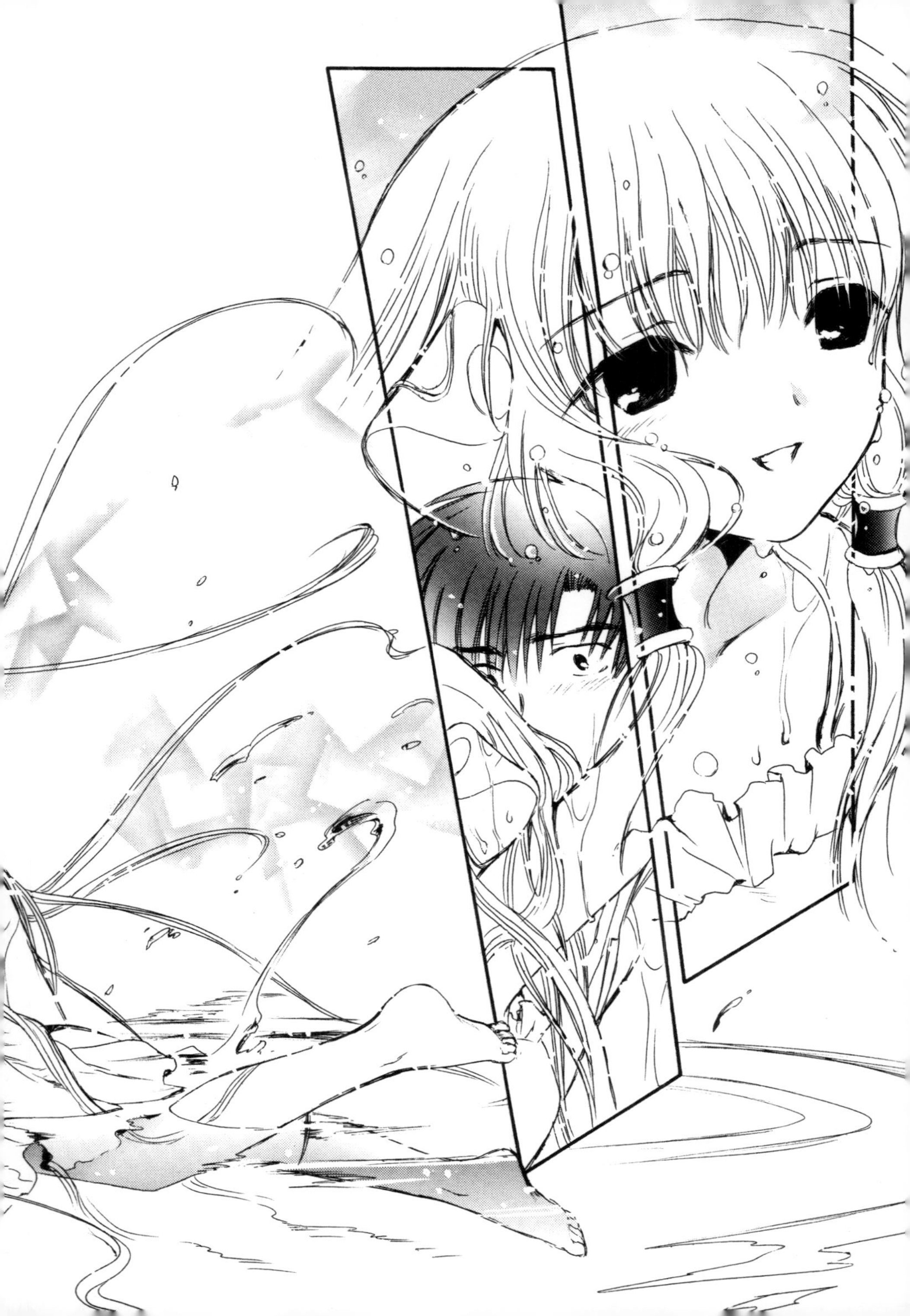

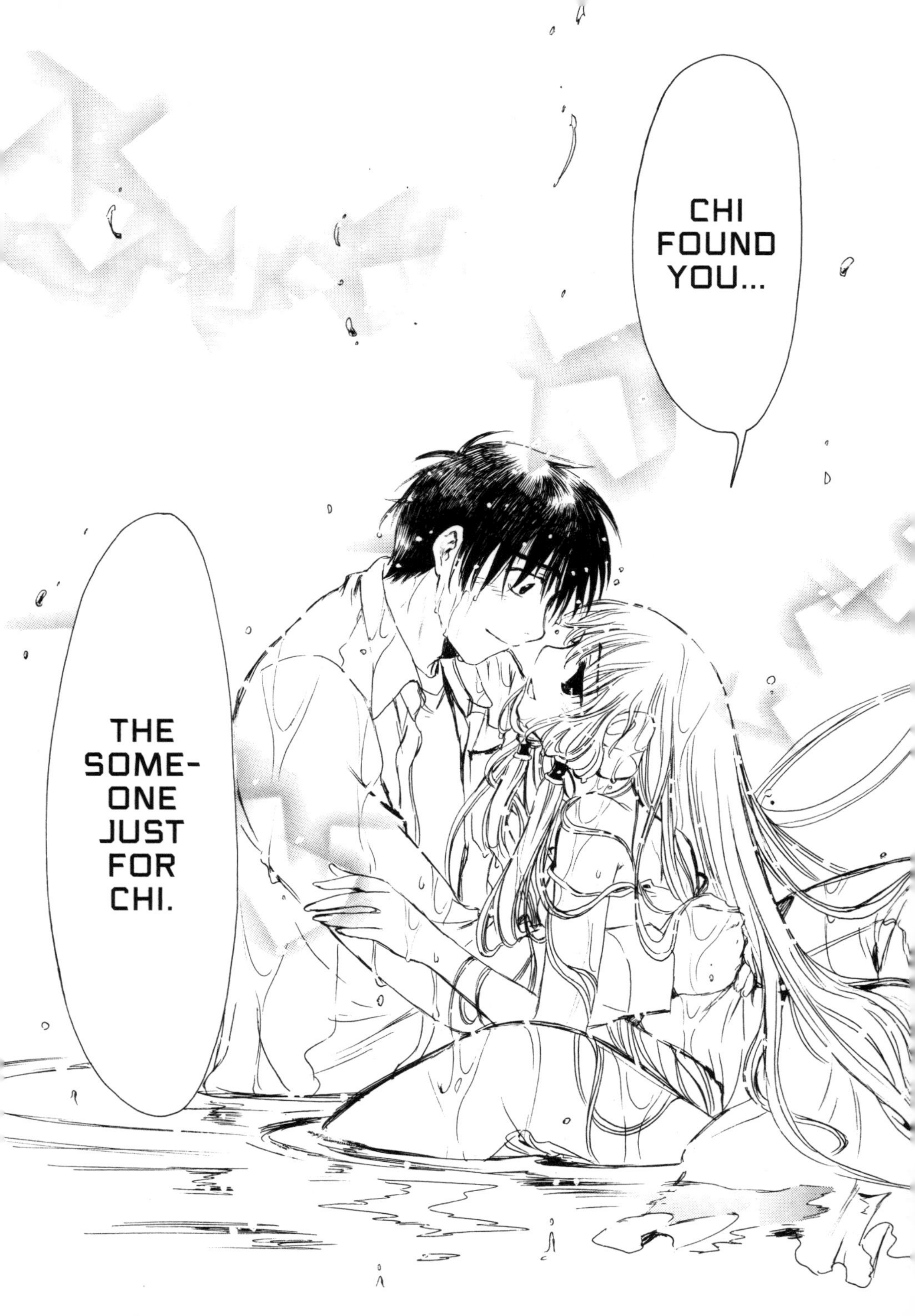
CHI FOUND YOU...
THE SOMEONE JUST FOR CHI.

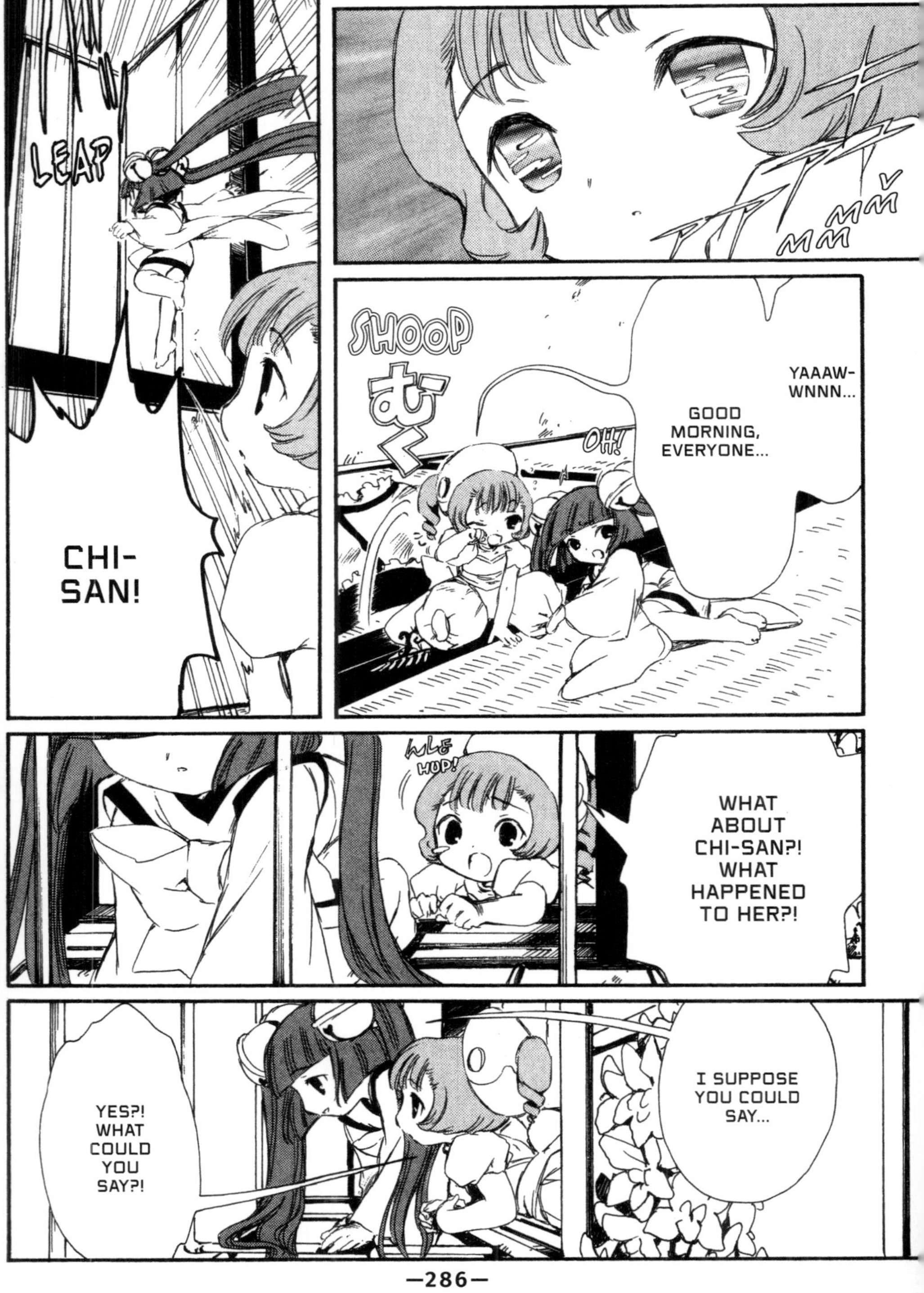
YAAAW-WNNN...
GOOD MORNING, EVERYONE...
SHOOP
むく
OH!
LEAP
CHI-SAN!
WHAT ABOUT CHI-SAN?! WHAT HAPPENED TO HER?!
HUP!
I SUPPOSE YOU COULD SAY...
YES?! WHAT COULD YOU SAY?!

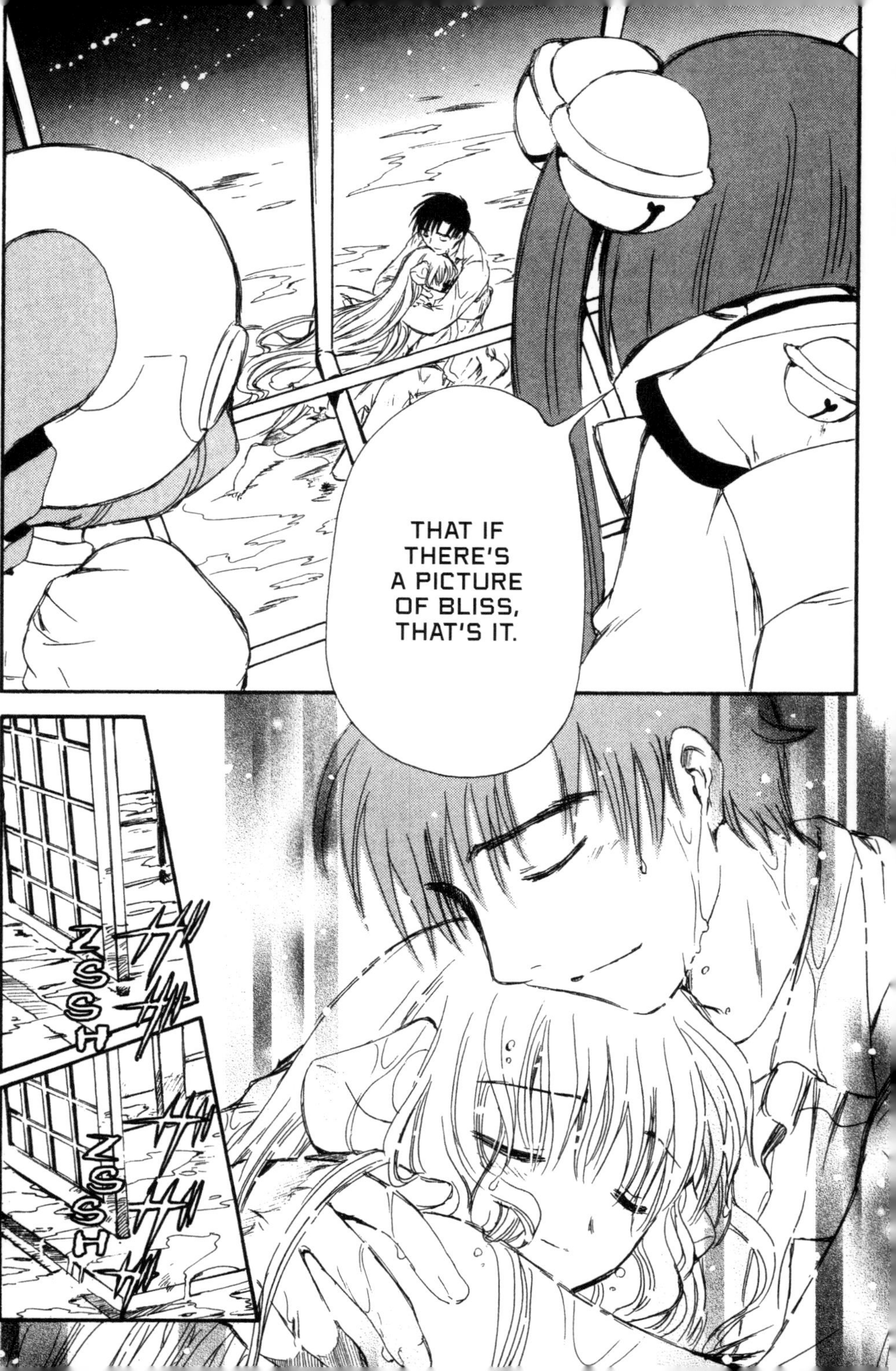
THAT IF THERE'S A PICTURE OF BLISS, THAT'S IT.
ZSSH
ZSSH

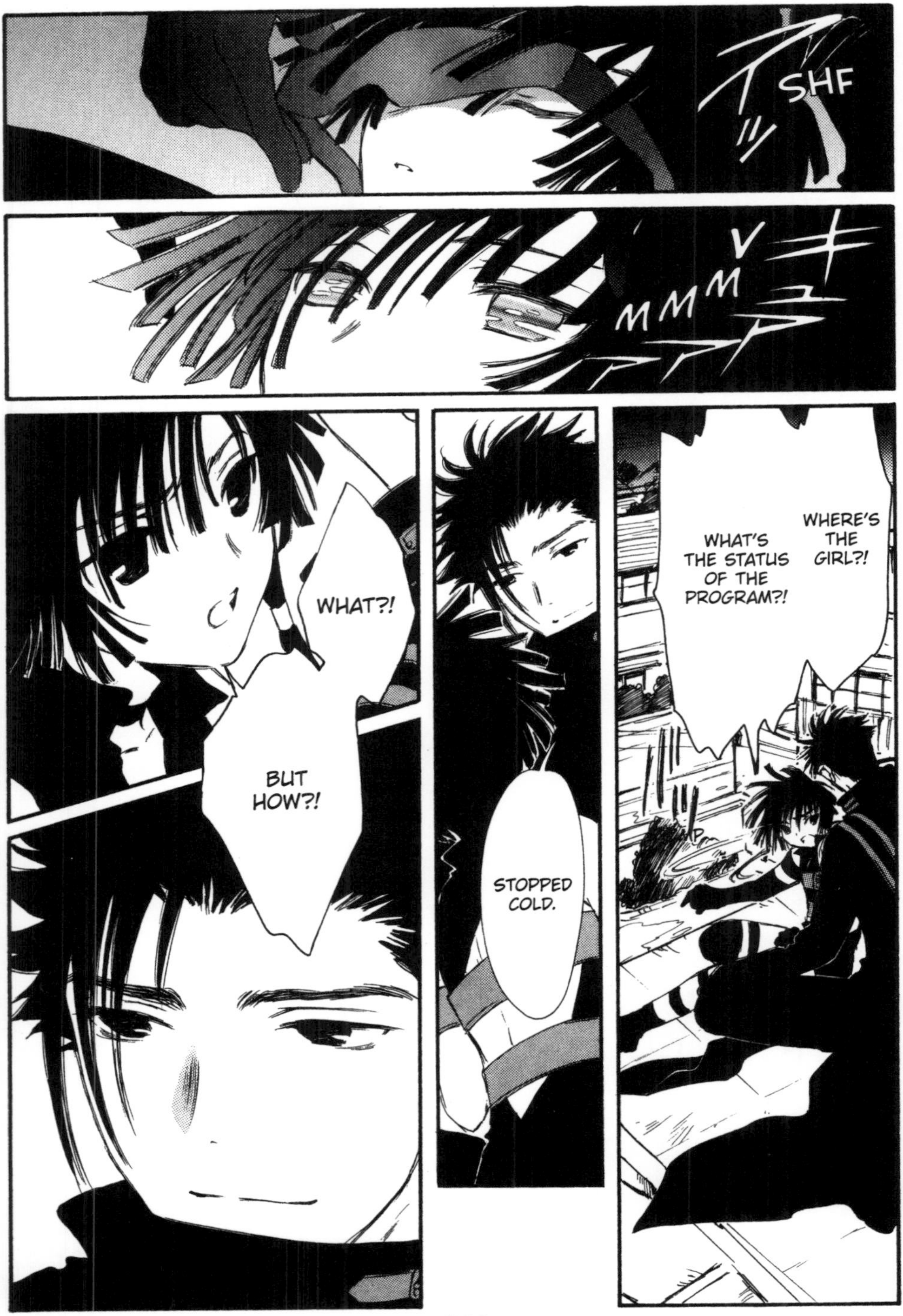
SHF
MMMV
WHERE'S THE GIRL?!
WHAT'S THE STATUS OF THE PROGRAM?!
STOPPED COLD.
WHAT?!
BUT HOW?!

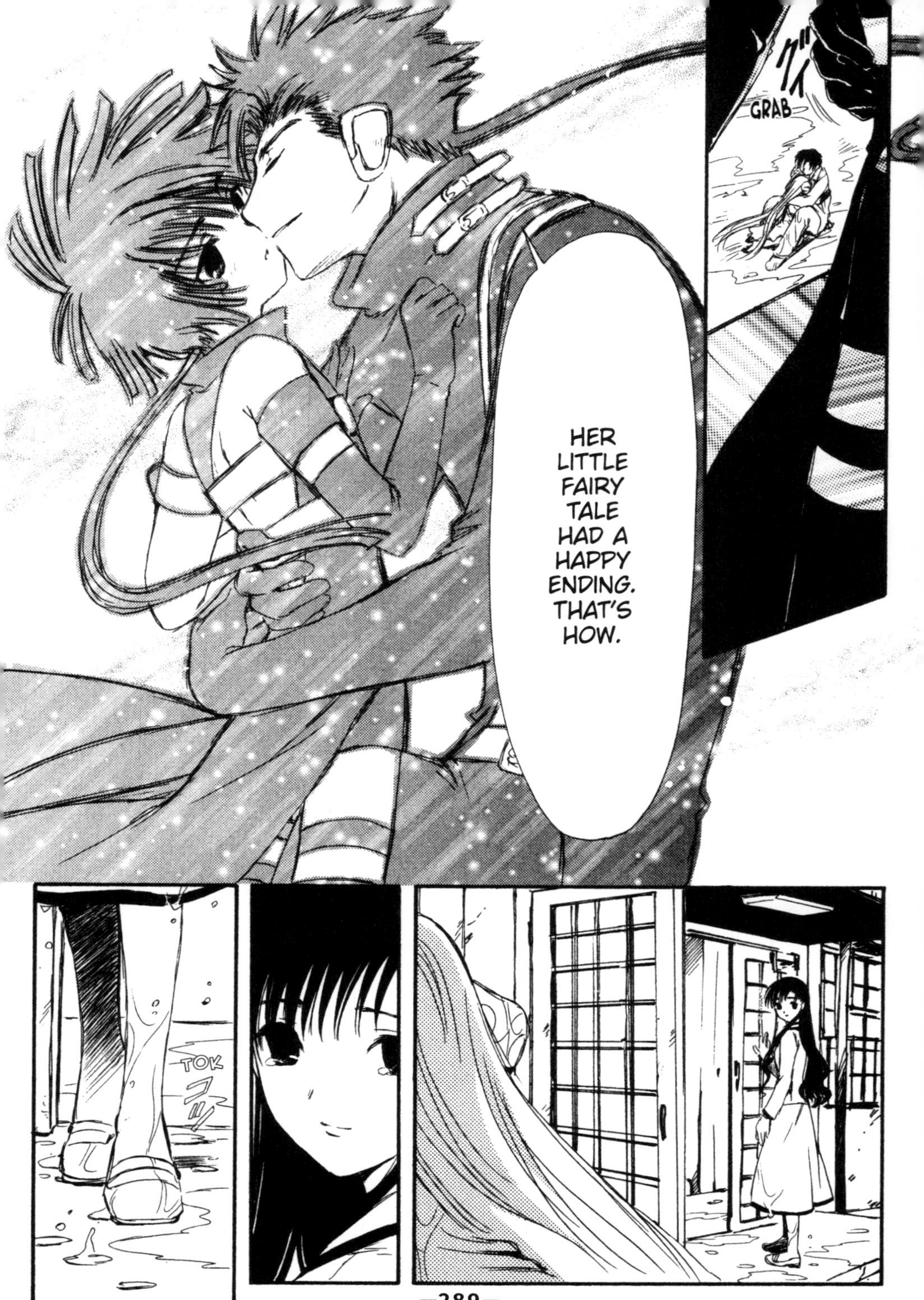
グイ
GRAB
HER LITTLE FAIRY TALE HAD A HAPPY ENDING. THAT'S HOW.
TOK

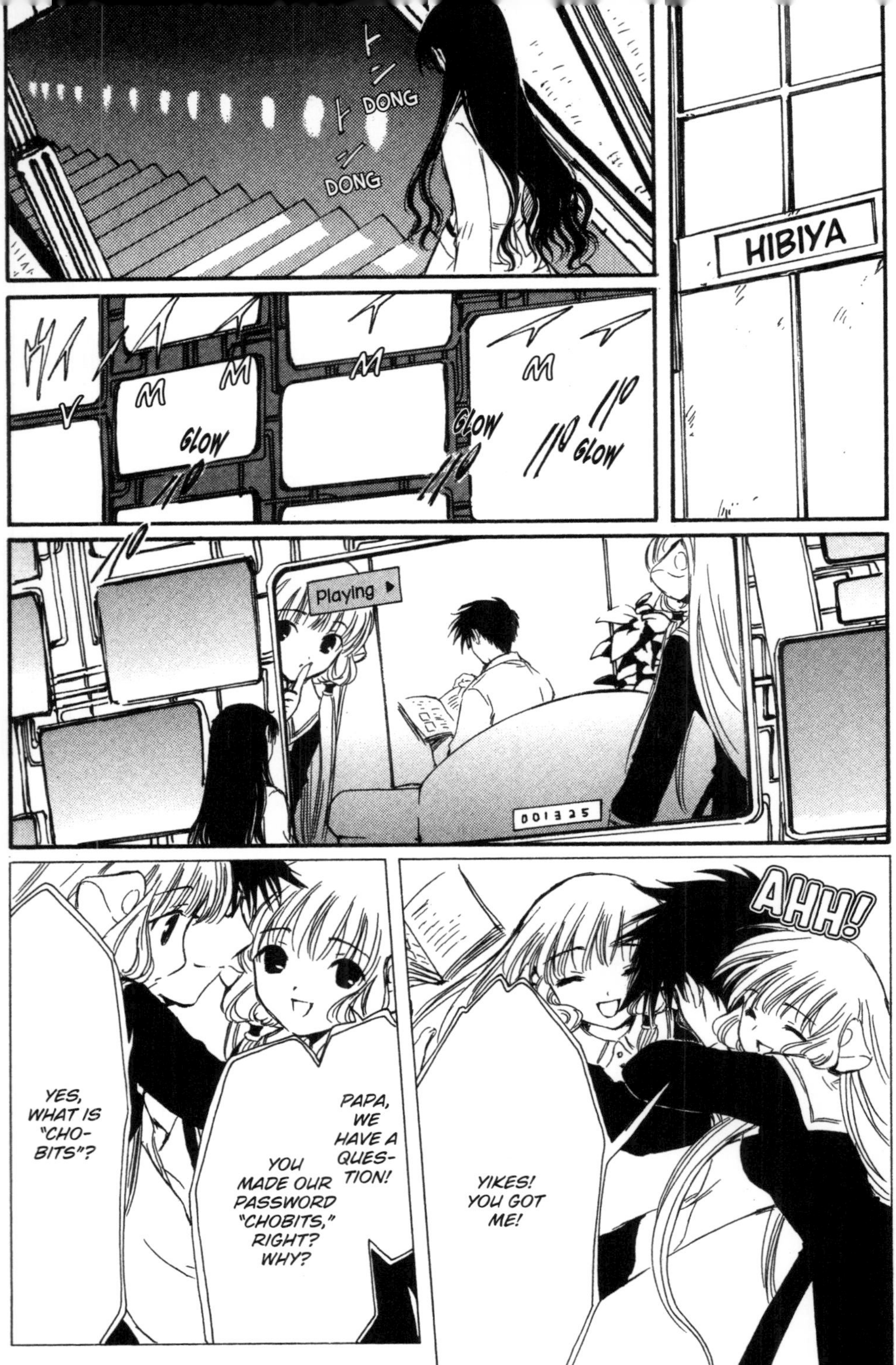
HIBIYA
トン
DONG
トン
DONG
M
M
M
M
GLOW
GLOW
GLOW
Playing
001325
AHH!
YIKES! YOU GOT ME!
PAPA, WE HAVE A QUESTION!
YOU MADE OUR PASSWORD "CHOBITS," RIGHT? WHY?
YES, WHAT IS "CHO-BITS"?

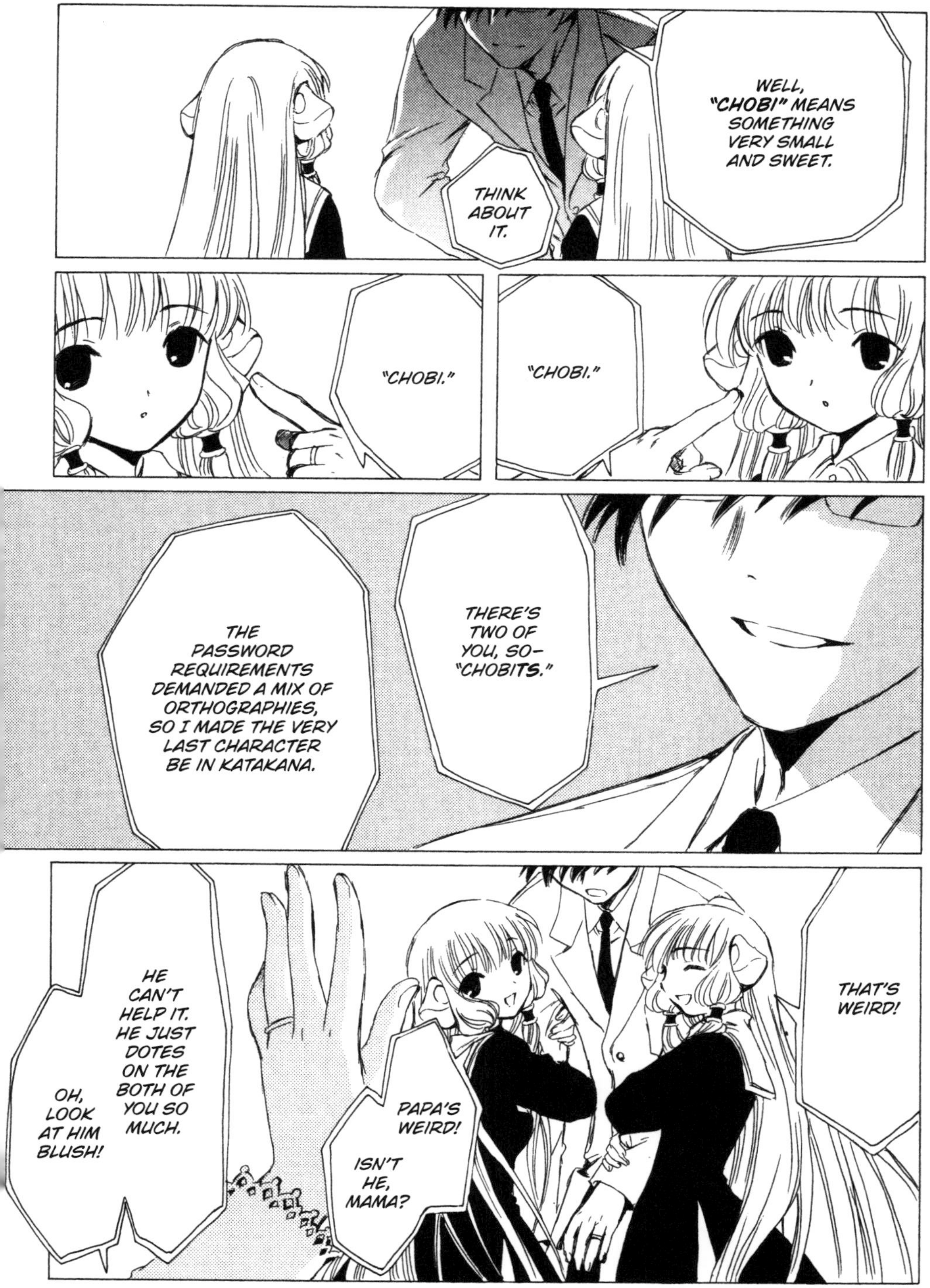
WELL, "CHOBI" MEANS SOMETHING VERY SMALL AND SWEET.
THINK ABOUT IT.
"CHOBI."
"CHOBI."
THERE'S TWO OF YOU, SO— "CHOBITS."
THE PASSWORD REQUIREMENTS DEMANDED A MIX OF ORTHOGRAPHIES, SO I MADE THE VERY LAST CHARACTER BE IN KATAKANA.
THAT'S WEIRD!
PAPA'S WEIRD!
ISN'T HE, MAMA?
HE CAN'T HELP IT. HE JUST DOTES ON THE BOTH OF YOU SO MUCH.
OH, LOOK AT HIM BLUSH!

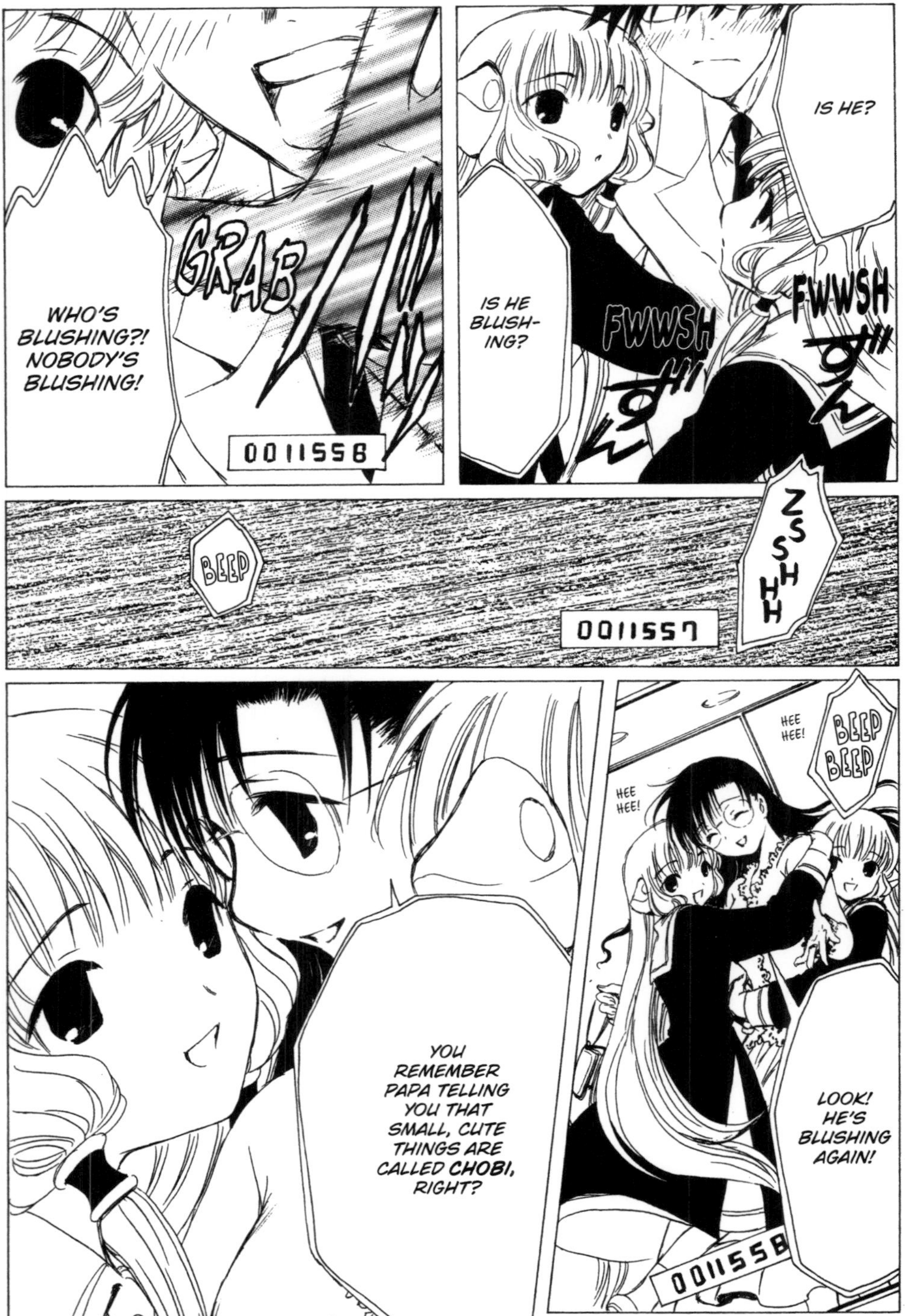
IS HE?
IS HE BLUSHING?
FWWSH
FWWSH
GRAB
WHO'S BLUSHING?! NOBODY'S BLUSHING!
0011556
ZSSHHH
0011557
BEEP
BEEP BEEP
HEE HEE!
HEE HEE!
LOOK! HE'S BLUSHING AGAIN!
0011558
YOU REMEMBER PAPA TELLING YOU THAT SMALL, CUTE THINGS ARE CALLED CHOBI, RIGHT?

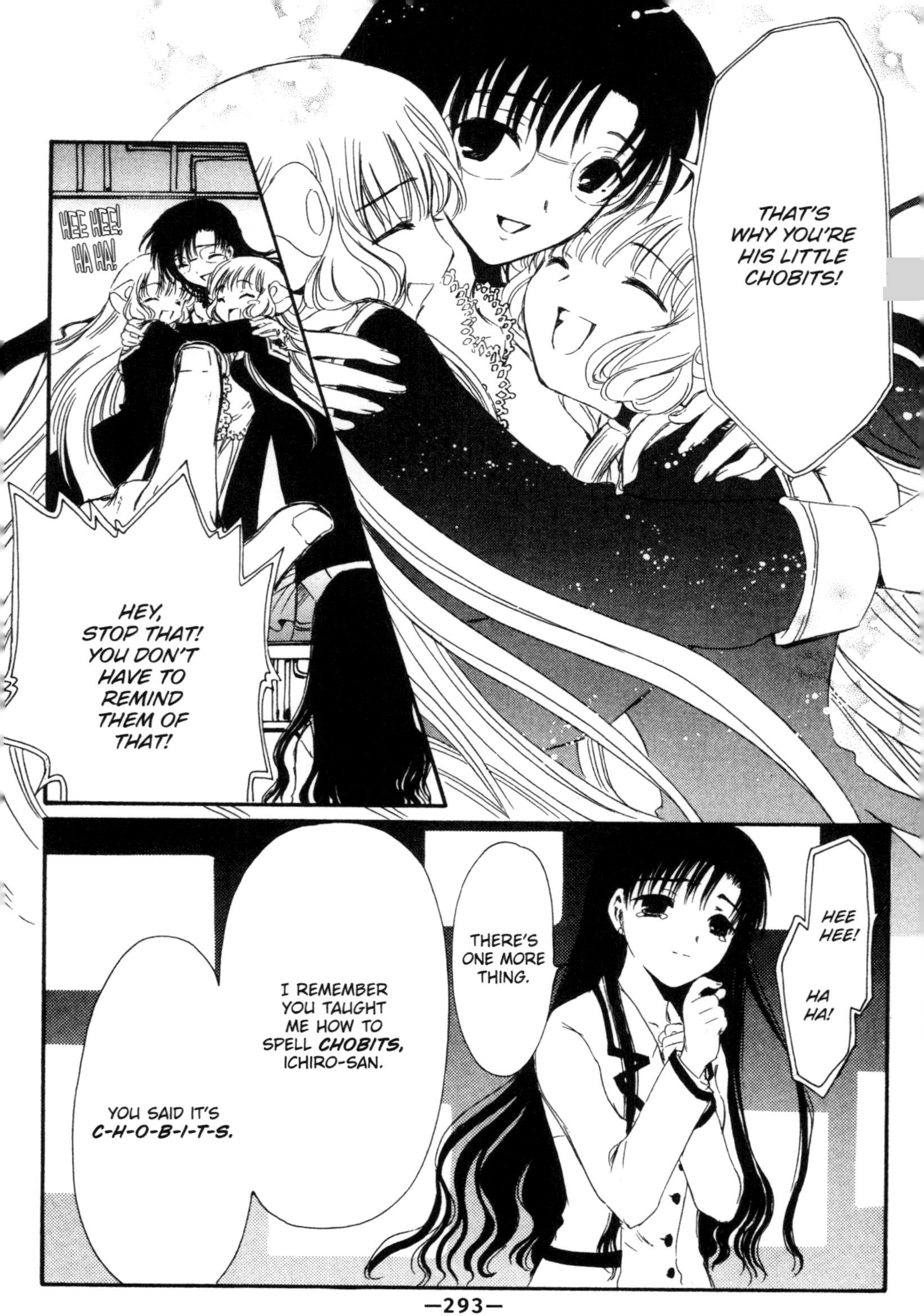
THAT'S WHY YOU'RE HIS LITTLE CHOBITS!
HEE HEE! HA HA!
HEY, STOP THAT! YOU DON'T HAVE TO REMIND THEM OF THAT!
HEE HEE!
HA HA!
THERE'S ONE MORE THING.
I REMEMBER YOU TAUGHT ME HOW TO SPELL ***CHOBITS***, ICHIRO-SAN.
YOU SAID IT'S ***C-H-O-B-I-T-S.***

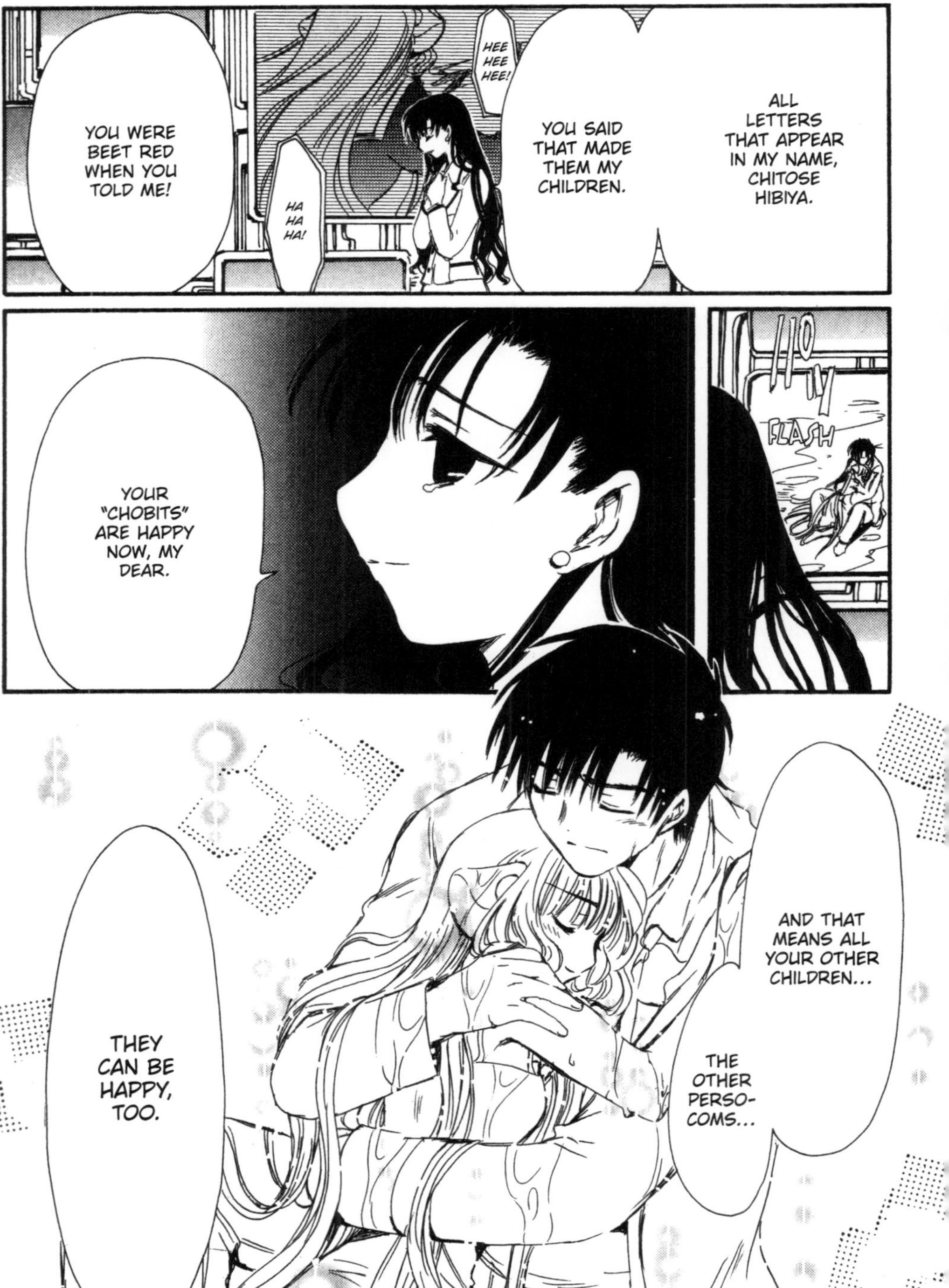
ALL LETTERS THAT APPEAR IN MY NAME, CHITOSE HIBIYA.
YOU SAID THAT MADE THEM MY CHILDREN.
HEE HEE HEE!
HA HA HA!
YOU WERE BEET RED WHEN YOU TOLD ME!
FLASH
YOUR "CHOBITS" ARE HAPPY NOW, MY DEAR.
AND THAT MEANS ALL YOUR OTHER CHILDREN...
THE OTHER PERSO-COMS...
THEY CAN BE HAPPY, TOO.

〈chapter.87〉 end

〈chapter.88〉

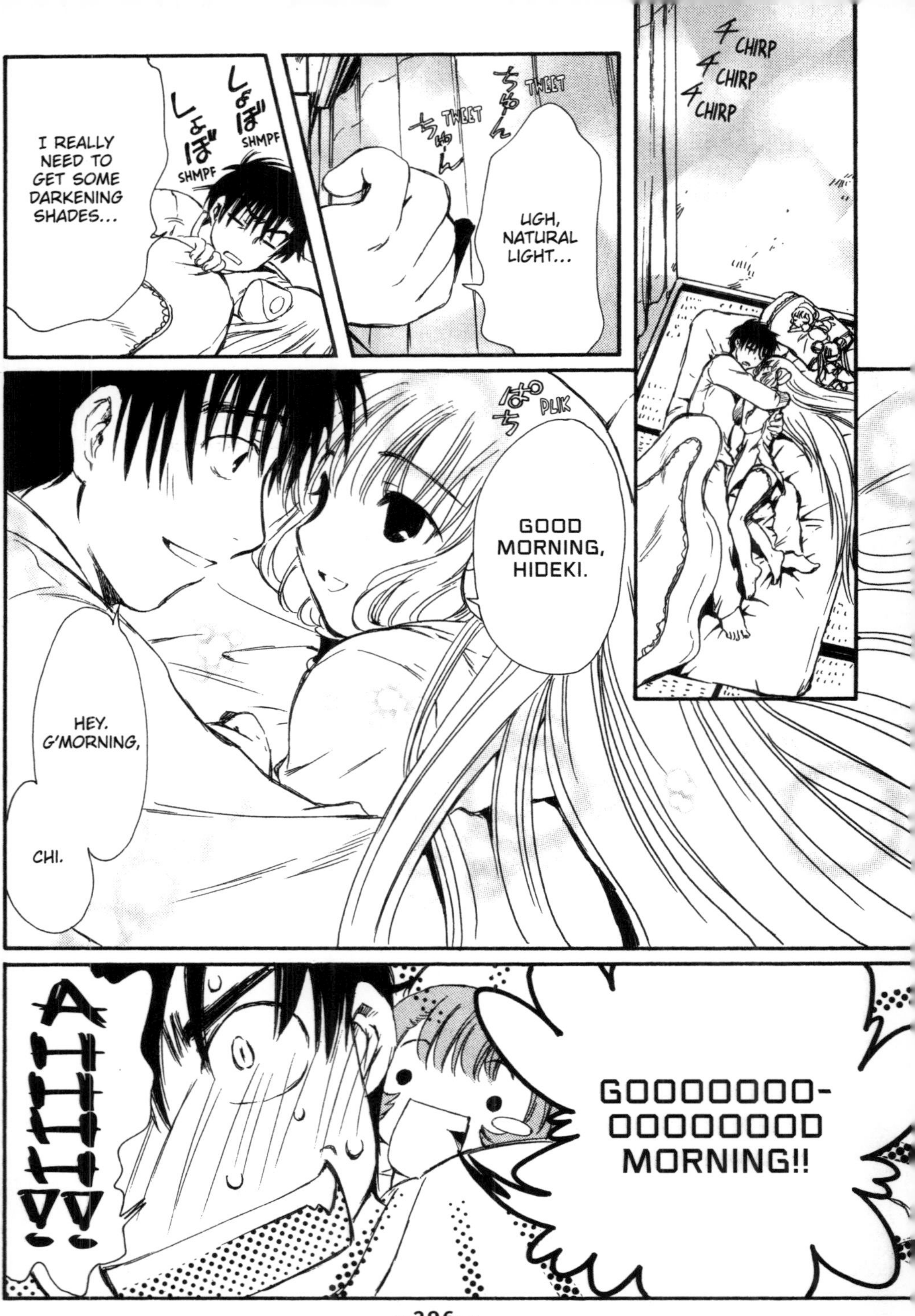
4 CHIRP
4 CHIRP
4 CHIRP
ちゅん TWEET
ちゅん TWEET
UGH, NATURAL LIGHT...
しょぼ SHMPF
しょぼ SHMPF
I REALLY NEED TO GET SOME DARKENING SHADES...
ぱち PLIK
GOOD MORNING, HIDEKI.
HEY. G'MORNING, CHI.
GOOOOOOO-OOOOOOOD MORNING!!
AIIII!!

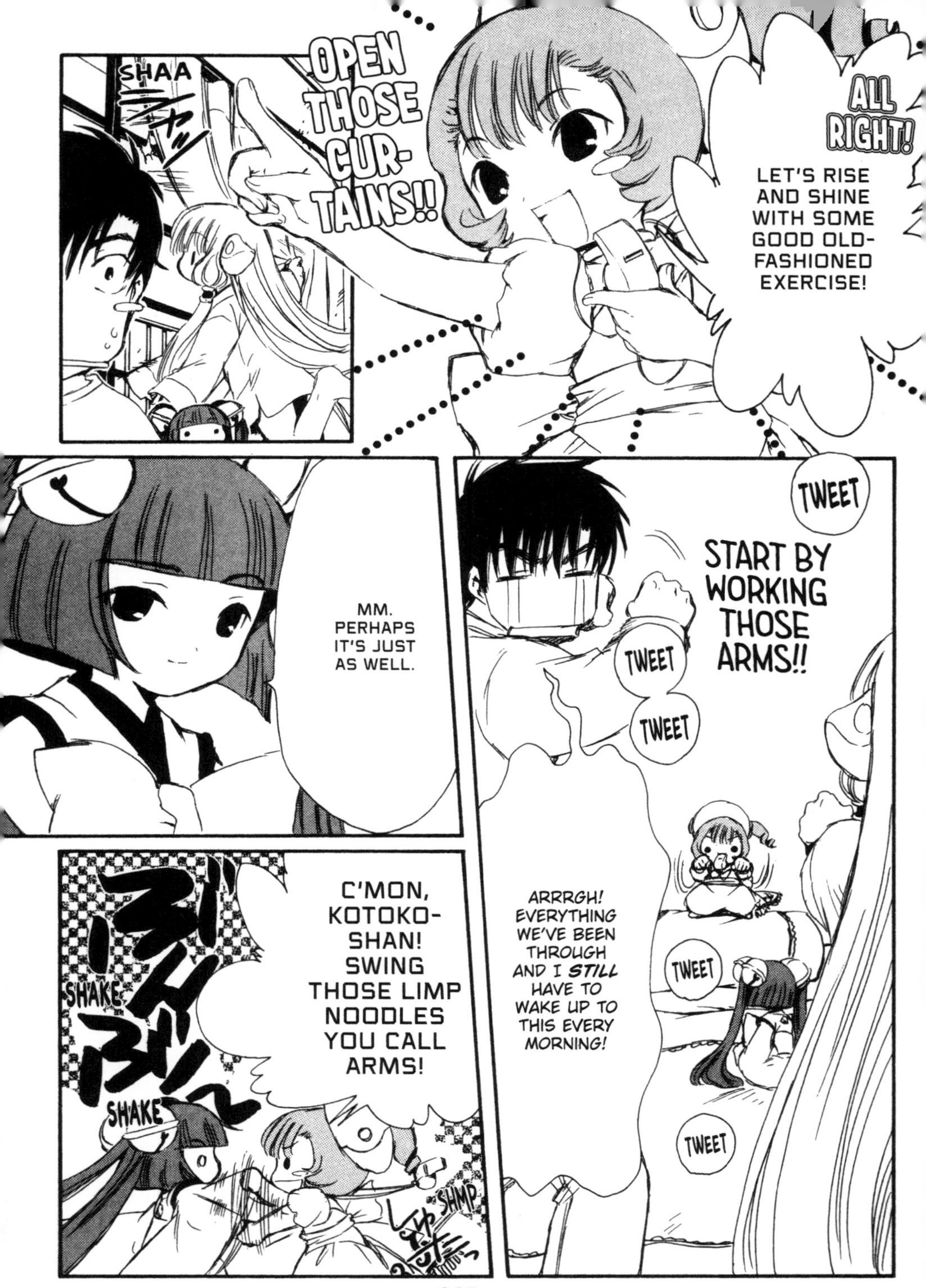
ALL RIGHT!
LET'S RISE AND SHINE WITH SOME GOOD OLD-FASHIONED EXERCISE!
OPEN THOSE CUR-TAINS!!
SHAA
TWEET
START BY WORKING THOSE ARMS!!
TWEET
TWEET
ARRRGH! EVERYTHING WE'VE BEEN THROUGH AND I *STILL* HAVE TO WAKE UP TO THIS EVERY MORNING!
TWEET
TWEET
MM. PERHAPS IT'S JUST AS WELL.
C'MON, KOTOKO-SHAN! SWING THOSE LIMP NOODLES YOU CALL ARMS!
SHAKE
SHAKE
SHMP

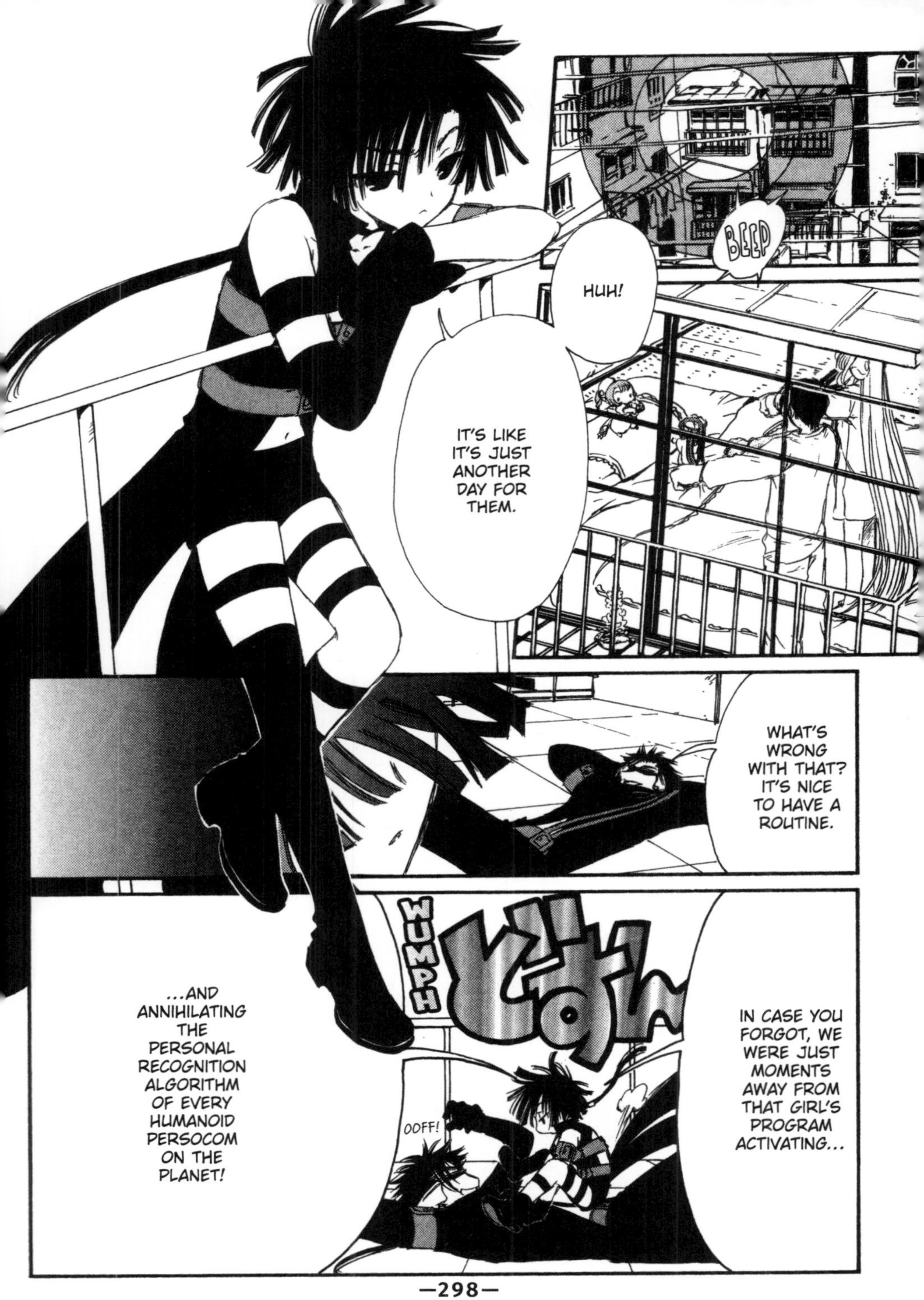
BEEP
HUH!
IT'S LIKE IT'S JUST ANOTHER DAY FOR THEM.
WHAT'S WRONG WITH THAT? IT'S NICE TO HAVE A ROUTINE.
IN CASE YOU FORGOT, WE WERE JUST MOMENTS AWAY FROM THAT GIRL'S PROGRAM ACTIVATING...
WUMPH
OOFF!
...AND ANNIHILATING THE PERSONAL RECOGNITION ALGORITHM OF EVERY HUMANOID PERSOCOM ON THE PLANET!

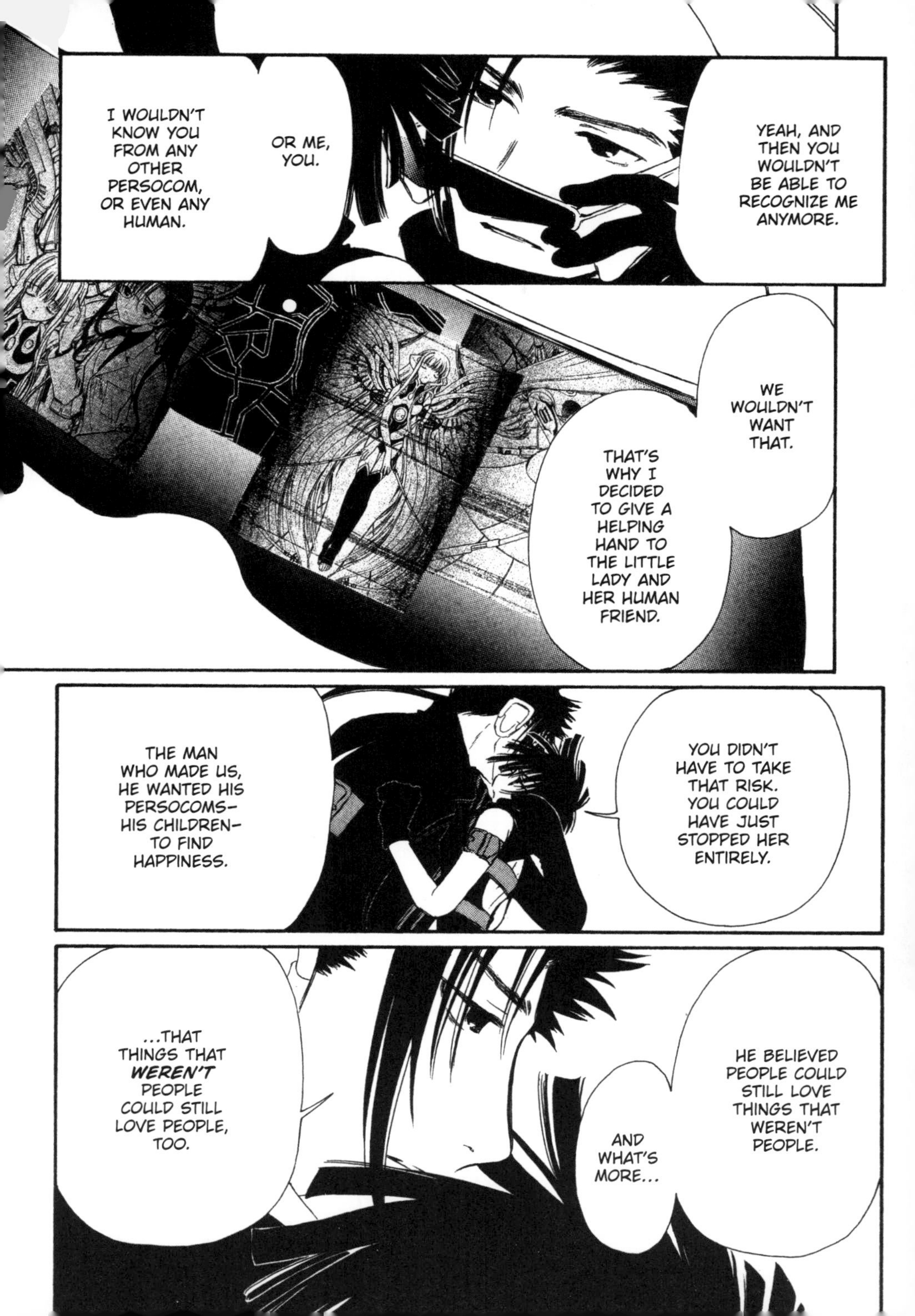
YEAH, AND THEN YOU WOULDN'T BE ABLE TO RECOGNIZE ME ANYMORE.
I WOULDN'T KNOW YOU FROM ANY OTHER PERSOCOM, OR EVEN ANY HUMAN.
OR ME, YOU.
WE WOULDN'T WANT THAT.
THAT'S WHY I DECIDED TO GIVE A HELPING HAND TO THE LITTLE LADY AND HER HUMAN FRIEND.
YOU DIDN'T HAVE TO TAKE THAT RISK. YOU COULD HAVE JUST STOPPED HER ENTIRELY.
THE MAN WHO MADE US, HE WANTED HIS PERSOCOMS– HIS CHILDREN– TO FIND HAPPINESS.
HE BELIEVED PEOPLE COULD STILL LOVE THINGS THAT WEREN'T PEOPLE.
AND WHAT'S MORE...
...THAT THINGS THAT ***WEREN'T*** PEOPLE COULD STILL LOVE PEOPLE, TOO.

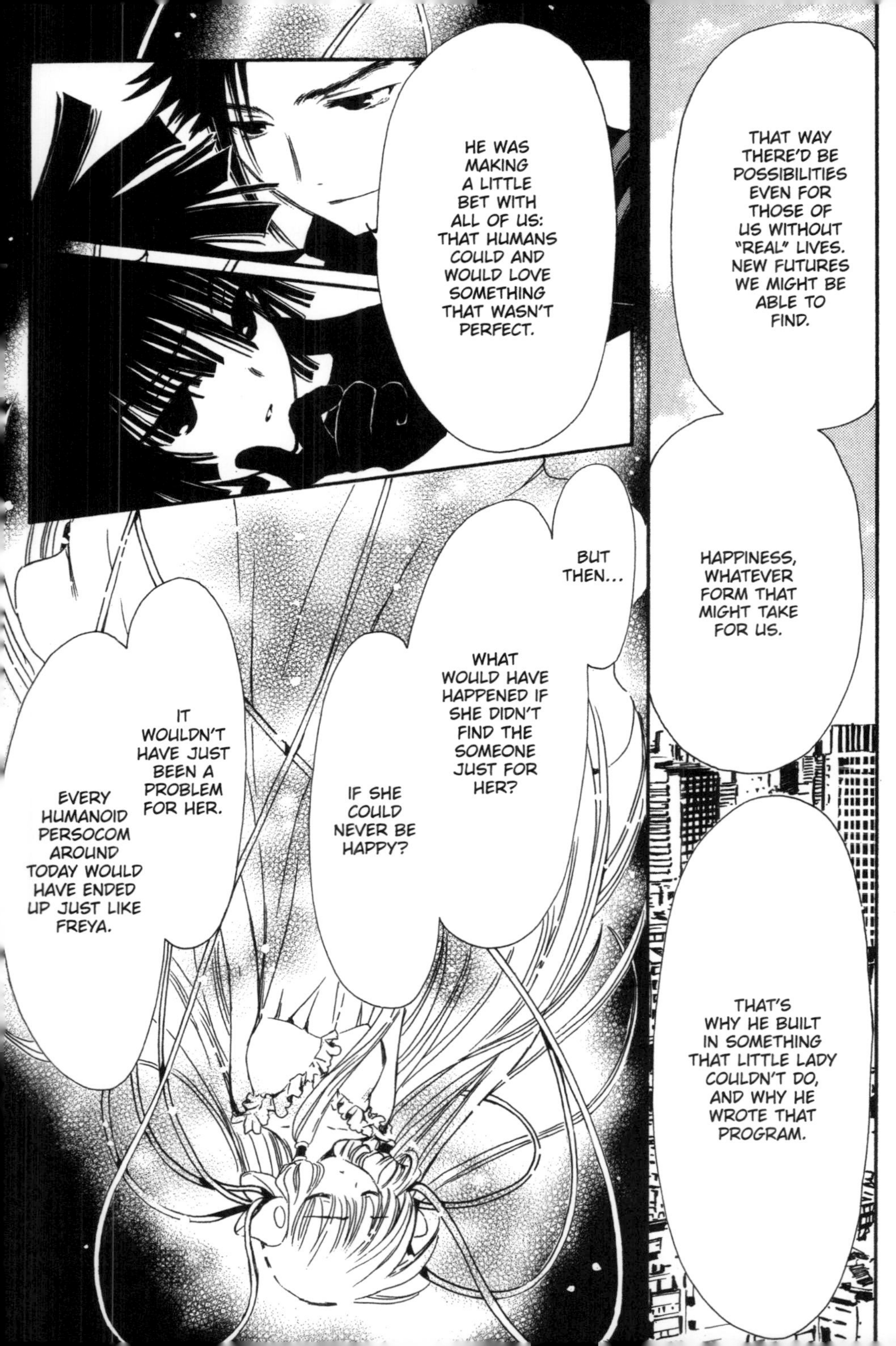
THAT WAY THERE'D BE POSSIBILITIES EVEN FOR THOSE OF US WITHOUT "REAL" LIVES. NEW FUTURES WE MIGHT BE ABLE TO FIND.
HAPPINESS, WHATEVER FORM THAT MIGHT TAKE FOR US.
THAT'S WHY HE BUILT IN SOMETHING THAT LITTLE LADY COULDN'T DO, AND WHY HE WROTE THAT PROGRAM.
HE WAS MAKING A LITTLE BET WITH ALL OF US: THAT HUMANS COULD AND WOULD LOVE SOMETHING THAT WASN'T PERFECT.
BUT THEN...
WHAT WOULD HAVE HAPPENED IF SHE DIDN'T FIND THE SOMEONE JUST FOR HER?
IF SHE COULD NEVER BE HAPPY?
IT WOULDN'T HAVE JUST BEEN A PROBLEM FOR HER.
EVERY HUMANOID PERSOCOM AROUND TODAY WOULD HAVE ENDED UP JUST LIKE FREYA.

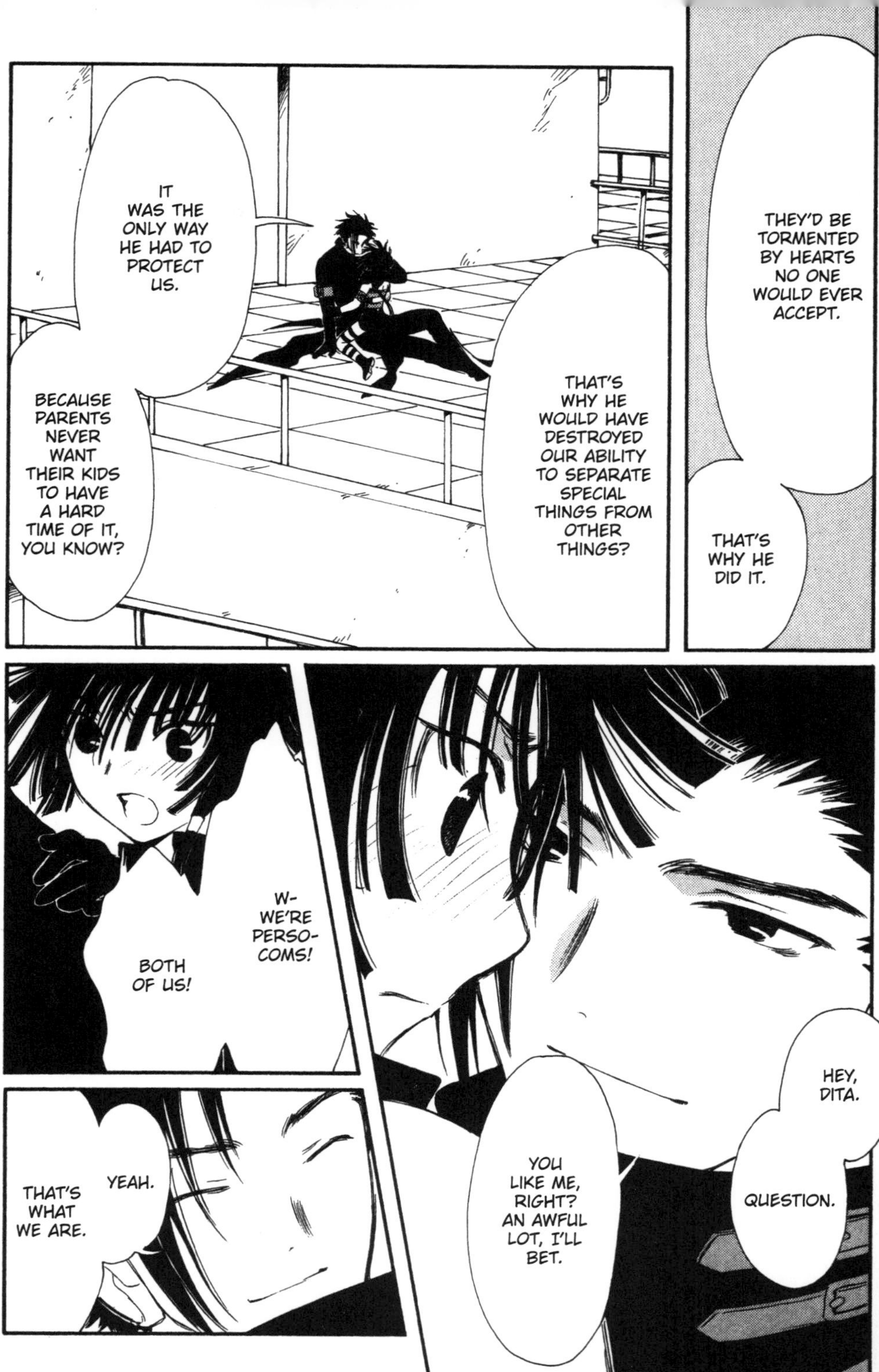
THEY'D BE TORMENTED BY HEARTS NO ONE WOULD EVER ACCEPT.
THAT'S WHY HE DID IT.
THAT'S WHY HE WOULD HAVE DESTROYED OUR ABILITY TO SEPARATE SPECIAL THINGS FROM OTHER THINGS?
IT WAS THE ONLY WAY HE HAD TO PROTECT US.
BECAUSE PARENTS NEVER WANT THEIR KIDS TO HAVE A HARD TIME OF IT, YOU KNOW?
HEY, DITA.
QUESTION.
YOU LIKE ME, RIGHT? AN AWFUL LOT, I'LL BET.
W-WE'RE PERSO-COMS!
BOTH OF US!
YEAH.
THAT'S WHAT WE ARE.

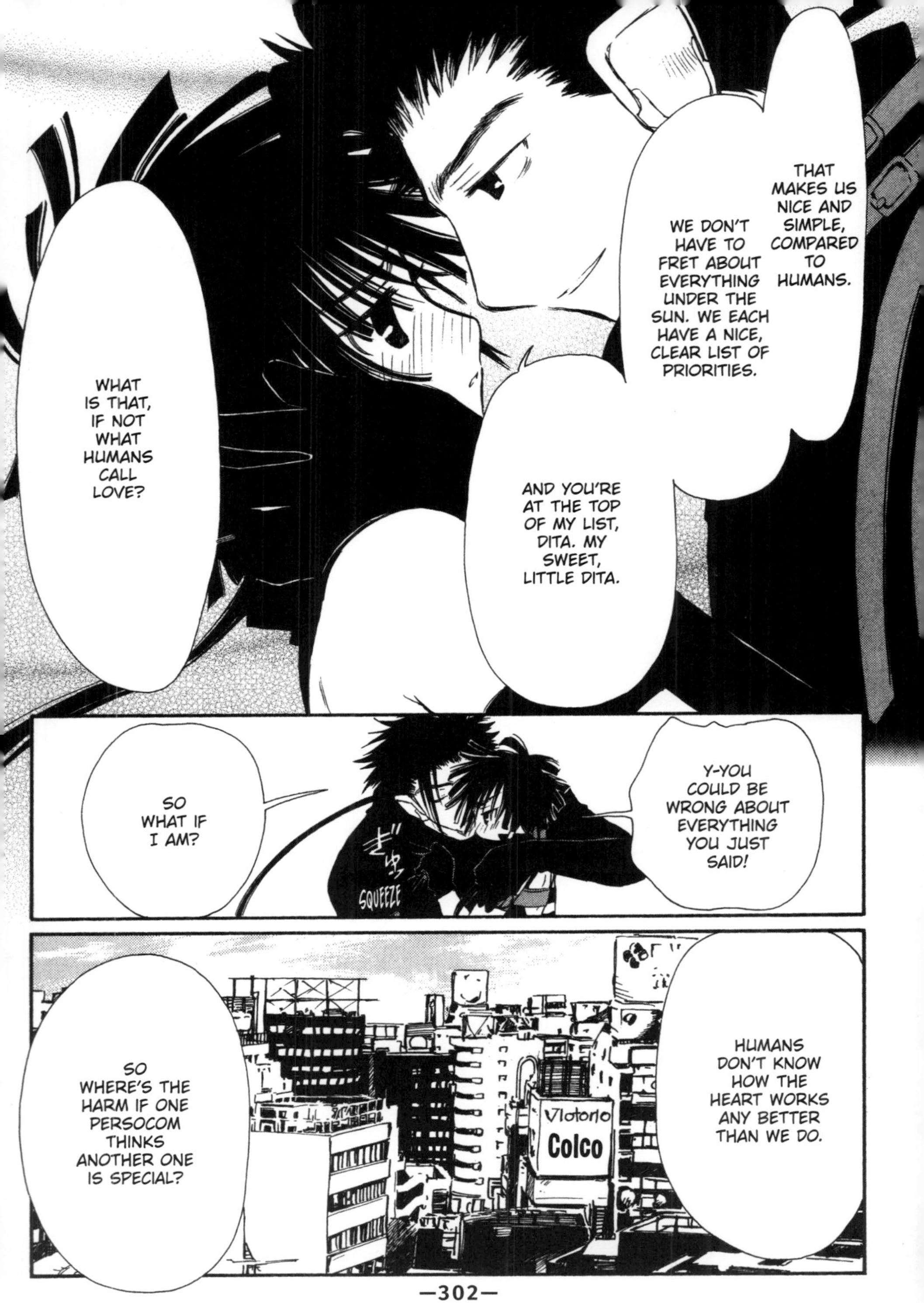
THAT MAKES US NICE AND SIMPLE, COMPARED TO HUMANS.
WE DON'T HAVE TO FRET ABOUT EVERYTHING UNDER THE SUN. WE EACH HAVE A NICE, CLEAR LIST OF PRIORITIES.
AND YOU'RE AT THE TOP OF MY LIST, DITA. MY SWEET, LITTLE DITA.
WHAT IS THAT, IF NOT WHAT HUMANS CALL LOVE?
Y-YOU COULD BE WRONG ABOUT EVERYTHING YOU JUST SAID!
SQUEEZE
SO WHAT IF I AM?
HUMANS DON'T KNOW HOW THE HEART WORKS ANY BETTER THAN WE DO.
Vlotorio
Colco
SO WHERE'S THE HARM IF ONE PERSOCOM THINKS ANOTHER ONE IS SPECIAL?

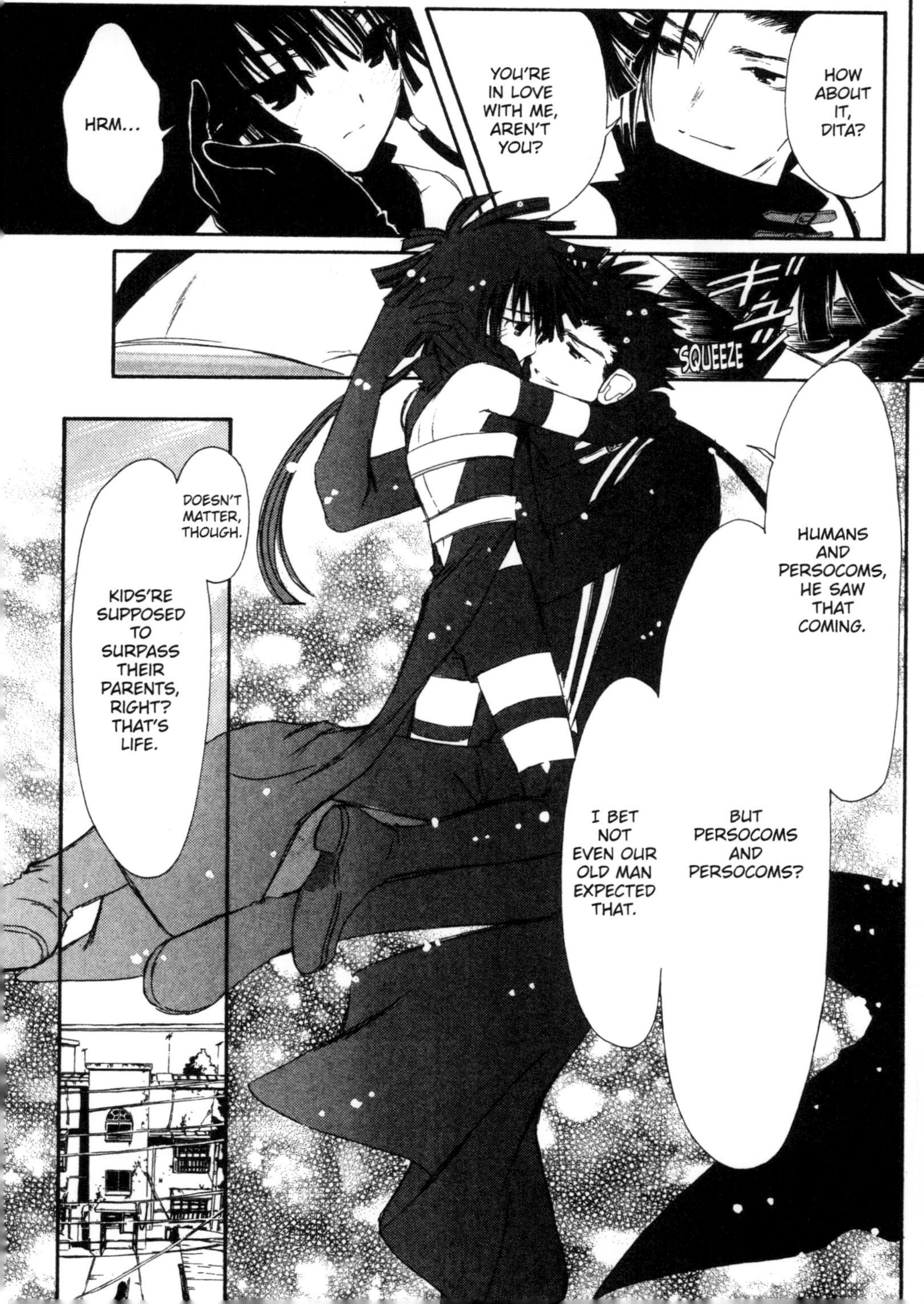
HOW ABOUT IT, DITA?
YOU'RE IN LOVE WITH ME, AREN'T YOU?
HRM...
SQUEEZE
HUMANS AND PERSOCOMS, HE SAW THAT COMING.
BUT PERSOCOMS AND PERSOCOMS?
I BET NOT EVEN OUR OLD MAN EXPECTED THAT.
DOESN'T MATTER, THOUGH.
KIDS'RE SUPPOSED TO SURPASS THEIR PARENTS, RIGHT? THAT'S LIFE.

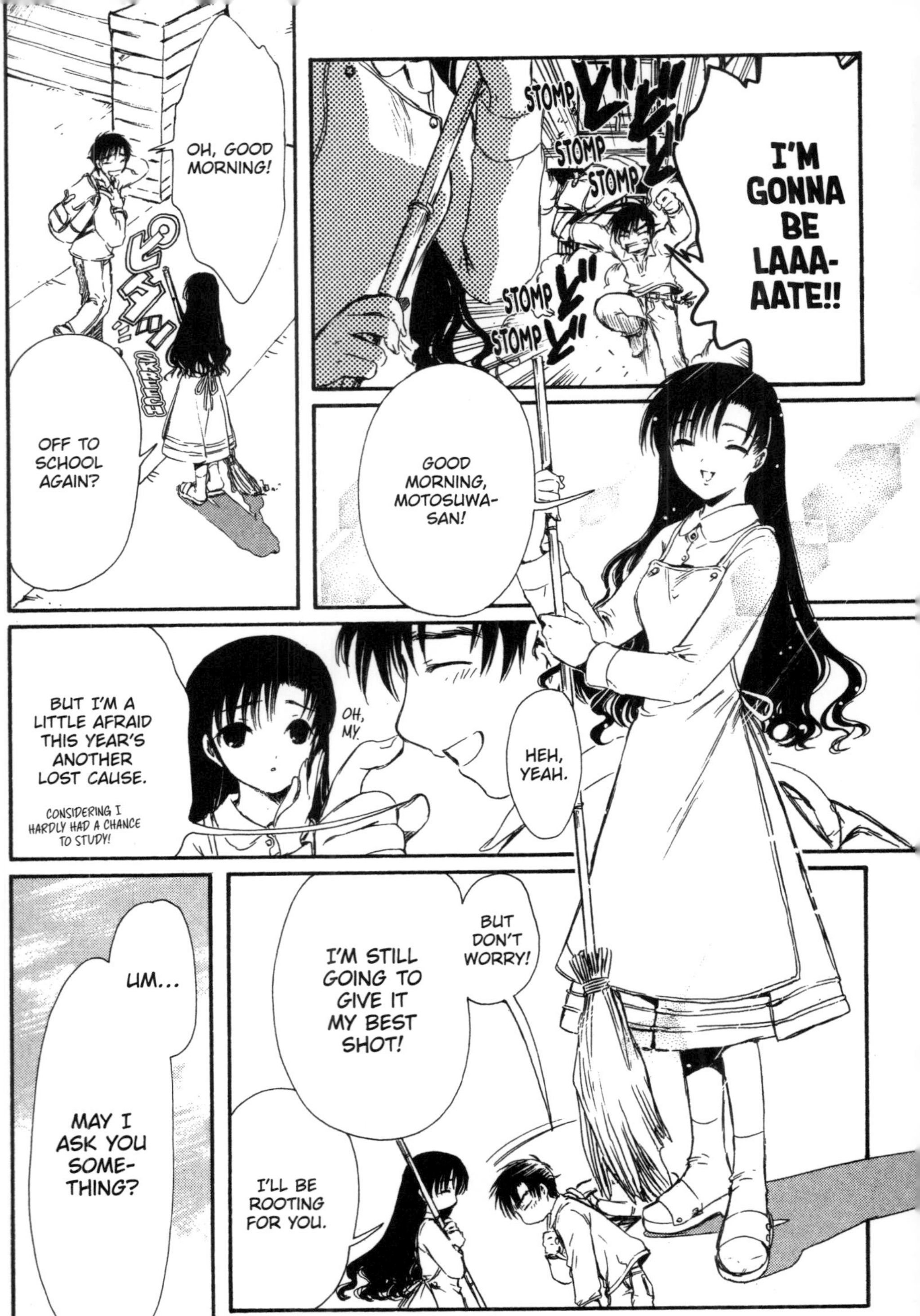
STOMP
STOMP
STOMP
STOMP
STOMP
I'M GONNA BE LAAAA-AATE!!
GOOD MORNING, MOTOSUWA-SAN!
OH, GOOD MORNING!
OFF TO SCHOOL AGAIN?
HEH, YEAH.
OH, MY.
BUT I'M A LITTLE AFRAID THIS YEAR'S ANOTHER LOST CAUSE.
CONSIDERING I HARDLY HAD A CHANCE TO STUDY!
BUT DON'T WORRY!
I'M STILL GOING TO GIVE IT MY BEST SHOT!
I'LL BE ROOTING FOR YOU.
UM...
MAY I ASK YOU SOMETHING?

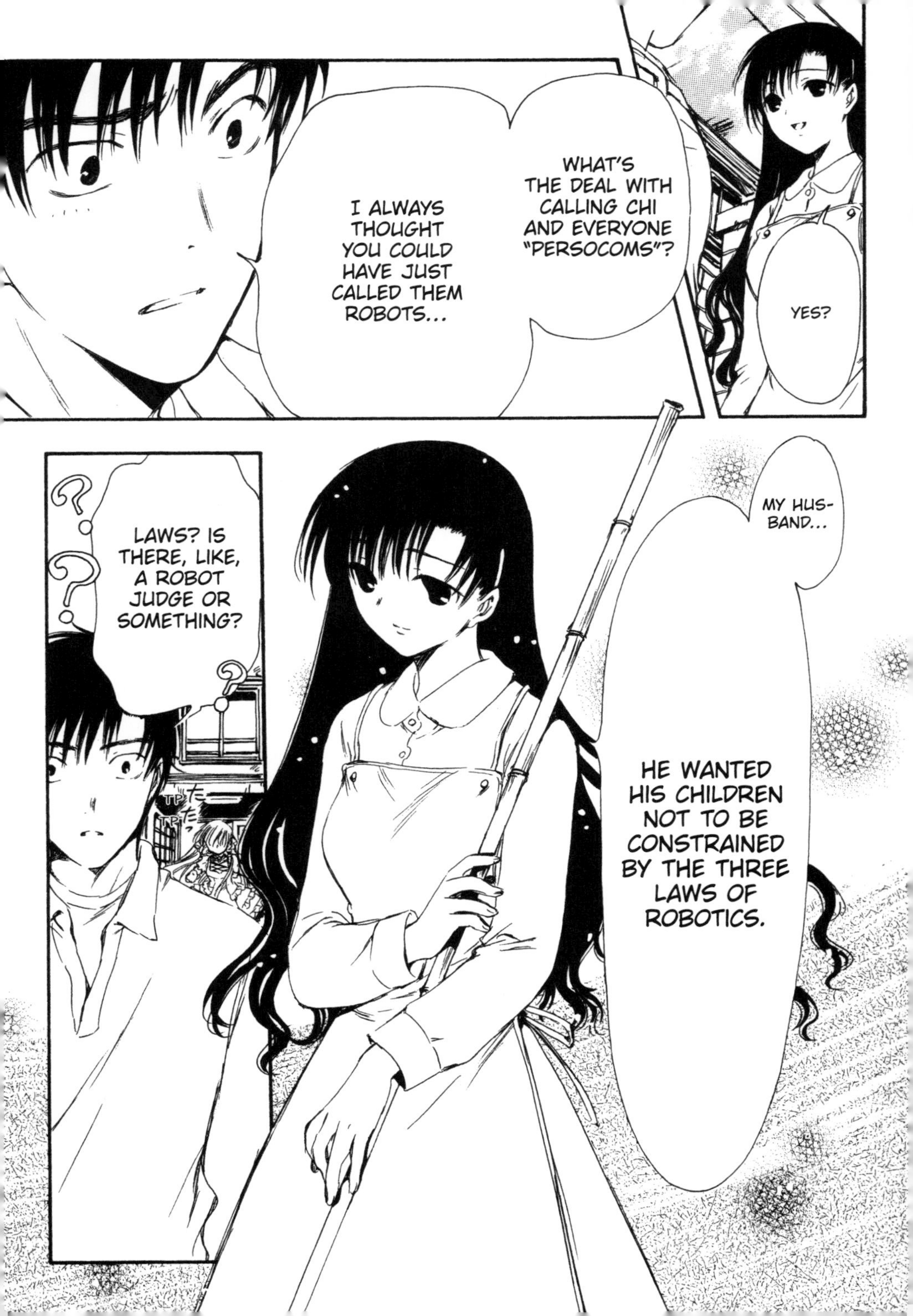
YES?
WHAT'S THE DEAL WITH CALLING CHI AND EVERYONE "PERSOCOMS"?
I ALWAYS THOUGHT YOU COULD HAVE JUST CALLED THEM ROBOTS...
MY HUS-BAND...
HE WANTED HIS CHILDREN NOT TO BE CONSTRAINED BY THE THREE LAWS OF ROBOTICS.
LAWS? IS THERE, LIKE, A ROBOT JUDGE OR SOMETHING?
TP
TP

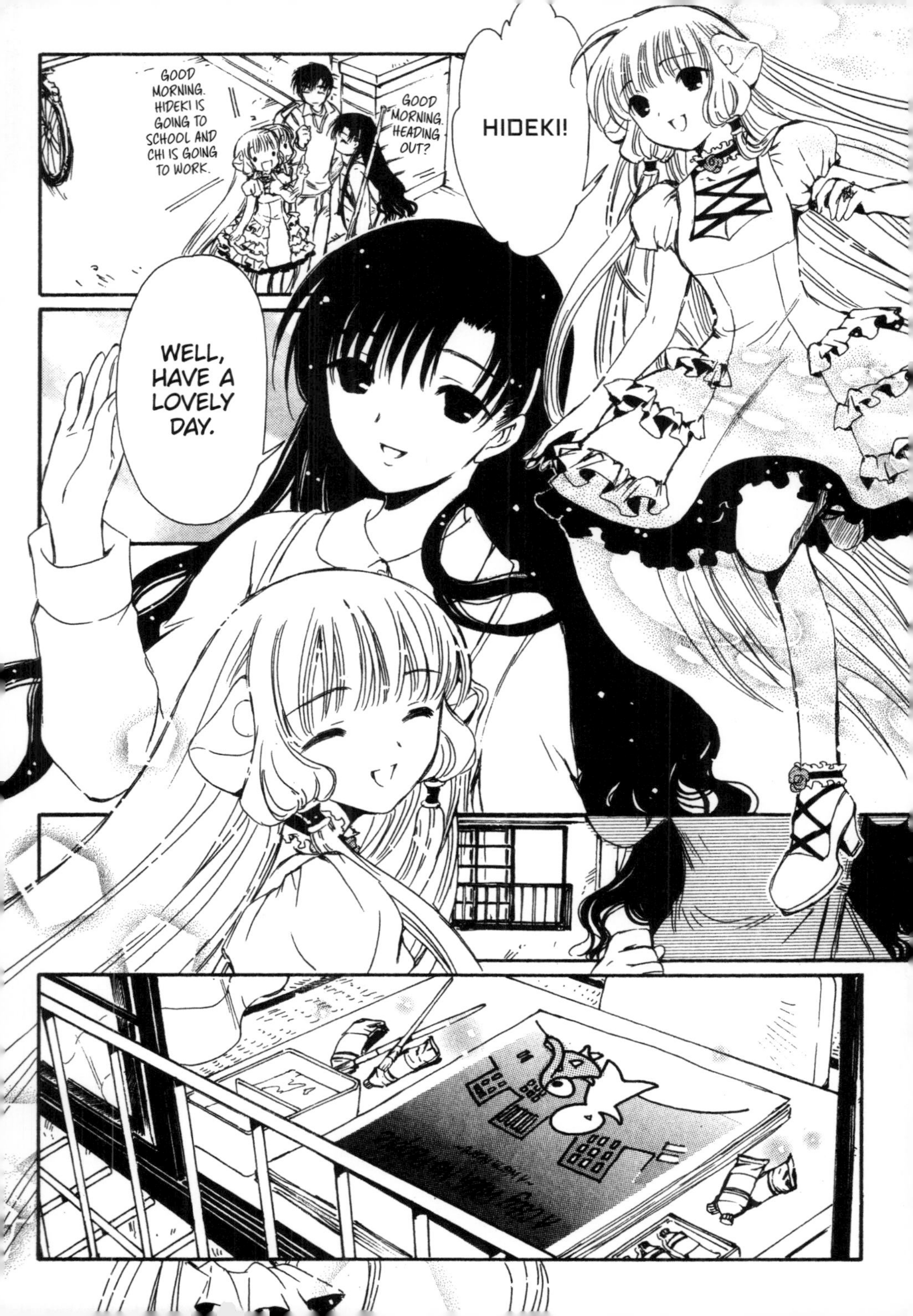
HIDEKI!
GOOD MORNING. HEADING OUT?
GOOD MORNING. HIDEKI IS GOING TO SCHOOL AND CHI IS GOING TO WORK.
WELL, HAVE A LOVELY DAY.

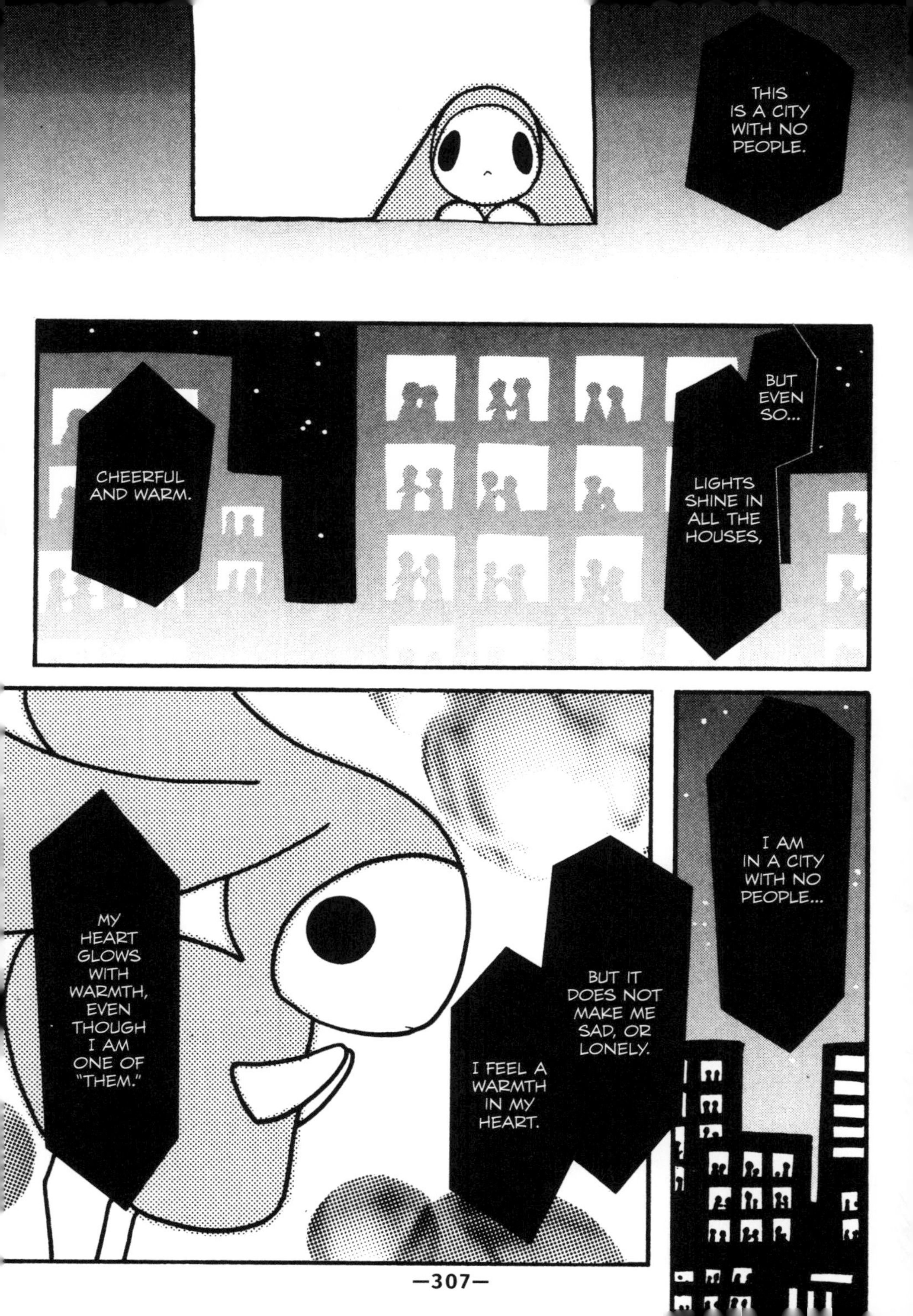
THIS IS A CITY WITH NO PEOPLE.
BUT EVEN SO...
LIGHTS SHINE IN ALL THE HOUSES,
CHEERFUL AND WARM.
I AM IN A CITY WITH NO PEOPLE...
BUT IT DOES NOT MAKE ME SAD, OR LONELY.
I FEEL A WARMTH IN MY HEART.
MY HEART GLOWS WITH WARMTH, EVEN THOUGH I AM ONE OF "THEM."

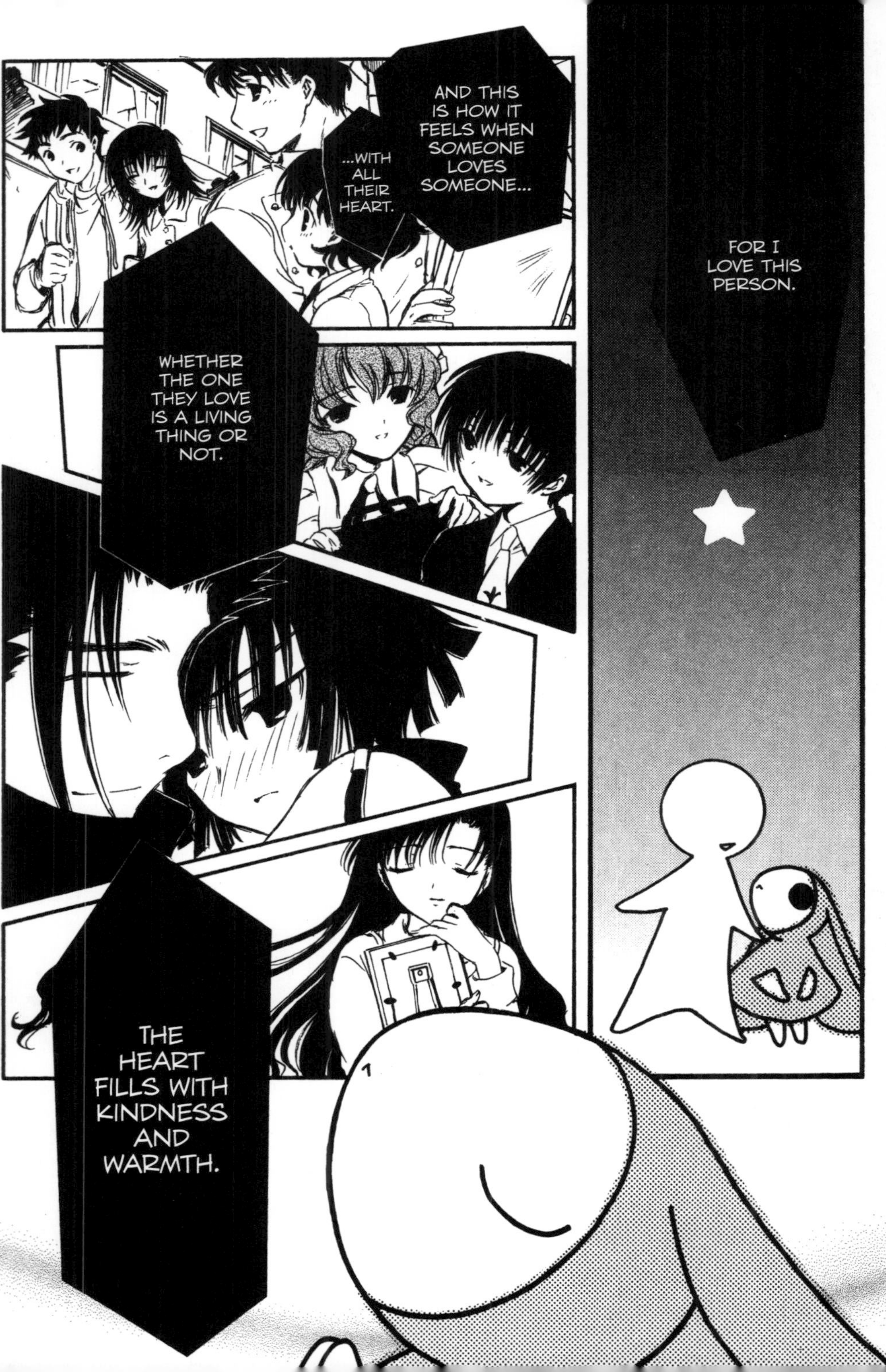
FOR I LOVE THIS PERSON.
AND THIS IS HOW IT FEELS WHEN SOMEONE LOVES SOMEONE...
...WITH ALL THEIR HEART.
WHETHER THE ONE THEY LOVE IS A LIVING THING OR NOT.
THE HEART FILLS WITH KINDNESS AND WARMTH.

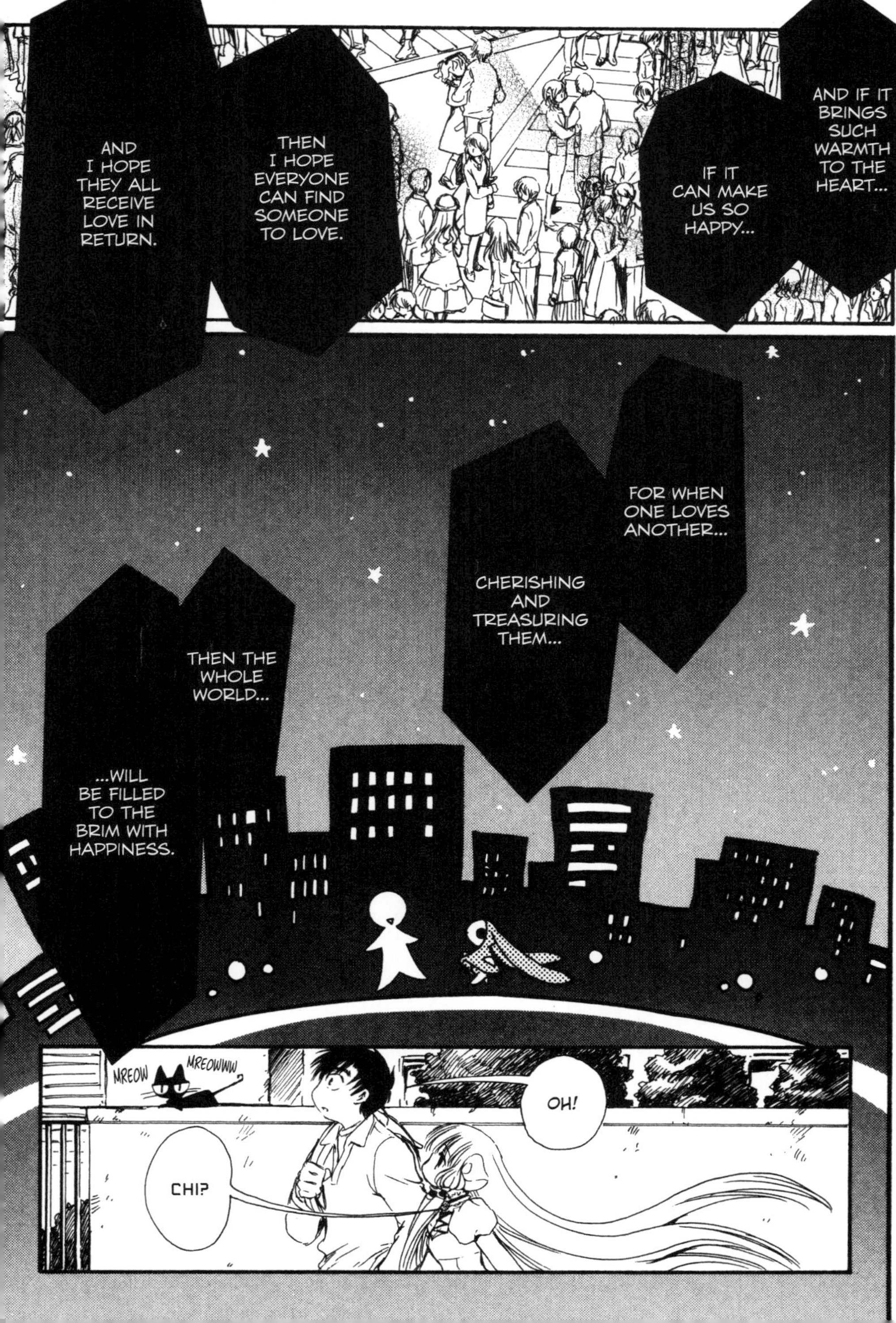
AND IF IT BRINGS SUCH WARMTH TO THE HEART...
IF IT CAN MAKE US SO HAPPY...
THEN I HOPE EVERYONE CAN FIND SOMEONE TO LOVE.
AND I HOPE THEY ALL RECEIVE LOVE IN RETURN.
FOR WHEN ONE LOVES ANOTHER...
CHERISHING AND TREASURING THEM...
THEN THE WHOLE WORLD...
...WILL BE FILLED TO THE BRIM WITH HAPPINESS.
MREOWWW
MREOW
OH!
CHI?

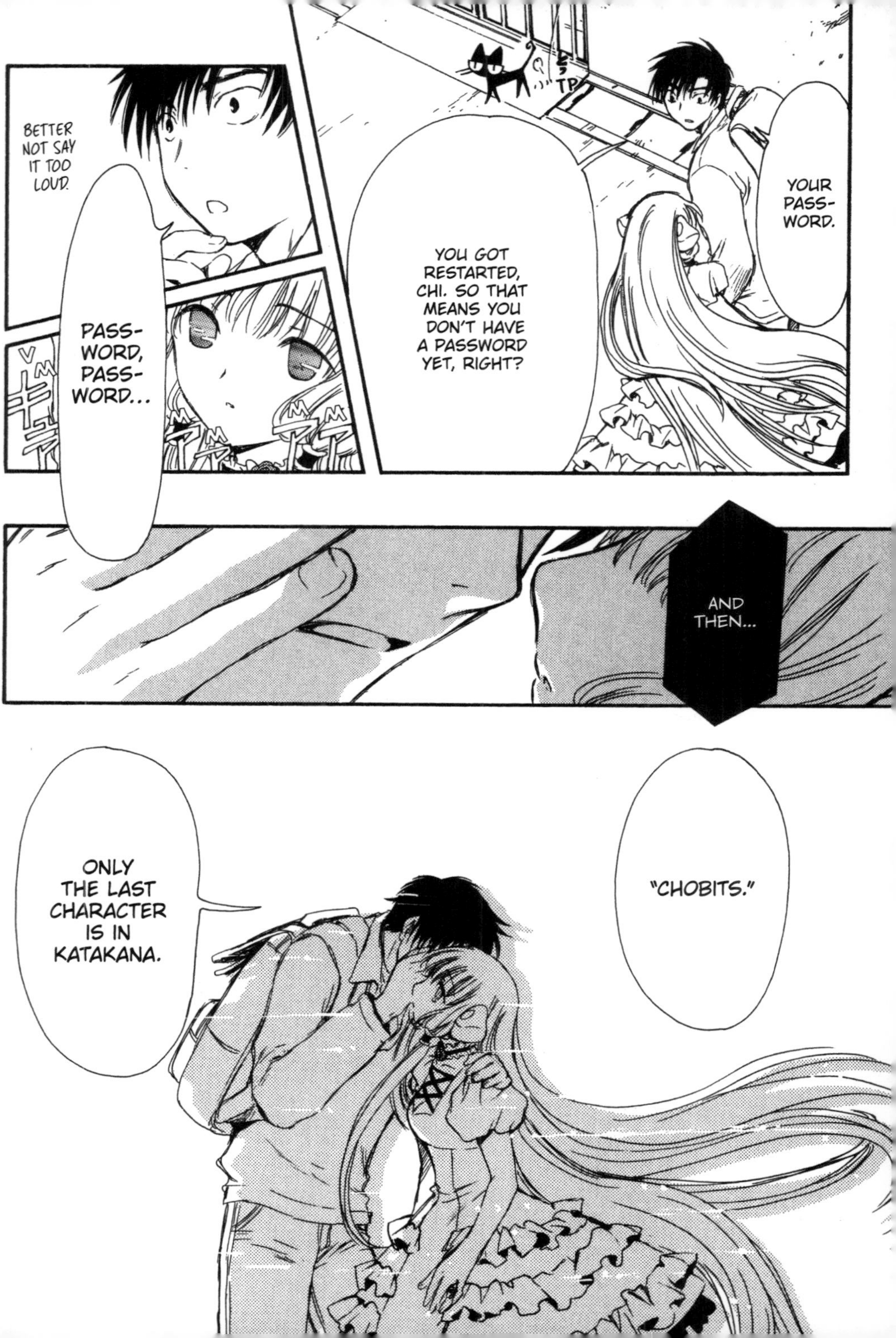
TP
YOUR PASSWORD.
YOU GOT RESTARTED, CHI. SO THAT MEANS YOU DON'T HAVE A PASSWORD YET, RIGHT?
BETTER NOT SAY IT TOO LOUD.
PASSWORD, PASSWORD...
AND THEN...
"CHOBITS."
ONLY THE LAST CHARACTER IS IN KATAKANA.

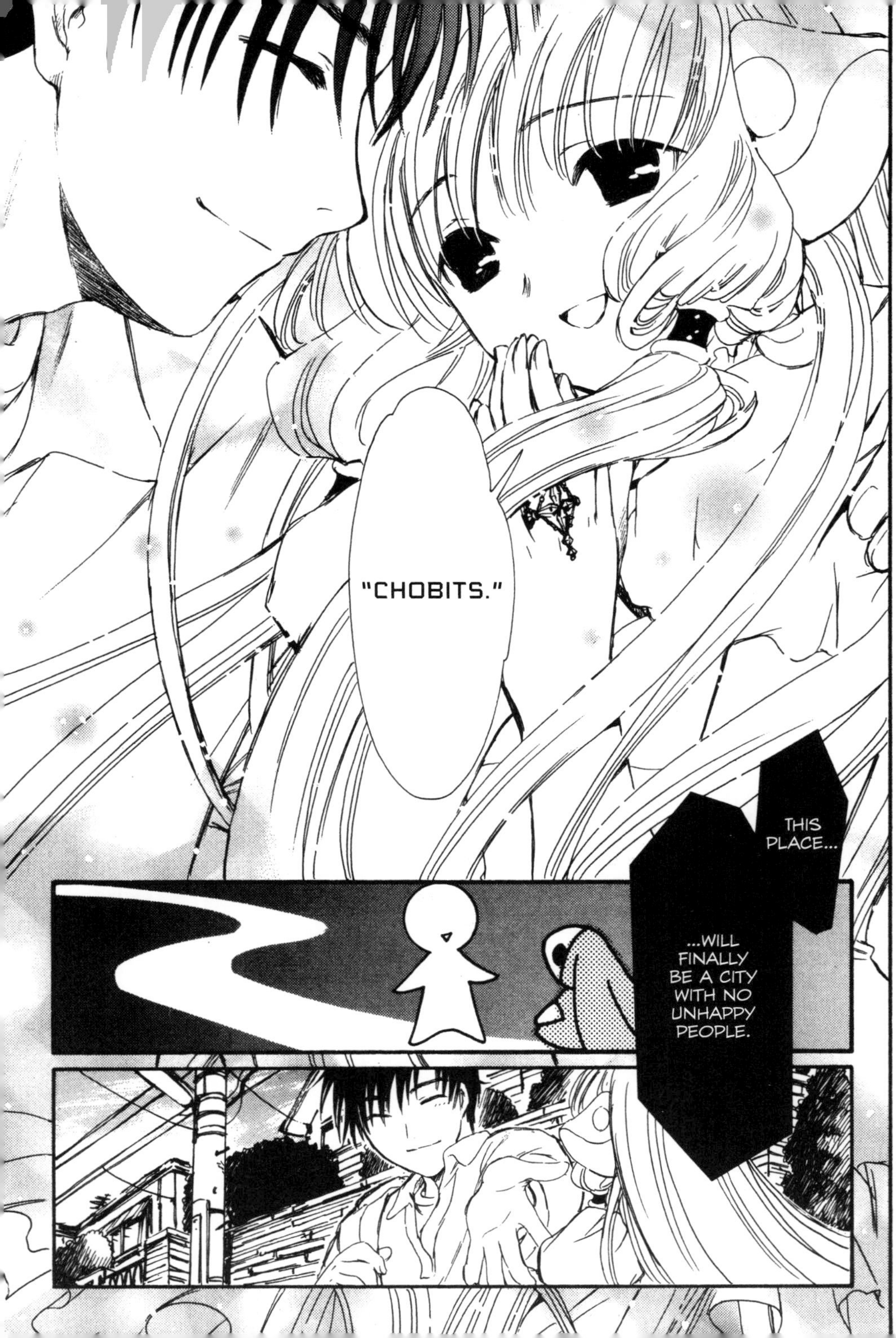
"CHOBITS."
THIS PLACE...
...WILL FINALLY BE A CITY WITH NO UNHAPPY PEOPLE.

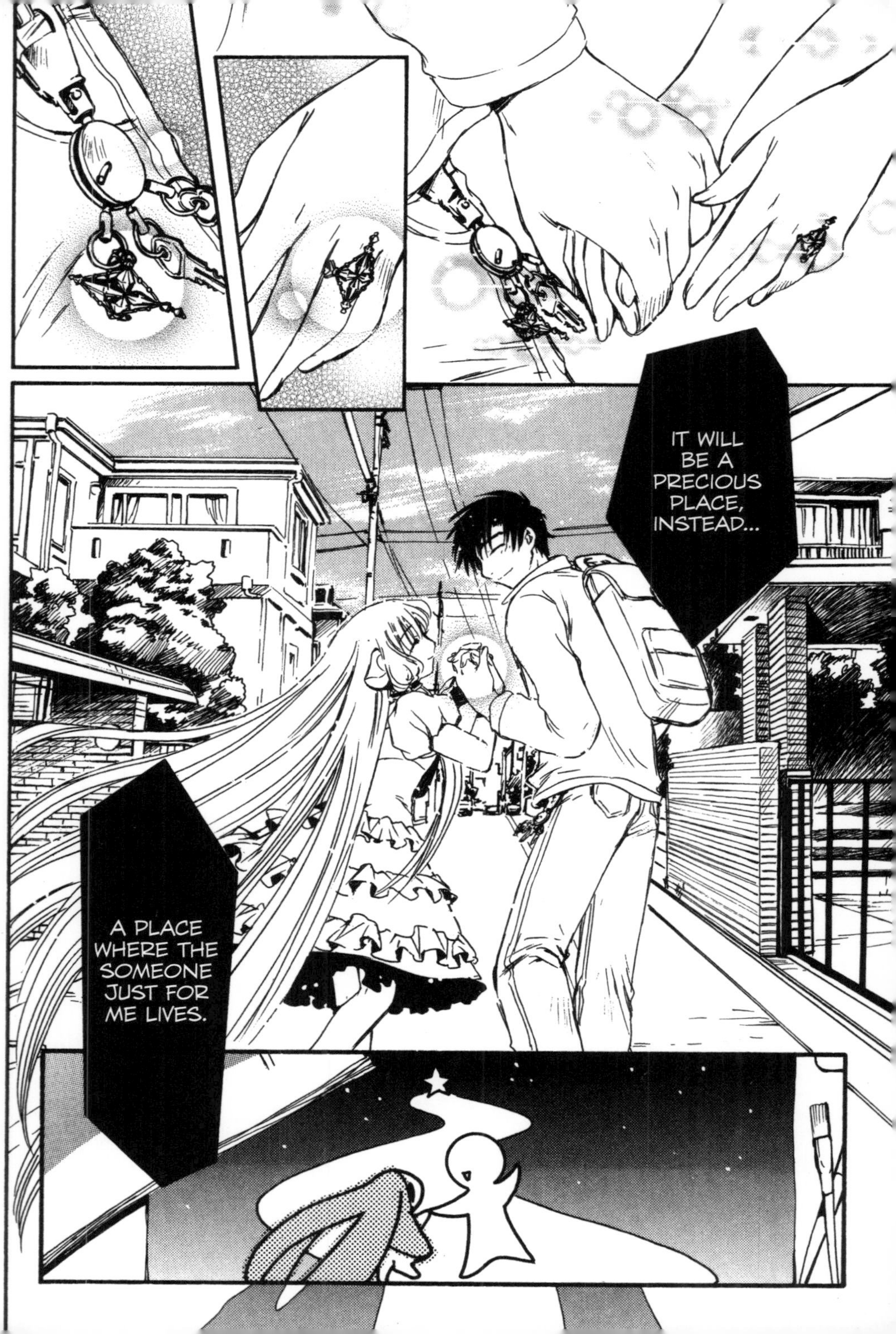
IT WILL BE A PRECIOUS PLACE, INSTEAD...
A PLACE WHERE THE SOMEONE JUST FOR ME LIVES.

Chobits

<end>

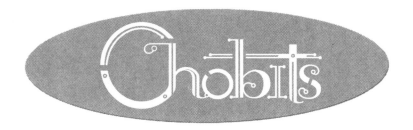

A Kodansha Comics Hardcover Original
*Chobits 20th Anniversary Edition* volume 4 copyright ©2002
CLAMP • ShigatsuTsuitachi CO.,LTD. / Kodansha Ltd.
English translation copyright ©2021
CLAMP • ShigatsuTsuitachi CO.,LTD. / Kodansha Ltd.

Published in the United States by Kodansha Comics, an imprint of
Kodansha USA Publishing, LLC, New York.

Publication rights for this English edition arranged through
Kodansha Ltd., Tokyo.

First published in Japan in 2002 by Kodansha Ltd., Tokyo
as *Chobittsu*, volumes 7 and 8.

ISBN 978-1-64651-019-1

Printed in China.

www.kodanshacomics.com

9 8 7 6 5 4 3 2 1
Translation: Kevin Steinbach
Lettering: Michael Martin
Editing: Tiff Ferentini
Kodansha Comics edition cover design: Phil Balsman

Publisher: Kiichiro Sugawara

Director of publishing services: Ben Applegate
Associate director of operations: Stephen Pakula
Publishing services managing editor: Noelle Webster
Assistant production manager: Emi Lotto, Angela Zurlo

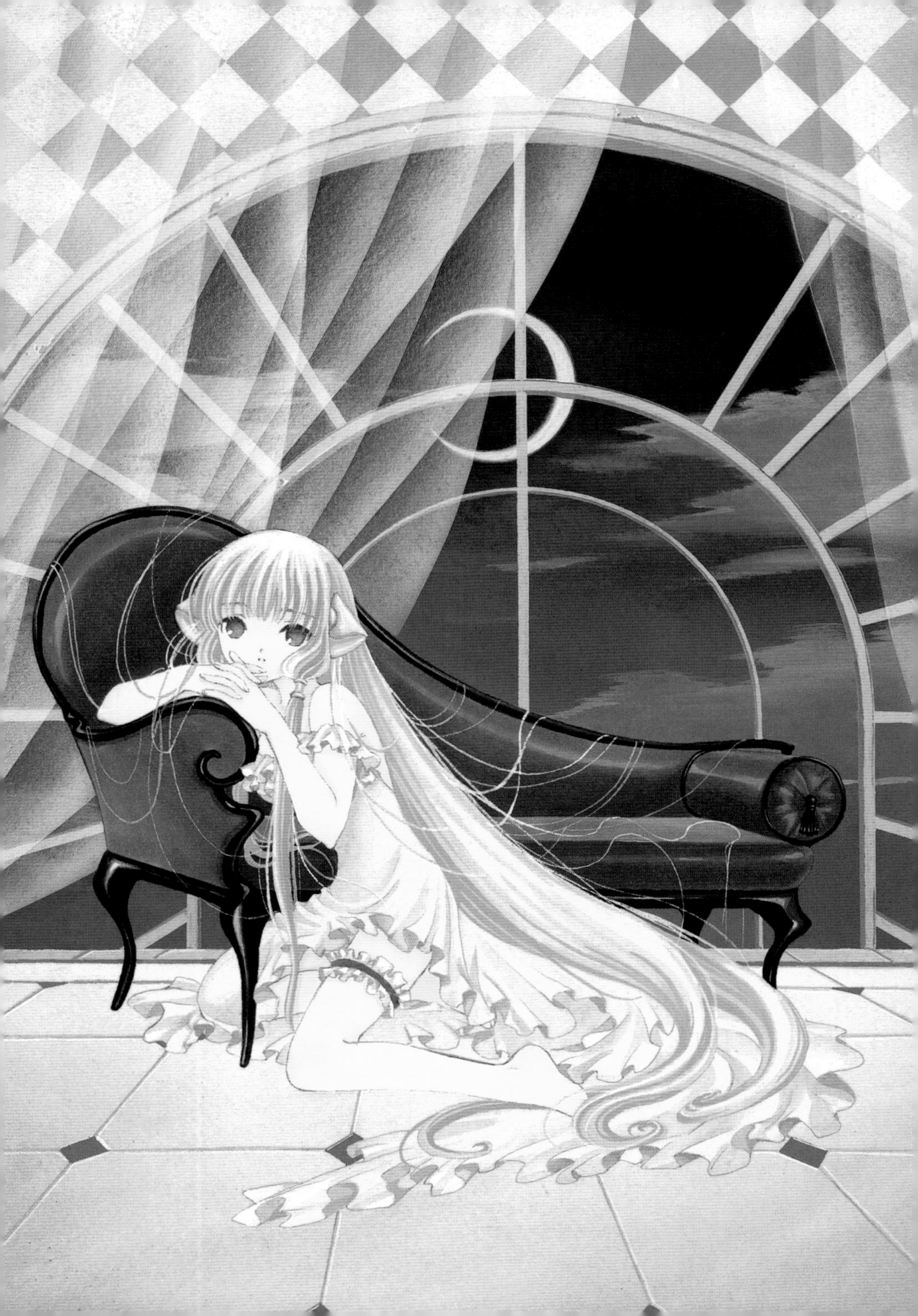

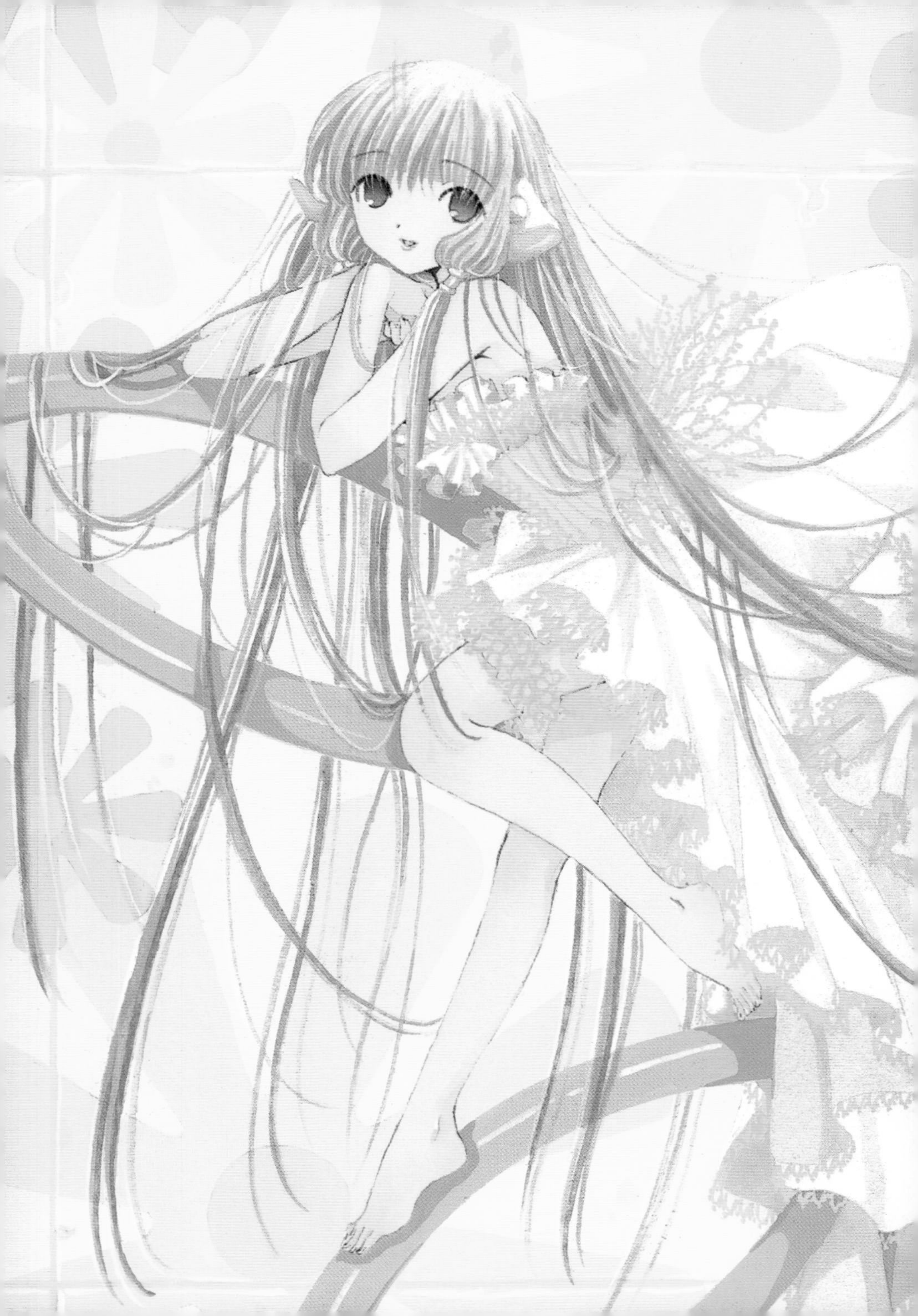

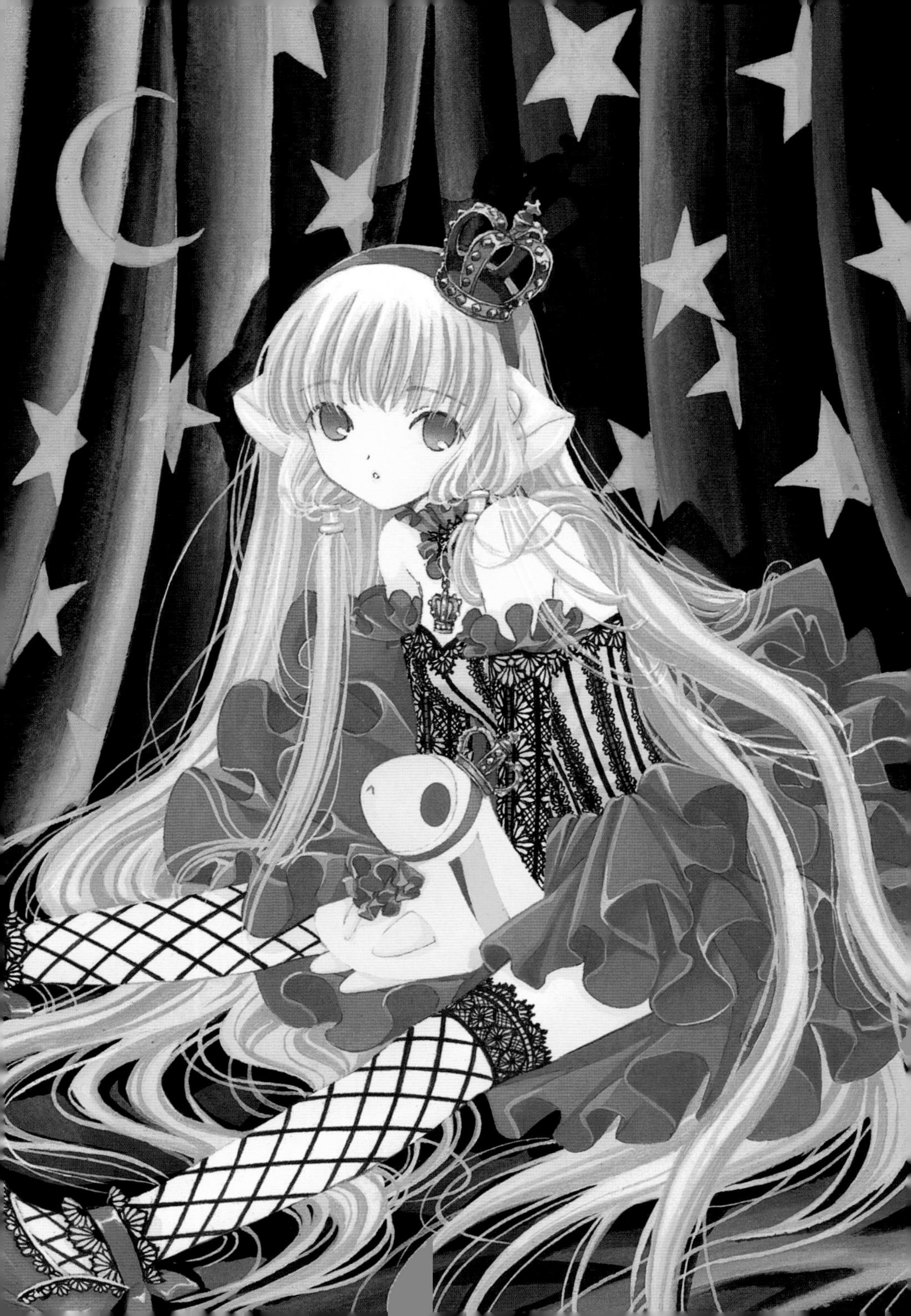

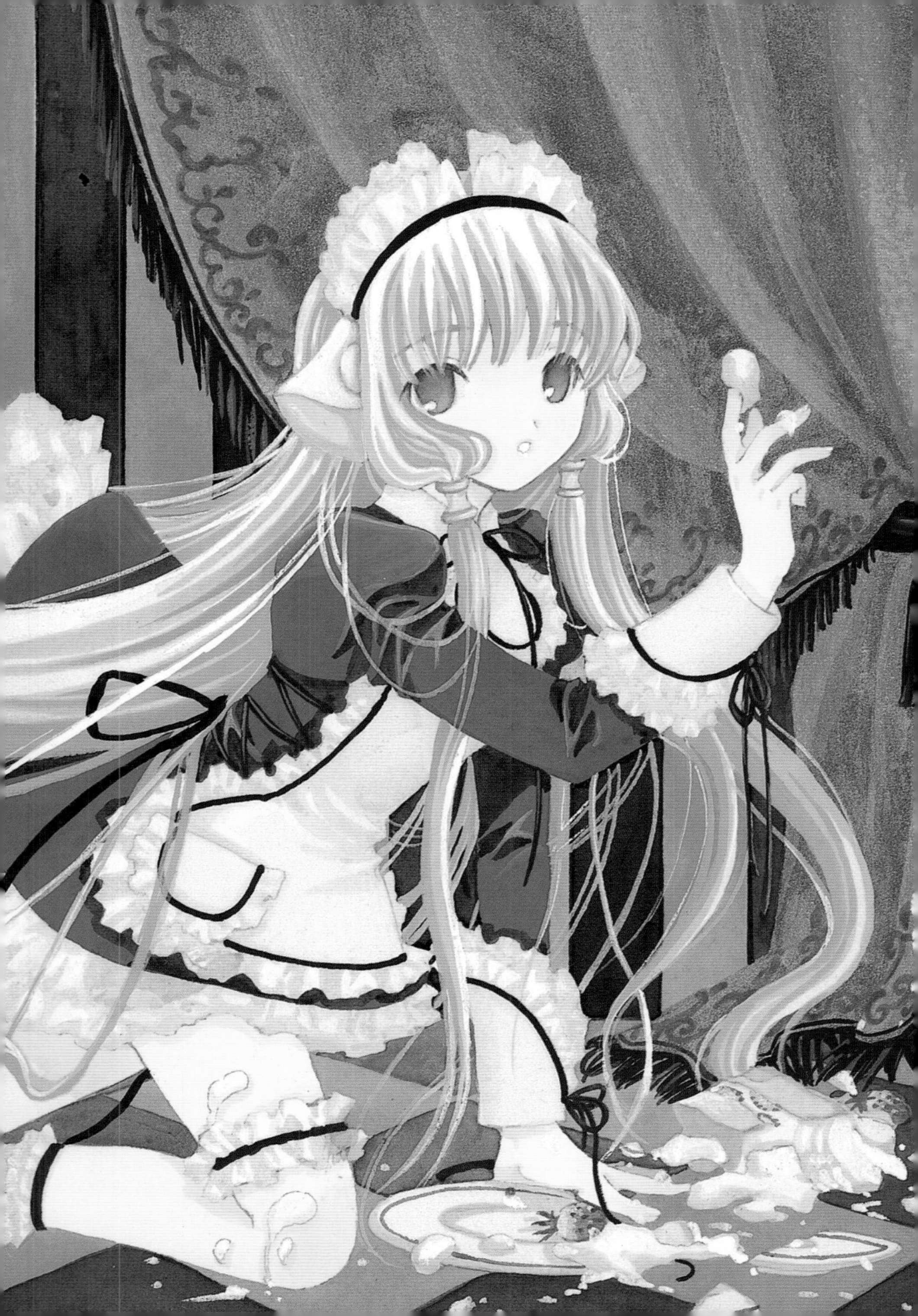

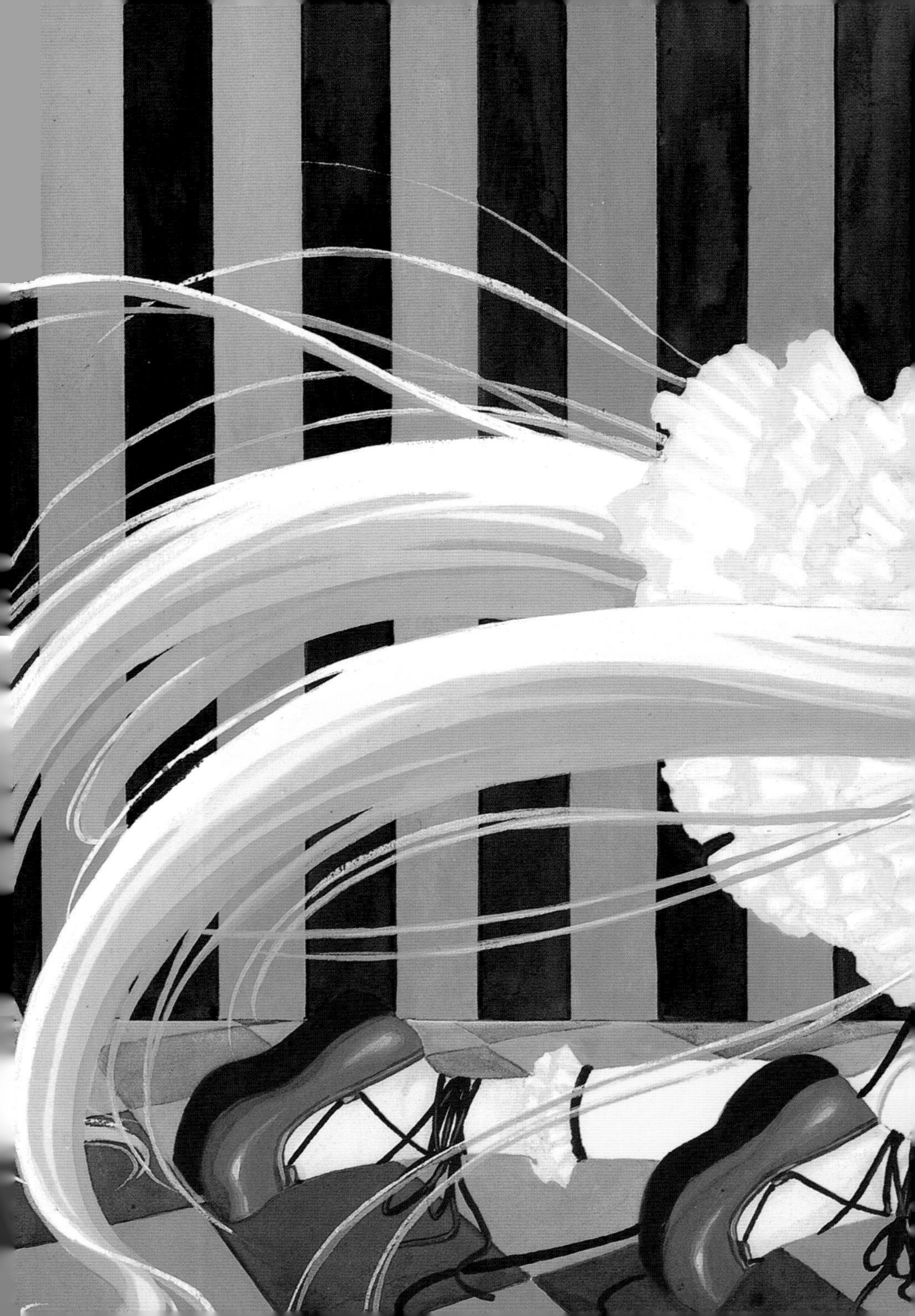

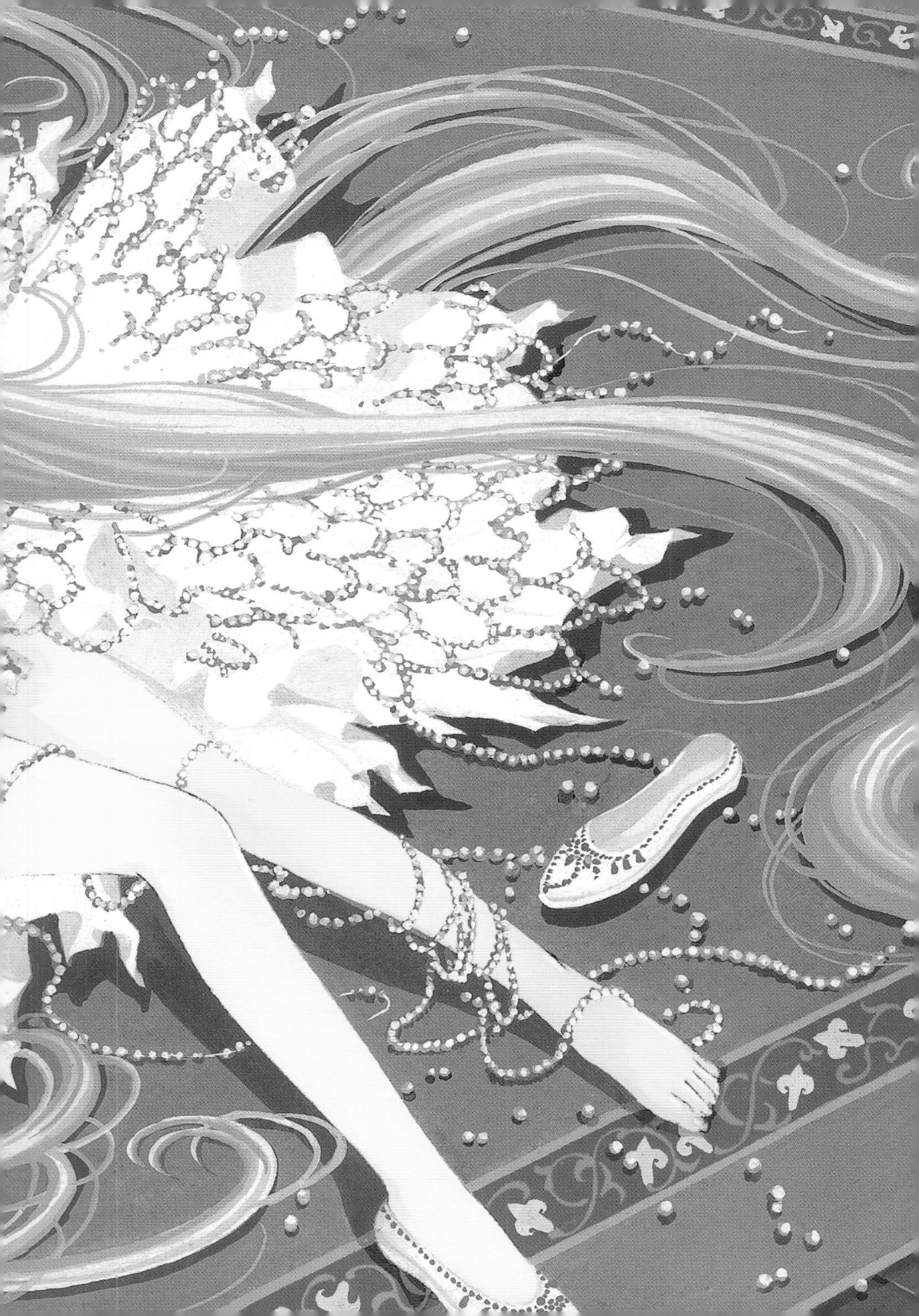

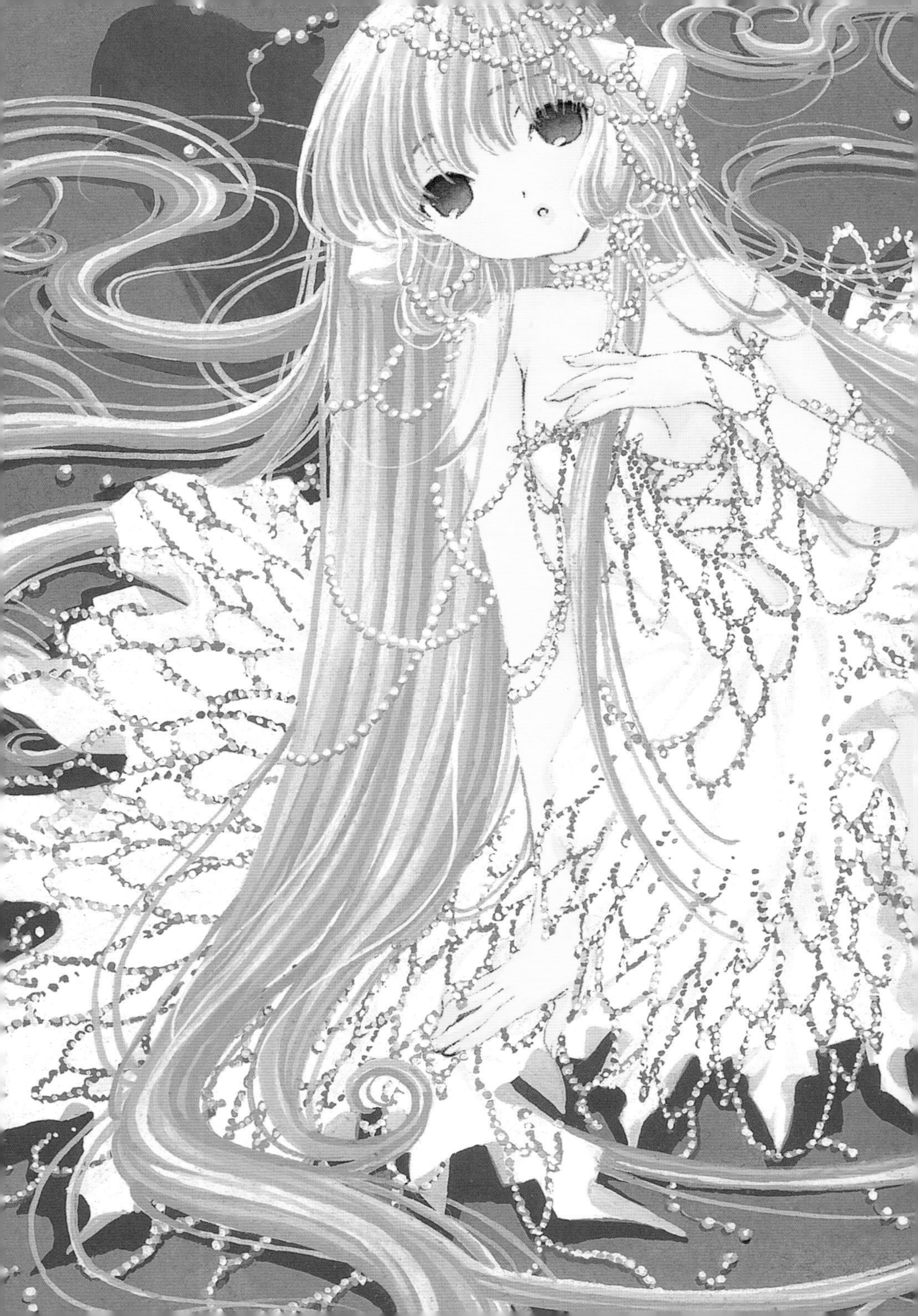

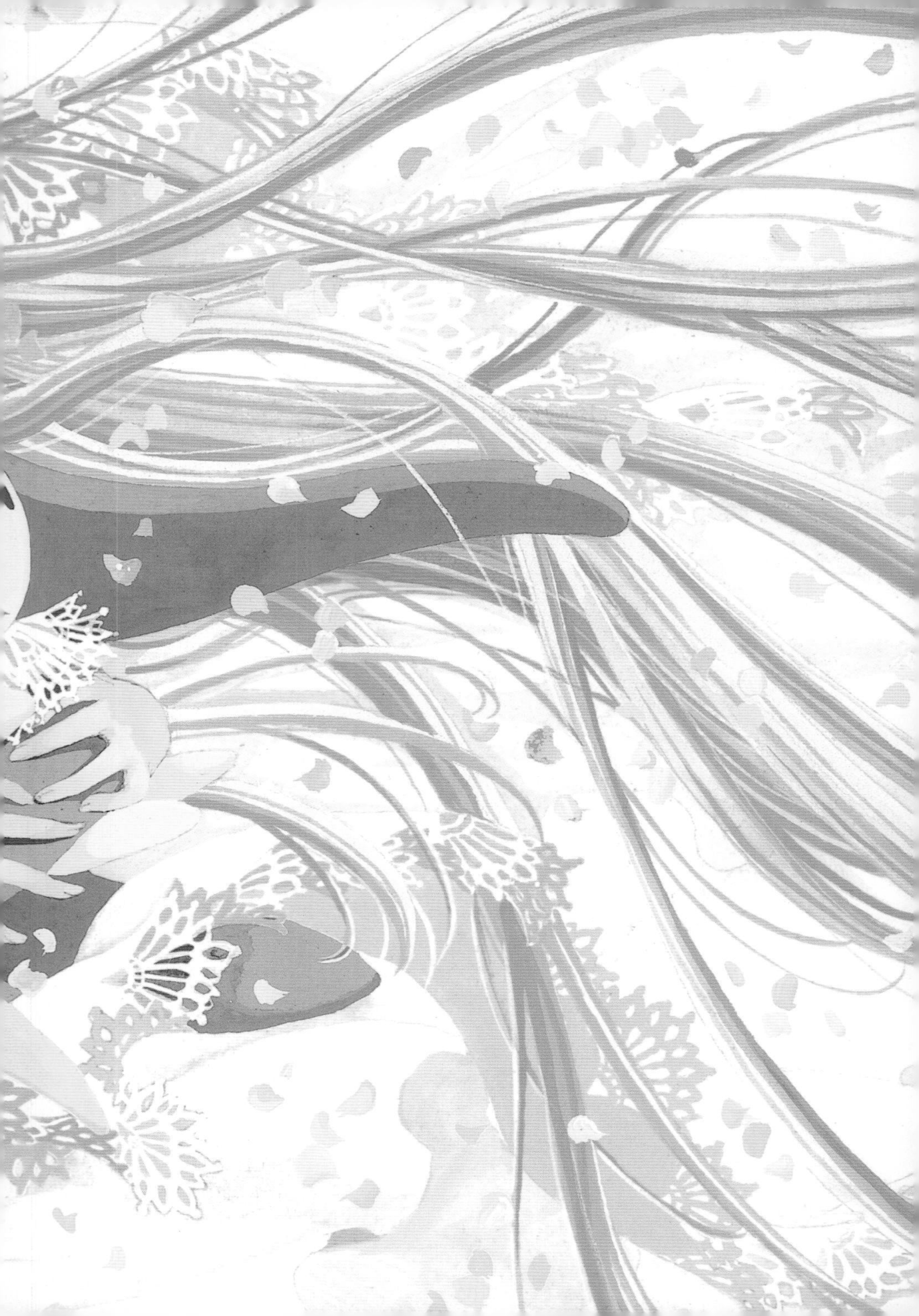

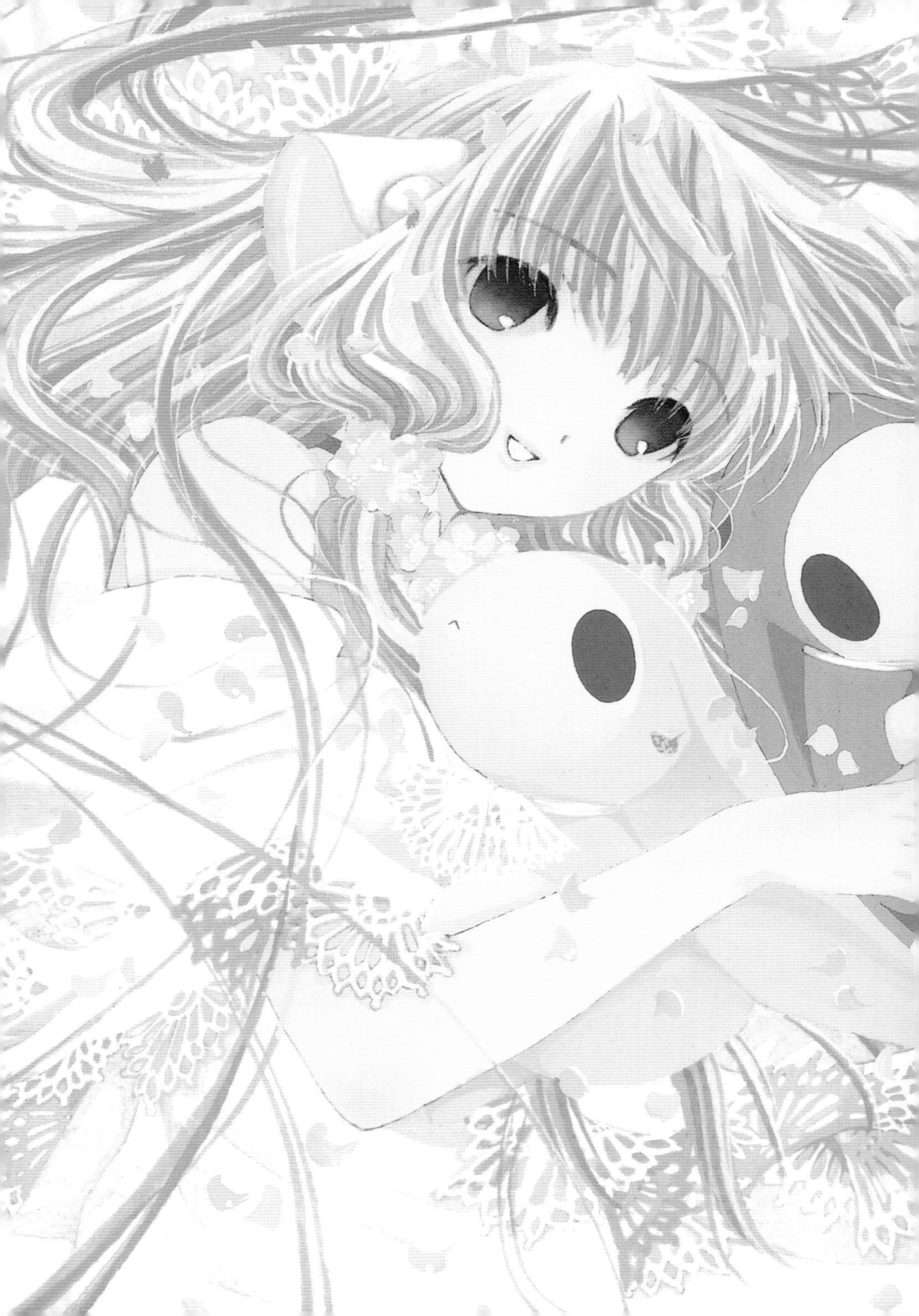

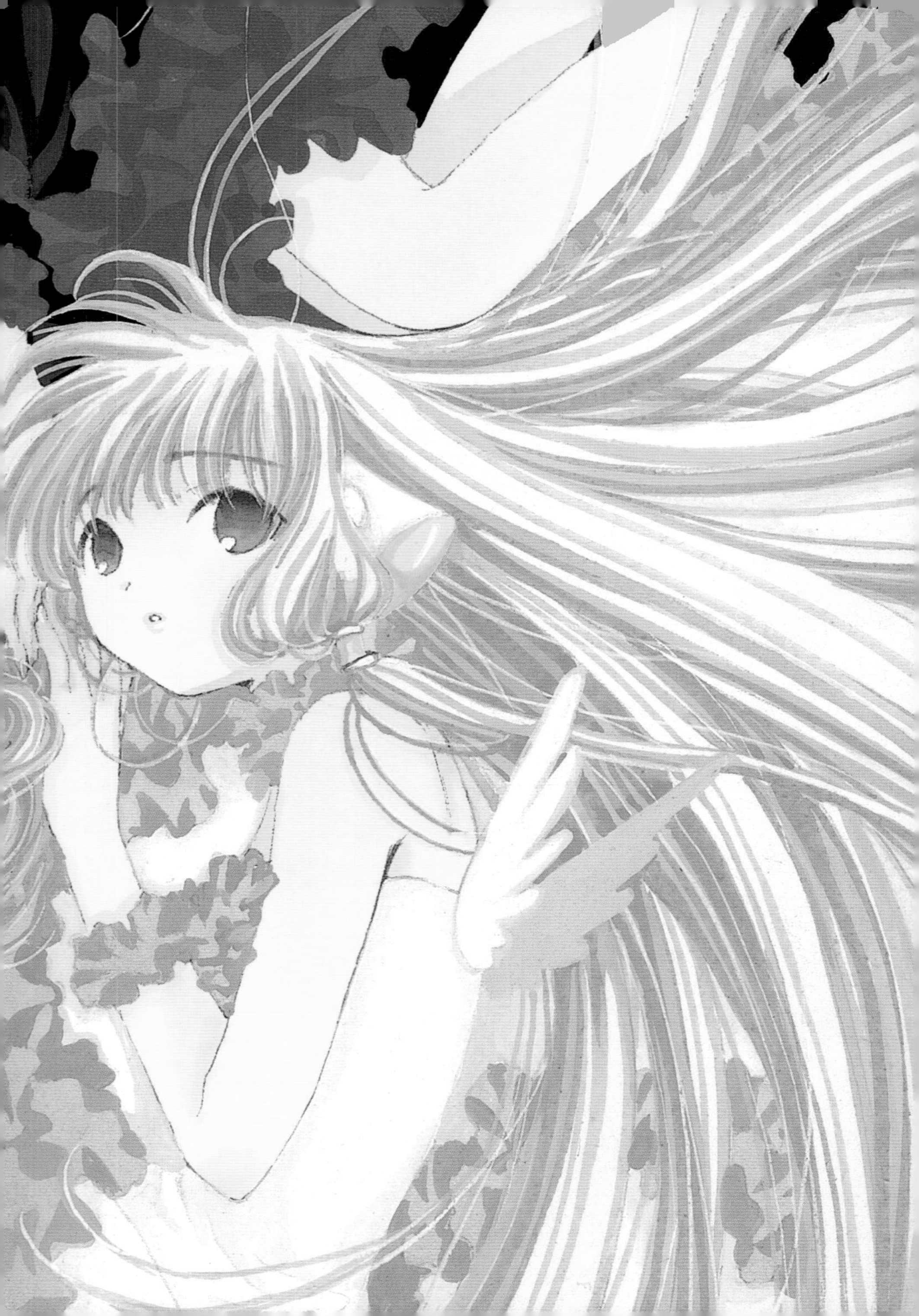

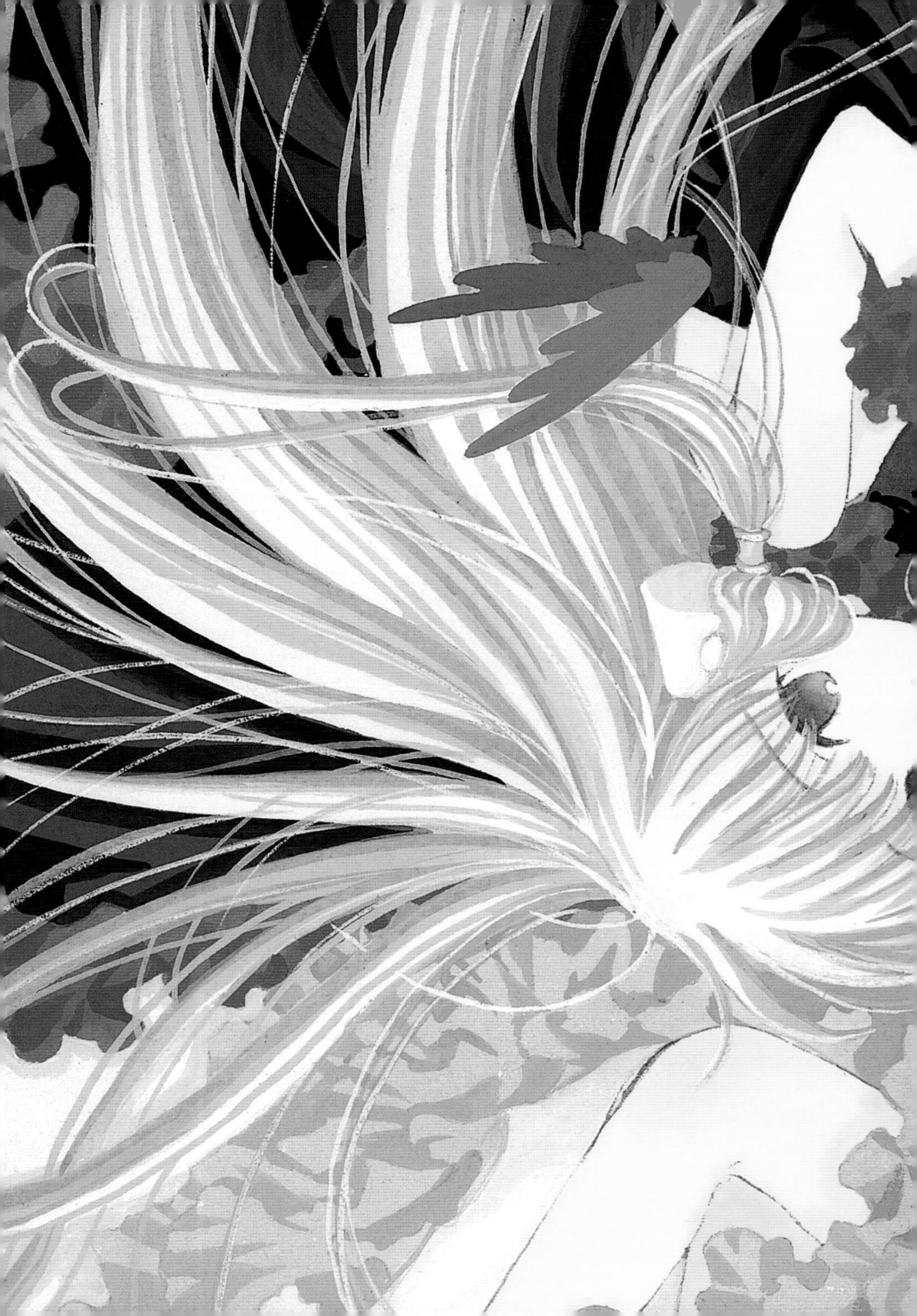

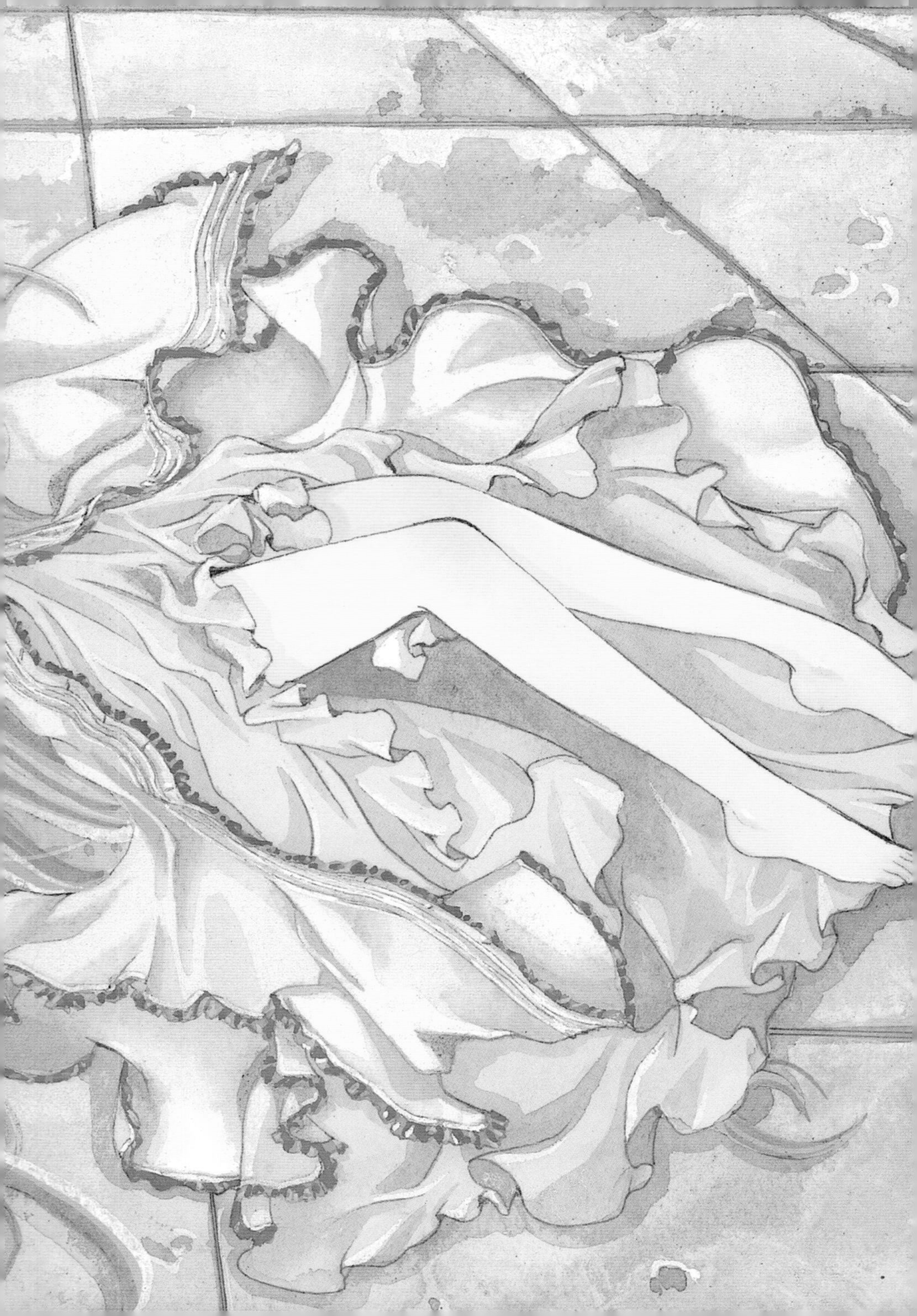

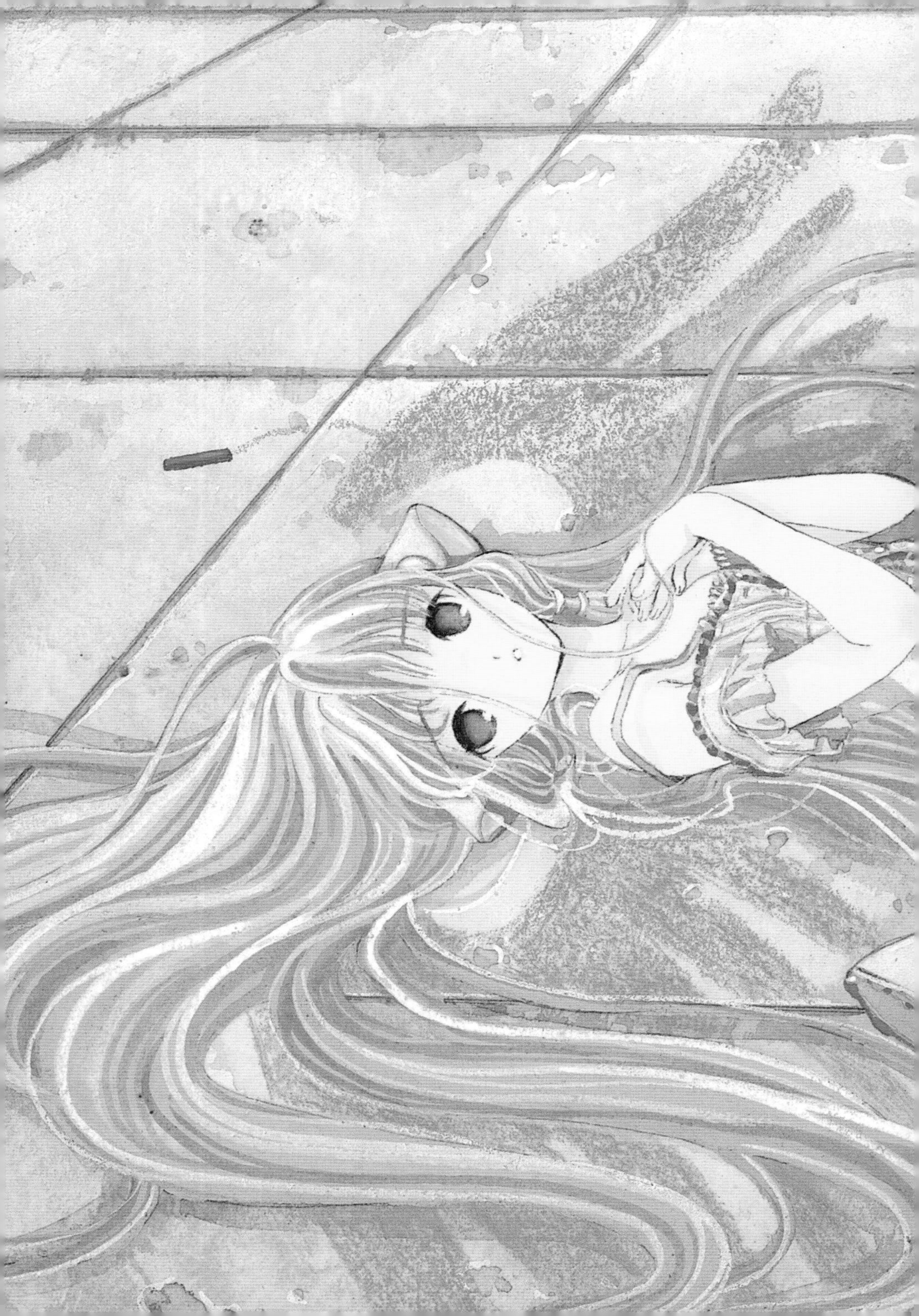

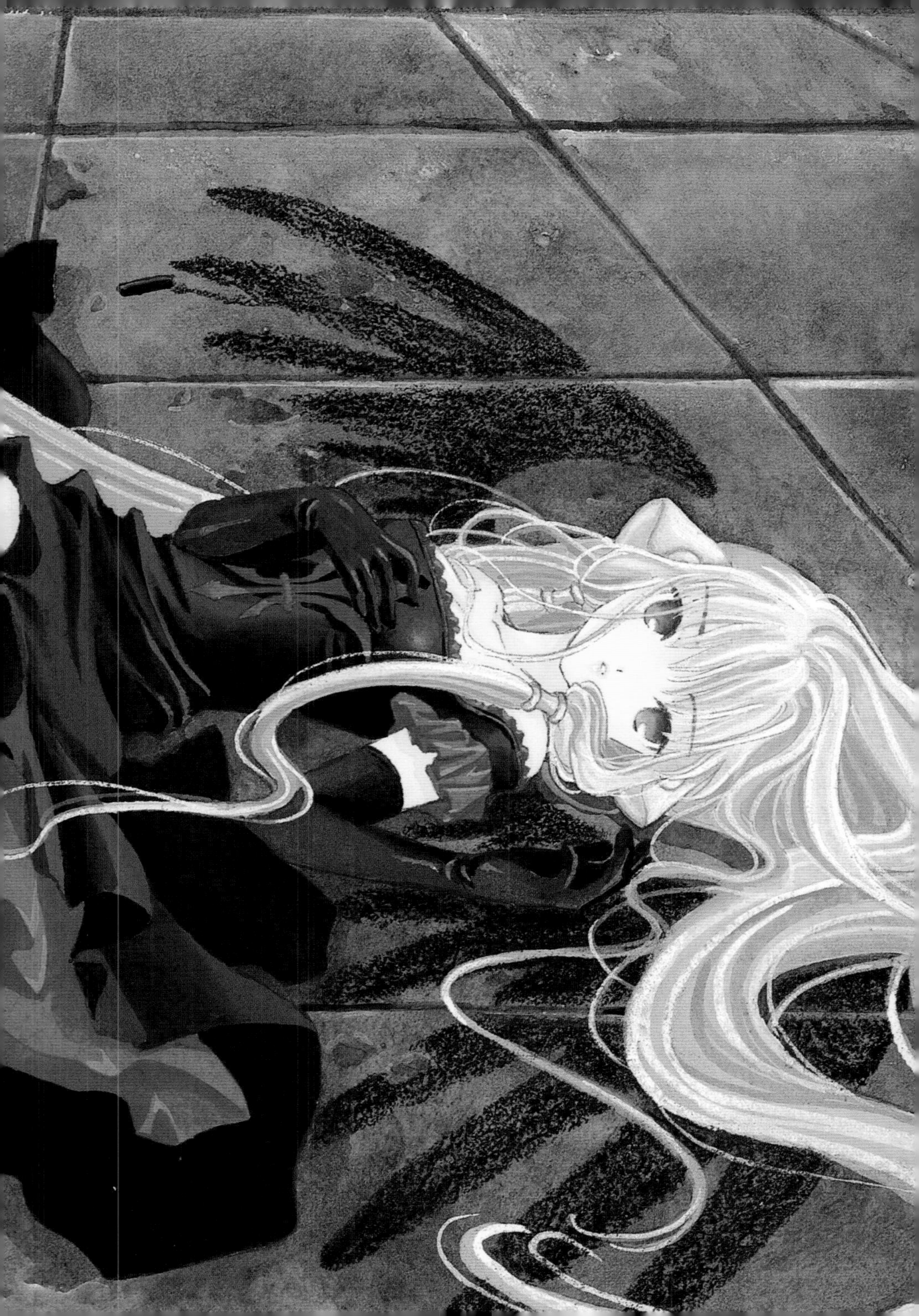

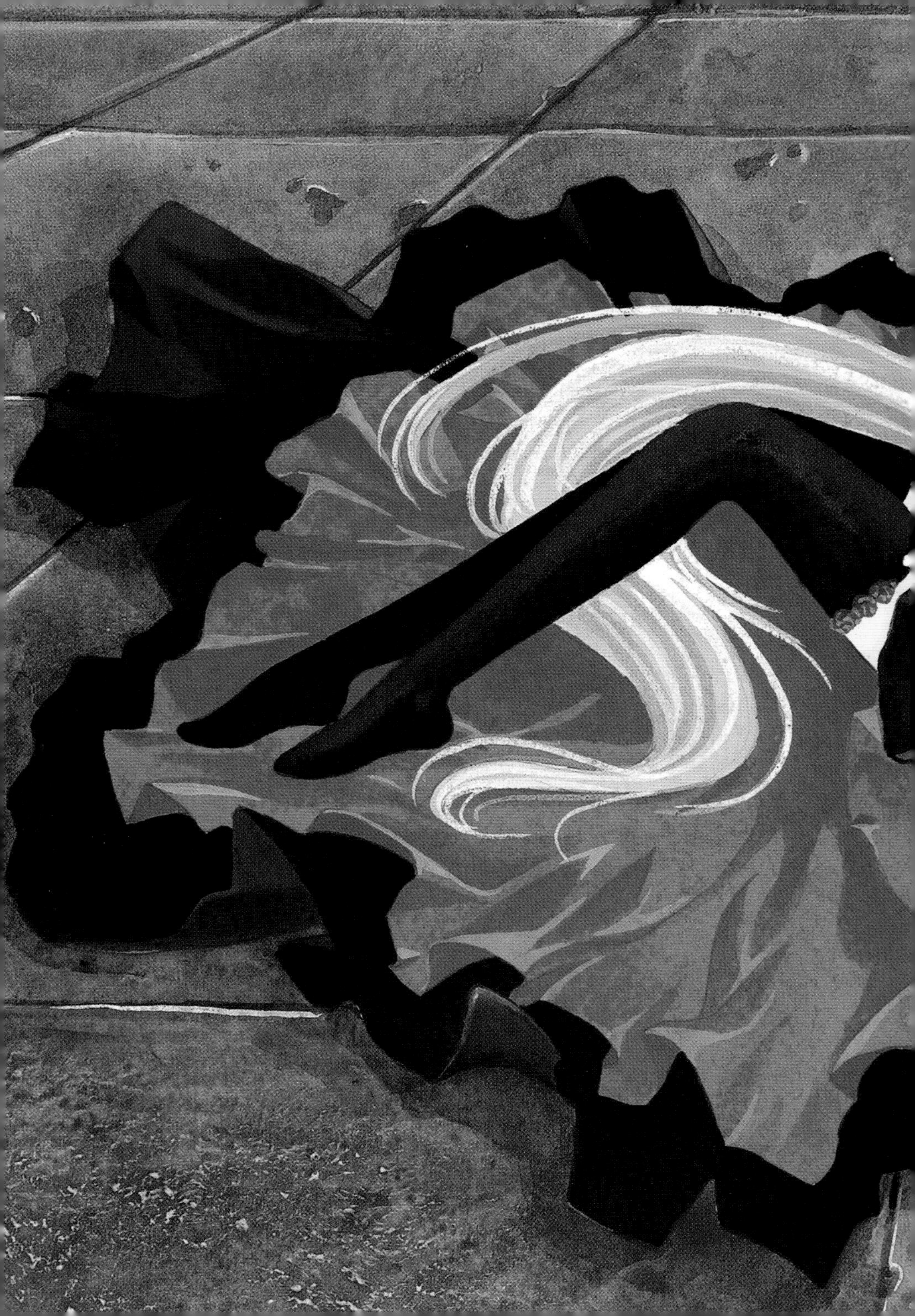

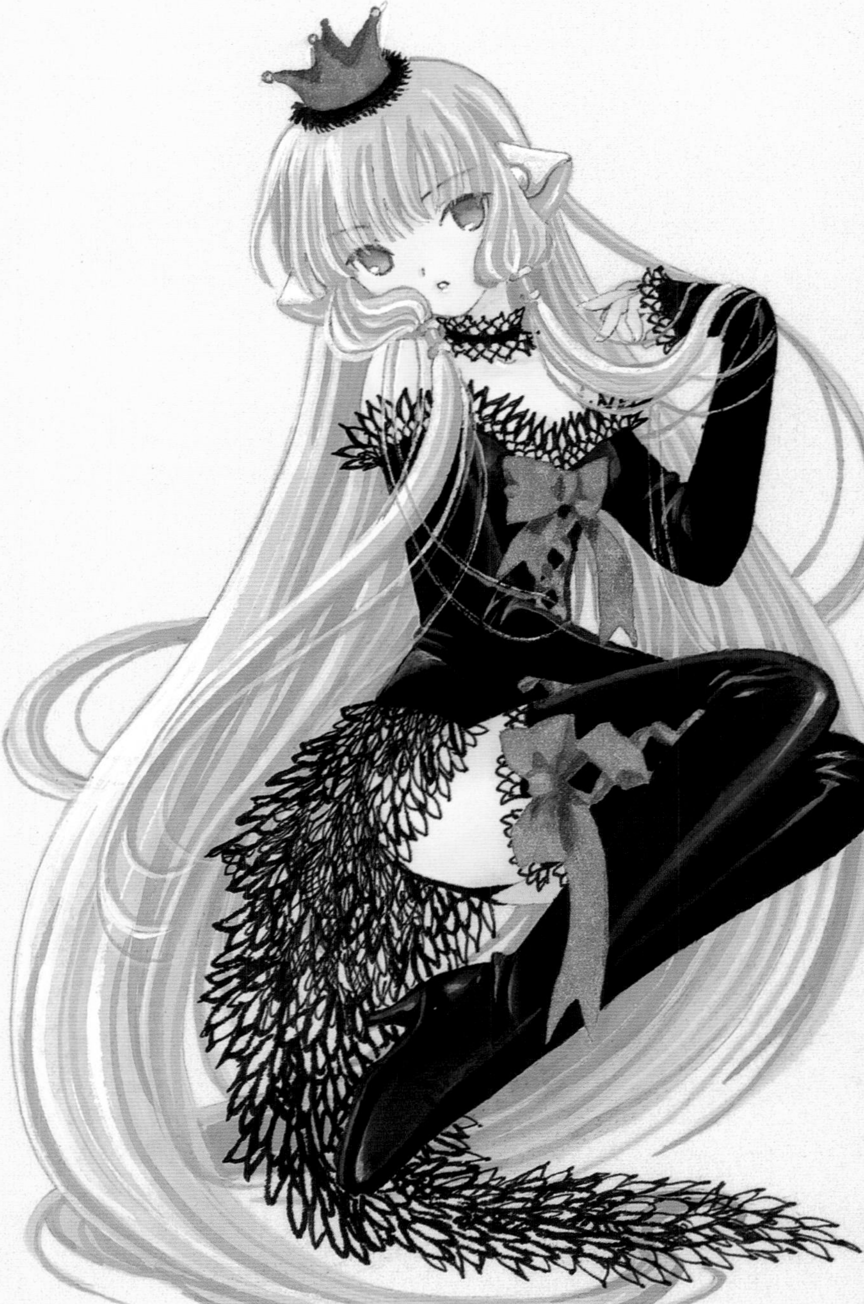

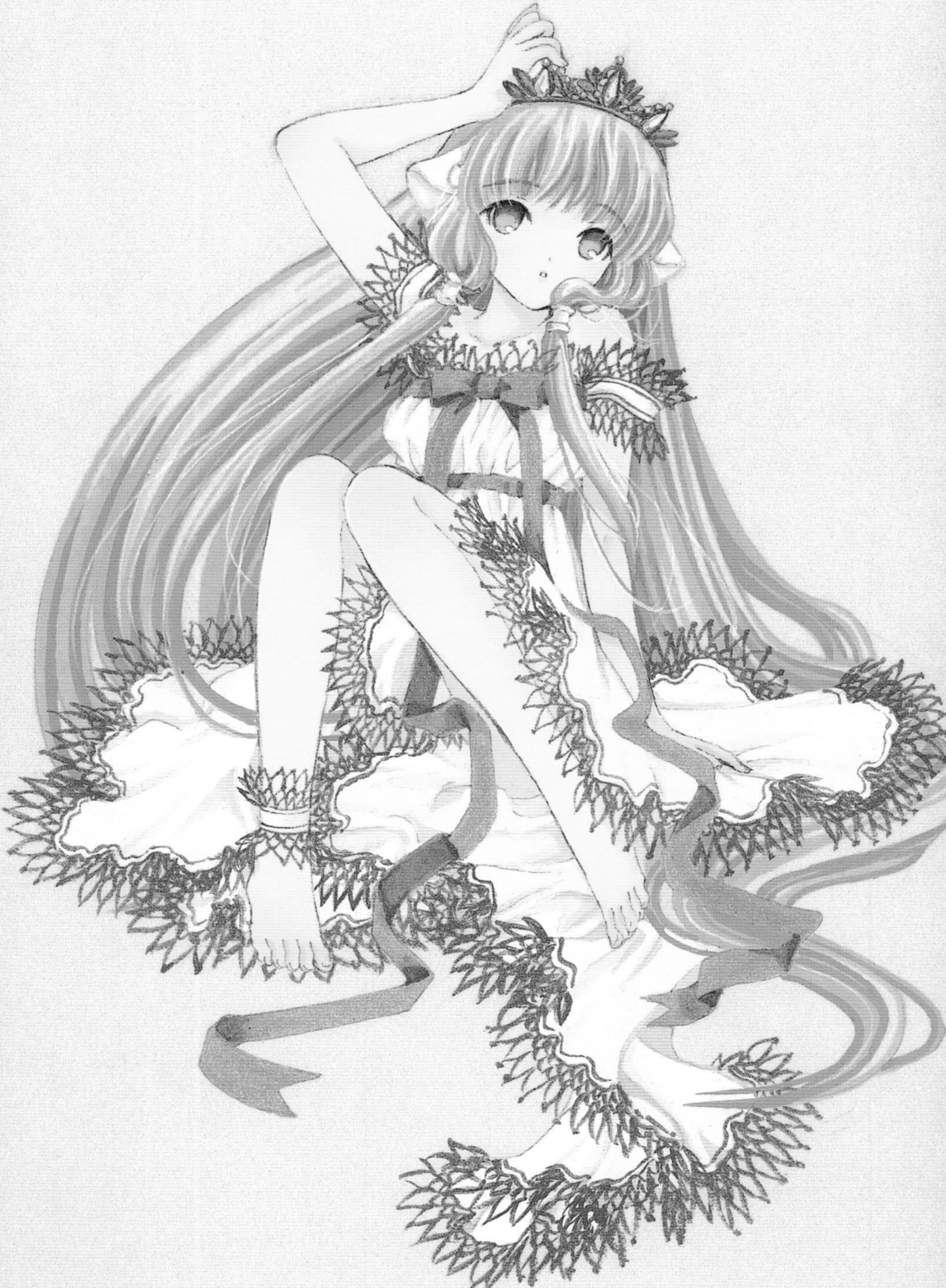

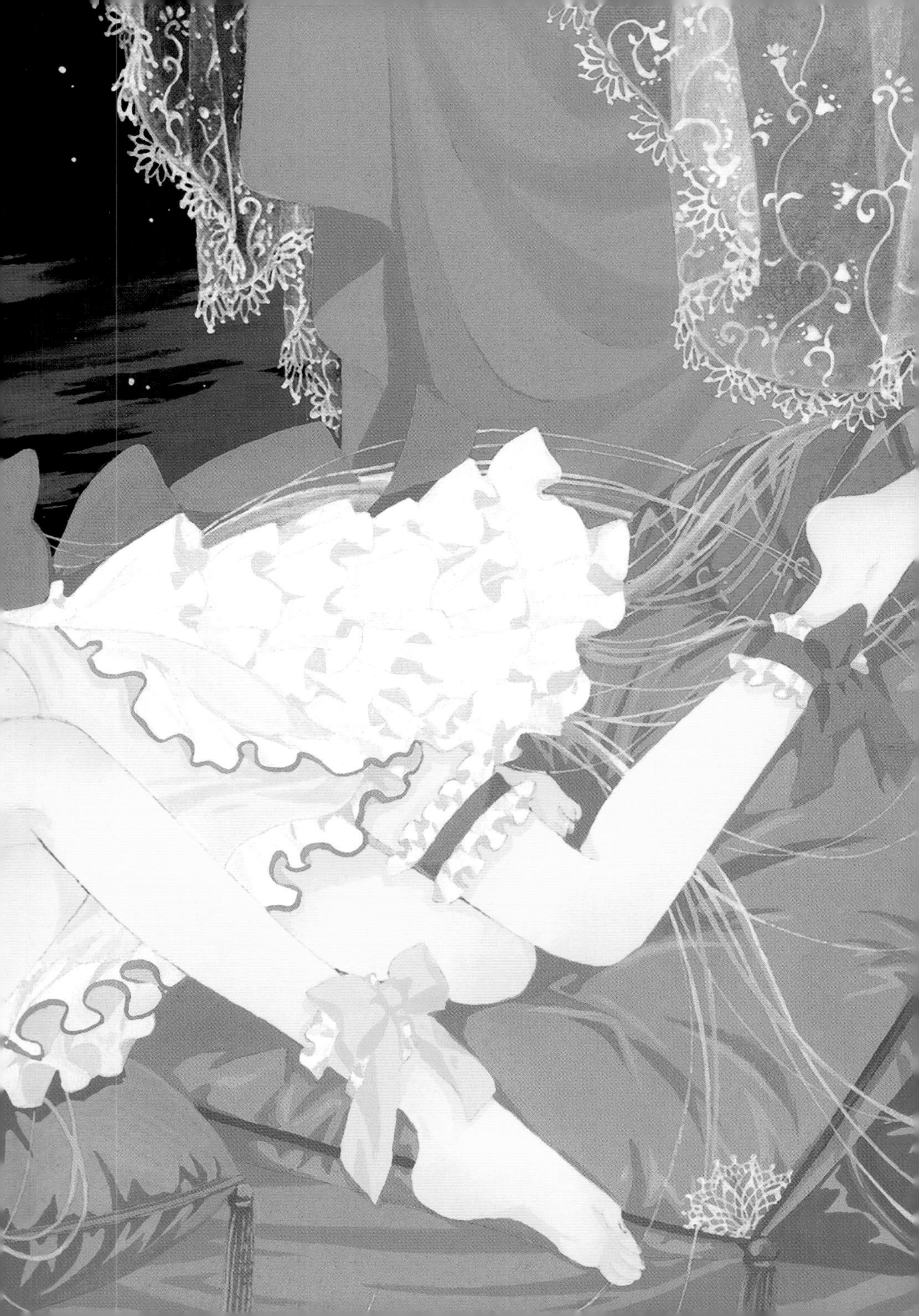

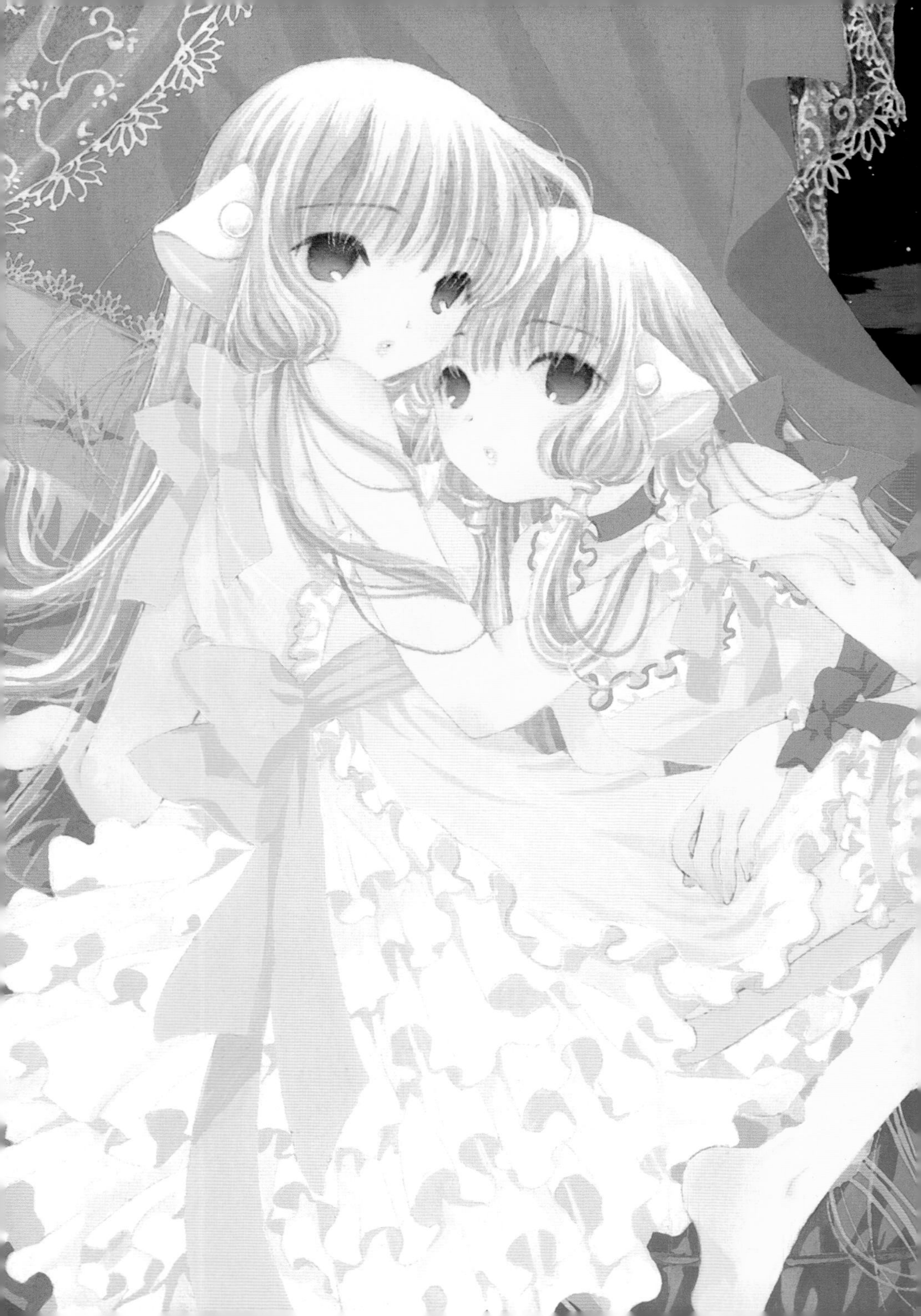

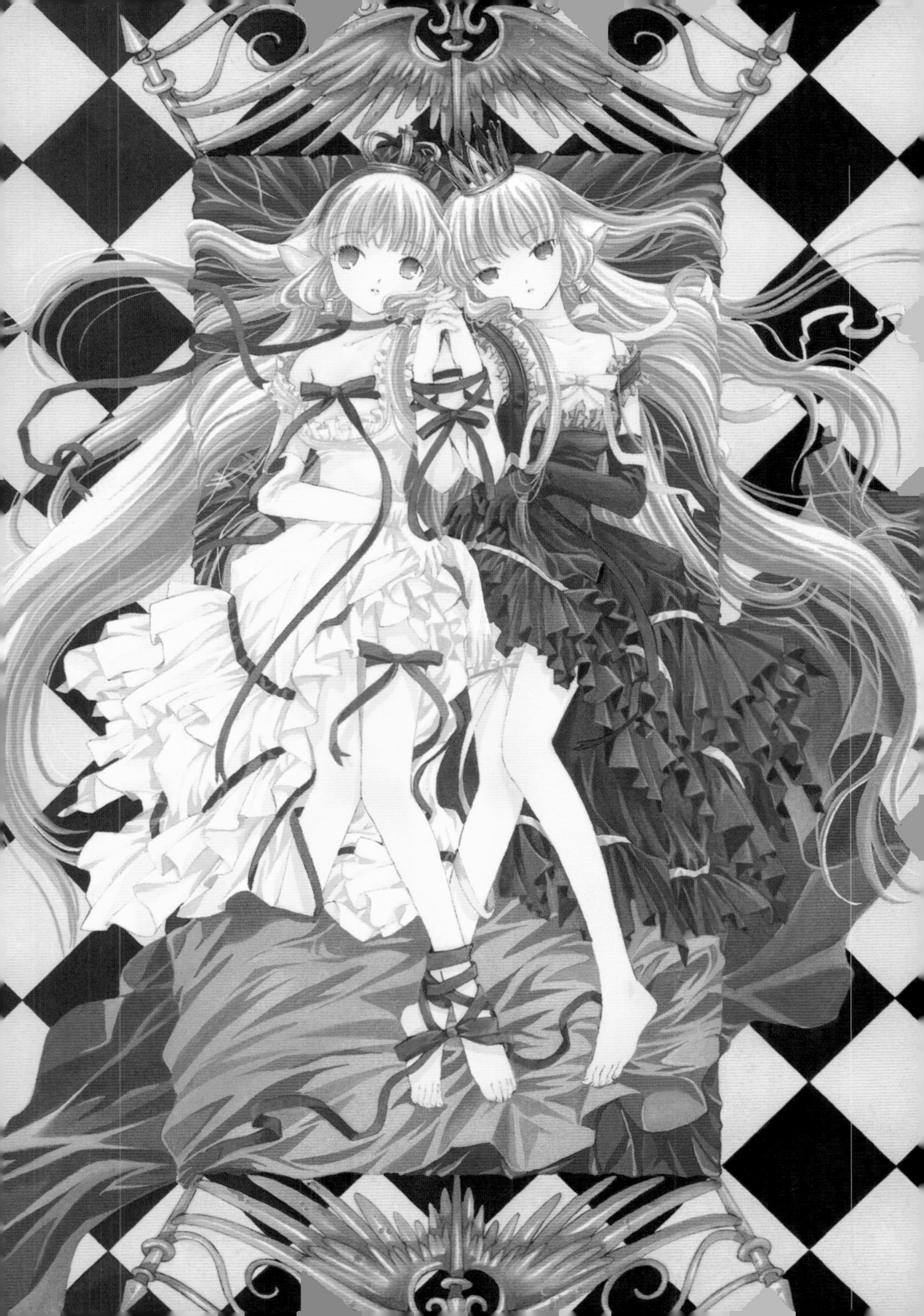